LANDMARKS IN Rhetoric and Public Address

LANDMARKS IN Rhetoric and Public Address

David Potter, *General Editor*

ADVISORY BOARD

THE

COLONIAL IDIOM

Edited by

DAVID POTTER

and

GORDON L. THOMAS

Carbondale and Edwardsville

SOUTHERN ILLINOIS UNIVERSITY PRESS

FEFFER & SIMONS, INC.

London and Amsterdam

For A. Craig Baird

Contents

PART III On *Occasional* Matters

PART IV On *Political* Matters

PART V   On *Religious* Matters

x   Contents

Preface

From the beginning, the American colonist was distinguished from his fellows by the fluency and the nature of his public speaking and by the extent of his listening. Particularly in New England where the town meeting and the congregationalist form of church organization were early features, local gatherings emphasized parliamentary speaking by the freemen and long and frequent sermons and lectures by the ministers.

Vigorous as well as long-winded speechmaking was not confined to the town halls and meeting houses of the "new Zions". Every colonial college stressed rhetoric in its curriculum, and regular exercises in oratory and disputation were features not only in the classroom and commencement hall but in the secret confines of the literary societies. In the cities and many of the towns, gentlemen pursued their love of conviviality, good talk, literature, and disputation in sodality, junto, philosophical society, and in the tavern. In courts of law, British trained as well as American prepared lawyers practiced a type of pleading which differed increasingly from the continental pattern. In legislative assemblies from Massachusetts to Georgia, thoughtful and often querulous colonials evaluated the directives and charges of the royal governors and, eventually, through caucus and debate helped set the stage for rebellion, a stage occupied by the delegates to the Continental Congress.

Throughout the seventeenth century, speech was the idiom of colonial communication. Not until the early decades of the eighteenth century did the local printing presses challenge the domination of public address as the disseminator of information and the agent of persuasion. And even in the years immediately preceding the Declaration of Independence, much of the widely circulated printed matter had its origin or instigation in the pulpit or in town meeting.

One might challenge the literary quality of much of the colonial speaking preserved on brittle sheets and eye-challenging microfilm or microcard. The television-adjusted citizen will certainly wonder how his lineal but hardly spiritual ancestors sat through the long sermons and endured the sometimes tightly constructed and "unworldly" lectures. But the sermons did not faze the better conditioned colonial New Englanders and that which is worldly changes with the times. From these talks and sermons and from the varied speaking of our colonial past, one can—if he attempts to reconstruct the times, issues, and personalities—gain a deeper insight and better understanding of what brought democratic America into being. Indeed, one might even learn how to cover his political tracks more cleverly after studying the life and oratory of a Benjamin Church or garner a time-tested formula for arousing raw emotion from an analysis of the Boston Massacre speeches.

In brief, a student of our culture and our history cannot savor the flavor of his chosen speciality unless he has at least a working knowledge of the speechmaking of the colonial period. To make such a working knowledge more available without resorting to the insult of capsulizing or predigesting, we have collected major and representative speeches as delivered by Americans from the earliest period of our colonial history to the signing of the Declaration of Independence. Whenever possible, each speech is reproduced in its entirety, and to it is appended a short sketch of the speaker and his speech situation when such information is available. Lengthy footnotes added to the published version of the speeches have been deleted in the interest of readability and economy.

Of course, scholars will observe notable omissions in our sampling. There is, for example, no sermon by that polished pulpit orator, Mather Byles. But the addition of one speech or sermon would have resulted in the dropping of an item of comparable length. Our preference excluded the sacrifice of a Davies, West, or Mayhew.

Less difficult to defend but equally painful to us was the exclusion of Edwards' "Sinners in the Hands of an Angry God" and Hamilton's "Argument in the Peter Zenger Trail." Both items can be located in excellent and readily accessible format—unlike the great majority of the lengthy addresses we have reprinted. Therefore we made the sacrifice to publishing costs and our contract.

In order to assist the student in initiating further study, we have included a short list of bibliographical material. By intent we have restricted ourselves to this minimum of commentary and introduction. There is no dearth of scholarly interpretation of the colonial period. There is a surplus of oversimplification. By reading the original speeches and digging into the welter of issues and ideas which occupied early Americans, one should develop a keen appreciation of the germinant period. We hope the reader will also experience the excitement that was ours as we assembled the contents of this volume.

We are indebted to many people for assistance in gathering and selecting material. Of particular assistance were Annette Mulvaney, Norman Halliday, and Bobbi Montross. We are grateful to A. Craig Baird, Orville Hitchcock, Lester Breniman and Ralph A. Micken for their suggestions and encouragement, to Phyllis Thomas and Marjorie Bond Potter for their understanding and forebearance, to Kaye Kopietz for assistance in proofreading, and to Southern Illinois University and Michigan State University for the grants which helped underwrite our research.

David Potter

Gordon L. Thomas

Carbondale, Illinois
August 1, 1968

I

On *Academic* Matters

EULOGIUM

William Smith

William Smith was born in Aberdeen, Scotland, on September 7, 1727. After attending the parish school he was taken in charge by the Society for the Education of Parochial Schoolmasters and educated under its care until 1741, when he entered the University of Aberdeen, from which he graduated A.M. in 1747. On March 3, 1751, he sailed for New York as a tutor and remained in this capacity until August, 1753. He went back to England and, on December 21, 1753, he was ordained deacon in the Established Church. Two days later he was elevated to the priesthood. In May of 1754, he returned to America and became teacher of logic, rhetoric, and natural and moral philosophy in the Academy and Charitable School of Philadelphia. In 1755, under a new charter, the Academy became the College, Academy and Charitable School, and Smith became provost. From 1766 to 1777, he acted as rector of Trinity Church, Oxford, Pennsylvania. He retired to Barbados Island when Howe advanced on Philadelphia and, after the evacuation of the city, he returned to the college. In 1779, the charter of the college was made void. Smith then became rector of Chester Parish, Chestertown, Kent County, and established Kent School. In 1789, the charter of the college was restored and Smith resumed his post as provost. In 1791 he lost this post. He died on May 14, 1803.

John Sargent, a merchant in London and member of Parliament, presented a gold medal to the College of Philadelphia. It was to be awarded to the student who wrote the best English essay on "the reciprocal advantages of a perpetual union between Great Britain and her American colonies."

The medal was conferred at a public commencement held on May 20, 1766. Smith, provost of the college, gave this speech at that time.

The text is from John Morgan and others. *Four Dissertations*. Philadelphia: William Thomas Bradford, 1766.

Sir,

AS the reward of your great merit in this elegant performance, I am, in the name of the Trustees and Faculty of this College, as well as in behalf of the worthy Donor, to beg your acceptance of this GOLD MEDAL—Its intrinsic value may not be an object of much consideration to you; but the truly honorable circumstances, by which it now becomes yours, must render it one of the most valuable jewels in your possession.

3

ADORNED tho' you have been with honors in distant lands, yet we trust those will not be the least acceptable to you, which your native country bestows.

THAT the first literary prize, contended for in this Institution, should fall to the share of one of its oldest sons, who, to much genius and application, has joined much knowledge of the world, will not seem strange. Yet still, for the honor of the Seminary, and what will not derogate from your honor, it will appear that you have obtained this pre-eminence over no mean competitors.

SOME of our younger sons (among whom we ought not to omit the name of the modest and candid WATTS, with some others even of inferior standing) have exhibited such vigorous efforts of genius, and tread so ardently on the heels of you and others their seniors, that it will require the utmost exertion of all your faculties, the continual straining of every nerve, if you would long wish to lead the way to them, in the great career of Fame.

O NOBLE contest! O Happy Feat of Science! to behold such a divine emulation among thy sons, kindled by the ardent desire of glory, and supported on those liberal principles which true literature alone can inspire!

MUCH do we owe to you, Gentlemen, on this occasion, much every way—much for the pains you have taken to do honor to the place of your education; and much for the public testimony you have given in its favor, declaring that *here* you have imbibed the true principles of Liberty, and have learned from your "early youth that your head, your heart and your hand should ever be at the service of your country"—

TRUE it is, Gentlemen, that we have publickly inculcated—and it was our duty to inculcate, on you, "that if there be any thing on this earth suited to the native dignity of the human mind, and worthy of contention, it must be to assert the cause of Religion and Truth, to support the fundamental rights and liberties of mankind; and to strive for the constitution of your country, and a government by known laws freely consented to by yourselves, or your certain delegates."

WE have exhorted you, "when your country calls, to be all eye and ear and heart and voice and hand, in a cause so glorious; proceeding with a manly and intrepid spirit, with a fervent and enlightened zeal; fearless of danger, undaunted by opposition, and convincing the world that Liberty is your unconquerable delight, and that you are sword foes to every species of bondage either of body or of mind."

BUT however much it might have been our duty to deliver lessons of this kind, small would have been the honour we should have derived from them, if you, Gentlemen had not nobly called those lessons forth into Action, demonstrating by your *living* example, that the education you received in this place, "was not a mere art of furnishing the Head, but a true discipline of the Life and Manners."

TRULY delicate and difficult, we confess was the subject prescribed to you—to treat of "the reciprocal advantages of a perpetual UNION between *Great Britain* and her *American* colonies," at a time when a fatal Misunderstanding had untwisted all the cords of that UNION, and the minds of many were too much inflamed. This difficulty was likewise encreased to us by other considerations.

Great-Britain, who, by her liberality, had raised this College from a helpless to a flourishing state, had an undoubted demand on us, in our particular capacity, for all the returns of gratitude. Yet we could not, we durst not, divert the streams of Learning from their sacred course. Our country, nay all *America,* had a right to demand that those streams should be directed pure along, to water the goodly TREE OF LIBERTY, nor ever be suffered to cherish any foul weed, that would shoak its growth.

IN this most difficult conjuncture, we rejoice to behold you, in your youth, exercising all the temper and prudence of the most experienced Patriots; freely and dutifully acknowledging in behalf of the mother country, that, "as the design of colonizing, was not to found a *new* empire, but to extend the *old,* the Colonies owe obedience under all constitutional and legal restrictions, and a due subordination in all commercial purposes" yet firmly asserting in behalf of the Colonies that they "are entitled, in return, to the full and free enjoyment of BRITISH LIBERTY, and necessary protection from all external violence—and that a policy which would ensure a small immediate revenue, at the expense of a great, though indirect, national gain, is *mean* and *sordid,* unworthy of the generous enterprizing spirit of a commercial nation;" and radically destructive of the mutual confidence.

WE rejoice that ever we had the least share in forming sentiments like these, which have led you to draw the true line, and powerfully to shew that on the everlasting basis of *reciprocal Interest,* and a participation of *constitutional privileges,* and on this alone, our UNION shall be perpetuated, and "our bleeding wounds healed up, without so much as a fear by way of remembrance."

HERE you have shewn yourselves entitled to the name of true SONS OF LIBERTY INDEED! neither betraying her sacred cause on the one hand, nor denegrating into *Licentiousness* on the other.—

THE occasion now calls me to address a few things to you, Gentlemen, who have just received your degrees in this Seminary; but I would not trespass on the patience of this candid audience.

YOU have observed the honors to which literary merit, and integrity of principles, have already advanced those who have gone before you in their studies here; and you cannot but be sensible, that of all the glories reflected on this Institution, we judge those the most solid and transporting which we derive from our own sons.

THE time is fast approaching, and I trust your bosoms now glow for it, when you too shall, in your turn, have an opportunity of doing honor to your education, by your conduct in public life. When that time shall come, educated as you have been in the principles of sound Liberty, permit us to promise ourselves, that you will ever think it your glory, to be enlisted under her banners, and follow her exalted call.

WHAT we have often given in solemn charge to those who have gone before you, and what you have often heard delivered in the course of your studies here, is I hope, engraven on your memories, and need not now be repeated.

YOU will consider all arts, all sciences, all eloquence, all philosophy, as intended to discipline the soul for eternity, and so far as they center not ultimately in this grand view, they are at best but empty trifles. Always look on the scriptures of God as that master system of knowledge, by which all other wisdom is to be regulated and perfected.

IN whatever station of life you are, we hope you never will forget your obligations to this seminary, which will travail, as it were in pain for you, till you appear on the theatre of action with dignity; and will expect to find its own children and sons, at least, among the number of its friends—We wish you every felicity, and bid you farewell.—

AND here I ought to conclude—But the joyous occasion calls me to return particular thanks to this splendid audience for the countenance they have given us this day; and to congratulate them on the glorious and happy turn in the affairs of *America,* whereof yesterday gave us the certain and confirmed accounts.

WHEN I look back on the dreadful state of suspence, in which these Colonies have been so long agitated; when, in the room of foreboding doubt and painful sollicitude, I behold joy in every look, the clouds dispersed, the sun breaking in upon us again, and an assembly around me in which every man, rejoices to salute his neighbour as *Free*—I *Feel,* I *Feel,* a sympathy unutterable, and an exultation of soul never felt before!

O GLORIOUS DAY! O happy *America!* if now we but know how to prize our happiness—The unguarded follies of intemperate zeal will soon be forgotten; but the stedfast, the noble, the patriotic efforts of cool and good men, in the indication of native and constitutional rights, will more and more claim the regard of all the Free, in every clime and age; and perhaps be consecrated by time into one of the brightest transactions of our story; asserting our pedigree, and shewing that we were worthy of having been descended from the illustrious stock of Britons!

THE cause of Liberty, Civil and Religious, is the cause of *Britain*—herself—nay it is the cause of heaven; and it was with inexpressible satisfaction that I beheld more than one of the gentlemen, who have written on the ties of UNION between *Great-Britain* and her colonies, deriving a very capital argument from the ties of a Common Religion.

WHEN I review the history of the world, and look on the progress of Knowledge, Freedom, Arts, and Science, I cannot but be strongly persuaded that Heaven has yet glorious purposes to serve thro' *America.*

CIVIL Liberty, the Protestant Religion, the principles of Toleration, in their purity, honorable as they are to human nature, subsist but in few places of the globe; and *Great-Britain* is their principal residence.

UNDER her auspices they were transplanted into *America;* where they have got firm root, and are flourishing into immense growth and will bring such an accession of strength to the general cause of liberty and Protestantism, that we trust no power on earth shall ever be able to prevail against their united strength.

THIS sentiment, it is hoped, will more and more gain ground among good men both here and in the mother country; convincing them that to check the spirit of Freedom, or discourage the propagation of knowledge here in *America*, would, on the part of *Great-Britain*, be to wound her own members, and weaken or destroy that glorious public system of Truth, Freedom and Happiness, whereof she is the Guardian and the head.

ANIMATED by these principles, and guided by an enlightened zeal, it will become us to manifest our gratitude and love to the mother country, by every means in our power. Let us make our moderation known to all the world; bending our whole thoughts to a virtuous industry, beneficial to ourselves and to *Great-Britain;* acting "as Free, but not using our liberty as a cloak of maliciousness" or of Licentioussness.

Prayse of Eloquence

EXCERPTS

Michael Wigglesworth

Michael Wigglesworth, Puritan preacher and poet, was born in Yorkshire, England, October 18, 1631. At the age of seven he was brought to New England. He was educated at Harvard and was later a tutor there. He studied theology and became pastor of the church at Malden, Massachusetts where he is presumed to have been ordained in 1656. He held this pastorate until his death in 1705.

The Day of Doom, Wigglesworth's best-known poem, was published in 1662. Rigidly Calvinistic, it was very popular in New England for over one hundred years. Other works which achieved recognition during Wigglesworth's lifetime are *Meat Out of the Eater* and *A Discourse on Eternity*.

The following long excerpts from "Prayse of Eloquence," written as a classroom oration in 1650, are indicative of contemporary oratorical composition at Harvard. The text is from the Student Notebook of Michael Wigglesworth, manuscript in the New England Historical and Geneological Society Archives.

How sweetly doth eloquence even inforce trueth upon the understanding, & subtly convay knowledge into the minde be it never so dull of conceiving, & sluggish in yeelding its assente. So that let a good Oratour put forth the utmost of his skill, & you shall hear him so lay open & unfould, so evidence & demonstrate from point to point what he hath in hand, that he wil make a very block understand his discourse. Let him be to giue a description of something absent or unknown; how strangely doth he realize & make it present to his hearers apprehensions, framing in their mindes as exact an idea of that which they never saw, as they can possibly have of any thing that they have bin longest & best acquainted with. Or doth he take upon him to personate some others in word or deedes? why he presents his hearers not with a lifeless picture, but with the living persons of those concerning whom he speaks. They see, they hear, they handle them, they walk they talk with them, & what not? Or is he to speak about such things as are already known? Why should he here discourse after the vulgar manner, & deliver his mind as a cobler would doe: his hearers might then have some ground to say they knew as much as their oratour could teach them. But

by the power of eloquence ould truth receivs a new habit. though
its essence be the same yet its visage is so altered that it may
currently pass & be accepted as a novelty. The same verity is again
& again perhaps set before the same guests but drest & disht up after
a new manner, & every manner season'd so well that the intel-
lectuall parts may both without nauseating receiv, & so oft as it
doth receiv it still draw some fresh nourishing virtue from it. So
that Eloq. giues new luster & bewty, new strength new vigour, new
life unto trueth; presenting it with such variety as refresheth,
actuating it with such hidden powerful energy, that a few languid
sparks are blown up to a shining flame.

And which is yet more: Eloquence doth not onely reviue
the things known but secretly convay life into the hearers understanding rousing it out of its former slumber, quickning it beyond
its naturall vigour, elevating it aboue its ordinary conception. There
are not onely objects set before it, but ey's (after a sort) giuen
it to see these objects in such wise as it never saw. yea it is strengthened as to apprehend that which is taught it, so of it self with
enlargment to comprehend many things which are not made
known unto it. Hence it comes to pass that after the hearing of a
welcomposed speech livelily exprest the understanding of the
Auditor is so framed into the mould of Eloquence, that he could
almost goe away & compose the like himself either upon the same
or another subject. And whats the reason of this? why his mind
is transported with a kind of rapture, & inspired with a certain
oratoric fury, as if the oratour together with his words had
breathed his soul & spirit into those that hear him.

These and the like effects hath Eloquence upon the understanding. But furthermore 'tis a fit bait to catch the will and
affections. For hereby they are not onely layd in wait for, but
surprized: nor onely surprized, but subdued; nor onely subdued,
but triumphed over. Yet Eloquence beguil's with such honesty,
subdues with such mildness, triumphs with such sweetness: that
here to be surprized is nothing dangerous, here to be subject is
the best freedom, this kind of servitude is more desireable then
liberty. For wᵣas our untractable nature refuseth to be drawn,
and a stiff will scorn's to be compel'd: yet by the power of welcomposed speech nature is drawn aḡ st the stream with delight,
and the will after a sort compelled with its owne consent. Altho:
for a time it struggle and make resistance, yet at length it suffer's
it self to be vanquish't and takes a secret contentment in being
overcome. In like manner, for the affections. Look as a mighty
river auḡmᵗed wᵗʰ excessiue rains or winter snows swelling above
its wonted channel bear's down banks and bridges, overflows
feilds & hedges, sweeps away all before it, that might obstruct
its passage: so Eloq. overturn's, overturn's all things that stand

in its way, & carrys them down wth the irresistible stream of its all controuling power. Wonderful it were to speak of the severall discoverys of the power in severall affections: wonderfull but to think in generall, how like a blustering tempest it one while driues before it the raging billow's of this troubled Ocean: how other whiles (as though it had them in fetters it curb's & calm's the fury at a word. And all this without offering violence to the party's so affected nay with a secret pleasure & delight it stirs men up to the greatest displeasure & distast. Doth it affect wth grief? why to be so grieved is no grievance. doth it kindle coales, nay flames of fiery indignation? why those flames burn not, but rather cherish. doth it draw tears from the eys? why even tears flow with pleasure. For as is wel sayd by one upon this point In omni animi motu etiam in dolore ets quaedam jucunditas. So potently, so sweetly doth Eloquence command. and of a skilfull orator in point of the affections that may be spoken really, which the Poet affirmeth fabulously of Æolus god of the winds.

But I need instance no more. some of you I hope will by this time assent unto what has bin hitherto prov'd that Eloq. is of such useful concernment & powerfull operation. But methinks I hear some still objecting. 'Tis very true Eloq. is a desirable thing, but what are we the better for knowing its worth unless we coud hope for selues to attain it? It is indeed a right excellent indowment: but 'tis not every capacity, nay scarce one of a hundreth that can reach it. How many men of good parts do we find that yet excel not here? Cicero indeed, a man in whom vast understanding & naturall fluent facility of speech conspire together; no marvail if he makes judges weep and princes tremble. But to what purpose is it for a man of weak parts & mean abilitys to labour after that which he is never like to compass? Had we not as good toss our caps against the wind as weary out our selves in the pursuit of that which so few can reach to?

An. To these I woud answer first, the reason why so few attain it is bec. there [are] few that indeed desire it. hence they run not as if they ment to win, they pursue not as if they hop't to overtake. But 2ly let me answer them with Turner's words upon this very argument Negligentiam nostram arguit, qui cum non possimus. quod debemus, optimus, nolumus quod possimus, benè. we cannot do what we woud therefore will not doe what we may. This savours of a slouthful sistem. Bec. we cannot keep pace with the horsemen, shall we sit down & refuse to goe? we cannot reach so far as our selues desire & as some others it may be attain, shall we not therefore reach as far as our endeavours may carry us? Bec. we cannot be Oratores optimi, do we content our selues to be Oratores Pessimi? And as for those that have most excell'd in this kind, whence had they their excellency? they did not come declaming into the world: they were not born with orations in their mouths: eloquence did not sit upon their lips whilest they lay in their cradles: neither did they suck it in from their mothers brests. But if you examine the matter you shall find that by incredible paines & daly exercise, they even turn'd the cours of nature into another channel, & cut out a way for the gentle stream of Eloquence, where naturall impediments seem'd altogether to deny it passage: thereby affecting as much as another could bragg, viam aut inveniam aut faciam: Eminent in this respect is the example of the 2 best oratours that fame has brought to our ears. Of Cicero, who when he had naturally a shrill, screaming, illtun'd voyce rising to such a note that it indanger'd his very life: yet by art & industry he acquired such a commendable habit, as none with ease could speak more sweetly than he. And Demosthenes, though he were naturally of a stammering tongue crasy-body'd & broken-winded, & withall had accustom'd himself to a jetting uncomely deportment of his body, or some part of it at least: when to conclude he had scarce any prt. of an oratour, saue onely an ardent desire to be an oratour: yet by his indefatigable paines he so overcame these naturall defects, as that he came to be reputed prince of the Graecian Eloquence. Though this was not gotten without some further difficulty & seeming vain attempts. Insomuch as he was severall times quite discouraged, and once threw all aside, dispairing ever to become an oratour bec. the people laught at his orations. yet notwithstanding being heartned to it again by some of his welwillers, he never left striving till he had won the prize.

Go too therefore my fellow-students (for to you I address my speech, my superiours I attempt not to speak to, desiring rather to learn of them more of this nature, but) to giue me leav to say: Let no man hereafter tel me I despair of excelling in the oratoricall faculty, therefore 'tis bootless to endeavour. Who more unlike to make an oratour than Demosthenes except it were one who had no tongue in his head? yet Demosthenes became orator optimus. Tell me not 'I have made trial once & again, but find my labour fruitless.' thou art not the first that hast made an onset, & bin repelled; neither canst thou presage what renew'd endeavors may produce. Would you then obtain this skill? take Demosthenes his course; gird up your loines, put to your shoulders, & to it again, & again, & agen, let nothing discourage you. Know that to be a dunce, to be a stammerer, unable to bring forth 3 or 4 sentences hanging well together, this is an easy matter: but to become an able speaker, hic labor, hoc opus est. Would you haue your orations pleas, such as need not be laughts at? why follow him in that also. Let them be such as smell of the lamp, as was sayd of his. not slovenly I mean, but elaborate, diurnam industriam et nocturnis lucubrationibus elaboratae, such as savour, of some paines taken with them. A good oration is not made at the first thought, nor scarce at the first writing over. Nor is true Eloquence wont to hurry it out thick & threefould, as if each word: were running for a wadger: nor yet to mutter or whisper it out of a book after a dreaming manor, with such a voyce as the oratour can scantly heare himself speak; but to utter it with lively affection, to pronounce it distinctly with audible voyce.

But I shall burden your patience no further at the present. Those and the like vices in declaming that are contrary to Eloquence, were the chief motives that drew me first into thoughts of this discourse. but I see I cannot reach at this season to speak of them particularly. wherefore with your good leav and gods assistance I shall rather treat of them at another opportunity.

FORENSIC DISPUTATIONS

James Mitchell Varnum, William Williams,
Theodore Parsons, and Eliphalet Pearson

Although English forensic disputations were not featured in the American college curriculum until the middle of the eighteenth century, graduating seniors were debating religious, academic, and secular questions on the commencement platform as early as 1760. Of particular interest to the modern student are the two disputations which follow. The first, performed by James Mitchell Varnum and William Williams at Rhode Island College (Brown University) at the commencement exercises, September 7, 1769, considered "Whether British America Can Under Present Circumstances Consistent With Good Policy, Affect to Become an Independent State." The text is taken from the *Collections of the Rhode Island Historical Society*, VII, 281–98. The second was exhibited by Theodore Parsons and Eliphalet Pearson at the commencement exercises of Harvard College on July 21, 1773 and considered "Whether the slavery, to which Africans are in this province, by the permission of law, subjected, be agreeable to the law of nature?" The text is taken from the edition printed by John Boyle, Boston, 1773.

Of the four disputants three, Eliphalet Pearson, James Varnum, and William Williams, achieved more than local importance. Born in Newbury, Massachusetts in 1752, Pearson prepared for Harvard at Dummer Academy. After graduate study at Harvard, he taught at Andover and assisted Samuel Phillips in drawing up the constitution of Phillips Academy. He served as the first principal of Phillips from 1778 until 1786 when he accepted an appointment as Hancock Professor of Hebrew and Oriental Languages at Harvard. Objecting to the trend toward Unitarianism at Harvard, he resigned in 1806 and was instrumental in founding the Andover Theological Seminary where he served first as a professor and later as president of the board of trustees. He resigned from Andover in 1821 and died five years later in Greenland, New Hampshire.

James Varnum was born in Dracut, Massachusetts in 1748. Expelled from Harvard, probably for involvement in the student disturbances of April, 1768, he entered the College of Rhode Island and was graduated with its first class in 1769. After a brief experience in teaching, he entered the law office of Oliver Arnold and was admitted to the bar in 1771. In 1775 he was commissioned a colonel of the First Regiment, Rhode Island Infantry. Commissioned brigadier general by General Washington in 1777, he served the colonial forces with distinction. After several terms as a member of the Continental Congress, he was appointed United States Judge for the Northwest Territory in 1787. He died in Marietta, Ohio in 1789.

William Williams, minister and teacher, was born in Hill-
town, Pennsylvania in 1752. He prepared for the College of Rhode
Island at the school of the Reverend Issac Eaton in Hopewell, New
Jersey and was graduated from Rhode Island in the first class of
1769. He was licensed to preach in 1773 and on July 3, 1776 was
ordained pastor of the Baptist Church of Wrentham, Massachusetts
where he preached for forty-eight years. Shortly after moving to
Wrentham, Williams founded an academy which sent eighty students to his alma mater including such notables as the Hon. David
R. Williams, Governor of South Carolina and Tristam Burgess,
Professor of Oratory and Belles-Lettres at Brown. For his service to
the College of Rhode Island, Williams recevied an honorary D.D.
and in 1789 was elected to the Board of Fellows. He died in September, 1823 at the age of seventy-one.

1 A DISPUTATION
on "Whether British America can under present
circumstances consistent with good policy, affect to become
an independent state."

Respondent

True patriotism is undoubtedly one of the noblest virtues that
ever inspired the human breast. There is something so grand in
its nature, so beneficial in its effects, that even the most despotic
themselves are obliged to admire, though with horror and reluctance. It fires the mind with an unshaken resolution, to promote
the supreme good of society, notwithstanding private interest
may be sacrificed in the effort. It is far from being the sudden
blaze of an intemperate zeal, neither is it the enthusiastic flight of
political craft, but that uniform deliberative principle, which
exictes us maturely to survey all the circumstances of our country—
to consider which of them is or probably may be an obstruction
to its growth or future prosperity; to examine thoroughly the
source from whence this calamity results; and to preserve with
unremitted activity and prudence, in the use of those means which
will ensure success, both in disappointing the mischievous designs
of its enemies, and in the security of its peace and tranquility upon
a basis the most permanent and immovable. In short, the true
patriot is warmed with every social virtue.

Such of late has been the situation of our own native land,
that ample scope has been afforded for the exercise of this principle; and to the immortal honor of North America, it has been
exerted in a most glorious manner. But as the powerful influences
of the solar rays are often diminished and greatly obstructed by
aqueous particles in our atmosphere, so our rational remonstrances

and powerful rhetoric, have been by the baleful influence of state ministers, counteracted and hitherto rendered abortive. But what may be our approaching destiny cannot be determined by human wisdom. However, as a fixed doom is the only just foundation of despair, we can in no wise consider our case as desperate; nay, we have the highest reason to expect redress, while we demonstrate by our conduct the most sacred regard for our privileges and firm attachment to our duty. Suffer me therefore, my benevolent auditors, to court your indulgence and candor, while I freely inquire, whether British America can, under her present circumstances, consistent with good policy, effect to become an independent state. An inquiry of so much importance as this, needs no apology for its introduction, especially as our own private interests, the good of our country, and the fate of posterity, are all comprised in it.

Had British America been left to the peaceful enjoyment of those privileges, which it could boast of in former reigns, the most romantic genius, in its wildest excursions, had not dreamt of independence. But the late alarming attacks of the parent state upon American freedom, by thrusting in that triple headed *Cerberus* of a Stamp Act, suspension of legislation in the provinces, and the imposition of duties on paper, glass, etc., has, with justice, roused the advocates of American liberty to the most vigorous exertions in defence of our rights; amongst whom, not a few will transmit their names, with growing honor, down the long tract of future time to latest posterity, every generation rising up and calling them blessed. But some less cautious and too soon discouraged, have rashly recommended an opposition, *vi et armis,* and an affectation of independence in the colonies—a thought so shocking that I tremble in relating it! A design, the prosecution of which, I think myself able to demonstrate, at once would be the most preposterous policy, and productive of the most injurious consequences.

With regard to this imposition of duties, it must be esteemed as taxation without our consent, and consequently a burden; very unnatural treatment from a parent, whom we exerted our utmost efforts to honor and obey! But let us inquire whether there is so much horror in this circumstance, as people are apt to imagine! All manner of taxation, say they, without our consent by ourselves or representatives, is an essential violation of the British Constitution, and therefore inconsistent with our rights as freemen. I fully grant it, and cordially wish that every American was sufficiently impressed with a just sense of it. But we are taxed without our consent, and consequently we are abject slaves to all intents and purposes. Wherefore, Rouse! Resist! Conquer!

But stop, and for a moment pause. We are not slaves. In order to do this, they must not only impose duties on a number of articles, but oblige us to purchase those articles. This they have not done, neither can they. It is true we are prohibited from purchasing them of other nations, but that by no means amounts to an absolute obligation to receive them from Britain. For there is not a single article restricted in this sort, but what we can manufacture in our own country, or do as well without. We have without dispute, a large quantity of raw materials, and can produce more. And as to our skill and manufacture, it is far from being contemptible, considering the short time of our application thereto. But from the late progress in different branches we may rationally expect improvements, which in the course of a few years will do honor to America. What then is the intolerable burden under which we labor? Truly we are obliged to prosecute industry and frugality. This is a burden indeed, but only to the indolent and lazy patricide. Every skillful politician esteems industry the glory of his country. How can this be applied to better advantage, under our present situation, than to the manufacturing of those articles, which have for the most part, through bad policy, been imported from Europe? This would secure among ourselves an immense quantity of cash, which otherwise must cross the Atlantic, and more effectually enable Great Britain to prosecute those oppressive measures which deservedly merit out utmost detestation. This would secure the balance of trade in our favor; a consideration essentially necessary to the growth and prosperity of America, and consequently it must be the grand object in the view of every one who is a friend to his country. From all which we may infer, that under the auspicious smiles of heaven, America will soon shine with redoubled splendor.

But some will probably object, that the author of this innovation, intended it as a precedent on which to establish further encroachments; for if Great Britain has a right to impose a penny, she has a pound, and so on as much as she pleases; therefore if we only submit to the first, we virtually give up all right to freedom. I answer, in the present inquiry, we are not concerned about futurity, or what may or may not be good policy *hereafter* but whether in our *present circumstances*, to affect independence is consistent with good policy? Should it ever be our unhappy case that we can no longer command our own property, but have it at the sole disposal of despotic rulers, then it will be time to resist, and for this reason, that death itself is the last refuge from abject slavery.

We have yet other sources to which we may resort for redress. We are indisputably favored with an excellent Prince, who, ever since his accession to the throne, has discovered the most tender regard for his numerous subjects. We have learned and powerful advocates in both Houses of Parliament, the thunder of whose eloquence has often stunned and silenced those venal sons of slavery, who pay their homage at ministerial shrines, and venerate no other God but gain. It is also equally certain that the popular clamor at home is in our favor, and the influence of the merchants is engaged in our cause. These are all favorable circumstances, and well deserve our serious consideration. For the very existence of the legislative authority of the British constitution, depends on the consent of the people. And when the majority of them is set in opposition to any act or law, it must of consequence fall to the ground; since the legislators act only by a delegated power, which also they derive from the people. We have therefore no reason at present to expect any further infringements, but a speedy deliverance from those of which we now complain. Doubtless we should long since have obtained redress, had we not been tormented by worms in our own bowels. We are misrepresented to our Sovereign, and that, too, by those very persons who are dependent on us for their very subsistence. We have also enemies in England, the worst of enemies, who make use of every possible opportunity to fill the Royal ear with suggestions of our disloyalty to his person and government. These obstacles may, and probably soon *will* be, removed out of the way; and then our mother country will return to her native smiles, and we to an entire confidence in her affection. I shall dismiss these considerations by repeating a few lines from the justly renowned author of "The Farmer's Letters."

"Let us withhold from Great Britain," he says, "all the advantages she has been used to receive from us. Then let us try if our ingenuity, industry, and frugality will not give weight to our remonstrances."

"Let us all be united with one spirit in one cause. Let us invent; Let us work; Let us save: Let us at the same time keep up our claims, and unceasingly repeat our complaints."

But supposing we could resist Great Britain with success, exclusive of foreign assistance, let us forestall some of the inevitable consequences; and this we may easily do without the spirit of prophecy. And here it will be allowed by all, that a single discharge from a British navy, would utterly demolish the strongest fortifications of which we can boast, and with infinite ease lay in ashes our principal trading towns. Consequently we must take refuge in the wilderness amongst the savage haunts of wild beasts, fabricate houses in the mountains, claim kindred with and court the society of the merciless savages of the desert. Who sees not, that in such a situation we should not only relinquish the superfluities, but bid an eternal farewell to the pleasures and comforts of life; forget the little politeness and humanity of which we now boast; and relapse into downright barbarity! We must depend entirely on the cultivation of land for subsistence! A precarious subsistence, attended with insuperable difficulties and labors! To which we must add the maintenance of a large standing army, in order to defend our habitations from the ravages of the enemy. But where are our finances? How could we support it? The half, at least, of our able hands, being detained in this manner from tillage, our soils would not produce, even a competency for the necessities of nature; consequently we must either submit to the rage of an incensed foe, or become an easy prey to famine and poverty. Dreadful alternative! Either of which, only in idea, harrows up my very soul.

It will also be confessed, that such have been the circumstances of America from her first settlement to the present time, that there has not been sufficient encouragement or leisure to rear the arts and sciences to that exalted height of which they are capable under the cultivation of those masterly geniuses, brighter than which Greece, Italy or Britain can boast of few. Advantages considered, her literary productions equal, if not rival the best in Europe. We are now arrived to that glorious era, in which science begins to display its charms. Should nothing impede its progress, America will soon shine as a star of the first magnitude in the firmament of literature. But such an animating prospect vanishes, when we are involved in the din of war, and affrighted by the groans of slaughter. What can we expect but ignorance, superstition and barbarity? What must become of the administration of justice, the only support of a regular society? Under the restraint of what laws should we be laid, but the wild propensions of our own breasts? Instead of civility and politeness, what could we expect but a rude set of barbarians, accosting and accosted in in the same frightful unpolished strain? Every man's strength must be his own defence, and when that fails, malice and rage will devour the miserable victims. These are consequences naturally resulting, even upon a presumption that we could resist our mother country with success. But this supposition is wild and chimerical, and by no means to be admitted.

From England we have received our existence, and to her are we indebted for protection. Were it not for her fostering wings, how easily should we be destroyed by an invading foe! We are not yet arrived to maturity. We are infants and stand in the greatest necessity of dandling on the knees of an indulgent parent. How could we confront with Gallic rage, Spanish cruelty, Italic inquisition? But what is most astonishing, and big with horror, WE talk of resisting Great Britain! A thought the most ridiculous that ever entered the mind of mortals. One paw of the British Parliament, as says my Lord Chatham, would crush America to atoms. Where are our fortifications? Where is our navy? Where are our regular disciplined troops? Where is our wealth to support a standing army? In short, have we one implement of war? O America! couldst thou hear the roaring thunder of that nation which made Europe tremble and recoil for anguish, the most inconsiderable nation of which as far exceeds thee in strength, as yon glorious luminary does the least satellite of Jupiter in splendor— Couldst thou see the red lightnings flash and the awful conflagration, where then would be thy thoughts of independence? Return, oh return, to thy senses and to thy manufactures! Shouldst thou lift a rebellious hand, blood would run down thy streets as a stream, and death in every dreary form, would stalk through the land. Who can bear the prospect? Who can behold the dying pangs of America? Stabbed in every vein, wrenched with inexpressible torture, sinking into oblivion.

Opponent

To appear an advocate for injured truth, to assert and vindicate the fights of mankind, when trampled on and violated in the most audacious and wicked manner, by men destitute of the common feelings of humanity, is an engagement worthy the gentleman, the scholar, and the Christian. Actuated, I trust, by this generous, disinterested principle, I solicit your attention and candor for a few moments, while I assert and by cogent arguments demonstrate "That British America under her present circumstances *can* consistent with good policy affect to become an independent state."

I am not insensible, gentlemen, of the disadvantages under which I labor, in the present controversy, notwithstanding the goodness of my cause, for it is no secret to the wise observers of human nature, that men in their present state, however upright in their intentions, are subject to strange prepossessions, so that when one side of a question is presented to their view, and supported by the appearance of argument, they yield their assent without due examination of the contrary opinion. It is this precipitancy in the forming of judgments, that has enslaved the world with error, and dragged on the generality of mankind from age to age in ignorance —for when the mind is settled in an opinion, however ill grounded, it is no easy matter to relinquish it, and that because it carries in it an impeachment of the understanding, at which the mind of man greatly revolts.

From the constitution of human nature you see the great advantage of which my antagonist has availed himself, by being put first in the cause; neither should I think any strange thing had happened if I should have none but the philosophic and more sensible part of my audience in favor of my opinion; and these without vanity I confide, will keep me in countenance, while I unravel and show the absurdity of his sophistical reasoning.

Therefore I proceed to an examination of his thesis—and I am willing my reasonings should be tried by the rules of sound argumentation. Attending to his introduction, I was greatly pleased at the many pretty things said in praise of patriotism, a virtue which can never be too much celebrated, or too heartily recommended, and which is deservedly deemed the bulwark of society. However, I could not but be surprised to find him prefacing a discourse of that kind, with a labored panegyric on a virtue, which his whole chain of reasoning tended totally to eradicate, and which forced upon me the droll conceit of a celebrated ancient, in the introduction to his "Art of Poetry," "of joining a mare's neck to a human head." Upon his principles, one would have expected him rather to have displayed his rhetoric in preaching up the salutary doctrine of non-resistance, and positive obedience, and to have endeavored to persuade us that the Americans were like other beasts of burden formed for the use of, and obliged to be obsequious to, their European masters. But this introduction he intended as a lure, effectually to captivate the audience, that they might readily swallow the gilded pills which he had prepared for them afterwards. In short, he seems to have studied Granvillian politics, and adopted the maxims in present vogue with British ministers. This surely will not be deemed speaking reproachfully of his education. However this artifice is quite transparent, and can answer no valuable purpose in gaining his point with you, gentlemen, who weigh arguments, and can be satisfied with nothing short of evidence.

I may therefore proceed next to the stating of the question, with which I have as little cause to be displeased, upon the whole, as with his introduction. He has indeed said the reverse of what I am about to prove, and together with it many agreeable things in a very agreeable manner; but as little to his purpose, as his encomiums on patriotism. He tells us that the late taxations first suggested the thought of independence to the Americans. That the Americans have in a glorious manner defended their rights, purchased immortality, etc., etc., all which I consider as making nothing to his purpose, but weakening in fact what he had before asserted. But if he has produced anything that may merit the appellation of arguments in this case, I imagine it must be the following:—"That a fixed doom is the only just foundation of despair, and that this is not the case with America."—"That an inviolable attachment to our duty, and incessant remonstrances to the throne, will give us redress from all our present grievances." —"That we can cease to use British manufactures, and compel

Britain to a compliance."—"That we reap great advantages from her, and are indebted to her for protection."—"That it would be our ruin, if it was in our power, to break her connections." And lastly: "That an attempt to resist her would be to the last degree chimerical and frantic, and in which we cannot possibly succeed." These I think contain everything in the performance that can be imagined argumentative.

As to the first, "That a fixed doom is the only just foundation of despair, and that this is not yet our case." I would beg leave to ask the gentleman what ideas he has connected with the words "fixed doom?" The British Parliament have more than once asserted in the strongest terms, their jurisdiction over the colonies in the affair of taxation; and have given us the most convincing proof that they were in earnest, by enacting those execrable laws relative to stamps, paper, glass, etc. The ministry have put these laws into execution, in their utmost rigor, when it was in their power. They have sent ships of war, and no inconsiderable armament, to enforce obedience, which have disturbed our peaceful trade, almost beggarded the greater part of our merchants, drained our country of cash, and subjected this vast continent to the cruel illiberal insults of a few imperious crown officers whose tender mercies are cruelty. The king has approved the conduct of his Parliament and ministry, and thanked them publicly for their signal services; and all this without most dutiful remonstrances and prayers in his ear. Nay, the last intelligence from England to be relied on, informs us that the Parliament will never give up their rights of taxation, that is, their right of enslaving their fellow subjects in America. And yet our "doom is not fixed!" But if it *is* not, we need never for the future dread slavery or tyranny, from any quarter. But he says, "We must *remonstrate,* and incessantly *petition the throne* for redress." What in this respect could have been done that we have left undone? Our prayers have not only been repeated, but have breathed the spirit of loyalty and affection to his Majesty and government. They have been the united voice of millions of distressed, injured, innocent people. But what have they availed us? Nay, have we not been severely punished for praying? And that too, when our prayers have not only been materially but formally good. After all this, what has reason to hope for, from this quarter? Nothing. Surely we are hopeless, degenerate slaves. And nothing remains but that we avail ourselves of those advantages with which nature has furnished us, and boldly vindicate our liberty, or lose our lives in the glorious cause. But he has hinted at a method compelling Great Britain into an compliance, by stopping all importation, and living as much as possible independent of them. So after all his noise and parade, we are happily agreed, and are pleading for precisely the same thing; for I had not intimated, nor indeed conceived, the least desire of shedding their blood, or of hazarding the shedding of ours. Far be it from me, or any of the advocates of my cause, to desire this of even the first cruel projectors, or the malicious executors, of those infernal plans. We choose to leave them to meet their deserts at the hand of Him who hears, and who will redress the groans of the oppressed.

The next thing he has urged has the greatest appearance of argument of anything hitherto mentioned, and is, "That we are indebted to her for protection; that we have received innumerable favors from her, and cannot possibly exist without her." If all this was *fact,* I should think it worthy a serious consideration; but I imagine it is much easier to assert than to prove. What child in England does not know that about a century and a half ago, our venerable ancestors, persecuted for religion in their native land, fled for refuge to the more hospitable wilds of America; and unassisted, unsupported by Britain, felt by turns the extremities of hunger, cold, and Indian barbarity, until by their own valor, and the kind interposition of heaven, they settled themselves in a peaceful habitation of this new found world. An inheritance which they bequeathed to their posterity, they to us, and we shall again transmit to ours, if we are but followers of them, who are translated to a better country. How little protection Old England afforded to, and with what almost entire neglect she treated those infant plantations, the annals of New England sufficiently prove; until she found that by affording us protection, she could be amply repaid. This she rationally expected, and has long since found verified, by the amazing increase of her trade. It may without an hyperbole be asserted, that it is in a great measure owing to America, that the British navy rides mistress of the main, which, before the plantation of these colonies was not only inconsiderable, but despicable in the eyes of Europe. And had they failed here, the prospect of having millions of faithful slaves in America to fill their coffers with treasure, might justly be esteemed an ample compensation for their assistance. And this from her late conduct, if Britons are uniform, seems to have been in her view.

That we are absolutely dependent on England for existence has never yet been sufficiently proved to me; for if a few thousands, who first planted this country, under the care and protection of heaven, could sustain all the fierce attacks of outnumbered tribes of barbarians, instigated and aided by the power of France, what may not the vastly augmented numbers of its present inhabitants be supposed able to achieve? As to any injury which our trade could receive by this measure, it would be impossible, we need not fear being worsted. Should Britain shut her ports against us, it does not follow that Holland, France, Spain and Portugal would. On the contrary, they would welcome us as their customers, and allow us to make the advantages of our markets, of which we are now totally deprived. And who would not rather feed at a stranger's than a mother's table, provided they could find better fare and kinder treatment?

Now the last of all, the most formidable argument, comes thundering in with the roar of cannon, cries of slaughter, and all the dire images that a poetic imagination can portray. But however noisy and terrific, I will venture near and give it a candid examination. It is this:—If independent of foreign aid, we could resist Great Britain with success, this our success would prove our certain ruin; our trading towns would be laid in ashes by one volley from a British squadron; we should be utterly impoverished by maintaining a large standing army; our hands would be taken from the tillage of land; and we should be driven back into the wilderness to seek a shelter, obliged to relinquish all literary pursuits, with many more conceits too chimerical to mention. What I have already said, sufficiently confutes the most forcible part of this argument. None, however, will deny, but that our seaport towns may with ease be reduced by the British navy; and let them be destroyed if they can find their account in it. Nay, I could with pleasure behold the scene, rather than see them stand as the dear purchase of American freedom. As to a standing army, all America would compose it. Like the first founders of Rome, we should all be soldiers, and if this would not suffice to guard us against our foes, the sons of liberty from Britain's isle, nay Corsica's would come in rafts across the wide Atlantic to our aid; for thousands there are now convinced that America is the only spot on this globe that can with propriety be called free.

The objection against the tillage of the earth for subsistence seems to militate directly against the wisdom of the Creator, who planted a garden for innocent man, ordered him to dress it, and subsist on the fruits thereof. And wise and virtuous men in all ages, have been lavish in their praises of this kind of life; and that with reason, for its simplicity, and freedom from temptations to vice. Amidst his vagaries and zeal for tyranny he would feign persuade us that it is the proper nursing of literature, the very reverse of which is abundantly evident from reason and fact.

Thus have I followed my antagonist through his labored performance, weighed it in the balance, and found it wanting. And now, my countrymen, let me, as a friend to American Liberty, stand forth and exhort you to be fast and immovable in defence of your rights. Let not the menaces of a British Parliament, in the least affright, nor their fair promises deceive you, into any base compliances. *Latet anguis in herba.* Their evident design is to make us slaves. They are wresting our money from us without our consent. Do not be charmed by the fascinating sounds, Parent-State, Mother-Country, Indulgent-Parent, etc. You are convinced that these are mere words, of course, without ideas, and might as well be adopted by Normandy, Saxony, Denmark, and Sweden, as by Britain, when they are used to reconcile us to slavery, for none will deny that we derive our pedigree from them.

Their menaces might terrify and subjugate servile, timid Asiatics, who peaceably prostrate their necks to be trampled on by every bold usurper. But my auditors, you have not so learned the principles of liberty. You know liberty is your birthright, and if this is taken away, we may in part adopt the language of Micah, "What have we more?" Besides, how unreasonable is it, that this wide extended continent, formed by nature for a kingdom of its own, should pay homage to the diminutive island of Britain, but a mere speck upon this huge globe? I have, as before observed, no aversion to a friendly alliance, a close union with Britain, provided we could enjoy that liberty wherewith God has made us free. But to purchase their friendship at so dear a rate as owning them our master, is worse than madness; it is patricide. How could we answer it to posterity, who must drag out a painful life in slavery? Nay, how shall we answer it to ourselves, when the galling yoke of slavery bears heavy on our necks?

On the other hand, view the liberty, the transporting liberty of America. View millions basking in its beams, and gratefully acknowledging their obligations to the venerable names that now stand as pillars to support our rights. View America, the largest and happiest empire on earth, the land of liberty, the seat of science, the refuge of religion. But my point is gained; your countenances indicate the patriotic feelings of your breasts, and with one voice you declare that AMERICA SHALL BE FREE.

Respondent

Liberty, Sirs, is the fair offspring of heaven, the inestimable property of man. And that inconsiderate wretch who can calmly resign it to a tyrant's lust, must be lost to the genuine feelings of humanity and deserves to be stained with the blackest infamy. For tyranny is naturally brutal, untamed by reason, unawed by religion. It proceeds from the foul embraces of pride and cruelty, and from them received its commission to spread devastation and havoc wherever human nature can be found. I see the infernal monster skulking at a distance; but with horror let me say it, under the specious garb of liberty, cloaking its execrable designs with the soothing epithets of good policy. For in that fatal hour when North America affects independence, she will inevitably involve herself in the worst of slavery. This is not the wild conjecture of a distempered brain, not the brat of cowardice, but the result of mature deliberation. And notwithstanding the many objections advanced by my antagonist, to my former cogent arguments, I am still convinced that good policy is consistent with itself, and loudly proclaim the absolute necessity of an indissoluble union between Great Britain and the colonies. Let us then, for a moment, suppress the premature affectation of independence, whilst we examine a little farther, the chimerical basis on which it is founded.

As to our "doom being fixed," it is impossible for the British Parliament to make us "hopeless, desperate slaves," by imposing duties on a number of their own articles, which we are under no absolute obligation to purchase—for, as I before observed, we can either manufacture these restricted articles in our own country, or dispense with the use of them. This argument, however, my opponent has not attempted to answer, for it is indeed impossible. Therefore what has been observed with regard to America's doom, and the determinations of the Parliament is nothing at all to the purpose. But supposing they were determined to enslave us, shall we precipitate ourselves into certain destruction in order to avoid an imaginary inconvenience? This is madness. It is worse—it is suicide!

But we are informed by my antagonist, that he has no desire of shedding European blood, or of hazarding the shedding of ours. And truly we believe him. However, this is giving up the question to all intents and purposes. And indeed he expressly asserts "that after all his noise and parade, he and I are pleading for precisely the same thing." Now in the name of wonder, why has he rallied all his artillery to confound me, if possible, for embracing his sentiments? I should imagine that persons "actuated by such generous, disinterested principles," as he tells us he is, would be fond of others vindicating the truth as well as themselves. But anon we hear him talking in quite a different strain, breathing the spirit of ingratitude, declaring that we have received scarce any advantages from Great Britain—which is egregiously repugnant to known facts, and these, too, the most incontestable.

Let us view North America from her first settlement down to the present time, and we shall find Great Britain continually affording her assistance. Permitted and encouraged by her it was planted by her own sons. Guarded by her powerful arms France has endeavored in vain to encroach upon her property and freedom. Had we been totally neglected, as this gentleman would insinuate, by the British court, what must have been our melancholy fate, when exposed, weak and defenceless in ourselves, to the inveterate rage of our malignant foes? Is it not conspicuous to all, that the dim traces of our existence would have proclaimed our wretchedness? Besides we have not only been defended against the attempts of our enemy to deprive us of our habitation, but enabled, by the commanding awe of British protection, to maintain, a valuable and extensive commerce. How inconsistent, therefore, is my antagonist to assert, that our "trade would receive no possible detriment," while he fully acknowledges that our principal trading towns would be utterly laid to the ground, at sight of a British squadron. If our seaports were wrested from us, what method could be devised for the continuation of commerce? Oh! says this patron of liberty, "the ports of Holland, France, Spain and Portugal would be open to our reception." Yes, but where shall we find harbors of egress and ingress? Why truly we must betake ourselves to aerial naviga- tion, build ships specifically lighter than the atmosphere, and soar above the reach of British cannon. A fine conceit indeed; for which one might rationally imagine he was indebted to the occult science of witchcraft.

"Thunder, lightning, conflagrations and dire alarms" start up in view and fill my opponent with terror. I protest by those British heroes, those invincible warriors, who have so often drawn their swords in defence of justice, that he is not affrighted without a cause. After all his incentives to rebellion he has come at length to this conclusion, that all North America must compose a standing army, men, women, and children, without exception; and upon his own principles, cut off from commerce "we must depend entirely on the cultivation of land for subsistence," and that too, without hands to till it.

Having therefore, my indulgent auditors, examined the prin- cipal objections exhibited against my former arguments, and found nothing in them of real weight, what remains but that I entreat you to strain every nerve to perpetuate that union, which is not only the cement of interest, and a never failing source of commerce between Great Britain and her dependencies, but the very bulwark of the protestant religion. A union on which depends the fate of millions. Of millions did I say? The fate of Europe depends upon it. I beseech you, my dear countrymen, I conjure you, as you regard your own private interest, as you value the prosperity of our coun- try, as you esteem the happiness of prosperity, as you prize the blessings of liberty, as you are concerned for the cause of religion and the cause of God, banish the fatal thought of affecting to become an independent state! Adopt and prosecute such measures, and in such manner, that it will be impossible to determine whether an American's character is most distinguishable for loyalty to his sovereign, duty to his mother country, love of freedom, or affection for his native soil.

2 A DISPUTATION
on "The Legality of Enslaving the Africans."

A. My friend, the last question has suggested another; which, as it is acknowledged by all to be far from unimportant, and, in the apprehensions of many, by no means improper to be attentively considered by this people at the present day; the candor of this truly venerable, this learned and polite assembly will excuse us in attempting, in a few words, to examine, *Whether the slavery, to which Africans are in this province, by the permission of law, subjected, be agreeable to the law of nature?* And since, fully persuaded of the truth of those principles, in which is founded the idea of natural equality, to the exclusion of a right in one individual of the human species to exercise any degree of authority over another without his consent, I am obliged to appear in favor of the negative of the proposition; and since, if I rightly remember, I have sometimes heard you express a very different sentiment, if you are disposed to join in the proposal, I will first attend to what may be offered on your part in support of it. And shall therefore only observe, that the strangely inconsistent conduct of mankind, respecting this matter, furnishes us with reflections upon the present state of human nature by no means the most agreeable. To me, I confess, it is matter of painful astonishment, that in this enlightened age and land, where the principles of natural and civil Liberty, and consequently the natural rights of mankind are so generally understood, the case of these unhappy *Africans* should gain no more attention;—that those, who are so readily disposed to urge the principles of natural equality in defence of their own Liberties, should, with so little reluctance, continue to exert a power, by the operation of which they are so flagrantly contradicted. For what less can be said of that exercise of power, whereby such multitudes of our fellow-men, descendants, my friend from the same common parent with you and me, and between whom and us nature has made no distinction, save what arises from the stronger influence of the sun in the climate whence they originated, are held to groan under the insupportable burden of the most abject slavery, without one chearing beam to refresh their desponding souls; and upon whose dreary path not only the feeblest ray of hope is permitted to dawn, and whose only prospect of deliverance is—in death. If indeed the law protects their lives, (which is all that can be said even here, and more—shame to mankind!—more than can be said in some of our sister colonies, the only favor these unhappy people receive, from such protection, is a continuation of their misery; the preservation of a life, every moment of which is worse than non-existence. A favor this, no doubt, that in a very special manner demands acknowledgement!

B.   Though conscious, my friend, of my inability, the most advantageously to represent the arguments in favor of this proposition, especially when circumscribed within the narrow limits the present occasion will allow; yet clearly convinced of the propriety of attentively considering this question, especially at a period when persons of every denomination are so justly affected with a sense of Liberty, I readily comply; rather hoping that if any present, are in doubt respecting this matter, they will take occasion from hence, so fully to examine it, as to procure satisfaction to themselves, than expecting what shall be now offered on my part will have so desirable an effect.

I am well aware of the difficulty of his task who attempts to defend a proposition of this nature. An heart replete with benevolence and compassion will hardly admit reasoning that involves principles seemingly incompatible with the happiness of *any*. Suffer me therefore to entreat you, that every tender sentiment, that even the feelings of humanity may be suspended, while we calmly attend to the voice of reason, which is the voice of nature's alwise and benevolent Author.

That Liberty to all is sweet I freely own; but still 'tis what, in a state of society at least, all cannot equally enjoy, and what even in a *free* government can be enjoyed in the most perfect sense by none. Such is the nature of society, that it requires various degrees of authority and subordination; and while the universal rule of right, *the happiness of the whole,* allows greater degrees of Liberty to some, the same immutable law suffers it to be enjoyed only in less degrees by others. And though my friend, I can most cordially join with you in the benevolent wish, that it were possible that these Africans, who I am free with you to call my brethren, and to whom, it is confessed, the principles of our civil constitution allow but a small degree of liberty, might enjoy it equally with us; yet 'till I am convinced it might comport with the rule above mentioned, to allow them more I am in duty bound to appear an advocate for those principles.

Let it therefore be remembered, that the question to be considered is, *"Whether the slavery, to which Africans are in this Province, by the permission of law, subjected, be agreable to the law of nature?"*

It is, I presume, scarcely necessary to observe to you, that by the law of nature is intended that law which is the measure of all our moral actions, and by which their fitness and propriety, and consequently their justice or injustice, are to be determined. In other words, that law to which whatever action is in it's nature fit and proper, just and right, is agreeable, and to which every action of an opposite nature is disagreeable. This, then being intended by the law of nature, whether the justice of *African slavery,* if found agreeable to this law, is defensible, will be needless to inquire. But it will be said, though this definition of the law of nature be admitted, we are still to be informed what those actions are, that are agreeable to this law, and consequently right. I answer, whatever action in it's nature, concomitant circumstances being considered; tends to *happiness on the whole,* is agreeable to this law, and every action of a contrary tendency is hereunto disagreeable. And hence it will follow, that whatever practical principle of society, (which is to be considered as the action of the community) hath this tendency, is to be reputed just, and approved and adopted, and those of a contrary tendency consequently disapproved.

To demonstrate this, it will be necessary only to observe, that as nothing in nature can possibly be of the least consequence but happiness or misery, so the difference in the tendency of the practical principles of any society to the production of these, is the only thing that can possibly render some eligible, fit and proper, rather than others; and was it not for this distinction, it must forever remain a matter of perfect indifference, what practical principles were in any society adopted. But without stopping more fully to demonstrate the truth of this principle, it having been recognized as well by the generality of ethic writers, as by the wisdom of all good governments, I shall proceed to enquire, how far it will operate to the determination of the present question.

And in the first place, I shall enquire into the agreement of the law of nature with the idea of slavery *in general,* in opposition to that principle of natural equality, which is so zealously contended for by the advocates for universal Liberty.

By slavery *in general* I mean the involuntary subordination of the will of one to that of another; whereby, independent of all compact, the actions of the former are in all things to be directed by the will of the latter. Now if slavery *in general,* according to this definition, be agreeable to the law of nature, the principle of natural equality must fall, and in order to determine the question in dispute, it will be necessary only to apply the general principle to the case of the *African* subordination, whereby it will be easy to discern if there is any thing in the nature of their particular case not agreeable hereto.

I am therefore now to shew, that slavery, as above defined, is not repugnant to the law of nature, and therefore that the principle of natural equality cannot be true.

That right of authority is to be found in some being involving subordination in others, independent of all voluntary contract on the part of the subordinate, is, as far as I know, universally acknowledged. Such is the right of the Governor of the universe to govern and direct the conduct of all finite existences, and such is the right of parents to govern and direct the conduct of their children. Now if it be found, that there is the same foundation for authority and subordination among different individuals of the human species, between whom no such relations as those abovementioned do subsist, as there is for authority and subordination in those cases where it is acknowledged to be just, it will follow, that degrees of rightful authority in some, involving degrees of subordination in others, must be admitted among them likewise. In other words if the *reason* and *foundation* of the *absolute* authority of the Governor of the universe over the creation, and the *limited* authority of parents over their children, be found to operate with equal strength in favor of a right of some individuals among mankind to exercise any degrees of authority over others, the exercise of such authority must be acknowledged just, i.e. agreeable to the law of nature. And now to determine this question, it is necessary to inquire, in what the right of authority, in the cases abovementioned, is founded: And here the answer is obvious, in *the greatest good of the whole*. For since the Governor of the universe is possessed of power, wisdom, and goodness in perfection of degree, it is impossible but that the greatest happiness to the creation should be the result of his exercise of the most absolute sovereignty. And though this right of absolute authority in the Creator over his creatures be inseparable from the relation between Creator and creature, yet it is not founded simply in that relation, that is, in the idea of derived existence; but in the natural imperfection and dependance of the creature, and the natural perfection of the Creator, and the reason of the necessarily absolute subjection of the creature does not consist merely in his having *received existence,* but in his having received it from *such* a Being; a Being by the perfection of his nature qualified for the most perfect government, and under whose administration it is impossible but that the beforementioned immutable law of nature, the greatest happiness of the whole, should operate to effect. Agreeable to this is the foundation of the natural authority of parents over their children; it by no means consisting in the notion of *derived existence;* but in the different qualifications of parents and children to execute this immutable law: For while parents so far excel their children in wisdom, and from natural affection are disposed to promote their happiness, it will follow, that more happiness will result to both, from the exercise of authority in parents, and subordination in children, than from the exercise of equal Liberty in each. And that this authority of parents over their children is derived from this source, and not from the natural relation subsisting between them, considered merely as parents and offspring, is moreover evident beyond all contradiction from this consideration, that whenever the parent is by any means disqualified, in the respects before mentioned, to direct the conduct of his child, the subordination of the child ceases. If this, which I think none will deny, be a just representation of the foundation in *nature* of authority and subordination; in order to justify involuntary slavery *in general,* in opposition to the notion of *natural* equality, it is necessary only to inquire, whether among different individuals, between whom there is no such natural relation as that of parent and offspring, there be not the same reason, ground, and foundation in nature for the exercise of authority in some, necessarily involving subordination in others, which there is in cases where such relation actually subsists. And concerning this, no one surely can remain a moment undetermined, who reflects with the least degree of attention, upon the vast inequality observable between different individuals of the human species, in point of qualification for the proper direction of conduct. Now whether this inequality be considered as arising from difference in natural capacity, difference in the means of improvement, or in disposition properly to employ such means; in a word, whether it arises from nature or education, or any other supposeable quarter, it matters not, while this is in fact the case, while some are actually found so far to excel others both in respect of wisdom and benevolence, both in the knowledge of the principles of propriety, and a disposition to practice such principles, that the general end, happiness, would be better promoted by the exercise of authority in the former, though necessarily involving subordination in the latter, than by the enjoyment of equal Liberty in each, the exercise of such authority must be right, and never the less so, though the individuals by such an economy subordinated, do not consent. It is fit that children should be subjected to the authority of their parents, whether they consent to such subjection or not; this is put beyond all possibility of doubt by the express declaration of wisdom which cannot err; not to mention the consent of all ages in their approbation of the principles of those civil societies which have warranted the exercise of such authority. Every law is applicable to all cases within the same reason; and since it cannot be denied that the reason of authority and subordination between parents and children, equally applies to the support of a distinction of the same kind among others not so related, it follows inevitably, that a distinction in the latter case is equally justifiable with one in the former; they are both supported by the same principle of natural law, and therefore must stand or fall together.

I have introduced these observations upon the foundation of the authority of the Governor of the universe over the creation, and of parents over their children, for the sake of example, rather than as necessary to support the general idea of inequality: I say as necessary, for while there is so manifestly great an inequality in the capacities and dispositions of mankind to direct their own as well as the conduct of others, to its only proper end, I think it demonstrable, that the principle of absolute equality could not be supported, even though we had no argument from fact by which it might be illustrated. And in truth, I think, before the principle of absolute equality can be maintained, it must be made to appear, that all mankind, in point of capacity and disposition to conduct properly, are equal.

It now remains only to apply these general principles to the particular case of *Africans* in this country, and see what degree of authority the people here are thereby warranted to exercise over them; and if it shall appear in fact, that they are not reduced by the law of this land to a degree of subordination beyond what the law of nature abovementioned, the happiness of both, requires, it will follow undeniably, that the law by which they are thus subjected is just.

A. Before you proceed to the application you mention, permit me to make an observation, that perhaps may render such application unnecessary. I think you have by no means supported the idea of slavery *in general;* but that your argument in favour of natural inequality, though ingeniously enough conducted, is manifestly inconclusive, and that the contrary, notwithstanding all you have alledged, may still be true. For though I acknowledge, that in every society the practical principle that in it's operation tends to the greatest happiness of the whole is right, i. e. agreeable to the law of nature, and that the *absolute* authority of the Governor of the universe, and the *limited* authority of parents over their children is founded in the reason you alledge; and also admit, among different individuals, all those different degrees of qualification for the proper direction of conduct for which you contend; yet that the natural right of independence is hence excluded, and the principle of natural equality consequently overthrown is by no means acknowledged. The reason is obvious, that the principle for which you contend is in the nature of things utterly impracticable; your conclusion therefore, from premises implying a false hypothesis, cannot be admitted.

The exercise of authority, only in cases where such exercise is productive of happiness, is undoubtedly right: But such is the constitution of things with regard to man, such his nature, state, and condition, as renders it absolutely impossible that a principle, warranting the exercise of authority in any particular case, independent of the consent of the subordinate, should be correspondent to this end. And for this good reason, that it is impossible for human wisdom to distinguish the cases where the exercise of such authority would be proper, from those where it would not be so; and could this be effected, it would still be utterly impossible for any *practical principle* of society, for any human *law* to make the distinction. The same law which would warrant the exercise of authority in one case, must of necessity warrant it in another; unless it could be suppoˆsed, that some infallible judge could be present at all times, and in all places, and direct the operation of law in every particular case. And were even this possible, it might still be doubted whether the principle of natural equality would be overthrown. Such are the weaknesses and imperfections, the passions and prejudices of the best of men, and so deeply are all impressed with a sense of Liberty and independence, that it may well be questioned, whether a law, warranting authority in those cases only where it would be most proper, were such law possible, would operate more to the general happiness, than a law establishing the principle of natural equality: For tho' in that case, many would conduct less foolishly than they now do; yet the idea of servitude, and dependence upon the will of another, would be a perpetual, and not unfruitful source of misery. But whatever might be the effect of such a constitution, since that is confessedly impossible, it is evident beyond all contradiction, that the principle of natural equality is infinitely better adapted to the general end, happiness, than any other practical principle that can possibly be established. Hence I think it is manifest, notwithstanding the plausible appearance of your reasoning in theory, since it will not endure the true touchstone of practice, that slavery, which many to their cost know to be a practical thing, is far from being supported thereby.

Your notion of the ground and foundation of natural authority, in the examples you have adduced, is undoubtedly just, and consent in those cases, is by no means necessary to subordination, but, unfortunately for your conclusion, the cases are far from being applicable to the point in hand: For as in one case, perfection of wisdom and goodness excludes the possibility of error, and renders the most perfect subjection necessarily best; so the principle of affection implanted by the Author of nature in the breast of the parent, inspiring such a tender concern for the welfare of his offspring, and so strongly operative to the production of kind offices towards him, together with the natural inability of the child, through weakness or inexperience, to be his own director, may well warrant a general rule of limited subordination in the other. And when you have shewn me the man, or number of men, capable of infallibly directing the conduct of others, the exercise of authority in them, shall not want my approbation. And when you shall point out to me any classes of men, between whom there is such a com-

parative difference in point of ability for the proper direction of
conduct, as between parents and children, and the *same* disposition
in the superior towards an inferior, that the Author of nature has
implanted in the hearts of parents towards their children, I will
readily acknowledge the exercise of a like degree of authority justifiable by the law of nature.

But I am much at a loss to conceive how your reasoning in
favor of slavery *in general,* were it ever so fully conclusive, could
possibly justify us in thus forcibly subjugating the *Africans,* between
whom and us nature seems to have made no such difference as that,
upon which you suppose the notion of *natural inequality* to be
founded: For I suppose you will hardly imagine the darkness of a
man's skin incapacitates him for the direction of his conduct, and
authorises his neighbours, who may have the good fortune of a
complexion a shade or two lighter, to exercise authority over him.
And if the important difference does not lay here, it seems not very
easy to determine where it does; unless perchance, it be in the
quality of their hair; and if the principle of subordination lies here,
I would advise every person, whose hair is inclined to deviate from
a right line, to be upon his guard. If indeed any should alledge,
that they are distinguished by the flatness of their noses, I can't
but think this circumstance against them, for if a man is to be led
and governed by the nose, it may well be questioned, whether a nose
of a different figure would not be better adapted to the purpose.

B. My friend, I am no enemy to humour, but I think it rarely
serves to illustrate a logical conclusion. I confess my argument,
as you have represented it, appears ridiculous enough; but if you
had deferred your reply till I had made an application of the principle to the point in hand, perhaps it would have saved you this
needless expence of wit. I have not pretended, as a consequence
from my principles, that every degree of superiority in point of
discretion would warrant to any individual of a community a right
to exercise authority over his neighbour: I have only contended,
that the notion of *equality,* in the strict sense, had no foundation
in nature; but as happiness is the only end of action, so superiority
in wisdom, goodness, &c. is in the nature of things a proper foundation of authority. And as nature has made differences among
creatures in these respects; so it is fit and proper, and agreeable
to nature's law, that different degrees of authority in point of
direction of conduction should be exercised by them; and that in
some cases, even among the human species, this difference is so
important, as to render the exercise of authority justifiable, even
without the consent of the governed: For this I have produced an
example from fact, in the case of parents and children. All this you
have implicitly allowed. I now go on to say, as a consequence from

the same acknowledged principle, that whenever such a connection of things takes place, that any number of men cannot, consistently with the good of the whole, have a residence in any community but in a state of involuntary subordination, and that their residence in such community notwithstanding such subordination, be in fact best for the whole, such subordination, though involuntary, is no violation of the law of nature; but on the contrary to all intents and purposes correspondent thereto. This is a true conclusion from premises incontestible, principles universally acknowledged, and which you yourself have but now admitted. Subordination in this case comes fully within the reason of the subordination of children, rests on precisely the same foundation, and is therefore justifiable on precisely the same principles. For whether the necessity of such subordination arises from natural incapacity, or from any other quarter, it matters not, if this is in fact the case; if the interest of the whole does require it; let the causes or reasons of such require-ment be what they may, such subordination is equally justifiable as in any other case whatever; not only in the case of children, but even in the case of consent; for the obligation to fulfil contracts; which obligation is ultimately founded in the good of society.

Now fully within this predicament lies, as I conceive, the particular case of *Africans* in this country. That it is only a state of limited subordination (I say *limited,* for it is to be remembered, that the authority of those to whom they are subordinate, is re-stricted by the superior authority of law, to which we are all sub-ordinate, and which provides that they, as well as other, shall be treated according to the general principles of humanity) that these people can *consistently* enjoy a residence among us is, I suppose, acknowledged by all. And whether it is not better for them to reside here, notwithstanding such subordination, even regard being had to *their* interest only, than in their native country, no one can doubt, at least no one, who has a tolerably adequate conception of their misery, and wretchedness there. Figure to yourself my friend, you are not unacquainted with *African* history; figure to yourself the delightful situation of a natural inhabitant of *Africa*. View him necessarily destitute of every means of improvement in social vir-tue, of every advantage for the cultivation of those principles of humanity, in which alone consists the dignity of the rational nature, and from which only source springs all that pleasure, that happiness of life, by which the human species is distinguished from the other parts of the animal creation. Consider his situation as a candidate for an eternal existence; view him as necessarily ignorant of every principle of that religion, through the happy influence of which alone the degenerate race of Adam can rationally form the most distant expectation of future felicity. View him moreover in a state of the most abject slavery, a slavery of the worst kind, a slavery

of all others most destructive of human happiness—an entire subjection of the tyrannizing power of lust and passion—wholly devoted to the governing influence of those irregular propensities,
which are the genuine offspring of depraved nature, when unassisted by philosophy or religion. Behold him actually clothed in
all that brutal stupidity, that savage barbarity which naturally
springs from such a source. Add to this, his condition of perpetual
insecurity, arising from the state of hostility and war that forever
rages in those inhospitable climes; and consider the treatment he
is to expect, whom the fortune of war has subjected to the power
of his enraged foe, whose natural cruelty is perpetually sharpened,
and whose desire of revenge is continually cherished, by a sense of
his own danger. Reflect, I say, a moment upon the condition of a
creature in human shape, (for in such a state of degradation one
can hardly call him a man) the misery, the wretchedness of whose
situation is by these expressions but faintly represented; and compare it with the condition of a slave in this country; and then see,
if you can hesitate one moment, which of the two is most eligible.
If peradventure a doubt should arise, if you will please to enquire,
whether you would rather choose one, for whose prosperity you
was tenderly concerned, should be educated in *Africa,* with all the
immunities of a native *African,* or in this country, though in that
state of subordination, to which *Africans* are here subjected, I will
venture to warrant you of every such doubt a speedy resolution.

Here then I rest the argument, for upon this point the present
question must infallibly determine. Notwithstanding all the uneasiness attending subordination, and all the miseries to which an
African is exposed in his removal from his native country; while
his condition here is so much more eligible than his condition there,
his removal is to be esteemed a favor: And the constitution of our
government, whereby such removal is countenanced and encouraged, is by no means to be esteemed reprehensible. It is in vain
to alledge here the want of consent on his part. It is evident from
the reasoning above, that consent, in order to subjection, is necessary in those cases only where the end of authority, the greatest
possible good, cannot be promoted without it: But who I beseech
you, ever thought the consent of a child, an ideot, or a madman
necessary to his subordination? Every whit as immaterial is the
consent of these miserable *Africans,* whose real character seems
to be a compound of the three last mentioned. What can avail his
consent, who through ignorance of the means necessary to promote his happiness, is rendered altogether incapable of choosing
for himself? And as the consent of such a being could by no means
involve subordination in a case where it would be otherwise improper, so the want of it can be no bar in a case where it would not.
In all such cases it is undoubtedly the duty of those, whom provi-

dence has favored with the means of improvement in understanding, and the wisdom resulting from such improvement, to make use of their discretion in directing the conduct of those who want it.

I am sensible that I have already dwelt too long upon this argument; you will however in this connexion, permit me to add, that were involuntary subjection, in all cases, contrary to the law of nature, it is impossible to suppose, that the Governor of the universe, whose wisdom is infinite, and whose will is eternally and immutably coincident with, and *when revealed to us, the measure* of, this law, should ever have expressly tolerated it in any particular instance. I mention this in the present connexion, the rather because I suppose the authority, the Israelites, when under a government absolutely theocratical, were permitted to exercise over strangers, was founded in the same reason with the authority, for which I contend, viz: that it was better for them to reside among a people, where they might have some opportunity for improvement in knowledge and virtue, though in a state of subordination, than to remain amongst the barbarous and idolatrous nations, whence they originated.

Were it necessary or expedient, it would be easy to shew, by comparison, in a great variety of instances not mentioned, the superiority of a slave in this country, in point of condition, to a natural inhabitant of *Africa.* And though it be too true, that these unhappy creatures are, in many particular cases, cruelly treated, yet, while their importation is to them a redemption from a condition on the whole so much more miserable, we must, as I said before, justify the government in tolerating such importation; and with regard to the particular instances of abuse, we can only say *caveant qui sunt conscii.*

I have omitted the right, sometimes pretended to be derived from purchase, because I look upon the argument to be trifling. For though right of authority, if it be well founded, be possibly, in some cases, transferable, yet it is well known, that all the authority any one of these miserable creatures can pretend to over another, is founded merely in the fortune of a brutal, savage war, conducted without the lest regard, on either side, to any principles of equity, justice, or national honor; and for the right of authority so founded I have no disposition to contend. But I think there is much more in their argument who contend that, by the purchase of these victims, their lives are preserved, which would otherwise undoubtedly be sacrificed to the cruelty of the captors. For though I am sensible, that to this is commonly replied, that the custom of purchasing captives is a perpetual source of war; yet if we consider that a people, so inhumanly savage as to dispose of their nearest relations for baubles, can never want matter of discord; and that, was it not for the advantages in this way made of them, the captives would generally perish, we shall have no reason to doubt whether the custom of purchasing may in this way be considered as a favor.

On the whole, since it is evident beyond all controversy, that the removal of the *Africans,* from the state of brutality, wretchedness, and misery, in which they are at home so deeply involved, to this land of light, humanity, and christian knowledge, is to them so great a blessing; however faulty any individuals may have been in point of unnecessary cruelty, practiced in this business; yet, whether the general state of subordination here, which is a necessary consequence of their removal, be agreeable to the law of nature, can by no means longer remain a question.

A. Notwithstanding all you have so ingeniously alledged in support of this question, I am still obliged to confess myself one of those in whom your reasoning has failed to produce conviction: And must be excused in saying that the justice of slavery *generally* understood, is still, for aught I am able to discern, far from being supported. It is true the Israelites when under a theocratical government were permitted, under certain circumstances, to exercise authority over strangers resident among them. And this is adduced as an argument, infallibly conclusive in favor of slavery. But is it certain that this conclusion is not drawn a little too hastily?

The Governor of the universe has, in a certain instance, expressly tolerated slavery. Nothing was ever by him tolerated but what was agreeable to the law of nature. Therefore, Slavery is lawful. The man must have a very extraordinary talent who can deduce this conclusion from such premises. It is readily granted, that thus much may be justly inferred from them, viz. that such a particular connexion of things *once* took place, as rendered slavery, under the *express permission* of the Governor of the universe, lawful. But will it follow from hence, that slavery is ever lawful *without such permission?* As well may we infer a right, by the law of nature, to put any who are unable to resist our power, under harrows and axes of iron, and in a word, make the *particular* precept in any case, given the *Israelites,* a measure, whereby to explain those *general* laws of nature, which are to regulate the conduct of *all mankind.* It is undoubtedly true, that every express declaration of the Governor of the universe is agreeable to, and justly explanatory of, the law of nature, as far as such declaration extends: And the conduct of any particular person, or people, which is agreeable to such declaration is most certainly right; but it can never be certainly inferred from hence, that a like conduct in others, not having the same warrant, is agreeable to this law: For the imperfection of human wisdom renders it forever uncertain, whether the cases are in all respects similar; and consequently, it can never be *certainly* determined, that the same conduct will, in both cases, have the same natural tendency to happiness; and hence the same conduct, that in the former case was right, *may* in the latter, be wrong. But could even this be ascertained, there would still remain an insuperable difficulty in determining the actions of one people to be right, *merely* from an express toleration of the same, or like actions in another: And this arises *solely* from the *want* of such toleration. If it be objected, that an action, in it's nature unfit, could not be tolerated; it may be answered, that the same action, *when so expressly* authorised, may be fit and proper, and in its nature right, which *without such toleration,* would not be so; and for this plain reason, that the same action, when by rightful authority permitted, may have on the whole a tendency to happiness, which without such permission, would have an opposite tendency.

If this reasoning be just (the validity of which, I am happily too well acquainted with your knowledge of the principles of argumentation, to doubt whether you will dispute) how far the lawfulness of the practice of slavery among the Israelites, when expressly tolerated by the Governor of the universe, will justify people in a like practice, to whom no such toleration has ever been granted, is by no means difficult to discern. And before the principle of natural equality can be overthrown, the tendency of slavery to the good of mankind, must, by arguments drawn from *the nature and constitution of things,* be made *evidently* to appear.

I have no disposition to contend for the support of principles not founded in sufficient reason; was I convinced, that the principle of natural equality, *universally* understood, was not founded in the general good of mankind, notwithstanding the consent of philosophers in all ages, I would readily give it up. And was I persuaded, that the practice of enslaving *Africans,* as tolerated in this province, was consonant to this end, I should no longer doubt of it's propriety: But unhappily for my apprehension this is far from being the case.

Was it possible to consider this case as standing alone, independent of it's connexions with practices of a like kind in other places, and the more extensive influence it may consequently have upon the happiness of mankind, it is at least doubtful if it would then be right. I am ready to allow, that was it *certain* that their condition here is happier on the whole, than in their own country, your premises, in this *independent view* of the matter, would well warrant your conclusion; but even this I apprehend is far from being true. You have represented the misery and wretchedness of these people in their native land, in a light indeed disagreeable enough: But I am still disposed from my apprehension of the dignity of the rational nature, at least to hope that your colouring is a little too strong; and that notwithstanding the unhappy state of degradation into which they are confessedly sunk, they are still some degrees

above brutes. It is acknowledged that they are extremely unacquainted with the politer arts, and almost wholly ignorant of every
thing belonging to science, and consequently strangers to all the
pleasures of a scholar and a philosopher; they are also confessedly
destitute of an acquaintance with the principles of urbanity and consequently want, in a great measure, the happiness resulting from a
well regulated civil society; their condition is allowedly not greatly
different from a state of nature; though it is to be remembered,
that if modern writers of the best reputation are to be credited,
their manners, in most parts of that extensive country, are far less
savage and barbarous; their conveniences and enjoyments much more
numerous, and in a word their manner of life much more agreeable
than has been heretofore represented. And indeed it is not to be
wondered that those who have been disposed to make a gain by this
iniquitous practice of enslaving their fellow men, should be careful,
for their justification, to represent them as nearly upon a level with
the brute creation as possible; not to mention the ridiculous attempts
that have, in this view, been made to prove them actually of another
species. But granting their condition to be, as in fact it is, comparatively low; that their sources of happiness, when compared with
those which the members of a well-ordered civil society enjoy, are
few; yet it is not to be forgotten, that their appetites and desires
are in some good measure proportional. *Nemo desiderat quae ig-
norat.* The benevolent author of our being has accommodated our
natural desires in a great measure to the *natural* means of gratification. And he who attentively considers the anxious and perplexing
cares; the fatiguing and often fruitless labors; the cravings of
unnatural appetites; the frequently disappointed views and expectations; and, in a word, the various and almost innumerable *new*
sources of infelicity *naturally,* and many of them *inseparably* connected with what is commonly called a state of civilization, will
perhaps perceive that the difference, in point of *real* happiness,
between the scholar, the courtier, and the simple child of nature,
is far from infinite. But allowing it to be very considerable, allowing
that the privileges and advantages of a *free* member, of a *free
society,* where useful sciences and the liberal arts are patronized and
flourish, and where all those principles that beautify and adorn the
rational nature are cultivated, are comparatively very great: What,
I beseech you has all this to do with the present question? What
advantage is all the learning of this country to those ignorant
wretches, who are now practising their ludicrous gambols on yonder
common, except indeed that it generally procures them one day in
the year, a dispensation from the severity of their servitude—What
is all our boasted acquaintance with science and the politer arts to
these miserable creatures, who, by their situation, have little more
concern in these matters than their brethren in the middle regions

of *Africa;* and which knowledge, could they obtain it, must serve only to increase their misery? What a blessing, for example, would a knowledge of the principles of civil Liberty be to a person perpetually doomed to a state of the most abject slavery? In their native country, though their condition be indeed contemptible enough, they have the blessing of *Liberty* to sweeten every pleasure, and give a relish to every enjoyment: But here, though their condition were in other respects much more favourable than it is, while conscious of perpetual and absolute dependance upon the will of others, this reflection, so opposite to the strong sense of Liberty implanted in the heart of every son of Adam, must necessarily mar the happiness of every gratification, effectually chill the sense of pleasure, and stop every natural source of felicity. A keen excruciating sense of liberty forever lost must still predominate, till, the spirit broken by the fatigue of incessant distress, they sink into a state of lifeless insensibility. And then for sooth we are presently disposed to tax them with natural stupidity; and make the very thing that our unnatural treatment has occasioned the ground of our justification. It is well known, that stupidity is by no means the natural characteristic of these people; and when we consider the nature of their condition in this country, how miserably dejected, depressed and despised, instead of marking their want of apprehension, we ought rather to admire that there are any the least appearances of sensibility remaining in them.

But it is alledged, "that at home they are in a perpetual state of war, and that by the purchase of captives many lives are preserved, that would otherwise be devoted to destruction." Surprizing indeed; that here, as in the former case, the very evil that this practice has occasioned should be alledged in excuse of it! One must have a favourable opinion indeed of that cause which needs the support of such arguments! These people are naturally peaceable, and less inclined to acts of hostility that the generality of mankind; the nature of their climate disposing rather to the softer pleasures, than the fiercer passions. This though long smothered is now a truth well known; and 'tis astonishing that the patience with which they endure the cruellest servitude, should not, long e're this time have rectified this mistake. But I may not enlarge here; the absurdity of this argument is too glaring to justify a serious confutation.

It is also alledged, that "in their own country they are unnecessarily ignorant of the principles of our holy religion." This indeed, generally understood, is confessedly a melancholy truth. The advantages they enjoy from revelation are not to be mentioned. Those feeble rays of nature's light which the fatal apostacy of our original parents has happily left unextinguished in their posterity, are their almost only guide: And the insufficiency of these, for the purposes of moral direction, is confessedly but too evident from the ignorance of those, who are unhappily favored with no other directors. But admitting this to be the case, that the advantages enjoyed by this people, of a religious nature, are extremely small; before an argument can be hence derived in favor of their removal to this country, it must be shewn that the advantages they here enjoy are greater. But if we examine the religious advantages of slaves in this country, I fear we shall find, to the dishonor of our profession, that they are not greatly superior to those of their brethren in *Africa,* at least the excess will fall far short of an equivalent for the excess of their misery.

It is true, that in most parts of *New-England,* slaves are some-times permitted to attend public worship, but how much is to be expected from this, without the addition of private instruction, which heaven knows is but sparingly afforded them, their acquaint-ance in general with the principles of christianity abundantly demon-strates. And if we consider their opportunities of instruction, in connexion with fixed prejudices against a religion, whose professors they naturally consider as avowedly violating one of the plainest laws of nature; and add to this, the strong temptations they are under, from the nature of their condition, to every species of iniquity, we shall hardly expect to find in them more of the spirit of true *practical* religion, than is to be found in those who never heard of the gospel. And whether this is not in fact generally the case, is by no means a question to those who are acquainted with them. But admitting the possibility that some individuals, may be benefited in this way; shall this be alledged as an equivalent for all the miseries to which these people are, by this practice, inevitably subjected, for the sure and certain destruction to which such multitudes are hereby devoted? As well may the design of propagating christian knowledge, be al-ledged in excuse of the shocking cruelties practised on the miserable Americans, by their merciless destroyers, the Spaniards and Portu-guese. Thus we see this formidable argument turns out upon ex-amination, not less deficient than those aforementioned; and this practice of enslaving our fellow men, though considered in this in-dependent view, notwithstanding all that can be alledged, must be acknowledged altogether unjustifiable.

But we must not stop here: Upon your own principles, we must consider this practice *in all its connexions*; we must not only regard the evils of slavery in *this* country, but must take in also the miseries and calamities that are by this means brought upon *any* of the human race. Before this practice can be justified, it must appear to be pro-ductive of *general* happiness; it must correspond with the general good of the *whole.* Now if we consider the practice of slavery in this country, it's tendency to countenance and encourage the same thing, as it is practised in the southern colonies, and West-Indies, it will appear much more glaringly iniquitous and unjust. Several hundred thousands of those unhappy creatures, are, by the best information, annually exported from the various parts of *Africa* to *America,* a great proportion of whom, thro' the shocking, the unparalleled sufferings of transportation, miserably perish on the voyage, and as to those who unhappily survive, to enter upon that state of perpetual servitude, to which they are destined, it is well known, that they are treated with less humanity, more merciless severity, and savage barbarity, than reason would warrant us to exercise towards the meanest of the brute creation. It would wring drops of blood from an heart of adamant to relate the cruel sufferings of these unhappy people, in those countries, who, at the same time, have less advantages for christian knowledge, than the natives of California, or the inhabitants of the antarctic circle. But I forbear—The person that can imagine the practice of slavery in this country, considered in all it's consequences, connexions and tendencies, productive of the happiness of mankind, must, I think, allow, that the direct way to encrease their happiness is by every possible means to encrease their misery.

B. As you have not now disputed the truth of the principle, but joined with me in resting the argument upon a matter of fact, I shall no farther pursue the dispute, but leave that point to be determined by the judgment of others.

Lecture V. On Eloquence

John Witherspoon

John Witherspoon, American educator and father of American Presbyterianism, was born in Yester, Scotland, February 5, 1723. He was educated at the University of Edinburgh, and held several pastorates in Scotland before he came to the United States in 1768 to assume the presidency of Princeton College. He despised any point of view which contained intellectual abstraction or subtlety. He particularly opposed Berkleyanism, which was popular in so many American circles, and eradicated it from Princeton. He was a strict empiricist, and is described as a founder of the philosophy of "common sense," which long dominated American thinking.

At the outbreak of the American Revolution he gave strong support to the colonies, despite his original position that the clergy should stay out of politics. He became a delegate from New Jersey to the Continental Congress, and was in Congress almost continuously from 1776 to 1782. He did much writing in support of the Revolution. He was a signer of the Declaration of Independence and the Articles of Confederation. He was one of the leaders of the Popular Party of the Presbyterian Church.

When he returned to his post at Princeton, he broadened the area of its curriculum, making of the college a place for training for civil leadership, rather than a purely theological institution.

Witherspoon was blind the last two years of his life and died on his farm near Princeton on November 15, 1794.

When the Reverend John Witherspoon, newly appointed President of the College of New Jersey, arrived in Princeton on August 12, 1768, the village consisted of only fifty crude houses strung along the high road and a campus composed of one general purpose building and the president's house. The building was Nassau Hall, newly constructed, and destined to be the first of three that were to be built on this same spot. A severely plain stone structure 176 feet long and 54 feet deep, it contained a basement and 3 stories. It was surmounted by a low belfry. Inside were dormitory rooms which would accommodate 147 students, classrooms, and a chapel. This "prayer hall," cool in summer and ice cold in winter, was the largest room in the building. Opposite a low gallery running along the north side of the hall was the rostrum, surmounted by a lifesize portrait of George II. It was from this rostrum that President Witherspoon presented his lectures on the Scriptures, on History, and on the "Eloquence of the Pulpit and the Bar." In addition he lectured on rhetorical theory, largely in the classical tradition, expressing a point of view that was to be followed closely by Chauncey Goodrich some years later. Not himself an accomplished speaker, Witherspoon had a "disappointing voice," a marked Scottish

44

accent, and a reputation that "here was a man who did not speak save when he had something worth saying."

The text of "Lecture V. On Eloquence" is taken from *The Works of Rev. John Witherspoon*. Philadelphia: William W. Woodward, 1800, pp. 406–13.

HAVING given you a short view of language in general, if it were not too long, I would consider the structure of particular languages; instead of which, take the few following short remarks.

1] The nature of things necessarily suggests many of the ways of speaking which constitute the grammar of a language, and in every language there is nearly the same number of parts of speech, as they are enumerated in the Latin grammar; noun, pronoun, verb, participle, adverb, preposition, interjection, conjunction.

2] In the use of these, there is a very great variety. Nouns to be sure, are declined nearly the same way in all by cases and numbers, though the Greeks in this differ a little, using three numbers, instead of two, having a particular inflection of the word, when there are but two persons meant; and another for the plural or more; but in the verbs, there is a very great diversity; in the active and passive signification they generally agree, but some express the persons by terminations, and some by pronouns and nominatives expressed. Some have modes which others have not. The Greeks have an optative mood; the Latins have gerunds; the Hebrews with fewer differences of moods, have conjugations that carry some variety of signification to the same word. In one word *maser,* he delivered, there is not only this and its passive, but another, he delivered diligently, and the passive; another, he made to deliver; another, he delivered himself. The Greeks, besides the active and passive, have a *media vox,* of which perhaps the use is not now fully understood; since some of the best grammarians say it signifies doing a thing to one's self; *Tupsomai* I shall strike myself. Most of the modern languages decline their verbs, not by inflection of the termination, as the Greek and Latin, but by auxiliary verbs, as the English and French. The Chinese language is perhaps the least improved of any language that has subsisted for any time; this probably is owing to their want of alphabetical writing; every word among them had a character peculiar to it, so that letters and words were the same in number in their language; this rendered it of immense difficulty to understand their writing among themselves, and quite impossible to foreigners: but they were vastly surprised to find, that the Jesuits from Europe, that came among them, could easily write their language by our alphabet: and as they use the same word in different tones, for different meanings, these fathers also soon found a way of distinguishing these in writing by certain marks and accents placed over the word, differing as it was to be differently taken.

3] Some have amused themselves, with inventing a language, with such a regular grammar as might be easily understood, and having this language brought into general use. We have a remark of this kind, in Father Lami's rhetorique, in French, and he says the grammar of the Tarter language come nearest to it. We have also had some schemes and propositions of this kind in English, but it seems wholly chimerical. I shall only observe further, that some few have imagined that the Hebrew language itself was originally, and when compleat, a perfect language, and that we now have it only maimed, and but a small part of it. These suppose the language to be generated thus, by taking the letters of the alphabet, and first going through them regularly by two, and then by three, *ab, ag, ad, etc. aba, abb, etc.* All these schemes are idle, because no person can possibly lay down rules before-hand, for every thing that may hereafter be thought and spoken, and therefore, when they are brought out, they will be expressed as those to whom they first occur shall incline, and custom will finally fix them, and give them their authority.

Leaving these things therefore, as matters of more curiosity than use, I proceed to speak of eloquent speech, and its history as an art. It is plain, that in the progress of society and the commerce of human life, it would soon appear that some spoke with more grace and beauty, and so as more to incline the hearers to their sentiments, than others; neither is it hard to perceive that it would be early in repute. In the first associations of mankind, they must have been chiefly governed by those who had the power of persuasion. In uncultivated societies, it is so still: In an Indian tribe, the sachem or wise man directs their councils. The progress of oratory towards perfection, must have been evidently in fact, like the progress of all other human arts, gradual, and in proportion to the encouragement given to its exercise. It prevailed, where the state of things and constitution of government favored it, but not otherwise.

It is to be observed here, that by the consent of all, and by the memorials of antiquity that are left, poetry was more ancient than oratory; or perhaps we may rather say, that the first exertions of genius in eloquent expression were in poetry, not in prose. It has frequently been made matter of critical inquiry, why poetry was prior to oratory, and why sooner brought to perfection? I do not perceive very clearly, what great advantage there is in determining this question, supposing we should hit upon the true reasons: one reason I take to be, that the circumstance in poetry that gives generally the highest pleasure, viz. a strong and vigorous fancy, is least indebted to application, instruction or time for its perfection: therefore poetical productions in general, and that species of them in

particular which have most of that quality, must be as easily produced in uncultivated times, as any other; and for some reasons
given in a former discourse, must appear then with the greatest
effect. Whereas, to success in oratory, some knowledge of the human
heart, and even some experience in the ways of men, is necessary.
Another difference is plain; poetical productions having generally
pleasure or immediate entertainment as their design, may produce
that effect in any age; whereas the circumstances that rendered the
orator's discourse interesting, are all gone.

Perhaps to this we may add, that the incitements to poetry are
more general. A poet pleases and obtains fame from every single
person who reads or hears his productions; but an assembly, business, and an occasion are necessary to the orator. This last is likewise
limited in point of place and situation. Oratory could not thrive in
a state where arbitrary power prevails, because then there is nothing left for large assemblies and a diffusive public to determine;
whereas poetry is pleasing to persons under any form of government whatever.

Those who have given the history of oratory have rather given
us the history of the teachers of that art than its progress and
effects. It must be observed, however, that in this as well as in poetry,
criticism is the child and not the father of genius. It is the fruit
of experience and judgment, by reflection upon the spontaneous
productions of genius. Criticism inquires what was the cause of things
being agreeable, after the effect has been seen. Ward brings a
citation from Cicero, to show that the orator's art was older than
the Trojan war. The purport of this is that Homer attributes force to
Ulysses' speeches, and sweetness to Nestor's; perhaps also he has
characterised Menelaus' manner as simple, short and unadorned.
There is not, however, any certainty in this art being much studied or
explained in these early times from this citation; for though Homer
is an excellent poet, of inimitable fire and great strength of natural
judgment, it is not certain that he kept so perfectly to propriety,
as to describe only the manner and style of things at the time of the
Trojan war, which was 250 years before his own. I should be more
apt to conclude that he had described manners, characters, and
speakers as they were in his own time, with a little air of antiquity.

We are, however, told by Pausanias, that the first school of
oratory in Greece was opened in the school of Theseus, the age
preceding that war. If there be any certainty in this, its being taught
in Greece has been very ancient indeed; but these being fabulous
times, it is scarcely to be depended upon. However, it is certain that
oratory flourished early, and was improved greatly in Greece. Many
circumstances concurred to produce this effect. The spirit and capacity of the people—the early introduction of letters—but chiefly
their political situation—the freedom of their states—the frequency

of public assemblies—and the importance of their decisions. There is much said of the spirit and capacity of the Greeks for all the arts, and to be sure their climate, so serene and temperate, might have all the effect that a climate can have: but I reckon the two other causes much more considerable. The introduction of letters is necessary to the improvement and perfection of a language, and as they were early blessed with that advantage, they had the best opportunity of improving. However, the last cause of all is much more powerful than both the former, though perhaps literature is necessary to be joined with it to produce any great effect. As to some of the other arts, particularly painting and statuary, an eminent modern critic says, the Greeks could not but excel, because they, of all others, had the best images from nature to copy. He says that the games in Greece, in which the best formed bodies for agility and strength in the whole country were seen naked, and striving and exerting themselves to the very utmost, must have presented to persons of genius originals to draw from, such as in most other nations never are to be seen. If this remark is just in the other arts, the influence of eloquence in the public assemblies of these free states must have had a similar effect in the art of speaking.

The art of speaking in Greece, however, does not seem to have risen high till the time of Pericles, and he is said to have been so powerful an orator that he kept up his influence in the city as much by his eloquence as tyrants did by their power. There is a passage of Cicero, which seems to say that he was the first who prepared his discourses in writing, and some have been simple enough to believe that he read them; but nothing can be a more manifest mistake, because action or pronunciation was by all the ancients considered as the great point in oratory. There were to be seen in Cicero and Quintilian's times, orations said to be of Pericles; but both these great orators seem to be of opinion that they were not his, because they did not at all seem to come up to the great fame of his eloquence. Mr. Bayle, a very eminent critic says justly that these great men might be mistaken in that particular; for a very indifferent composition may be the work of a very great orator. The grace of elocution and the power of action might not only acquire a man fame in speaking, but keep up his influence in public assemblies. Of this we have two very great British examples, Mr. Whitefield in the pulpit, and Mr. Pitt in the senate.

After Pericles there were many great orators in Greece, and indeed all their statesmen were orators till the time of Demosthenes, when the Grecian eloquence seems to have attained its perfection. The praises of this great speaker are to be so generally met with, that I shall not insist upon them at all, further than reminding you, that though no doubt eminently qualified by nature, he needed and received great improvement from art.

The Roman eloquence was of much shorter duration. It is true that the Roman state being free, and the assemblies of the people having much in their power, it seems, according to the principles we have gone upon, that public speaking must have been in esteem; but there is something peculiar. The Romans were for many ages a plain, rough, unpolished people. Valor in war was their idol, and therefore though to be sure from the earliest times the assemblies must have managed in their deliberations by their speakers, yet they were concise and unadorned, and probably consisted more of telling them their story, and showing their wounds which was of frequent practice among them, than any artful or passionate harangues. The first speakers of any eminence we read of in the Roman history, were the Gracchi. Cicero I believe makes little mention even of them. Anthony and Crassus were the first celebrated orators among the Romans, and they were but in the age immediately before Cicero himself, and from his time it rather fell into decay.

I have said above that genius and excellence was before criticism. This is very plain; for though we read of schools and rhetoricians at different times and places, these are considered by the great masters as persons quite contemptible. Of this kind there is a remarkable passage in Cicero in his *Brutus*. At hunc (speaking of Pericles) non declamator, etc. The first just and truly eminent critic in Greece was Aristotle, who flourished as late as the time of Demosthenes. And Cicero himself was the first eminent critic among the Romans. Aristotle has laid open the principles of eloquence and persuasion as a logician and philosopher, and Cicero has done it in a still more masterly manner, as a philosopher, scholar, orator, and statesman; and I confess unless he has had many authors to consult that we know nothing of, his judgment and penetration are quite admirable, and his books de Oratore, etc. more finished in their kind, than any of his orations themselves.

As to the effects of oratory, they have been and are surely very great, but as things seen through a mist, or at a great distance, are apt to be mistaken in their size, I am apt to think many say things incredible, and make suppositions quite contrary to nature and reason, and therefore to probability. Some speak and write as if all the ancient orators had a genius more than human, and indeed by their whole strain seem rather to extinguish than excite an ardor to excel. Some also seem to me to go upon a supposition as if all the people in the ancient republics had been sages, as well as their statesmen orators. There is a remark to be found in many critics upon a story of Theophrastus the philosopher, from which they infer the delicacy of the Athenians. That philosopher it seems went to buy something of an herb-woman, at a stall, and she in her answer to him it seems called him stranger. This they say shows that she knew him by his accent not to be a native of Athens, although he had lived there thirty years. But we are not even certain that her calling him stranger implied any more than that he was unknown to her. Besides, though it were true, that she discovered him not to be an Athenian born, this is no more than what happens in every populous country that there is something in the accent which will determine a man to be of one country or province, rather than another, and I am somewhat of opinion that this would be more discernible in Greece than any where else. The different dialects of the Greek tongue were not reckoned reproachful, as many local differences are in Britain, which therefore people will endeavor to rid themselves of as well as they can. In short I take it for granted, that an assembly of the vulgar in Athens was just like assembly of common people among us, and a senate at Athens in understanding and taste was not superior to the senate of Great Britain, and that some of them were but mere mobs; and that they were disorderly is plain from what we read of Plato being pulled down from the desk, when he went up to defend Socrates.

The most remarkable story of the effect of oratory is that told of Cicero's power over Caesar in his oration for C. Ligarius. This is very pompously told by some critics, that Caesar came to the judgment seat determined to condemn him, and even took the pen in his hand to sign his condemnation, but that he was interested by Cicero's eloquence, and at last so moved that he dropped the pen and granted the orator's request. But supposing the facts to have happened, I am very doubtful of the justness of the remark. Caesar was a great politician, and as we know he did attempt to establish his authority by mercy, it is not unlikely both that he determined to pardon Ligarius, and to flatter Cicero's vanity by giving him the honor of obtaining it. In short, oratory has its chief power in promiscuous assemblies, and there it reigned of old, and reigns still, by its visible effect.

A VALEDICTORY ORATION

Barnabas Binney

Barnabas Binney, whose father, Captain Barnabas Binney, was a wealthy Boston merchant and an active and prominent "son of liberty," was born in Boston in the spring of 1751. He was graduated from Rhode Island College (now Brown University) in 1774, presenting the valedictory address, "A Plea for the Right of Private Judgment in Religious Matters."

Binney studied medicine in London and in Philadelphia, receiving his medical degree from the University of Pennsylvania. In 1776 he entered the Revolutionary War as a hospital physician and surgeon and remained in the army until it was disbanded in 1783. His unstinting efforts on behalf of the American cause undermined his health and caused his death on June 20, 1787.

As George Bohman points out in his chapter on the colonial period in the *History and Criticism of American Public Address*: "at the annual public commencements, college students publicly performed declamations, orations, dialogues, and disputatious exercises which were the essential parts of the program of speech training during this period. . . . The commencements, at first held in the fall but later advanced to midsummer, attracted large crowds of alumni, friends, and townspeople."

The text of Binney's address is taken from Barnabas Binney, *An Oration Delivered On The Late Public Commencement At Rhode-Island College In Providence; September 1774. Being A Plea, For the Right Of Private Judgment In Religious Matters. . . .* Boston: John Kneeland, 1774.

THE constant and candid attendance, which this numerous and judicious assembly has already granted to the preceding exercises, has been sufficient gratefully to affect every ingenuous mind, justly to merit the warmest acknowledgements, and pleasingly to deter every youth present from attempting to transgress on their indulgent patience. It is therefore with hesitancy and reluctance that we presume still to detain you: Yet, being appointed to conclude the day, by an Oration and the Valedictions of the class, may we be permitted to beg your attention a few minutes longer? On a subject, which, *at this* period we hope will not seem altogether improper or unacceptable; we mean *religious Liberty;* or, a plea for it; corroborated by the fatal consequences of its prohibition or abridgment, and the glorious effects of its protection or toleration, so abundantly evident in the history of every age and nation, both ecclesiastic and civil.

AMERICA, hitherto the infant state of glorious freedom, on which surrounding nations, while still enslaved, gaze with envy, love, and wonder; *America,* no doubt the future, spacious Theatre for actions yet unthought of with the ancient worthies; by her adequate conceptions, and her loyal defense of her *civil* rights, has already illustriously exalted her fame and greatness, and increased the esteem and veneration of her friends to no common pitch. Her latest babes all learn her wrongs and lisp for justice; while her eldest sons, more strong to wield all science, make her presses teem with the justest descriptions of the nature, consequences, and glory of that *civil* liberty, which her delivering God did at first invest her with, and her ancient parent swore to protect her in. But, does the enjoyment and security of her *religious* rights less merit her attention than her civil? Or, are they not so nearly allied that a deprivation of the former in any degree is an absolute incroachment on the latter? The answer, to every honest man, must be obvious; *religious liberty* itself is the first, most sacred, and unalienably natural right of man.

INSTEAD, therefore of offering any elaborate apologies for speaking on such a subject, To You, most benevolent and discerning auditors we appeal; whether, if, (as the most celebrated historians unitedly assert) *religious* liberty, is a subject the most important and interesting imaginable, to individuals and society; a subject pregnant with the grandest events to kingdoms, nations, empires; and therefore, can never be too well understood, too highly prized, or too often inculcated by us on our posterity: If, (which they all *as* unitedly assert) the most extensive liberty conceivable, exclusive of *that,* of choosing our own religion, is but mere vassalage: And if, a full toleration of *that,* has ever immortalized the nation which has granted it; has ever proved the happy means of sweetly uniting the different interests and communities of such a nation in a peaceful harmony; has ever been found the *only* effectual method, of diffusing useful and extensive knowledge; of softening and refining the manners of the people; of cherishing every virtuous, social passion; of reclaiming from monkish slavery, and exalting the human mind above the low, detestable superstitions, which, ravage upon priest-ridden multitudes: If also, a toleration of *that sacred right,* is the *only* true way, to suppress and *keep* under all the viperish brood of tyrannizing ecclesiastics; and to *establish* permanent as the sun, immutable as the laws of truth, or God himself, a government equal and salutary through its various branches: If moreover, a prohibition or abridgment of it, has always been attended with the most deplorable consequences; and has been the grand cause of nine-tenths of all the bloodshed which has ever happened upon this globe: In short, if there is *now* any such thing as persecution for *religion's* sake; or, if it is probable, or even possible, that there *may* be, either against or among us Americans: We say, to YOU, most benevolent auditors we appeal, whether, if these are facts, every person who has the interest either of church or state at heart; every person who wishes well to his fellow creatures, his posterity, or himself; finally, whether, every person who is an enemy to despotism, tyranny or carnage, must not think every well-meant effort to establish just ideas of *such* liberty, laudable, useful and desirable; especially at the present juncture.

WE flatter ourselves, that the bare proposing the subject will procure us the attention of the *Clergy, auribus erectis*; as they are all deeply interested, and especially, as they all love to enjoy this liberty *themselves,* however reluctantly many of them allow it to those who subscribe not to their creeds. And we beg, as an *uncommon* favor, that we may have the *candid* attention of those, who are so exceedingly jealous and tenacious of the sacred dignity of that order, as to deem it the worst of blasphemy to say even so much truth, as they themselves declare, through all their different denominations, one of another, namely, *That woe is to the people when the priests get the power.*

BY RELIGIOUS LIBERTY *we mean a free, uncontroled liberty of thinking, worshipping and acting in all religious matters as we please,* provided *thereby, we are not prejudicial to the state.*

A HINT of the equity of tolerating and enjoying this liberty, and of the folly and impolicy of prohibiting it; together with a short historical retrospect of the fatal consequences attending such prohibition, and the glorious effects attending such toleration, we propose as the method of enforcing our plea for it.

WHAT can be plainer than the justice of equity of this liberty? Indeed, it seems so self-evident, that did not daily experience convince us, that the amazing force of education, prejudice, and pride is so great as to make some think, it is rather just to give up private judgment to public dictates, or the decrees of convocations, than to enjoy it themselves, it would seem needless to say a word about it. It is plain that the justice or equity of it, consists in the equal, the natural, unalienable, and inherent right or claim, resulting invariably from the nature and fitness of things, which every individual of the human race has to it. Now, if it is not just or equitable that every individual should have this liberty; supposing every individual *should insist* upon taking it, there would be injustice, or iniquity somewhere: But as we cannot conceive of injustice or iniquity without injury or wrong, we ask who would be injured or wronged thereby? None? Then they would insist upon nothing but what it is equitable they should have. But if any are wronged thereby, we then ask *how?* Are they wronged because *all* assume that which *they only* have the privilege of? If so, we ask who give them this exclusive privilege of judging in matters of religion, not only for themselves, but for others also? God, or man? If God, then let them produce some sufficient testimony, by which their pretention may be justified: If man, or men; we still ask who gave *them* authority to confer this exclusive privilege? Did it originate in councils and associations of *Divines*? If it is said yes; (as it often has been) we must still follow up, and ask, who gave *them* the monopoly of wisdom, judgment, and power? Or, did they only *divine* that they had it? BY what authority do *they* become the standard of orthodoxy? And above all, by whose commands, do they hereticate, anathematize and persecute those, who cannot help thinking different from them? We will not say who; 'tis enough for us to demonstrate that no priest, or set of priests; no man, or set of men; whether lords temporal or *spiritual;* whether those who are subject to majesty, or *majesty itself;* ever did, or ever can, with the least shadow of justice, prohibit or abridge this right of private judgment in religious matters. It is plain, that, none *can* control this liberty, but those who have superior *power:* But if superior *power* alone can sufficiently authorize, or justify the controlment; we are resolved into a state of nature; to talk of justice, right, and equity is mere cant; persecution has no existence; they who have most power have most right; and every one may do whatever his inclination suggests, if his strength is sufficient! But surely this can never be, where there is a cry of government, law, and a free state! But, if superior *power* cannot justify any man, or men in dictating what shall be the faith of their fellow creatures, neither can superior *learning* or *knowledge:* Because, *all* human knowledge does but manifest that all men are fallible, and therefore, incapable of assuming the prerogative of judging for others in matters of religion. Since therefore, neither human power, nor human knowledge can justify the abridgment, or exclusive enjoyment of this liberty; but it still remains as much the right of the beggar as of the prince; of the savage *Hottentot,* as the orthodox precisian; of the rankest deist, as of the greatest saint: Because it is the inherent, unalienable gift of God to all; and since moreover, God himself cannot give it exclusively; because it would be directly contrary to the very first and the most essential principle in the whole system of intelligences, namely, that the dictates of our *own* consciences, and not those of another's must be forever followed; we must conclude that the full enjoyment, toleration, and protection of it are highly equitable; and the prohibition of it most unjust and iniquitous.

THERE never was an Era in history, in which, persecution was not used, *pretendedly* at least, as the means, of working *conviction* in dissenters; or, somehow, of forcing the assent of the *mind.* There can scarcely be found a period, in which, the wheel, the sword, and the fagot; or any other corporeal constraints, were used, barely, for the purpose of gaining *professors* of a religion, and not *believers* of it. Indeed, if the bare external, organic, or corporeal profession, confession, or assent to any religion, is all that is aimed at; it must be acknowledged, that *corporeal* pains or penalties are not void and foolish; but well adapted to that end: But the folly of attempting to alter the *judgment, sentiments,* or *mental* language, by corporeal, coercive measures, is strange indeed! How inadequate, how useless to accomplish the end! While the mind is an inaccessable queen, who is secluded in some invisible, unknown recess of an elegant, beautiful, and august structure; a queen, who has determined what God she will worship, and in what manner; a queen, who can baffle, or render ineffectual, all the compulsive stratagems of her united enemies to alter that determination; either by causing her prime minister to give out that she conforms to the popular cry when she does not, merely to prevent the rude rabble from damaging her palace; or, by mysteriously eluding through some unknown outlet, when they shall ruin or destroy it: What brutal folly, and what savage madness is it, to attempt to alter her *faith* or *secret* practice, by such diabolical methods? We say, that there is no religion without faith of some sort or other. By faith, we mean, the belief of some certain fact, truth, principle or principles, which, we think ought to be credited. Now, can any person ever believe any of those principles, facts, &c. which, are proposed for his credit, unless, he sees sufficient evidence attending them to gain his assent? Never. Will the penalties and punishments of nonconformity to those who demand his assent, ever produce evidence? Never; unless of a bloodthirsty disposition. Will the still more severe punishments of supposed Heretics, such as imprisonment, whipping, racking, hanging, &c. ever conquer the *mind,* (the body they may) alter its *judgment* for the better, reclaim it from its supposed error, or afford any signs of truth or goodness in a religion *thus* established? Never. Must not, then, the dictates of every man's conscience, who is untainted by the curst inebriating instigations of *priestly* cruelty, join to affirm, that it is the height of folly *thus* to attempt it? And since no way is so likely to produce evidence and conquer the mind, as a dispassionate, deliberate discussion of that which is proposed for credit; must not reason herself, that voice of God in man, forever declare, that when no evidence is produced by that method, nothing can be so disagreeable to her, nothing so unbecoming the human soul divine, nothing so contrary to the will of heaven, as to refuse any man the liberty of peaceably believing, what he *can* see evidence for? She must. Hence, we must conclude, that as all possible attempts to alter men's religious sentiments, except that of free and candid disquisition, are means, no ways adapted to the end; or calculated to produce their desired effect; they must forever be esteemed, in the minds of the honest, the rational, and generous, attempts as vain and foolish, as unjust and tyrannic.

IF, as we have asserted, the common aim in prohibiting or abridging this liberty, or in persecuting, is the conviction of the mind; the great *impolicy* of it, must be no less evident than the injustice and absurdity. Degenerate as mankind are, there is universally no small degree of sensibility, pity, and commiseration apparent among them, when men are murdered, tortured, or maltreated for their *religious heterodoxy;* whether real or supposed. And this, almost, infallible mark of true magnanimity; this noble, generous sympathy, has often warmed and inflamed the kindred passions in mere spectators; and roused to righteous deeds of heroic vengeance on the persecuting herd; 'till *priestly Neros* have trembled to the centre, at the just retortion of their own bloody acts. The narrowminded souls, who never knew the godlike glory of forbearing, have often blush'd, and sunk in shame, to think how far they shot beyond their mark. Never was there a cause persecuted yet, whether christian or pagan; whether, rational and righteous, or absurd and devilish, but it grew; for an experimental confirmation of this, search all antiquity; but especially look back to the reformation from popery; then, extend your view still farther, to the commencement of christianity; enquire of the *reverend* Pharisees; ask of the *sage,* jewish Rabbies; of *Pilate;* the *Roman soldiers;* of the infamously famous tyrants, who during the ten persecutions wallowed in human blood, and clouded the heavens with the smoke of consuming martyrs; ask *them,* who have gibbited their names for posterity to gaze at, with detestation and horror; ask *Nero, Domitian, Trajan, Adrian, Antonius Pius, Severus, Maximin, Decius, Valerian, Dioclesian,* and *Galeirus;* ask them all, how much they suppressed christianity? And whether, in the end, ten christians did not arise at the burning of one? Then come back and ask of all the popes, bishops, cardinals, priors, priests, monks and friars, from the time the papal throne was first erected, 'till the noble JOHN WICKLIFF, dared to dissent from the whole world, and at one stroke, to lop off the immense body of papal trumpery; we say, ask of all those *holy Gentlemen,* whether their unutterable barbarites did not turn of good account to the reformers? And amount to a demonstrative proof that their cause was bad? It cannot be denied. Let that tygris *bloody* Mary, her attending inflammatory zealots, and biggoted successors; let the monsters *Gardiner* and *Bonner;* let the flames of Smithfield; and the still more exquisite and ingenious tortures of Scotland; all, from their long-tried experience, impartially declare the true merit of prohibiting the sacred right of private judgment; and say, whether they will not unitedly cry, *impolitic! impolitic!* Come nearer home, and ask the same question of those cruel statutes, and the intolerant spirit of the times, which first drove our faithful ancestors to this land of freedom; and say, whether they also, must not join the common cry, *impolitic! impolitic!* Indeed, if experience, that best of teachers, did not point out the impolicy of such conduct; a moderate degree of common sense might. Nothing is more common among men, than to treat with entire and sovereign neglect, all the multitude of little, nibling cavillers, and injudicious, silly opponents, as unworthy their notice: And yet nothing is more common among men, than to be very angry at the *truth;* and especially, if it strikes against any part of their conduct or prepossessions; and above all, if it strikes at their faith or practice in *religious matters;* and hence the world have learned, to look upon the persecution of a religion, as no indifferent voucher for its veracity, or authority. For they are apt to reason in this manner, if reason, argument, or ridicule could confute; they, i.e. the opposers, would never be at the expence of confuting, or trying to confute with the sword and fagot. Indeed, as a noble author has made, pretty plain, so strangely are men attached to a cause that is bitterly persecuted; so apt are they to think, that it has arguments irrefutable by reason; so prone to look upon it, as, great and grand, to attract such attention; that a hot persecution of *Poets* would raise an *Arcadia,* in a wilderness. Poetry would be looked upon as something divine; and thousands would long to die martyrs to the glorious cause. How great then, is the *impolicy* of those thoughtless bigots, who exhibit so grand a proof of the badness of their own cause, and of the goodness of that they run down!

ALTHOUGH, by our hinting the injustice, absurdity, and *impolicy* of the thing itself, (that is, the prohibiting this *religious liberty*) we are insensibly brought to see one of its consequences; (namely, that it rather hardens in *error,* than convinces of *truth*) yet, as we proposed glancing at the *consequences* of this prohibition, as separate, and distinct from the point of light, in which, the prohibition itself, must appear to every reasonable man; (namely, *unjust, absurd,* and *impolitic*) permit us, previously, to advert a minute to the judicious precautions of this *Colony:* by which, we shall be led, first, to that fountain-head of all wickedness, that *Hydra-mischief,* UNION OF CHURCH AND STATE; and then, to what we proposed, the *consequences* of this *union,* prohibition or abridgment, for the former ever produces the latter.

THIS COLONY, is justly renowned for the impartiality, with which, she treats men of all religions and denominations. Indeed, in her very *Charter,* the floodgates of persecution are forever effectually shut; for by *Charles* the IId. it is expresly said, "We have thought fit, and do hereby publish, grant, ordain and declare, that our royal will and pleasure is, that no person within the said *Colony,* at any time hereafter, shall be anywise molested, punished, disquieted, *or called in question,* for any differences in matters of religion; and that every person and persons, from time to time, and at all times hereafter, do freely and fully have and enjoy, his and their own judgment and conscience, in matters of religious concernment, throughout the *said Colony*." Such a glorious sentence as *this,* reflected honor upon the British throne: And the men, who nobly petitioned for it, well knew, that truth, or the christian religion, could both exist and flourish *without* the intervention of any civil sword whatever. And hence we see, as long as her charter endures, and is adhered to, *persecution,* that offspring of darkness, envy and spite; that infallible mark of an ignorant head and a wicked heart; that last shift of a poor baffled enemy; *persecution,* that infernal fury! is forbidden, under any shape or pretence whatever, to enter *here;* forbidden, not only by the law of nature, and revealed religion; but, by an express law of the *state*. And moreover, to her immortal glory, so catholic and discerning has this *Colony* been, as not only to preserve the spirit of her *charter,* but also to provide an act, by her assembly, which, in union with her *charter,* will forever secure her religious rights, as long as they shall be in force; we mean, that act, which forbids the support of *ministers,* in every manner, except that of *voluntary* contribution. Thus it is expressed: "Be it enacted by the general assembly, that what maintainance, or salary may be thought needful, or necessary, by any churches, congregations, or societies of people now inhabiting, or that hereafter shall, or may inhabit this Colony, for the support of their respective minister or ministers, shall be raised by *free* contribution, *and no other way*." This sentence also will forever honor the men who enacted it.

BY the two sentences now rehearsed, it is evident, that, in the first place, all petty tyrants, whether priests or laymen, are utterly prevented from lording it over the human mind, by making use of any irrational, external, or, corporeally coercive, or compulsive measures to effect, or bring about, any sort of religious uniformity whatever: And in the second, that, all persons within this Colony are, not only at full liberty, to hear any preacher they please, as little as they please, or none if they please; but at full liberty *to pay,* or *bestow their property* upon any preacher they please, in as sparing a manner as they please; or in no manner at all, if they please. It is moreover evident, that under such laws, regulations, or restrictions, the *true* Clergy, the *honest, undesigning, non-usurping* preachers of the gospel, stand as fair a chance of being treated civilly, and supported comfortably, as the primitive apostles and

disciples did; nay a fairer, for, although the oppressing and avaricious, the controller and the wolf are excluded; yet, argument and
reason, courtesy and beneficence, are not. It is still further evident,
that by those laws there is only a dissolution of what ought never to
be put together; *church* and *state*: And that by them, the *Clergy* have
only lost what they *never* had a right to, the use of the civil sword;
while the people have preserved what they *ever* had a right to, the
exercise of their own judgment. From these several steps, it is still
further evident yet, that where there is no union of church and state,
that is, where there is no civil power put into the hands of the
Clergy, (and if the magistrate meddles with, or enforces religion,
we shall still look upon *him* as the *Clergy,* or the servant of the
Clergy, whether it be in Constantinople, in Rome, or in England) by
which, they may establish their creeds, and decrees, or exact their
extravagant demands; there can be no such thing as religious
tyranny; or persecution for religion's sake. Consequently the
UNION of *church* and *state* is the cause that produces, the very
fountain whence proceeds, the supporter and nourisher of persecution, tyranny, and almost all the long catalogue of black enormities
which *that* order of men have been guilty of. Reason herself, unassisted, did predict, that the coition of bodies so very contrary,
and heterogeneous, must necessarily beget monsters indeed: But
when experience comes after, *she* confirms the prophesy; she declares, that it ever has been, is, and most certainly ever will be, like
the trojan horse, big with unthought of mischiefs: Although it ever
has been, is, and ever will be, like that ancient destroyer, caress'd
by deluded zealots, as the progeny of heaven; as defensive of the
church and state, and as well-pleasing to the Deity; 'till to their
cost they find, as the Mistaken Trojans did, that they have taken
unutterable pains to destroy themselves, and set the world on fire.
To speak plain, it is a scheme, first contrived by aspiring politicians,
then consented to by still more aspiring monarchs, urged on by
greedy, ravening *priests,* and at last completed and established by
the united band.

PROBABLY it will be readily allowed, that whatever religion any
nation, as such, chooses for itself, it chooses to *establish*. And it
must be, *as* readily allowed, by every *reasonable* man, that the
establishment of any religion whatever, *without* any toleration, or
exemption, is the most detestable usurpation and tyranny. We must
hence consequently and justly infer, that, since a toleration, or exemption from an establishment, is that alone which renders it, in
any degree, sufferable; the toleration is the most amiable part of the
establishment. And since the more extensive the toleration is, the
more amiable is the establishment: We must as justly infer, that a
full toleration is *most* amiable: But where there is a *full* toleration,

there can be no establishment; (unless an establishment of toleration) for, they are not only inconsistent, but utterly exclusive of each other.

IT is common for some people, who rather than say nothing, say any thing, to raise many bugbears in their own imaginations, and then tell us they are the consequences of a *full* toleration of this religious liberty. But notwithstanding, what any may barely *assert,* we shall still think that it is just, prudent, politic, and therefore reasonable, to allow this toleration to every human creature under the sun; even to those whom true Englishmen have most aversion to, *Papists.* For what are we pleading for? a toleration of licentiousness? a toleration of what is *prejudicial* to the state? No; far from it: But for a toleration of religious liberty, which never can be so, either to states, or individuals. We are not pleading that any nation, state or people, should ever tolerate the destruction of those whom pagans, papists, or protestants dogmatize infidels or heretics; very far from it. If any members of a civil community, or persons under the same civil government, out of a mistaken zeal for God, or their own cause; think it their duty to destroy, molest, or persecute those who dissent from them in their religious sentiments, let the civil magistrate as guardian of the peace of that community, or government, take care of them; let him punish them by virtue of the *civil* laws, not of *ecclesiastic canons;* let him punish them with all the severity those laws direct. And in so doing, he has no business to ask whether the criminals are Atheists, Deists, Pagans, Papists, Jews or Christians; whether Churchmen, Presbyterians, Baptists, Quakers, Calvinists, Arminians, Universalists or Sandemanians. It is enough for him to know that they are guilty; to know the specific nature of their crime and the punishment by civil law annexed; and to see that they get it. If there are any whose religious principles teach them to kill whom they think heretics; or to be seditious or rebellious; or anyhow dangerous to society; let the civil magistrate watch, and when the civil law will take hold of them, let him punish them: And *that,* without ever asking them whether their religion led them to such crimes, or not; which is none of his business. As to the *Clergy,* whether in their own person, or in the person of the magistrate, they have no more right, or business to be intrusted with the civil sword; than a madman has to be intrusted with a firebrand in a magazine of powder; nor so much, for, (if experience may determine) even in populous places, the devastations of the former will ever be greater than those of the latter.

HOWEVER easy it is to say, it will not be so easy to make probable, that the establishment of any religion, can be either eligible or necessary. The veracity, or authority of any religion, with *thinking* people, will never be a grain more apparent for its being *established;* and consequently it cannot gain one more *real* friend upon *that* account. Indeed it will become a fine nest for vermin to breed in; and hence we find every religion upon earth, which has the shadow of an establishment so full of them. It cannot contribute to the peace, safety, and good order of society; nor to the making individuals more honest: For, unless the laws of the state, or the magistrates are weak and deficient, *they* are sufficient for that purpose. A little reflection must inevitably teach us, that, TRUTH would stand a far better chance of finding admirers and advocates, if every state, as such, was to leave her to herself, and her divine protector; and only take care to punish its own bad subjects, and reward its good, without meddling with the religion of any.

BUT since it is so difficult to find the *good* effects of this *union* of *church* and state, lamb and tyger, dove and serpent; bodies, which are as essentially different, and as unconnected as fire and water; let us apply to history to know whether it is really productive of any *bad* effects.

DISTINCT from its being a detestable usurpation of that sacred right which every individual should have in legislation, or in making the laws by which himself is to be governed; the *first* bad consequence of this prolific union is, that it produces and ratifies that unmanly dispiritedness, and pusilanimity; that tame and shameful resignation of private judgment, though supported by equity, reason, and truth, to public edicts and decrees, though founded in caprice or custom, and supported by arbitrary power: Which pusilanimity and resignation, are the most infallible means of raising and cherishing the most designing, usurping, and grasping despots that ever had existence; both in church and state. The *second* consequence is, that it almost entirely excludes all that is excellent, great, or glorious in man, namely, the use of his reason, or of his own intellectual abilities; eclipses every beam of light and knowledge; and spreads a universal veil of error, superstition, and midnight darkness, beneath whose secret covert, continually lurk secure, the horrid beasts of prey, which roam at large and gorge their ruthless appetites unhurt, unsought, unseen. The *third* is, that in process of time it often makes the wise grow mad and fills the world with intestine broils, and foreign wars. These are the three principal limbs, which with their innumerable branches, overspread the nations, and shut out the light of life. Such an infinitude of evils is this union fraught with, that thousands of volumes do but partly contain them; but a very few therefore, and in a very general manner too, can we possibly mention, in the few minutes we have to spare.

WHAT but the basest pusilanimity, what but the most accursed acquiescence in the infernal dictates of the sacred *associations* of artful, avaricious *priests;* and their cruel, blood-thirsty copartners, the *civil* rulers; could ever have plunged whole nations into those horrible enormities, which make the blood dance cold, but at the shocking recollection? Let EGYPT, that house of *gods,* that mother of idolatry and superstition, from time immemorial declare, how immediately consequent upon this union, this combination of priests and civil rulers to promote each others tyrannic schemes, the dictates of reason and common sense were rejected, while their pretendedly divine illuminations and commands were universally adhered to. And let that same Egypt declare, what worse than licentious, worse than atheistical effects *that* adherence produced. Let CARTHAGE, that supporter of cruelty, that cherisher of the flames of the valley of Hinnon, declare, how tenfold worse than brutal was the dastardly, abominable, the astonishing submission to the religion she patronized in her brightest days; because it was thus by establishment made *orthodox.* Let the Assyrians, the Babylonians, the Medes, Persians, and Macedonians. Let especially the Phoenicians, Gauls, Scythians, and even the illustrious and refined GRECIANS and ROMANS, all stand as eternal monuments of the inexpressible darkness, superstition, confusion, and misery, immediately consequent upon that servile acknowledgement of whatever passes current for orthodoxy in religion. Even Israel itself, though its government was *theocratical,* had its sons of Eli, and its priests of Baal.

BUT lest what has been said should seem to be invalidated by reflecting that those nations were heathens; let us come down to the christian Era. And permit us to mention, previous to our hinting at some of the manifold evils, under which the church and state have groaned, for ages, throughout all Christendom; that we disdain the thought of barely exposing the infirmities of the *Clerical* order; or of rehearsing aught against any, because of *that* order. For, notwithstanding gowns, and bands, and prayers, and rigid austerities, and solemn countenances have deluded, and led captive in every age and nation more than ten times ten thousands; notwithstanding that order of men has done more mischief in the world than all the rest put together, yet we know, that they have done very great good; and we know, that, in almost every age they have had some of the best of men among them; some HONEST men; emphatically so, a character, which contains the sum of all eulogies. We love and admire *that* character; we can't but speak well of it; and we desire ever to esteem and honor it: Though we hold ourselves still bound to maintain, that no man or men whatever, can have any right to impose their *credenda* or *agenda* upon their fellow creatures; or to dictate to them what set of articles they shall believe; or to demand their property for teaching them, or pretending to teach them, without some *mutual contract.* Because, as soon as *this* is done, we are no longer freemen, but under the most galling spiritual tyranny; and thereby the widest door is opened for every audacious imposition that can enter the heart of man.

CHRISTIANITY, when first introduced, was so far from containing any thing in it destructive of public peace, or private liberty, that it was nothing but lenity and good will to man: And while it utterly forbad violence of every sort and degree, it proclaimed nothing but the glad tydings of joy and peace.

THE opinion of its heavenly author concerning sacerdotal power and incorporation of church and state, is recorded in few words; *MY kingdom is not of THIS world.* When they would have made him a king, he hid himself. When his mistaken servants would have called fire from heaven to destroy a whole city because it did not think as they did; he taught them, that the spirit of *his* religion, was to bless and save, not to persecute and destroy. Thus, rejecting all sublunary pomp and power, he displayed, brighter than yonder sun, the simple majesty and effulgent glory of an incarnate God. As to his pupils, they thought indeed at first, pretty much the same as many of their *professed* brethren have since, and do now; that it was a very clever thing to be called Rabbi, Rabbi; and to have one greatest among them: But, they had a master who taught them ere he left them, that they were not to be called Rabbi, Rabbi; and that the ready way to become greatest of all, was to be least of all, and servant of all.

AND through the efficacy of such teaching, we find, it was but a little after, before they manifested the most generous conceptions of *religious liberty:* For then it was, in the days of the apostles, that it flourished among all who professed him to be their master, in its full extent; while christianity in the morning of her existence, like some delightsome, fragrant garden, subsisting solely by the influence of the sun, and expanding to it, all its buds, blossoms, and fruits for warmth, for life and beauty; was supported alone by the rays of the SUN *of* RIGHTEOUSNESS. She found *then* while uncorrupted, and directed by the best of precepts, that although she was bitterly opposed, it would be but a poor alternative to fly to human, or diabolical authority to establish her cause. Although she was denied this liberty herself, and scourged from country to country for her faith and doctrines; yet, she denied it not to others; but, with a heavenly simplicity, declared the simple, glorious truth, and left every individual to make what use of it he pleased; to embrace it, or discard it, at his pleasure, or his peril. She *then* neither had, nor claimed, any power to make men profess, worship, or act in religious matters different from what they chose.

Happy! O happy for the inhabitants of earth, had this golden age still continued. But, that the nations yet unborn might learn to keep as watchful an eye on their *religious,* as civil rights; on their *ministers,* as magistrates; and that the prowling herd of *usurping, sacred despots* might be forever blasted with shame, confusion, and infamy; hear it! O Americans! Hear it! O ye unborn millions; and hearing, feel; and feeling, swear by heaven's great fire, that what *he* gave, you'll still preserve; scarce had these first promulgators laid their weary heads at rest, before high flying professors, grasping at wealth and power, the sanctimonious sons of Beelsebub, began to exercise their spiritual dominion, to turn priesthood into priestcraft, and to make merchandize of souls.

THE first successful stratagem was, to persuade the people, that since their *teachers* were by far the likeliest to understand the true meaning of the scriptures, they should strictly abide by *their* interpretations of them. Thus they were sottishly to relinquish their *own* judgments; and thereby shamefully to lay a broad foundation for the support of whatever innovations the prolific inventions of such ingenious gentlemen might happen to introduce. Such a plan as this, must necessarily have been (as we see it was) the mother of gross ignorance; that again, of the meanest cowardice; that again of a numerous brood of pilfering, pillaging, ravaging knaves; and those again the creators of poverty, misery, and death. A discovery of the utility of such a plan as this, together with the fine, consequent opportunity of cliping, interpolating, and construing the scriptures to their own vile purposes, was what first induced many great, and ambitious statesmen to patronize and incorporate christianity.

So unanimously was this *fundamental* measure fallen into, that in less than a century and a half after the ascension; by far the greatest part of the jewish christian preachers brought back just as many of the institutions, rites, and ceremonies of that nation, as they thought convenient: And the greatest part of the several gentile preachers, as many of the religious rites of *their* respective nations, as *they* thought convenient. How conscientious, upright and pious they were, in first making use of these dazling trinkets and gewgaws, which so well suited the common people who had been used to them, is not for us to say: *This,* we know, that as soon as ever *secular* power was thought of, to confirm and establish the use of them, they brought in something very handsome; a very pretty interest indeed. But these rites were not so numerous, glaringly absurd, and burdensome, 'till the *reverend Clergy,* in the third century, thought it best to court the favor of the civil rulers for the benefit of the cause of God and truth; because, after that, so powerful were the gifts, the posts of profit, favors and honors; the penalties, the punishments, indignities, and depositions; the smiles and courtesies; the frowns and threats of the great men in office, that near all those, who before resolutely opposed their impudent impositions, were now hushed to silence.

'TILL the middle of the second century, the different christian churches or societies were independent of each other; united neither by confederacies, *associations,* nor any other bond than christian charity. Each assembly was governed by its own laws, as a little state by itself: But by degrees the Greeks, and then the Latins, formed all the different churches of a province into one ecclesiast-ical body or association. These associations and convocations of *divines,* though they have ever proved abundantly fruitful in every work of darkness, containing in themselves, the foundation and seeds of popery, with all popery's effects; did not, however, bring forth any thing very remarkable, 'till united to that generating husband, *secular power.*

IN the third century the emperor CONSTANTINE arose; a professed friend to christianity. Out of his great zeal, he thought he could never be a too liberal father to the church; and in the abundance of his kindness, like a silly, fondling ape, overlaid, and choaked his child in the nursing. *He* moddled the church as a body politic; took to himself the grand power of directing her universal discipline in faith and manners; of constituting, ordering, protecting and exalting as many bishops, and dignified prelates as he thought fit. There is a historical tradition, that a voice was heard from heaven, on the very day those great donations, and church-revenues were given, crying out, 'this day is poison poured into the church.' Whether this tradition is true or false, it was not long after, before all his munificence proved poison with a witness; hence the common proverb of that period, *'Religion brought forth wealth, and the daughter devoured the mother.'*

BEFORE *his* time, few fallible councils thought of forming *creeds;* much less of consigning to destruction, the bodies and souls of all the dissenters from them: But as soon as they got CIVIL POWER upon their side, they exhibited, pretty feelingly, to others, what sort of *advice* they would give. *There* was the main point, the chief and most efficacious ingredient. CIVIL POWER. Before they had *that* in their hands; all their success depended upon the arts of insinuation and deceit; but after, upon the edge of the sword. *Then* the edicts of their assemblies, became sacred and permanent. And not only the people felt the good effects of their new strength; but they, themselves often felt it, whenever they opposed one another; (and they never agreed very well.) Hear the opinion of that singu-lar, reputable, and memorable father Gregory Nazianzene; "I am desirous of avoiding all *synods,* because, I never saw a good effect, or happy conclusion, from any one of them: They rather increase than lessen the evils they were designed to prevent; for, there the lust of power, and love of contention, are manifested in instances innumerable."

A GLANCE at two or three of the first of those general councils may give us some pretty adequate idea of near all the rest; since in the main they differed but little. *Eusebius* tells us, that "in anno domini 325, at the council of Nice, above 300 bishops were brought together, some by the hope of gain, and others to see such a miracle of an emperor as Constantine;" and it seems, they met with very good encouragement; for he abundantly rewarded them with rich presents, long and sumptuous entertainments, and posts of grandeur on their return. All history agrees, that they were the most litigious, and contentious men; insomuch that they began to quarrel through envy and spleen, and to accuse one another even before the emperor. And when they met in council to do business, their conduct was not dissimilar; for, the party accused having a written list of the articles which they were commanded to believe laid before them, immediately tore it all to pieces; and a great tumult arising, those priests who presented the paper, creed, or confession for the other party to sign, were cryed out on, as betrayers of the faith, and were so terrified, that they all arose, except two, and were the very first in condemning the sentiments and party they had just before espoused; and this very council also was upon the very brink of decreeing the celibacy of the Clergy, as agreeable to the divine will. So much for the cart-loads of scholastic terms, and circumlocutory, perplexing, intricate definitions of faith, and endless, blind explanations of inexplicable mysteries, enforced by the mere dint of human authority!

THE next general council of Constantinople, in anno domini 381, was called to confirm the decisions of that at Nice, but only encreased the rage of the controversy. Previous to it, the emperor ordered the "people of his city to embrace the religion which Peter, prince of the apostles had delivered to the Romans;" and *that,* was, always, whatever the head pontiff pleased to call it; and all know, that light and darkness differ not more, than the different pontiffs did in their different creeds. The worthy father just now mentioned says concerning this second council, "that those conveyers of the *holy ghost,* those preachers of *peace* to all men, grew so bitterly outrageous and clamorous against one another, in the midst of the church bandying into parties, mutually accusing each other, leaping about as if they were mad, under the impulse of a lust of power and dominion, that you would have thought they would have rent the world in pieces." And yet, by such godly *vi et armis* was *orthodoxy* established: Though in the end "THRONES, and not *orthodoxy,* was what they were after."

The fourth general council of Chalcedon, A. D. 451, was occasioned by the extraordinary transactions of a council of Ephesus in the year 449, of which Dioscorus, bishop of Alexandria, was president; and in which the doctrine of the two natures in Christ after the incarnation was condemned, and the contrary doctrine of Eutyches affirmed. The menaces of the president, together with the soldiers and monks, who surrounded the council, terrified the whole assembly. And Flavianus, bishop of Constantinople, who had condemned Eutyches, being accused by the president, and declared to be anathematized and deposed; and appealing therefore from him, and some bishops at the same time interposing in his behalf; the president started up, and sternly called for the emperor's commissioners, by whose command the proconful of Asia came in with the military, and a confused mob with chains and clubs and swords. And some bishops not willing to declare, and others flying away, he cried out, "If any one refuses to sign, with me he hath to contend;" and then he and another bishop carried about a *blank* paper, and obliged them all to sign it. *After* which it was filled up with the charge of heresy against Flavianus, and the sentence of his deposition. Flavianus still excepting against the president, he and others fell furiously upon him, beating him barbarously, throwing him down, kicking and trampling upon him, insomuch that three days after he died of the bruises he had received in the council. Hence we see, as a merry writer observes, "Twas *thus they* prov'd their doctrine orthodox, / By apostolic *blows* and *knocks.*" And indeed, in most of such councils, convocations, or associations since, the hardest first has made the soundest creed.

HAD there never been a kind emperor, Constantine, 'tis highly probable, that 'till this day, there had never been one cruel pope. *His* unboundedly liberal *temporalities* led the way, and never ceased, 'till they raised the papal chair, above all principalities, and at last, completed the whole fabric of POPERY in all its enormous hierarchy. If ever money appeared to be the root of all evil, it was *then.* The *emperor* rul'd the money; the money rul'd the priests; the priests rul'd the people; and, to speak the truth, the devil seem'd to rule them all.

SECULAR POWER, in concert with the wisdom of spiritual men, did wonders indeed! It made the exalted pontiffs infallible; it plucked up all bounds to their dominions; and bid the world adore them: It made their authority unquestionable and divine; it converted real bread into real flesh; it constituted carved wood, and molten metals, and pain'ed canvass, objects of fear, of love, and homage; it spread the doleful regions of purgatories in the bowels of the earth; it justified the vending of masses for the dead and damned; it made eternal bliss to depend upon the absolutions of popes; it made necessary the tortures of inquisitions for the terror for the living; it covered the earth with Crusades for the honor of the lamb of God; it stagnated the atmospheres with the smoak of burning heretics; and, finally introduced that artful lady superstition, with all her host of countless spectres dancing at her heels.

IN the reign of Constantine, that *unmerciful* kind emperor, it is well known, that, the bishop of Rome was far supereminent to all the other officers and dignitaries in the church: But Constantine, (who although he nobly delivered the church from the dreadful external frying pan of persecution, threw her into the still more dreadful, internal fire of contentions) by trying to make Constantinople the metropolis of his empire, and the glory of the world, bestowed the most liberal donations, and illustrious marks of royal favors, on the bishop of this new and august city, thereby enabling him to contend with the roman pontiff for the greatest share of revenues and submission: The horrible and bloody contest for many years hung doubtful; 'till, after blinding the poor multitude and making them think, that all possible reverence and passive obedience should be shewn to their spiritual leaders; and after stopping the mouths of the more discerning with gold and preferment, these two rivals, (for it was the fashion of bishops then, who were not too great cowards, to fight it out at the head of their own numerous armies) with all the magnificent, splendid marks of human greatness, contended with each other in a manner—too bad to be described; 'till having condemned, excommunicated, anathematized, ruined, and massacred thousands in the shameful contest, and compleatly separated the latin and greek churches, through the interposition of that monster Phocas, who waded through brother's blood, to the imperial honors, the scale canted FOR THE SEE of ROME; and satan has never wanted prime ministers of state upon earth since.

THE grandest stroke that was ever given towards universal despotism in the church was in A.D. 372, when Valentinian enacted, that the bishop of Rome, as God's viceregent, should applaud or condemn, all preachers, preaching, and religious matters throughout the empire. And to finish the whole plan, for fear the common people should be uneasy and doubt the equity of this unlimited power; the ingenious pontiffs ordered some of their most accomplished artisans to forge proper CREDENTIALS, containing a full delegated authority, from St. Peter the apostle, to their primitive ancestors in the *papal chair;* while they taught them that, according to appointment, the lineal succession had been strictly kept up! Astonishing! And what is still more astonishing, is, that *this artifice,* in conjunction with civil power, proved effectual to stop all murmurs! Indeed, after all their cunning, some of the poor people who were obliged to pay for the release of the souls of their relations in purgatory, could not help observing, that if *they* could not recollect ten relations that ever they had, yet, the *priests* could; and were sure to tell them, that they had relations *there* too, as long as they had any money in their pockets. Had we a hundred tongues, an iron voice, and years at our command to tell them in; the innumerable, the unutterable consequences of these gradual infringements, which finally shut out every spark of light, and shadow of liberty; insomuch, that even *princes* could not tell, whether their crowns, their thrones, their wives, their children, or their lives, would be their own in the succeeding hours; nay, could *we* add to these the most extensive historic knowledge, and the smoothest eloquence to roll it off in; while *you* were blest with the most enduring patience to hear, we could not unfold the thousandth part of those, dark horrors, which upon the riveting of the chains, for more than ten dark ages, did overspread all Europe.—And is it not a pity that the *british* annals should be stained? And even with the worst of crimes? *Overboiling priestly zeal?* Is it not a pity that *she,* the *reformed,* should ever let it be said she loved, in the dark, to hug that ugly hag, persecution? But we forbear—and above all, is it not a pity, O! YE AMERICANS, that *we,* or any of *our* ancestors, who fled *from* persecution, should leave it for posterity to say, *'they themselves became persecutors?*—Forgive us heaven!—O! my fellow countrymen! trembling, we are ashamed to turn over New England's history! But, for the future, while we have a moment's reflection, or a spark of sensibility left us, let us blush for our fathers conduct, and solemnly unite to expiate it, by a better of our own.—O! how strange is that epidemic disease, which hitherto, in every nation, has been the ruin of reformers! They nearly all dance the same giddy round!—First, as they ought, throw off the intollerable burden of ecclésiastical hierarchies; then, emerging from obscurity, ignorance and poverty, display all their powers in defence of equity and truth: While the people charmed and captivated, in grateful return, love, fear, obey, honor, defend and exalt them; 'till the poor mortals, intoxicated with ingratitude, pride and madness, and looking down from such lofty eminences, forget who they were, become giddy and tumble headlong from justice, affability and amity, into austerity, cruelty and devilishness! Strange indeed! Yet *this,* is the beaten track. Scarce can we find an eminent reformer from it, but what at last himself has trod in it: Be ye therefore ready, WATCH and OPPOSE. Oppose while you may, the very first appearance of slavery, especially, *priestly* slavery. Almost every human calamity is gradually progressive, to oppose, to repulse, to apply a remedy before the disease is irresistible and incurable, is rational, manly, just and noble; but to sit sucking our fingers, 'till our burdens press so hard that we can neither support them, nor throw them off, is characteristic rather, of asses than of men.

WE should now attempt to hint the glorious effects of a *toleration,* of this liberty; were we not apprehensive, that we have already transgressed upon your unexampled patience: Suffice it then just to observe, that in the first place, by it, we are delivered from the numerous, dreadful consequences attending the *prohibition* of it; in the second, it cannot possibly have, any concomitant evils of its own; and in the third, even in a political view, it is the grandest, surest and best cement of the various protestant communities and interests; consequently an increaser of their wealth, strength and honor: For it is the only universal encourager of the arts, sciences, and useful knowledge; and the most efficacious promoter of contentment, peace and concord: In short, it is the GLORY of a nation. Traverse all the mighty empires of the earth, and say, without a toleration of *this* liberty, what are they better than *Procrustes* himself? By his bed he commands every guest to be measured; if too long, lop them; if too short, stretch them: So, by their established orthodoxy, every mind must be measured; if it believes too much, punish the body for it; if it believes too little, punish the body for it! Behold, Britain, she who was late the beauty, and the wonder of the world; say, did ever her army, her navy, her commerce, her manufactures, her arts, her learning, her senatorial eloquence, or her state policy, gain her half the esteem and reverence that her TOLERATION did? Never. It was THAT, in conjunction with her CIVIL CONSTITION, [sic] which *once* made the world tremble and adore. O! ye Americans, *religious liberty* was the diadem which first enticed your fathers hither; remember it; and still hold it dearer than life. Remember also, the easy methods by which its destruction has ever been brought about. Watch, and nip the damning apple in the bud. Now, while you *may* prevent every usurping wretch from threatning that his little finger shall be thicker than his father's loins. Now, while you *may* destroy the whip of scorpions; and let our land be a jubilee; while the etherial concave rings with ceaseless, grateful shouts of praise, for that most inestimable blessing.

AND finally, since this America bids fair for beings as great an empire as ever the sun lighted, may millions yet unborn rise up and call this generation *blessed*, who, through the King of kings, by their *undaunted resolution, unremitted vigilance,* and *salutary provisions*, secured for their posterity the *greatest blessings*, and most *invaluable privileges* which human creatures can enjoy. Thus, with our sincere thanks for your animating attention, permit us to bid you FAREWELL.

Valedictions

To the CORPORATION

GENTLEMEN of the Corporation, it is with the highest pleasure, we embrace this public opportunity of expressing our unfeigned gratitude for your noble assiduity, and indefatigable attempts to spread over this land, the happy influences, and salutary effects, of true learning; that sovereign antidote against jesuistical invasions. And it is with no small satisfaction, I now return you, in behalf of my Class, our most hearty thanks, for being admitted to the honors of the seminary in this place. Gentlemen, may you still be encouraged in your benevolent design, while yon *alma mater,* like

some prolific dame, with an annual increase, brings forth her sons
of genius and virtue; 'till she has covered the earth with a glorious
race of american Homers, Ciceros and Newtons, who shall bless
mankind, raise her fame above old Athens, and render your names
as immortal as the sun; with these, our wishes, permit us, Gentlemen, to bid you FAREWELL.

To the PATRONS *of the* COLLEGE, *and* FRIENDS *of* LEARNING

LEARNING was the glory of Rome, the pride of Greece, and the
renown of Egypt; though unhappy for the glorious subject, we have
been speaking on, it was, in each of these celebrated nations, too
much confined to the priests and the opulent: But, as the times are
changed, it is with pleasure we hope to see learning the glorious
characteristic of this town and colony. True learning is the friend of
liberty and religion; for the happy souls who have once felt her
irradiating charms, will hardly ever after be enslaved by tyrants
or vice; by laymen or priests. And as a blessed presage that it shall
prevail, how are our happy eyes saluted with numbers, in this
audience, of the most illustrious characters, not only from different
towns in this colony, but from almost every colony on this wide, extended continent, who are all, well known, patrons and assistants
in this glorious cause! Ye Mecaenases of our age! Ye public-
spirited friends of light and knowledge! It is with heart-felt joy we
return you our warmest thanks, for your manly efforts to cherish
the study of literature through this continent; and especially are
we bound by the deepest gratitude to thank, esteem and honor the
town of Providence: It is to YOU principally the institution in this
place owes her present strength; it was solely by *your* unequalled
generosity that the simply grand and elegant building was erected
on yon eminence to gladen the eyes of every magnanimous be-
holder; and it shall be for you same shall blow her trump in future
time. You have already signalized yourselves by your prudent and
uncommon liberality in support of the greatest ornament, honor
and advantage society can enjoy, learning; your names have already reached the most distant parts of this extensive country, and
often reechoed from the other side the atlantic. The men of letters
now esteem you, the illiterate bless you, and all posterity, in succession, shall declare, *you* were the men who heroically assisted to
scatter the clouds of ignorance from this land; by causing the sun
of knowledge to shine forth. You see, Gentlemen, that you have the
greatest encouragement to persevere in your laudable benefactions;
for not only knowledge increases; but the most learned and wealthy
of every colony on the continent, with many also in Europe, are
daily assisting in your grand design. And *such* are the men whose
worthy labors can never be too often rehearsed; or too much

imitated. May you, Gentlemen, and your worthy coadjutors, far and near, long flourish and succeed, 'till late, very late, you cease your grateful efforts here, to take your feat where life and knowledge are the same, and *God himself* shall say, FAREWELL.

To the COMPANY *of* CADETS

WE desire now to return our thanks to the most respectable company of Cadets, who this day have escorted our honorable Governor and Corporation. Gentlemen, with a grateful sense of the honor you have already done us, together with a full conviction, that next to our heavenly General himself, a good standing militia, is the only security for our rights and privileges; we can't but wish you all imaginable success; that you may be the grand means of diffusing a true spirit of martial heroism through this colony and continent; and long receive, as you justly merit, for the generous example of military glory which you have this day exhibited; and especially for the uncommon and astonishing progress which you have so lately made in that most noble and necessary art; the honor, esteem and plaudit of the present and future generations, who with us are obligated to wish, that you may forever FARE WELL.

To the RESIDENTS *at* COLLEGE

> YE, *happy youth!—at length the* day's *roll'd on!—*
> *With mutual joy, and mutual gain, no more!*
> *In concert sweet, like birds of various note,*
> *And age, and plume, in one harmonious grove;*
> *Shall we together rove the healthful rounds*
> *Of studious life!—As friendly villagers,*
> *On some fair summer's morn, with jocund mirth,*
> *In numbers trip, to rifle all the sweets,*
> *And beauties of the spacious dewy meads;*
> *So we, in nature's ample field, where fruits,*
> *And flowers, and roots, for* mental *food, and health*
> *Luxuriant grow, began to crop; but now!—*
> *And yet, with envious love, ye favour'd still,*
> *We still congratulate.* We *quit yon feat*
> *Of knowledge, forc'd the world's rude waves to tempt,*
> *And with our slender, shallow, untry'd skiff;*
> *Her dang'rous seas to course, and buffet through*
> *The thick and frequent storms of noisy life;*
> *Yet, may the muses grant* YOU *kindest aid,*
> *And young imagination stutt'ring, nurse*
> *On high Parnassus: Still supply rich draughts*
> *From the castalion font, your tender minds,*

To raise, to fire, to cherish and instruct
In all the mazy-running labyrinths
Of nature's secret-working mysteries.
In skilful depths of commerce, government,
Arts, arms and agriculture, may you dive.
And since, by heav'n, you thus surrounded stand
With rarest blessings mortals know on earth;
Still show to all around, your Hearts replete
With love and gratitude to God and man;
Still heed your skilful, faithful, kindest guides,
Who constant lead you, to the greatest good;
While virtuous diligence marks all your ways,
And conscious friends, with pleasure cry, FAREWELL.

To the PRESIDENT and PROFESSOR

WITH joy, with grief, while common justice pleads,
Though loath to be a panegyrist's boast,
And sure to show the live carnation's blush,
If but a part of all your kindness drops
From grateful lips—in one short parting word
Permit e'en here, dear Sirs, to ease our hearts
Which groan with thankfulness, for all your care;
Your gen'rous, constant care, and vigilance
To open Natures's volume wide, and teach
The import of its various characters,
To all not legible. Your labors - - - - - But—
Your acquisitions, and your parts, we leave
To be determin'd by the public's watchful eye;
Nor tempt the envious to deny the truth:
Howe'er, for one and all, for once and all,
Though why, the world, we dare not, will not tell,
We thank you, Sirs; and hence our hearts unite,
That heav'n's rich blessings on your heads may rest,
And long success your noble efforts follow:
While peace, and joy, and plenty laugh around,
'Till angels wast you from your labors here,
To yon celestial scenes where knowledge, love,
Transport and virtue fill your blissful minds,
And all forever cease to bid FAREWELL.

To his CLASS-MATES, *Messir's* JOHN DORRANCE, DWIGHT FOSTER, TIMOTHY JONES, JACOB MANN, *and* ELIAS PENNIMAN

WITH tardy pace - - - - - declining long the task,
(Such is the parting with the souls we love!)

At length my mates, the last dissolving stroke
Comes home to us! - - - - - The pleasing circle's run!—
With landskips gay, and smiling brows, while nought,
But chearful friendship sparkles in the eye,
No more!—at ease reclin'd on yonder hill,
Where verdent grass perfum'd with sweetest flowers,
By faithful nature's provident command
Prepares a couch unknown to rankling care;
While o'er contented heads, those shady trees,
By faithful nature's provident command
Prepares a couch unknown to rankling care;
While o'er contented heads, those shady trees,
Seem pleas'd to spread their num'rous, waving bows.
Or sweetly blushing in their vernal bloom,
Or gently bending, with their ripen'd fruit!
Alas! no more, in those fair, fertile fields,
Where zephyrs gently fan the sultry heat,
Shall we in harmless jolity and mirth,
And converse free, of all the mighty minds
Of ancient times, talk down the summer's fun!
In wint'ry storms, by gen'rous fires, no more
Together turn the grave historian's page!
Nor search the greek and roman classics more!
Nor swell with rapture at the poet's song!
No more together snuff the midnight lamps,
To catch celestial flames from dying Catos!
No more in quest of sweet instruction's aid,
Shall we together wait our teachers kind!
But, like the feather'd young, push'd from their nests,
Though scarcely fledg'd, we singly *hence must shift,*
Toss'd by the tempests of the blust'ring world! - - - - -
With recollection emulous, let's oft
Look back on all the pleasing hours we've past;
While taste for sciences, virtue, truth, still prompt
To seek the noblest end of souls, increase
Of knowledge, love of God, and love of man.
Still let a grateful sense of favors, oft
Receiv'd on yonder hill, glow in our breasts;
While friendship steady as the rolling sun
Strikes light and life through all our scatter'd ways,
And animates to deeds of amity;
Deeds of reciprocal benevolence;
While each to other crys, though far, or near,
My mate, my friend, my brother, FARE THOU WELL.

II

On *Legal* Matters

THE SPEECH, &c.

Samuel Chew

Samuel Chew was a member of a prominent Virginia and Maryland family, his grandparents coming to the colonies in the *Seaflower* in 1622. Biographical data about Samuel Chew is vague and conflicting but one source (Appleton's *Cyclopedia of American Biography*) asserts that he was born in Maryland about 1690.

A practicing physician, Chew was elected chief justice of the district court of Newcastle, Pennsylvania. His mother, a devout Quaker, influenced her husband and her children to become members of the Society of Friends. Chief Justice Chew continued his membership in the Society until the Governor of Pennsylvania recommended a Militia Law to the state legislature in 1741. Quaker members appealed to the court over which Chew presided. When the chief justice declared that "self-defense was not only lawful but obligatory upon God's citizens," he was expelled from the meeting. In reply, Chew declared that the "Bulls of Excommunication" of his late brethren were "as full fraught with fire and brimstone and other church artillery, as even those of the Pope of Rome."

It was common practice in the American colonies for the chief justice of any court to deliver a speech to the grand jury, at the opening of the court session, "calculated," as Chew explains in the example given below, "to the best of our Judgments to the Occasion of the Times, his Majesty's Service, and the Good of the Publick." Typically a straightforward explanation of the duties of a grand jury and of the nature of various crimes that might come before it, the charge occasionally was used by more politically minded judges as vehicles for speeches about liberty, freedom of religion and conscience, the necessity for combatting tyranny. The speech given here is an example of this latter kind.

The text is from the Philadelphia edition printed in 1742 by Benjamin Franklin.

Gentlemen of the GRAND-JURY,

IT was said from the Bench, the last time I had the Honour to sit here, That no other End than the Happiness of Mankind in their Creation could consist with the natural Notions Men entertain of GOD; and consequently, that the Use of all the Means necessary to that End for which Men were created, must needs be lawful and right. And indeed to affirm the contrary, would in Effect be making GOD to defeat his own Purposes, and be charging Infinite Wisdom with the greatest Folly: A Blasphemy not to be conceived without Horror! It being then premised and supposed, that the Use of all necessary Means is lawful to a good End, I shall beg Leave to suppose for Argument sake, That Civil Government makes up some Part of the Means absolutely necessary to Human Happiness; and of Course that it is likewise lawful and right. I say I beg Leave to suppose it for Argument sake only: For I am far from being confident, that the Proposition, That Civil Government is lawful, to Christians at least, self-evident as it is, will not be disputed by some; because I find other Points equally evident, if they happen to concern religious Systems, are frequently made the Subjects of Controversy. And as most religious Societies would be thought infallible, Men seldom care to yield up favourite Opinions or Hypotheses in Religion even to the clearest Evidence. Indeed all Protestants have thought it expedient to disclaim the Pretence to Infallibility, in Words; but notwithstanding outward Professions, when we see religious Communities impatient of Contradiction, boil with Anger, and persecute to the utmost of their Power those that call in Question the Truth of any Part of their System; in a Word, when Men arrogate to themselves a Right to act in a Manner becoming Infallibility alone, it is clear to a Demonstration, that they do virtually lay Claim to it, and either foolishly think themselves infallible, or wickedly and impudently would be thought so by others. And I defy any Man living to give a good Reason for his being angry with another for differing in Opinion from him concerning Religion or any thing else, but this, that he is himself infallible.

THE End of all Civil Government being Happiness, that Happiness consists in the Security and Protection of the Lives, Liberties and Properties of the People who form or constitute the Community. The Security of Life and Property is commonly well enough understood, and therefore needs no Explanation. But to know wherein true Liberty consists, and what is meant by the Security of it, requires more Consideration. "True and impartial Liberty has been justly defined to be the Right of every Man to pursue the natural, reasonable and religious Dictates of his own Mind; to think what he will, and act as he thinks, provided he acts not to the Prejudice of another." This Right is inherent to all Men: Every Man is born with it, nor can he be debarred the Exercise of it but by the Means of Tyranny and Usurpation. And so dear is it to Mankind, that they will frequently risque all other Things for its sake, and sacrifice even Life itself rather than part with it. To secure this invaluable Blessing, was, as has been said, one of the main Ends of the Institution of Civil Government. And whenever those who are intrusted with the Execution of the Powers of Government, go about to deprive the People of the free Exercise of this Liberty, they cease to be properly Governours, and are Tyrants; and that Government may justly be pronounced the most perfect, where the Preservation of the Lives of the People, the Right of every Man to dispose of the Produce of his own Labour, and to be of that Religion he thinks best, are the most effectually secured from the Attempts of such as would take them away. And it is for this Reason that the Constitution of our Mother-Country claims the Preference of all others, and has ever been the Glory of *Englishmen,* and the Admiration and Envy of Foreigners.

YOU will easily perceive, *Gentlemen,* from what has been said, that I profess myself an Advocate for Liberty of Conscience: But then it is to be taken under proper Restrictions. And tho' Liberty of Conscience, or the being of such a Religion as a Man thinks best, is the undoubted and unalienable Right of every Man, it hath notwithstanding in common with every other Species of Liberty, this tacit Condition annexed to it, *Namely,* Provided that it does no Hurt to others. In all Governments the private ought to yield to the publick Good, whenever they come in Competition with each other. And in the Regulation of our temporal Affairs, notwithstanding it is most true that every Man ought to be left to his own Direction to act as he pleases for his own proper Interest, so long as he hurts not his Neigbour, nor injures the Common-Wealth under which he lives; yet, as soon as he acts otherwise, it is lawful to restrain and punish him: So in Matters of Religion, tho' every Man ought to have the Liberty of enjoying his private Opinions and of worshipping GOD in his own Way, be they ever so whimsical or wrong, while they affect only himself, and have not a bad Influence upon his own or his Neighbour's Morals, or are attended with Consequences dangerous to the publick Safety; yet, whenever that happens to be the Case, *That is to say,* When Men's religious Principles have a manifest Tendency to corrupt their own or their Neighbour's Morals, to sap, overturn or render insecure the particular Civil Government under which they live, or to destroy the very Being and End of all Government, and consequently the Happiness of Mankind in general, they have no Right to enjoy them, and it is lawful to restrain them from the publick Exercise of such a Religion, and from being admitted to a Participation of the Offices and Emoluments of Civil Government, which seems to be all the Punishment the Nature of the Case will admit of. I confess that all Things that are lawful, are not always expedient. And as false Opinions and Errors in Judgment, are Men's Misfortunes, and not their Faults, they ought to excite Compassion and Pity in us. And whatever Tendency in their own Natures Men's Errors or Mistakes in Religion may have with regard to others; yet if there is Reason to believe that they are not themselves aware of the Tendency of the Opinions they hold; if they behave peace-

ably, and do no immediate Hurt to their Neighbours, and their
Number is too inconsiderable to endanger the Safety of the Civil
Government or to disturb the publick Peace, it may be better to
leave them in the Enjoyment of their visionary Schemes and idle
senseless Reveries, than to give them any disturbance about them.

IN *Great-Britain*, so remarkable for the Justice and Lenity
of its Laws, and for none more than that Liberty of Conscience and
Toleration allowed to tender scrupulous Minds, we see under what
Disqualifications and legal Restraints the *Roman* Catholicks labour
upon the Score of their Religion. Is it for any other Reason than
that the avowed Principles of that Religion are supposed to be inconsistent with the Safety of a Protestant State? And the same
Reason ought and will always prevail to lead every wise Government to do the same Thing with regard to any other religious Society, whenever it shall become necessary for its own proper
Security. In the last Century a Sect of mad Enthusiasts appeared
in the World, who preached up a Fifth-Monarchy, as it was called,
and publickly taught, That the Time being then come that Christ
was to return to the Earth and reign over the Faithful a Thousand
Years before the End of the World, no Obedience was due to any
King, saving only to King Jesus. Will any Man be so hardy, as to
affirm, that the propagators of such a Doctrine, which manifestly
tended to the unhinging of all Government, and the utter demolish-
ing of all Civil Authority, would claim a Right to Toleration, however sincere they might be? And I defy the World, or any Man
breathing in it, to shew wherein a doctrine that teaches the absolute
Unlawfulness of Resistance to Christians against armed Enemies,
and that a miraculous divine Interpolition is indispensibly to be
waited for and expected in such Cases, doth essentially differ from
that Doctrine which denies the Obligation of Civil Obedience in
general. He that denies the Lawfulness of Means, condemns the
End: And therefore, to deny the Lawfulness of Government or
Political Society; to deny the Lawfulness of the Means necessary
to its Preservation and Defense; to deny the Obligation of Civil
Obedience, and the Lawfulness of such Means as are requisite to
enforce Civil Obedience, all amount to the same Thing.

I expect it will be objected, that the Toleration granted in
England by Act of Parliament to those very People who assert the
Unlawfulness of War and all Resistance, is an Evidence that the
Legislature did not think their Principle of that dangerous Consequence to Civil Society, as I now affirm it to be. But this will not
be admitted to be a fair Deduction from the Act of Toleration. A
religious Society may hold Principles that in their remote Consequences may be destructive of all Government, and yet may be so
circumstanced as to create no Apprehension or Danger from it to
the particular Government under which it is found. This was the

Case of the People called *Quakers* at the Time of passing the Act
of Toleration. The Legislature could not be ignorant that the
Doctrine that teaches the Unlawfulness of War and all manner
of Resistance to Christians, tended in its Consequences to the Dissolution of the Government, by rendering the Kingdom, for want
of Soldiers, a Prey to *France,* or any other Invader. When therefore
it is considered how small the Number of the People called *Quakers*
was at that Time; the Meanness of their Appearance, and the
Contempt they were generally held in; the Experience that every
Thing that looks like Persecution, commonly serves more firmly
to rivet and fix People in their Errors, whereas when left to themselves, they frequently come to discover their Mistakes; the little
Probability that such an absurd Principle, as that of the Unlawfulness of Defence, should gain much Ground; but above all, when we
further consider their professed Submission to the Higher Powers,
and their patient, inoffensive, non-resisting Deportment under
Sufferings, which made them Objects of Commiseration, it is easy
to discover that these were the natural Inducements that procured
them the Favour of a Toleration. I call it a Favour; for I deny
that either They, or any other religious Society that hold any
Principle inconsistent with the Security of Government, can upon
any just Maxims of Liberty claim such a Toleration, of Right.
And so sensible were these People of the Favour and Indulgence
derived to them by the Means of this Act, that they expressed their
Gratitude by the strongest Declarations of Thanks and Acknowledgment for it. But can it be imagined, *Gentlemen*, that if these
People holding a Principle inconsistent with the very Nature of
Government in general, had at the same time shewn themselves to
be of turbulent, factious Spirits; had they aspired to thrust themselves into the House of Commons as a sure Means of imposing
upon the Nation their religious Scheme; had they assumed an
Authority as a religious Society to intermeddle in judicial Affairs;
to hector and domineer over the King's Judges and Ministers of
Justice, in order to awe and restrain them from doing their Duty to
their King and Country under Pretences of Unity or Church-Discipline: Can it be imagined, I say, that if they had behaved in this
Manner, that they would have been deemed worthy of any Incouragement or Toleration? Or that on the contrary they would
not have been punished as licentious Invaders of the Civil Authority? It may indeed be said, that as *Quakers* have never been admitted to enjoy civil Offices in *England,* they could have no Pretence
or Colour at any Time for intruding their Church-Discipline to the
Purposes supposed. Be it so. But then, if in any other Part of the
British Dominions, where, by a very singular Indulgence, they have
been admitted to participate in common with the rest of their
Fellow-Subjects in the Enjoyment of Offices judicial and ministerial,

they have played the same Game, I hope it will be allowed to be an Incroachment upon the Civil Authority, a tyrannical Usurpation upon the common Rights of their Fellow-Subjects, and a most ungrateful Return for the peculiar Favours to which they have been admitted by the Indulgence of that Constitution under which they lived.

And now methinks, I see some starched and formal Cavillers ready to break forth, and ask, What is all this to the Purpose? "This whole Paragraph is but hypothetical, nothing is directly affirmed by it." Have a little Patience, *Gentlemen*. I wish it were only true in Theory or barely hypothetical. But I believe I shall be able to convince you, that Matters are carrying further than mere Speculation. It is Part of the Office of a Judge, upon the convening and swearing Grand-Juries immediately before their Entrance upon the Business for which they are called together, not only to give them in Charge such Things as are the proper Subjects of their Enquiry, but also to admonish and excite them to a faithful and conscientious Discharge of their Duty to their King and Country; and moreover to recommend to their Consideration whatever else shall be thought necessary for his Majesty's Service, and the publick Utility. This is as much a judicial Act as any other Court-Transaction can possibly be. I am, *Gentlemen,* (however unworthy the Honour) by the Authority of his Majesty's Commission, constituted Chief Justice of this Government, which gives me a Right to sit in this Place. And in *November* last, at a Court of Oyer and Terminer, held here, I did, according to Custom and the Duty of my Office, deliver from the Bench, as the Act of the Court, a Speech to the Grand-Jury, calculated to the best of our Judgments to the Occasion of the Times, his Majesty's Service, and the Good of the Publick. Had we committed any Mistakes therein, or exceeded the Limits of our Duty, or the Bounds of the Law; I take it we were accountable to his Majesty alone, and subject to no other Controul than the Laws of the Land which to his Majesty's Glory he makes the Measure of his Government. But I am mistaken, it seems, and am accountable for what I shall transact in the King's Courts as one of his Majesty's Judges, to a paultry ecclesiastical Jurisdiction, that calls itself a *Monthly Meeting*. Tell it not in *Gath*, publish it not in *Askalon!* Yes, *Gentlemen*, a *Monthly Meeting* of the People called *Quakers* (and sorry I am for the Occasion to mention it) under a Notion or Pretence of my being of their Society, and consequently subject to their Government, forsooth, have by their Ambassadors formally and insolently dealt with me, for presuming to utter any Thing from the Bench which they can't approve; and signified to me, that that Part of the Speech, wherein I assert the Lawfulness of Self-Defence to Christians, being not consonant to their Principles, unless I will publickly recant, they will expel me their Society, or in other Words, thunder out their Excommunication against me. An amazing Instance this, of the intoxicating Nature of Power, and of the voracious unbridled Appetite these meek self-denying Christians have after it. Is it not extraordinary, that these People, who, solely upon Account of their religious Principles, are almost every where kept under and excluded from civil Offices; and who take it as a Favour and Indulgence, that they are barely permitted to the Exercise of their Religion, should here, where by a singular Instance of Favour they have been admitted to an Equality with their Fellow-Subjects, thus grow rampant, take it into their Heads, that they have an Authority, as a religious Society, to intermeddle in judicial Affairs, to affront and brave the King's Courts, to lord it and domineer over his Majesty's Supream Judges, and other Ministers of Justice, in order to intimidate them from doing their Duty to their King and Country? In short, to act a Part, which, if it could have been foreseen, would justly have excluded them from all civil Offices, and left them upon the same Footing with their Brethren in other Places. Is their *Boasted Humility,* their Submission to the higher Powers come to this? They are content to be subject to their Superiors, provided they may have the supream Direction and Government of them.

IT was for Want of a timely Check to such Beginnings as these, that the Church of *Rome* extended by Degrees her wide Dominion, and usurped such an enormous Power over the Christian World, as to be able to govern it with an arbitrary and irresistible Sway. Nothing was able to withstand the spiritual Thunders of the Vatican. Princes were deposed, Subjects absolved from their Allegiance; and often both Princes and People excommunicated, and prohibited all Manner of religious Exercise, for Years together, by the apostolical Vicar of the meek and humble Jesus. And tho' the Constitution of *England* was the best calculated for Freedom and human Happiness of any Government in the known World, it was not able to stem the Torrent of that Church-Power, that like a Whirlpool drew all Things into its Vortex. And a moderate Acquaintance with History will furnish any one with numerous Instances, wherein the Crowns were made to totter upon the Heads of our Princes; and the civil Estate frequently reduced to the Brink of Ruin by the ecclesiastical. In fine, we may easily discover, that while the Church in any Shape was suffered to intermeddle with the civil Authority, so long there was neither Peace nor Safety for it. And it is worthy of Observation, that this stupendous Dominion proceeded not from any real Power in the Tyrants, but resulted intirely from an imaginary Authority in the Church, which had captivated and enslaved Men's Minds.

IT is therefore no light Matter, *Gentlemen*, but ought to alarm every Man, who has the Good of his Country and consequently his own Happiness at Heart, when ecclessiastical Judicatures, whether under the Constitution of his Holiness at *Rome*, or the Forms of *Synods, Presbyteries, Monthly-Meetings,* or any other religious Convocations, take upon them to insult Courts of Justice: For it is more than probable, that when Men are daring enough, in this Manner to attack the Judges themselves, in Relation to Matters merely judicial, they don't intend to stop there, but will endeavour to extend their Dominion to inferior Officers, to Jurymen, and perhaps to Witnesses. And if they have a Right to exercise their spiritual Domination over Judges, for Speeches to Grand-Jurys, I don't see what should tye up their Hands or restrain them from extending their Jurisdiction to Matters of private Property, or from intermeddling in the Prosecution of Criminals at the Suit of the Crown, whenever, for Reasons of State, or any political Considerations, they shall think it proper. The King's Courts, and all concerned in the Administration of Justice therein, ought to be perfectly free and at full Liberty to act according to the Laws, the Dictates of their Consciences, and the Right and Equity of Cases: But if these Attempts prevail, and Men are to be terrified from doing their Duty to their King and Country, by the Fear of Church Censures and Ecclesiastical Bugbears, there will soon be an End to all Law, and we may bid farewell to publick Justice: For it will always be in the Power of some prevailing Faction in Religion, as often as the Interest o the Brotherhood or Party are thought to be concerned in the Event of Causes, to give a favourable Turn to the Decision of them. Grand-Jurymen will not dare to find Bills, nor Petit-Jurymen Verdicts, whatever Cause there may be for them, against noted Zealots or sanctified Villains.

As for this Audacious, this daring Attempt, to wound the civil Authority tho' my Sides, I have good Reason to believe it did not spring originally from any Part of the lower Counties: But be that as it will, and whether it is a native Production of our own Soil, or that these People have been inspired and set on by their Friends above, who have already embroiled their own Government, and kindled Flames that will not easily be extinguished, it alters not the Case; tho' indeed this further may be apprehended from it, that the greater the Number of rich considerable People there is ingaged in the Confederacy, the greater is the Danger and Influence, and the more extensive will the spreading Mischief be.

For my own Part in this Affair, I thank God that he has given me Courage and Resolution to act according to the Duty of my Station to the best of my Understanding; and that I am not to be intimidated by vain and empty Threats, or impotent Censures, from discharging, with Uprightness and Integrity, that Trust which is reposed in me. And could I persuade myself, that Men in general held Church Anathemas in the same Derision and Contempt that I do, when they come in Competition with the Duty we all owe to God, to our King and to our Country. I would not have troubled you with this Discourse, but I am too well convinced the contary [sic] is true; and that many well-meaning People, thro' the Prejudice of Education, and for want of duely considering, that the Persons who compose these Kinds of Judicatories are weak and fallible Men like themselves, the Result of whose Consultations are not infrequently the Effects of Pride, Envy, Hatred and Wrath covered with the specious Cloathing of Humility, are too apt to entertain high and mistaken Notions of Unity and Church Power, and thereby to render themseves [sic] Slaves to an Hierarchy and ecclesiastical Fantoms.

I would not be understood to condemn all Church-Discipline, nor would I dissuade any Man from a reasonable Conformity to the Rules of the particular Society he thinks fit to join himself to: But as Civil Government is absolutely essential to human Happiness, and as there are certain Relations and Duties subsisting between one Man and another, and between every Man and the Civil Government under which he lives and by which he is protected, which are of prime Obligation antecedent to all Church-Government or private Compacts whatsoever, I would have every Man to be upon his Guard against Incroachments upon the Civil Authority, and keep a watchful Eye upon the Measures of such as would enervate moral Obligations and political Power by craftily setting up something else in their Places, and gilding it with the Name of Religion. There can be but one supream independant Power in any Society, and that supream independant Power must necessarily reside in the Civil Government: Amy Claim therefore of a Right to the Exercise of a Power in its Consequences paramount to the Civil Authority, must be founded on Usurpation, and tends to the Dissolution of the State.

AFTER what has been said to you in general, *Gentlemen*, I hope I have no need to say much to you to excite you to a resolute and faithful Discharge of your Duty, as Grand-Jurymen in particular. The same high Motives that should incite Judges and other Ministers of Justice to execute the Laws without Favour or Partiality, and to discharge the Duty of their several Stations, will, I doubt not, induce you to acquit yourselves with a Probity suitable to the Importance of the Office, and the great Trust reposed in you. The Oath and Affirmation you have now severally taken, exact of you Diligence and Impartiality: The Laws of the Land are to guide you in the Course of your Enquiries for the Good of your Country. If therefore you pay a proper Regard to These, you will be in no Danger from Tamperings or private Influences of religious Societies, but against all other Combinations of artful Men to turn you aside from your Duty.

I would not give just Cause of Offense to any, and therefore cannot hold myself excused from saying, That however infatuated and violent some of the People called *Quakers* amongst us may seem to be, and how much soever they may appear to have deviated from that peaceable and humble Disposition which rendered their primitive Brethren so remarkable, I am yet well assured it is by no means the Case of all the *Quakers*. I have the Honour to be personally acquainted with great Numbers of them, who entertain just Notions of true Liberty in the full Extent of it; who have just Ideas of the Nature of Civil Government, and of the Duty and Decorum they owe to it; who reject the Tenet which condemns the Lawfulness of defensive War to Christians as an idle untenable Whim; and who are not only worthy of all Favour and Toleration, but have also a Right to be ranked in the Number of his Majesty's best Subjects, and to share in all Civil Employments. And I am firmly perswaded, that the sensible *Quakers* in *England*, who have constantly guarded with great Prudence and Circumspection against every Thing that might give Umbrage to the Civil Government, are too wise to approve the inordinate and rash Measures of their Brethren here.

I think it necessary further to add, with regard to the Principles of the *Quakers* in general, that I know of none they publickly profess, that are not perfectly consistent with the Safety and Happiness of Civil Society, that of the Unlawfulness of defensive War only excepted. And if they are mistaken in that Point, and Defense is not only lawful but necessary, nothing can be more clear than that Persons perswaded of the Unlawfulness of it, are unfit to be trusted with the Power of making Laws; seeing Defence can no otherwise be effectually provided for. And as the Quakers are not all agreed as to the Point of Defence; if some Test was instituted to distinguish those amongst them who believe it lawful, from those who are perswaded of the contrary, I profess, I know no Reason why such of them as are perswaded of its Lawfulness, should not be employed in Legislation in common with other of their Fellow-Subjects.

I shall take up but little more of your Time, *Gentlemen*, but briefly enumerate and explain some of the particular Subjects of your present Enquiry; and,

First, HIGH-TREASON: which is the compassing and imagining the Death of the King, and must be manifested by some Overt-Act. Providing Arms to kill the King, levying War against him, assembling Persons in order to depose him or get him into their

Power, are all construed into compassing and imagining his Death, and make a Man guilty of High-Treason. Adhering to the King's Enemies, counterfeiting the Great Seal or Privy Seal, forging or counterfeiting the King's Coin, impairing it, or lightening it by clipping it, or otherwise, are likewise several Species of High-Treason. There are other Offences that amount to High-Treason; but as they be such as cannot well be committed here, I have no need to mention them to you.

Secondly, MISPRISION OF TREASON: Which is a Negligence in not revealing Treason where a Person is privy to it. But where such Concealment is attended with Circumstances that denote the Approbation of the Party, it then changes its Nature and becomes High-Treason.

Thirdly, PETIT-TREASON: Where one out of Malice takes away the Life of a Subject, to whom he owes special Obedience. It may be committed where a Servant kills his Master, a Wife her Husband, or a Secular his Prelate or Superior.

Fourthly, SODOMY: All unnatural Copulations, whether with Man or Beast, seem to come under the Notion of Sodomy, and are punished in the Manner of other Felonies which are excluded Clergy.

Fifthly, RAPE, or RAVISHMENT: Which is the carnal Knowledge of a Woman by Force and against her Will. This Offence is likewise punished with Death without Benefit of Clergy.

Sixthly, HOMICIDE: Which signifies the slaying of a Man, and is distinguished into voluntary and casual. Voluntary Homicide is that which is done with Deliberation, and a set Purpose to kill, which is Murder. And casual Homicide is when the Death of a Man happens by Chance, without any previous Intention to kill; and is either Manslaughter or Chance-medley. Murder is strictly and properly the wilful killing of any Subject whatsoever, through Malice forethought. Which Malice is of two kinds, *To Wit,* Either expressed or implied. Express Malice, where there is a previous Purpose to do some personal Injury to the Party slain. Implied Malice is where any Person in the Execution of an unlawful Action happens to kill a Man. Here altho' there were no Intent to do any personal Injury to the Party slain, yet the Law will supply the Malice, and make it Murder; so that whoever will undertake any Action in its own Nature unlawful, shall be chargeable with the Consequences of it, and therefore does it at his Peril.

MANSLAUGHTER is the unlawful Killing of a Man, without any preconceived Malice. As when two Persons meet, and upon falling out, one kills the other. It is done in present Heat, on a sudden

Quarrel, and upon a just Provocation; and differs from Murder only in this, that it is not done with Malice Foregoing.

CHANCE-MEDLEY is when a Man is doing a lawful Act, without Intention of Hurt to another, and the Death of some Person doth by Chance ensue. It is said, that if a Schoolmaster in correcting his Scholar, a Father his Son, a Master his Servant, or an Officer in whipping a Criminal in a reasonable Manner, happens to occasion his Death, it is Chance-Medly [sic] or Misadventure: But if they exceed the Bounds of Moderation, they are guilty of Manslaughter. And if they correct with an improper Instrument for Correction, as with a Sword, an Iron Bar; or if they kick the Party to the Ground and stamp upon him, so as by any of these Means to occasion Death, it is then said to be Murther, because of the Cruelty and Barbarity of the Action. Upon this I shall make a short Observation, that if the Cruelty and Barbarity of the Action by which one of the King's Subjects is killed, constitutes the Offence and makes it Murder in the particular Cases mentioned, it should seem by a clear Analogy, that whenever a Person loses his Life from a Series or Course of Cruelty and hard Usage practised towards him by another in whose Power he might happen to be, the Offence cannot be less heinous.

Seventhly, MAIHEM: Where any Person shall on Purpose and of Malice-Fore-thought, and by lying in wait, unlawfully cut out or disable the Tongue, put out an Eye, slit the Nose, cut off a Nose or Lip, or cut off or disable any Limb or Member of any Subject of his Majesty, with Intention, in so doing, to maim or disfigure, in any the said Members, such his Majesty's Subject; in every such Case, the Person or Persons so offending, their Counsellers, Aiders and Abettors, are by Act of Parliament declared Felons, and are made liable to suffer Death without Benefit of Clergy.

Eighthly, BURGLARY: Which is the breaking and entering into the Mansion-House of another in the Night Time, to the Intent to commit some Felony within the same, whether such felonious Intent be executed or not: And here, if the Thief break the Window, draw or lift the Latch, unlock the Door, or break the Wall or any other Part of the House; any of these amount to a Breaking in Law. So again, even the setting a Foot over the Threshold, putting the Hand or a Hook in at the Window, are to all Intents and Purposes in Law entering the House.

Ninthly, And by a late Act of Assembly of this Government, the Printing, Making, Signing or importing any Bills of Credit, in Imitation of those made current by Law, or the being aiding and assisting therein, with an Intent to defraud any Person, is made Felony of Death without Benefit of Clergy.

AND by another late Act of our Government, the Stealing of any Negro or Mulatto Slaves, Horse, Gelding, Mare or Colt, or the aiding or abetting such Theft, are made Felony of Death. So also, if any Tenant, Lodger, &c. in any Dwelling House, shall steal thence Goods, Wares or Merchandize, to the Value of *Five Pounds*; or if any Person shall enter into any Mansion or Dwelling House, by Day or by Night, without breaking the same, with an Intent to commit Felony, or being in such House shall commit any Felony, and shall in the Night Time break the said House to get out of it: These are declared to be Burglary and made Felony of Death.

To conclude, *Gentlemen*, all such Offences as are either Capital, or are of too high a Nature to fall under the Cognizance of the County Courts, are the proper Subjects of your Enquiry.

SPEECH

Against the Writs of Assistance

James Otis

Member of a distinguished Colonial family, James Otis was born in West Barnstable, Massachusetts on February 5, 1725. He was educated at Harvard and studied law with Jeremiah Bridley, who was not only an excellent lawyer but a fine classical scholar as well.

Otis first began the practice of law in Plymouth but soon moved to Boston where he shortly earned a reputation for his keen mind and ready wit. As a result of his efforts in opposition to the Writs of Assistance, Otis was elected to the state legislature in May of 1761. He soon found himself speaking and writing against the actions of Governor and Council. One such remonstrance, when read in the House, resulted in its being denounced as treason, much in the manner of Patrick Henry's famous speech to the Virginia House of Burgesses.

In 1766, James Otis was selected by his colleagues as speaker of the Massachusetts legislature but this selection was vetoed by Governor Bernard. Speeches, letters, circulars now followed each other in rapid pace as Otis plunged into the activities of those who dared to stand against established authority. Such actions soon earned for him the enmity of many who held high position. One such, John Robinson, a Commissioner of the Customs, meeting him in a coffee house, assaulted him with a cane and inflicted head wounds from which Otis seemingly never recovered completely. Never an especially stable person, he experienced only periods of lucidity after this event. One observer remarked: "He rambles and wanders like a ship without a helm. . . . The nervous, concise, and pithy were his character till lately; now the verbose, roundabout, and rambling, and long-winded."

On May 23, 1783, as he stood at the doorway of a farmhouse where he was then living, he was struck by lightning and instantly killed. Tradition has it that some time previously he had told his sister that this was the way he wished to die.

In 1755, the British government began to employ general writs of assistance to enable colonial officers to suppress smuggling that was widespread in the colonies. In 1761 Otis was selected by his fellow townsmen to lead the attack on these general warrants. Although, at the time, he was Advocate General, he resigned from this position and appeared before the Massachusetts Supreme Court in Boston on February 24–25 to plead the case of the colonists. The cause of the government was argued by Oxenbridge Thacher, who had been his law mentor only brief months before.

The text of the "Speech Against the Writs of Assistance" is taken from *The Massachusetts Spy Or, Thomas's Boston Journal,* Thursday, April 29, 1773.

May it Please Your Honours,

I was desired by one of the Court to look into the books, and consider the question now before the court, concerning Writs of Assistance. I have accordingly considered it, and now appear, not only in obedience to your order, but also in behalf of the inhabitants of this town, who have presented another petition, and out of regard to the liberties of the subject. And I take this opportunity to declare, that whether under a fee or not, (for in such a cause as this I despise a fee) I will to my dying day oppose, with all the powers and faculties God has given me, all such instruments of slavery on the one hand, and villainy on the other, as this writ of assistance is. It appears to me (may it please your honours) the worst instrument of arbitrary power, the most destructive of English liberty, and the fundamental principles of the constitution, that ever was found in an English law-book. I must therefore beg your honours patience and attention to the whole range of an argument, that may perhaps appear uncommon in many things, as well as to points of learning, that are more remote and unusual, that the whole tendency of my design may the more easily be perceived, the conclusions better descernd, and the force of them be better felt.

I shall not think much of my pains in this cause as I engage in it from principle. I was sollicited to engage on the other side. I was sollicited to argue this cause as Advocate-General, and because I would not, I have been charged with a desertion of my office; to this charge I can give a very sufficient answer. I renounced that office, and I argue this cause from the same principle; and I argue it with the greater pleasure as it is in favor of British liberty, at a time when we hear the greatest monarch upon earth declaring from his throne that he glories in the name of Briton, and that the privileges of his people are dearer to him than the most valuable prerogatives of his crown. And as it is in opposition to a kind of power, the exercise of which in former periods of English history, cost one King of England his head and another his throne. I have taken more pains in this cause, than I ever will take again: Although my engaging in this and another popular cause has raised much resentment; but I think I can sincerely declare, that I cheerfully submit myself to every odious name for conscience sake; and from my soul I despise all those whose guilt, malice or folly has made them my foes. Let the consequences be what they will, I am determined to proceed. The only principles of public conduct that are worthy a gentleman or a man are, to sacrifice estate, ease, health and applause, and even life itself to the sacred calls of his country. These manly sentiments in private life make the good citizen, in

public life, the patriot and the hero. I do not say, when brought
to the test, I shall be invincible; I pray God I may never be brought
to the melancholy trial; but if ever I should, it would be then
known, how far I can reduce to practice principles I know founded in
truth—In the mean time I will proceed to the subject of the writ. "In
the first, may it please your Honours, I will admit, that writs of one
kind, may be legal, that is, *special writs, directed to special officers,*
and to search *certain houses, &c. especially set forth in the writ,* may
be granted by the Court of Exchequer at home, *upon oath made before the Lord Treasurer by the person* who asks, *that he suspects such
goods to be concealed in* THOSE VERY PLACES HE DESIRES TO
SEARCH. The act of 14 Car. II. which Mr. Gridley mentions
proves this. And in this light the writ appears like a warrant from
a justice of peace to search for stolen goods. Your Honours will
find in the old book, concerning the office of a justice of peace,
precedents of general warrants to search suspected houses. But in
more modern books you will find only special warrants to search
such and such houses specially named, in which the complainant has
before sworn he suspects his goods are concealed; and you will find it
adjudged *that special warrants only are legal.* In the same manner
I rely on it, that the writ prayed for in this petition being general
is illegal. It is a power that places the liberty of every man in the
hands of every petty officer. I say I admit that *special* writs of assistance to search *special* places, may be granted to certain persons
on oath; but I deny that the writ now prayed for can be granted,
for I beg leave to make some observations on the writ itself before
I proceed to other Acts of Parliament.

In the first place the writ is UNIVERSAL, being directed 'to
all and singular justices, sheriffs, constables and all other officers
and subjects &c,' so, that in short it is directed to every subject in
the King's dominions; every one with this writ may be a tyrant:
if this commission is legal, a tyrant may, in a legal manner also,
controul, imprison or murder any one within the realm.

In the next place, IT IS PERPETUAL; there's no return, a
man is accountable to no person for his doings, every man may
reign secure in his petty tyranny, and spread terror and desolation
around him until the trump and the archangel shall excite different
emotions in his soul.

In the third place, a person with this writ, IN THE DAY TIME
may enter all houses, shops, &c. AT WILL, and command all to
assist.

Fourthly, by this not only deputies, &c. but even THEIR
MENIAL SERVANTS ARE ALLOWED TO LORD IT OVER US. What is
this but to have the curse of Canaan with a witness on us, to
be the servant of servants, the most despicable of GOD's creatures.
Now one of the most essential branches of English liberty,

is the freedom of one's house. A man's house is his castle; and whilst he is quiet, he is as well guarded as a prince in his castle. This writ, if it should be declared legal, would totally annihilate this privilege. Custom-house officers may enter our houses when they please—we are commanded to permit their entry—their menial servants may enter—may break locks, bars and every thing in their way—and whether they break through malice or revenge, no man, no court can inquire—bare suspicion without oath is sufficient. This wanton exercise of this power is no chimerical suggestion of a heated Brain. I will mention some facts. Mr. Pew had one of these writs, and when Mr. Ware succeeded him, he endorsed this writ over to Mr. Ware, so that THESE WRITS ARE NEGOTIABLE from one officer to another, and so your Honours have no opportunity of judging the persons to whom this vast power is delegated. Another instance is this. Mr. Justice Wally had called this same Mr. Ware before him by a constable, to answer for a breach of Sabbath-day acts, or that of profane swearing. As soon as he had done, Mr. Ware asked him if he had done, he replied, yes. Well then, says he, I will shew you a little of my power—I command you to permit me to search your house for unaccustomed goods; and went on to search his house from the garret to the cellar, and then served the constable in the same manner. But to shew another absurdity in this writ, if it should be established, I insist upon it EVERY PERSON by the 14 Car. II. HAS THIS POWER as well as Custom-house officers: the words are, 'It shall be lawful for any person or persons authorized &c.' What a scene does this open! Every man, prompted by revenge, ill humor or wantonness to inspect the inside of his neighbor's house, may get a writ of assistance; others will ask it from self defense; one arbitrary exertion will provoke another, until society be involved in tumult and in blood—again these writs ARE NOT RETURNED. Writs in their nature are temporary things; when the purposes for which they are issued are answered, they exist no more; but these monsters in the law live forever, no one can be called to account. Thus reason and the constitution are both against this writ. Let us see what authority there is for it. Not more than one instance can be found of it in all our law books, and that was in the zenith of arbitrary power, Viz. In the reign of Car. II. when star-chamber powers were pushed to extremity by some ignorant clerk of the Exchequer. But had this writ been in any book whatever, it would have been illegal. ALL PRECEDENTS ARE UNDER THE CONTROUL OF THE PRINCIPLES OF LAW. Lord Talbot says it is better to observe these than any precedents though in the House of Lords, the last resort of the subject.—No Acts of Parliament can establish such a writ: Though it should be made in the very words of the petition it would be void. 'AN ACT AGAINST

THE CONSTITUTION IS VOID.' Vid. Viner. But these prove no more than what I before observed, that *special* writs may be granted *on oath and probable suspicion.* The Act of 7th, and 8th of William III. that the officers of the plantations shall have the same powers, &c. is confined to this sense, that an officer should show probable ground, should take his oath on it, should do this before a magistrate, and that such magistrate, if he think proper should issue a *special warrant* to a constable to search the places. That of 6th Anne can prove no more.

SPEECH

in Defence of the Soldiers

Josiah Quincy, Jr.

Josiah Quincy, Jr. was born in Boston on February 23, 1744. He
attended grammar school at Braintree, Massachusetts under the
tutelage of Joseph Marsh. He entered Harvard University in
1759, receiving his A.B. degree in 1763 and his A.M. in 1766. For
this occasion, he was assigned the responsibility of delivering the
English oration, the highest academic honor given by the university.

Quincy began the study of law with Oxenbridge Thacher
and shortly after found himself in charge of the law office on the
death of his mentor. Early fame came to him when he consented,
along with John Adams, to defend the British soldiers who were
accused of murder in the Boston massacre.

He early became interested in politics, writing articles for the
Boston Gazette and publishing pamphlets urging opposition to
British colonial policies. He became part of the inner councils of
the Boston patriots and it was arranged for him to go to England to
present the case of the colonists. He left Boston in Sepember of
1774 and consulted with the leading Whigs in England regarding
the situation in America. His efforts, however, produced no results.

He began the return journey to America on March 16, 1775,
and died on board ship a few hours before arriving in Gloucester
harbor, April 26.

Courageous and tireless in the patriot cause, Quincy was an
ardent defender of the liberty of man—no matter which one—and
an effective enough speaker and agitator so that he was viewed by
the British as a "pestilent Fellow" who went "brandishing [the
lighted Torch] . . . up and down the Country, in hopes of kindling
the Flame of Civic Discord and Fury."

The "Speech in Defence of the Soldiers" was delivered at
the trial of William Wemms, James Hartegan, and others, soldiers
in his Majesty's Twenty-ninth Regiment, for the murder of
Crispus Attucks, Samuel Gray, and others on Monday evening, the
5th of March, 1770. The text is taken from the J. Fleeming edition
printed in Boston, 1770.

May it please your Honours and you Gentlemen of the Jury,

WE have at length gone through the evidence in behalf of
the prisoners. The witnesses have now placed before you, that
state of facts, from which results our defence. The examination has
been so lengthy, that I am afraid some painful sensations arise,
when you find that you are now to sit and hear the remarks of

the council. But you should reflect, that no more indulgence is shown to the Prisoners now on trial, than has ever been shown in all capital causes: the trial of one man has often taken up several days; when you consider, therefore, that there are eight lives in issue, the importance of the trial will show the necessity of its length. To each of the prisoners different evidence applies, and each of them draw their defence from different quarters.

I stated to you, Gentlemen, your duty, in opening this cause—do not forget the discharge of it. You are paying a debt you owe the community for your own protection and safety: by the same mode of trial are your own rights to receive a determination; and in your turn, a time may come, when you will expect and claim a similar return from some other jury of your fellow subjects.

In opening, I pointed to the dangers to which you were exposed; I trust your own recollection will now preclude a recapitulation of them. The reasons of what I then said, I trust have in some measure appeared: the propriety of some of those observations has been corroborated by succeeding evidences; and you must have traced yourselves, some of these consequences, turning out in evidence, which have had intimate relation, if not their origin, with some or all of those opinions, notions, sentiments or passions (call them what you will) which I took occasion to observe, as clues, aids, and leading-strings, in our intended examination and decision.

How much need was there for my desire, that you should suspend your judgment till the witnesses were all examined? How different is the complexion of the cause? Will not all this serve to show every honest man, the little truth to be attained in partial hearings? We have often seen communities complain of *ex parte* testimonies: individuals, as well as societies of men, are equally susceptible of injuries of this kind: this trial ought to have another effect; it should serve to convince us all, of the impropriety, nay injustice, of giving a latitude in conversation upon topicks, likely to come under a judicial decision; the criminality of this conduct is certainly enhanced, when such loose sallies and discourses are so prevalent as to be likely to touch the life of a citizen. Moreover there is so little certainty to be obtained by such kind of methods, I wonder we so often find them practiced. In the present case, how great was the prepossession against us? And I appeal to you, Gentlemen, what cause there now is to alter our sentiments. Will any sober, prudent man countenance the proceedings of the people in *King-Street*—can any one justify their conduct—is there any one man, or any body of men, who are interested to espouse and support their conduct? Surely no. But *our* inquiry must be confined to the *legality* of their conduct, and here can be no difficulty. It was certainly illegal, unless many witnesses are directly perjured: Witnesses who have no apparent interest to falsify—witnesses, who have given their testimony with candor and accuracy—witnesses, whose credibility stands untouched—whose credibility, the council for the King, do not pretend to impeach; or hint a suggestion to their disadvantage.

I say, Gentlemen, by the standard of the law are *we* to judge the actions of the people who were the assailants, and those who were the assailed, and then on duty. And here, Gentlemen, the rule, we formerly laid down, takes place. To the *facts,* Gentlemen, apply yourselves. Consider them as testified: weigh the credibility of the witnesses—balance their testimony—compare the several parts of it—see the amount of it—and then according to your oaths—"Make *true* deliverance according to your *evidence.*" That is, Gentlemen, having settled the facts—bring them truly to the standard of the law; the king's judges who are acquainted with it, who are presumed best to know it, will then inspect this great standard of right and wrong, truth and justice; and they are to determine the degree of guilt to which *the* fact rises.

But before we come to those divisions of enquiry, under which I intend to consider the evidence, let me once more carefully distinguish between the transactions in *Cornhill* and those by the *Custom House.*

The conduct of the soldiers in *Cornhill* may well be supposed to have exasperated the minds of all who beheld their behaviour. Their actions accumulated guilt as it flew—at least, we may well suppose, the incensed people who related them, added new colours to the scene. The flame of resentment imperceptibly enkindles, and a common acquaintance with human nature will shew, that it is no extravagant supposition, to imagine many a moderate man might at such a season, with such sentiments, which I have more than once noticed, hearing such relations and complaints; I say do I injure any one, in supposing, that under all these circumstances, a very moderate person, who in ordinary matters acted with singular discretion, should now be drawn imperceptibly away, or rather transported into measures, which in a future moment he would condemn and lament. What more natural supposition, than to suppose many an honest mind might at this time fluctuate thus. The soldiers are here—we wish them away: we did not send for them—they have cut and wounded the peaceable inhabitants, and it may be my turn next. At this instant of time, he has a fresh detail of injuries— resentment redoubles every successive moment—huzza! for the *Main-guard*: we are in a moment before the *Custom-House.* No time is given for recollection. We find, from the king's evidence, and from our own, the cry was "Here is a soldier!" Not here is *the soldier* who has injured us—here is the fellow who wounded the man in *Cornhill.* No, the reasoning or rather ferment seems to be, the soldiers have committed an outrage, we have an equal right to inflict punishment—or rather revenge, which they had to make an assault. They said right, but never considered, that *those* soldiers *had no* right at all. These are sentiments natural enough to persons in this state of mind—we can easily suppose even good men thinking and acting thus. Very similar to this is the force of Dr. *Hirons's* testimony, and some others. But our enquiry is—What says the law? We must calmly enquire, whether this, or any thing like it, is countenanced by the law. What is *natural* to the *man*—what are his feelings are one thing: what is the *duty* of the *citizen* is quite another. Reason must resume her seat—and then we shall hear, and obey the voice of the law.

The law indulges no man in being his own avenger. Early, in the history of jurisprudence, we find the sword taken from the party injured, and put into the hands of the magistrate. Were not this the case, punishment would know no bounds in extent or duration. Besides, it saps the very root of distributive justice, when any individual invades the prerogative of law, and snatches from the civil magistrate the balance and the rod. How much more are the pillars of security shaken, when a mixt body, assembled as those in *King-street,* assume the province of justice, and invade the rights of the citizen? For it must not be forgot, that the soldier is a citizen, equally entitled with us all to protection and security. Hence all are alike obliged to pay obedience to the law: For the price of this protection is that of obedience.

Let it not be apprehended, that I am advancing a doctrine, that a soldier may attack an inhabitant, and he not allowed to defend himself. No Gentlemen! if a soldier rush violently through the street and presents a weapon of death, in a striking posture; no doubt the person assailed may defend himself, even to taking the life of the assailant. Revenge and a sense of self Preservation instantly take possession of the person thus attacked; and the law goes not upon the absurd supposition, that a person can in these circumstances, unman himself. Hence we find a husband, taking his wife in the act of adultery, instantly seizes a deadly weapon and slays the adulterer; it is not murder. Nay a fillip upon the nose or forehead, in anger, is supposed by the law to be sufficient provocation to reduce killing to Manslaughter. It is, therefore, upon principles like these, principles, upon which those, who now bear the hardest against us, at other times, so much depend; it is, I say, upon the right of self-defence and self-preservation we rely for our acquittal.

Here again it should be kept in view, that whenever the party injuring has escaped by flight, and time sufficient for the passions to cool, in judgment of law, hath elapsed; however great the injury, the injured party must have recourse to law for his redress. Such is the wisdom of the law; of that law, than which we are none of us to presume ourselves wiser; of that law, which is found in the experience of ages, and which in condescension to the infirmities of flesh and blood (but to nothing else) extenuates the offence.

For "no man, says the learned Judge *Foster, under the protection of the law* is to be the *avenger* of his own wrongs. If they are of such a nature for which the laws of society will give him an adequate remedy, *thither* he ought to resort. But be they *of what nature soever,* he *ought* to bear his lot *with patience* and remember, *that vengeance belongeth to the Most High."* Crown Law 296.

Now, Gentlemen, those, whoever they were, who committed the outrage in *Cornhill, had absconded*—the soldiers, who are supposed to have done them, were confined in their barracks. People were repeatedly told this, and assured by the military officers, that they should not go unpunished. But what followed? Are all present appeased? We are constrained, by the force of the evidence, to affirm they were not. But to get regular and right ideas, we must consider all the commotions of the season, and endeavour to come at truth by analyzing the evidence, and arranging it, under distinct heads of enquiry. [Mr. *Quincy* now entered, at large, upon a review of the appearances in several parts of the town: he was copious upon the expressions and behaviour sworn to.

He, then, more particularly recapitulated the evidence touching *Murray's Barracks, Dock-square,* and the *Market-place.*

He next pursued several parties, through the several lanes and streets, till they centered at the scene of action.

The testimonies of the witnesses, who swore to the repeated information given the people—that the Sentry and party were on duty; that they were desired to withdraw and warned of the consequences; were in their order considered.

Under the next three heads, was remarked "the temper of the *Sentry,* of the *party of soldiers,* and of the *people surrounding them."*

The words, *insult* and *gestures* of the same persons were next pointed out: and from thence was collected the designs of the persons *assaulting,* and the reasonable apprehensions of those *assaulted.*

Mr. *Quincy* then came to the *attack* itself; considering who the persons were (namely *some* sailors;) remarking minutely the words and actions immediately preceeding the onset; the weapons used; the violence of the assault and battery; and the danger of the soldiers.

Mr. *Quincy* next exhibited those parts of the testimonies, which evidenced the attack continued *after the firing.*

Under all these heads, there was methodically stated the number of the witnesses to each point, and by a comparative view of all the proofs, conclusions drawn as to the force of the whole.

The next consideration, in this mode of enquiry, was the evidence as severally pertaining to *each* prisoner, with such observations, on the one hand, as served to shew a defect of legal proof as to *fact;* on the other, such matters as served to *justify, execuse* (sic) or *extenuate* the offence, in law.

And particularly with regard to *Killroy*, Mr. *Quincy* cited and commented on the following passages from Judge Foster's Crown law, and the Marquiss of *Beccaria's* Essay on Crimes and punishments.

"WORDS are often misrepresented, whether through ignorance, inattention, or malice, it mattereth not the defendant, he is equally effected in either case; and they are extremely liable to misconstructions. And withall, this evidence is not in the ordinary course of things to be disproved by that sort of negative evidence by which the proof of plain facts may be and often is confronted." Crown Law, 243.

"Finally, the CREDIBILITY of a witnesses is NULL when the question relates to the WORDS of a *criminal;* for the tone of voice, the gesture, all that preceds, accompanies and follows the different ideas which men annex to the same words, may so alter and modify a man's discourse, that it is almost impossible to repeat them precisely in the manner in which they were spoken. Besides, violent and uncommon actions, such as real crimes, leave a trace in the multitude of circumstances that attend them, and in their effects; but *Words* remain only in the memory of the hearers, who are commonly negligent or prejudiced. It is infimitely (sic) easier then to found an accusation on the *Words,* than on the *actions* of a man; for in these, the number of circumstances, urged against the accused, afford him variety of means of *justifications*."]

May it please your Honours, and you Gentlemen of the Jury,

AFTER having thus gone through the evidence, and considered it as applicatory to *all* and *every* of the prisoners, the next matter in order seems to be the consideration of the law pertinent upon this evidence.

And here, Gentlemen, let me again inform you, that the law which is to pass upon these prisoners, is a law adapting itself to the human species, with all their feelings, passions and infirmities; a law which does not go upon the absurd supposition, that men are stocks and stones; or that in the fervour of the blood, a man can act with the deliberation and judgment of a philosopher. No Gentlemen—the law supposes that a principle of resentment, for wise and obvious reasons, is deeply implanted in the human heart; and not to be eradicated by the efforts of state policy. It, therefore, in some degree conforms itself to all the workings of the passions, to which it pays a great indulgence, so far as not to be wholly incompatible, with the wisdom, good order and the very being of government.

Keeping therefore this full in view, let us take once more, a very brief and cursory survey of matters supported by the evidence. And here, let me ask sober reason—What language more more approbrious—What actions more exasperating, than those used on this occasion? Words, I am sensible are no *justification* of blows, but they serve as the grand clues to discover the temper and the designs of the agents: they serve also to give us light in discerning the apprehensions and thoughts of those who are the objects of abuse.

"You lobster," "You bloody-back," "You coward" and "You dastard," are but some of the expressions proved. What words more galling? What more cutting and provoking to a soldier? To be reminded of the colour of his garb, by which he was distinguished from the rest of his fellow citizens; to be compared to the most despicable animal, that crawls upon the earth, was touching indeed a tender point. To be stigmatized with having smarted under the lash, at the halbert, to be twited with so infamous an ignominy; which was either wholly undeserved, or a grievance which should never have been repeated—I say to call up and awaken sensations of this kind, must sting even to madness. But accouple these words with the succeeding actions—"You dastard"—"You coward!"—A soldier and a coward! This was touching, (with a witness) *"The point of honour,* and the pride of virtue." But while these are as yet fomenting the passions, and swelling the bosom, the attack is made: and probably the latter words were reitterated at the onset; at lest, were yet sounding in the ear. Gentlemen of the jury, for heaven's sake, let us put ourselves in the same situation! Would you not spurn at that spiritless institution of society, which tells you to be a *subject* at the expence of your *manhood?*

But does the soldier step out of his ranks to seek his revenge? Not a witness pretends it: Did the people repeatedly come within the points of their bayonets, and strike on the muzzels of the guns? You have heard the witnesses.

Does the law allow one member of the community to behave in this manner towards his fellow-citizen, and then bid the injured party be calm and moderate? The expressions from one party were —"Stand off—stand off!" "I am upon my station"—"if they molest me *upon my post,* I will fire."—"Keep off!" These were words likely to produce reflection and procure peace. But had the words on the other hand a similar tendency?—Consider the temper prevalent among all parties at this time. Consider the then situation of the soldiery; and come to the heat and pressure of the action. The materials are laid, the spark is raised, the fire inkindles, the flame rages, the understanding is in wild disorder, all prudence and true wisdom are utterly consumed. Does common sense, does the law expect impossibilities? *Here,* to expect equanimity of temper, would be as irrational, as to expect discretion in a madman. But was anything done on the part of the assailants, similar to the conduct, warnings and declarations of the prisoners? Answer for yourselves, Gentlemen. The words reiterated, all around, stabbed to the heart, the actions of the assailants tended to a worse end: To awaken every passion of which the human breast is susceptible. Fear, anger, pride, resentment, revenge, alternately, take possession of the whole man. To expect, under these circumstances, that such words would asswage the tempest, that such actions would allay the flames—You might, as rationally, expect the inundations of a torrent would suppress a deluge; or rather, that the flames of Etne would extinguish a conflagration!

Prepare, Gentlemen of the Jury, now to attend to that species of law, which will adapt itself to this trial, with all its singular and aggravating circumstances. A law full of benignity, full of compassion, replete with mercy.

And here, Gentlemen, I must, agreeable to the method we formerly adopted, first tell you by what law the prisoners are *not* to be tried, or condemned. And they most certainly are *not* to be tried by the *Mosaic* law: a law, we take it, peculiarly designed for the government of a peculiar nation, who being in a great measure under a theoretical form of government, it's institutions cannot, with any propriety, be adduced for our regulation in these days. It is with pain, therefore, I have observed any endeavour to mislead our judgment on this occasion; by drawing our attention to the precepts delivered in the days of *Moses;* and by disconnected passages of Scriptures, applied in a manner foreign to their original design or import, there seems to have been an attempt to touch some peculiar sentiments, which we know are thought to be prevalent; and in this way, we take it, an injury is like to be done, by giving the mind a biass, it ought never to have received; because it is not warranted by our laws.

We have heard it publicly said of late, oftener, than formerly, "Whosoever shedeth man's blood, by man shall his blood be shed." This is plainly, Gentlemen, a general rule, which, like all others of the kind must have its exceptions. A rule, which if taken in it's strict litteral lattitude, would imply, that a man killing another in self defence, would incur the pains of death. A doctrine, which no man in his senses would ever embrace: a doctrine that certainly never prevailed under the *Mosaical* institution. For we find, the *Jews* had their six cities of refuge, to which the manslayer might flee, from the avenger of blood. And something analogous to this, (if it did not originate from it) is our benefit of clergy.

And so, that "the murderer shall flee to the pit" comes under the same consideration. And when we hear it asked, as it very lately has been, "Who DARE stay him?" I answer, if the laws of our country stay him, you ought to do likewise; and every good subject *dares* to do what the law allows. But the very position is *begging the question*: for the question, now in issue, is, whether either of the prisoners is a murderer, in the sense of our laws; for you recollect, that what is murder and what not, is *a question of law,* arising upon facts stated and allowed.

But to go on; "You shall take no satisfaction for the life of a *murderer,* which is *guilty of death.*" Here again, is a begging the question; and moreover the words *"guilty of death,"* if rightly rendered from the original, must be one of those general rules, I just now mentioned; which always have their exceptions. But those words seem to be wrong translated: for in the margin of our great bible, we find them rendered *"faulty to die."* Against a position of this kind we have no objection. If we have committed *a fault,* on which *our laws* inflict the punishment of *death,* we must suffer. But what fault we have committed you are to enquire: or rather you, Gentlemen, are to find the *facts proved in Court against us,* and the judges are to see and consider what the law pronounces touching our offence, and what punishment is thereby inflicted as a penalty.

In order to come at the whole law resulting from the facts which have been proved, we must enquire into the LEGALITY of the *assemblies.* For such is the wisdom and policy of the law, that if any assembly be *lawful,* each individual of that assembly is answerable *only for his own act,* and *not for any other.* On the contrary, if an assembly be *unlawful, the act of any one* of the company, to the particular purpose of assembling, is *chargeable on all.* This is law, which no lawyer will dispute; it is a law founded in the security of the peace of society, and however little considered, by people in general, it ought now steadily to be kept in mind.

Was the assembly of the soldiers lawful?

For What did the soldiers assemble?

Was the Sentinel insulted and attacked?

Did he call for assistance, and did the party go to assist him?

Was it lawful for them so to do?

Was the soldiers when thus lawfully assembled, assaulted, &c. by a great number of people assembled, &c.

Was this last assembly lawful?

Was anything done by this unlawful assembly, that will, in law, justify, excuse, or extenuate the offence of killing, so as to reduce it to manslaughter?

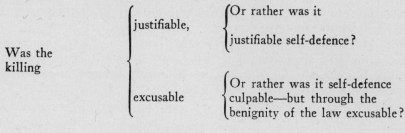

Was the killing
justifiable, { Or rather was it justifiable self-defence?

excusable { Or rather was it self-defence culpable—but through the benignity of the law excusable?

Or felonious?

If felonious, was it { with or / without } Malice?

Under each of these heads of enquiry, in their order, Mr. *Josiah Quincy* arranged his arguments; and as he separated and compared, and settled the facts, he applied, his law, with explanatory comments. In the course of which he necessarely run over again facts, that had been before cited, which occasions our omission of this part of his defence. But for the sake of those, who would chuse to inspect, at their leisure, the authorities. They are here subjoined in the order, in which they were cited.

Hawkin's Vol. II, p. 29. 9. *ibid*—Mutiny Act p. 115, 116, 117, 118 § 78.8—Blackstone's Com. Vol. 1. p. 147. 262. 335, 336—Blackstone Vol. IV. p. 194, 195—3d Institute p. 51. 57—Blackstone Vol. IV. p. 191, 192—Foster's Crown Law 276, 277, 278. 262, 267—Blackstone Vol. IV. p. 200 top.

Blackstone Vol. IV. p. 180. 280—Foster's Crown Law p. 298—3d Institute, 56 top—Hawkins Vol. 1. 75—*ibid* 71 bot. *ibid* 72 top—Foster's Crown Law 273, 274—Keil 128, 129 51.

Foster's Crown Law 278. 277. 276. 295.

Blackstone Vol. I. p. 191—Foster's Crown Law p. 277—Blackstone Vol. IV. p. 192—Foster's Crown Law p. 298. 296. 292—3d Institute p. 55 bot.—Hawkins Vol. 1. p. 82 bot. 84 mid.—Hawkins pleas of the Crown Vol. 1 p. 484—Hawkins Vol. 1. 85 mid.—Cro. Car. p. 537 Cooks case—Hale Vol. II. p. 274—Blackstone Vol. IV. p. 183—Hawkins Vol. I. p. 82 bot.—Keil p. 135 bot.

Foster p. 261, 262—Blackstone Vol. IV. p. 27—Hawkins Vol. I. p. 84 § 44—Foster p. 350 § 5.

Hawkins Vol. 1 Chap. 31, § 21—cites Bulstrode p. 86, 87—Keil p. 51—Lord Bacon's Eleut. 25.

The law laid down in Foster, 261, 2. before cited, being indisputable law, not denied or controverted; and being very material in the trial, and much relied on by the prisoners, is here set down at large.

"I will mention a case, (says the learned Judge,) which through the ignorance or lenity of juries hath been sometimes brought within the rule of accidental death. It is where a blow aimed at *one* person lighteth upon *another* and killeth him. This, in a loose way of speaking, may be called accidental *with regard to the person who dieth by a blow not intended against* HIM. But the law considereth this case in a quite different light. If from circumstances it appeareth that the injury intended to A be it by poison, blow, or ANY OTHER MEANS OF DEATH, would have amounted to murder, supposing *him* to have been killed by it, it will amount to the same offence if B. happeneth to fall by the same means. Our books say, that in this case the malice *egreditus personam.* But to speak more intelligibly, where the injury intended against A. proceeded from a wicked, murderous, or mischievous motive, the party is answerable for all the consequences of the action, if death ensues, from it, though it had not its effect upon the person whom he intended to destroy. The *malitia* I have already explained, the heart regardless of social duty DELIBERATELY bent upon mischief, consequently the guilt of the party is just the same in one case as the other. *On the other hand,* if the blow intended against A. and lighting on B. *arose from a sudden trasport of passion* which in case A. had died by it, *would have been reduced to manslaughter,* the fact will admit of the SAME ALLEVIATION if B. should happen to fall by it." To the same effect are other authorities.

May it please your Honours, and you Gentlemen of the Jury,

I have now gone thro' those authorities in law, which I thought pertinent to this trial. I have been thus lengthy, not for the information of the Court, but to satisfy you, Gentlemen, and all who may chance to hear me, of that law, which is well known to those of us, who are conversant in courts, but not so generally known, or attended to, by many, as *it ought to be*—A law which extends to each of us, as well as to any of the prisoners; for it knows *no distinction of persons.*

And the doctrines which have been thus laid down are for the safeguard of us all. Doctrines which are founded in the wisdom and policy of ages; which the greatest men, whoever lived, have adopted and contended for. Nay, the matter has been carried, by very wise men, much farther than we have contested for. And that you may not think the purport of the authorities read, are the rigid notions of a dry system, and the contracted decisions of municipal law, I beg leave to read to you a passage from a very great, theoretic, writer: a man whose praises have resounded through all the known world, and probably will, through all ages, whose sentiments are as free air, and who has done as much for learning, liberty, and mankind, as any of the Sons of *Adam,* I mean the sagacious Mr. *Locke*: He will tell you, Gentlemen, in his Essay on Government, p. 2. c: 3. That *all manner of force without right* puts man in a state of *war* with the *aggressor;* and of consequence, that, being in such a state of *war,* he may LAWFULLY KILL him, who put him under this *unnatural* restraint. According to this doctrine, we should have nothing to do, but enquire, whether here was *"force without right:"* if so, we were *in such a state,* as rendered it LAWFUL TO KILL the aggressor, who "put us under so *unnatural* a *restraint.* Few, I believe will say, after hearing *all* this evidence, that we were under no *unnatural restraint."* But we don't want to extend matters so far. We cite this author to show the world, that the greatest friends to their country, to universal liberty, and the immutable rights of all men, have held tenets, and advanced maxims favourable to the prisoners at the bar. And although we should not adopt the sentiments of Mr. *Locke* in their most extensive latitude, yet there seems to be something very analogous to his opinion, which is countenanced in our laws.

There is a spirit which pervades the whole system of *English* jurisprudence, which inspires a freedom of thought, speech, and behaviour. Under a form of government like ours, it would be in vain to expect, that pacific, timid, obsequious, and servile temper, so predominant in more despotic governments. From our happy constitution there results it's very natural effects—an impatience of injuries, and a strong resentment of insults: (and a very wise man has said, "He who *tamely* beareth insults *inviteth* injuries.") Hence, I take it, that attention to the "feelings of humanity"—to "humanity and imperfection"—"the infirmities of flesh and blood;" that attention to "the indelible rights of mankind"—that lenity to "the passions of man"—that "benignity and condescention of the law" so often repeated in our books.

And, indeed, if this were not the case, the genius of our civil constitution and the spirit of our municipal law would be repugnant —that prime defect in any political system—that grand solecism in state-policy.

Gentlemen of the Jury,

This cause has taken up much of your time, and is likely to take up so much more, that I must hasten to a close: indeed I should not have troubled you, by being thus lengthy, but from a sense of duty to the prisoners; they, who, in some sense, may be said to have put their lives in my hands; they whose situation was so peculiar, that we have necessarily taken up more time, than ordinary cases require: they, under all these circumstances, placed a confidence, it was my duty not to disappoint; and which I have aimed at discharging with fidelity. I trust you, Gentlemen, will do the like: that you will examine and judge with a becoming temper of mind; remembering that they who are *under oath* to declare the *whole truth,* think and act very differently from by-standers, who, being under no ties of this kind, take a latitude, which is by no means admissible in a *court of law.*

I cannot close this cause better, than by desiring you to consider well the genious and spirit of the law, which will be laid down, and to govern yourselves by this great standard of truth. To some purposes, you may be said, Gentlemen, to be *Ministers of justice:* and "Ministers (says a learned Judge) "appointed for the ends of public justice, should have written on their *hearts* the solemn engagements of his Majesty, (at his coronation) to cause law and justice IN MERCY to be executed in *all* his judgments."

> *The quality of mercy is not strained;*
> *It droppeth like the gentle rain from heaven . . . .*
> *It is twice blessed;*
> *It blesses* him that gives, *and* him that takes.

I leave you, Gentlemen, hoping you will be directed in your enquiry and judgment; to a right discharge of your duty. We shall all of us, Gentlemen, have an hour of cool reflection—when the feelings and agitations of the day shall have subsided; when we shall view things through a different, and a much juster medium. It is, *then,* we all wish an absolving conscience. May you, Gentlemen, now act such a part, as will hereafter ensure it; such a part as may occasion the prisoners to rejoice. May the blessing of those, who were in jeopardy of life, come upon you—may the blessing of him who is *"not faulty to die,"* discend and rest upon you and your posterity.

SPEECH

in Defence of the Soldiers

John Adams

John Adams, second President of the United States, was born in
Braintree, Massachusetts (in a section of the town that later became
the separate town of Quincy) on October 19, 1735. He was
graduated from Harvard College in 1755, and taught school for a
while in Worcester while preparing himself for law. He was admitted to the bar in 1758. As his law practice grew, he took an increased interest in town matters, and wrote for newspapers on
public affairs. In October, 1764, he married Abigail Smith.

Adams first proved his jurisprudential ability with his arguments against the Stamp Act. He became one of the leaders of the
Boston Bar, and was elected to the General Court.

In 1774, Adams was elected delegate to the First Continental
Congress, and remained a member of the Congress till 1778. Dur-
ing this time, he wrote his *Novangius* papers and outlined his
"Thoughts on Government," written to counteract Thomas Paine's
Common Sense. On June 7, 1776, Adams seconded the motion of
Richard Henry Lee that the Colonies should be "free and in-
dependent states;" a proposition he debated before the Congress. He
was selected as a member of the committee to draft the Declaration
of Independence. He was chosen head of the Board of War and
Ordnance, Minister Plenipotentiary for Peace Treaties with
Britain, and minister to Holland.

In 1785, Adams was appointed ambassador to the court of
St. James. While in London, he published *A Defense of the Con-
stitution of the United States of America Against the Attack of Mr.
Turgot,* which appeared in three volumes in 1787.

In April, 1790, he began his *Discourses on Davila,* published
in the *United States Gazette* in 1791. These were expositions on
the tragedy of civil wars. He had watched the progress of the
French Revolution, and could envision nothing but failure in civil
matters when a proper government was absent. He became recognized
as one of the leaders of the Federalists. In 1796, when Washington
refused to accept another election, Adams was chosen president, defeating Jefferson.

Adam's four years as president, 1797–1801, were marked with
intrigue and national emotional upheaval. The passage of the Alien
and Sedition Acts has generally been laid to him and to other leaders
of the Federalist party.

But despite the national militant spirit aroused by the French
crisis, Adams staunchly kept himself to maintaining the peace with
France.

Immediately upon the end of his term of office in 1801, Adams
retired to Quincy, Massachusetts, where he consoled himself with

his library. He continued close correspondence with Jefferson and spoke freely on public affairs, even though by this time he had no party affiliation.

On July 4, 1826, John Adams died at age ninety, very nearly at the hour of Jefferson's death.

The "Speech in Defense of the Soldiers" was delivered at the trial of William Wemms, James Hartegan, and other soldiers in His Majesty's Twenty-ninth Regiment for the murder of Crispus Attucks, Samuel Gray, and others on the fifth of March, 1770. The text is from John Hodgson. *The Trial of William Wemms, James Hartegan, William McCanley, Hugh White, Matthew Killroy, William Warren, John Carrol, and Hugh Montgomery.* Boston: Fleeming, 1770.

May it please your Honours and you Gentlemen of the Jury,

I am for the prisoners at the bar, and shall apologize for it only in the words of the Marquis *Beccaria*: "If I can but be the instrument of preserving one life, his blessing and tears of transport, shall be a sufficient consolation to me, for the contempt of all mankind." As the prisoners stand before you for their lives, it may be proper, to recollect with what temper the law requires we should proceed to this trial. The form of proceeding at their arraignment, has discovered that the spirit of the law upon such occasions, is conformable to humanity, to common sense and feeling; that it is all benignity and candor. And the trial commences with the prayer of the Court, expressed by the Clerk; to the Supream JUDGE of Judges, empires, and worlds: "God send you a good deliverance."

We find, in the rules laid down by the greatest English judges, who have been the brightest of mankind: we are to look upon it as more beneficial, that many guilty persons should escape unpunished, than one innocent person should suffer. The reason is, because it's of more importance to community, that innocence should be protected, than it is, that guilt should be punished; for guilt and crimes are so frequent in the world, that all of them cannot be punished; and many times they happen in such a manner, that it is not of much consequence to the public, whether they are punished or not. But when innocence it self, is brought to the bar and condemned, especially to die, the subject will exclaim, it is immaterial to me, whether I behave well or ill; for virtue itself, is no security. And if such a sentiment as this, should take place in the mind of the subject, there would be an end to all security whatsoever. I will read the words of the law itself.

The rules I shall produce to you from Lord Chief Justice *Hale,* whose character as a lawyer, a man of learning and philosophy, and as a christian, will be disputed by nobody living; one of the greatest and best characters, the English nation ever produced:

his words are these. 2. H.H.P.D. *Tutius semper est errare, in acquietando, quam in puniendo, exparte misericordiae, quam ex parte justitiae,* it is always safer to err in acquitting, than punishing, on the part of mercy, than the part of justice : The next is from the same authority, 305 *Tutius erratur ex parte mitiori,* it is always safer to err on the milder side, the side of mercy, H.H.P.C. 509, the best rule in doubtful cases, is, rather to incline to acquital than conviction : and in page 300 *Quod dubitas ne feceris,* Where you are doubtful never act; that is, if you doubt of the prisoners guilt, never declare him guilty; this is always the rule, especially in cases of life. An other rule from the same Author, 289, where he says, In some cases, presumptive evidence go far to prove a person guilty, though there is no express proof of the fact, to be committed by him; but then it must be very warily pressed, for it is better, five guilty persons should escape unpunished, than one innocent person should die.

The next authority shall be from another Judge, of equal character, considering the age wherein he lived; that is Chancellor *Fortescue,* in praise of the laws of England, page 59, this is a very ancient writer on the English law : his words are, "Indeed one would rather, much rather, that twenty guilty persons escape the punishment of death, than one innocent person be condemned, and suffer capitally." Lord Chief Justice *Hale,* says, It is better five guilty persons escape, than one innocent person suffer. Lord Chancellor *Fortescue,* you see, carries the matter farther, and says, Indeed one had rather, much rather, that twenty guilty persons should escape, than one innocent person suffer capitally. Indeed, this rule is not peculiar to the English law, there never was a system of laws in the world, in which this rule did not prevail; it prevailed in the ancient Roman law, and which is more remarkable, it prevails in the modern Roman law, even the Judges in the Courts of Inquisition, who with racks, burnings and scourges, examine criminals, even there, they preserve it as a maxim, that it is better the guilty should escape punishment, than the innocent suffer. *Satius esse nocentem absolvi quam insentem damnari,* this is the temper we ought to set out with; and these the rules we are to be governed by. And I shall take it for granted, as a first principle, that the eight prisoners at the bar, had better be all acquitted, though we should admit them all to be guilty, than, that any one of them should, by your verdict, be found guilty, being innocent.

I shall now consider the several divisions of law, under which the evidence will arrange itself.

The action now before you, is homicide; that is the killing of one man by another, the law calls it homicide, but it is not criminal in all cases, for one man to slay another. Had the prisoners been on the *Plains of Abraham,* and slain an hundred *Frenchmen* apiece, the *English* law would have considered it, as a commendable action, virtuous and praiseworthy: so that every instance of killing a man, is not a crime in the eye of the law; there are many other instances which I can not enumerate, an officer that executes a person under sentence of death, &c. So that, Gentlemen, every instance of one man's killing another, is not a crime, much less a crime to be punished with death. But to descend to some more particulars.

The law divides homicide into three branches; the first, is justifiable, the second excusable, and the third felonious; felonious homicide, is subdivided into two branches; the first is murder, which is killing with malice aforethought, the second is manslaughter, which is killing a man on a sudden provocation: here Gentlemen, are four sorts of homicide, and you are to consider, whether all the evidence amounts to the first, second, third, or fourth of these heads. The fact, was the slaying five unhappy persons that night; you are to consider, whether it was justifiable, excusable, or felonious; and if felonious, whether it was murder or manslaughter. One of these four it must be, you need not divide your attention to any more particulars. I shall however, before I come to the evidence, show you several authorities, which will assist you and me in contemplating the evidence before us.

I shall begin with justifiable homicide; if an officer a sheriff execute a man on the gallows, draws and quarters him, as in case of high treason, and cuts off his head, this is justifiable homicide, it is his duty. So also, Gentlemen, the law has planted fences and barriers around every individual; it is a castle round every man's person, as well as his house. As the love of God and our neighbor, comprehends the whole duty of man, so self-love and social, comprehend all the duties we owe to mankind, and the first branch is self-love, which is not only our indisputable right, but our clearest duty, by the laws of nature, this is Interwoven in the heart of every individual; God almighty, whose laws we cannot alter, has implanted it there, and we can annihilate ourselves, as easily as root out this affection for ourselves. It is the first, and strongest principle in our nature, Justice *Blackstone* calls it, "The primary cannon in the law of nature." That precept of our holy religion which commands us to love our neighbor as ourselves doth not command us to love our neighbor better than ourselves, or so well, no Christian Divine hath given this interpretation. The precept enjoins, that our benevolence to our fellowmen, should be as real and sincere, as our affections to ourselves, not that it should be as great in degree. A man is authorised therefore by common sense, and the laws of England, as well as those of nature, to love himself better than his fellow subject: If two persons are cast away at sea, and get on a plank, (a case put by Sir Francis *Bacon*) and the plank is insufficient to hold them both, the one hath a right to push the other off to save himself. The rules of the common law therefore, which authorize a man to preserve his own life at the expence of another's, are not contradicted by any divine or moral law. We talk of liberty and property, but, if we cut up the law of self-defence, we cut up the foundation of both, and if we give up this, the rest is of very little value, and therefore, this principle must be strictly attended to, for whatsoever the law pronounces in the case of these eight soldiers will be the law, to other persons and after ages, all the persons that have slain mankind in this country, from the beginning to this day, had better have been acquitted, than that a wrong rule and precedent should be established.

I shall now, read to you a few authorities on this subject of self defence. Foster 273 in the case of justifiable self-defence, "The injured Party may repell force with force in defence of his person, habitation, or property, against one who manifestly intendeth and endeavoureth with violence, or surprize to commit a known felony upon either."—"In these cases, he is not obliged to retreat, but may pursue his adversary, till he findeth himself out of danger; and if in a conflict between them he happeneth to kill, such killing is justifiable." Keiling, 128, 129. I must intreat you, to consider the words of this authority, the injured person may repell force by force against any who endeavours to commit any kind of felony on him or his, here the rule is, I have a right to stand on my own defense, if you intend to commit felony; if any of the persons made an attack on these soldiers, with an intention to rob them, if it was but to take their hats feloniously, they had a right to kill them on the spot, and had no business to retreat; if a robber meets me in the street, and commands me to surrender my purse, I have a right to kill him without asking questions; if a person commits a bare assault on me, this will not justify killing, but if he assaults me in such a manner, as to discover an intention, to kill me, I have a right to destroy him, that I may put it out of his power to kill me. In the case you will have to consider, I do not know that there was any attempt to steal from these persons; however, there were some persons concerned, who would probably enough have stolen, if there had been any thing to steal; and many were there who had no such disposition, but this is not the point we aim at, the question is are you satisfied, the people made the attack in order to kill the soldiers? If you are satisfied that the people, whoever they were, made that assault, with a design to kill or maim the soldiers, this was such an assault, as will justify the soldiers killing in their own defence. Further it seems to me, we may make another question, whether you are satisfied that their real intention was to kill or maim or not? If any reasonable man, in the situation of one of these soldiers, would have had reason to believe in the time of it, that the people came with an intention to kill him, whether you have this satisfaction now, or not in your own minds, they were justifiable, at least excusable in firing; you and I, may be suspicious that the people who made this assault on the soldiers, did it to put them to flight, on purpose that they might go exulting about the town afterwards in triumph; but this will not do, you must place yourselves in the situation of *Wemms* or *Killroy*—consider yourselves, as knowing that the prejudices of the world about you, were against you, that the people about you, thought you come to dragoon them into obedience to statutes, instructions, mandates and edicts, which they thoroughly detested; that many of these people were thoughtless and inconsiderate, old and young, sailors and landmen, negroes and molattos; that they, the soldiers had no friends about them, the rest were in opposition to them; with all the bells ringing, to call the town together to assist the people in *King street;* for they knew by that time, that there was no fire; the people shouting, huzzaing, and making the mob whistle, as they call it, which when a boy makes it in the street, is no formidable thing, but when made by a multitude, is a most hideous shriek, almost as terrible as an Indian yell; the people crying, Kill them! Kill them! Knock them over! heaving snowballs, oyster shells, clubs, white birch sticks of three inches and an half diameter, consider yourselves, in this situation, and then judge whether a reasonable man in the soldiers situation, would not have concluded they were going to kill him. I believe, if I was to reverse the scene, I should bring it home to our own bosoms; suppose Colonel *Marshall,* when he came out of his own door, and saw these grenadiers coming down with swords, &s. had thought it proper to have appointed a military watch; suppose he had asembled *Gray* and *Attucks* that were killed, or any other person in town, and applanted them in that station as a military watch, and there had come from Murray's barracks, thirty or forty soldiers, with no other arms than snow-balls, cakes of ice, oyster-shells, cinders and clubs, and attacked this military watch in this manner, what do you suppose would have been the feelings and reasonings of any of our householders; I confess I believe they would not have borne the one half of what the witnesses have sworn the soldiers bore, till they had shot down as many as were necessary to intimidate and disperse the rest; because, the law does not oblige us to bear insults to the danger of our lives, to stand still with such a number of people round us, throwing such things at us, and threatening our lives, until we are disabled to defend ourselves.

"Where a known felony, is attempted upon the person, be it to rob, or murder, here the party assaulted may repel force with force, and even his own servant then attendant on him, *or any other person present,* may interpose for preventing mischief, and if death ensues, the party so interposing will be justified. In this case nature and social duty co-operate." Foster, 274.

Hawkins P. C. Chap. 28, 25. towards the end, "Yet it seems that a private person, *a fortiori,* an officer of justice, who happens unavoidably to kill another in endeavouring to defend himself from, or suppress dangerous rioters, may justify the fact, in as much as he only does his duty in aid of the public justice." Section 24. "And I can see no reason why a person, who without provocation is assaulted by another in any place whatsoever, in such a manner as plainly shews an intent to murder him, as by discharging a pistol, or pushing at him with a drawn sword, &s. may not justify killing such an assailant, as much as if he had attempted to rob him: For is not he who attempts to murder me, more injurious than he who barely attempts to rob me? And can it be more justifiable to fight for my goods than for my life; and it is not only highly agreeable to reason that a man in such circumstances, may lawfully kill another, but it seems also to be confirmed by the general tenor of our law books, which speaking of homicide *se defendo,* suppose it done in some quarrel or affray."

"And so perhaps the killing of dangerou rioters, may be justified by any private persons, who cannot otherwise suppress them, or defend themselves from them; in as much as every private person seems to be authorized by the law, to arm himself for the purposes aforesaid." Hawkins, p. 71. § 14.—Here every private person is authorized to arm himself, and on the strength of this authority, I do not deny the inhabitants had a right to arm themselves at that time, for their defence, not for offence, that distinction is material and must be attended to.

Hawkins, p. 75. § 14.—"And not only he who on an assault retreats to the wall or some such streight, beyond which he can go no further, before he kills the other, is judged by the law to act upon unavoidable necessity; but also he who being assaulted in such a manner, and in such a place, that he cannot go back without manifestly endangering his life, kills the other without retreating at all." —§ 16. "And an officer who kills one that insults him in the execution of his office, and where a private person, that kills one who feloniously assaults him in the high way, may justify the fact without ever giving back at all."

There is no occasion for the Magistrate to read the Riot act. In the case before you, I suppose you will be satisfied when you come to examine the witnesses, and compare it with the rules of the common law, abstracted from all mutiny-acts and articles of war, that these soldiers were in such a situation, that they could not help themselves; people were coming from *Royal exchange lane,* and other parts of the town, with clubs, and cord wood sticks; the soldiers were planted by the wall of the *Custom House;* they could not retreat, they were surrounded on all sides, for there were people behind them, as well as before them; there were a number of people in *Royal-exchange lane,* the soldiers were so near to the *Custom-house,* that they could not retreat, unless they had gone into the brick wall of it. I shall shew you presently, that all the party concerned in this unlawful design, were guilty of what any one of them did; if any body threw a snow-ball, it was the act of the whole party; if any struck with a club, or threw a club, and the club had killed any body, the whole party would have been guilty of murder in law.

Ld. C. J. HOLT, in Mawgrige's Case, Keyling 128, says, "Now it hath been held, that if A of his malice prepensed assaults B, to kill him, and B draws his sword and attacks A and pursues him, then A for his safety gives back, and retreats to a wall, and B still pursuing him with his drawn sword, A in his defence kills B. This is murder in A. For A having malice against B, and in pursuance thereof endeavouring to kill him, is answerable for all the consequences, of which he was the original cause. It is not reasonable for any man that is dangerously assaulted, and when he perceives his life in danger from his adversary, but to have liberty for the security of his own life, to pursue him that maliciously assaulted him; for he that hath manifested that he hath malice against another, is not fit to be trusted with a dangerous weapon in his hand. And so resolved by all the Judges when they met at Seargeant's inn, in preparation for my *Lord Morley's* trial."

In the case here we will take *Montgomery,* if you please, when he was attacked by the stout man with a stick, who aimed it at his head, with a number of people round him, crying out, Kill them! Kill them! had he not a right to kill the man. If all the party were guilty of the assault made by the stout man, and all of them had discovered malice in their hearts, had not *Montgomery* a right, according to Lord Chief Justice *Holt,* to put it out of their power to wreak their malice upon him. I will not at present, look for any more authorities in the point of self-defence; you will be able to judge from these, how far the law goes, in justifying or excusing any person in defence of himself, or taking away the life of another who threatens him, in life or limb: the next point is this, That in case of an unlawful assembly, all and every one of the assembly is guilty of all and every unlawful act, committed by any one of that assembly, in prosecution of the unlawful design they set out upon.

Rules of law should be universally known, whatever effect they may have on politics; they are rules of common law, the law of the land, and it is certainly true, that where ever there is an unlawful assembly, let it consist of many persons or a few, every man in it is guilty of every unlawful act committed by any one of the whole party, be they more or be they less, in pursuance of their unlawful design. This is the policy of the law: to discourage and prevent riots, insurrections, turbulence, and tumults.

In the continual vicissitudes of human things, amidst the shocks of fortune and the whirls of passion, that take place at certain critical seasons, even in the mildest government, the people are liable to run into riots and tumults. There are Church-quakes and state-quakes, in the moral and political world, as well as earth-quakes, storms, and tempests in the physical. Thus much however must be said in favour of the people and of human nature, that it is a general, if not universal truth, that the aptitude of the people to mutinies, seditions, tumults and insurrections, is in direct pro-portion to the despotism of the government. In governments com-pletely despotic, i.e., where the will of one man is the only law, this disposition is most prevalent. In Aristocracies, next—in mixed Monarchies, less than either of the former—in compleat Republic's the least of all—and under the same form of government as in a limited monarchy, for example, the virtue and wisdom of the administration may generally be measured by the peace and order, that are seen among the people. However this may be, such is the imperfection of all things in this world, that no form of govern-ment, and perhaps no wisdom or virtue in the administration, can at all times avoid riots and disorders among the people.

Now it is from this difficulty, that the policy of the law hath framed such strong discouragements, to secure the people against tumults; because when they once begin, there is danger of their running to such excesses, as will overturn the whole system of gov-ernment. There is the rule from the reverend sage of the law, so often quoted before.

1. H.H.P.C. 437. "All present, aiding and assisting, are equally principal with him that gave the stroke, whereof the party died. For tho' one gave the stroke, yet in interpretation of law, it is the stroke of every person, that was present aiding and assist-ing."

1. H.H.P.C. 440. "If divers come with one assent to do mis-chief, as to kill, rob, or beat, and one doth it, they are all principals in the felony. If many be present, and one only give the stroke whereof the party dies, they are all principal, if they came for that purpose."

Now if the party at *Dock-square,* came with an intention only to beat the soldiers, and began the affray with them, and any of them had been accidentally killed, it would have been murder, because it was an unlawful design they came upon; if but one does it, they are all considered in the eye of the law to be guilty, if any one gives the mortal stroke, they are all principal here, therefore there is a reversal of the scene; if you are satisfied, that these soldiers were there on a lawful design and it should be proved any of them shot without provocation and killed any body, he only is answerable for it. First Hales's pleas of the crown.

1. H.H.P.C. 444. "Although if many come upon an unlawful design, and one of the company kill one of the adverse party, in pursuance of that design, all are principals; yet if many be together upon a lawful account, and one of the company, kill another of an adverse party, without any particular abetment of the rest to this fact of homicide they are not all guilty that are of the company, but only those that gave the stroke or actually abetted him to do it."

1. H.H.P.C. 445. "In the case of a riotous assembly to rob or steal deer, or do any unlawful act of violence, there the offence of one, is the offence of all the company."

In an other place, 1. H.H.P.C. 439. "The *Lord Dacre* and divers others went to steal deer in the park of one Pelham. Raydon one of the company, killed the keeper in the park, the *Lord Dacre* and the rest of the company being in the other part of the park. Yet it was adjudged murder in them all, and they died for it. And he quotes Crompton 25, Dalton 93 p. 241. "So that in so strong a case as this, where this nobleman set out to hunt deer in the ground of another, he was in one part of the park, his company in another part, yet they were all guilty of murder."

The next is *Hale's* Pleas of the Crown, 1. H.H.P.C. 440. "The case of *Drayton Bassit;* diverse persons doing an unlawful act, all are guilty of what is done by one."

Foster, 353, 354. "A general resolution against all opposers, whether such resolution appears upon evidence to have been actually and implicitly entered into by the confederates, or may reasonably be collected from their number, arms or behavior, at or before the scene of action, such resolutions, so proved, have always been considered as strong ingredients in cases of this kind. And in cases of homicide, committed in consequence of them, every person present; in the sense of the law, when the homicide hath been committed, hath been involved in the guilt of him that gave the mortal blow."

Foster. "The cases of Lord *Dacre* mentioned by *Hale,* and of *Pudsey,* reported by *Crompton,* and cited by *Hale,* turned upon this point. The offences they respectively stood charged with as principals, were committed far out of their sight and hearing; and yet both were held to be present. It was sufficient, that at the instant the facts were committed, they were of the same party and upon the same pursuit, and under the same engagements and expectations of mutual defence and support, with those that did the facts."

Thus far I have proceeded, and I believe it will not be hereafter disputed by any body, that this law ought to be known to every one who has any disposition to be concerned in an unlawful assembly, whatever mischief happens in the prosecution of the design they set out upon, all are answerable for it. It is necessary we should consider the definitions of some other crimes, as well as murder; sometimes one crime gives occasion to another, an assault is sometimes the occasion of man slaughter, sometimes of excusable homicide. It is necessary to consider what is a riot. 1. *Hawk.* c. 65. § 2. I shall give you the definition of it. "Wheresoever more than three persons uses force or violence, for the accomplishment of any design whatever, all concerned are rioters."

Were there not more than three persons in *Dock-Square?* Did they not agree ot go to *King-Street,* and attack the *Main guard?* Where then, is the reason for hesitation, at calling it a riot? If we cannot speak the law as it is, where is our liberty? And this is law, that wherever more than three persons, are gathered together, to accomplish any thing with force, it is a riot.

1] *Hawk.* c. 65, § 2. "Wherever more than three, use force and violence, all who are concerned therein are rioters. But in some cases wherein the law authorises force, it is lawful and commendable to use it. As for a sheriff, 2. *And.* 67 *Poph.* 121, or constable, 3. H. 7, 10. 6. or perhaps even for a private person, *Poph.* 121, *Moore* 656. to assemble a competent number of people, in order with force, to oppose rebels, or enemies, or rioters, and afterwards with such force, actually to suppress them."

I do not mean to apply the word rebel on this occasion; I have no reason to suppose that ever there was one in *Boston,* at least among the natives of the country; but rioters are in the same situation, as far as my argument is concerned, and proper officers may suppress rioters, and so may even private persons.

If we strip ourselves free from all military laws, mutiny acts, articles of war and soldiers oaths and consider these prisoners as neighbours, if any of their neighbours were attacked in *King-street,* they had a right to collect together to suppress this riot and combination. If any number of persons meet together at a fair, or market, and happen to fall together by the ears, they are not guilty of a riot, but of a sudden affray: here is another paragraph which I must read to you, 1. *Hawkins,* c. 65, § 3. "If a number of persons, being met together at a fair or market, or on any other *lawful* and *innocent occasion,* happen on a sudden quarrel, to fall together by the ears, they are not guilty of a riot, but of a sudden affray only, of which none are guilty, but those who actually engage in it," &c. End of the § . It would be endless, as well as superfluous, to examine, whether every particular person engaged in a riot, were in truth one of the first assembly, or actually had a previous knowledge of the design thereof.

I have endeavoured to produce the best authorities, and to give you the rules of law in their words, for I desire not to advance any thing of my own. I chuse to lay down the rules of law, from authorities which cannot be disputed. Another point is this, whether, and how far, a private person may aid another in distress? Suppose a press gang should come on shore in this town, and assault any sailor, or householder in *King street,* in order to carry them on board one of his Majesty's ships and impress him without any warrant, as a seaman in his Majesty's service, how far do you suppose the inhabitants would think themselves warranted by law, to interpose against that lawless press gang? I agree that such a press gang would be as unlawful an assembly, as that was in *King street.* If they were to press an inhabitant, and carry him off for a sailor, would not the inhabitants think themselves warranted by law to interpose in behalf of their fellow citizens? How Gentlemen, if the soldiers had no right to interpose in the relief of the Sentry, the inhabitants would have no right to interpose with regard to the citizen, for whatever is law for a soldier, is law for a sailor, and for a citizen, they all stand upon an equal footing, in this respect. I believe we shall not have it disputed, that it would be lawful to go into *King street,* and help an honest man there against the press master. We have many instances in the books which authorize it, which I shall produce to you presently.

Now suppose you should have a jealousy in your minds, that the people who made this attack on the Sentry, had nothing in their intention more than to take him off his post, and that was threatened by some; suppose they intended to go a little farther, and tar and feather him, or to ride him, (as the phrase is in *Hudibras*) he would have had a good right to have stood upon his defence, the defence of his liberty and if he could not preserve that without hazard to his own life, he would be warranted in depriving those of life, who were endeavouring to deprive him of his; that is a point I would not give up for my right hand, nay, for my life.

Well, I say, if the people did this, or if this was only their intention, surely the officers and soldiers had a right to go to his relief, and therefore they set out upon a lawful errand, they were therefore a lawful assembly, if we only consider them as private subjects and fellow citizens, without regard to Mutiny Acts, Articles of War, or Soldiers Oaths; a private person, or any number of private persons, have a right to go to the assistance of their fellow subject in distress and danger of his life, when assaulted and in danger from a few or a multitude. *Keyl.* 136. "If a man perceives another by force to be injuriously treated, pressed and restrained of his liberty, tho' the person abused doth not complain, or call for aid or assistance; and others out of compassion shall come to his rescure [sic], and kill any of those that shall so restrain him, that is manslaughter. *Keyl*—A and others without any warrant, impress B to serve the King at sea, B quietly submitted and went off with the press master: *Hugett* and the others pursued them, and required a sight of their warrant; but they shewing a piece of paper that was not a sufficient warrant, thereupon *Hugett* with the others drew their swords, and the press-masters theirs, and so there was a combat, and those who endeavored to rescue the pressed man killed one of the pretended press-masters. This was but manslaughter, for when the liberty of one subject is invaded, it affects all the rest: It is a provocation to all people, as being of ill example and pernicious consequences."

2] Lord *Raymond*, 1301. The Queen *versus* Tooley *et alios*. Lord Chief Justice *Holt* says, 3d. "The prisoner (*i.e.*, *Tooley*) in this case had sufficient provocation; for if one be imprisoned upon an unlawful authority, it is a sufficient provocation to all people out of compassion; and where the liberty of the subject is invaded, it is a provocation to all the subjects of England, &c. and sure a man ought to be concerned for magna charta and the laws; and if any one against the law imprisons a man, he is an offender against magna charta."

I am not insensible of Sir *Michael Foster's* observations on these cases, but apprehend they do not invalidate the authority of them as far as I now apply them to the purpose of my argument. If a stranger, a mere fellow subject may interpose to defend the liberty, he may to defend the life of another individual. But according to the evidence, some imprudent people before the Sentry, proposed to take him off his post, others threatened his life, and intelligence of this was carried to the *Main-guard,* before any of the prisoners turned out: They were then ordered out to relieve the Sentry, and any of our fellow citizens might lawfully have gone upon the same errand; they were therefore a lawful assembly.

I have but one point more of law to consider, and that is this: In the case before you, I do not pretend to prove that every one of the unhappy persons slain, were concerned in the riot; the authorities read to you just now, say, it would be endless to prove, whether every person that was present and in a riot, was concerned in planning the first enterprise or not: nay, I believe it but justice, to say, some were perfectly innocent of the occasion. I have reason to suppose, that one of them was Mr. *Maverick*; he was a very worthy young man, as he has been represented to me, and had no concern in the riotous proceedings of that night; and I believe the same may be said, in favour of one more, at least, Mr. *Caldwell* who was slain; and therefore many people may think, that as he, and perhaps another was innocent, therefore innocent blood having been shed, that must be expiated by the death of somebody or other. I take notice of this, because one gentleman nominated by the sheriff, for a Juryman upon this trial, because he had said he believed Captain *Preston* was innocent, but innocent blood had been shed, and therefore somebody ought to be hanged for it, which he thought was indirectly giving his opinion in this cause. I am afraid many other persons have formed such an opinion; I do not take it to be a rule, that where innocent blood is shed, the person must die. In the instance of the *Frenchmen* on the *Plains of Abraham,* they were innocent, fighting for their King and country; their blood is as innocent as any, there may be multitudes killed, when innocent blood is shed on all sides, so that it is not an invariable rule. I will put a case, in which, I dare say, all will agree with me: Here are two persons, the father and the son, go out a hunting, they take different roads, the father hears a rushing among the bushes, takes it to be game, fires and kills his son through a mistake; here is innocent blood shed, but yet nobody will say the father ought to die for it. So that the general rule of law, is, that whenever one person hath a right to do an act, and that act by any accident, takes away the life of another, it is excusable, it bears the same regard to the innocent as to the guilty. If two men are together, and attack me, and I have a right to kill them, I strike at them, and by mistake, strike a third and kill him, as I had a right to kill the first, my killing the other, will be excusable, as it happened by accident. If I in the heat of passion, aim a blow at the person who has assaulted me, aiming at him, I kill another person, it is but manslaughter. *Foster,* 261, § 3. "If an action unlawful in itself be done deliberately and with intention of mischief or great bodily harm to particulars, or of mischief indiscriminately, fall it where it may, and death ensues against or beside the original intention of the party, it will be murder. But if such mischievous intention doth not appear, which is matter of fact and to be collected from circumstances, and the act was done heedlessly and inconsiderately, it will be manslaughter; not accidental death, because the act upon which death ensued was unlawful."

Supposing in this case, the molatto man was the person made the assault, suppose he was concerned in the unlawful assembly, and this party of soldiers endeavoring to defend themselves against him, happened to kill another person who was innocent, though the soldiers had no reason that we know of, to think any person there, at least of that number who were crouding about them innocent, they might naturally enough presume all to be guilty of the riot and assault, and to come with the same design; I say, if on firing on these who were guilty, they accidentally killed an innocent person, it was not their faults, they were obliged to defend themselves against those who were pressing upon them, they are not answerable for it with their lives, for upon supposition it was justifiable or excusable to kill. *Attucks* or any other person, it will be equally justifiable or excusable if in firing at him, they killed another who was innocent, or if the provocation was such as to mitigate the guilt to manslaughter, it will equally mitigate the guilt, if they killed an innocent man undesignedly, in aiming at him who gave the provocation, according to Judge *Foster,* and as this point is of such consequence, I must produce some more authorities for it. 1. *Hawkins,* 84. "Also, if a third person accidentally happen to be killed, by one engaged in a combat with another upon a sudden quarrel, it seems that he who kills him, is guilty of manslaughter only, &c." H.H.P.C. 442, To the same point, and 1. H.H.P.C. 484. and 4. *Black,* 27.

I shall now consider one question more, and that is concerning provocation. We have hitherto been considering self-defence, and how far persons may go in defending themselves against aggressors, even by taking away their lives, and now proceed to consider, such provocations as the law allows to mitigate or extenuate the guilt of killing, where it is not justifiable or excusable.

An assault and battery, committed upon a man, in such a manner as not to endanger his life, is such a provocation as the law allows to reduce killing, down to the crime of manslaughter. Now the law has been made on more considerations than we are capable of making at present; the law considers a man as capable of bearing any thing, and every thing, but blows. I may reproach a man as much as I please, I may call him a thief, robber, traitor, scoundrel, coward, lobster, bloody back, &c. and if he kills me it will be murder, if nothing else but words preceed; but if from giving him such kind of language, I proceed to take him by the nose, or fillip him on the forehead, that is, an assault! that is a blow; the law will not oblige a man to stand still and bear it; there is the distinction; hands off, touch me not; as soon as you touch me, if I run you thro' the heart it is but Manslaughter; the utility of this distinction, the more you think of it, the more you will be satisfied with it; it is an assault when ever a blow is struck, let it be ever so slight, and sometimes even without a blow. The law considers man as frail and passionate, when his passions are touched, he will be thrown off his guard, and therefore the law makes allowances for this frailty, considers him as in a fit of passion, not having the possession of his intellectual faculties, and therefore does not oblige him to measure out his blows with a yard stick, or weigh them in a scale; let him kill with a sword, gun or hedge stake, it is not murder, but only manslaughter, Keyling's Reports 135. *Regina versus* Mawgrige. "Rules supported by authority and general consent, shewing what are always allowed to be sufficient provocations. First, if one man, *upon any words shall make an assault* upon another, either by *pulling him by the nose, or filliping upon the forehead,* and he that is so assaulted, shall draw his sword, and immediately run the other through, that is but manslaughter; for the peace is broken by the person killed, and with an indignity to him that received the assault. Besides, he that was so affronted, might reasonably apprehend, that he that treated him in that manner, might have some further design upon him." So that here is the boundary, when a man is assaulted, and kills in consequence of that assault, it is but manslaughter; I will just read as I go along the definition of an assault. 1. Hawkins, Chap. 62. § 1. "An assault is an attempt or offer, with force or violence, to do a corporal hurt to another; as by stricking at him, with or without a weapon, or presenting a gun at him, at such a distance to which the gun will carry, or pointing a pitchfork at him, or by any other such like act done in an angry, threatening manner, &c. But no words can amount to an assault." Here is the definition of an assault, which is a sufficient provocation to soften killing down to manslaughter. 1. Hawkins, Chap. 31. § 36. "Neither can he be thought guilty of a greater crime, than manslaughter, who finding a man in bed with his wife, or being actually *struck by him,* or *pulled by the nose, or filliped upon the forehead,* immediately kills him, or in the defence of his person from an unlawful arrest; or in the defence of his house, from those who claiming a title to it, attempt forcibly to enter it, and to that purpose shoot at it, &c." Every snow-ball, oyster shell, cake of ice, or bit of cinder that was thrown that night, at the Sentinel, was an assault upon him; every one that was thrown at the party of soldiers, was an assault upon them, whether it hit any of them or not. I am guilty of an assault, if I present a gun at any person, whether I shoot at him or not, it is an assault, and if I insult him in that manner, and he shoots me, it is but manslaughter. Foster, 295. 6. "To what I have offered with regard to sudden rencounters, let me add, that the blood, already too much heated, kindleth afresh at every pass or blow. And in the tumult of the passions, in which mere instinct self-preservation, hath no inconsiderable share, the voice of reason is not heard. And therefore, the law in condesension to the infirmities of flesh and blood doth extenuate the offence." Insolent, scurrilous, or slanderous language, when it preceeds an assault, aggravates it. Foster 316. "We all know that words of reproach, how grating and offensive soever, are in the eye of the law, no provocation, in the case of voluntary homicide, and yet every man who hath considered the human frame, or but attended to the workings of his own heart, knoweth, that affronts of that kind, pierce deeper, and stimulate in the veins more effectually, than a slight injury done to a third person, tho' under colour of justice, possibly can." I produce this to show the assault, in this case, was aggravated by the scurrilous language which preceeded it. Such words of reproach, stimulate in the veins, and exasperate the mind, and no doubt if an assault and battery succeeds them, killing under such provocation, is softened to manslaughter, but killing without such provocation, makes it murder.

FIVE o'Clock, P.M. the Court adjourned till *Tuesday* morning, nine o'Clock.

Tuesday, NINE o'Clock, the Court met according to adjournment, and Mr. ADAMS proceeded.

May it please your Honours, and you Gentlemen of the Jury,

I yesterday afternoon produced from the best authorities, those rules of law which must govern all cases of homicide, particularly that which is now before you; it now remains to consider the evidence, and see whether any thing has occurred, that may be compared to the rules read to you; and I will not trouble myself nor you with laboured endeavours to be methodical, I shall endeavour to make some few observations, on the testimonies of the witnesses, such as will place the facts in a true point of light, with as much brevity as possible; but I suppose it would take me four hours to read to you, (if I did nothing else but read) the minutes of evidence that I have taken in this trial. In the first place the Gentleman who opened this cause, has stated to you, with candour and precision, the evidence of the identity of the persons.

The witnesses are confident that they know the prisoners at the barr, and that they were present that night, and of the party; however, it is apparent, that witnesses are liable to make mistakes, by a single example before you. Mr. *Bass,* who is a very honest man, and of good character, swears positively that the tall man, *Warren,* stood on the right that night, and was the first that fired; and I am sure you are satisfied by this time, by many circumstances, that he is totally mistaken in this matter; this you will consider at your leisure. The witnesses in general did not know the faces of these persons before; very few of them knew the names of them before, they only took notice of their faces that night. How much certainty there is in this evidence, I leave you to determine.

There does not seem to me to be any thing very material in the testimony of Mr. *Aston,* except to the identity of *McCauley,* and he is the only witness to that. If you can be satisfied in your own minds, without a doubt, that he knew *McCauley* so well as to be sure, you will believe he was there.

The next witness is *Bridghem,* he says he saw the tall man *Warren,* but saw another man belonging to the same regiment soon after, so like him, as to make him doubt whether it was *Warren* or not; he thinks he saw the *Corporal,* but is not certain, he says

he was at the corner of the *Custom house,* this you will take notice
of, other witnesses swear, he was the remotest man of all from
him who fired first, and there are other evidences who swear the
left man did not fire at all; if *Wemms* did not discharge his gun
at all, he could not kill any of the persons, therefore he must be
acquitted on the fact of killing; for an intention to kill, is not
murder nor manslaughter, if not carried into execution: The witness saw numbers of things thrown, and he saw plainly sticks strike
the guns, about a dozen persons with sticks, gave three cheers, and
surrounded the party, and struck the guns with their sticks several
blows: This is a witness for the crown, and his testimony is of
great weight for the prisoners; he gives his testimony very sensibly
and impartially. He swears positively, that he not only saw ice or
snow thrown, but saw the guns struck several times; if you believe
this witness, of whose credibility you are wholly the judges, as
you are of every other; if you do not believe him, there are many
others who swear to circumstances in favour of the prisoners; it
should seem impossible you should disbelieve so great a number,
and of crown witnesses too, who swear to such variety of circumstances that fall in with one another so naturally to form our
defence; this witness swears positively, there were a dozen of
persons with clubs, surrounded the party; twelve sailors with clubs,
were by much an overmatch to eight soldiers, chained there by
the order and command of their officer, to stand in defence of the
Sentry, not only so, but under an oath to stand there, *i.e.,* to obey
the lawful command of their officer, as much, Gentlemen of the
Jury, as you are under oath to determine this cause by law and
evidence; clubs they had not, and they could not defend themselves
with their bayonets against so many people; it was in the power
of the sailors to kill one half or the whole of the party if they
had been so disposed; what had the soldiers to expect, when twelve
persons armed with clubs, (sailors too, between whom and soldiers,
there is such an antipathy, that they fight as naturally when they
meet, as the elephant and Rhinoceros) were daring enough, even
at the time when they were loading their guns, to come up with
their clubs, and smite on their guns; what had eight soldiers to
expect from such a set of people? Would it have been a prudent
resolution in them, or in any body in their situation, to have stood
still, to see if the sailors would knock their brains out, or not?
Had they not all the reason in the world to think, that as they
had done so much, they would proceed further? their clubs were
as capable of killing as a ball, a hedge stake is known in the law
books as a weapon of death, as much as a sword, bayonet or
musket. He says, the soldiers were loading their guns, when the
twelve surrounded them, the people went up to them within the
length of their guns, and before the firing; besides all this he

swears, they were called cowardly rascals, and dare to fire; he says these people were all dressed *like* sailors; and I believe, that by and bye you will find evidence enough to satisfy you, these were some of the persons that came out of *Dock-square,* after making the attack on *Murray's barracks,* and who had been arming themselves with sticks from the butchers stalls and cord wood piles, and marches up round Cornhill under the command of *Attucks.* All the bells in town were ringing, the ratling of the blows upon the guns he heard, and swears it was violent; this corroborates the testimony of *James Bailey,* which will be considered presently. Some witnesses swear a club struck a soldier's gun, *Bailey* swears a man struck a soldier and knocked him down, before he fired, "the last man that fired, levelled at a lad, and moved his gun as the lad ran:" You will consider, that an intention to kill is not murder; if a man lays poison in the way of another, and with an express intention that he should take it up and die of it, it is not murder: Suppose that soldier had malice in his heart, and was determined to murder that boy if he could, yet the evidence clears him of killing the boy, I say, admit he had malice in his heart, yet it is plain he did not kill him or any body else, and if you believe one part of the evidence, you must believe the other, and if he had malice, that malice was ineffectual; I do not recollect any evidence that ascertains who it was that stood the last man but one upon the left, admitting he discovered a temper ever so wicked, cruel and malicious, you are to consider his ill temper is not imputable to another, no other had any intention of his deliberate kind, the whole transaction was sudden, there was but a very short space of time between the first gun and the last, when the first gun was fired the people fell in upon the soldiers and laid on with their weapons with more violence, and this served to increase the provocation, and raised such a violent spirit of revenge in the soldiers, as the law takes notice of, and makes some allowance for, and in that fit of fury and madness, I suppose he aimed at the boy.

The next witness is *Dodge,* he says, there were fifty people near the soldiers pushing at them; now the witness before says, there were twelve sailors with clubs, but now here are fifty more aiding and abetting of them, ready to relieve them in case of need; now what could the people expect? It was their business to have taken themselves out of the way; some prudent people by the *Town house,* told them not to meddle with the guard, but you hear nothing of this from these fifty people; no, instead of that, they were huzzaing and whistling, crying damn you, fire! why don't you fire? So that they were actually assisting these twelve sailors that made the attack; he says the soldiers were pushing at the people to keep them off, ice and snow-balls were thrown, and I heard ice rattle on their guns, there were some clubs thrown from a considerable distance across the street. This witness swears he saw snow-balls thrown close before the party, and he took them to be thrown on purpose, he saw oyster-shells likewise thrown. Mr. *Langford* the watchman, is more particular in his testimony, and deserves a very particular consideration, because it is intended by the council for the crown that his testimony shall distinguish *Killroy* from the rest of the prisoners, and exempt him from those pleas of justification, excuse or extenuation, which we rely upon for the whole party, because he had previous malice, and they would from hence conclude, he aimed at a particular person; you will consider all the evidence with regard to that, by itself.

Hemmingway, the sheriff's coachman, swears he knew *Killroy,* and that he heard him say, he would never miss an opportunity of firing upon the inhabitants: this is to prove that *Killroy* had pre-conceived malice in his heart, not indeed against the unhappy persons who were killed, but against the inhabitants in general, that he had the spirit not only of a *Turk* or an *Arab,* but of the devil; but admitting that this testimony is litterally true, and that he had all the malice they would wish to prove, yet, if he was assaulted that night, and his life in danger, he had a right to defend himself as well as another man; if he had malice before, it does not take away from him the right of defending himself against any unjust aggressor. But it is not at all improbable, that there was some misunderstanding about these loose expressions, perhaps the man had no thoughts of what his words might import; many a man in his cups, or in anger, which is a short fit of madness, hath uttered the rashest expressions, who had no such savage disposition in general! So that there is but little weight in expressions uttered at a kitcheng fire, before a maid and a coachman, where he might think himself at liberty to talk as much like a bully, a fool, and a madman as he pleased, and that no evil would come of it. Strictly speaking, he might mean no more than this, that he would not miss an opportunity of firing on the inhabitants, if he was attacked by them in such a manner as to justify it: soldiers have sometimes avoided opportunities of firing, when they would have been justified, if they had fired. I would recommend to them, to be tender by all means, nay, let them be cautious at their peril; but still what he said, amounts in strictness, to no more than this, "If the inhabitants make an attack on me, I will not bear from them what I have done already;" or I will bear no more, than what I am obliged by law to bear. No doubt it was under the fret of his spirits, the indignation, mortification, grief and shame, that he had suffered a defeat at the Ropewalks; it was just after an account of an affray was published here, betwixt the soldiers and inhabitants at *New York.* There was a little before the 5th of *March,* much noise in this town, and a pompuous account in the newspapers, of a victory obtained by the inhabitants there over the soldiers; which doubtless excited the resentment of the soldiers here, as well as exultations among some sorts of the inhabitants: and the ringing of the bells here, was probably copied from *New York,* a wretched example in this, and in two other instances at least: the defeat of the soldiers at the Rope-walks, was about that time too, and if he did, after that, use such expressions, it ought not to weigh too much in this case. It can scarcely amount to proof that he harboured any settled malice against the people in general. Other witnesses are introduced to show that *Killroy* had besides his general ill-will against every body, particular malice against Mr. *Gray,* whom he killed, as *Langford* swears.

Some of the witnesses, have sworn that *Gray* was active in the battle at the Rope walks, and that *Killroy* was once there, from whence the Council for the Crown would infer, that *Killroy;* in *King street,* on the 5th of *March* in the night, knew *Gray,* whom he had seen at the Rope-walks before, and took that opportunity to gratify his preconceived malice; but if this is all true, it will not take away from him his justification, excuse, or extenuation, if he had any. The rule of the law is, if there has been malice between two, and at a distant time afterwards they met, and one of them assaults the other's life, or only assaults him, and he kills in consequence of it, the law presumes the killing was in self-defence, or upon the provocation, not on account of the antecedent malice. If therefore the assault upon *Killroy* was so violent as to endanger his life, he had as good a right to defend himself, as much as if he never had before conceived any malice against the people in general, or Mr. *Gray* in particular. If the assault upon him, was such as to amount only to a provocation, not to a justification, his crime will be manslaughter only. However, it does not appear, that he knew Mr. *Gray;* none of the witnesses pretend to say he knew him, or that he ever saw him. It is true they were both at the Rope-walks at one time, but there were so many combatants on each side, that it is not even probable that *Killroy* should know them all, and no witness says there was any rencounter there between them two. Indeed, to return to Mr. *Langford's* testimony, he says, he did not perceive *Killroy* to aim at *Gray,* more than at him, but he says expressly, he did not aim at *Gray. Langford* says, "*Gray* had no stick, was standing with his arms folded up." This witness, is however most probably mistaken in this matter and confounds one time with another, a mistake which has been made by many witnesses, in this case, and considering the confusion and terror of the scene, is not to be wondered at—

Witnesses have sworn to the condition of *Killroy's* bayonet, that it was bloody the morning after the 5th of *March.* The blood they saw, if any, might be occasioned by a wound given by some of the bayonets in the affray, possibly in Mr. *Fosdick's* arm, or it might happen, in the manner mentioned by my brother before. One bayonet at least was struck off and it might fall, where the blood of some person slain afterwards flowed. It would be doing violence to every rule of law and evidence, as well as to common sense and the feelings of humanity, to infer from the blood on the bayonet, that it had been stabbed into the brains of Mr. *Gray,* after he was dead, and that by *Killroy* himself who had killed him.

Young Mr. *Davis* swears, that he saw *Gray* that evening, a little before the firing, that he had a stick under his arm, and said he would go to the riot, "I am glad of it, (that is that there was a rumpus) I will go and have a slap at them, if I lose my life." And when he was upon the spot, some witnesses swear, he did not act that peaceable inoffensive part, which *Langsford* thinks he did. They swear, they thought him in liquor—that he run about clapping several people on the shoulders, saying, "Dont run away"—"they dare not fire" *Langford* goes on "I saw twenty or five and twenty boys about the Sentinel—and I spoke to him, and bid him not be afraid." How came the Watchman *Langford* to tell him not to be afraid? Does not this circumstance prove, that he thought there was danger, or at least that the Sentinel in fact, was terrified and did think himself in danger. *Langford* goes on "I saw about twenty or five and twenty boys that is young shavers"—We have been entertained with a great variety of phrases, to avoid calling this sort of people a mob. Some call them shavers, some call them genius's. The plain English is gentlemen, most probably a motley rabble of saucy boys, negroes and mulattoes, Irish teagues and outlandish jack tarrs. And why we should scruple to call such a set of people a mob, I can't conceive, unless the name is too respectable for them: The sun is not about to stand still or go out, nor the rivers to dry up because there was a mob in *Boston,* on the 5th of *March* that attacked a party of soldiers. Such things are not new in the world, nor in the British dominions though they are comparatively, rareties and novelties in this town. *Carr* a native of *Ireland* had often been concerned in such attacks, and indeed, from the nature of things, soldiers quartered in a populous town, will always occasion two mobs, where they prevent one. They are wretched conservators of the peace!

Langford "heard the rattling against the guns, but saw nothing thrown." This rattling must have been very remarkable, as so many witnesses heard it, who were not in a situation to see what caused it—Those things which hit the guns made a noise, those which hit the soldiers persons, did not. But when so many things were thrown and so many hit their guns, to suppose that none struck their persons is incredible. *Langford* goes on "*Gray* struck me on the shoulder and asked me what is to pay? I answered, I don't know but I believe something will come of it, by and bye." Whence could this apprehension of mischief arise, if *Langford* did not think the assault, the squabble, the affray, was such as would provoke the soldiers to fire?—"a bayonet went through my great coat and jacket," yet the soldier did not step out of his place—This looks as if *Langford* was nearer to the party than became a watchman. Forty or fifty people round the soldiers, and more coming from *Quaker lane,* as well as the other lanes—The soldiers heard all the bells ringing and saw people coming from every point of the compass to the assistance of those who were insulting, assaulting, beating and abusing of them—what had they to expect but destruction, if they had not thus early taken measures to defend themselves?

Brewer saw *Killroy,* &c. saw Dr. *Young,* &c. "he said the people had better go home." It was an excellent advice, happy for some of them had they followed it, but it seems all advice was lost on these persons, they would harken to none that was given them in *Dock square, Royal exchange lane,* or *King street,* they were bent on making this assault, and on their own destruction.

The next witness that knows any thing was *James Bailey,* he saw *Carrol, Montgomery,* and *White,* he saw some around the Sentry, heaving pieces of ice, large and hard enough to hurt any man, as big as your fist: one question is, whether the Sentinel was attacked or not. If you want evidence of an attack upon him there is enough of it, here is a witness an inhabitant of the town, surely no friend to the soldiers, for he was engaged against them at the Rope-walks; he says he saw twenty or thirty round the Sentry, pelting with cakes of ice, as big as one's fist; certainly cakes of ice of this size may kill a man, if they happen to hit some part of the head. So that, here was an attack on the Sentinel, the consequence of which he had reason to dread, and it was prudent in him to call for the *Main Guard:* he retreated as far as he could, he attempted to get into the *Custom house,* but could not; then he called to the *Guard,* and he had a good right to call for their assistance; "he did not know, he told the witness, what was the matter, but he was afraid there would be mischief by and bye"; and well he might, with so many shavers and genius's round him, capable of throwing such dangerous things. *Bailey* swears, *Montgomery* fired the first gun, and that he stood at the right, "the next man to me. I stood behind him, &c." This witness certainly is not prejudiced in favour of the soldiers, he swears, he saw a man come up to *Montgomery* with a club, and knock him down before he fired, and that he not only fell himself, but his gun flew out of his hand, and as soon as he rose he took it up and fired. If he was knocked down on his station, had he not reason to think his life in danger, or did it not raise his passions and put him off his guard; so that it cannot be more than manslaughter.

When the multitude was shouting and huzzaing, and threatening life, the bells all ringing, the mob whistle screaming and rending like an Indian yell, the people from all quarters throwing every species of rubbish they could pick up in the streets, and some who were quite on the other side of the street throwing clubs at the whole party, *Montgomery* in particular, smote with a club and knocked down, and as soon as he could rise and take up his firelock, another club from a far struck his breast or shoulder, what could he do? Do you expect he should behave like a Stoick Philosopher lost in Apathy? Patient as *Epictatus* while his master was breaking his leggs with a cudgel? It is impossible you should find him guilty of murder. You must suppose him divested of all human passions, if you don't think him at the least provoked, thrown off his guard, and into the *furor brevis,* by such treatment as this.

Bailey "Saw the Molatto seven or eight minutes before the firing, at the head of twenty or thirty sailors in *Cornhill,* and he had a large cord wood stick." So that this *Attucks,* by this testimony of *Bailey* compared with that of *Andrew,* and some others, appears to have undertaken to be the hero of the night; and to lead this army with banners, to form them in the first place in *Dock square,* and march them up to *King-street,* with their clubs; they passed through the main-street up to the *Main* guard, in order to make the attack. If this was not an unlawful assembly, there never was one in the world. *Attucks* with his myrmidons comes round *Jackson's* corner, and down to the party by the Sentry-box; when the soldiers pushed the people off, this man with his party cried, do not be afraid of them, they dare not fire, kill them! kill them! knock them over! And he tried to knock their brains out. It is plain the soldiers did not leave their station, but cried to the people, stand off: now to have this reinforcement coming down under the command of a stout Molatto fellow, whose very looks, was enough to terrify any person, what had not the soldiers then to fear? He had hardiness enough to fall in upon them, and with one hand took hold of a bayonet, and with the other knocked the man down: This was the behavior of *Attucks;* to whose mad behaviour, in all probability, the dreadful carnage of that night, is chiefly to be ascribed. And it is in this manner, this town has been often treated; a *Carr* from *Ireland,* and an *Attucks* from *Framingham,* happening to be here, shall sally out upon their thoughtless enterprizes, at the head of such a rabble of Negroes, &c. as they can collect together, and then there are not wanting, persons to ascribe all their doings to the good people of the town.

Mr. *Adams* proceeded to a minute consideration of every witness produced on the crown side; and endeavored to shew, from the evidence on that side, which could not be contested by the council for the crown, that the assault upon the party, was sufficiently provoking to reduce to manslaughter the crime, even of the two who were supposed to be proved to have killed. But it would swell this publication too much, to insert his observations at large, and there is the less necessity for it, as they will probably occur to every man who reads the evidence with attention. He then proceeded to consider the testimonies of the witnesses for the prisoners, which must also be omitted: And concluded,

I will enlarge no more on the evidence, but submit it to you. Facts are stubborn things; and whatever may be our wishes, our inclinations, or the dictates of our passions, they cannot alter the state of facts and evidences nor is the law less stable than the fact; if an assault was made to endanger their lives, the law is clear, they had a right to kill in their own defence; if it was not so severe as to endanger their lives, yet if they were assaulted at all, struck and abused by blows of any sort, by snow-balls, oyster-shells, cinders clubs, or sticks of any kind; this was a provocation, for which the law reduces the offence of killing, down to manslaughter, in consideration of those passions in our nature, which cannot be eradicated. To your candour and justice I submit the prisoners and their cause.

The law, in all vicissitudes of government, fluctuations of the passions, or flights of enthusiasm, will preserve a steady undeviating course; it will not bend to the uncertain wishes, imaginations, and wanton tempers of men. To use the words of a great and worthy man, a patriot, and an hero, an enlightened friend of mankind, and a martyr to liberty; I mean ALGERNOON SIDNEY, who from his earliest infancy sought a tranquil retirement under the shadow of the tree of liberty, with his tongue, his pen, and his sword, "The law (says he) no passion can disturb. 'Tis void of desire and fear, lust and anger. 'Tis *mens sine affectu;* written reason; retaining some measure of the divine perfection. It does not enjoin that which pleases a weak, frail man, but without any regard to persons, commands that which is good, and punishes evil in all, whether rich, or poor, high or low—'Tis deaf, inexorable, inflexible." On the one hand it is inexorable to the cries and lamentations of the prisoners; on the other it is deaf, deaf as an adder, to the clamours of the populace.

III

On *Occasional* Matters

———

LITTLE SPEECH

John Winthrop

John Winthrop, Puritan leader, was the first governor of the Massachusetts Bay Colony. His *Journal*, also called *History of New England*, is one of the most valuable sources of early American history.

Winthrop was born January 12, 1587 (1588?), in Edwardstone, Suffolk, England. His family was well-to-do. He was educated at Cambridge University and later studied law. He became a successful lawyer in London but was not satisfied there. He had been interested in the Puritan faith since boyhood and decided that he should be with the colonists in America. In 1629 he decided to move to New England with his family and associated himself with the Massachusetts Bay Company. As a member of this Company, he favored the move to New England, and was chosen the first governor in 1630 in place of Matthew Craddock, who stayed in England.

Winthrop arrived at Salem, Massachusetts in June, 1630, with eleven ships and about seven hundred colonists. He was one of the founders of Boston, and was reelected governor at the end of his term. He served in that capacity or as deputy governor for the rest of his life. While deputy governor, he took part in the banishment of Anne Hutchinson. He had previously been rebuked by the clergy for being too lenient. He organized the New England Confederation in 1643, and was its first president. He died March 26, 1649.

In 1645, Winthrop, then lieutenant governor, was impeached by the lower house of the General Court. On July 3, 1645, he was acquitted. He then delivered the "little speech" to the people to justify his position that they must "quietly and cheerfully submit into that authority which is set over them" for their own good. The text of the speech is taken from the James Kendall Hosmer edition of the *Journal* published in New York by Charles Scribner's Sons, 1908, II, 237–39.

I suppose something may be expected from me, upon this charge that is befallen me, which moves me to speak now to you; yet I intend not to intermeddle in the proceedings of the court, or with any of the persons concerned therein. Only I bless God, that I see an issue of this troublesome business. I also acknowledge the justice of the court, and, for mine own part, I am well satisfied, I was publicly charged, and I am publicly and legally acquitted, which is all I did expect or desire. And though this be sufficient for my justification before men, yet not so before the God, who hath seen so much amiss in my dispensations (and even in this affair) as calls me to be humble. For to be publicly and criminally charged in this court, is matter of humiliation, (and I desire to make a right use of it,) notwithstanding I be thus acquitted. If her father had spit in her face, (saith the Lord concerning Miriam,) should she not have been ashamed seven days? Shame had lien upon her, whatever the occasion had been, I am unwilling to stay you from your urgent affairs, yet give me leave (upon this special occasion) to speak a little more to this assembly. It may be of some good use, to inform and rectify the judgments of some of the people, and may prevent such distempers as have arisen amongst us. The great questions that have troubled the country, are about the authority of the magistrates and the liberty of the people. It is yourselves who have called us to this office, and being called by you, we have our authority from God, in way of an ordinance, such as hath the image of God eminently stamped upon it, the contempt and violation whereof hath been vindicated with examples of divine vengeance. I entreat you to consider, that when you choose magistrates, you take them from among yourselves, men subject to like passions as you are. Therefore when you see infirmities in us, you should reflect upon your own, and that would make you bear the more with us, and not be severe censurers of the failings of your magistrates, when you have continual experience of the like infirmities in yourselves and others. We account him a good servant, who breaks not his covenant. The covenant between you and us is the oath you have taken of us, which is to this purpose, that we shall govern you and judge your causes by the rules of God's laws and our own, according to our best skill. When you agree with a workman to build you a ship or house, etc., he undertakes as well for his skill as for his faithfulness, for it is his profession, and you pay him for both. But when you call one to be a magistrate, he doth not profess nor undertake to have sufficient skill for that office, nor can you furnish him with gifts, etc., therefore you must run the hazard of his skill and ability. But if he fail in faithfulness, which by his oath he is bound unto, that he must answer for. If it fall out that the case be clear to common apprehension, and the rule clear also, if he transgress here, the error is not in the skill, but in the evil of the will: it must be required of him. But if the case be doubtful, or the rule doubtful, to men of such understanding and parts as your magistrates are, if your magistrates should err here, yourselves must bear it.

For the other point concerning liberty, I observe a great mistake in the country about that. There is a twofold liberty, natural (I mean as our nature is now corrupt) and civil or federal. The first is common to man with beasts and other creatures. By this, man, as he stands in relation to man simply, hath liberty to do what he lists; it is a liberty to evil as well as to good. This liberty is incompatible and inconsistent with authority, and cannot endure the least restraint of the most just authority. The exercise and maintaining of this liberty makes men grow more evil, and in time to be worse than brute beasts: *omnes sumus licentia deteriores.* This is that great enemy of truth and peace, that wild beast, which all the ordinances of God are bent against, to restrain and subdue it. The other kind of liberty I call civil or federal, it may also be termed moral, in reference to the covenant between God and man, in the moral law, and the politic covenants and constitutions, amongst men themselves. This liberty is the proper end and object of authority, and cannot subsist without it; and it is a liberty to that only which is good, just, and honest. This liberty you are to stand for, with the hazard (not only of your goods, but) of your lives, if need be. Whatsoever crosseth this, is not authority, but a distemper thereof. This liberty is maintained and exercised in a way of subjection to authority; it is of the same kind of liberty wherewith Christ hath made us free. The woman's own choice makes such a man her husband; yet being so chosen, he is her lord, and she is to be subject to him, yet in a way of liberty, not of bondage; and a true wife accounts her subjection her honor and freedom, and would not think her condition safe and free, but in her subjection to her husband's authority. Such is the liberty of the church under the authority of Christ, her king and husband; his yoke is so easy and sweet to her as a bride's ornaments; and if through forwardness or wantonness, etc., she shake it off, at any time, she is at no rest in her spirit, until she take it up again; and whether her lord smiles upon her, and embraceth her in his arms, or whether he frowns, or rebukes, or smites her, she apprehends the sweetness of his love in all, and is refreshed, supported, and instructed by every such dispensation of his authority over her. On the other side, ye know who they are that complain of this yoke and say, let us break their bands, etc., we will not have this man to rule over us. Even so, brethren, it will be between you and your magistrates. If you stand for your natural corrupt liberties, and will do what is good in your own eyes, you will not endure the least weight of authority, but will murmur, and oppose, and be always striving to shake off that yoke; but if you will be satisfied to enjoy such civil and lawful liberties, such as Christ allows you, then will you quietly and cheerfully submit unto that authority which is set over you, in all the administrations of it, for your good. Wherein, if we fail at any time, we hope we shall be willing (by God's assistance) to hearken to good advice from any of you, or in any other way of God; so shall your liberties be preserved, in upholding the honor and power of authority amongst you.

A FUNERAL ORATION

John Lovell

John Lovell, father of James, was born in Boston April 1, 1710. Because of his wide and vast intellectual powers, he was appointed a Hollis scholar his first year at Harvard. He received his A.B. in 1731.

In April 1929, he left Cambridge to become usher at the South Grammar School in Boston. He made frequent contributions to the *Weekly Rehearsal* (1731–35), a spirited literary paper. Because of his fluency in French, he was made French interpreter for the Boston selectmen.

He was unanimously chosen master of South Grammar School May 21, 1734, and though he was praised as a good scholar and a sharp critic, he was criticized by some pupils for his "barbarous discipline." Some who came under his tutelage as boys were Samuel Adams, Samuel Langdon, James Bowdoin, Robert Treat Paine, Andrew Oliver, John Hancock, Thomas Brattle, Jeremy Belknap, Francis Dana, Henry Knox, William Phillips, William Eustis, Christopher Gore, and Harrison Gray Otis. He excelled in oratory, wrote poetry, and published political and theological pamphlets.

He minimized the colonial troubles of the time, and urged that the Crown equate the rights of Colonials with the rights of Englishmen. A dedicated loyalist, Lovell left Boston for Halifax March 14, 1776, where he died about mid-July, 1778.

At the request of the inhabitants of Boston, Lovell delivered at the opening of the annual meeting of the town, March 14, 1742, at Faneuil Hall, the funeral oration occasioned by the death of Peter Faneuil. The text is from the Kneeland and Green edition published in Boston in 1743.

I STAND in this Place, my *Fellow Townsmen, and my worthy patrons,* at the Call of those to whom you have committed the Direction of your *public Affairs,* to condole with you for the *Loss* of your late *generous Benefactor,* THE FOUNDER OF THIS HOUSE. Certain I am, there are Numbers in this great Assembly, who could upon this Occasion have done *more Justice* to his *Memory,* and have *better* discharg'd the Office that is enjoin'd me. But the *Commands* of those (for such I must always esteem their *Desires*) who have devolved this Charge upon me, and the Veneration I have for the Vertues of the Deceas'd, oblige me to bear what little Part I can, in a grateful Acknowledgement of the just

138

Regard due to the Memory of a Man, whose Name, I am sure, will never be forgotten among us.

How soon, alas! is our Joy for having found such a Benefactor, chang'd into Mourning for the Loss of him! But a few Months are pass'd since we were framing Votes, and consulting the best Measures to express our Gratitude for his unexampled Favours; and the first *annual* Meeting within these Walls that were rais'd by his *Bounty,* finds us assembled in the deepest Sorrow for his Decease.

Instances of Mortality are never more affecting than in those whose Lives have been public Blessings. Surely then, every Breast must feel a more than common Distress, for the Loss of One, whose *Largeness of Heart* equal'd, great as it was, his *Power to do Good.* Honest Industry must mourn, for which the Exercise of his Bounty found an almost constant Employment: And they that know how to pity the *Calamities* of *human Nature* themselves, will mourn for him that *always* reliev'd them.

So soon as he arriv'd to the Possession of his large and plentiful Estate; instead of fruitlessly *hoarding up his Treasures,* tho' no Man manag'd his Affairs with greater *Prudence* and *Industry;* instead of *wasting* them in *Luxury,* tho' *Plenty* always crown'd his Board; instead of *neglecting the Wants* of his Fellow-Creatures, an unhappy Circumstance too often attending the Possession of Riches, He made it manifest that he understood the *true Improvement of Wealth,* and was determin'd to *pursue* it. It was to him the *highest Enjoyment* of *Riches,* to relieve the *Wants* of the *Needy,* from which he was *himself* exempted, to see *Mankind* rejoicing in the *Fruits* of his Bounty, and to feel that divine Satisfaction which results from communicating Happiness to *others.* His Acts of *Charity* were so *secret* and *unbounded,* that none but they who were the *Objects* of it, can compute the Sums which he annually distributed among them. His Alms *flow'd* like a *fruitful River,* that diffuses it's *Streams* thro' a *whole Country.* He *fed the Hungry,* and he *cloath'd the Naked,* he *comforted the Fatherless,* and the *Widows* in their Affliction, and his *Bounties* visited the *Prisoner.* So that ALMIGHTY GOD in giving *Riches* to THIS MAN, seems to have scattered *Blessings* all abroad among the People.

But these *private Charities* were not the only Effects of his *public Spirit,* which, not contented with distributing his Benefactions to *private Families,* extended them to the *whole Community.* Let THIS STATELY AEDIFICE which bears his Name witness for him, what Sums he expended in public Munificence. This *Building* erected by him at an immense Charge, for the *Convenience* and *Ornament* of the Town, is incomparably the *greatest Benefaction* ever yet known to our *western Shoar.* Yet *this Effect* of his Bounty,

however great, is but the *first Fruits* of his Generosity, a *Pledge*
of what his Heart, *always devising liberal Things,* would have done
for us, had his Life been spar'd. It is an *unspeakable Loss* to the
Town, that he was taken away in the *midst of his days,* and in so
sudden a Manner, as to prevent his making *Provision* for what his
generous Heart might design. For I am well assur'd, from those
who were acquainted with his Purposes, that he had *many more
Blessings in Store* for us, had *Heaven* prolong'd his Days.

But he is gone! The *Town's Benefactor,* the *Comforter of the
Distress'd,* and the *poor Man's Friend.*

He is gone! And all his *Plans* of *future Bounties* with him,
they are buried in the Grave together. He shall be *rais'd* to Life
again: And his *intended Charities,* tho' they are lost to us, will
not be lost to him. *Designs* of *Goodness* and *Mercy,* prevented as
these were, will meet with the *Reward* of *Actions.*

He is gone! And must *such Men* die! Die in the midst of their
Days! Must the *Protectors* and *Fathers* of the Distress'd be taken
away, while their *Oppressors* are continued, and *increase in Power!*
GREAT GOD! *How unsearchable thy Ways! We confess* our *Sins,
but just and righteous art* THOU.

To express your *Gratitude* to your generous *Benefactor,* you
have pass'd the most *honorable Resolves,* and to preserve his
Memory, you have call'd this House by his Name. But in vain, alas,
would you *perpetuate* his Memory by such *frail Materials!* These
Walls, the present *Monuments* of his *Fame,* shall moulder into
Dust: These Foundations, however deeply laid, shall be forgotten.
But his *Deeds,* his *Charities,* shall survive the *Ruins* of Nature.
And to have *reliev'd the Miseries of the Distress'd,* to have *still'd
the Cries of Orphans,* and to have *dry'd the Widow's Tears,* are
Acts that shall embalm his *Memory* for many Generations on
Earth, and shall follow him beyond the *Limits of Mortality,* into
those *blissful Regions* where endless *Charity* dwells.

What now remains, but my *ardent Wishes* (in which, I know
you will concur with me) That *this Hall* may ever be sacred to the
Interests of *Truth,* of *Justice,* of *Loyalty,* of *Honor,* of *Liberty.*
May no *private Views* nor *party Broils* ever enter within these
Walls; but may the same *public Spirit* that glow'd in the Breast of
the *generous Founder, influence* all your Debates, that Society may
reap the Benefit of them.

May LIBERTY always spread its *joyful Wings* over this Place:
Liberty that opens *Men's Hearts* to *Beneficence,* and gives the
Relish to those who enjoy the *Effects* of it. And may LOYALTY
to a KING, under whom we enjoy this *Liberty,* ever remain *our
Character.* A Character always *justly due to this Land,* and of
which our *Enemies* have in vain *attempted to rob us.*

May those who are the *Inheriters* of the large Estate of our *deceased Benefactor,* inherit, likewise *the Largeness of his Soul.* May the *Widow,* the *Orphan,* and the *Helpless,* find in them a *Protector,* a *Father,* and a *Support.* In a Word, to sum up all, *May* FANEUIL *live in them.*

May CHARITY, that most excellent of *Graces* that *Beam* from the Breast of the FATHER OF MERCIES, which, so soon as ever it enters our *Bosom* begins our *Happiness, Charity,* the Joy of *Men,* of *Angels,* of ALMIGHTY GOD; which compleats the *Felicity* of Earth and Heaven: May *Charity* more abound among us. May it *warm* the Hearts of those who are like to our departed Friend in their *Fortunes,* to resemble him too in his *Bounties:* May there be rais'd up some new *Benefactors* in the room of him we have lost, who shall, if possible, rival FANEUIL's Spirit. And may there always remain in this Town the same grateful Sentiments, the same vertuous Dispositions to remember their Benefactors with Honor.

AN ORATION, &c.

David Rittenhouse

David Rittenhouse, astronomer, mathematician, and instrument maker, was born at Paper Mill Run near Germantown, Pennsylvania, on April 8, 1732. He taught himself clockmaking and worked at this trade while he studied astronomy. He constructed mathematical and astronomical instruments, including a telescope which he completed in 1756.

He was elected treasurer of Pennsylvania in 1777, and became the first director of the United States Mint in Philadelphia. He was frequently employed in making boundary surveys and was a member of a commission which determined the boundaries of Pennsylvania.

Rittenhouse was active in the Revolutionary war. He supervised the casting of cannon and the manufacture of saltpetre. He was President of the Council of Safety in 1777, and a member of the General Assembly. After the War, he became president of the Philosophical Society and in 1795, was elected a fellow of the Royal Society of London. He died June 26, 1796.

It was as a member of the American Philosophical Society that Rittenhouse gave the following lecture on Astronomy to that society on February 24, 1775, and dedicated it to the members of Congress then assembled in Philadelphia.

The text of the address or oration is from the Philadelphia edition printed by John Dunlap in 1775.

Gentlemen,

IT was not without being sensible how very unequal I am to the undertaking, that I first consented to comply with the request of several gentlemen for whom I have the highest esteem, and to solicit your attention on a subject which an able hand might indeed render both entertaining and instructive, I mean ASTRONOMY. But the earnest desire I have to contribute something towards the improvement of *Science* in general, and particularly of *Astronomy,* in this my native country, joined with the fullest confidence that I shall be favoured with your most candid indulgence, however far I may fall short of doing justice to the noble subject, enables me chearfully to take my turn as a member of the society on this annual occasion.

THE order I shall observe in the following discourse is this: In the first place I shall give a very short account of the rise and progress of Astronomy, then take notice of some of the most important discoveries that have been made in this science, and conclude with pointing out a few of its defects at the present time.

AS, on this occasion, it is not necessary to treat my subject in a strictly scientific way, I shall hazard some conjectures of my own; which, if they have but novelty to recommend them, may perhaps be more acceptable than retailing the conjectures of others.

THE first rise of Astronomy, like the beginnings of other sciences, is lost in the obscurity of ancient times. Some have attributed its origin to that strong propensity mankind have discovered, in all ages, for prying into futurity; supposing that Astronomy was cultivated only as subservient to judicial Astrology. Others with more reason suppose Astrology to have been the spurious offspring of Astronomy; a supposition that does but add one more to the many instances of human depravity, which can convert the best things to the worst purposes.

THE honour of first cultivating Astronomy has been ascribed to the Chaldeans, the Egyptians, the Arabians, and likewise to the Chinese; amongst whom, it is pretended, astronomical observations are to be found of almost as early a date as the flood. But little credit is given to these reports of the Jesuits, who it is thought, were imposed on by the natives; or else perhaps from motives of vanity, they have departed a little from *truth,* in their accounts of a country and people among whom they were the chief European travellers.

NOT to mention the prodigious number of years in which it is said the Chaldeans observed the heavens, I pass on to what carries the appearance of more probability; the report that when Alexander took Babylon, astronomical observations for one thousand nine hundred years before that time were found there and sent from thence to Aristotle. But we cannot suppose those observations to have been of much value; for we do not find that any use was ever after made of them.

THE Egyptians too, we are told, had observations of the stars for one thousand five hundred years before the Christian aera. What they were is not known; but probably the Astronomy of those ages consisted in little more than remarks on the rising and setting of the fixed stars, as they were found to correspond with the seasons of the year; and, perhaps, forming them into constellations. That this was done early, appears from the book of Job, which has by some been attributed to Moses, who is said to have been learned in the sciences of Egypt. "Canst thou bind the sweet influences of Pleiades, or loose the bands of Orion? Canst thou bring forth Massaroth in his season, or canst thou guide Arcturus with his sons?" Perhaps too, some account might be kept of eclipses of the sun and moon, as they happened, without pretending to predict them for the future. These eclipses are thought by some to have been foretold by the Jewish prophets in a supernatural way.

As to the Arabians, though some have supposed them the first inventors of Astronomy, encouraged to contemplate the heavens by the happy temperature of their climate, and the serenity of their skies, which their manner of life must likewise have contributed to render more particularly the object of their attention; yet it is said nothing of certainty can now be found to induce us to think they had any knowledge of this science amongst them before they learned it from the writings of Ptolemy, who flourished one hundred and forty years after the birth of Christ.

BUT notwithstanding the pretensions of other nations, since it was the Greeks who improved Geometry, probably from its first rudiments, into a noble and most useful science; and since we cannot conceive that Astronomy should make any considerable progress without Geometry, it is to them we appear indebted for the foundations of a science, that (to speak without a metaphor) has in latter ages reached the astonishing distant heavens.

AMONGST the Greeks Hipparchus deserves particular notice; by an improvement of whose labours Ptolemy formed that system of Astronomy which appears to have been the only one studied for ages after, and particularly (as was said before) by the Arabians; who made some improvements of their own, and, if not the inventors, were at least the preservers of Astronomy. For with them it took refuge, during those ages of ignorance which involved Europe, after an inundation of northern people had swallowed up the Roman Empire; where the universally prevailing corruption of manners, and false taste, were become as unfavourable to the cause of Science, as the ravages of the Barbarians themselves.

FROM this time, we meet with little account of astronomical learning in Europe, until Regiomontanus, and some others, revived it in the fourteenth century; and an hundred years afterwards, appeared the celebrated Copernicus, whose vast genius, assisted by such lights as the remains of antiquity afforded him, explained the true system of the universe, as at present understood. To the objection of the Aristotelians, that the sun could not be the centre of the world, because all bodies tended to the earth, Copernicus replied, that probably there was nothing peculiar to the earth in this respect; that the parts of the sun, moon and stars likewise tended to each other, and that their spherical figure was preserved amidst their various motions, by this power; an answer that will at this day be allowed to contain sound philosophy. And when it was further objected to him, that, according to his system, Venus and Mercury ought to appear horned like the moon, in particular situations; he answered as if inspired by the spirit of prophecy, and long before the invention of telescopes, by which alone his prediction could be verified, "That so they would one day be found to appear."

NEXT follows the noble Tycho, who with great labour and perseverance, brought the art of observing the heavens, to a degree of accuracy unknown to the ancients; though in theory he mangled the beautiful system of Copernicus. The whimsical Kepler too (whose fondness for analogies frequently led him astray, yet sometimes happily conducted him to important truths) did notable services to Astronomy. And from his time down to the present, so many great men have appeared amongst the several nations of Europe, rivalling each other in the improvement of Astronomy, that I should tresspass on your patience were I to enumerate them. I shall therefore proceed to what I proposed in the second place, and take notice of some of the most important discoveries in this science.

ASTRONOMY, like the Christian religion, if you will allow me the comparison, has a much greater influence on our knowledge in general, and perhaps on our manners too, than is commonly imagined. Though but few men are its particular votaries, yet the light it affords is universally diffused among us; and it is difficult for us to divest ourselves of its influence so far, as to frame any competent idea of what would be our situation without it. Utterly ignorant of the heavens, our curiosity would be confined solely to the earth, which we should naturally suppose a vast extended plain; but whether of infinite extent or bounded, and if bounded, in what manner—would be questions admitting of a thousand conjectures, and none of them at all satisfactory.

THE first discovery then, which paved the way for others more curious, seems to have been the circular figure of the earth, inferred from observing the meridian altitudes of the sun and stars to be different in distant places. This conclusion would probably not be immediately drawn, but the appearance accounted for, by the rectilinear notion of the traveller; and then a change in the apparent situations of the heavenly bodies would only argue their nearness to the earth: and thus would the observation contribute to establish error, instead of promoting truth, which has been the misfortunes of many an experiment. It would require some skill in Geometry, as well as practice in observing angles, to demonstrate the spherical figure of the earth from such observations.

BUT this difficulty being surmounted, and the true figure of the earth discovered, a free space would now be granted for the sun, moon, and stars to perform their diurnal motions on all sides of it; unless perhaps at its extremities to the north and south; where something would be thought necessary to serve as an axis for the heavens to revolve on. This Mr. Crantz in his very entertaining history of Greenland informs us is agreeable to the philoso-

phy of that country, with this difference perhaps, that the high
latitude of the Greenlander makes him conclude one pole only,
necessary: He therefore supposes a vast mountain situate in the
utmost extremity of Greenland, whose pointed apex supports the
canopy of heaven, and whereon it revolves with but little friction.

A FREE space around the earth being granted, our Infant
Astronomer would be at liberty to consider the diurnal motions
of the stars as performed in intire circles, having one common
axis of rotation. And by considering their daily anticipation in
rising and setting, together with the sun's annual rising and falling
in its noon day height, swiftest about the middle space, and sta-
tionary for some time when highest and lowest, he would be led
to explain the whole by attributing a slow motion to the sun, contrary to the diurnal motion, along a great circle dividing the
heavens into two equal parts, but obliquely situated with respect
to the diurnal motion. By a like attention to the moon's progress
the Zodiac would be formed, and divided into its several constellations or other convenient divisions.

THE next step that Astronomy advanced I conceive must have
been in the discovery attributed to Pythagoras; who it is said first
found out that Hesperus and Phosphorus, or the Evening and
Morning Star, were the same. The superior brightness of this
planet, and the swiftness of its motion, probably first attracted the
notice of the inquisitive: And one wandering star being discovered,
more would naturally be looked for. The splendor of Jupiter, the
very changeable appearance of Mars, and the glittering of Mercury
by day light, would distinguish them. And lastly, Saturn would be
discovered by a close attention to the heavens. But how often would
the curious eye be directed in vain, to the regions of the north and
south, before there was reason to conclude that the orbits of all
the planets lay nearly in the same plane; and that they had but
narrow limits assigned them in the visible heavens.

FROM a careful attendance to those newly discovered celestial
travellers, and their various motions, direct and retrograde, the
great discovery arose, that the sun is the center of their motions;
and that by attributing a similar motion to the earth, and supposing
the sun to be at rest, all the Phoenomena will be solved. Hence a
hint was taken that opened a new and surprizing scene. The earth
might be similar to them in other respects. The planets too might
be habitable worlds. One cannot help greatly admiring the sagacity
of minds, that first formed conclusions so very far from being
obvious; as well as the indefatigable industry of Astronomers, who
originally framed rules for predicting eclipses of sun and moon,
which is said to have been done as early as the time of Thales;
and must have proved of singular service to emancipate mankind
from a thousand superstitious fears and notions, which jugling

impostors (the growth of all ages and countries) would not fail to turn to their own advantage.

FOR two or three centuries before and after the beginning of the Christian AEra, Astronomy appears to have been held in considerable repute; yet very few discoveries of any consequence were made, during that period and many ages following.

THE ancients were not wanting in their endeavours to find out the true dimensions of the Planetary System. They invented several very ingenious methods for the purpose; but none of them were at all equal, in point of accuracy, to the difficulty of the problem. They were therefore obliged to rest satisfied with supposing the heavenly bodies much nearer to the earth than in fact they are, and consequently much less in proportion to it. Add to this, that having found the earth honoured with an attendant, while they could discover none belonging to any of the other planets, *they* supposed it of far greater importance in the Solar System than it appears to *us* to be: And the more praise is due to those few, who nevertheless conceived rightly of its relation to the whole.

TYCHO took incredible pains to discover the parallax of Mars in opposition; the very best thing he could have attempted in order to determine the distances and magnitudes of the sun and planets. But telescopes and micrometers were not yet invented! so that not being able to conclude any thing satisfactory from his own observations, he left the sun's parallax as he found it settled by Ptolemy, about twenty times too great. And even after he had reduced to rule the refraction of the atmosphere, and applied it to astronomical observations, rather than shock his imagination by increasing the sun's distance, already too great for *his* hypothesis, he chose to attribute a greater refraction to the sun's light, than that of the stars, altogether contrary to reason; that so an excess of parallax might be balanced by an excess of refraction. Thus when we willingly give room to one error, we run the risk of having a whole troop of its relations quartered upon us. But Kepler afterwards, on looking over Tycho's observations, found that he might safely reduce the sun's parallax to one minute; which was no inconsiderable approach to the truth. Alhazen, an Arabian, had some time before, discovered the refraction of light in passing through air; of which the ancients seem to have been entirely ignorant. They were indeed very sensible of the errors it occasioned in their celestial measures; but they with great modesty, attributed them to the imperfections of their instruments or observations.

I MUST not omit, in honour of Tycho, to observe that he first proved, by accurate observations, that the comets are not meteors floating in our atmosphere, as Aristotle, that tyrant in Philosophy, had determined them to be, but prodigious bodies at a vast distance from us in the planetary regions; a discovery the lateness of which we must regret, for if it had been made by the ancients, that part of Astronomy (and perhaps every other, in consequence of the superior attention paid to it) would have been in far greater perfection than it is at this day.

I HAD almost forgot to take notice of one important discovery made in the early times of Astronomy, the precession of the equinoxes. An ancient astronomer, called Timocharis, observed an appulse of the Moon to the Virgins Spike, about 280 years before the birth of Christ. He thence took occasion to determine the place of this star, as accurately as possible; probably with a view of perfecting the lunar theory. About four hundred years afterwards Ptolemy comparing the place of the same star, as he then found it, with its situation determined by Timocharis, concluded the precession to be at the rate of one degree in an hundred years; but later astronomers have found it swifter.

WHATEVER other purposes this great law may answer, it will produce an amazing change in the appearance of the heavens; and so contribute to that endless variety which obtains throughout the works of Nature. The seven stars that now adorn our winter skies, will take their turn to shine in summer. Sirius, that now shines with unrivalled lustre, amongst the gems of heaven, will sink below our horizon, and rise no more for very many ages! Orion too, will disappear, and no longer afford our posterity a glimpse of glories beyond the skies! glittering Capella, that now passes to the north of our zenith, will nearly describe the equator: And Lyra, one of the brightest in the heavens will become our Polar Star: Whilst the present Pole Star, on account of its humble appearance, shall pass unheeded; and all its long continued faithful services shall be forgotten! All these changes, and many others, will certainly follow from the precession of the equinoxes; the cause of which motion was so happyily discovered and demonstrated by the immortal Newton: A portion of whose honors was nevertheless intercepted by the prior sagacity of Kepler, to whom I return.

KEPLER'S love of harmony encouraged him to continue his pursuits, in spite of the most mortifying disappointments, until he discovered that admirable relation which subsists between the periodic times of the primary planets, and their distances from the sun; the squares of the former being as the cubes of the latter. This discovery was of great importance to the perfection of Astronomy; because the periods of the planets are more easily found by observation, and from them their several relative distances may be determined with great accuracy by this rule. He likewise found from o' vation, that the planets do not move in circles, but in elipses, having the sun in one focus. But the causes lay hid from him, and it was left as the glory of Sir Isaac, to demonstrate that both these things must necessarily follow from one simple principle, which almost every thing in this science tends to prove does really obtain in Nature: I mean, that the planets are retained in their orbits by forces directed to the sun; which forces decrease as the squares of their distances encrease.

KEPLER also discovered that the planets do not move equally in their orbits, but sometimes swifter, sometimes slower; and that not irregularly, but according to this certain rule, That in equal times the areas described by lines drawn from the planet to the sun's center, are equal. This Sir Isaac likewise demonstrated must follow, if the planet be retained in its orbit by forces directed to the sun, and varying with the distance in any manner whatsoever. These three discoveries of Kepler, afterwards demonstrated by Newton, are the foundation of all accuracy in astronomical calculations.

WE now come to that great discovery, which lay concealed from the most subtle and penetrating geniuses amongst mankind, until these latter ages; which so prodigiously enlarged the fields of astronomy, and with such rapidity handed down one curiosity after another, from the heavens to astonished mortals, that no one capable of raising his eyes and thoughts from the ground he trod on, could forbear turning his attention, in some degree, to the subject that engages us this evening.

GALILEO, as he himself acknowledges, was not the first inventor of the telescope, but he was the first that knew how to make a proper use of it. If we consider that convex and concave lenses had been in use for some centuries, we shall think it probable that several persons might have chanced to combine them together, so as to magnify *distant* objects; but that the small advantage apparently resulting from such a discovery, either on account of the badness of the glasses or the unskilfulness of the person in whose hands they were, occasioned it to be neglected.

BUT Galileo, by great care in perfecting his telescope, and by applying a judicious eye, happily succeeded; and with a telescope magnifying but thirty times, discovered the moon to be a solid globe, diversified with prodigious mountains and vallies like our earth; but without seas or atmosphere. The sun's bright disk, he found frequently shaded with spots, and by their apparent motions proved it to be the surface of a globe, revolving on its axis in about five and twenty days. This it seems was a mortifying discovery to the followers of Aristotle; who held the sun to be perfect without spot or blemish. Some of them, it is said, insisted that it was but an illusion of the telescope and absolutely refused to look through one, lest the testimony of their senses should prove too powerful for their prejudices.

GALILEO likewise discovered the four attendants of Jupiter, commonly called his satellites: Which at first did not much please that great ornament of his age, the sagacious Kepler. For by this addition to the number of the planets, he found their creator had not paid that veneration to certain mystical numbers and proportions, which he had imagined. Let us not blush at this remarkable instance of philosophical weakness, but admire the candour of the man who confessed it.

GALILEO not only discovered these moons of Jupiter but suggested their use in determining the longitude of places on the earth; which has since been so happily put in practice, that Fontenelle does not hesitate to affirm, that they are of more use to Geography and Navigation, than our own moon. He discovered the phases of Mars and Venus; that the former appears sometimes round and sometimes gibbous, and that the latter puts on all the shapes of our moon: And from this discovery, he proved to a demonstration, the truth of the Copernican System. Nor did that wonderful ring, which surrounds Saturn's body, without touching it, and which we know nothing in nature similar to, escape his notice; though his telescope did not mignify [sic] sufficiently to give him a true idea of its figure.

AMONGST the fixed stars too, Galileo pursued his enquiries. The Milky-Way, which had so greatly puzzled the ancient Philosophers, and which Aristotle imagined to be vapours risen to an extraordinary heighth, he found to consist of an innumerable multitude of small stars; whose light appears indistinct and confounded together to the naked eye. And in every part of the heavens, his telescope shewed him abundance of stars, not visible without it. In short, with such unabated ardour did this great man range through the fields of Astronomy, that he seemed to leave nothing for others to glean after him.

NEVERTHELESS, by prodigiously encreasing the magnifying powers of their telescopes, his followers made several great discoveries; some of which I shall briefly mention. Mercury was found to become bisected, and horned near its inferior conjunction, as well as Venus. Spots were discovered in Mars, and from their apparent motion, the time of his revolution on an axis nearly perpendicular to his orbit, was determined. A sort of belts or girdles, of a variable or fluctuating nature, were found to surround Jupiter, and likewise certain spots on his surface, whence he was concluded to make one revolution in about ten hours on his axis; which is likewise nearly perpendicular to his orbit. Five moons or satellites were found to attend Saturn, which Galileo's telescope, on account of their prodigious distance, could not reach: And the form of his ring was found to be, a thin circular plane, so situated as not to be far from parallel to the plane of our equator; and always remaining paralled to itself. This ring, as well as Saturn, evidently derives its light from the sun, as appears by the shadows they mutually cast on each other.

BESIDES several other remarkable appearances, which Hugenius discovered amongst the fixed stars, there is one in Orion's Sword, which, I will venture to say, whoever shall attentively view, with a good telescope and experienced eye, will not find his curiosity disappointed. "Seven small stars, says he, of which three are very close together, seemed to shine through a cloud, so that a space round them appeared much brighter than any other part of heaven, which being very serene and black looked here as if there was an opening, through which one had a prospect into a much brighter region." Here some have supposed old night to be entirely dispossessed, and that perpetual daylight shines amongst numberless worlds without interruption.

THIS is a short account of the discoveries made with the telescope. Well might Hugenius congratulate the age he lived in, on such a great acquisition of knowledge: And recollecting those great men, Copernicus, Regiomontanus, and Tycho, so lately excluded from it by death, what an immense treasure, says he, would they have given for it. Those ancient philosophers too, Pythagoras, Democritus, Anaxagoras, Philolaus, Plato, Hipparchus; would they not have travelled over all the countries of the world, for the sake of knowing such secrets of Nature, and of enjoying such sights as these.

THUS have we seen the materials collected, which were to compose the magnificent edifice of astronomical Philosophy; collected, indeed, with infinite labour and industry, by a few volunteers in the service of human knowledge, and with an ardour not to be abated by the weaknesses of human nature, or the threatened loss of sight, one of the greatest of bodily misfortunes! It was now time for the great master builder to appear, who was to rear up this whole splendid group of materials into due order and proportion. And it was, I make no doubt, by a particular appointment of Providence, that at this time the immortal Newton appeared. Much had been done preparatory to this great work by others, without which if he had succeeded we should have been ready to pronounce him something more than human. The doctrine of atoms had been taught by some of the ancients. Kepler had suspected that the planets gravitated towards each other, particularly the earth and moon; and that their motion prevented their falling together: And Galileo first of all applied geometrical reasoning to the motion of projectiles. But the solid spheres of the ancients, or the vortices of Des Cartes, were still found necessary to explain the planetary motions; or if Kepler had discarded them, it was only to substitute something else in their stead, by no means sufficient to account for those grand movements of nature. It was Newton alone that extended the simple principle of gravity, under certain just regulations, and the laws of motion, whether rectilinear or circular, which constantly take place on the surface of this globe, throughout every part of the solar system; and from thence, by the assistance of a sublime geometry, deduced the planetary motions, with the strictest conformity to nature and observation.

OTHER systems of Philosophy have been spun out of the fertile brain of some great genius or other; and for want of a foundation in nature, have had their rise and fall, succeeding each other by turns. But this will be durable as science, and can never sink into neglect, until "universal darkness buries all."

OTHER systems of Philosophy have ever found it necessary to conceal their weakness, and inconsistency, under the veil of unintelligible terms and phrases, to which no two mortals perhaps ever affixed the same meaning: But the Philosophy of Newton disdains to make use of such subterfuges; it is not reduced to the necessity of using them, because it pretends not to be of Nature's privy council, or to have free access to her most inscrutable mysteries; but to attend carefully to her works, to discover the immediate causes of visible effects, to trace those causes to others more general and simple, advancing by slow and sure steps towards the great first cause of all things.

AND now the Astronomy of our planetary system seemed compleated. The telescope had discovered all the globes whereof it is composed, at least as far as we yet know. Newton with more than mortal sagacity had discovered those laws by which all their various, yet regular, motions are governed, and reduced them to the most beautiful simplicity. Laws to which not only their great and obvious variety of motions are conformable, but even their minute irregularities; and not only planets but comets likewise. The busy mind of man, never satiated with knowledge, now extended its views further, and made use of every expedient that suggested itself, to find the relation that this system of worlds bears to the whole visible creation. Instruments were made with all possible accuracy, and the most skilful observers applied themselves with great diligence to discover an annual parallax, from which the distances of the fixed stars would be known. They found unexpected irregularities, and might have been long perplexed with them to little purpose, had not Dr. Bradley happily accounted for them, by shewing that light from the heavenly bodies strikes the eye with a velocity and direction, compounded of the proper velocity and direction of *light,* and of the *eye,* as carried about with the earth in its orbit; compared to which the diurnal motion, and all other accidental motions of the eye, are quite inconsiderable. Thus instead of what he aimed at, he discovered something still more curious, the real velocity of light, in a way intirely new and un-thought of.

ALL Astronomical knowledge being conveyed to us from the remotest distances, by that subtle, swift and universal messenger of intelligence, LIGHT; it was natural for the curious to enquire into its properties, and particularly to endeavour to know with what velocity it proceeds, in its immeasurable journeys. Experimental Philosophy, accustomed to conquer every difficulty, undertook the arduous problem; but confessed herself unequal to the task. Here Astronomy herself revealed the secret; first in the discovery of Roemer, who found that the farther Jupiter is distant from us, the later the light of his satellites always reaches us; and after-wards in this of Dr. Bradley, informed us, that light proceeds from the sun to us in about eight minutes of time.

As the apparent motion of the fixed stars, arising from this cause, was observed to complete the intire circle of its changes in the space of a year it was for some time supposed to arise from an annual parallax, notwithstanding its inconsistency in other respects with such a supposition. But this obstacle being removed, there followed the discovery of another apparent motion in the heavens, arising from the nutation of the earth's axis; the period whereof is about nineteen years. Had it not been so very different from the period of the former, the causes of both must have been almost inexplicable. This latter discovery is an instance of the superior advantages of accurate observation: For it was well known that such a nutation must take place from the principles of the New-tonian Philosophy, yet a celebrated astronomer had concluded from hypothetical reasoning, that its quantity must be perfectly insen-sible.

THE way being cleared thus far, Dr. Bradley assures us, from his most accurate observations, that the annual parallax cannot ex-ceed two seconds, he thinks not one; and we have the best reason to confide in his judgment and accuracy. From hence then we draw this amazing conclusion, That the diameter of the earth's orb bears no greater proportion to the distance of the stars which Bradley observed, than one second does to radius; which is less than as one to 200,000. Prodigiously great as the distance of the fixed stars from our sun appears to be, and probably their distances from each other are no less, the Newtonian Philosophy will furnish us with a reason for it: That the several systems may be sufficiently removed from each other's attraction, which we are very certain must require an immense distance; especially if we consider that the cometic part, of our system at least, appears to be the most considerable tho' so little known to us. The dimensions of the several parts of the planetary system, had been determined near the truth by the astronomers of the last age, from the parallax of Mars. But from that rare phenomenon the transit of Venus over the sun's disk, which has twice happened within a few years past, the sun's parallax is now known beyond dispute to be 8 seconds and an half nearly, and consequently the sun's distance above 10,000 diameters of the earth.

IF from the distances of the several planets, and their apparent diameters taken with that excellent instrument, the micrometer, we compare their several magnitudes we shall find the moon, Mercury, and Mars, to be much less than our earth, Venus a little less, but Saturn many hundred times greater, and Jupiter above one thousand times. This prodigious globe, placed at such a vast distance from the other planets, that the force of its attraction might the less disturb their motions, is far more bulkey and ponderous than all the other planets taken together. But even Jupiter, with all his fellows of our system, are as nothing compared to that amazing mass of matter the sun. How much are we then indebted to Astronomy for correcting our ideas of the visible creation: Wanting its instruction we should infallibly have supposed the earth by far the most important body in the universe, both for magnitude and use. The sun and moon would have been though two little bodies nearly equal in size, though different in luster, created solely for the purpose of enlightening the earth; and the fixed stars, so many sparks of fire, placed in the concave vault of heaven, to adorn it, and afford us a glimmering light in the absence of the sun and moon.

BUT how does Astronomy change the scene! Take the miser from the earth, if it be possible to disengage him; he whose nightly rest has been long broken by the loss of a single foot of it, useless perhaps to him, and remove him to the planet Mars, one of the least distant from us: Persuade the ambitious monarch to accompany him, who has sacrificed the lives of thousands of his subjects to an imaginary property in certain small portions of the earth, and now point it out to them, with all its kingdoms and wealth, a glittering star "close by the moon," the latter scarce visible and the former less bright than our Evening Star. Would they not turn away their disgusted sight from it, as not thinking it worth their smallest attention, and look for consolation in the gloomy regions of Mars.

BUT dropping the company of all those, whether kings or misers, whose minds and bodies are equally affected by gravitation, let us proceed to the orb of Jupiter; the earth and all the inferior planets will vanish, lost in the sun's bright rays, and Saturn only remain: He too sometimes so diminished in lustre as not to be easily discovered. But a new and beautiful system will arise. The four moons of Jupiter will become very conspicuous; some of them perhaps appearing larger, others smaller than our moon; and all of them performing their revolutions with incredible swiftness, and the most beautiful regularity. Varying their phases from full to new and from new to full, and frequently eclipsing the sun and each other, at least to the equatoreal parts of Jupiter; and almost in every revolution suffering eclipses themselves by falling into Jupiter's shadow; excepting that the outermost will seem, like a traveller fond of the sun-beams, cautiously to avoid the shadow for whole years together. Since we are advanced so far, if not tired of the journey, let us proceed a step further; it is but 400 millions of miles to the globe of Saturn. Here again all will be lost but Jupiter itself. The sun will put on something of a starlike appearance, but with excessive brightness. The five satellites of Saturn will exhibit appearances similar to those of Jupiter, but they will very rarely eclipse the sun, or suffer eclipses themselves. The particular phoenomena of Saturn's ring, we cannot explain, unless we knew the time and plane of Saturn's revolution on his axis. But this we know, that it must sometimes appear, by night, like a prodigious luminous arch, almost equal to one quarter of the heavens; and at other times, dark, so as to afford no light itself, but to intercept the light of every star beyond it, by night, and of the sun itself by day. And to conclude, if borne on the wings of a comet we should travel with it to the remotest part of its orbit, our whole planetary system would disappear, and the sun become a star, only more refulgent than Sirius perhaps, because less distant.

The opinion of the earth's rotation on its axis was once violently opposed, from a notion of its dangerous tendency with respect to the interests of religion: But, as truth is always consistent with itself, so many new proofs were furnished from time to time by new discoveries, that a mistaken interpretation of some passages in the bible was compelled to give way to the force of astronomical evidence. The doctrine of a plurality of worlds, is inseparable from the principles of Astronomy; but this doctrine is still thought, by some pious persons, and by many more I fear, who do not deserve that title, to militate against the truths asserted by the Christian religion. If I may be allowed to give my opinion on a matter of such importance, I must confess that I think upon a proper examination the apparent inconsistency will vanish. Our religion teaches us what Philosophy could not have taught; and we ought to admire with reverence the great things it has pleased divine Providence to perform, beyond the ordinary course of Nature, for man, who is undoubtedly the most noble inhabitant of this globe. But neither Religion nor Philosophy forbids us to believe that infinite wisdom and power, prompted by infinite goodness, may throughout the vast extent of creation and duration, have frequently interposed in a manner quite incomprehensible to us, when it became necessary to the happiness of created beings of some other rank or degree.

How far indeed the inhabitants of the other planets may resemble man, we cannot pretend to say. If like him they were created liable to fall, yet some, if not all of them, may still retain their original rectitude. We will hope they do: The thought is comfortable. Cease Galileo to improve thy optic tube. And thou great Newton, forbear thy ardent search into the distant mysteries of nature; lest ye make unwelcome discoveries. Deprive us not of the pleasure of believing that yonder radient orbs, traversing in silent Majesty the etherial regions, are the peaceful seats of innocence and bliss. Where neither natural nor moral evil has ever yet intruded; where to enjoy with gratitude and adoration the creator's bounty, is the business of existence. If their inhabitants resemble man in their faculties and affections, let us supose that they are wise enough to govern themselves according to the dictates of that reason their creator has given them, in such manner as to consult their own and each others true happiness on all occasions. But if on the contrary they have found it necessary to erect artificial fabrics of government, let us not suppose that they have done it with so little skill, and at such an enormous expence, as must render them a misfortune instead of a blessing. We will hope that their statesmen are patriots, and that their Kings, if that order of beings has found admittance there, have the feelings of humanity. Happy people! and perhaps more happy still, that all communication with us is denied. We have neither corrupted you with our vices nor injured you by violence. None of your sons and daughters, degraded from their native dignity, have been doomed to endless slavery by us in America, merely because *their* bodies may be disposed to reflect or absorb the rays of light, in a way different from *ours*. Even you, inhabitants of the moon, situated in our very neighbourhood, are effectually secured, alike from the rapacious hand of the haughty Spaniard, and of the unfeeling British nabob. Even British thunder impelled by British thirst of gain, cannot reach you: And the utmost efforts of the mighty Frederick, that tyrant of the north and scourge of mankind, if aimed to disturb *your* peace, becomes inconceivably ridiculous and impotent.

PARDON these reflections; they rise not from the gloomy spirit of misanthropy. That being before whose piercing eye, all the intricate foldings and dark recesses of the human heart become expanded and illuminated, is my witness with what sincerity, with what ardor, I wish for the happiness of the whole race of mankind: How much I admire that disposition of lands and seas, which affords a communication between distant regions, and a mutual exchange of benefits: How sincerely I approve of those social refinements which really add to our happiness, and induce us with gratitude to acknowledge our great creator's goodness. How I delight in a participation of the discoveries made from time to time in nature's works, by our Philosophie brethren in Europe.

BUT when I consider, that *luxury* and her constant follower *tyranny*, who have long since laid in the dust, never to rise again, the glories of Asia, are now advancing like a torrent irresistible, whose weight no human force can stem, and have nearly compleated their conquest of EUROPE; luxury and tyranny, who by a vile affectation of virtues they know not, pretend at first to be the patrons of science and philosophy, but at length fail not effectually to destroy them; agitated I say by these reflections, I am ready to wish—vain wish! that nature would raise her everlasting bars between the new and old world; and make a voyage to Europe as impracticable as one to the moon. I confess indeed, that by our connections with Europe we have made most surprizing, I had almost said unnatural, advances towards the meridian of glory; But by those connections too, in all probability, our fall will be premature. May the God of knowledge inspire us with wisdom to prevent it: Let our harbours, our doors, our hearts, be shut against luxury. But I return to my subject, and will no longer indulge these melancholy thoughts.

SOME have observed, that the wonderful discoveries of the microscope ought to go hand in hand with those of the telescope; lest whilst we contemplate the many instances of the wisdom and power of divine Providence, displayed in the great works of creation, we should be tempted to conclude that man, and other less important beings of this lower world, did not claim its attention. But I will venture to affirm, without at all derogating from the merits of those who have so greatly obliged the world with the success of their microscopical enquiries, that no such danger is to be apprehended. Nothing can better demonstrate the immediate presence of the deity in every part of space, whether vacant or occupied by matter, than astronomy does. It was from an astronomer St. Paul quoted that exalted expression, so often since repeated, *"In God we live, and move, and have our being."* His divine energy supports that universal *substratum* on which all corporal substances subsist, that the laws of motion are derived from, and that wings *light* with angelic swiftness.

IF the time would permit, how agreeable the task to dwell on the praises of Astronomy: To consider its happy effects as a science, on the human mind. Let the sceptical writers forbear to lavish encomiums on their cobweb Philosophy, liable to be broken by the smallest incident in Nature. They tell us it is of great service to mankind, in banishing bigotry and superstition from amongst us. Is not this effectually done by Astronomy. The direct tendency of this science is to dilate the heart with universal benevolence, and to enlarge its views. But then it does this without propagating a single point of doctrine contrary to common sense, or the most cultivated reason. It flatters no fashionable princely vice, or national depravity. It encourages not the libertine by relaxing any of the precepts of morality; nor does it attempt to undermine the foundations of religion. It denies none of those attributes, which the wisest and best of mankind, have in all ages ascribed to the deity: Nor does it degrade the human mind from that dignity, which is ever necessary to make it contemplate itself with complacency. None of these things does Astronomy pretend to; and if these things merit the aim of Philosophy, and the encouragement of a people, then let scepticism flourish and Astronomy lie neglected; then let the names of Berkeley and Hume become immortal, and that of Newton be lost in oblivion.

I SHALL conclude this part of my discourse with the words of Dr. Barrow—It is to Astronomy we owe "that we comprehend the huge fabric of the universe, admire and contemplate the wonderful beauty of the divine workmanship, and so learn the invincible force and sagacity of our own minds, as to acknowledge the blessings of heaven with a pious affection."

I NOW come, in the last place, to point out some of the defects of Astronomy at this day. Which I am induced to undertake by the hopes I entertain that some of those defects may be removed under the auspices of this society and of you my fellow citizens who have so zealously promoted its institution. "The advantages arising from Astronomy, the pleasure attending the study of it, the care with which it was cultivated by many great men amongst the ancients, and the extraordinary attention paid to it in Europe by the present age," all contribute to recommend it to your protection, under which we have the best reason to expect that it will flourish.

THE mildness of our climate and the serenity of our atmosphere, perhaps not inferior to that of Italy, and likewise our distant situation from the principal observatories in the world (Whence many curious phaenomena must be visible here that are not likely to be observed any where else) are so many circumstances greatly in our favour.

AND I trust there will not be wanting men of genius, to arise in this new world, whose talents may be particularly adapted to astronomical enquiries. Indeed I am persuaded that nature is by no means so nigardly in producing them as we are apt to imagine. Some are never tempted forth from obscurity, some are untimely snatched away by death, a striking instance whereof we have in Horrox, and many are accidentally led to other pursuits.

THE Astronomy of comets is still in its infancy; not that the attention of the learned and ingenious has at all been wanting for more than a century past; but because it will necessarily require many ages to bring it to perfection. I wish we were in a condition to promote it in some degree, by carefully observing such comets as may appear. As yet we scarce dare affirm that any one has or will return a second time. It has never that I know of been certainly proved by observation, that a comet has descended within a parabolic orbit, and until that is done we have only a coincidence of periods and orbits (none of which have been very precise) to depend on for their return. Far less are astronomers able to determine the changes that may, and probably do, happen in their orbits and velocities in every period, so as to predict their nearer or more remote approach to the earth or any planet. Whether their business be to repair or to destroy, whether they are worlds yet in formation or once habitable worlds in ruins; whether they are at present habitable and regular attendants of our Sun only, or whether they are the vast links that connect the distant parts of creation by surrounding more suns than one, we know not.

IF we descend to the Planetary System, there are still many things wanting to compleat Astronomy.

THE orbits of the primary planets have at one time been supposed moveable with various irregularities, at other times fixed and permanent. It seems now generally granted that according to the theory of gravity they must change their situations; yet not long since some great astronomers warmly contended that this change was altogether insensible.

ACCORDING to the best tables we now have, the planes of the orbits of Jupiter, the earth and Mercury are immoveable, though the orbits themselves have a progressive motion in their planes. On the contrary, the poles of the orbits of Saturn, Mars and Venus are supposed to revolve about the poles of the earth's orbit, with such velocities as at present nearly reconciles calculation to appearances. But there is good reason to apprehend that such a supposition is not true in fact, and a mistake in this matter will have some important consequences. More probable is it that the poles of the orbits of all the planets, the earth not excepted, revolve about some common centre. The several quantities of these motions, I am confident, are to be had from observation, and not from theory alone. If such a motion of the Earth's orbit be admitted, it will account for the diminution of the obliquity of the eliptic, which seems now incontestible; and that in whatever manner we divide the forces producing such motion, amongst the two superior planets and Venus, or even amongst all of them. And I should suspect the further diminution of obliquity, from this cause, will amount to about one degree and an half.

BUT as Astronomy now stands it seems doubtful whether this change is owing to a deviation in the diurnal or annual motion of the earth; which introduces a very disagreeable uncertainty in conclusions drawn from some nice and useful observations.

THE Lunar Astronomy has been brought so much nearer to

perfection, by the celebrated MAYER, than could have been expected, that I shall mention no deficiency in it but this. We do not certainly know whether that apparent acceleration of the moon's motion, which Mayer with other great astronomers has admitted, ought to be attributed to a real increase of velocity in the moon, or to a diminution of the earth's diurnal motion. If to the former, the destruction of this beautiful and stupendous fabric, may from thence be predicted with more certainty than from any other appearance in Nature: But if to the latter, it may be prettily accounted for, by Dr. Halley's ingenious hypotheses concerning the change of variation in the magnetical needle. The Doctor supposes the external crust or shell of the earth to contain a nucleus detached from it, and that the impulse which first caused the diurnal motion, was given to the external parts, and from thence in time communicated to the internal nucleus, by means of an intervening fluid; but not so as perfectly to equal the velocity of the superficial parts of the globe. Whence it will follow, that the external shell of the earth is still communicating motion to the internal parts, and losing motion itself proportionably. The diurnal motion must therefore become slower and slower, yet can never be retarded, by this cause, beyond certain limits; nor can we conceive that any inconvenience will follow.

THERE is another physical question relating to the moon which to me appears extremely curious, it is this—Whence is it that the moon always turns the same side to us? or, which is the same thing, How comes the moon's rotation on her axis, and her monthly revolution about the earth, to be performed in the same time? None I believe will suppose it to be accidental, nor will the astronomer be easily satisfied with a final cause. Was it not originally brought about by a natural cause which still subsists? Can the attraction of any foreign body change a rotatory motion into a libratory one, and a libratory motion into rest, in spaces so very free from all resistance as those wherein the planets move? There are other defects in Astronomy that are purely optical. Removing of those depends on the further improvement of telescopes, or rather on the more judicious use of them, at times and places the most favourable.

IN speaking of telescopic discoveries I purposely reserved those made on Venus for this place, because they are still uncertain. Burratini in Poland first discovered spots in Venus, then Cassini in Italy; and afterwards Bianchini got a sight of them. But from all their observations it is uncertain whether Venus revolves on its axis once in 23 hours, or once in 24 days. Perhaps it does neither. Nor is their determination of the axis' situation much more satisfactory. These spots on Venus are not to be seen but through an excellent telescope and a pure atmosphere.

IN the year 1672 and 1676 Cassini saw a small star near Venus, which he thought might be a satellite attending on her. It appeared to have the same phase with Venus. In 1740 Mr. Short with a telescope of 16 inches saw a small star at the distance of ten minutes from Venus, which from its apparent shape he likewise thought might be a satellite. And in 1761 Mr. Montaigne, in France, saw what he took to be the satellite of Venus on the 3d, 4th, 7th and 11th of May. But whether Venus has a satellite or not, must still be left amongst the doubtful things of Astronomy.

THE spots on the sun, and those on the surfaces of several planets, have been many years observed without our approaching any nearer towards discovering their nature and cause. Dr. Wilson of Glasgow, has lately succeeded in advancing one step at least, with respect to those of the sun. He has proved from observation that those spots are vast cavities, whose bottoms lie far below the general surface of the sun, and whose sloping sides form the border which we generally see surrounding them. If I should venture to add one conjecture of my own, to those of this ingenious gentleman, I would suppose that those prodigious cavities in the surface of the sun, some of them capable of containing half our earth, are not repeatedly formed by unaccountable explosions of a semifluid substance, but permanent and solid, like the cavities within the moon. And that it is the dark matter sometimes lodging in them, that distinguishes them, and is only accidental.

THE diurnal rotations of Saturn and Mercury are yet unknown; but when further improvements shall be made in the art of using telescopes, this circumstance will hardly escape the vigilance of astronomers.

THESE are a few of the many things that are still left to the industry of the ingenious in this science.

BUT if all higher and more sublime discoveries are not reserved for us in a future and more perfect state; if Astronomy shall again break those limits that now seem to confine it, and expatiate freely in the superior celestial fields; what amazing discoveries may yet be made amongst the fixed stars! That grand phaenomenon the Milkey-Way seems to be the clue that will one day guide us. Millions of small stars compose it, and many more bright ones lie in and near it, than in other parts of heaven. Is not this a strong indication that this astonishing system of worlds beyond worlds innumerable, is not alike extended every way, but confined between two parallel planes, of *immeasurable*, though not *infinite* extent? Or rather, is not the Milkey-Way a vein of a closer texture, running through this part of the material creation? Great things are sometimes best explained by small and small by great. Material substances, such as we daily handle, have been thought composed of impenetrable particles in actual contact: Then again it has seemed necessary to suppose them at a distance from each other, and kept in their relative situations by *attraction* and *repulsion*. Many appearances require that those distances should be very great in proportion to the size of the particles. Hence some, with no small reason, have concluded that matter consists of indivisible points endued with certain powers. Let us compare these smaller portions of it with that great aggregate of matter which is the object of Astronomy; *Light* will then appear to have as free passage through a piece of glass, as the comets have in the planetary regions; and several other new considerations will arise.

IF instead of *descending* we *ascend* the scale. If we consider that infinite variety which obtains in those parts of Nature with which we are most intimate: How one order of most curiously organized bodies, infinitely diversified in other respects, all agree in being fixed to the earth, and receiving nourishment from thence: How another order have spontaneous motion, and seek their food on different parts of the earth, whilst by gravity they are confined to its surface, but in other respects diversified like the former. How a *Third* float in, and below the surface of, a dense fluid, of equal weight with their bodies, which would soon prove fatal to both the others. And a *Fourth* consisting of a vast variety too, have this property in common, that by a peculiar mechanism of their bodies, they can soar to great heights above the earth, and quickly transport themselves to distant regions in a fluid so rare as to be scarcely sensible to us. But not to pursue this boundless subject any further, I say, when we consider this great variety so obvious on *our* globe, and ever connected by some degree of uniformity, we shall find sufficient reason to conclude, that the visible creation, consisting of revolving worlds and central suns, even including all those that are beyond the reach of human eye and telescope, is but an inconsiderable part of the whole. Many other and very various orders of things unknown to, and inconceiveable by us, may, and probably do exist, in the unlimited regions of space. And all yonder stars innumerable, with their dependencies, may perhaps compose but the leaf of a flower in the creator's garden, or a single pillar in the immense building of the divine architect.

HERE is ample provision made for the all-grasping mind of man!

IF it shall please that almighty Power who hath placed us in a world, wherein we are only permitted *"to look about us and to die;"* should it please him to indulge us with existence throughout that half of eternity which still remains unspent, and to conduct us through the several stages of his works, here is ample provision made for employing every faculty of the human mind, even allowing its powers to be constantly enlarged through an endless repetition of ages. Let us not complain of the vanity of this world, that there is nothing in it capable of satisfying us: Happy in those wants, happy in those restless desires, forever in succession to be gratified; happy in a continual approach to the Deity.

I MUST confess that I am not one of those sanguine spirits who seem to think that when the whithered hand of death hath drawn up the curtain of eternity, almost all distance between the creature and creator, between finite and infinite, will be annihilated. Every enlargement of our faculties, every new happiness conferred upon us, every step we advance towards the perfection of the divinity, will very probably render us more and more sensible of his inexhaustible stores of communicable bliss, and of his inaccessible perfections.

WERE we even assured that we shall perish like the flowers of the garden, how careful would a wise man be to preserve a good conscience during the short period of his existence; because by his very constitution, which he cannot alter, this is his pride and glory, and absolutely necessary to his present happiness; because this would insure to him at the approach of death, the soothing reflection, that he was going to restore, pure and uncorrupted, that drop of divinity within him, to the original ocean from whence it was separated. How much more anxiously careful ought we to be if we believe, as powerful arguments compel us to believe, that a conduct in this life depending on our own choice, will stamp our characters for ages yet to come. Who can endure the thought of darkening his faculties by an unworthy application of them here on earth, and degrading himself to some inferior rank of being, wherein he may find both his power and inclination to obtain wisdom and exercise virtue, exceedingly diminished? On the other hand, if that humble admiration and gratitude, which sometimes rises in our minds when we contemplate the power, wisdom and goodness of the deity, constitutes by far the most sublimely happy moments of our lives, and probably will forever continue to do so, there cannot be a stronger incitement to the exercise of virtue and a rational employment of those talents we are entrusted with, than to consider that by these means we shall in a few years be promoted to a more exalted rank amongst the creatures of God, have our understandings greatly enlarged, be enabled to follow truth in all her labyrinths with a higher relish and more facility, and thus lay the foundation of an eternal improvement in knowledge and happiness.

ACCEPTANCE

of the Command of the Continental Armies

George Washington

George Washington was born on February 22, 1732, in Westmore-
land County, Virginia. His father and his elder half-brother seem
to have been his principal, if not his only, teachers in the seven or
eight years of schooling he received. In 1749, Washington was
appointed county surveyor for Culpepper. In the fall of 1755, he
was appointed colonel and commander-in-chief of all Virginia forces
in the French and Indian War. He resigned this post in 1758, and
was elected a burgess from Frederick in the same year; he served in
this capacity for fifteen years. From 1760 to 1774, he was justice of
Fairfax. He was a delegate to both the First and Second Continental
Congresses and, on June 15, 1775, was chosen by the Second
Continental Congress to command the armies of the American
colonies in their war with Great Britain. After the war, he returned
to Mount Vernon. He was president of the Constitutional Convention. Elected the first President of the United States, he took
the oath of office on April 30, 1789. He was unopposed in his
re-election for a second term. Retiring in 1797, from the Presidency,
he became commander of the army that was being raised in expectation of war with France in 1798. He died December 14, 1799.

On Thursday, June 15, 1775, the Continental Congress, meeting in Philadelphia, nominated George Washington as general to
command all the continental forces. On Friday, June 16, Washington was unanimously chosen commander-in-chief of the Continental
forces. The president of the Congress informed him of the vote
and asked his acceptance. Washington then gave this acceptance
speech.

The text is from Peter Force. *American Archives*. 4th ser.;
Vol. II. Washington: M. St. Claire Clarke and Peter Force,
1839, 1848.

Mr. President,

Though I am truly sensible of the high honor done me, in this
appointment, yet I feel great distress, from a consciousness that
my abilities and military experience may not be equal to the extensive and important trust. However, as the Congress desire it, I will
enter upon the momentous duty, and exert every power I possess
in their service, for the support of the glorious cause. I beg they
will accept my most cordial thanks for this distinguished testimony
of their approbation.

But, lest some unlucky event should happen, unfavorable to

my reputation, I beg it may be remembered, by every gentleman in the room, that I this day declare, with the utmost sincerity, I do not think myself equal to the command I am honored with.

As to pay, Sir, I beg leave to assure the Congress, that as no pecuniary consideration could have tempted me to accept this arduous employment, at the expense of my domestick ease and happiness, I do not wish to make any profit from it. I will keep an exact account of my expenses. Those, I doubt not, they will discharge, and that is all I desire.

IV

On *Political* Matters

SPEECH

to the Virginia House of Burgesses

Sir William Berkeley

A member of the celebrated family which flourished at the English
court for several centuries, William Berkeley was born in London
in 1606. He matriculated at Queen's College, Oxford, in 1623,
and received the degrees of A.B. from St. Edmund Hall in 1624,
and A.M. from Merton College in 1629.

Berkeley demonstrated a variety of talents early in his career.
While a young man, he was appointed to a seat in the Privy Chamber
and was recognized as a polished courtier at Whitehall and an
accomplished playwright in London. In 1638, he was knighted by
Charles I.

Berkeley's first colonial appointment was a commissionership
of Canadian affairs. In 1641, he was appointed governor of Virginia,
a post he held until 1677. He quickly aligned himself with the small
but powerful group of planters of the tidewater area and earned
their continued support for his advancement of manufacturing,
building, and military defence. But his apparent disregard for the
welfare of the less fortunate classes and his relentless persecution of
Puritans and Quakers earned him the reputation of a tyrant and
triggered Bacon's Rebellion.

Recalled from office by Cromwell in 1652, Berkeley retired to
his plantation in Virginia until the Restoration. In 1660, he again
assumed the governorship. Popular reaction augmented by his
defiance of a royal commission which arrived with pardons for
Bacon's followers, brought on his final discrediting. He died in
Twickenham in 1677.

The Speech to the Virginia House of Burgesses was delivered
on March 15, 1650 (1651?). The text is from the *Virginia Magazine
of History and Biography*, I, 75 ff.

Gentlemen you perceave by the Declaration that the men of
Westminster have set out, which I beleave you have all scene, how
they means to deale with you hereafter, who in the time of their
wooing and courting you propound such hard Conditions to be
performed on your parts, & on their owne nothing but a benigne
acceptance of your duties to them.

Indeed me thinks they might have proposed something to us
which might have strengthned us to beare those heavy chaines they
are making ready for us, though it were but an assurance that we
shall eat the bread for which our owne Oxen plow, and with our
owne sweat we reape; but this assurance (it seems) were a franchise

beyond the Condition they have resolu'd on the Question we ought to be in: For the reason why they talke so Magisterially to us is this, we are forsooth their worships slaves, bought with their money and by consequence ought not to buy, or sell but with those they shall Authorize with a few trifles to Coszen us of all for which we toile and labour.

If the whole Current of their reasoning were not as ridiculous, as their actions have been Tyrannicall and bloudy; we might wonder with what browes they could sustaine such impertinent assertions: For it you looke into it, the strength of their argument runs onely thus: we have laid violent hands on your Land-Lord, possess'd his Manner house where you used to pay your rents, therefore now tender your respects to the same house you once reverenced: I call my conscience to witness, I lie not, I cannot in all their Declaration perceave a stronger argument for what they would impose on us, than this which I have now told you: They talke indeed of money laid out on this Country in its infancy: I will not say how little, nor how Centuply repaid, but will onely aske, was it theirs? They who in the beginning of this warr were so poore, & indigent, that the wealth and rapines of three Kingdomes & their Churches too, cannot yet make rich, but are faine to seeke out new Territories and impositions to sustaine their Luxury amongst themselves. Surely Gentlemen we are more slaves by nature, than their power can make us if we suffer our selves to be shaken with these paper bulletts, & those on my life are the heaviest they either can or will send us.

'Tis true with us they have long threatned the Barbados, yet not a ship goes thither but to beg trade, nor will they do to us, if we dare Honourably resist their Imperious Ordinance. Assuredly Gentlemen you have heard under what heavy burthens, the afflicted English Nation now groanes, and calls to heaven for relief: how new and formerly unheard of impositions make the wifes pray for barreness and their husbands deafnes to exclude the cryes of their succourles, starving children: And I am confident you do believe, none would long endure this slavery, if the sword at their throats Did not Compell them to Languish under the misery they howrely suffer. Looke on their sufferings with the eyes of understanding, and that will prevent all your teares but those of Compassion. Consider with what prisons and Axes they have paid those that have served them to the hazard of their soules: Consider your selves how happy you are and have been, how the Gates of wealth and Honour are shut on no man, and that there is not here an Arbitrary hand that dares to touch the substance of either poore or rich: But that which I would have you chiefly consider with thankfullnes is: That God hath separated you from the guilt of the crying bloud of our Pious Souveraigne of ever blessed memory:

But mistake not Gentlemen part of it will yet staine your garments if you willingly submit to those murtherers hands that shed it: I tremble to thinke how the oathes they will impose will make those guilty of it, that have long abhor'd the traiterousness of the act: But I confesse having had so frequent testimonies of your truths and courages, I cannot have a reasonable suspition of any cowardly falling of from the former resolutions, and have onely mentioned this last, as a part of my duty and care of you, not of my reall doubts and fears: or if with untryed men we were to argue on this subject, what is it can be hoped for in a change, which we have not allready? Is it liberty? The sun looks not on a people more free than we are from all oppression. Is it wealth? Hundreds of examples shew us that Industry & Thrift in a short time may bring us to as high a degree of it, as the Country and our Conditions are yet capable of: Is it securety to enjoy this wealth when gotten? With out blushing I will speake it, I am confident theare lives not that person can accuse me of attempting the least act against any mans property? Is it peace? The Indians, God be blessed round about us are subdued; we can onely feare the Londoners, who would faine bring us to the same poverty, wherein the Dutch found and relieved us; would take away the liberty of our consciences, and tongues, and our right of giving and selling our goods to whom we please. But Gentlemen by the Grace of God we will not so tamely part with our King, and all these blessings we enjoy under him; and if they oppose us, do but follow me, I will either lead you to victory, or loose a life which I cannot more gloriously sacrifice than for my loyalty, and your security.

SPEECH

at the Boston Town Meeting

Increase Mather

Increase Mather was born in Dorchester, Massachusetts, on June 21, 1639. He was graduated from Harvard College in 1656, and then attended Trinity College, Dublin. Disapproving of the Restoration's effect on religion, he returned to Massachusetts in 1661, and became pastor of Boston's North Church. In 1662, he married Maria Cotton.

Mather was elected a fellow of Harvard in 1675, and ten years later became president of the college. He held this position until 1701.

In 1689, Mather was sent to England as agent of the Province of Massachusetts, his function to secure redress for grievances. He had conferences with Charles II and with William and Mary. In 1692, he returned to Boston with a new crown charter which settled the matter of the government of the province.

After 1701, Mather devoted his time to writing and to the religious matters of the Congregational Church. Though his power in the Puritan colonies was indisputable, his attitude toward other sects became increasingly tolerant.

Mather published ninety-two volumes, one of which, *Cases of Conscience*, 1693, spoke his attitude toward the civil prosecution of witches in Massachusetts and was influential in bringing the witchcraft trials to a halt. He died in Boston on August 23, 1723.

In reply to a declaration from Charles II that "except they would make a *full Submission, and entire Resignation* of their Charter to his Pleasure, a *Quo Warranto* against it should be Prosecuted," the freemen of Boston met in the Town House on January 23, 1683, to give instructions to their Deputies for the General Court. The Reverend Increase Mather was urged to speak on the subject of submission. This he did so effectively that "many of the freemen fell into tears, and there was a General Acclamation, *We Thank you, Syr: We Thank you, Syr.*"

The text of this brief address is from Cotton Mather. *Parentator.* Boston: Nathaniel Belknap, 1724, pp. 91–92.

As the Question is now Stated, *Whether you will make a full Submission and entire Resignation of your Charter and the Priviledges of it, unto his Magisties Pleasure,* I verily Believe, We shall Sin against the GOD of Heaven if we know what Jephthah said, *That which the Lord our GOD has given us, shall we not Possess it!* And though *Naboth* ran a great Hazard by the Refusal, yet he said, GOD *forbid that I should give away the Inheritance of my*

Fathers. Nor would it be *Wisdom* for us to Comply. We know, David made a Wise Choice, when he chose to fall into the *Hands of* GOD rather than into the *Hands of Men*. If we make a *full Submission and entire Resignation to Pleasure*, we fall into the *Hands of Men* Immediately. But if we do it not, we still keep ourselves in the *Hands of* GOD*;* we trust ourselves with his Providence: and who knows, what GOD may do for us? There are also Examples before our Eyes, the Consideration where of should be of Weight with us. Our Brethren hard by us; what have [they] gain'd by being so Ready to part with their *Liberties*, but an Acceleration of their *Miseries?* And we hear from *London*, that when it came to, the Loyal Citizens would not make a *full Submission and entire Resignation to Pleasure*, lest their Posterity should Curse them for it, And shall *We* then do such a Thing? I hope, there is not one Freeman in *Boston*, that can be guilty of it! However I have Discharged my Conscience, in what I have thus Declared unto you.

SPEECH

to the Assembly at New-York

Samuel Mulford

Samuel Mulford, son of one of the earliest settlers of Easthampton, Massachusetts, was born in Salem, Massachusetts, in 1645. Throughout his life, Mulford was an active participant in public affairs and an equally active critic of British colonial government. The first of these concerns saw him appointed justice of the peace for Suffolk County and elected a member of the New York Assembly from 1705 to 1720. From the latter office he was twice expelled, first in 1715 for "printing, without Leave of the House, a Speech formerly made to the Assembly, in which are many false and scandalous Reflections upon the Governor," and again in 1720 when he protested the legality of the Assembly.

During these years of public service, Samuel Mulford visited England to protest the colonial governor's right to demand a share of all oil and bone procured from whales taken at sea, was defendant in several matters of litigation, and was a constant thorn in the side of Governor Robert Hunter who was so provoked by Mulford's attacks on him that he referred to the irrascible captain as "a crazed man." Mulford died in 1725.

The speech given here, complaining of unjust duties and taxes, was delivered before the Assembly on April 2, 1714. After this speech was printed and published, Mulford was expelled from the House.

The text is from the edition printed in New York by William Bradford, 1714.

Gentlemen;

THE ill Measures that have been taken, and the Foundation laid within this Colony, which may bring the Subjects within the same to be Tenants at Will, both Persons and Estates, causeth me to make this Speech to this House; Requesting them to Consider well what they do: and not Sell a Birth-right Privilege for Fear, Favour, Affection or Lucre of Gain; but prove true to the Trust reposed in them not to make ill Presidents and Laws, pernicious to the Publick: But to endeavour the Government may be carried on, for Her Majesties Benefit, and the Good of the Subjects; according to the Laws and Constitutions of *English* Government.

It is not unnecessary to mention the ill Circumstances the Colony was under in the time when a Duty was settled on the importation of Goods, for the Support of Government; there was not any Port or

Officers appointed, where to make Entry of their Vessels, and get Clearing when Outward Bound except at *New-York;* where there was so many Officers and Subtil Fellows to Inspect into every nice Point in the Law, and if they were not fulfilled and observed in every particular, their Vessels were Seised: So that not any man was fit for Master of a Vessel to go to *New-York,* except he were a lawyer; and then they should not escape, except it was by Favour. As I was informed, several were made Sufferers, as followeth; One Vessel coming from the *West Indies,* had some Barrels of Pomento on Board, in which, one Barrel had some Prohibited Goods in it, unknown to the Master: A Sailor makes Information, the Vessel was Seised; altho' the Master proffer'd to make Oath he knew not any thing of it, yet the Vessel and Cargo was Condemned. A Coaster coming to *New-York,* made Entry at the Office, amongst other Goods Twelve Bridles; but he was favoured so much, that for the Sum of *Twenty* or *Thirty Pounds,* he got his Sloop Clear. Another Coaster coming to New-York; it seems a Woman sent a Hat by the Master, a Present to a Boy Related to her, Living in *New-York;* the Sloop was Seized about bringing of that Hat: But (as I was informed) was Favoured, that for the value of about *Twenty Pounds* got Clear. These and several other such like Measures being taken, much discouraged men to come to *New-York.* But in this time, we of the County of *Suffolk,* Namely *Southold, South Hampton* and *East Hampton,* were the greatest Sufferers; we not having an Office to Enter and Clear at: we having some small Coasting Vessels, not suffered to Load and Unload, except they went to *New-York* to Enter and Clear. And Three Sloops, Namely *Benjamin Horton, James Petty* and *Joseph Petty* Masters, coming from *Boston* to *New-York,* there made Entry of their Vessels and Cargo, was detained Thirteen Days before they could procure a Clearing to go home to *Southold.* Such hard Measures discouraged Men to go to *New-York.* And part of the Money granted Their Majesties for Support of Government, was improved to hire Men & Vessels to come down under a pretence of hindering *Indian*-Trade with *Boston*; and to Search our Houses. They Seised *Edward Petty's* Sloop, that had not been out of the Countrey in about Four Months before (lay at the Oyster Pond all Winter) in *March* fitted to Load for *New-York,* was Seised, carried to *New-York,* there Condemned, because he presumed to take Mr. *Nathaniel Silvester's* Family and Houshold Goods on Board his Sloop, and carry them to *Rhoad-Island* the Fall before; and so the Poor Man was destroyed, because he did not go 120 Miles for a Permit, to carry him and his 60 Miles. Another Sloop, Namely *John Pune* Master, coming from *Boston* with a Clearing for *New-Haven,* being near Plumgut, the Officer went on Board him, Seised his Sloop, carried her to *New-York,* where she was Condemned because he had a Pillow of Six Pounds of Cotton Wool for his Bolster in his Cabbin, which he did not make it appear he had given Bond for. Another Sloop. *James Rogers* Master, (which he upon Terms had of Capt. *Cyprian Southack*) coming from *Boston* to *Shelter-Island,* was Boarded by the Officer from *New-York*, Seised, Carried away and Condemned, for having no Register. [It seems Capt. *Southack* had a Register when went in her himself and when he put a Master in and went not himself, that Register would pass; but when *Rogers* hath it at *New-York*, it is called no Register.] Another small Sloop. Built up *Connecticut*-River, belonging to *John Davis* of *East Hampton*, took in the River a Load of Boards, went to *Rhoad-Island*, there took in Two Barrels of Molasses, and a Remnant in a Hogshead, went to the Custom-House for a Clearing to go to *New-York,* spoke to the Officer to do it Authentickly; Davis depending it was so, never looked into it until the Officer came on Board him, in or near Plumgut, demanding his Clearing, and read Two Barrels of Sugar and a Hogshead; the Master made answer, Not so; it is Molasses; there was never any Sugar on Board: It seems the Officer of *Rhoad-Island* mistook, and put in Sugar when it was Molasses; and sent under his Hand to *New-York* that it was his mistake; but all would not do, the Vessel was Condemned. So that almost all the Vessels belonging to our Towns were either Seised or Drove out of the Colony. There came a Boat from *Fairfield*, which a Young Man hired to bring him over to be Married; to carry his Wife and Portion home: the Boat was Seised, carried to *New-York* there lies and rots, as I am informed: The Young Man went up the Island, so got home with his Wife; and was compelled to Pay the Owner of the Boat *Thirty Pounds* for it. Our Vessels being thus carried and drove away, we had not Vessels to carry the Growth of the Countrey to a Market; nor bring us such Goods as we wanted: And if any come from *New-York*, with Vessel and Goods, and the People would deal with them, the Trader would set the Price on his Goods, and also on what the People had of the Growth of the Countrey: And if the People would have sent their Effects to *New-York,* to have got Money to have Paid their Taxes or Bought Goods, they were denied to have Fraight carried to *New-York*, or Goods brought from thence in their Vessels: So that they were Compelled to take what they were proffered or keep their Goods by them. *Southold* People being much Oppressed, as they informed me: Wheat then being at *Boston Five Shillings* and *Six-pence* per Bushel, and at *New-York* but *Three Shillings* and *Four-pence*; they had not liberty to carry or send it to *Boston*: Nor any Vessel suffer'd to come at them from thence; and not any coming to them from *New-York*, their Wheat and Grain lay by them, until the Vermin Eat and Spoil'd it; and they were much Impoverished thereby. So that by

these and several other severe Measures being taken, whereby
several were Destroyed, and much Impoverishing others: to the
great Grievance of Their Majesties Leige People; Discouragement to the Inhabitants to Manure their Land, and causing several
to Sell their Land, Move out of the Government; because they
could not see how they should Live within the same. For where
Trade is so Clogg'd, Navigation Discourag'd, Strangers Deter'd
to come, causeth Goods Imported to be Scarce and Dear, and the
Growth of the Countrey Low; which was the Misery of many in
this Colony. Whereby in all probability, the Countrey was twice
so much dampnified in settling that Duty, as it would be in a
Land-Tax; besides the Flood of Debts which are endeavoured to be
put on the Countrey, the greatest part of them created by settling
that Duty, running in that Channel. And notwithstanding all the
hardship those were under, whereby several Persons was Compelled
to Sell part of their Necessary Food, to get Money to Pay their
Taxes; the Money that did arise thereby, to the Sum of *Five
Thousand Pounds per Annum*, and also several *Hundred Pounds*
of the Countreys Money were imbezel'd, so that it was not applied
to the Uses it was Granted for; and now endeavoured to be turned
upon the Countrey; as if they were their Debts. This Duty was
Granted to Their Majesties, for Support of Government; put into
Their Majesties Officers Hands, to be issued out by Warrant under
the Governour's Hand, by and with the Consent of the Council;
it was not put into the Treasurer's Hands: if it had, the one half
of it might have prevented any Crying Debts of the Government
or Countrey. No doubt but Their Majesties did depend on the
Fidelity of their Officers, not to imbezel the Monies: But it was
otherwise; it was miserably imbezel'd: Part applied to disturb their
Majesties Leige People. So that when there was Sufficient put into
their Majesties Officers hands, for the Support of Government, and
the fame is imbezel'd, it cannot in Justice be a Debt of the Countrey; neither are they liable to make it good. If it had been in a
Countrey Treasurer's Hands, appointed by the Countrey, and he
had imbezel'd the Money; in such case the Countrey might be
answerable for the same. So that in this case concerning these
Debts before us, there is not any of them the Countreys Debts,
but such as are made so by this House: And now to make such the
Countreys Debts which they never created, but have already
allowed sufficient to have made Satisfaction for the same, is great
Injustice, and a matter of ill Consequence: For if the Governour for
the time being may put in whom, and so many Officers as he will; to
allow them what Salary he pleaseth; to make so many Debts in the
Colony as he will: and the Commissioners at *Albany* to make what
Debts they please (as many of these are such) and all these must
be the Countreys Debts, then the Assembly may do for Assessors;

lay Taxes on the Countrey, and shall not judge for themselves what part of their Estates they must part with for the Support of Government, but leave it to the Governour's good Nature, to let them have such part of their Estates to live upon as he pleaseth. And if I am not mistaken, this is the Foundation laid to bring us to this Condition; and if this House will Build on the Foundation laid, it will certainly do to bring us to be no more Free men, but Tenants at Will, both Persons and Estates: And making those the Debts of the Countrey, which was never created by them, is a large step to bring it to pass. Besides the Injustice to make them so, it is an encouragement to have more Debts made of the same Nature; and likewise makes a President for time to come; so becomes a matter of ill Consequence to swallow up all the Money that shall arise by the Excise: And not passing Bills to put Money into the Treasurer's Hands, so that there shall be little or no Money there for any Uses. But to settle a Duty upon importing of Goods, and let it pass in the same Channel it did formerly, which was so Pernicious to the Prosperity of this Colony. And I know not how it will be better now than it was formerly: We have not any assurance of it; but leave it to his Excellency's Good Nature, the event thereof may better inform you, It is good to hope for the best; and that there will be no more Crying Debts: but there is but small reason for it; For if 5000 *Pounds per Annum* would not prevent them, I know not how 2800 should do it. By what hath been said, is sufficient to Convince any impartial Man, that the Subjects within this Colony have been lamentably Oppressed, if not Destroyed: Which caused the Assembly to Address Her Majesty that we might have a Treasurer; the Return to our House was by My Lord Cornbury, viz. 'I have received Letters from the Right Honourable the Lords Commissioners for Trade and Plantations, containing Her Most Sacred Majesties Commands to me, to permit the General Assemble of this Province to Name their own Treasurer, when they Raise Extraordinary Supplies for Particular Uses; and which are no part of Her Majesties standing and constant Revenue; but the Treasurer so Nominated must be Accountable to the Governour, Council and Assembly: Warrants may be issued by the Colonels, Captains, or other Persons, as the Act shall be directed.' By this we appointed our Treasurer; and several Years he received the Publick Monies (not having to do with Her Majesties standing and constant Revenue) being issued out by an Act, of Governour Council and Assembly, to the great Satisfaction of the Countrey. But I fear it is working about so, that our Treasurer shall be but as a Cypher; and we shall lose the Benefit that we might have had by him, as we had for some Years when the Money was in his hands: For I perceive the Countrey shall not employ or hire a Servant to do any Business for them, but he must be the Queens

Officer, and so brought about to be Appointed and Commissioned by the Governour; and have a Salary from him: Neither shall the Bill pass for the Treasurer to Pay the Officers of the Assembly, and the Printer for Printing the Minutes of the House and Act passed into Law (altho' Passed by the Council without any amendments yet Rejected by his Excellency) to the great Damage of those Officers, and keep the Subjects in Ignorance, whom should be Subject to Law, and shall be Ignorant what they be. But these are Measures that the greater Advantage may be taken against them, and shall know what Law is, when they are Prosecuted for Transgressing the same. So that by such Methods as have been lately taken, would make a Man think, as if it were purposed that the Countrey should not have any Officers, nor to do with any Money, but what the Governour and Council pleaseth. It is true, it is worded in Her Majesties Instructions, viz. *That you shall not suffer the Publick Monies to be issued out, but by Warrant under your Hand, by and with the Consent of the Council.* I am of Opinion, that it cannot be understood that Her Majesty put those words into the Instruction, purposely to Empower his Excellency to make as many Debts in the Government as he pleaseth; and to have the whole Disposing of all the Publick Monies, with the Advice and Consent of the Council: Which in effect is to say, his Excellency hath the whole Disposing of the same at his Will. For if he may put in Office, whom and as many as he will; and allow them what Salary he pleaseth, and make so many Debts as he see cause; in such case, what Member of the Council will gainsay his Paying such Debts as he pleaseth? So that in Reason the Sense must be taken, that it should be so issued that it might not be imbezel'd; but applied to the Uses it was granted for: and not for the Governour to appropriate it at his Pleasure, taking to himself an inherent Right to dispose of the Publick Money, altho' it be never so Pernicious to the Publick. I will not believe that Her Majesty ever intended those words should be Construed to alter *English* Government; not to deprive the Subject of Property and Liberty. For by Her Command to my Lord *Cornbury*, that the Treasurer should issue it out as the Act directs; which was done by Act of Governour, Council and Assembly: And I am apt to be of Opinion, that it is the most Just way it can be issued; and nothing against the intent of Her Majesties Instructions, as is pretended. I look on such Pretences, only to divert it from coming into the Treasurer's hands; that so it may run in the old Channel that hath been so Pernicious to the Publick; and deprive the Countrey of having any thing to do about the issuing it: But it shall go according to Pleasure. The Injury that the Publick sustained (as before mentioned) was the Occasion of my being against settling it: Not as some pretend, because I was a Merchant. I defy that man that shall make it appear, that I prefer my own Interest to do the Publick and Injury. But I am apt to think, Those that make that pretence are just on the contrary; and care not how they Injure the Publick for their own Interest. They are very like to be the Libellers, that Charge those that speak Truth, and would prevent the Subjects of this Colony to be Tenants at Will, Persons and Estates, with flying in Her Majesties Face, and Charging Her with Tyrany: As tho' speaking Truth, and mentioning matter of Fact was a Crime. It was rather a Crime in the Libellers, to perswade the People that Her Majesty would alter the Constitution of *English* Government, & cause Her Subjects in this Colony to be under Arbitrary Government; their Persons and Estates, at the Pleasure of the Governour for the time being; and so give the Subject an ill Opinion of Her Majesty. I know that within the Realm of *England*, for any man by Speaking, Writing or Printing, to declare any thing that should give the People an ill Opinion of Their Majesties, is Treason by Act of Parliament: But here they do their Pleasure. And I am of the Opinion, that there is some amongst us that would have made Notable Counsellors in King *James* the Second's time: And I wish his Excellency had not any ill Counsellors now, that Bills do not pass now of the same Nature, as they did since he came to the Government.

We have an Undoubted Right and Property by the Law of God and Nature, settled upon the Subject by Act of Parliament; which is not to be taken from them by the Supream Power, without due Course of Law. The End of Law is to Secure our Persons and Estates; the End of Government to put the same in Execution, to that purpose that Justice be done: According to the Words in his Excellency's Instruction, viz. *You shall carry on the Government for Our Benefit, and Good of Our Subjects; according to the Laws and Customs of the Colony.* Now Gentlemen, I am not of the Opinion, that it is for the Good of the Subject, that the Governour should have liberty to make so many Debts in the Government as he pleaseth; and all the Publick Money run that Channel, that he should have the sole disposing of the same to what Uses he pleaseth, without the Consent of them that granted the same for Particular Uses. There hath been Money given to some Officers within this Colony, that instead of doing good, have improved all their Wit and Cunning to destroy, molest and disturb Her Majesties Subjects.

Seeing we have the Priviledge to be an Assembly, granted by her Majesty, let us not Betray the Trust reposed in us: But Assist in having the Government carried on for Her Majesties Benefit, and the Good of the Subject; and Oppose all Measures taken to bring us and Posterity to be Tenants at Will, lest by degrees we are brought to it. Be not drove by Threats, nor drawn by flattering: But discharge a good Conscience towards GOD and Men. Although a

Complaint went Home against us, and Threatned that if we would
not settle a Revenue, the Parliament would do it for us; and many
Libels to Scandalize, Vilify and Reproach us: and Scandalous Reports raised, as if we had not done our Duty; and would not do any
thing for Support of Government, but would let it Starve. Which
drew several to Consent to what they did not Well Understand, or
else I am much mistaken; for I hope better of them, than to do an
Injury to the Publick (tho' some for their own Interest might do
it.) If we must be Enslaved, it were better to have it Forc'd upon
us, than for us to bring it upon our Selves. And what Justice have
any Person or People, when judgment is given against them before
they are called to Answer for themselves: but shall not be suffered
to speak. And for those Libellers, they may Write what they please,
when Ashamed to set their Names to what they Assert: So I pass
them to be such Spirit as would be Troublers of Her Majesties good
Subjects. And for those that Report we would Starve the Government, is but a False Narration to make Clamour, and spread a False
Report: For how is the Government Starved? When we have helped
the Governour to 3110 pounds, for Three Years towards his
Salary (besides what he hath had in the *Jerseys.*) Which is more
than the *Three Governours* of *Boston, Connecticut* and *Rhode-
Island* have had for all Three of their Salaries, for the same time.
And the other Officers of the Government might have had their
Salaries, if his Excellency would have Pleased to Assented to the
Bills for that purpose. And seeing we have a Right to Sit here a
General Assembly, let us think what Governour Dungan use to say;
viz. *I cannot do you any Harm, if you can keep your own Dogs from
Biting you.* It will be Well if there be not any such amongst us; I
hope there is not so many that shall make us Tenants at Will; and
make a Man Ashamed to have his Name mentioned to be in such
an Assembly. I can but Do or Suffer: but am in hopes, you will
Consider well what you do, for the Time Present and to Come.

Much more might have been said, but this may be Sufficient to
put you in mind of the *Ill Measures* that was taken, and the *Ill
Consequences thereof;* and if it may be Prevented for the future.
Although We are Compared to a *Pevish Child,* that Cried for Salt
Beef for its own Hurt; yet I hope, you will have the Sense of the
Burn't Child, which Dreads the Fire: and not be like Persons *Non
Compos Mentus,* to Wilfully Run into the same.

SPEECH AGAINST

the Petition to Change the Form of Government

John Dickinson

John Dickinson was born on November 8, 1732, in Talbot County,
Maryland. He was educated at home by a tutor. In 1750, he
became a student in the law office of John Moland. Three years
later, he went to London to continue his studies in the Middle
Temple and remained there until 1757. In October, 1760, he was
elected to the Assembly of the Lower Counties of Delaware and
became speaker. Two years later, he was elected representative from
Philadelphia to the Pennsylvania legislature. In October, 1765, he
was appointed as one of the Pennsylvania delegates to the Stamp Act
Congress. In 1770, he was reelected to the Pennsylvania legislature.
He was a member of the First and Second Continental Congresses.
He took up arms when the fighting came, but when the new members of Congress were elected and his name was rejected, he resigned
his commission and soon afterward resigned from the Pennsylvania
Assembly. In 1779, he was again elected to Congress from Delaware, but resigned in the autumn. In 1781, he was elected president
of the Supreme Executive Council of Delaware. He was a delegate
from Delaware to the convention to frame the Federal Constitution
in 1787. He died on February 14, 1808.

Provoked by the Governor's refusal to give his assent to a new
supply bill, the Pennsylvania Assembly drafted a petition to the
King requesting him to change the Colony from a proprietary to
a royal one. The measure to draft this petition had been passed and
the petition drafted when John Dickinson gave his speech before the
Assembly on May 24, 1764. Once a measure is resolved by a legislative body it is contrary to rule to object to the measure. However,
Dickinson was allowed to make his speech opposing the measure,
either because he had not been in attendance previously or because
he had gone to the trouble of preparing the speech.

The text is from the edition printed in Philadelphia by William
Bradford, 1764.

Mr. Speaker,

WHEN honest men apprehend their country to be injured, nothing is more natural than to resent and complain: but when they enter
into consideration of the means for obtaining redress, the same
virtue that gave the alarm, may sometimes, by causing too great a
transport of zeal, defeat its own purpose; it being expedient for
those who deliberate of public affairs, that their minds should be
free from all violent passions. These emotions blind the under-

standing: they weaken the judgment. It therefore frequently happens, that resolutions form'd by men thus agitated, appear to *them* very wise, very just, and very salutary; while others, not influenced by the same heats, condemn those determinations, as weak, unjust, and dangerous. Thus, Sir, in councils it will always be found useful, to guard against even that indignation, which arises from integrity.

MORE particularly are *we* bound to observe the utmost caution in our conduct, as the experience of many years may convince us, that all our actions undergo the strictest scrutiny. Numerous are the instances, that might be mentioned, of rights vindicated and equitable demands made in this province, according to the opinions entertained here, that in *Great-Britain,* have been adjudged to be illegal attempts and pernicious pretensions.

THESE adjudications are the acts of persons vested with such dignity and power, as claim some deference from us: and hence it becomes not unnecessary to consider, in what light the measures now proposed may appear to those, whose sentiments from the constitution of our government, it will always be prudent to regard.

BUT on this important occasion we ought not to aim only at the approbation of men, whose authority may censure and control us. More affecting duties demand our attention. The honour and welfare of *Pennsylvania* depending on our decisions, let us endeavour so to act, that we may enjoy our own approbation, in the cool and undisturbed hours of reflections; that we may deserve the approbation of the impartial world; and of posterity who are so much interested in the present debate.

NO man, Sir, can be more clearly convinced than I am, of the inconveniences arising from a strict adherence to proprietary instructions. We are prevented from demonstrating our loyalty to our excellent Sovereign, and our affection to our destrest fellow-subjects, unless we will indulge the Proprietors, with a distinct and partial mode of taxation, by which they will have perhaps four or five-hundred pounds a year, that ought to go in case of our constituents.

THIS is granted on all sides to be unequal; and has therefore excited the resentment of this House. Let us resent—but let our resentment bear proportion to the provocation received; and not produce, or even expose us to the peril of producing, effects more fatal than the injury of which we complain. If the change of government now meditated, can take place, with all our privileges preserved; let it instantly take place: but if *they* must be consumed in the blaze of royal authority, we shall pay too great a price for our approach to the throne; too great a price for obtaining (if we should obtain) the addition of four or five hundred pounds to the proprietary tax; or indeed for any emolument likely to follow from the change.

I HOPE, I am not mistaken when I believe, that every member

in this House feels the same reverence that I do, for these *inestimable rights.* When I consider the spirit of liberty that breathes in them, and the flourishing state to which this province hath risen in a few years under them, I am extremely desirous, that they should be transmitted to future ages; and I cannot suppress my solicitude, while steps are taking, that tend to bring them all into danger. Being assured, that this house will always think an attempt to change this government too hazardous, unless these privileges can be *perfectly secured,* I shall beg leave to mention the reasons by which I have been convinced, that such an attempt ought not *now* to be made.

IT seems to me, Sir, that a people who intend an innovation of their government, ought to chuse the most proper *time,* and the most proper *method* for accomplishing their purposes; and ought seriously to weigh all the probable and possible *consequences* of such a measure.

THERE are certain periods in public affairs, when designs may be executed much more easily and advantageously, than at any other. It hath been by a strict attention to every interesting circumstance; a careful cultivation of every fortunate occurrence; and patiently waiting till they have ripened into a favourable conjuncture, that so many great actions have beeen performed in the political world.

It was through a rash neglect of this prudence, and too much *eagerness* to gain his point, that the Duke of *Monmouth* destroyed his own enterprize, and brought himself dishonourably to the block, tho' every thing then verged towards a revolution. The Prince of Orange with a *wise delay* pursued the same views, and gloriously mounted a throne.

IT was through a like neglect of this prudence, that the commons of *Denmark,* smarting under the tyrany of their nobility, in a fit of revengeful fury, *suddenly* surrendered their liberties to their king; and ever since with unavailing grief and useless execrations, have detested the *mad moment,* which slipt upon them the shackles of slavery, which no struggles can shake off. With *more deliberation* the *Dutch* erected a stadholdership, that hath been of signal service to their state.

THAT excellent historian and statesman *Tacitus,* whose political reflections are so justly and universally admired, makes an observation in his third annal, that seems to confirm those remarks. Having mentioned a worthy man of great abilities, whose ambitious ardour hurried him into ruin, he used these words, "quod Multos etiam bonos pessum dedit, qui spretis qua tarda cum securitate, praematura vel cum exitio properant." "Which misfortune hath happened to many good men, who despising those things which they might *slowly* and *safely* attain, seize them too hastily, and with fatal speed rush upon their own destruction."

IF then, Sir, the best intentions may be disappointed by too rapid a prosecution of them, many reasons induce me to think, that this is not the *proper time* to attempt the change of our government.

IT is too notorious and too melancholy a truth, that we now labour under the disadvantage of royal and ministerial displeasure. The conduct of this province during the late war, hath been almost continually condemned at home. We have been covered with the reproaches of men, whose stations give us just cause to regard their reproaches. The last letters from his majesty's secretary of state prove, that the reputation of the province has not yet revived. We are therein expressly charged with double dealing, disrespect for his Majesty's orders, and in short, accusations, that show us to be in the utmost discredit. Have we the least reason to believe, when the transactions of this year, and the cause of our application for a change, are made known to the King and his ministers, that their resentment will be waived? Let us not flatter ourselves. Will they not be more incensed, when they find the public service impeded, and his majesty's dominions so long exposed to the ravages of merciless enemies, by our inactivity and obstinacy, as it will be said? For this, I think, hath been the constant language of the ministry on the like occasions. Will not their indignation rise beyond all bounds, when they understand that our hitherto denying to grant supplies, and our application for a change, proceed from the governor's strict adherence to the terms of the stipulations, so solemnly made, and so repeatedly approved, by the late and present King?

BUT I may perhaps be answered, "that we have agreed to the terms of the stipulations, according to their true meaning, which the Governor refuses to do." Surely, Sir, it will require no slight sagacity in distinguishing, no common force of argument, to persuade his Majesty and his Council, that the refusal to comply with the true meaning of the stipulations proceeds from the Governor, when he insists on inserting in our bill the very words and letters of those stipulations.

"BUT these stipulations were never intended to be inserted *verbatim* in our bills, and our construction is the most just." I grant it appears so to us, but much I doubt, whether his Majesty's Council will be of the same opinion. That Board and this House have often differed as widely in their sentiments. *Our* judgment is founded on the knowledge we have of facts, and, of the purity of our intentions. The judgment of *others* is founded on the representations made to them, of those facts and intentions. These representations may be erroneous. If we are rightly informed, we are represented as the mortal enemies of the proprietors, who would tear their estates to pieces, unless some limit was fixed to our fury. For *this purpose* the second and third articles of the stipulations were formed. The inequality of the mode was explained and enlarged upon by the provincial counsel; but in vain. I think, I have heard a worthy member who lately returned from *England*, mention these circumstances.

IF this be the case, what reasonable hope can we entertain, of a more favorable determination *now?* The proprietors are still living. Is it not highly probable that they have interest enough, either to prevent the change, or to make it on such terms, as will fix upon us *forever,* those demands that appear so extremely just to the *present Ministers?* One of the Proprietors appears to have great intimacy and influence, with some very considerable members of his Majesty's Council. Many men of the highest character, if public reports speak truth, are now endeavouring to establish proprietary governments, and therefore probably may be more readily inclined to favour proprietary measures. The very gentlemen who *formed* the articles of the stipulations, *are now in power,* and no doubt will inforce their *own acts* in the strictest manner. On the other hand, every circumstance that now operates against us, may in time turn in our favour. We may perhaps be fortunate enough, to see the present prejudices against us worn off: to recommend ourselves to our Sovereign: and to procure the esteem of some of his ministers. I think I may venture to assert, that such a period will be infinitely more proper than the present, for attempting a change of our government.

WITH the permission of the House, I will now consider the manner in which this attempt is carried on: and I must acknowledge, that I do not in the least degree approve of it.

THE time may come, when the weight of this government may grow too heavy for the shoulder of a subject; at least, too heavy for those of a woman, or an infant. The proprietary family may be so circumstanced, as to be willing to accept of such an equivalent for the government from the crown, as the crown may be willing to give. Whenever this point is agitated, either on a proposal from the crown or proprietors, this province may plead the cause of her privileges with greater freedom, and with greater probability of success, than at present. The royal grant; the charter founded upon us; the public faith pledged to the adventurer, for the security of those rights to them and their posterity, whereby they were encouraged to combat the dangers, I had almost said, of another world; to establish the British power in remotest regions, and add inestimable dominions with the most extensive commerce to their native country; the high value and veneration we have for these privileges; the afflicting loss and misfortune we should esteem it, to be deprived of them, and the unhappiness in which his majesty's faithful subjects in this province would thereby be involved; our inviolable loyalty and attachment to his Majesty's person and illustrious family, whose sovereignty hath been so singularly distinguished by its favourable influence on the liberties of mankind. All these things may then be properly insisted on. If urged with that modest heart-felt energy, with which good men should always vindicate the interests of their country, before the best of sovereigns, I should not despair of a gracious attention, to our humble requests. Our petition in such a case, would be simple, respectful, and perhaps affecting.

BUT in the present mode of proceeding, it seems to me, that we preclude ourselves from every office of decent duty to the most excellent of Kings; and from the right of earnestly defending our privileges, which we should otherwise have. The foundation of this attempt, I am apprehensive, will appear to others, *peculiarly unfortunate*. In a sudden passion, it will be said against the proprietors, we call out for a change of government. Not from reverence for his Majesty; not from a sense of his paternal goodness to his people; but because we are angry with the Proprietors; and tired of a dispute founded on an order approved by his Majesty, and his royal grandfather.

OUR powerful friends on the other side of the *Atlantic,* who are so apt to put the kindest construction, on our actions, will no doubt observe, "that the conduct of the people of *Pennsylvania,* must be influenced by very extraordinary councils, since they desire to come *more immediately* under the King's command, BECAUSE they will *not obey* those royal commands, which have been already signified to them."

BUT here it will be said; nay it has been said; and the petition before the House is drawn accordingly; "we will not alledge this dispute with the Governor on the stipulations, but the general inconveniences of a proprietary government as the cause of our desiring a change." 'Tis true we may act in this artful manner, but what advantages shall we gain by it? Though *we* should keep the secret, can we seal up the lips of the Proprietors? Can we recal our messages to the Governor? Can we annihilate our own resolves? Will not all—will not any of these discover the *true cause* of the present attempt?

WHY then, should we unnecessarily invite fresh invective in the very beginning of a most important business, that to be happily concluded, requires all the favour we can procure, and all the dexterity we can practice?

WE intend to surround the throne, with petitions that our government may be changed from proprietary to royal. At the same time we mean to preserve our privileges: But how are these two points to be reconciled?

IF we express our desire for the preservation of our privileges, in so general or faint a manner, as may induce the King to think, they are of no great consequence to us, it will be nothing less than to betray our country.

IF on the other hand we inform his Majesty, "that tho' we *request* the laws and liberties framed and delivered down to us by

our careful ancestors: or we may tell his Majesty with a surly discontent, that we will not submit to his *implored protection,* but on
such conditions, as we please to impose on him." Is not this the
inevitable and dreadful alternative, to which we shall reduce ourselves?

IN short, Sir, I think the farther we advance in the path we are
now in, the greater will be the confusion and danger in which we
shall engage ourselves. Any body of men acting under a charter,
must surely tread on slippery ground, when they take a step that
may be deemed a surrender of that charter. For my part, I think
the petitions that have been carried about the city and country to
be signed, and are now lying on the table, can be regarded in no
other light, than as a surrender of the charter, with a short indifferent hint annexed of a desire, that our privileges may be spared,
if it shall be thought proper. Many striking arguments may in my
opinion be urged, to prove that any request made by this House for
a change, may with still greater propriety be called a surrender.
The common observation "that many of our privileges do not depend on our charter only, but are confirmed by laws approved by the
Crown," I doubt will have but little weight with those, who will
determine this matter.

IT will readily be replied, "that these laws were founded on
the charter; that they were calculated for a proprietary government,
and for no other; and approved by the Crown in that view alone:
that the proprietary government is now acknowledged by the people
living under it to be a bad government; and the Crown is intreated
to accept a surrender of it: that therefore by abolishing the proprietary government, every thing founded upon it, must of consequence be also abolished."

HOWEVER if there should be any doubts in the law on these
points, there is an easy way to solve them.

THESE reflections, Sir, naturally lead me to consider the *consequences* that may attend a change of our government; which is the
last point, I shall trouble the House upon at this time.

IT is not to be questioned, but that the Ministry are desirous
of vesting the immediate government of this Province, advantageously in the Crown. Tis true, they don't chuse to act arbitrarily, and
tear away the present government from us, without our consent.
This is not the age for such things. But let *us* only furnish them with
a pretext, by pressing petitions for a change; let us only relinquish
the hold we now have, and in an instant we are precipitated from
that envied height where we now stand. The affair is laid before
the parliament, the desires of the Ministry are insinuated, the
rights of the Crown are vindicated, and an act passes to deliver us
at once from the government of Proprietors, and the privileges we
claim under them.

THEN, Sir, we who *in particular* have presented to the authors of the fatal change, this *long-wish'd* for opportunity of effecting it, shall for our *assistance* be entitled to their thanks—THANKS! which I am persuaded, every worthy member of this House *abber* to deserve, and would *stern* to receive.

IT seems to be taken for granted, that by a change of government, we shall obtain a change of those measures which are so displeasing to the people of this Province—that justice will be maintained by an equal taxation of the proprietary estates—and that our frequent dissentions will be turned into peace and happiness.

THESE are effects indeed sincerely to be wished for by every sensible, by every honest man: but reason does not always teach us to expect the warm wishes of the heart. Could our gracious Sovereign take into consideration, the state of every part of his extended dominions, we *might* expect redress of every grievance: for with the most implicit conviction I believe, he is as just, benevolent, and amiable a Prince, as heaven ever granted in its mercy to bless a people. I venerate his virtues beyond all expression. But *his* attention to our particular circumstances being impossible, we must receive our fate from ministers; and from *them*, I do not like to receive it.

WE are not the subjects of ministers; and therefore it is not to be wondered at, if they do not feel that tenderness for us, that a good prince will always feel for his people. Men are not born ministers. Their ambition raises them to authority; and when possessed of it, one established principle with them seems to be, "never to deviate from a precedent of power."

DID we not find in the late war, tho' we exerted ourselves in the most active manner in the defence of his Majesty's dominions, and in promoting the service of the Crown, every point in which the Proprietors thought fit to make any opposition, decided against us? Have we not also found, since the last disturbance of the public peace by our savage enemies, the conduct of the late Governor highly applauded by the ministry, for his adherence to those very stipulations now insisted on; and ourselves subjected to the *bittered reproaches,* only for attempting to avoid burthens, that were thought extremely grievous. Other instances of the like kind I pass over, to avoid a tedious recapitulation.

SINCE then, the gale of ministerial favour has in *all seasons* blown propitious to proprietary interest, why do we now fondly flatter ourselves, that it will suddenly shift its quarter? Why should we with an *amazing credulity,* now fly for *protection* to *those* men, trust *every thing* to *their* mercy, and ask the most distinguishing *favours* from *their* kindness, from whom we complained a few months ago, that we could not obtain the most reasonable request? Surely, Sir, we must acknowledge one of these two things: either, that our *complaint* was then *unjust;* or, that our *confidence* is now *unwarranted*. For my part, I look for a rigid perseverance in former measures. With a new government, I expect new disputes. The experience of the royal colonies convinces me, that the immediate government of the Crown, is not a security for that tranquility and happiness we promise ourselves from a change. It is needless for me to remind the House, of all the frequent and violent controversies that have happened between the King's Governors in several provinces, and their assemblies. At this time, if I am rightly informed, *Virginia* is struggling against an instruction relating to their paper currency, that will be attended as that colony apprehends, with the most destructive consequences, it carried into execution.

INDEED, Sir, it seems vain to expect, where the spirit of liberty is maintained among a people, that public contests should not *also* be maintained. Those who *govern,* and those who *are governed,* seldom think they can gain too much on one another. *Power* is like the *ocean;* not easily admitting limits to be fixed on it. It must be in motion. Storms indeed are not desirable: but a long dead calm is not to be looked for; perhaps, not to be wished for. Let not *us* then, in expectation of *smooth seas,* and an *undisturbed course,* too rashly venture our *little vessel* that hath safely sailed round *our own well known* shores, upon the *midst* of the *untry'd deep,* without being first fully convinced, that her *make* is strong enough to bear the *weather* she may meet with, and that she is well *provided* for so long and so dangerous a voyage.

NO man, Sir, amongst us hath denied, or will deny, that this Province must *stake* on the event of the present attempt, liberties that ought to be immortal—*Liberties!* founded on the acknowledged rights of human nature; and restrained in our mother-country, only by an unavoidable necessity of adhering in some measure, to established customs. Thus hath been formed between old errors and hasty innovations, an entangled chain, that our ancestors either had not moderation or leisure enough to untwist.

I WILL now briefly enumerate, as well as I can recollect, the particular privileges of Pennsylvania.

IN the first place, we here enjoy that best and greatest of all rights, a *perfect religious freedom*.

POSTS of honour and profit are unfettered with *oaths* or *tests;* and therefore are open to men, whose abilities, strict regard to their conscientious persuasion, and unblemished characters qualify them to discharge their duties with credit to themselves, and advantage to their country. Thus justice is done to merit; and the public loses none of its able servants.

THE same wisdom of our laws, has guarded against the absurdity of granting greater credit even to villains, if they will swear, than to men of virtue, who from religious motive cannot. Therefore those who are conscientiously scrupulous of taking an oath, are admitted as witnesses in criminal cases. Our legislation suffers no checks, from a council instituted, in fancied limitation of the House of Lords. By the right of sitting on our own adjournments, we are being dismist, when private passions demand it. At the same time, the strict discharge of the trust committed to Us, is inforced by the short duration of our power, which must be renewed by our constituents every year.

NOR are the people stript of all authority, in the execution of laws. They enjoy the satisfaction of having some share, by the appointment of provincial commissioners, in laying out the money which they raise; and of being in this manner assured, that it is applied to the purposes, for which it was granted. They also elect sheriffs and coroners; officers of so much consequence, in every determination that affects honour, liberty, life or property.

LET any impartial person reflect, how contradictory some of those privileges are to the most antient principles of the English constitution, and how directly opposite other of them are to the settled prerogatives of the crown; and then consider, what probability we have of retaining them on a *requested* change: that is of continuing in fact a proprietary government, though we humbly pray the King to change this government. Not unaptly, in my opinion, the connection between the proprietary family and this Province, may be regarded as a marriage. Our privileges may be called the fruits of that marriage. The domestic peace of this family, it is true, has not been unvexed with quarrels, and complaints: But the pledges of their affection ought always to be esteemed: and whenever the parent on an *imprudent request* shall be *divorced,* much I fear, that their issue will be declared *illegitimate. This* I am well persuaded of, that surprizing must our behaviour appear to all men, if in the instant when we apply to his *Majesty* for relief from what we think oppression, we should discover a resolute disposition to deprive him of the uncontroverted prerogatives of his royal dignity.

AT this period, when the administration is regulating new colonies and designing, as we are told the *strictest reformations* in the old, it is not likely that they will grant an invidious distinction in our favour. Less likely is it, as that distinction will be liable to so many, and such strong *constitutional* objections; and when we shall have the weight both of the clergy and ministry, and the universally received opinions of the people of our mother country to contend with. I mean not, Sir, the least reflection on the church of *England*. I reverence and admire the purity of its doctrine, and the moderation of its temper. I am convinced, that it is filled with learned and with excellent men: but all zealous persons, think their own religious tenets the best, and would willingly see them embraced by others. I therefore apprehend, that the dignified and reverend gentlemen of the church of *England,* will be extremely desirous to have *that* church as well secured, and as much distinguished as possible in the American colonies: especially in those colonies, where it is overborne, as it were, by dissenters. There can never be a more critical opportunity for this purpose than the present. The cause of that church will besides be connected with that of the crown, to which its principles are thought to be more favourable, than those of the other professions.

WE have received certain information, that the conduct of this Province which has been so much censured by the ministry, it attributed to the influence of a society, that holds warlike measures at all times to be unlawful. We also know, that the late tumulous and riotous proceedings, which are represented in so strong a light by the petition now before the House, have been publicly ascribed to the influence of another society. Thus the blame of every thing disreputable to this province, is cast on one or the other of these dissenting sects. Circumstances! that I imagine, will neither be forgot, nor neglected.

WE have seen the event of our disputes concerning the *Proprietary* interests; and it is not to be expected, that our success will be greater, when our opponents become more numerous; and will have more dignity, more power, and as they will think, more law on their side.

THESE are the dangers, Sir, to which we are now about to expose those privileges, in which we have hitherto so much gloried. Wherefore? To procure two or three, perhaps four or five hundred pounds a year, (for no calculation has carried the sum higher) from the Proprietors, for two or three or four or five years, for so long and something longer, perhaps, the taxes may continue.

BUT are we sure of gaining this point? *We are not.* Are we sure of gaining any other advantage? *We are not.* Are we sure of preserving our privileges? *We are not.* Are we under a necessity of pursuing the measure proposed at this time? *We are not.*

HERE, Sir, permit me to make a short pause. Permit me to appeal to the heart of every member in this House, and to entreat him to reflect, how far he can be justifiable in giving his voice, thus to hazard the liberties secured to us by the wise founders of this Province; peaceably and fully enjoyed by the present age, and to which posterity is so justly entitled.

BUT, Sir, we are told there is no danger of losing our privileges, if our government should be changed, and two arguments are used in support of this opinion. The first is, "That the government of the Crown is exercised in *Carolina* and the *Jerseys.*" I cannot perceive the least degree of force in this argument. As to *Carolina,* I am not a little surprized, that it should mentioned on this occasion, since I never heard of one privilege that colony enjoys, more than all the other royal governments in America. The privileges of the *Jerseys,* are of a different nature from many of which we are possest; and are more consistent with the royal prerogative.

INDEED I know of none they have, except that Quakers may be witnesses in criminal cases, and may bear offices. Can this indulgence shewn to them for a particular reason, and not contradictory to the rights of the crown, give us any just cause to expect the confirmation of privileges directly opposite to those rights, and for confirming which no such reason exists. But perhaps the gentlemen, who advance this argument, mean, that *we* shall purchase a change at a cheap price, if we are only reduced to the same state with the *Jerseys*—Surely, Sir, if this be their meaning, they entirely forget those extraordinary privileges, which some time ago were mentioned.

HOW many must we in such a case renounce? I apprehend, it would prove an argument of little consolation to these gentlemen, if they should lose three fourths of their estates, to be told, that they still remain as rich as their neighbours, and have enough to procure all the necessaries of life.

IT is somewhat remarkable, that this single instance of favour in permitting an affirmation instead of an oath, in a single province, should be urged as so great an encouragement to us, while there are so many examples of another kind to deterr us. In what *royal government* besides the *Jerseys,* can a *Quaker* be a witness in criminal cases, and bear office? (a) *In no other.* What can be the reason of this distinction in the *Jerseys?* Because of the instance of that colony, when it came under the government of the crown, there was, as appears from authentic vouchers, an ABSOLUTE NECESSITY from the scarcity of other proper persons, to make use of the people called *Quakers* in public employments. Is there such a necessity in this province? Or can the ministry be *persuaded,* that there is such a necessity? No, Sir, those from whom they will receive their information, will grant no such things; and therefore I think there is the *most imminent danger,* in case of a change, that the people of *this society* will lost the exercise of those rights, which, tho' they are intitled to as men, yet such is the situation of human affairs, they with difficulty can find a spot on the whole globe where they are allowed to enjoy them. It will be an argument of some force I am afraid, that the church of *England* can never expect to raise its head among us, while we are encouraged, as it will be said, in dissension; but if an *oath* be made necessary for obtaining offices of honour and profit; it will then be expected that any Quakers who are tempted to renounce their principles, will undoubtedly make an addition to the established church.

IF any other consideration than that which has been mentioned, was regarded in granting that indulgence in the *Jerseys,* tho' no other is exprest, it seems not improbable, that the nearness of this Province might have had some weight, as from its situation it afforded such strong temptations to the inhabitants of the *Jerseys* to remove hither, had they been treated with any severity.

THEIR government in some measure was formed in imitation of our government; but when this is altered, the *English* constitution must be the model, by which it will be formed.

HERE it will be said "this cannot be done but by the Parliament; and will a British Parliament do such an act of injustice, as to deprive us of our rights?" This is the second argument, used to prove the safety of the measure now proposed.

CERTAINLY the *British* Parliament will not do, what they think an unjust act: but I cannot persuade myself, that *they* will think it unjust, to place us on the same footing with themselves. It will not be an easy task to convince them, that the people of *Pennsylvania* ought to be distinguished from all other subjects, under his Majesty's *immediate* government; or that such a distinction can answer any good purpose. May it not be expected, that they will say "No people can be freer than ourselves; every thing more than we enjoy, is licentiousness, not liberty: any indulgences shewn to the colonies heretofore, were like the indulgences of parents to their infants; they ought to cease with that tender age; and as the colonies grow up, to a more vigorous state, they ought to be carefully disciplined, and all their actions regulated by strict laws. Above all things it is necessary, that the prerogative should be exercised with its full force in our American provinces, to restrain them within due bounds, and secure their dependance on this kingdome."

I AM afraid, that this will be the opinion of the Parliament, as it has been in every instance, the undeviating practice of the ministry.

BUT, Sir, it may be said "these reasons are not conclusive, they do not demonstratively prove, that our privileges will be endangered by a change. I grant the objection: but what stronger reasons, what clearer proofs are there, that they *will not be* endangered by a change."

THEY are fast now; and *why* should we engage in an enterprize that will render them *uncertain?* If nothing will content us but a revolution brought about by ourselves, surely we ought to have made the strictest enquiries what terms we may expect; and to have obtained from the ministry some kind of security for the performance of those terms.

THESE things might have been done. They are not done. If a merchant will venture to travel with great riches into a foreign country, without a proper guide, it certainly will be adviseable for him to procure the best intelligence he can get, of the climate, the roads, the difficulties he will meet with, and the treatment he may receive.

I PRAY the House to consider, if we have the slightest security that can be mentioned, except opinion (if that is any) either for the preservation of our present privileges, or gaining a single advantage from a change. Have we any writing? have we a verbal promise from any Minister of the Crown? We have not. I cannot therefore conceal my astonishment, that gentlemen should require a less security for the invaluable rights of *Pennsylvania,* than they would demand for a debt of five pounds. Why should we press forward with this unexampled hurry, when no benefit can be derived from it? Why should we have any aversion to deliberation and delay, when no injury can attend them?

IT is scarcely possible, in the present case, that we can spend too much time, in forming resolutions, the consequences of which are to be *perpetual.* If it is true as some averr, that we can *now* obtain an advantageous change of our government, I suppose it will be also true next week, next month, and next year: but if *they* are mistaken, it will be early enough, whenever it happens, to be disappointed, and to repent. I am not willing to run risques in a matter of such prodigious importance, on the credit of *any man's opinion,* when by a small delay, that can do no harm, the steps we are to take may become more safe. *Gideon,* tho' he had conversed with an "angel of the lord" would not attempt to relieve his countrymen, then sorely opprest by the *Midianites* lest he should involve them in greater miseries, until he was convinced by two miracles that he should be successful. I do not say, we ought to wait for *miracles;* but I think we ought to wait for something, which will be next kin to a miracle; I mean, some *sign of a favourable disposition* in the *ministry* toward us. I should like to see an *olive leaf* at least brought to us, before we quit the *ark.*

PERMIT me, Sir, to make one proposal to the House. We may apply to the Crown now, as freely as if we were under its immediate government. Let us desire his Majesty's judgment on the point, that has occasioned this unhappy difference between the two branches of the legislature. This may be done without any violence, without any hazard to our constitution. We say the justice of our demands, is clear as light: every heart must feel the equity of them.

IF the decision be in our favour, we gain a considerable victory; the grand obstruction of the public service is removed; and we shall have more leisure to carry our intentions coolly into execution. If the decision be against us, I believe the most zealous amongst us will grant it would be madness to expect success in any other contest. This will be a single point, and cannot meet with such difficulties, as the procuring a total alteration of the government.

Therefore by separating it from other matters, we shall *soon* obtain a determination, and know *what chance* we have of succeeding in things of greater value. Let us try our fortune. Let us take a cast or two of the dice for smaller matters, before we dip deeply. Few gamesters are of so sanguine a temper, as to stake their *public happiness*, let us act at least with as *much* deliberation, as if we were *betting* out of our private purses.

PERHAPS a little delay may afford us the pleasure of finding our constituents more unanimous in their opinions on this interesting occasion: and I should chuse to see a vast majority of them join with a calm resolution in the measure, before I should think myself justifiable in voting for it, even if I approved of it.

THE present question is utterly foreign from the purposes, for which we were sent into this place. There was not the least probability at the time we were elected, that this matter could come under our consideration. We are not debating how much money we shall raise: what laws we shall pass for the regulation of property; for on any thing of the same kind, that arises in the usual parliamentary course of business. We are now to determine, WHETHER A STEP SHALL BE TAKEN THAT MAY PRODUCE AN ENTIRE CHANGE OF OUR CONSTITUTION.

IN forming this determination, one striking reflection should be preserved in our minds; I mean, "that we are the servants of the people of *Pennsylvania*"—of *that people*, who have been induced by the excellence of the present constitution, to settle themselves under its Protection.

THE inhabitants of remote countries, impelled by that love of liberty which all wise providence has planted in the human heart, deserting their native soils, committed themselves with their helpless families to the mercy of winds and waves, and braved all the terrors of an unknown wilderness, in hopes of enjoying in these woods, the exercise of those invaluable rights, which some unhappy circumstance had denied to mankind in every other part of the earth.

THUS, Sir, the people of *Pennsylvania* may be said to have purchased an inheritance in its constitution, at a prodigious price; and I cannot believe, unless the strongest evidence be offered, that they are now willing to part with that, which has cost them so much toil and expence.

THEY have not hitherto been disappointed in their wishes. They have obtained the blessings they fought for.

WE have received these feats by the free choice of this people, under this constitution; and to preserve it in its utmost purity and vigour, has always been deem'd by me, a principal part of the trust committed to my care and fidelity. The measure now proposed has a direct tendency to endanger this constitution; and therefore in my opinion, we have *no right* to engage in it, without the *almost universal* consent of the people, exprest in the plainest manner.

I THINK, I should improperly employ the attention of this House, if I should take up much time in proving, that the deputies of a people have not a right by any law divine or human, to change the government under which their authority was delegated to them, without such a consent as has been mentioned. The position is so consonant to natural justice and common sense, that I believe it never has been seriously controverted. All the learned authors that I recollect to have mentioned this manner, speak of it as an indisputable maxim.

IT may be said perhaps in answer to this objection "that it is not intended to change the government, but the governor." This, I apprehend, is a distinction only in words. The government is certainly to be changed from proprietary to royal; and *whatever may be intended,* the question is, whether such a change will not expose our present privileges to danger.

IT may also be said "that the petitions lying on the table, are a proof of the people's consent." Can petition so industriously carried about, and after all the pains taken, signed only by about thirty five hundred persons, be look'd on as the *plainest expressions of the almost universal consent* of the many thousands that fill this Province? No one can believe it.

IT cannot be denied, Sir, that much the greatest part of the inhabitants of this Province, and among them men of large fortunes, good sense, and fair characters, who value very highly the interest they have in the present constitution, have not signed these petitions, and as there is reason to apprehend, are extremely averse to a change at this time. Will they not complain of such a change? And if it is not attended with all the advantages they now enjoy, will they not have reason to complain? It is not improbable, that this measure may lay the foundation of more bitter, and more lasting dissentions among us, than any we have yet experienced.

BEFORE I close this catalogue of unhappy consequences, that I expect will follow our request of a change, I beg leave to take notice of the *terms* of the petition, that is now under the consideration of the House.

THEY equally excite in my breast—surprize, and grief, and terror. This poor Province is already sinking under the weight of the discredit and reproaches, that by *some fatality* for several years past, have attended our public measures; and we not only seize this unfortunate season to engage her in new difficulties, but prepare to put on her devoted head, a load that must effectually crush her. We inform the King by this petition, that *Pennsylvania* is become a scene of confusion and anarchy: that armed mobs are marching from one place to another: that such a spirit of violence and riot prevails, as exposes his Majesty's good subjects to constant alarms and danger: and that this tumultuous disposition is so general, that it cannot be controuled by any powers of the present government; and that we have not only hopes of returning to a state of peace and safety, but by being taken under his Majesty's immediate protection.

I CANNOT think this a proper representation of the present state of this Province. Near four months are elapsed, since the last riot: and I do not perceive the least probability of our being troubled with any more. The rioters were not only successfully opposed, and prevented from executing their purpose; but we have reason to believe, that they were convinced of their error, and have renounced all thoughts of such wild attempts for the future. To whose throat is the sword now held? What life will be saved by this application; Imaginary danger! Vain remedy! Have we not *sufficiently felt* the effects of royal resentment? Is not the authority of the Crown *fully enough exerted* over does it become us to paint in the strongest colours, the folly or the crimes of our *countrymen?* To require unnecessary protection against men who intent us no injury, in such *loose* and *general* expressions, *as may produce even the establishment of an armed force among us?*

WITH unremitting vigilance, with undaunted virtue, should a free people *watch* against the encroachments of power, and remove every pretext for its extension.

WE are a dependant colony; and we need not doubt, that means will be used to secure that dependance. But that we ourselves should furnish a reason for settling a *military establishment* upon us, must exceed the most extravagant wishes of those, who would be most pleased with such a measure.

WE may introduce the innovation, but we shall not be able to stop its progress. The precedent will be pernicious. If a specious pretence is afforded for maintaining a small body of troops among us now, equally specious pretences will never be wanting hereafter, for adding to their numbers. The burthen that will be imposed on us for their support, is the most trifling part of the evil. The poison will soon reach our vitals. Whatever struggles we may make to expell it, *"Haeret lateri letbalis aerundo"*—

THE dart with which we are stuck, will still remain fixed—too firmly fixed, for our feeble hands to draw it out. Our fruitless efforts will but irritate the wound; and at length we must tamely submit to————I quit a subject too painful to be dwelt upon.

THESE, Sir, are my sentiments on the petition that has occasioned this debate. I think this neither the *proper season,* nor the *proper method,* for obtaining a change of our government. It is *uncertain,* whether the measure proposed will place us in a better situation, than we are now in, with regard to the point lately controverted: with respect to other particulars it may place us in a worse. We shall run the *risque* of *suffering* great *losses*. We have *no certainty* of *gaining* any thing. In seeking a *precarious, hasty, violent* remedy for the present *partial* disorder, we are *sure* of exposing the whole *body* to danger. I cannot perceive the necessity of applying such a remedy. If I did, I would with the greatest pleasure pass over to the opinion of some gentlemen who differ from me, whose integrity and abilities I so much esteem, that whatever reasons at any time influence me to agree with them, I always receive a satisfaction from being on their side. If I have erred now, I shall comfort myself with reflecting, that it is an *innocent error*. Should the measures pursued in consequence of this debate, be opposite to my opinion; and should they procure a change of government with all the benefits we desire; I shall not envy the praise of others, who by their *fortunate* courage and skill have conducted us unhurt through the midst of such threatening *dangers,* to the wished for port. I shall cheerfully submit to the censure of having been too *apprehensive* of injuring the people of this Province. If any severer sentence shall be passed upon me by the worthy, I shall be sorry for it: but this truth I am convinced of; that it will be much easier for me to bear the unmerited reflections of *mistaken zeal*, than the just reproaches of a *guilty mind*. To have concealed my real sentiments, or to have counterfeited such as I do not entertain, in a deliberation of *so much consequence* as the present, present, would have been the *basest hypocricy*. It may perhaps be thought that this however would have been the most *politic* part for me to have acted. It might have been so. But if *policy* requires, that our words or actions should *belye* our hearts, I thank God that I *detest* and *despise* all its *arts,* and all its *advantages*. A good man *ought* to serve his country, even tho' she *resents* his services. The great reward of honest actions, is not the fame or profit that follows them, but the *consciousness* that attends them. To discharge on this important occasion, the *inviolable duty* I owe the public, by obeying the *unbiassed dictates* of my *reason* and *conscience,* hath been my sole view; and my only wish now is, that the resolutions of this House, whatever they are, may promote the happiness of *Pennsylvania*.

SPEECH FOR

the Petition to Change the Form of Government

Joseph Galloway

Joseph Galloway was born about 1731, at West River, Maryland. He entered the law and rose to prominence. He was elected as assemblyman in 1756, a post he held continuously until 1776, with the single exception of one year, 1764 to 1765. From 1766 to 1775, he was annually elected to the speakership of the Assembly. He was selected to be a delegate to the First Continental Congress in 1774. He refused to be a delegate to the Second Congress. When the Revolution started and Philadelphia was occupied by Howe, Galloway became civil administrator, cooperating with the British. Upon the capture of Philadelphia by the Continental forces, in 1778, he went to England and became the spokesman of the American Loyalists. With the American victory, his estates were confiscated. In 1793, his petition to the Pennsylvania authorities for permission to return was refused. After twenty-five years of exile, he died on August 29, 1803.

This speech was given in answer to John Dickinson's speech of May 24, 1764. As soon as Mr. Dickinson had concluded his speech, Mr. Galloway rose to answer the objections raised against the petition to change the form of government.

The text is from the edition printed in Philadelphia by Dunlap, 1764.

Mr. Speaker,

IN this important Debate, I shall not take up the Time of the House in making large Protestations of my Sincerity, or that my Conduct is actuated by an ardent Desire to restore the almost expiring Liberties of my Country. Should any Person question those Polits, I shall make them to be determined by my past and present actions, which will have more weight for or against me, than all that I can say on the Occasion. Should those fail of demonstrating the rectitude of my Conduct, I am sensible, the most solemn Professions will not produce that effect; and by avoiding them, I spare myself the Blush, and you the Pain that must arise from an Eulogy made by a Man on his own Actions. I therefore recommend it to the Gentleman whose long Performance I now raise to answer, to consider that a steady Uniformity of Conduct, in support of Public Liberty, would have stood in no need of such Aids, and that a contrary Behaviour, with the Judicious and Impartial, will not receive the least Advantage from them. And it will also be but just in him to reflect, that if any thing disagreeable to him, should fall from me in the Course of my Observations on what he has said, he ought to impute it to the manner in which he has treated a great Number of honest prudent Men, the long Supporters of the Rights of the People.

THE Censure he has so liberally bestow'd on a very great Majority of the House, is too indecent to be passed over in Silence. When this important Affair had been fully considered and debated; viewed in all Lights, and fully determined by so great a Majority as nine Tenths in favor of the Measure, is it not surprising to hear our Conduct represented as flowing from a "Transport of Zeal and Resentment, and violent Passions." I know of nothing that can justify so unbecoming a Charge. This House, Sir, has long submitted to Proprietary Injustice, and from a melancholy impelling Necessity, has given up many important Points of the Liberties of the People. They have seen one Privilege after another, sacrificed without the least Hopes of Recovery, and new Demands and Exactions every Day made. And at Length tired out with the continually increasing Mischiefs constantly flowing from a Union of great Wealth, with extensive Power; and after having in vain attempted every other Measure for saving their Country from Ruin, they have resolved to petition his Majesty to resume the Powers of Government into his own Royal Hands.

AND certainly, Sir, this Resolution was far from being hasty or precipitate: The Measure had been often thought of and proposed by the same Members in preceding Assemblies. At the last Sitting, it was frequently moved, and solemnly debated. And yet so cooly and deliberately did they proceed, that they would not absolutely determine on this important Point, without first adjourning to consult their Constituents. The Adjournment was accordingly made, for six Weeks; and we are not returned to these Seats, fully convinced that our Conduct is approved of by all the Friends of Liberty, and Lovers of Order and Government. Hence I conclude, that the Resolution of this House is not founded in Passion or Precipitation, but in cool Reflection, and solid Judgment; and that the Charge the Gentleman has made against it is as groundless as it is indecent.

I OWN, Sir, all Passion and undue Attachment, of every Kind, should be banished from Public Councils. And that there are Passions which do not arise from "Resentment," yet are equally dangerous to the public Weal, and to which it has frequently fallen a Sacrifice. Such is the Passion of Ambition: A restless Thirst after Promotion, a Fondness to serve the Purposes of Power, from an Expectation of being rewarded with Posts of Honor and Profit. These equally blind the Understanding, captivate the Judgment, and destroy the pure Operations of Reason. And I cannot but wish, the Gentleman was as free from these mischievous Passions, so frequently destructive of Public Liberty, as the Majority of this House is from those with which he has charged them with so little Respect and Reserve.

BUT, Sir, I will proceed to the Merits of this Debate. The Gentleman contends, That this is not the proper Time to petition for Relief from our Distress, by a Change of Governors. But agrees, if the Change can take Place with our Privileges preserved, "Let it take Place instantly." Thus confessing that a Change is necessary, and yet in a few Minutes after, he positively affirms our Privileges are "all safe now," and that "we are in the full and peaceable Enjoyment of them." A Declaration of this Kind, Sir, from a Stranger to Proprietary Usurpations, would have been scarcely excusable; Because a Man ought to be acquainted with Facts before he positively determines on them. But in a Gentleman who has seen so many of our Rights fading and expiring under the baleful influence of Proprietary Ambition and Interest, it is utterly unpardonable. There are but few, very few indeed, even of those who are most dependant on Proprietary Favor, but will acknowledge in private, where they dare to own what they think, that our Rights are deeply wounded by the Attempts of Power—But permit me to ask the Gentleman, if the Liberties are in such a State of perfect Security, why is a Change necessary at all? Why should it take place even now or hereafter?—I leave this Contradiction to him to reconcile—I confess, Sir, I cannot do it.

IT is a stale and common Device, where Men are destitute of Arguments to support an Opposition to a necessary Measure, to use all their Force in persuading to put off and procrastinate. But, Sir, I am confident this Art will not succeed now; for all that has been said, has not tended to alter, but to confirm my Judgment, and now is the only proper Time to forward the Petition.

THAT there are "certain Periods, when Designs may be executed much more easily and advantageously, than at any other; That a strict Attention to every interesting Circumstance is necessary; And that we ought to wait until they have ripen'd into a favorable Conjecture;" I agree. All this has been done by the Assemblies of this Province, who, like the Parliament of *England,* after having long opposed the most arbitrary Measures in vain, and essayed every domestic Expedient to restore the lost Liberties of their Country, found nothing would save her, but a Revolution. We have often attempted to obtain Relief from Oppression, from the Proprietaries, but in vain—They have forbid us even to address them—They have refused to hear us—We have opposed their Measures before the Privy-Council—We have been but partially relieved, occasioned entirely by their Misrepresentations—and now we find, from their increasing Interest, unless we can effect a Change at this Time, any future Attempt must be ineffectual. We have considered every "Interesting Circumstance," and find them all, "Ripen'd up to this favorable Conjuncture." And in my Opinion, this is the only Time of Petitioning with a Prospect of Success. My Reasons are—The Proprietors, if they should incline to oppose this Change (as it is not certain they will, since it is a Part of the Proposal, that a full Equivalent be made them) have not probably so great an Interest now to support their Pretensions as they have had heretofore, Death having removed two of their principal Friends in the Privy Council: Then as to our being deprived of any of our Privileges in the Change, I apprehend, there is not the least Danger of it: The present Ministry, besides the Disposition to mild and equitable Measures which they have already manifested, will undoubtedly be very cautious how they give any Handle to a virulent Opposition, by so great an Act of Injustice, as the depriving a *free People* of those Privileges they have so dearly bought. Were they disposed to do it, they can only do it through the Parliament, which is composed in Part of that very Opposition: Their Prudence therefore, as well as their Justice, will prevent the Attempt. Again, at this Time, the Nation has immense Tracts of Territory to form into new Colonies: By an easy and expeditious Settlement of those Colonies, the Wealth and Commerce of the Nation will be increased and extended. This can only be done by granting to the Settlers particular Privileges, and greater Liberties than the People of our Mother Country and of foreign Nations enjoy in their present State. Sound Reason undoubtedly will recommend this Policy. And should they even attempt to deprive of its Rights this Colony, which has so remarkably flourished, and now takes off such fast Quantities of *English* Manufactures, from no other Cause but her extensive Privileges; it will require but little Discernment to perceive, how great a Damp such Measure must give to all the Schemes for new Settlements, and how sensibly the true Interest and Welfare of the Nation will be affected.

THIS, Sir, is not an imaginary Conjecture: It is founded on Reason, and on Experience. The Colony of *Barbados* had, in the Opinion of the ablest Council, forfeited her Charter Privileges— And yet upon this Policy only, her Privileges were preserved, as appears from the Extract read by a learned and worthy Member, from the Life of Lord *Clarendon*.

BUT it is said, "Men of the highest Character (if reports say true) are endeavouring to establish Proprietary Governments; and therefore probably may more readily incline to favor Proprietary Measures." I much doubt the Truth of this Report. I rather think Proprietary Governments are, by the Obstructions to his Majesty's Service and fatal Consequences to his Subjects, rendered so odious, that the Crown will choose to retain the Government of the Territories granted, in its own Hands, whatever Liberties it may confer to promote the Settlements. This certainly is the most probable Conjecture—founded on a positive Declaration of his Majesty's Ministers. The Declaration was to this Effect—"That his Majesty's Royal Prerogatives were not to be trusted to the feeble Hands of private Individuals; who were ever ready to sacrifice them to their private Emolument."

BUT, Sir, should this Report be true; would not common Prudence or what is more powerful, private Interest, induce these Gentlemen to obtain as many Privileges for all Sects of People, as would safely tend to encourage the Settlement of the Land granted them? Wou'd they not consider, that the more Privileges they could publish to the World, the more People would flock to their new Country, and the sooner their Estate would become Valuable. This was the Policy of our first Proprietor. This enabled him to sell his Lands at twice as much as they are sold in any other Government. It was this that has so remarkably advanc'd, and so speedily perfected the Province we now represent.

ANOTHER Circumstance unites to make this Conjuncture the most favorable: We have a Sovereign whom the Member himself allows, is as "just, benevolent and amiable a Prince, as Heaven ever granted in his Mercy to bless a People?" It is to him we petition: It is his Justice we implore, and his Virtue on which we rely for a Protection against the Oppression of his private Subjects. To him we have never applied before for Redress: And is he such a Cypher in the Government, that this important Transaction, in which the Rights of Thousands of his Loyal Subjects, are concerned, will not come to his Notice? Is he possessed of so much Justice and Benevolence, and will he permit such Injustice to be done us, witout Interfering?—I cannot believe it. He has not made this Charge: He has not appeared this Nothing in the Constitution: He has enquired into the Aggrievances of the Subject: He has redressed them: And the Minister on whom he much relies is a Man of acknowledged Virtue and Morality. In short, he has hitherto, and will still hear and redress the Complaints of his Subjects upon every Principle of Justice and Reason. Will such a Father of his People, when we ask him to separate Power from Property; to take the Nomination of the Governor who is to rule his People into his Royal Hands, for the Delivery and Safety of that People; will he deprive them of their Liberties granted by his Royal Predecessors for a valuable Consideration? "Will he when we ask Bread give us a Stone? When we ask a Fish will he for a Fish give us a Serpent? or, If we ask an Egg, will he give us a Scorpion?"

WHAT then are we to fear from such a Sovereign, and such a

Minister? When will the Period arrive, productive of such a Number of fortunate Circumstances for our Deliverance? When will Proprietary Power and Influence again receive such a Shock as to lose in a short time two of its principal Pillars? When are we again to expect such extensive Plans for the forming of new Colonies and extending the *English* Dominions? When will the Safety of our Privileges be so naturally supported by the Nation's Welfare? and when (look History through) can we promise ourselves so just, so good, and so virtuous a Sovereign, to do us Justice?

AFTER what I have said, how foreign must the Case of the D. of *Monmouth* appear to that of the present Assembly; and how much at a loss for Arguments must the Gentleman be, who if driven to such inapposite Instances to support his Cause? That Duke being a Refugee in *Holland,* was made a Tool to the Art and Policy of others. He set up an idle Pretension to the Crown of JAMES II. and he landed with 80 private Gentlemen at *Lime,* in a Time when the King was supported in the warmest Manner by the Parliament, and no one single Circumstance to promise him Success. In the Attempt he failed, and no wonder. More apposite Instances might be produced which happened near the same Period to shew the Danger of Delays, from the Mischiefs that arose to the Nation, by the Parliament's *omitting* to seize the fortunate Time of restoring the lost liberties of *England:* But these did not suit the Gentleman's Purpose.

AT the End of the Civil War, the King was ready to secure the Liberties of the Nation, which then like the Liberties of *Pennsylvania* were near expiring: But the Art and Policy of wicked Men interfered and prevented. At the Time of the Restoration, Cha. II. would have complied with any Terms for preventing the Abuse of Power, and Settling the Constitution on a rational and lasting Foundation. But the *Presbyterians,* out of Hatred to the *Independants,* joined the *Royalists* in all their Measures of Power: This gave them such additional strength, that Instead of restoring the Liberties of their Country, they renewed and continued their former Tyranny. I hope, Sir, the same Sect in this Province, will not act the Same indiscreet Part: That they will not attempt to sacrifice the Liberties of *Pennsylvania* to their private Animosity: Or, if they do, that the same fatal Effects will not attend their Actions: The Spirit of Liberty, if Properly exerted, will be strong enough to support this Struggle for our Preservation.

BUT it seems, under these distressing Circumstances, when we have no prospect of enjoying either Security of Person or Property, the grand and important Objects of all Government, we ought patiently to wait until *Proprietary Influence* shall be at an End. Had the Gentleman, who makes this Proposal, in the long Piece he has read in the House, offer some Reason to shew when that lucky Period would happen, or that it will ever happen while Proprietary Power and Property are united; or that it will happen before our invaluable Liberties, and all that *Englishmen* hold in Esteem, will be "consumed, not in the Blaze of Royal Authority" as he asserts, but in the Sink of Proprietary Injustice and Ambition, he would have afforded some small Comfort to the expiring Liberties of *Pennsylvania*. But this he has not attempted, conscious of the Vanity and Folly of such an Attempt. Let us but consider, that the Experience of Ages, fully demonstrates Wealth to be the Parent of Power, the Nurse of Influence: And that an Increase in Wealth, will as naturally beget an Increase of Power and Influence, as an Increase of Velocity in the falling Stone will produce more certain Death.

LET us take a View of the Proprietary Estate, what it was fifty, what twenty Years ago, and what it is now, and we must be convinced, that nothing can prevent their being the richest Subjects in the *English* Nation: And therefore Subjects of the greatest Influence and Power, and more likely in future to oppose with Success, any Measures that may be taken against their Oppression. Are we to expect the same Cause will not produce the same Effect, and that Wealth, by some Magick Charm in future, will, instead of producing Power and Influence, bring forth its contraries? If not, how vain and chimerical is the Expectation that Proprietary Power and Influence will ever cease? As vain and chimerical as the Expectations of a future Messiah to the deluded *Jews*.

AND as to the Royal and Ministerial Prejudices, we have heard of these in a Light the most terrible and frightful to us, and the most irreverant and disrespectful to his Majesty: they are represented as so ineradicably fixt, that nothing can remove them; I own I entertain very different Sentiments of the Royal and Ministerial Justice. Will his Majesty and Ministry, upon a solemn Representation and Proof of Facts, refuse to lay aside Prejudices, which can be easily made appear to be founded on Proprietary Misrepresentations? Will the Royal Ear be deaf to Truth? or will it not hear at all? If we are heard, I am confident, nothing is more easy than to shew the Conduct of this House has been founded on the strictest Loyalty to his Majesty, and Regard for the People we represent; and that the Obstructions which His Service has hereto met with, are entirely owing to Proprietary Oppression and Injustice. Our Proceedings will demonstrate, that the Assemblies of this Province have ever been the first to vote a Compliance with his Majesty's Requisitions. That the subsequent Obstructions to his Service have flowed from Proprietary Instructions, made in favor of their private Interest. That notwithstanding those Obstructions, in order to comply with the Royal Orders, the Rights of the People have been often wav'd, the Aids have been always granted, and even upon Terms abhorrent to common Justice. Upon these Facts being fully proved, the Opinion I have of the Royal Goodness and Virtue, will not permit me to doubt, but all Prejudices, if any now remain, will be easily overcome, and the Province restored to her former Credit.

BESIDES, when I consider the Province of *Pennsylvania* as the only Colony that has fully complied with the General's last Requisition, notwithstanding the unjust Opposition given to it on the Part of the Proprietary: That many have not complied in any Degree; some but in Part, none fully but this Assembly may Hope is not unreasonable, that former Prejudices will vanish, and our Conduct stand high in the Royal Esteem.

SHOULD so great a Reflection be thrown on his Majesty and his Ministry, as assert, they are thus irascible, thus blind to Justice and the Complaints of the Subject, in plain Terms. (For it has been very fully insinuated, that their present Prejudices, if any there be, cannot be overcome.) I answer, Sir, if this cannot be done now, there is not the least Prospect that it ever can be done. Every Day hereafter will bring on new Difficulties, and encrease the Power of Opposition—and to use the Gentleman's own Words, "It is not to be expected that our Success will be greater, when our Opponents will have more Dignity, more Power, and, as they will think, more Law on their side." This consideration alone points out the propriety of the present Time.

HERE, Sir, permit me to observe, the Gentleman entangles himself in another Contradiction. He first contends, this is not the proper Time to petition, because Proprietary Influence and Opposition, will at this Period, be too heavy for us; and then he confesses, we are not to expect more Success hereafter, because the Proprietaries "will have more Dignity, more Power, and, as they will think, more Law on their side."

IT is notorious, the late ministerial Censures, have not arisen from any unjust Conduct on our Parts—But entirely from Proprietary Misrepresentations. The Attachment of Human Nature to its private Interest is too obvious in the Course of Human actions to be denied—And the Degrees of this Attachment always encrease in proportion to the Wealth possessed—*crescit—nummi quantum ipsa pecunia crescit.* This is not Speculation, but what the Experience of many Years plainly discovers with respect to the Proprietaries. From this Source ever will arise Proprietary Instructions, arbitrary and unjust. A virtuous Legislature, I hope ever will fill these Seats, to the latest Ages. Their Virtue and Integrity will ever compel them to oppose Oppression. That Opposition will create Delays and Obstructions to his Majesty's Service, and the People's Welfare. And will Ambitious Men grasping at arbitrary Power, in Case of any Dispute respecting those Obstructions, lay aside their Endeavours, in support of their own Actions, to misrepresent our Conduct? Will they forget the Arts of Deception? They certainly will not; but will exert them with more Ardor and Success, in proportion to their Increase of Wealth, which will serve as a Weapon of Influence to encrease our Discredit, and the Ministerial Displeasure. Hence, Sir, I have not the Vanity to hope, that if we cannot now succeed in removing the Prejudices occasioned by Proprietary Misrepresentations, we never shall see the Day, while the Powers of Government are united with immense Property, that Proprietary Influence or Ministerial Prejudices against us will cease. But I much fear a little Time will shew us in the ridiculous Light that *Horace* shews his Clown, "who meeting a River in his Road, sat down on the Bank, to wait till the Stream should pass him."

> *Rusticus exspectat dum defluat amnis; at ille*
> *L'abitur; et labetur in omne valubilis avum.*

THE Gentleman further proceeds in his Possibilities and Conjectures (for of them, and of his Doubts, his Piece is entirely composed) and has attempted to point out the Time when he wou'd advise the Prosecution of the Measure resolved on—The Time "*may* come (says he) when the Weight of this Government *may* grow too heavy for the Shoulder of a Subject; at least too heavy for a Woman or an Infant." This House would have been obliged to him, had he pointed out when these *may-be's* will come to pass. And does he advise us then to submit to our present State of Thraldom and Insecurity, until the Government *may* grow too heavy for the Proprietaries? Were I, with the Gentleman, obliged to use such flimsey Arguments, for want of better, I might reply, this Time *may* never happen; and thus oppose possibility with possibility. But Sir, I am not reduced to this sad Necessity—I have evident Reasons to offer, why it will not happen—Will not Proprietary Wealth and Influence daily encrease with the Weight of the Government, in the fame, if not a greater proportion? The Weight of Government cannot be encreased but by an additional Number of Inhabitants. An Increase of People must necessarily accumulate the Proprietaries Revenues and Estate. An increase of Wealth will produce an Increase of Power and Influence; and these will consequently encrease the Breadth of the Proprietaries Shoulders, and ever enable him the better to bear the Weight of Government by procuring more Assistance and Support.

BUT "this Government *may* be too heavy at least for a Woman, or an Infant." But how long are we to wait for these fortunate Periods—future Generations may expect them in vain—and what will become of all that the Good and Virtuous in the mean Time hold dear and valuable? Mr. T. PENN *may* die—and what then? RICHARD is alive—But he may die—But has he no Heirs? He has several of Age, full of Health and Vigor, and as likely to live as most Men. But they *may* all die, unmarried, and without Issue. Will not there yet remain the Children of T. PENN? But they, and every of them, may also die without Issue; and in such Case, the Government must devolve on the Widow of some of them. Is this what the Gentleman means? for he has not explained himself. If I am wrong, 'tis his fault, not mine. And after all these glaring Improbabilities, scarcely Possibilities, shall happen, then it seems is the proper Time for a Change.

I CONFESS I cannot discover the Force of this Mode of Reasoning; but perhaps his own Mode may convince the Gentleman, and therefore for once I will use it. Is it not more than probable this Woman may have as much, if not more, Art, Cunning, and Influence, than our present Parties? May she not marry a Person of equal Weight, and superior Distinction? How then can this Period, shou'd it ever arrive, be more proper than the present? Proprietary Wealth and Influence will be encreased, and therefore the Thing more difficult, and of Course the Time more improper.

BUT, Sir, if those Possibilities should not happen, we are to wait till all the Male part of the Proprietary Family arrived at Age, save one, shall die—And the Powers of Government shall devolve on an Infant. I own, Sir, this Period seems as distant and improbable as the other. But when it arrives, how is the Change to be effected. Here the Gentleman is again defective in Explanation. Is it to be by a violent Resumption on the part of the Crown, without the Consent of the Infant? for he cannot consent. If so, our Privileges will be left in the Confusion and Violence, with the Government. Is it to be done by a Suit in Chancery, to enforce a specific Performance of the subsisting Contract between the first Proprietor and the Crown? A Court of Chancery cannot make a final Decree in any Case against an Infant, till he is of Age. Is it to be by a Parliamentary Enquiry, and an Act of the *British* Legislature, in Consequence of such Enquiry? If it is, the Rights of the People may be involved in the Enquiry, which the Mode intended by the House is calculated to avoid. Hence, Sir, it appears, that this Period of all others, will be attended with most Difficulty to the Crown, and Danger to the Privileges we wish to have restored from the Bonds of Proprietary Captivity.

AGAIN it is contended, "that the Proprietary Family *may* be so circumstanced, as to be willing to accept of such an Equivalent for the Government from the Crown, as the Crown may be willing to give." What these Circumstances are, remains also a secret to be unfolded. I conclude, Sir, for I can think of no others, that they are, when the Government shall be become of ten Times greater

Value than at present, and when the Estate of the Proprietary
Family shall be encreased in a Ten-fold proportion to what it is
now. But can the Gentleman tell us, why they may not possibly be
now willing to accept such an Equivalent?

AT any of these Times, we are told, "this Province may plead
the Cause of her Privileges with greater Freedom, and with greater
Probability of Success, than at present—The Royal Grant, the
Charter founded upon it: the public Faith pledged to the Adventurers, etc. etc. may be all properly insisted on." I should be glad
to learn, why these Things may not now be pleaded with equal
Freedom and Success. Will it be indecent to lay a true State of
Facts before his Majesty and Ministry? Will it be treasonable
to inform them—That his Majesty's Royal Predecessors, to encourage the Extension of their Dominions, granted certain Privileges to the first Adventurers. That those Privileges were enlarged,
were ratified and confirmed by the Crown. That the Royal Faith
was pledged as a Security of the Enjoyment of them. That in
Consequence of these Grants, his *British* Dominions have been
greatly extended, and the *English* Nation benefited. That notwithstanding all this, the Proprietaries and Sons of the first Grantee,
actuated by Motive of Private Interest only, and in Violation
of the Royal Faith thus plighted, had so highly presumed, as
arbitrarily to usurp and dissolve the most valuable of those Rights.
That these Things had created so great Disrespect and Contempt
for a Proprietary Government, that there was not longer any
Security under it; whence his Majesty's good Subjects were not
only deprived of those invaluable Blessings so fully granted and
confirmed to them, but that all Government was at an End, and
the very Design of Society destroyed. And therefore, to intreat his
Majesty to restore his good Subjects to their lost Liberties and
Freedom thus arbitrarily usurped; by separating Proprietary
Power from Property, and by resuming the Nomination of the
Governor into his own Royal Hands, by enforcing a specific Performance of a Contract, now *bona fide* subsisting between him and
the Proprietaries. This is a true State of the Facts, unperverted,
and not misrepresented. And will this be, as the Member, has
asserted, "precluding ourselves from every Office of decent Duty
to the Most excellent of Kings?" Will this be treating his Majesty
with Irreverence and Disrespect? This, or tantamount, has been
done to the most absolute Monarch. Can a People give a more
irrefragable demonstration of their Loyalty and Affection for
their Sovereign, than to petition to be under his immediate Care,
and to implore his immediate Protection. And can an Application
like this, be disagreeable to his Majesty, or to his Ministry, so
evidently for the Advantage of the Crown, and the good of its
Subjects? No, Sir, There is not the least Danger or Probability of

the Member's Prediction coming to pass—That all will be imputed to a "sudden Passion and Resentment against the Proprietors."

I SHOULD not, Sir, treat the Member with the Freedom he deserves, if I did not assert that he has wilfully and disengenuously mistated, in more Parts than one, the Ground and Cause of this Petition to the Crown. He has represented it as arising only from our differing with the Governor in Sentiments, on the Stipulation respecting the Proprietaries located and uncultivated Lands. And as if all we complained of was not of more Value than two or three Hundred Pounds per Annum, for a few Years. Nothing can be more unfair and destitute of candor; And nothing more evident of the highest Inattention and Indiscretion, than to appeal to "our Resolves," so full of different Aggrievances, to support this Representation. Though this Aggrievance, Sir, itself, is a Thing extremely unjust, and what a free people must with great Reluctance yield to; and yet was this all, I am confident this House would give up such a Sum, and an Hundred Fold added, to restore our Constituents to their lost Liberty. But this is not the Burthen of our Complaints, and our Oppressions—They are Things that affect the very existence of our Privileges and Safety. The very Resolves he appeals to, must, when they are considered, cover him with confusion. 'Tis arbitrary Proprietary Instructions, inforced on our Governors, in manifest Violation of the Royal Grant, subversive of the Powers of Legislature, our first and most essential Privilege, we complain of. Instructions that prevent our affording that Protection to the People committed to our Care, which it is our Duty to give, and their Right to receive. Instructions which prevent our passing any salutary Regulations for the Public Safety, or the People's Benefit. To which should we submit in Part, we shall soon be obliged to give up the whole, and be reduced to the servile Condition of the Parliament of *Paris,* or of the worst of Slaves of the most absolute Monarcch.

WE further complain, That the Increase of public Houses, to an enormous Degree, merely to augment the Income of the Proprietaries Deputy, has corrupted the Morals of the People, to the great Scandal of Religion and Government; has enervated and untimely destroyed Numbers of his Majesty's Subjects; whereby the People are diminished, and the Government weakened; and that all our reasonable Bills which have been presented to Proprietary Governors, for a Redress, have been continually refused, from Motives of private Interest and Proprietary Instructions.

THAT the Liberties and Properties of the People are render'd precarious, and dependant on the Will of the Proprietaries, by their insisting on the Nomination of the Judges, during their Pleasure, who are to determine all Causes between them and their Tenants, the Good People of this Province.

THAT no Military Force can be obtained for the Protection of the Subject from internal Tumults, and Insurrections at Home, or from the common Enemy Abroad, but upon Terms the most arbitrary and unjust, that will surrender both the lives and Properties of the People to the Will and Mercy of the Proprietaries and their Deputies.

THESE intolerable Mischiefs, with a Multitude of others well known to this House; all arising from the Nature of Proprietary Interest and Government, are the true Causes of our Petition to the Crown. Mischiefs which are daily increasing and will continue to do so, while Power and Property remain in the same Hands; and which will soon, unless speedily remedied, reduce this poor Province to a Condition infinitely worse than any of the Royal Governments in *America*, so much decried by the Gentleman, and the People to a State little better than absolute Slavery. In these Governments none of these Mischiefs exist. We find in them, a full Freedom and Power of Legislation—No obstructions to his Majesty's Service, a perfect Administration of Justice, no legally established Source of Vice and Immorality, and a sufficient Protection against all Tumults, Insurrections, and Invasions. Why should we dread a Change, even supposing all his chimerical Fears should prove absolute Realities.

LET us suppose, says the Gentleman, that his Majesty will not accept of the Government, clogged, as it will be said, with Privileges inconsistent with the Royal Rights. I cannot think with him, this Supposition is reasonable: But suppose it reasonable, the worse Consequence is, that we must then remain, where he would have us remain, yet longer in our present situation; for the Crown cannot take our Privileges from us, without an Act of Parliament. But were it in his Majesty's Power, to deprive us of our Rights, He would certainly reflect, that those Privileges, whatever they are, were granted and ratify'd by his Royal Predecessors—That they are the Purchase of the People, never yet forfeited—That it will be an Act of Injustice and Violation of the Royal Faith to resume them without the Assent of the Owners—That such Resumption will deeply affect the Welfare of the Nation, and wise Policy of settling the extensive newly-acquired Dominions. And has his Majesty less Justice and Goodness of heart, than his Royal Predecessors, who granted and confirmed these Privileges? Will he violate their Covenants and Acts, which remain in Full Force and Virtue? Or has he less Wisdom, and will therefore damp the new Settlements intended of his now more than ever extensive Dominions, for the Sake of depriving an affectionate People of a few Privileges most solemnly granted and confirmed to them?

THE Gentleman thinks "the Petitions from the People to the Crown, which have been laid before the House can be regarded in no other Light than a Surrender of the Charter." I am at a Loss, Sir, to know what Idea he fixes to the Word *surrender:* It imports some Act of yielding up something we are in Possession of. But no Words of that Import are to be found in the Petitions. The former Part of them mentions the Mischiefs and Aggrievances the People labour under in the present Form of Government, arising from the Nature of that Government. And in the Conclusion makes the very Design and End of petitioning the enjoyment of those "Privileges granted them by his Majesty's Royal Predecessors, freed from the Inconveniences incident to Proprietary Governments;" and not a Word, nor even a Hint is contain'd in them, that the Petitioners would surrender, or even wave them. Hence it appears, that the Petitions cannot be construed into a Surrender, by the most tortured Interpretation, and without violating the Words, the Sense, the very End and Design of them; and that this will be done, either by his Majesty or his Ministry, the Opinion I entertain of their Justice, forbids me to suppose. And therefore I shall leave this invidious Reflection on his Majesty and his Servants, to be nursed and propagated by the Gentleman who has so freely published it.

TO answer particularly all the suppositious Reasons and conjectural Arguments that have been offered by the Gentleman, to prove that his Majesty and Ministry will act with Violence, and desert the Principles of Justice and Law, to take away our Rights without our Consent, would be taking up your Time very unnecessarily. These Reflections so groundlessly bestowed on them, with so little Decency and Reserve, must, in every loyal Breast, create Disgust against the Author, not a Fear of becoming his Majesty's immediate Subjects. And as to the Ministry, whatever Opinion has been entertained of a former one, the present is composed of many different Members, who are now under the Influence of the best of Sovereigns—We have made no Appeals to them—We have had no Experience of their Injustice. But should they be regardless of Justice; should they incline to deprive us of our Liberties against our Consent, we have the Satisfaction to know, with indisputable Certainty, that they cannot, unless a *British* Parliament should ratify their Injustice.

OUR Privileges do not depend on a Proprietary Charter—They are all confirmed by Laws of this Province; those Laws have received the Royal Approbation, and are become thereby of equal Solidity with an Act of Parliament, and therefore they cannot be repealed by any Power, but that of the King, Lords and Commons.

AND have we not here, Sir, all the Security Reason can desire, that our Privileges, thus solemnly confirmed and never forfeited, will be preserved on a Change? I agree we have not, if we implicitly believe the prophetical Conjectures of this Gentleman,

"For, says he, this Affair is laid before the Parliament, the Desires of the Ministry are insinuated, the Rights of the Crown vindicated, and an Act passes to deliver us *at once* from the Government of Proprietors and the Privileges we enjoy." Is not this an amazing Supposition, contradicted by Reason and Experience? Is not this a most indecent Reflection on a *British* Parliament? I shudder at the Explanation; but it is necessary. According to this Doctrine, Sir, the King, Lords, and Commons, are the servile Dupes of the Ministry. Without Consideration, without the least Reason, in an Instant a law passes the whole *British* Parliament, at the Desire of the Ministry, to blast our Liberties. The Royal Faith pledged to the Subject, is violated by Royalty itself—and private Injustice is done by the wisest Legislature in the World, renowned for their Justice in all Nations.

A SUPPOSITION so invidious, so destructive of the public Reputation of the *British* Government, cannot gain Credit with the most Credulous. Many Instances might be produced, wherein that honorable Body, the House of Commons, have rejected the unjust Attempts of particular Ministers, on the Liberties of *America.* I will mention two—In the Year 1718, influenced by Misrepresentations, there was an Attempt to inforce Royal Instructions on the Governors and Assemblies of the Colonies, as Laws; but the latter conceiving them inconsistent and destructive of their Powers of Legislation, did not pay that Regard to them that was required. Application was therefore made to the House of Commons, for a Law, to give them the same Force with an Act of Parliament. But that Body, thought it extremely unjust, as it really was, to deprive *British* Subjects of those Privileges which had been granted to them, and under which they had settled—and rejected the Application. In the Year 1748, the like Attempt was again made, and it met with the same Fate, and Success. Thus, Sir, we see a *British* House of Commons, the Guardians of *British* Liberties, have not been found on Experience, so lost to Justice and Public Faith, as has been represented. And we have no Reason to believe they are now grown more Corrupt, or less Virtuous.

AND, Sir, should an Application be made to Parliament, to new model our Constitution, when it is found that illegal Proprietary Instruction, disannulling the Powers of Legislation, contrary to the Privileges granted by the Royal Charter, is one of the Causes of our Petition. That these Instructions have been the sole Impediments to his Majesty's Measures, and the Protection of his Colonies, will they not justify the Legislature that opposed them? Will they not countenance a Conduct so familiar to their own? Will they refuse enforcing the Instructions of the Crown, as a Thing illegal, unjust, and inconsistent with the Rights of the Freemen of *America;* and yet approve and enforce the Instructions of private Subjects, founded on an unjust Attachment to their own private Interest? The absurdity, Sir, is too glaring to admit of a Supposition.

BUT further to paint our Royal and Ministerial Injustice, in the blackest Colours, and to aggravate the dreadful Consequences we are to expect from it, the Gentleman affirms, that "We find, during the late War, every Point, in which the Proprietaries thought fit to make any Opposition, decided against us." Here, Sir, the Gentleman has wandered widely from the facts. In the Year 1759, the Time he alludes to, nineteen Acts, passed by this Legislature, were presented for the Royal Approbation; thirteen of them were confirmed, though five of the thirteen were warmly opposed by the Proprietaries, as inconsistent with the Royal Prerogatives.

THEY earnestly contended that the Nomination of Commissioners, in Supply Bills, to dispose of the public Money, was an invasion of his "Majesty's Prerogatives and the Power and Privileges vested in them by the Royal Charter:" and yet this important Point was determined in our Favor, though contrary to the Practice of Ages, in our Mother Country, where all the public Monies are disposed of by the Crown alone.

THEY opposed, for some Reason, the Confirmation of the Law to prevent the Exportation of bad and unmerchantable Slaves, etc. because their Deputy Governor had not the Nomination of the Officer to put the Act in Execution; and yet this Act was confirmed and approved by the Crown.

THE Act to prevent the Exportation of unmerchantable Bread and Flour, was opposed on the same Principle, but with as little Success, on the Part of the Proprietaries.

THESE, with many other Points, too tedious to enumerate, were opposed with all the Proprietary Power and Influence, before the Ministry; and yet, Sir, the Assembly succeeded, and Justice was done the People of *Pennsylvania*. After these irrefragable Proofs of Royal and Ministerial Justice, if they should not succeed in prevailing on the Gentleman to alter his Sentiments and free Method of censuring them, I cannot doubt, but that they will at least wipe away these groundless Fears and frightful Apprehensions he has endeavoured to inculcate of the Loss of our Privileges by their unjust Measures.

I DO not expect, upon a Change of Governors, that a perpetual Calm will ensue, or that no Contests will ever arise between the Ruler and the People. That would be vain indeed; an Expectation contradicted by evident Experience and the very Nature of human Affairs. But, Sir, what I expect, and what every sensible Man must naturally foresee, is, that public Disputes will be very rare and uncommon. With what Ease and Expedition was the public Business, and his Majesty's important Service carried on, during the late War, in all the Royal Governments? Not a Dispute of Murmur subsisted between the Governors and the Governed; in their several legislatures. But in the two only Proprietary Governments, in *America,* Proprietary Contests were as constant and certain as the Meeting of their Legislatures. In one, his Majesty's Measures for the Protection of his Colonies, received little or no Assistance at all; in the other, it met with great and pernicious Obstructions. From whence does this between Royal and Proprietary Governments spring? From whence do these Mischiefs arise? I appeal, Sir, to the unbiassed and impartial, whether they do not proceed from the very Nature of Proprietary Governments. In the former, the Ruler has no sinister Motive, no undue Bias to reduce his Attention from the public Weal, and the good of the People. But in the latter, private Interest, like some restless Fiend, is always alive, is ever active: Active in perpetual Opposition to the true interest of the Colony. Hence it is, that incessant Contentions must ever exist, until the Spirit of Liberty is worn out, and the People fatigued with Controversy and Oppression, shall servilely submit to the Will and Pleasure of the Proprietor. From these Mischiefs, not to be avoided under our present Form of Government, I hope to be one of the happy Instruments of relieving my Country, by the Petition for a Change: And of conducting my fellow Subjects to a secure Haven, where, tho' a Storm may once in an Age arise, they shall remain in Safety, nor dread the fatal Rocks of Proprietary private Interest, or Proprietary Influence.

PERMIT me next, Sir, to attend the Gentleman in his Remarks on our Privileges; on which Head I shall be brief—

"WE here enjoy (we are told) that best and greatest of all Rights, a perfect religious Freedom." So do all Protestants in every Royal Government under his Majesty.

"PROVINCIAL Commissioners dispose of our public Money." So they do in *New York, New Jersey, Virginia,* and *Carolina;* and so they may in every other Colony on the Continent.

"THE Posts of Honor and Profit are unfetter'd with Oaths or Tests." The People of *Jersey* enjoy the same Privileges as to Oaths; and in my Opinion, the same might be obtained in every other Government, on a proper Application: And as to Tests, except the usual test required by Act of Parliament, and common to all the Kings Dominions, such a Thing is not known in *America,* unless imposed by the Legislature of any Colony.

"THOSE who are conscientiously scrupulous of taking an Oath, are admitted as Witnesses in Criminal Cases." Where this Scruple is rare in proportion to the Number of Inhabitants, a Government may, without great Inconvenience, refuse to indulge it. But where so great a part of the People as In *Pennsylvania,* are subject to it, Necessity will oblige a Government to allow an Affirmation, for its own Sake, if not for that of the Scrupulous, as otherwise Justice, one main End of Government, could be obtained. I have never seen a Calculation, but I apprehend, the Numbers in this Province, scrupulous in this Point, may be justly computed one Third of the People: There being the People called *Quakers,* the *Moravians, Menonists, Dumplers,* and great Number of the *Irish* and *Dutch* Presbyterians, who have those Doubts. Shou'd they be deprived of the Privileges of an Affirmation, in lieu of an Oath, in all Probability, one Offender out of three, in every Kind of Crime, would escape with Impunity, for want of Testimony to convict the Criminal. For should one of these People be robbed alone, or should he be robbed or murdered, in the presense of another of them, the Offender must Escape the Penalty of the Law, because the Witness cannot swear. The like Inconvenience to the Public must happen, where any other person is murdered in their Presence; to the great Encouragement of Offenders, and the Obstruction of Justice. Hence, Sir, there can be no Danger, that a Colony, thus circumstanced, will ever be deprived of this Privilege. Common Policy, in the Administration of Justice, and the Safety of the People, in both Life and Property, forbid it.

"OUR Legislation suffers no Checks from a Council, instituted in fancied Imitation of a House of Lords." But, Sir, have we not a Council dependant on the Will and Pleasure of our Oppressors, infinitely more mischievous: And is it possible, that the Gentleman is so little acquainted with the pernicious Effects of Proprietary Instructions, which not only check, but destroy, the Powers of Legislation, and chain down the Discretion of both Branches so effectually, as to make them Cyphers in the Constitution? Instructions which render them the Resemblance of the *French* Parliament, with only the Power of forming and registering their Master's Edicts—differing only in this imbittering Circumstance, that *they* are obliged to submit to the Edicts of Royalty, but *we* to those of private Men, no ways superior to us in Birth, Education, Merit, or Dignity.

"BY the Right of Sitting on our own Adjournments, we are secure of meeting when the public Good requires it." But, Sir, let me ask, what Public Good, what Service to our Country can we do, when Proprietary Instructions, and Proprietary private Interest, is to inslave our Judgments, and to rule in our Councils. Has not long Experience taught us, that we must sit Month after Month, spending and wasting our Constituents Money, fruitless and ineffectual? In short, Sir, these Privileges of Legislature, with that of our annual Elections, of which the Gentleman so much boasts, are all swallowed up and sacrificed at the Shrine of Proprietary Instructions, and the Measures of Power. They are now, Sir, but *Ideal* Shadows, and chimerical Notions.

UNDER these unfortunate Circumstances, arising entirely from Proprietary Government, what Man that ever tasted of the Sweets of Liberty, that has the least Idea of Freedom remaining, can lay his hand on his Heart, and dare whisper the Assertion, that we "Peaceably and fully enjoy our Rights and Privileges." Surely, Sir, no greater Mistake was ever affirmed, than that "They are safe now;" and no Truth more evident than that were we to lose all our Charter Privileges, and only enjoy those of the Royal Governments, our Situation then would be infinitely preferable to our present State.

BUT, Sir, we are told, some of these Privileges are contrary to the settled Prerogatives of the Crown, and therefore will be resumed on an Application for a Change. I know of but one of them that is so, which is that of Sitting on our own Adjournments, without a Power in the Governor to prorogue or dissolve us; and I have already shewn that the King and Ministry cannot resume it without the Aid of Parliament, and; Sir, I am confident, there Justice and Policy will ever secure to us, Privileges which we have dearly bought and never forfeited, and which are as much our Right as the Money in our Pockets, or any other Property we enjoy.

AGAIN, the Gentleman conjectures, that the Members of the established Church will be very active in this Affair, and will exert themselves to deprive the Dissenters of their religious Rights and Freedom. For my Part I cheerfully confess, I entertain a very different Opinion of their Moderation and Benevolence. Gratitude to that Church, which has so long held the Helm of Power, which has had, without using them, so many Opportunities of oppressing the Dissenters, forbids me to entertain so malevolent an Idea of them. Instead of oppressing them, they have, in many Instances, been extending their Rights and increasing their Privileges, ever since the Revolution. In the Case of *Carolina*, when both Proprietaries and People petitioned for a Change, no such violent Measures were prosecuted, either by the King, the Ministry, the Parliament, or the Church of *England*. His Majesty and Ministry, did not attempt to alter the Laws, or vary the Constitution. The Matter was laid before the Parliament, and such was their Justice, which has been so much oppugned and traduced, that they did not make the least Alteration, but granted his Majesty the Sum required to purchase the Government and Soil. Very similar were the Circumstances of that Government at that Time, to those of *Pennsylvania* now. A Savage Enemy, united with the *Spaniards*, were invading their Frontiers, the People wanted Protection, and his Majesty's Service was obstructed by Proprietary Measures and Interests. The Colony was settled principally by Persons of the established Church, more than sufficient to fill all the Offices of

Government; and yet, Sir, so far was the Royal Justice, or Ministerial Designs, from depriving the Dissenters of their liberties, that immediately on the Change, they repealed the only Law of the Province, imposing a Test on Dissenters, or that affected their Liberties. After this so late an Instance of Royal and Ministerial Goodness, what have we to fear from our Petition? Are we to be intimidated, and frightened from pursuing the only Measure that can save our Privileges, by such wild Conjectures, such imaginary Possibilities?

THE Gentleman's knowledge and Foresight, carries him still further. For he not only undertakes to foretell the Actions, but speaks the very Words of the Parliament, when this Affair shall come before them. He intimates, that they will say, "Any Indulgencies shewn to the Colonies heretofore, were like the Indulgencies of *Parents* to their *Infants*. They ought to *cease* with that *tender Age*." Did they say or act in this Manner, on any of the Antecedent Changes from Proprietary to Royal Governments. A Charge this, full of the highest Indignity and Affront. And will that wise Body countenance such arrant Deception, such unparalleled Fraud? They have not, they will not. This is the second Time I have seen this Doctrine published in *Pennsylvania*. I hope I may never see it again. It never took its Origin, nor ever was thought of in our Mother Country. The Author of the *Brief State,* that common Enemy to the Liberties of *America,* built his slavish Superstructure for depriving her of her Privileges upon this Principle. The Crown, Sir, in 1681, with this sole View to settle this Colony, and to extend the Commerce of the Nation, granted to our Ancestors the Privileges we ought now to enjoy. Those good People left their Mother Country, and every social Connection, and with infinite Toil, Expence, and Danger, unassisted by the Crown, settled this remote Wilderness—To the great Increase of the National Commerce. And thus have fulfilled their Contract with the utmost Punctuality on their Parts. At first, Sir, our Privileges were of little Value; they could be scarcely exercised or enjoyed. And now we are arrived at a Capacity to enjoy them, will our Mother Country retain the benefit of our Labor, and deprive us of the Consideration? Honor, Reason, Justice, Virtue, forbid it. Let me suppose, by Way of Illustration, That a Father sends his Son into a distant Country, to perform for him some essential Service: And he grants him a Consideration, which he is to have for the Performance. The Son performs the Service with great Toil and Danger, and at his own Expence. But when he should enjoy the Reward of his Fatigue —His Parent arbitrarily deprives him of the Consideration. What Words, Sir, shall we find in any Language, to describe the Idea of a Conduct so base and fraudulent? And how groundless and affrontive must such an Imputation be to a *British* Parliament?

OUR Right to petition for a Change, calls next for my Consideration. This, Sir, it is contended, we "have no Right to do without the *almost universal* Consent of the People, exprest in the plainest Manner." This Position appears to me as strange as it is absurd. It is contradicted by the Experience and Practice of all Ages and Nations. There is scarcely one Government in the civilized World, that now retains its original Form. And I believe none, Sir, that has been changed by the expressed universal Consent of the People. Innumerable Instances might be adduced of this Truth, from ancient and modern History; but a few from the latter may suffice. Was the glorious WILLIAM, the Deliverer of the *English* Nation from Bigotry, Superstition, and Slavery, vested with *British* Regality by the declared universal Assent of the People? Was the Stadtholder elected without considerable Opposition in the *States of Holland?* They were not.

THIS Province, Sir, was originally governed by a Governor, a Provincial Council of Seventy, and a House of Representatives, consisting of two Hundred. And in this Council the Governor had but a "treble Vote." This was our original Form of Government established in 1682, by the Proprietor and Adventurers. And yet we find that in 1701, this Frame of Government was, after it had undergone various Changes, finally surrendered by six Parts, in seven of the Assembly met, *without consulting their Constituents,* and our present Charter accepted. This Change then is either valid or it is not. In either Case the Doctrine of universal Consent is absurd or mischievous. If it is valid, then the Resolutions of this House for a Change, assented to by nine Tenths of the Members met, must be valid also. If it is not valid, then all our Privileges, derived under our present Charter, so much boasted of by the Gentleman, vanish, being founded on no Authority, and we must recur to the old inconvenience and scarcely practicable Form of Government.

BESIDES, Sir, the Right in this House to petition for a Change, whenever they think it necessary for the Welfare of their Constituents is founded on, and established by the very Terms of our present Charter. Six Parts in seven of the Assembly met, have Authority to *Alter, change,* diminish the Form and Effect thereof, without consulting or taking the opinion of the People.

FURTHER to expose the Absurdity of this Assertion; Arbitrary Power will ever have Numbers to support it; without this, Power could not become arbitrary. And should People oppressed, wait for this universal Assent, Changes never would happen, and their Slavery never end. What is right and necessary for the Safety of the People, virtuous Men, entrusted with their welfare, will ever pursue, tho' Millions and Mountains oppose. *Salus Papuli Oft Supreme Lex.* Let this Principle, and this alone, freed and unshackled with any other Consideration, actuate our Conduct, and we shall ever secure a self-approving Conscience, which is of higher Estimation than the greatest Wealth, the most invaluable Jewels.

BUT, Sir, I should be glad to learn what is meant by this almost *universal Consent.* Is it the Consent of two Thirds, nine Tenths, or of ninety-nine out of an Hundred of the People? Where will this vague and indeterminate Rule end. We have the Satisfaction to know that our Conduct is supported, and the Measure we are taking approved of, by a very great Majority of the People, and all the independant Lovers of Liberty; not merely from the Petitions to his Majesty, now before the House, but by our mixing among them, during our Recess, and various other Means of consulting their Inclinations. It is to them we are accountable; and if we have their Approbation, it is all we ought to expect; their Disapprobation is all we ought to fear.

BEFORE I conclude, I will endeavour, Sir, to remove the "Suprize, Grief, and Terror," with which the *Form* of our intended Petition to the Crown has struck him. If, Sir, a true Representation of the uncommon Mischiefs which attend the Liberties of a free People, arising from the very Nature of Proprietary Governments. If a true State of our present Confusion, both in and out of our public Councils—if a just Account of our present insecurity of Life and Estate, given to the Crown, be a just Cause of Terror, then the Gentleman's Pannick is just. But, Sir, these Things I conceive are rather Causes of Joy than Fear. 'Tis from hence we must hope to be relieved from our present unhappy Circumstances.

BUT we should not have informed his Majesty "that *Pennsylvania* is a Scene of Confusion; that armed Mobs are marching from one Place to another," etc. And are not these Things true? Armed Mobs, not only one, but three, in the Space of a few Months, have marched from Place to Place, broke open the public Gaol, and perpetrated with Impunity, the most horrid Murders in cool Blood—in the Face of the Magistracy, and defiance of the Government. And to add to their villainy they came to the capital City, with the same black Design, determined, if we may judge from their Threats, to wreak their Vengeance not only on the *Indians,* but upon some of the Members of Government itself. Nor was the Government capable of defending itself, or the People under its Care. No, Sir, our present Safety, and for aught I know, our present Existence, is owing to the King's Troops, and a few brave Volunteers, the Friends of Liberty, of public Virtue, and of Government. And shall we be afraid to reveal such imminent Danger! Such extreme Distress? to the best of Kings? And when such Confusion, such horrid Guilt, such heinous Offences, take Place in a dependant Colony, with Impunity; when the Government itself refuses or neglects, or is incapable to afford Redress, does it not become a matter of the highest Necessity and Wisdom? Is it not our indispensable Duty, to represent these Things in their true Light to the Crown, who alone can preserve us from such inexpressible Evils?

BUT, Sir, should we waive these Things, and draw our Petition in a different Dress, can we annihilate the Messages between the Governor and Assembly? Can we withdraw the Governor's Proclamations? Can we hold the Hands of his Majesty's General, whose Aid we were obliged to accept, from giving the Intelligence? Can we stop the Mouths, and close the Eyes of all *England* and *America,* or prevail on his Majesty, or the Ministry, to bury in Oblivion what they have, e'er now, so often read and heard? If we cannot do these Things how vain and ridiculous must our Attempt be, to hide these Tumults and Murders from the Royal Knowledge, should it be though prudential or useful? But, Sir, that cannot be; for the Assembly of *Carolina* represented their Government in the same State of Confusion, and want of Protection, in their Petition for a Change; and no ill, but very good Consequences attended it.

IF the Gentleman has been struck with Terror at the Form of our Petition, I own, Sir, I am struck with more Amazement at his Conduct in endeavouring to palliate the horrid Murders committed by these Insurgents. I have heard him in this House, express himself with genuine Warmth and Indignation against them. I have heard him denominate these first of Crimes by their proper names—I have heard him paint them in their strongest Colours. But he seems now afraid to call them *Crimes,* and adopts the soft and palliating Term, *"Folly," "of their Errors,"* and the Conduct of the House as unbecoming, in calling them "armed Mobs," which he represents as "painting them in the strongest Colours." He wou'd persuade us to believe "they have renounced all Thoughts of such wild Attempts for the future."

IS it not astonishing, that a Gentleman, who so lately could paint these Offences in the most aggravated Light, should now soften them into nothing more than an Act of Folly: And should charge this House with Indecency, in describing with so much Moderation, a Set of Villains, who in Defiance of the Laws, the Magistracy, the Government, and Heaven itself, had murdered a Number of innocent Men, Women, and Children, in cool Blood: Who exulting and glorying in the Act—attempted to add to their Crime, by resolving to massacre a Hundred and fifty more, together with some of the best Men in the Government; For such was their Design, if we may rely on their own Declarations, and Threats. What Wind has occasioned this sudden tack in the Gentleman's Conduct, I shall not precisely determine. Thus much I will add, That it must be some erroneous Policy, not Reason or Virtue; for Murders of the highest Rank cannot be palliated on either of those Principles.

THE first Riot in this Province, that I can recollect, was spirited up by the Tools of Power, to destroy the Freedom of Elections; the second by the same Persons, to intimidate the House of Representatives into the arbitrary Measures of the Government; the third to murder and destroy innocent People, his Majesty's Allies, on their Settlements, under the Protection of the Government; the fourth, still more aggravated, to murder, in cool Blood, Men, Women, and Children, under the immediate Care of the Magistracy, and in their Presence; and the fifth still more heinous and aggravated than all the others, to murder a Number of People under the immediate Eye of the Governor, and the Protection of his Majesty's Troops; nor were the Members of Government itself to have been free from the horrid Massacre, had not these Insurgents been stopped in their Career; not by any Power in the Government, for that was ineffectual, but by the King's Troops, and the voluntary Aid of the Citizens of Philadelphia. Let us take a serious View of these Facts, and then determine what Reason we have to expect these dangerous Tumults are at an End. Are not the Murderers still ranging the Country with Impunity? Has the Government made the least Enquiry after the Criminals; lifted a Finger, or given an Order for their Punishment, tho' requested to do it by this House; and are not these Things the most evident Proofs of our Insecurity, and of the greatest Disrespect to a Proprietary Government, and that it has not either Power sufficient, or Inclination, to afford Protection to his Majesty's Subjects.

BUT, Sir, the Gentleman would persuade us to believe he is well acquainted with their Conduct, their Penitence, and their future Designs, and that they, by some uncommon Attonement, have wiped away the Guilt of their heinous Offences, and never intend to commit them more.

WHAT Communication the Gentleman has with them, or what private Intelligence he has received of their Penitence, are yet unknown, as he has not communicated them. But Riots and Murders, Sir, when once begun, encouraged and supported by such Numbers as these have been, seldom cease, till the Offenders are punished, or their Designs succeed: But like the raging Flame, once kindled, will consume all before them, unless extinguished by some superior Force. And the daily Threats of these lawless People, with the infamous Pamphlets continually published, to justify and encourage them, do not demonstrate the least Intention in them to alter their Conduct, or the least Wish in their wicked Abettors, that they should do so.

"BUT (he says) that we shall furnish a Reason for settling a Military establishment upon us, etc. by thus representing the Government in Confusion. A Military Establishment is already, and will be more effectually established in the Colonies. This seems the determined unalterable Resolution of a *British* Parliament. Nothing less will ever secure them Protection in their present disunited State. There is no Alternative between this Measure and a general Union, to insure us Protection against the foreign Invader. Such an Union has been already rejected, and such an one we shall now never enjoy; Our Superiors think it convenient to keep us in another State; and therefore we shall undoubtedly have this Measure, which has struck the Gentleman with so much Terror and Pannick, established, whether the Government is changed or not. The Question then arises, whether we had rather have a Military Establishment in a Government under the Crown or the Proprietaries— Impartial Reason, free from Proprietary Attachment, will soon determine. The Crown has no private Interest to promote; the public Good will be its great Object, and therefore will never make use of it to our Disadvantage. All the Inconveniency we shall suffer by being immediately under the Crown, will be a proportionable Part of the Aids to support the Troops. But the Proprietaries have great private Interest; an Idol to which they have been long sacrificing the public Weal, without Fear or Remorse. They will undoubtedly then endeavour to make use of the Military Men to serve that Interest, to dragoon the People into their Measures; the Measures of Slavery and Oppression. Experience hath already convinced us of this Truth; the Conduct of the Government in the beginning of the late War, sufficiently proves it. Should the Military Power, in a Government under the Crown, misbehave, we should, upon complaint, be redressed. No Person of Influence there, would find it their Interest to interfere in Support of them, contrary to the Rights of the People. But if such a Power is made subservient to Proprietary Measures, will not the Principals in those Measures support that Power; and will not that Support ever prevent our obtaining Relief? Hence, Sir, it is clear, since we must have a military Power established in *America;* nay, since it is done already, it will be infinitely less mischievous to us, less fatal to our Liberties to become the immediate Subjects of his Majesty, than to remain under our present Government.

THE Gentleman asserts, that "With unremitting Vigilance and undaunted Virtue, should a free People watch against the Encroachments of Power," (meaning the Power of the Crown.) I agree, Sir, we ought to guard against the Encroachments of all Kind of Power. The Power of the Proprietaries, as well as of the Crown. The Extent of the latter we know; the Royal Government shews its Limits; they are known and confined; and rare it is, that any Attempts are made to extend them. But where Proprietary Power will terminate, where its Limits will be fixt, and its Encroachments end, is uncertain. It has already been extended to a most dangerous Length, and our Liberties are daily consuming before it. And, Sir,

I am fully persuaded, was the Gentleman a Friend to the Liberties of *Pennsylvania*, he would, with equal Zeal, have recommended this Vigilance and Virtue, to watch against, and remove the illegal Usurpations of Proprietary Tyranny.

PERMIT me, Sir, to answer a few Questions the Gentleman has put, by seriously asking him a few other. "Have we not (says he) sufficiently felt the Effects of Royal Resentment?" Royal Resentment, Sir, indecently described by the Gentleman in such aggravated Colours, has been dispensed with Royal Moderation. But why do much Rancour against the Royal Conduct? And why so tender of Proprietary Misrepresentations, Proprietary Hatred and Ill-will against the good People of this Province, the true Causes of the Royal Displeasure? Here, Sir, if Justice took Place, would the Shafts and Darts of the Gentleman be pointed. Here it would be just. But let me ask, what ill Effects have flowed from the Royal Resentment? What Liberties has it deprived us of? What Privileges has it destroyed? None. But, Sir, have we not felt the Iron Rod of Proprietary Instructions, and Proprietary private Interest, wounding and destroying the most essential Rights a People can enjoy?

"IS not the Authority of the Crown fully enough exerted over us?" I have seen no undue Exertions of the Royal Authority in this Province. But has not the private Authority of the Proprietaries, been so exerted, that the People have often wanted Protection, and Thousands been sacrificed to their Arbitrary Usurpation? If Sir, the Gentleman was truly concerned for the Welfare of his Country, would he not be more concerned to remove the arbitrary Attempts of Proprietary Interest, instead of abusing the Authority of Royalty? From whence, tho' we have received a fatherly Reproof, we have received no Injury—He certainly wou'd.

TO conclude, Sir, I have not heard one solid Argument drop from the Gentleman, to alter my Opinion. Nor do I believe his Eloquence has changed the Sentiments of one Member in the House. We are too well acquainted with the Facility, and Security to our Privileges, with which this Measure may be carried into Execution. And therefore we have too great a Regard for our Country to lay it aside. It has been often mentioned in this House, and sufficient Documents to prove it, have been laid on the Table, That Mr. PENN, the first Proprietor, conscious that the Powers of Government could not be always retained in his Family, actually made a Contract with the Crown, to resign them for a Sum of Money, of which he received Part. That this Contract still subsists in full force. That by this Contract, the equitable Right is, beyond Controversy, in the Crown. And that his Majesty may readily obtain the legal Right, upon paying the Residue of the Money, by a Suit in Chancery, should the present Proprietaries have the Presumption in so plain a Case, to enter into a Contest with the King about it. Besides, Sir, I have seen the Opinion of some very great Men, his Majesty's Servants, and often near his Person, That the Powers of Government is an Interest that cannot be transfer'red or alien'd. If this Opinion be a good one, as I am clear it is, the Right of Government cannot be in our Present proprietaries, but in the elder Branch of their Family. And further, It is certain, that the Proprietaries stand indebted to the Crown for one Moiety of the rents, Issues, and Profits of the lower three Counties, Ordinary and Extraordinary, every since the Year 1682, which, upon a moderate Calculation, must amount to fifty Thousand Pounds, Sterling, clear of all Expences and Deductions. Under these Circumstances, will it not be the highest Presumption in the Proprietaries, to oppose the Royal Resumption of the Nomination of the Governor of this Province. These are the Weapons which I am confident will be used for the Restoration of our Liberties, and for saving his Majesty's faithful Subjects in this Province, from that Thraldom and Bondage, which Proprietary Instructions, and private Interest have imposed upon them.

WITH great Propriety, a Political Body has often been compared to a human Constitution. Let us suppose then, That a human Constitution is attacked by a violent Disease, the Effect whereof has nearly destroyed the Powers of Life, and vital Motion, and Nature is no longer capable of struggling for Relief. Is not this the Time to apply the Remedy? and would any but a Quack, wait in Hopes of some lucky Crisis, until the Disorder grew too powerful for Nature and Medicine? The Powers of Legislature truly resemble the Soul which animates and directs the Conduct and Behavior of the political Institution. An upright Administration of Justice resembles the active Blood, which, by its pure and uninterrupted Course, preserves and supports its Health and Vigor. In these two vital Parts, with many others, the Fever of Ambition and arbitrary Power is, and has been continually raging with unremitting Violence. The Powers of Legislation are so check'd and controlled, that they are almost annihilated—The Courts of Judicature are so dependant on Proprietary Influence, that wherever Proprietary Interest is in Question, the Stream of Justice becomes so turbid and thick, that it can no longer discharge its Duty, Security of Life and Estate is become an empty Name, and the Spirit of Liberty distrest and worn out, by ineffectual Efforts for her Preservation, is verging fast to a Dissolution. Nothing but a Royal Medicine expeditiously administered, can possible revive or restore her. And if such a Medicine can be obtained, shall we not even attempt to obtain it, before the midnight Gloom approaches, and fatal Death puts an End to our Struggles? This, Sir, is not an Aggravation of our Circumstances; it is the true and unfortunate State of *Pennsylvania*.

SPEECH

to the Council and House of Representatives

Sir Francis Bernard

Francis Bernard was born in July, 1712. He became a scholar of St. Peter's College in 1725 and then entered Christ's Church, Oxford. In 1733 he became a member of the Middle Temple, was called to the bar in 1737, and settled at Lincoln as a provincial counsel. In 1740, he was made a commissioner.

Bernard was appointed governor of New Jersey in 1758, largely through the influence of his wife's cousin, the second Lord Barrington. In 1760, he was transferred to the governorship of Massachusetts where he built an early reputation for promoting colonial solidarity and establishing the colony's defenses in the French and Indian War.

The necessity of his enforcing the Stamp Act and other laws and regulations repugnant to many influential New Englanders led to a rapid decline in his popularity. Eventually a rebellious assembly dispatched charges against him to England, causing his removal in 1769.

Despite his varied talents and interests, Bernard never regained his early status. In 1774, he resigned the post of commissioner of customs for Ireland after a short tenure. On June 16, 1779, he died at Aylesbury.

The "Speech to the Council and House of Representatives" of Massachusetts was delivered on November 8, 1765. The text is from *Speeches of the Governors of Massachusetts, from 1765 to 1775* . . . . Boston: Russell and Gardner, 1818, pp. 56–59.

Gentlemen of the Council, and Gentlemen of the House of Representatives,

I was so determined to let the business of this part of the session pass on without any interruption from me, that I have postponed doing myself justice in a matter in which I think I have been much injured. But as it has not been my intention to pass it over in silence, and therefore seem to admit the justice of the charge, I take this opportunity to make the following expostulation.

Gentlemen of the House of Representatives,

Your answer to my speech is conceived in terms so different from what you have been used to address me with, that I know not how to account for it, but from the disordered state of the province, which affects its very councils. I shall therefore avoid

227

reasoning upon the unfair arguments and groundless insinuations which have been made use of to misrepresent me. Time and their own insufficiency will effectually confute them. Time will make you, gentlemen, sensible how much you were deceived when you were prevailed upon to give a sanction to so injurious a treatment of me.

What have I done to deserve this? I have happened to be the Governor of this province at a time when the Parliament has thought proper to enact a taxation of the colonies. It is not pretended that I have promoted this tax; nor can it with any truth be pretended that I have had it in my power to have opposed it by any means whatsoever. However, when the act was passed it brought upon me a necessary duty, which, it seems, did not coincide with the opinions of the people. This is my offence; but it is really the offence of my office; and against that, you should have expressed your resentment, and not against my person. If I could have dispensed with my duty, perhaps I might have pleased you; but then I must have condemned myself, and been condemned by my Royal Master. I cannot purchase your favor at so dear a rate.

I will however own, if it will please you, that I acted with more zeal for you, than prudence towards myself: I have thought it your duty to submit to this act until you could get it repealed; I have thought that a submission to it would be the readiest means to obtain a repeal; I have thought that a disobedience of it would be productive of more hurt to you than a submission to it; I have urged these things earnestly, because I thought them of great importance to you; but still I have acted with a regard to truth and with an upright intention. I may be mistaken in my apprehension of this matter; but the time is yet to come when it shall appear that I am so. If it should be so, as I heartily wish it may, an error of judgment, with a good will and fair meaning, does not deserve a severe reprehension; much less does it deserve it before it really appears to be an error.

You seem to be displeased with my making the opposition to the execution of the act of Parliament a business of the provincial legislature. But gentlemen, you should consider that it was in pursuance of the unanimous advice of a very full Council that I called you together for this very purpose. It was necessary for me to explain the cause of your meeting; and I could not avoid being explicit upon the subject, consistent with my sense of duty. I should have thought myself very inexcusable if I had foreseen danger to the province like to arise from the behavior of the people and not have warned you against them; but I could not be so indifferent about the welfare of this government. I have therefore acquitted myself; I have delivered my own soul; and you will remember, that, if any consequences disagreeable to you shall happen, I have not been wanting in guarding you against them. If there shall be none such, so much the better; I shall be well pleased to find myself mistaken.

To justify your unkind treatment of me, you charge me with unkindness towards the province. This is no uncommon practice; but let us see in the present case how it is founded. You intimate that if I had had the love and concern for the people which I profess, I should have expressed my sentiments of the act early enough to those whose influence brought it into being. But from whence do you learn that I have had any opportunity to express such sentiments? Do you imagine that I take the liberty of obtruding my advice to his Majesty's ministers unasked and unexpected, and in a business belonging to a department with which I have not the honor to correspond? I have never neglected any opportunity to serve the province in those offices to which I have a right to apply, and have taken as great liberty in so doing as perhaps any Governor whatsoever; but in this business I have had no pretence to interpose; nor do I believe any Governor in America has presumed to express his sentiments against the act in question.

You charge me with casting a reflection on the loyalty of the province, by wresting my words to a meaning which it is not easy to conceive how they could be thought to bear. No one, gentlemen, has been louder in proclaiming the loyalty of this province than I myself have. I have boasted of it; I have prided myself in it; and I trust the time will come when I shall do so again; for I hope the estimate of this people will not be formed from a review of the present times, which, in my opinion, have been made much more difficult than they need have been. But this fermentation must subside, though it is not easy to say when, or in what manner; and the province will be restored to its former peace and reputation.

If I wanted to apologize for my general conduct in this government, I need only to apply to your registers, where I shall find frequent instances of the approbation of my administration. And, so far as an upright intention, and a diligent exercise of my abilities will go, I have deserved them. It is not much above a year since you thought proper, by a special request, to desire me to be your advocate for particular purposes. If I was at liberty to make public my execution of that commission, I should make those blush who would persuade you that I am not a real friend to the interests, and especially to the trade of this people. Nothing is better understood at home than my attachment to this province. The public offices, where my letters are filed, are full of proofs of it; and there is not a minister of state, whom I have had the honor to correspond with, who does not know I am far from being unfriendly to the province, or indifferent to its interests.

But, gentlemen, you will make me cautious how I force my

services upon you. Not that I intend to desert the cause of the province; I shall still serve it by all means in my power. And really, gentlemen, if you will permit me to give you one piece of advice more, you may possibly stand in such need of advocates as to make it not prudent for you to cast off any of your natural and professed friends: for such I am, and shall always be, in wishes and private offices, whether you will allow me to appear publicly in that character or not. The pains which are taken to disunite the General Court, must have bad consequences, more or less; but they shall not prevent me pursuing such measures as I shall think most conducive to the general welfare of the province.

BOSTON MASSACRE ORATION

James Lovell

James Lovell, son of John Lovell, principal of the Boston Latin school, was the first orator to be chosen from among the citizens of Boston to commemorate the massacre which had occurred on March 5, 1770.

Born on October 31, 1737, James Lovell was graduated from Harvard College in 1756. He became an usher in the Latin school of which his father was principal, and taught there until the beginning of the war. An ardent supporter of the Revolution, Lovell was suspected by the British of being a "Rebel spy" and was imprisoned in Boston and later sent to Halifax where he became a fellow prisoner of Colonel Ethan Allen.

On his release from prison and his return to Boston, he was elected to the Continental Congress. In later years he became the collector for the port of Boston. He died on July 14, 1814.

On Tuesday, March 12, 1771, the Selectmen of the Town of Boston appointed a committee which included John Hancock, Dr. Joseph Warren, and Dr. Benjamin Church to take under consideration the Article, "Whether the Town will determine upon some suitable Method to perpetuate the memory of the horrid Massacre perpetrated on the Evening of the 5. of March 1776—by a Party of Soldiers of the 29. Regiment." A week later the committee duly reported its recommendation, "that for the present the Town make choice of a proper Person to deliver an Oration at such Time as may be Judged most convenient." James Lovell was unanimously elected and a Committee was appointed to wait upon him and acquaint him with the fact that the Town had chosen him to deliver such an oration in Faneuil Hall on Thursday, April 2 at 10 o'clock in the morning. At that time, however, it was found necessary to adjourn to the Old South Church because the Hall was not large enough to accommodate the crowd. Here, after a prayer by the Rev. Dr. Chauncey, James Lovell delivered the first Boston Massacre oration.

The text of the oration is taken from the edition printed by Edes and Gill in Boston, 1771.

YOUR design in the appointment of this ceremony, *my Friends, and Fellow-Townsmen,* cannot fail to be examined in quite different lights at this season of political dissention. From the principles I profess, and in the exercise of my common right to judge with others, I conclude it was *decent, wise, and honorable.*

The certainty of being favoured with your kindest partiality

231

and candor, in a poor attempt to execute the part to which you have invited me, has overcome the objection of my inability to perform it in a proper manner; and I now beg the favor of your animating countenance.

The horrid bloody scene we here commemorate, whatever were the causes which concurred to bring it on that dreadful night, must lead the pious and humane of every order to some suitable reflections. The pious will adore the conduct of that BEING who is unsearchable in all his ways, and without whose knowledge not a single sparrow falls, in permitting an immortal soul to be hurried by the flying ball, the messenger of death, in the twinkling of an eye, to meet the awful Judge of all it's secret actions. The humane, from having often thought with pleasing rapture on the endearing scenes of social life, in all it's amiable relations, will lament with heart-felt pangs their sudden dissolution by the indiscretion, rage, and vengeance of unruly human passions.

But, let us leave that shocking close of one continued course of rancor and dispute from the first moment that the troops arrived in town: that course will now be represented by your own reflexions to much more solid, useful purpose than by any artful language. I hope, however, that Heaven has yet in store such happiness, for this afflicted town and province, as will in time wear out the memory of all our former troubles.

I sincerely rejoice with you in the happy event of your steady and united effort to prevent a second tragedy.

Our fathers left their native land, risqued all the dangers of the sea, and came to this then-savage desert, with that true undaunted courage which is excited by a confidence in GOD. They came that they might here enjoy themselves, and leave to their posterity the best of earthly portions, full *English Liberty*. You showed upon the alarming call for tryal that their brave spirit still exists in vigor, tho' their legacy of rights is much impaired. The sympathy and active friendship of some neighboring towns upon that sad occasion commands the highest gratitude of this.

We have seen and felt the ill effects of placing standing forces in the midst of *populous* communities; but those are only what individuals suffer. Your vote directs me to point out the fatal tendency of placing such an order in *free* cities—fatal indeed! *Athens* once was free; a citizen, a favorite of the people, by an artful story gained a trifling guard of fifty men; ambition taught him ways to enlarge that number; he destroyed the commonwealth and made himself the tyrant of the *Athenians*. *Caesar* by the length of his command in *Gaul* got the affections of his army, marched to *Rome,* overthrew the state, and made himself perpetual dictator. By the same instruments, many less republics have been made to fall a prey to the devouring jaws of tyrants—But, this is a subject which should never be disguised with figures; it chuses the plain stile of dissertation.

The true strength and safety of every commonwealth or limited monarchy, is the bravery of its freeholders, its militia. By brave militias they rise to grandeur, and they come to ruin by a mercenary army. This is founded on historical facts; and the same causes will, in similar circumstances, forever produce the same effects. Justice *Blackstone,* in his inimitable clear commentaries, tells us, that "it is extremely dangerous in a land of liberty, to make a distinct order of the profession of arms; that such an order is an object of jealousy; and that *the laws and constitution of England are strangers to it.*" One article of the Bill of Rights is, that the raising or keeping a standing army within the kingdom in a time of peace, unless it be with consent of parliament, is against law. The present army there-fore, tho' called the peace *establishment,* is kept up by one act, and governed by another; both of which expire *annually.* This circum-stance is valued as a sufficient *check* upon the army. A less body of troops than is now maintained has, on a time, destroyed a King, and fought under a parliament with great success and glory; but, upon a motion to disband them, they turned their masters out of doors, and fixed up others in their stead. Such wild things are not again to happen, because the parliament have power to stop pay-ment once a year: but, *arma tenenti quis neget?* which may be easily interpreted, "who will bind *Sampson* with his locks on?"

The bill which regulates the army, the same fine author I have mentioned says, "is *in many respects hastily penned,* and reduces the soldier to a state of slavery in the midst of a free nation. This is impolitick: for slaves envy the freedom of others, and take a malicious pleasure in contributing to destroy it."

By this scandalous bill a justice of peace is empowered to grant, *without a previous oath* from the military officer, a warrant to break open any (freeman's) house, upon *pretence* of searching for deserters.

I must not omit to mention one more bad tendency: 'tis this—a standing force leads to a total neglect of militias, or tends greatly to discourage them.

You see the danger of a standing army to the cause of freedom. If the *British* Parliament consents from year to year to be exposed, it doubtless has good reasons. But when did *our* assembly pass an act to hazard all the property, the liberty and lives of their con-stituents? What check have we upon a *British* army? Can *we* dis-band it? Can *we* stop it's pay?

Our own assemblies in *America* can raise an army; and *our* Monarch, George the 3d. by our constitution takes immediate com-mand. This army can *consent* to leave their native provinces. Will the royal chief commander send them to find barracks at *Brunswick*

or *Lunenberg,* at *Hanover,* or *the commodious hall of Westminster?*
Suppose the last—Suppose this army was informed, nay *thought* the
parliament in actual rebellion, or only on the *eve* of one against
their King, or against *those who paid and cloathed them*—for there
it pinches:—We are *rebels against parliament*—we adore the King.

Where, in the case I have stated, would be the value of the
boasted *English* Constitution?

Who are a *free* people? Not those who do not suffer actual
oppression; but those who have a *constitutional check upon the
power* to oppress.

We are slaves or freemen; if, as we are called, the last, where
is our check upon the following powers, *France, Spain,* the *States
of Holland,* or *the British Parliament?* Now if any one of these
(and it is quite immaterial which) has right to make the two acts
in question operate within this province, they have right to give us
up to an unlimited army, under the sole direction of one *Saracen*
Commander.

Thus I have led your thoughts to *that* upon which I formed
my conclusion, that the design of this ceremony was *decent, wise,*
and *honorable.* Make the bloody 5th of *March* the Era of the resurrection of your birthrights, which have been murdered by the
very strength that nursed them in their infancy. I had an eye solely
to parliamentary supremacy; and I hope you will think every other
view beneath your notice in our present most alarming situation.

Chatham, Cambden and others, gods among men, and the
Farmer, whom you have addressed as the friend of *Americans,* and
the common benefactor of mankind; all these have owned that
England has right to exercise every power over us, but that of taking
money out of our pockets without our consent. Tho' it seems almost
too bold therefore in us to say "we doubt in every single instance
her *legal* right over this province" yet *we must assert it.* Those I
have named are mighty characters, but *they* wanted one advantage
providence has given *us.* The *beam* is carried off from our eyes
by the flowing blood of our fellow citizens, and now we may be
allowed to attempt to remove the *mote* from the eyes of our exalted
patrons. That more, we think, is nothing but *our obligation to England first, and afterwards Great Britain, for constant kind protection of our lives and birthrights against foreign danger.* We all
acknowledge that protection.

Let us once more look into the early history of this province.
We find that our *English* Ancestors disgusted in their native country
at a *Legislation,* which they saw was sacrificing all their rights,
left its Jurisdiction, and sought, like wandering birds of passage,
some happier climate. Here at length they settled down. The King
of *England* was said to be the royal landlord of this territory; with
Him they entered into mutual sacred compact, by which the price

of tenure and the rules of management were fairly stated. It is in this compact that we find OUR ONLY TRUE LEGISLATIVE AUTHORITY.

I might here enlarge upon the character of those first settlers, men of whom the world was little worthy; who, for a long course of years, assisted by no earthly power, defended their liberty, their religion and their lives against the greatest inland danger from the savage natives—but this falls not within my present purpose. They were secure by sea.

In our infancy, when not an over-tempting jewel for the *Bourbon* Crown the very *name* of ENGLAND saved us; afterwards her *fleets and armies*. We wish not to depreciate the worth of that protection. Of our gold, yea of our most fine gold, we will freely *give* a part. Our fathers would have done the same. But, must we fall down and cry "let not a stranger rob and kill me, O my father! let me rather dye by the hand of my brother, and let him *ravish* all my portions?"

It is said that disunited from *Britain* "we should bleed at every vein." I cannot see the consequence. The *States of Holland* do not suffer thus. But grant it true, SENACA, would prefer the LAUN-CETS of *France, Spain* or any other power to the BOW-STRING, tho' applied by the fair hand of *Britannia*.

The declarative vote of the *British Parliament* is the death-warrant of *our* birthrights, and wants only a Czarith King to put it into execution. Here then a door of salvation is open. *Great Britain* may raise *her* fleets and armies, but it is only *our own* King that can direct their fire down upon our heads. He is gracious, but not omniscient. He is ready to hear our APPEALS in their proper course; and knowing himself, tho' the most powerful prince on earth, yet, a subject under a divine constitution of LAW, that law he *will* ask and receive from the twelve Judges of England. These will prove that the claim of the *British Parliament* over *us* is not only ILLEGAL IN ITSELF, but a DOWN-RIGHT USURPATION OF HIS PREROGATIVE as KING OF *America*.

A brave nation is always generous. Let us appeal therefore, at the same time, to the generosity of the PEOPLE of *Great-Britain,* before the tribunal of Europe, not to envy us the full enjoyment of the RIGHTS OF BRETHREN.

And now, *my Friends and Fellow Townsmen,* having declared myself an *American* Son of Liberty of true charter-principles; having shewn the critical and dangerous situation of our birthrights, and the true course for speedy redress; I shall take the freedom to recommend with boldness one previous step. Let us show we understand the true value of what we are claiming.

The patriot *Farmer* tells us, "the cause of LIBERTY is a cause of too much dignity to be sullied by turbulence and tumult. Anger produces anger; and differences, that might be accommodated by kind and respectful behaviour, may by imprudence be enlarged to an incurable rage. In quarrels—risen to a certain height, the first cause of dissention is no longer remembered, the minds of the parties being wholly engaged in recollecting and resenting the mutual expressions of their dislike. When feuds have reached that fatal point, considerations of reason and equity vanish; and a blind fury governs, or rather confounds all things. A People no longer regard their interest, but a gratification of their wrath."

We know ourselves subjects of common LAW; to *that* and the worthy *executors* of it let us pay a steady and conscientious regard. Past errors in this point have been written with gall by the pen of MALICE. May our future conduct be such as to make even that vile IMP lay her pen aside.

The *Right* which imposes *Duties* upon us is in dispute; but whether they are managed by a *Surveyor General, a Board of Commissioners, Turkish Janizaries* or *Russian Cossacks,* let them enjoy, during our time of fair tryal, the common personal protection of the laws of our constitution. Let us shut our eyes, for the present, to their being *executors of claims subversive of our rights.*

Watchful hawkeyed JEALOUSY ever guards the portal of the temple of the GODDESS LIBERTY. This is known to those who frequent her altars. Our whole conduct therefore. I am sure, will meet with the utmost candor of her VOTARIES: but I am wishing we may be able to convert even her basest APOSTATES.

We are SLAVES 'till we obtain such *redress* thro' the justice of our King as our happy *constitution leads us to expect.* In that condition, let us behave with the propriety and dignity of FREEMEN; and *thus* exhibit to the world a new character of a people which no history describes.

May the allwise and beneficent RULER OF THE UNIVERSE preserve our *lives* and *health,* and prosper all our lawful *endeavours in the glorious cause of* FREEDOM.

BOSTON MASSACRE ORATION

Joseph Warren

Joseph Warren was born at Roxbury, Massachusetts, on June 11, 1741. Prepared at the school at Roxbury, he entered Harvard College at the age of 14. After graduation in 1759, he was appointed master of the Roxbury Grammar School, where he taught one year. Deciding to become a physician, he studied under Dr. James Lloyd and then established a medical practice in Boston. He soon became deeply interested in politics, making speeches at Fanueil Hall and contributing to the press.

In 1772, he delivered the Boston Massacre Commemoration Address. He continued to be a member of the important committees of Boston, and on March 6, 1775, he made a second Boston Massacre Oration. As the war approached he entered the army. On May 31, 1775, he was chosen president pro tempore of the Provincial Congress. On June 14, the Provincial Congress elected him a major general. Three days later, even before he had received his commission, he was killed at the Battle of Bunker Hill.

John Adams was asked to give the Boston Massacre Oration in 1772. When he declined, Joseph Warren agreed to make the address. It was delivered in Old South Church on March 5. In his *History of the Colony of Massachusetts-Bay,* Hutchinson remarks: "Though he gained no great applause for his oratorical abilities, yet the fervor, which is the most essential part of such compositions, could not fail of its effect upon the minds of the great concourse of people present." The text of the speech is from the Edes and Gill edition, Boston, 1772.

When Dr. Warren delivered his second Boston Massacre oration in the Old South Meetinghouse on March 5, 1775, the pulpit stairs and the pulpit itself were occupied by officers and soldiers of the garrison. Warren entered the rear of the church by the pulpit window. Although it was thought that the soldiers might be there to prevent the meeting from proceeding, the oration was delivered.

The text of the oration is from the edition printed in Newport, Rhode Island by S. Southwick, 1775.

I

WHEN we turn over the historic page, and trace the rise and fall of states and empires; the mighty revolutions which have so often varied the face of the world strike our minds with solemn surprize, and we are naturally led to endeavor to search out the causes of such astonishing changes.

THAT Man is formed for *social life,* is an observation which upon our first enquiry presents itself immediately to our view, and our reason approves that wise and generous principle which actuated the first founders of civil government; an institution which hath its origin in the *weakness* of individuals, and hath for its end, the *strength and security* of all; And so long as the means of effecting this important end, are thoroughly known and religiously attended to, Government is one of the richest Blessings to mankind, and ought to be held in the highest veneration.

IN young and new-formed communities, the grand design of this institution is most generally understood, and the most strictly regarded; the motives which urged to the social compact cannot be at once forgotten, and *that* equality which is remembered to have subsisted so lately among them, prevents those who are clothed with authority from attempting to invade the freedom of their Brethren; or if such an attempt be made, it prevents the community from suffering the offender to go unpunished: Every member feels it to be his interest, and knows it to be his duty, to preserve inviolate the constitution on which the public safety depends, and is equally ready to assist the Magistrate in the execution of the laws, and the *subject* in defence of his right; and so long as this noble attachment to a constitution, founded on free and benevolent principles exist in full vigor in any state, *that* state must be flourishing and happy.

IT was *this* noble attachment to a free Constitution, which raised ancient Rome from the smallest beginnings to that bright summit of happiness and glory to which she arrived; and it was the loss of *this* which plunged her from *that* summit into the black gulph of infamy and slavery. It was *this* attachment which inspired her senators with wisdom; it was *this* which glowed in the breasts of her heroes; it was *this* which guarded her liberties, and extended her dominions, gave peace at home and commanded respect abroad: And when *this* decayed, her magistrates lost their reverence for justice and the laws, and degenerated into tyrants and oppressors —her senators forgetful of their dignity, and seduced by base corruption, betrayed their country—her soldiers, regardless of their relation to the community, and urged *only* by the hopes of plunder and rapine, unfeelingly committed the most flagrant enormities; and hired to the trade of death, with relentless fury they perpetrated the most cruel murders, whereby the streets of imperial Rome were drenched with her *nobles* blood—Thus *this empress* of the world lost her dominions abroad, and her inhabitants dissolute in their manners, at length became contented *slaves;* and she stands to this day, the scorn and derision of nations, and a monument of this eternal truth, that PUBLIC HAPPINESS DEPENDS ON A VIRTUOUS

AND UNSHAKEN ATTACHMENT TO A FREE CONSTITUTION.

IT was *this* attachment to a constitution, founded on free and benevolent principles, which inspired the first settlers of this country: They saw with grief the daring outrages committed on the free constitution of their native land—they knew that nothing but a civil war could at that time, restore it's pristine purity. So hard was it to resolve to embrue their hands in the *blood* of their brethren, that they chose rather to quit their fair possessions and seek another habitation in a distant clime—When they came to this new world, which they fairly purchased of the Indian natives, the only rightful proprietors, they cultivated the then barren soil by their incessant labor, and defended their dear-bought possessions with the fortitude of the christian, and the bravery of the hero.

AFTER various struggles, which during the tyrannic reigns of the house of STUART, were constantly kept up between right and wrong, between liberty and slavery, the connection between Great Britain and this Colony was settled in the reign of King William and Queen Mary by a compact, the conditions of which were expressed in a Charter; by which all the liberties and immunities of BRITISH SUBJECTS were confided to this Province, as fully and as absolutely as they possibly could be by any human instrument which can be devised. And it is undeniably true, that the greatest and most important right of a British subject is, that *he shall be governed by no laws but those to which he either in person or by his representative* hath given his consent: And this I will venture to assert, is the grand basis of British freedom; it is interwoven with the constitution; and whenever this is lost, the constitution must be destroyed.

THE *British constitution* (of which ours is a copy) is a happy compound of the three forms (under some of which all governments may be ranged) viz. Monarchy, Aristocracy, and Democracy: Of these three the *British Legislature* is composed, and without the consent of each branch, nothing can carry with it the force of a law: In most cases, either the aristocratic or the democratic branch may prepare a law, and submit it to the deliberation of the other two; but, when a law is to be passed for raising a tax, that law can originate only in the democratic branch, which is the House of Commons in Britain, and the House of Representatives here— The reason is obvious: They, and their constituents are to pay much the largest part of it, but as the aristocratic branch, which in Britain is the House of Lords, and in this province, the Council, are also to pay some part, THEIR consent is necessary; and as the monarchic branch, which in Britain is the King, and with us, either the King in person, or the Governor whom he shall be pleased to appoint in his stead, is supposed to have a just sense of his own *interest,* which is *that* of all the subjects in general, HIS consent is also necessary, and when the consent of these three branches is obtained, the taxation is most certainly legal.

LET us now allow ourselves a few moments to examine the *late acts of the British Parliament for taxing America*—Let us with candor judge whether they are constitutionally binding upon us: If they are, IN THE NAME OF JUSTICE let us submit to them, without one murmuring word.

FIRST, I would ask whether the members of the British House of Commons are the Democracy of this Province? if they are, they are either the people of this province, or are elected by the people of this province, to represent them, and have therefore a constitutional right to originate a Bill for taxing them: It is most certain they are neither; and therefore nothing done by *them* can be said to be done by the democartic branch of our constitution. I would next ask, whether the Lords who compose the aristocratic branch of the British Legislature, are Peers of America? I never heard it was (even in these extraordinary times) so much as pretended, and if they are not, certainly no act of *theirs* can be said to be the act of the aristocratic branch of our constitution. The power of the monarchic branch we with pleasure acknowledge, resides in the King, who may act either in person or by his representative; and I freely confess that I can see no reason why a PROCLAMATION *for raising money in America* issued by the King's sole authority, would not be equally consistent with our constitution, and therefore equally binding upon us with the *late acts of the British Parliament for taxing us*; for it is plain, that if there is any validity in *those acts*, it must arise altogether from the monarchical branch of the legislature: And I further think that it would be at least as equitable: for I do not conceive it to be of the least importance to us by *whom* our property is taken away, so long as it is taken without our consent; and I am very much at a loss to know by what figure of rhetoric, the inhabitants of this province can be called FREE SUBJECTS, when they are obliged to obey implicitly, such laws as are made for them by men three thousand miles off, whom they know not, and whom they never impowered to act for them; or how they can be said to have PROPERTY, when a body of men over whom they have not the least controul, and who are not in any way accountable to them, shall oblige them to deliver up any part, or the whole of their substance, without even asking their consent: And yet, whoever pretends that the late acts of the British parliament for taxing America ought to be deemed binding upon us, must admit at once that we are absolute SLAVES, and have no property of our own; or else that we may be FREE-MEN, and at the same time under the

necessity of obeying the *arbitrary commands of those* over whom we
have no controul or influence; and that we may HAVE PROPERTY
OF OUR OWN, which is entirely at the disposal of another. Such
gross absurdities, I believe will not be relished in this enlightened
age: And it can be no matter of wonder that the people quickly
perceived, and seriously complained of the inroads which these
acts must unavoidably make upon their *liberty,* and of the hazard
to which their *whole property* is by *them* exposed; for, if they may
be taxed without their consent even the smallest trifle, they may
also without their consent be deprived of everything they possess,
although never so valuable, never so dear. Certainly it never entered the hearts of our ancestors, that after so many dangers in
this then desolate wilderness, their hard-earned property should
be at the disposal of the British parliament; and as it was soon
found that this taxation could not be supported by reason and
argument, it seemed necessary that one act of oppression should
be enforced by another, and therefore, contrary to our just rights
as possessing, or at least having a just title to possess, all the
liberties and IMMUNITIES of British subjects, a standing army
was established among us in time of peace; and evidently for the
purpose of effecting *that,* which it was one principal design of the
founders of the constitution to prevent (when they declared a
standing army in a time of peace to be AGAINST LAW) namely,
for the enforcement of obedience to acts which upon fair examination appeared to be unjust and unconstitutional.

THE ruinous consequences of standing armies to free communities may be seen in the histories of SYRACUSE, ROME, and
many other once flourishing STATES; some of which have now
scarce a name! Their baneful influence is most suddenly felt,
when they are placed in populous cities; for, by a corruption of
morals, the public happiness is immediately affected; and that this
is one of the effects of quartering troops in a populous city, is a
truth, to which many a mourning parent, many a lost, despairing
child in this metropolis, must bear a very melancholy testimony.
Soldiers are also taught to consider arms as the only arbiters by
which every dispute is to be decided between contending states;
they are instructed *implicitly* to obey their commanders, without
enquiring into the justice of the cause they are engaged to support:
hence it is, that they are ever to be dreaded as the ready engines
of tyranny and oppression. And it is too observable that they are
prone to introduce the same mode of decision in the disputes of
individuals, from thence have often arisen great animosities between *them* and *the inhabitants,* who whilst in a naked defenseless
state, are frequently insulted and abused by an armed soldiery.
And this will be more especially the case, when the troops are in-

formed, that the intention of their being stationed in any city, is to OVERAWE THE INHABITANTS. That, *this* was the avowed design of stationing an armed force in this town, is sufficiently known; and WE, my fellow-citizens have seen, WE have felt the tragical effects! —THE FATAL FIFTH OF MARCH, 1770, CAN NEVER BE FORGOTTEN —The horrors of THAT DREADFUL NIGHT are but too deeply impressed on our hearts—Language is too feeble to paint the emotions of our souls, when our streets were stained with the BLOOD OF OUR BRETHREN—when our ears were wounded by the groans of the *dying,* and our eyes were tormented with the sight of the mangled bodies of the *dead.* When our alarmed imagination presented to our view our houses wrapt in flames—our children subjected to the barbarous caprice of a raging soldiery—our beauteous virgins exposed to all the insolence of unbridled passion—our virtuous wives, endeared to us by every tender tie, falling a sacrifice to worse than brutal violence, and perhaps like the famed LUCRETIA, distracted with anguish and despair, ending their wretched lives by their own fair hands. When we beheld the authors of our distress parading in our streets, or drawn up in a regular *battalia,* as though in a hostile city; our hearts beat to arms; we snatched our weapons, almost resolved by one decisive stroke, to avenge the death of our SLAUGHTERED BRETHREN, and to secure from future danger, all that we held most dear: But propitious heaven forbade the bloody carnage, and saved the threatened victims of our too keen resentment, not by their discipline, not by their regular array— no, it was royal GEORGE's livery that proved their shield—it was that which turned the pointed engines of destruction from their breasts. The thoughts of vengeance were soon buried in our inbred affection to Great-Britain, and calm reason dictated a method of removing the troops more mild than an immediate resource to the sword. With united efforts you urged the immediate departure of the troops from the town—you urged it, with a resultion which insured success—you obtained your wishes, and the removal of the troops was effected, without one drop of *their blood* being shed by the inhabitants!

THE immediate actors in the tragedy of THAT NIGHT were surrendered to justice. It is not mine to say how far they were guilty! they have been tried by the country and ACQUITTED of murder! And they are not to be again arraigned at an earthly bar: But, surely the men who have promiscuously scattered *death* amidst the *innocent* inhabitants of a populous city, ought to see well to it, that they are prepared to stand at the bar of an OMNISCIENT JUDGE! And all who contrived or encouraged the stationing troops in this place, have reasons of eternal importance, to reflect with deep contrition on their base designs, and humbly to repent of their impious machinations.

THE infatuation which hath seemed for a number of years to prevail in the British councils with regard to us, is truly astonishing! What can be proposed by the repeated attacks made upon our freedom, I really cannot surmise; even leaving justice and humanity owt [sic] of the question, I do not know one single advantage which can arise to the British nation, from our being enslaved: I know not of any gains, which can be wrung from us by oppression, which they may not obtain from us by our own consent, in the smooth channel of commerce: We wish the wealth and prosperity of *Britain;* we contribute largely to both. Doth what we contribute lose all its value, because it is done voluntarily? The amazing increase of riches to *Britain,* the great rise of the value of her lands, the flourishing state of her navy; are striking proofs of the advantages derived to her, from her commerce with the Colonies; and it is our earnest desire that she may still continue to enjoy the same emoluments, until her streets are paved with AMERICAN GOLD; only, let us have the pleasure of calling it our own, whilst it is in our hands; but this it seems is too great a favor—we are to be governed by the *absolute commands of others, our property is to be taken away without our consent*—if we complain, our complaints are treated with contempt; if we assert our rights, that assertion is deemed insolence; if we humbly offer to submit the matter to the impartial decision of reason, the SWORD is judged the most proper argument to silence our murmurs! But this cannot long be the case—surely, the *British* nation will not suffer the reputation of their justice, and their honor to be thus sported away by a *capricious ministry;* no, they will in a short time open their eyes to their true interest: They nourish in their own breasts a noble love of Liberty, they hold her dear, and they know that all who have once possessed her charms had rather die than suffer her to be torn from their embraces—They are also sensible that Britain is so deeply interested in the prosperity of the Colonies, that she must eventually feel every wound given to their freedom; they cannot be ignorant that more dependence may be placed on the affections of a BROTHER, than on the forced services of a SLAVE—They must approve your efforts for the preservation of your rights; from a sympathy of soul they must pray for success: And I doubt not but they will e'er long exert themselves effectually to redress your grievances. Even in the dissolute reign of CHARLES II. when the house of *Commons* impeached the Earl of Clarendon of high treason, the first article on which they founded their accusation was, that *"he had designed a standing army to be raised, and to govern the kingdom thereby."* And the eighth article was, that *"he had introduced an arbitrary government into his Majesty's plantations."* A terrifying example, to those who are now forging *chains* for this COUNTRY!

YOU have my friends and countrymen, frustrated the designs of your enemies, by your unanimity and fortitude: It was your union and determined spirit which expelled those troops, who polluted your streets with INNOCENT BLOOD. You have appointed this anniversary as a standard memorial of the BLOODY CONSEQUENCES OF PLACING AN ARMED FORCE IN A POPULOUS CITY, and of your deliverance from the dangers which then seemed to hang over our heads; and I am confident that you never will betray the least want of spirit when called upon to guard your freedom. None but they who set a just value upon the blessings of liberty are worthy to enjoy her—your illustratious fathers were her zealous votaries—when the blasting frowns of tyranny drove her from public view, they clasped her in their arms, they cherished her in their generous bosoms, they brought her safe over the rough ocean, and fixed her seat in this then dreary wilderness; they nursed her infant age with the most tender care; for her sake, they patiently bore the severest hardships; for her support, they underwent the most rugged toils: In her defence, they boldly encountered the most alarming dangers; neither the ravenous beast that ranged the woods for prey; nor the more furious savages of the wilderness; could damp their ardor! Whilst with one hand, they broke the stubborn glebe; with the other, they grasped their weapons, ever ready to protect her from danger. No sacrifice, not even their own blood, was esteemed too rich a libation for her altar! God prospered their valour, they preserved her brilliancy unsullied, they enjoyed her whilst they lived, and dying, bequeathed the dear inheritance, to your care. And as they left you this glorious legacy, they have undoubtedly transmitted to you some portion of their noble spirit, to inspire you with virtue to merit her, and courage to preserve her; you surely cannot, with such examples before your eyes, as every page of the history of this country affords, suffer your liberties to be ravished from you by lawless force, or cajoled away by flattery and fraud.

THE voice of your Fathers blood cries to you from the ground; MY SONS, SCORN TO BE SLAVES! In vain we met the frowns of tyrants—In vain we left our native land—In vain, we crossed the boisterous ocean, found a new world, and prepared it for the happy residence of LIBERTY—In vain, we toiled—In vain, we fought—We bled in vain, if you, our offspring, want valour to repel the assaults of her invaders! Stain not the glory of your worthy ancestors, but like them resolve, never to part with your birth-right; be wise in your deliberations, and determined in your exertions for the preservation of your liberties. Follow not the dictates of passion, but enlist yourselves under the sacred banner of reason: Use every method in your power to secure your rights:

At least prevent the curses of posterity from being heaped upon your memories.

IF you with united zeal and fortitude oppose the torrent of oppression; if you feel the true fire of patriotism burning in your breasts; if you from your souls despise the most gaudy dress that slavery can wear; if you really prefer the lonely cottage (whilst blest with liberty) to gilded palaces surrounded with the ensigns of slavery; you may have the fullest assurance that tyranny, with her whole accursed train will hide their hideous heads in confusion, shame, and despair—If you perform your part, you must have the strongest confidence that THE SAME ALMIGTHY BEING who protected your pious and venerable fore-fathers, who enabled them to turn a barren wilderness into a fruitful field, who so often *made bare his arm* for their salvation, will still be mindful of you their offspring.

MAY THIS ALMIGHTY BEING graciously preside in all our councils. May he direct us to such measures as he himself shall approve, and be pleased to bless. May we ever be a people favored of GOD. May our land be a land of Liberty, the seat of virtue, the asylum of the oppressed, *a name and a praise in the whole earth,* until the last shock of time shall bury the empires of the world in one common undistinguished ruin!

II

My Ever-Honored Fellow-Citizens

IT is not without the most humiliating conviction of my want of ability that I now appear before you; but the sense I have of the obligation I am under to obey the calls of my country at all times, together with an animating recollection of your indulgence, exhibited upon so many occasions, has induced me, once more, undeserving as I am, to throw myself upon that candor which looks with kindness on the feeblest efforts of an honest mind.

YOU will not now expect the elegance, the learning, the fire, the enrapturing strains of eloquence, which charmed you when a LOVELL, a CHURCH, or a HANCOCK spake; but you will permit me to say, that with a sincerity equal to theirs I mourn over my bleeding country. With them I weep at her distress, and with them deeply resent the many injuries she has received from the hands of cruel and unreasonable men.

THAT personal freedom is the natural right of every man, and that property, or an exclusive right to dispose of what he has honestly acquired by his own labor, necessarily arises therefrom, are truths which common sense has placed beyond the reach of contradiction. And no man or body of men can, without being guilty of flagrant injustice, claim a right to dispose of the persons or acquisitions of any other man, or body of men, unless it can be proved that such a right has arisen from some compact between the parties, in which it has been explicitly and freely granted.

IF I may be indulged in taking a retrospective view of the first settlement of our country, it will be easy to determine with what degree of justice the late Parliament of Great Britain has assumed the power of giving away *that property,* which the Americans have earned by their labor.

OUR fathers, having nobly resolved never to wear the yoke of despotism, and seeing the European world, at that time, through indolence and cowardice, falling a prey to tyranny, bravely threw themselves upon the bosom of the ocean, determined to find a place in which they might enjoy their freedom, or perish in the glorious attempt. Approving Heaven beheld the favorite ark dancing upon the waves, and graciously preserved it until the chosen families were brought in safety to these western regions. They found the land swarming with savages, who threatened death with every kind of torture. But savages, and death with torture, were far less terrible than slavery. Nothing was so much the object of their abhorrence as a tyrant's power. They knew it was more safe to dwell with man in his most unpolished state than in a country where arbitrary power prevails. Even *anarchy itself,* that bugbear held up by the tools of power, though truly to be deprecated, is infinitely less dangerous to mankind than *arbitrary government. Anarchy* can be but of a short duration; for, when men are at liberty to pursue that course which is more conductive to their own happiness, they will soon come into it; and from the rudest state of nature order and good government must soon arrive. But *tyranny,* when once established, entails its curses on a nation to the latest period of time; unless some daring genius, inspired by heaven, shall, unappalled by danger, bravely form and execute the arduous designs of restoring liberty and life to his enslaved, murdered country.

THE tools of power, in every age, have racked their inventions to justify the FEW in sporting with the happiness of the MANY; and, having found their sophistry too weak to hold mankind in bondage, have impiously dared to force *religion,* the daughter of the king of *Heaven,* to become a prostitute in the service of *Hell.* They taught, that princes, honored with the name of Christian, might bid defiance to the founder of their faith, might pillage pagan countries and deluge them with blood, only because they boasted themselves to be the disciples of that teacher who strictly charged his followers to *do to others as they would that others should do unto them.*

THIS country having been discovered by an English subject, in the year 1620, was (according to the system which the blind superstition of those times supported) deemed the property of the Crown of England. Our ancestors, when they resolved to quit their native soil, obtained from King James a grant of certain lands in North America. This they probably did to silence the cavils of their enemies; for it cannot be doubted but they despised the pretended right which he claimed thereto. Certain it is, that he might, with equal propriety and justice, have made them a grant of the planet Jupiter. And their subsequent conduct plainly shows that they were too well acquainted with humanity, and the principles of natural equity, to suppose that the grant gave them any right to take possession; they, therefore, entered into a treaty with the natives, and bought from them the lands. Nor have I ever yet obtained any information that our ancestors ever *pleaded,* or that the natives ever *regarded,* the grant from the English crown: the business was transacted by the parties in the same independent manner that it would have been had neither of them ever known or heard of the island of Great Britain.

HAVING become the honest proprietors of the soil, they immediately applied themselves to the cultivation of it; and they soon beheld the virgin earth teeming with richest fruits, a grateful recompense for their unwearied toil. The fields began to wave with ripening harvests, and the late barren wilderness was seen to blossom like the rose. The savage natives saw, with wonder, the delightful change, and quickly formed a scheme to obtain *that* by fraud or force, *which* nature meant as the reward of industry alone. But the illustrious emigrants soon convinced the rude invaders that they were not less ready to take the field for battle than for labor; and the insidious foe was driven from their borders as often as he ventured to disturb them. The Crown of England looked with indifference on the contest; our ancestors were left alone to combat with the natives. Nor is there any reason to believe that it ever was intended by the one party, or expected by the other, that the *grantor* should defend and maintain the *grantees* in the peaceable possession of the lands named in the patents. And it appears plainly, from the history of those times, that neither the prince nor the people of England thought themselves much interested in the matter. They had not then any idea of a thousandth part of those advantages which they since have, and we are most heartily willing they should *still continue* to reap from us.

BUT *when,* at an infinite expense of toil and blood, this widely extended continent had been cultivated and defended; *When* the hardy adventurers justly expected that they and their descendants should peaceably have enjoyed the harvest of those fields which they had sown, and the fruit of those vineyards which they had planted; this country was *then* thought worthy the attention of the British ministry; and the only justifiable and only successful means of rendering the colonies serviceable to Britain were adopted. By an intercourse of friendly offices the two countries became so united in affection that they thought not of any distinct or separate interests; they found both countries flourishing and happy. Britain saw her commerce extended, and her wealth increased; her lands raised to an immense value; her fleets riding triumphant on the ocean; the terror of her arms spreading to every quarter of the globe. The colonist found himself free, and thought himself secure: He dwelt *under his own vine, and under his own fig-tree, and had none to make him afraid:* He knew, indeed, that by purchasing the manufactures of Great Britain he contributed to its greatness; he knew that all the wealth that his labor produced centered in Great Britain; But *that,* far from exciting his envy, filled him with the highest pleasure; *that thought* supported him in all his toils. When the business of the day was past, he solaced himself with the *contemplation,* or perhaps entertained his listening family with the *recital,* of some great, some glorious, transaction which shines conspicuous in the history of Britain; or, perhaps, his elevated fancy led him to foretell, with a kind of enthusiastic confidence, the glory, power and duration of an empire which should extend from one end of the earth to the other. He saw, or thought he saw, the British nation risen to a pitch of grandeur which cast a veil over the Roman glory; and, ravished with the preview, boasted a race of British kings whose names should echo through those realms where Cyrus, Alexander, and the Caesars were unknown; *Princes* for whom millions of grateful subjects redeemed from slavery and pagan ignorance, should, with thankful tongues, offer up their prayers and praises to that transcendently great and beneficent Being *by whom kings reign and princes decree justice.*

THESE pleasing connections might have been continued; these delightsome prospects might have been every day extended; and even the reveries of the most warm imagination might have been realized; but, unhappily for us, unhappily for Britain, the madness of an avaricious minister of state has drawn a sable curtain over the charming scene, and in its stead has brought upon the stage discord, envy, hatred, and revenge, with civil war close in their rear.

SOME demon, in an evil hour, suggested to a short-sighted financier the hateful project of transferring the whole property of the king's subjects in America to his subjects in Britain. The claim of the British Parliament to tax the colonies can never be supported but by such a TRANSFER; for the right of the House of Commons of Great Britain to originate any tax or grant money is altogether derived from their being elected by the people of Great Britain to act for them; and the people of Great Britain cannot confer on their *representatives* a right to give or grant anything which they *themselves* have not a right to give or grant *personally.*

Therefore, it follows, that if the members chosen by the people of Great Britain to represent them in Parliament have, by virtue of their being so chosen, any right to give or grant American property, or to lay any tax upon the lands or persons of the colonists, it is because the lands and people in the colonies are bona fide owned by, and justly belonging to, the people of Great Britain. But (as has been before observed) every man has a right to personal freedom, consequently a right to enjoy what is acquired by his own labor; and it is evident that the property in this country has been acquired by our own labor. It is the duty of the people of Great Britain to produce some compact in which we have explicitly given up to them a right to dispose of our *persons* or *property*. Until this is done, every attempt of theirs, or of those whom they have deputed to act for them, to give or grant any part of our property, is directly repugnant to every principle of reason and natural justice. But I may boldly say that such a compact never existed; no, not even in imagination. Nevertheless, the representatives of a nation, long famed for justice and the exercise of every noble virtue, have been prevailed on to adopt the fatal scheme; and although the dreadful consequences of this wicked policy have already shaken the empire to its centre, yet still it is persisted in. Regardless of the voice of reason—deaf to the prayers and supplications—and unaffected with the flowing tears of suffering millions, the British ministry still hug the darling idol; and every rolling year affords fresh instances of the absurd devotion with which they worship it. Alas! how has the folly, the distraction, of the British councils blasted our swelling hopes, and spread a gloom over this western hemisphere. The hearts of Britons and Americans, which lately felt the generous glow of mutual confidence and love, now burn with jealousy and rage. Though but of yesterday, I recollect (deeply affected at the ill-boding change) the happy hours that passed whilst Briton and American rejoiced in the prosperity and greatness of each other. Heaven grant those halcyon days may soon return! But now the Briton too often looks on the American with an envious eye, taught to consider his just plea for the enjoyment of his earnings as the effect of pride and stubborn opposition to the parent country; whilst the American beholds the Briton as the ruffian, ready *first* to take away his property, and *next,* what is still dearer to every virtuous man, the liberty of his country.

WHEN the measures of administration had disgusted the colonies to the highest degree, and the people of Great Britain had, by artifice and falsehood, been irritated against America, an army was sent over to enforce submission to certain acts of the British Parliament, which reason scorned to countenance, and which place men and pensioners were found unable to support.

MARTIAL law and the government of a well-regulated city are

so entirely different, that it has always been considered as improper
to quarter troops in populous cities. Frequent disputes must necessarily arise between the citizen and the soldier, even if no previous
animosities subsist. And it is further certain, from a consideration
of the nature of mankind, as well as from constant experience, that
standing armies always endanger the liberty of the subject. But
when the people, on the one part, considered the army as sent to
enslave them, and the army, on the other, were taught to look on
the people as in a state of rebellion, it was but just to fear the most
disagreeable consequences. Our fears, we have seen, were but too
well grounded.

THE many injuries offered to the town I pass over in silence.
I cannot now mark out the path which led to that unequaled scene
of horror, the sad remembrance of which takes the full possession
of my soul. The sanguinary theatre again opens itself to view. The
baleful images of terror crowd around me; and discontented ghosts,
with hollow groans, appear to solemnize the anniversary of the
FIFTH of MARCH.

APPROACH we then the melancholy walk of death. Hither let
me call the gay companion; here let him drop a farewell tear upon
that body which so late he saw vigorous and warm with social mirth.
Hither let me lead the tender mother to weep over her beloved son.
Come, widowed mourner, here satiate thy grief; behold thy murdered husband gasping on the ground; and to complete the pompous
show of wretchedness, bring in each hand thy infant children, to
bewail their father's fate. Take heed, ye orphan babes, lest, whilst
your streaming eyes are fixed upon the ghastly corpse, *your feet
slide on the stones bespattered with your father's brains!!* Enough;
this tragedy need not be heightened by an infant weltering in the
blood of him that gave it birth. Nature, reluctant, shrinks already
from the view, and the chilled blood rolls slowly backward to its
fountain. We wildly stare about, and with amazement ask, Who
spread this ruin around us? What wretch has dared deface the image
of his God? Has haughty France or cruel Spain sent forth her
myrmidons? Has the grim savage rushed again from the far distant
wilderness; or does some fiend, fierce from the depth of hell, with
all the rancorous malice which the apostate damned can feel, twang
his destructive bow, and hurl his deadly arrows at our breast? No,
none of these—but, how astonishing! It is the hand of Britain that
inflicts the wound! The arms of George, our rightful king, have
been employed to shed that blood, when justice, or the honor of his
crown, had called his subjects to the field.

BUT pity, grief, astonishment, with all the softer movements
of the soul, must now give way to stronger passions. Say, fellow-
citizens, what dreadful thought now swells your heaving bosoms.
You fly to arms—Sharp indignation flashes from each eye—Revenge

gnashes her iron teeth—Death grins a hideous smile, secure to drench his greedy jaws in human gore—Whilst hovering furies darken all the air.

BUT stop, my bold, adventurous country-men; stain not your weapons with the blood of Britons. Attend to reason's voice—Humanity puts in her claim—and sues to be again admitted to her wonted seat, the bosom of the brave. Revenge is far beneath the noble mind. Many, perhaps, compelled to rank among the vile assassins, do from their inmost souls detest the barbarous action. The winged death, shot from your arms, may chance to pierce some breast that bleeds already for your injured country.

THE storm subsides—a solemn pause ensues—You spare upon condition they depart. They go—they quit your city—they no more shall give offence—Thus closes the important drama.

AND could it have been conceived that we again should have seen a British army in our land, sent to enforce obedience to acts of Parliament destructive of our liberty? But the royal ear, far distant from this western world, has been assaulted by the tongue of slander; and villains, traitorous alike to king and country, have prevailed upon a gracious prince to clothe his countenance with wrath, and to erect the hostile banner against a people ever affectionate and loyal to him and his illustrious predecessors of the house of Hanover. Our streets are again filled with armed men; our harbor is crowded with ships of war. But these cannot intimidate us; our liberty must be preserved; it is far dearer than *life*—we hold it even dear as our *allegience;* we must defend it against the attacks of *friends* as well as *enemies;* we cannot suffer even BRITONS to ravish it from us.

NO longer could we reflect with generous pride on the heroic actions of our American forefathers; no longer boast of our origin from that far-famed island whose warlike sons have so often drawn their well-tried swords to save her from the ravages of tyranny—could we, but for a moment, entertain the thought of giving up our liberty. The man who meanly will submit to wear a *shackle* condemns the noblest gift of heaven, and impiously affronts the God that made him free.

IT was a maxim of the Roman people, which eminently conduced to the greatness of that state, never to despair of the commonwealth. The maxim may prove as salutary to us now as it did to them. Short-sighted mortals see not the numerous links of small and great events, which form the chain on which the fate of kings and nations is suspended. Ease and prosperity, though pleasing for a day, have often sunk a people into effeminacy and sloth. Hardships and dangers, though we forever strive to shun them, have frequently called forth such virtues as have commanded the applause and reverence of an admiring world. Our country loudly calls you to be circumspect, vigilant, active, and brave. Perhaps (all gracious Heaven avert it!)—perhaps the power of Britain, a nation great in war, by some malignant influence, may be employed to enslave you; but let not even this discourage you. Her arms, 'tis true, have filled the world with terror, her troops have reaped the laurels of the field; her fleets have ridden triumphant on the sea; and *when* or *where* did *you,* my countrymen, depart inglorious from the field of fight? *You,* too, can show the trophies of your fore-fathers' victories and your own; can name the fortresses and battles you have won; and many of you count the honorable scars of wounds received whilst fighting for your king and country.

WHERE justice is the standard, heaven is the warrior's shield; but conscious guilt unnerves the arm that lifts the sword against the innocent. Britain, united with these colonies by commerce and affection, by interest and blood, may mock the threats of France and Spain; may be the seat of universal empire. But should America, either by *force,* or those more dangerous engines, *luxury* and *corruption,* ever be brought into a state of vassalage, Britain must lose her freedom also. No longer shall she sit the *empress* of the sea; her ships no more shall waft her thunders over the wide ocean; the *wreath* shall wither on her temple; her weakened arm shall be unable to defend her coasts; and she, at last, must bow that venerable head to some proud foreigner's despotic rule.

BUT if, from past events, we may venture to form a judgment of the future, we justly may expect that the devices of our enemies will but increase the triumphs of our country. I *must* indulge a hope that *Britain's* liberty, as well as *ours,* will eventually be preserved by the virtue of America.

THE attempt of the British Parliament to raise a revenue from America, and our denial of their right to do it, have excited an almost universal inquiry into the right of mankind in general, and of British subjects in particular; the necessary result of which must be such a liberality of sentiment, and such a jealousy of those in power, as will, better than an adamantine wall, secure us against the future approaches of despotism.

THE malice of the Boston Port-Bill has been defeated, in a very considerable degree, by giving you an opportunity of *deserving* and *our brethren* in this and our sister colonies an opportunity of *bestowing* those benefactions which have delighted your friends and astonished your enemies, not only in America, but in Europe also. And, what is more valuable still, the sympathetic feelings for a brother in distress, and the grateful emotions excited in the breast of him who finds relief, must forever endear each to the other, and form those indissoluble bonds of friendship and affection on which the preservation of our rights so evidently depend.

THE mutilation of our charter has made every other colony

jealous for its own; for *this*, if once submitted to by us, would set on float the property and government of every British settlement upon the continent. If Charters are not deemed sacred, how miserably precarious is everything founded upon them!

EVEN the sending troops to put those acts in execution, is not without advantage to us. The exactness and beauty of their discipline inspire our youth with ardor in the pursuit of military knowledge. Charles, the *Invincible,* taught Peter the *Great* the art of war. The battle of Pultown convinced Charles of the proficiency Peter had made.

OUR Country is in danger but not to be despaired of. Our enemies are numerous and powerful; but we have many friends, determining to BE FREE, and Heaven and Earth will aid the RESOLUTION. On *you* depend the fortunes of America. *You* are to decide the important question on which rest the happiness and liberty of millions yet unborn. Act worthy of yourselves. The faltering tongue of hoary age calls on you to support your country. The lisping infant raises its suppliant hands, imploring defence against the monster, slavery. Your fathers look from their celestial seats with smiling approbation on their sons who, to secure the loaves and fishes to himself, would breed a serpent to destroy his children.

BUT, pardon me, my fellow citizens; I know you want not zeal nor fortitude. You will maintain your rights, or perish in the generous struggle. However difficult the combat, you never will decline it when freedom is the prize. An independence of Great Britain is not our aim. No, our wish is, that Britain and the colonies may, like the oak and ivy, grow and increase in strength together. But whilst the infatuated plan of making one part of the empire slaves to the other is persisted in, the interests and safety of *Britain,* as well as the *Colonies,* require that the wise measures recommended by the honorable Continental Congress be steadily pursued; whereby the unnatural contest between a parent honored and a child beloved may probably be brought to such an issue as that the peace and happiness of both may be established upon a lasting basis. But if these pacific measures are ineffectual, and it appears that the only way to safety is through fields of blood, I know you will not turn your faces from your foes, but will undauntedly press forward, until tyranny is trodden under foot, and you have fixed your adored goddess, LIBERTY, fast by a BRUNSWICK'S side, on the American Throne.

YOU *then,* who have nobly espoused your country's cause who generously have sacrificed wealth and ease—*who* have desposed the pomp and show of tinselled greatness—refused the summons to the festive board; been deaf to the alluring calls of luxury and mirth; *who* have forsaken the downy pillow, to keep your vigils by the midnight lamp for the salvation of your invaded country, that you might break the fowler's snare, and disappoint the vulture of his prey, *you,* then, will reap that harvest of renown which you so justly have deserved. Your country shall pay her grateful tribute of applause. Even the children of your most inveterate enemies, ashamed to tell from whom they sprang, while they in secret curse their stupid, cruel parents, shall join the general voice of gratitude to those who broke the fetters which their fathers forged.

HAVING redeemed your Country, and secured the blessing to future generations, *who,* fired by your example, shall emulate your virtues, and learn from you the heavenly art of making millions happy—with heart-felt joy, with transports all your own, you cry, the GLORIOUS WORK IS DONE. Then drop the mantle to some young ELISHA, and take your seats with kindred spirits to your native skies.

BOSTON MASSACRE ORATION

Benjamin Church

One of the leaders in the Boston Tea Party, a member of the Provincial Congress, and surgeon general of the Revolutionary Army, Benjamin Church was to be court-martialed, sentenced to life imprisonment, and finally banished from his native land.

Born in Newport, Rhode Island, on August 24, 1734, Church was graduated from Harvard University in 1754 and later attended the London Medical College. He was held in high esteem by the patriot leaders but in the latter part of 1775 several letters in cipher written by him, were intercepted by Elbridge Gerry. These letters revealed that for some time he had been in the pay of the British, supplying them with information possessed by only a few loyalists. On being allowed to leave the country, he embarked for the West Indies, but his ship was never heard from again.

Dr. Church was selected to present the oration celebrating the third anniversary of the Boston Massacre. Delivered in the Old South Church on March 5, 1773, it was received "with universal applause." So big a crowd attended the ceremony that John Hancock, acting as moderator, had to be helped through a window so that he might reach his place on the platform.

The text of the oration is from Benjamin Church. *An Oration, Delivered March Fifth, 1773.* Boston, 1773.

FROM a consciousness of inability, MY FRIENDS AND FELLOW COUNTRYMEN, I have repeatedly declined the duties of this ANNIVERSARY. Nothing but a firm attachment to the tottering *liberties* of *America* added to the irresistable importunity of some valued friends; could have induced me (especially with a very short notice) so far to mistake my abilities, as to render the utmost extent of your candor truly indispensable.

WHEN man was unconnected by social obligations; abhorrent to every idea of dependence; actuated by a savage ferocity of mind, displayed in the brutality of his manners; the necessary exigencies of each individual naturally impelled him, to acts of treachery, violence and murder.

THE miseries of mankind thus proclaiming eternal war with their species, led them probably to consult certain measures to arrest the current of such outrageous enormities.

A SENSE of their wants and weakness in a state of nature, doubtless inclined them to such reciprocal aids and support, as eventually established society.

MEN then began to incorporate; subordination succeeded to independence; order to anarchy; and passions were disarmed by civilization: Society lent its aid to secure the weak from oppression, who wisely took shelter within the sanctuary of law.

ENCREASING society afterwards exacted, that the tacit contract made with her by each individual at the time of his being incorporated, should receive a more solemn form to become authentic and irrefragable; the main object being to add force to the laws, proportionate to the power, and extent of the body corporate, whose energy they were to direct.

THEN *society* availed herself of the sacrifice of that *liberty*, and that *natural equality* of which we are all conscious: superiors and magistrates were appointed, and mankind submitted to a civil and political subordination. This is truly a glorious inspiration of reason, by which influence, notwithstanding the inclination we have for independence, we accept controul, for the establishment of order.

ALTHOUGH, unrestrained power in one person may have been the first and most natural recourse of mankind from rapine and disorder; yet all restrictions of power, made by laws ,or participation of sovereigns, are apparent improvements upon what began in unlimited power.

IT would shock humanity, should I attempt to describe those barbarous and tragic scenes, which crimson the historic page of this wretched and detestable constitution, where absolute dominion is lodged in one person: Where *one* makes the *whole,* and the *whole* is *nothing.* What motives, what events, could have been able to subdue men, endowed with reason, to render themselves the mute instruments and passive objects of the caprice of an individual!

MANKIND apprized of their privileges, in being rational and free; in prescribing civil laws to themselves, had surely no intention of being enchained by any of their equals: and although they submitted voluntary adherents to certain laws for the sake of mutual security and happiness; they no doubt intended by the original compact, a permanent exemption of the subject body, from any claims, which were not expressly surrendered, for the purpose of obtaining the security and defence of the whole: Can it possibly be conceived that they would voluntarily be enslaved, by a power of their own creation?

THE constitution of a *magistrate,* does not therefore take away that lawful defence against force and injury, allowed by the law of nature; we are not to obey a Prince, ruling above the limits of the power entrusted to him: for the *Common-wealth* by constituting a head does not deprive itself of the power of its own preservation.

Government or *Magistracy* whether supreme or subordinate is a mere *human ordinance,* and the laws of every nation are the measure of magistratical power: And Kings, the servants of the state, when they degenerate into tyrants, forfeit their right to government.

A BREACH of trust in a governor, or attempting to enlarge a limited power; effectually absolves subjects from every bond of covenant and peace; the crimes acted by a King against the people, are the highest treason *against the highest law among men.*

"IF the King (says Grotius) hath one part of the supreme power, and the other part is in the senate or people, when such a King shall invade that part which doth not belong to him, it shall be lawful to oppose a just force to him, because his power doth not extend so far."

THE question in short turns upon this single point, respecting the power of the civil magistrate: Is it the end of that office, that one particular person may do what he will without restraint? or rather that society should be made happy and secure? the answer is very obvious—And it is my firm opinion that the *equal justice* of GOD, and *natural freedom of mankind* must stand or fall together.

WHEN rulers become tyrants, they cease to be Kings; they can no longer be respected as GOD's *vicegerents,* who violate the laws they were sworn to protect: The preacher may tell us of *passive obedience,* that tyrants are scourges in the hands of a righteous GOD to chastise a sinful nation, and are to be submitted to like plagues, famine and such like judgments: such doctrine may serve to mislead ill-judging Princes into a false security; but men are not to be harangued out of their senses; human nature and self preservation will eternally arm the brave and vigilant, against slavery and oppression.

AS a despotic government is evidently productive of the most shocking calamities, whatever tends to restrain such inordinate power, though in itself a severe evil, is extremely beneficial to society; for where a degrading servitude is the detestable alternative, who can shudder at the reluctant ponyard of a *Brutus,* the crimsoned ax of a *Cromwell,* or the reeking dagger of a *Ravilliac?*

TO enjoy life as becomes rational creatures, to possess our souls with pleasure and satisfaction we must be careful to maintain that inestimable blessing, LIBERTY. By *liberty* I would be understood, the happiness of living under laws of our own making, by our personal consent or that of our representatives.

WITHOUT this, the distinctions among mankind, are but different degrees of misery; for as the true estimate of a man's life consists in conducting it according to his own just sentiments and innocent inclinations, his being is degraded below that of a free agent, which heaven has made him, when his affections and passions are no longer governed by the dictates of his own mind, and the interests of human society, but by the arbitrary, unrestrained will of another.

I THANK GOD we live in an age of rational inquisition, when the unfettered mind dares to expatiate freely on every object worthy its attention, when the privileges of mankind are thoroughly comprehended, and the rights of distinct societies are objects of liberal enquiry. The rod of the tyrant no longer excites our apprehensions, and to the frown of the DESPOT which made the darker ages tremble, we dare oppose demands of right, and appeal to that constitution, which holds even Kings in fetters.

IT is easy to project the subversion of a people, when men behold the ignorant or indolent victims of power; but it is extremely difficult to effect their ruin, when they are apprized of their just claims, and are sensibly and seasonably affected with thoughts for their preservation. GOD be thanked, the alarm is gone forth, the people are universally informed of their CHARTER RIGHTS; they esteem them to be the ark of GOD TO NEW-ENGLAND, and like that of old, may it deal destruction to the profane hands, that shall dare to touch it.

IN every state of society of men, personal liberty and security must depend upon the collective power of the whole, acting for the general interest. If this collective power is not of the whole, the freedom and interest of the whole is not secured: If this confluent power acts by a partial delegation, or for a partial interest: it's operation is surely determinable where it's delegation ends.

THE constitution of England, I revere to a degree of idolatry; but my attachment is to the common weal: The magistrate will ever command my respect, by the integrity and wisdom of his administrations.

JUNIUS well observes; when the constitution is openly invaded, when the first original right of the people from which all laws derive their authority is directly attacked; inferior grievances naturally lose their force, and are suffered to pass by without punishment or observation.

NUMBERLESS have been the attacks made upon our free constitution, numberless the grievances we now resent: But the *Hydra* mischief, is the violation of my right, as a BRITISH AMERICAN freeholder; in not being consulted in framing those statutes I am required to obey.

THE authority of the BRITISH monarch over this colony was established, and his power derived from the *provincial* CHARTER; by that we are entitled to a distinct legislation. As in every government there must exist a power superior to the laws, *viz.* the power that makes those laws, and from which they derive their authority: therefore the liberty of the people is exactly proportioned to the share the body of the people have in the legislature and the check placed in the constitution on the executive power. That state only is free, where the people are governed by laws which they have a share in making; and that country is totally enslaved, where one single law can be made or repealed, without the interposition or consent of the people.

THAT the members of the British Parliament are representatives of the whole British Empire, expressly militates with their avowed principles: Property and residence within the Island, alone constituting the right of election; and surely he is not my delegate in whose nomination or appointment I have no choice: But however the futile and absurd claim of a virtual representation, may comport with the Idea of a political visionary; he must (if possible) heighten the indignation, or excite the ridicule of a free born American, who by such a fallacious pretext would despoil him of his property.

An American freeholder according to the *just* and *judicious* conduct of the present ministry, has no possible right to be consulted, in the disposal of his property. When a lordly, though *unlettered British Elector,* possessed of a turnip garden; with great propriety may appoint a legislator, to assess the ample domains, of the most sensible oppulent *American* planter.

BUT remember my *Brethren!* When a people have once sold their liberties, it is no act of extraordinay generosity, to throw their lives and properties into the bargain, for they are poor indeed when enjoyed at the mercy of a master.

THE late conduct of Great-Britain so inconsistent with the practice of former times, so subversive of the first principles of government, is sufficient to excite the discontent of the subject: The *Americans* justly and decently urged, an exclusive right of taxing themselves; was it indulgent conciliating or parental conduct in that state, to exaggerate such a claim, as a concerted plan of rebellion in the wanton *Americans?* And by a rigorous and cruel exercise of power to enforce submission, excite such animosities, as at some future period may produce a bitter repentance.

CAN such be called a legal tax or free gift? It is rather levying contributions on grudging enslaved *Americans* by virtue of an act framed and enforced, not only without, but against their consent; thereby rendering the provincial assemblies a useless part of the constitution.

WHERE laws are framed and assessments laid without a legal representation, and obedience to such acts urged by force, the despairing people robbed of every constitutional means of redress, and that people brave and virtuous; must become the admiration of ages, should they not appeal to those powers, which the immutable laws of nature have lent to all mankind. *Fear* is a slender tye of subjection, we detest those whom we fear, and wish destruction to those we detest; but humanity, uprightness and good faith, with an apparent watchfulness for the welfare of the people, constitute the permanency, and are the firmest support of the *sovereign's* authority; for when violence is opposed to reason and justice, courage never wants an arm for it's defence.

WHAT dignity, what respect, what authority, can *Britain* derive from her obstinate adherence to error? She stands convicted of violating her own principles, but perseveres with unrelenting severity; we implore for *rights* as a grace, she aggravates our distress, by lopping away another and another darling privilege; we ask for *freedom* and she fends the *sword!*

TO the wisdom, to the justice, to the piety of his most sacred Majesty, I unite in my appeal with this unbounded Empire; GOD grant he may attend to the reiterated prayer, instead of the murmurs of discontent, and the frowns of louring disaffection, we would universally hail him with those effusions of genuine joy, and dutious veneration, which the proudest DESPOT will vainly look for, from forced respect or ceremonial homage.

PARTIES and actions since the days of the detested *Andross,* have been strangers to this land; no distinctions of heart-felt animosity disturbed the peace and order of society till the malignant folly of a late rancorous *commander in chief* conjured them from the dead: When shall this unhappy clime be purged of its numberous plagues? When will our troubles, our feuds, our struggles cease? *When will the locusts leave the land?* Then, and not till then, peace and plenty shall smile around us; the husbandman will labour with pleasure; and honest industry reap the reward of it's toil.

But let us not forget the distressing occasion of this anniversary: The sullen ghosts of murdered *fellow-citizens,* haunt my imagination. "and harrow up my soul," methinks the tainted air is hung with the dew of death, while *Ate'* hot from hell cries havock, and lets fly the dogs of war. Hark! The wan tenants of the grave still shriek for vengeance on their remorseless butchers: Forgive us *heaven!* Should we mingle in voluntary execrations, while hovering in idea over the guiltless dead. Where is the amiable, the graceful *Maverick?* the opening blossom is now withered in his cheek, the sprightly fire that once lightened in his eyes is quenched in death; the savage hands of brutal *ruffians,* have crushed the unsuspecting victim and in an evil hour snatched away his gentle soul.

WHERE is the friendly, the industrious *Caldwell?* he paced innoxious through the theatre of death; unconscious of design or danger; when the winged fate gored his bosom, and stript his startled soul for the world of spirits. Where are the refines of *active citizens* that were wont to tread these sacred floors? Fallen by the hand of the vindictive assassins, they swell the horrors of the sanguinary scene. Loyalty stands on tiptoe at the shocking recollection; while justice, virtue, honor patriotism become suppliants for immoderate vengeance: The whole soul clamours for arms, and is on fire to attack the brutal *banditti*, we fly agonizing to the horrid *aceldama;* we gaze on the mangled corses of our *brethren,* and grinning *furies* glotting over their carnage; the hostile attitude of the miscreant *murderers,* redoubles our resentment, and makes revenge a virtue.

BY *heaven they die!* Thus nature spoke, and the swoln heart leap'd to execute the dreadful purpose; dire was the interval of rage, fierce was the conflict of the soul. In that important hour, did not the stalking ghosts of our *stern fore-father's,* point us to bloody deeds of vengeance? did not the consideration of our *expiring* LIBERTIES, impel us to remorseless havoc? But hark! The guardian GOD of New-England issues his awful mandate. "PEACE, BE STILL;" hush'd was the bursting war, the louring tempest frowned it's rage away. Confidence in that God, beneath whose wing ever shelters all our cares, that blessed confidence released the dastard the cowering prey: With haughty scorn we refused to become their executioners, and nobly gave them to the wrath of heaven: But words can poorly print the horrid scene—Defenceless, prostrate, bleeding countrymen—the piercing, agonizing groans—the mingled moan of weeping relatives and friends—These best can speak; to rouse the luke-warm into noble zeal, to fire the zealous into manly rage; against the *foul oppression* of *quartering troops, in populous cities, in times of peace.*

> *Thou who yon bloody walk shalt traverse, there*
> *Where troops of* Britain's *King, on* Britain's *Sons,*
> *Discharged the leaden vengeance; pass not on*
> *E'er thou hast blest their memory, and paid*
> *Those hallowed tears, which sooth the virtuous dead:*
> *O stranger! Stay thee, and the scene around*
> *Contemplate well, and if perchance thy home,*
> *Salute thee with a father's honor'd name,*
> *Go call thy Sons—instruct them what a debt*
> *They owe their ancestors, and make them swear*
> *To pay it, by transmitting down entire*
> *Those sacred rights to which themselves were born.*

BOSTON MASSACRE ORATION

John Hancock

First President of the Provincial Congress and first to sign the
Declaration, John Hancock was born in Quincy, Massachusetts,
on January 23, 1737. Member of an old and wealthy colonial family,
he attended, as had his grandfather and father before him, Harvard
University, from which institution he was graduated at the age
of seventeen.

He soon became a leader in Massachusetts as a result of his
wealth, his power, and his convictions. He served as selectman for
the town of Boston, as a member from Boston in the provincial
assembly, and in 1774 as president of the Massachusetts Provincial
Congress. He was sent to the Continental Congress from 1775 to
1780 and from May, 1775 to October, 1777, was its president. In
1780, Hancock was elected Governor of his state, holding that
office until 1785. He was elected again in 1787 and served continuously until his death on October 8, 1793.

In 1774, John Hancock was selected to deliver the third
annual oration commemorating "the Memory of the Horrid Massacre perpetrated on the Evening of the Fifth of March 1770 . . . ."
The oration was duly delivered at 12 o'clock noon on March 5,
1774 in the Old South Meeting House "to a large and crowded
Audience and received by them with great Applause." Reading a
speech variously attributed to the pen of Sam Adams, Dr. Samuel
Cooper, and "leading Whigs," he gave what John Adams described
as an "elegant, a pathetic, a spirited performance." Adams, who was
present, went on to remark in his diary: "A vast crowd, rainy eyes,
&c. The composition, the pronunciation, the action, all exceeded the
expectations of everybody. They exceeded even mine, which were
considerable."

The text of the oration is taken from the Edes and Gill edition
published in Boston, 1774.

Men, Brethren, Fathers, and Fellow-Countrymen!

THE attentive gravity, the venerable appearance of this crowded
audience, the dignity which I behold in the countenances of so
many in this great Assembly, the solemnity of the occasion upon
which we have met together, join'd to a consideration of the part I
am to take in the important business of this day, fill me with an
awe hitherto unknown; and heighten the sense which I have ever
had, of my unworthiness to fill this sacred desk; but, allur'd by the
call of some of my respected fellow-citizens, with whose request

it is always my greatest pleasure to comply, I almost forgot my
want of ability to perform what they required. In this situation, I
find my only support in assuring myself that a generous people will
not severely censure what they know was well intended, though
it's want of merit, should prevent their being able to applaud it.
And I pray, that my sincere attachment to the interest of my
country, and hearty detestation of every design formed against her
liberties, may be admitted as some apology for my appearance in
this place.

I HAVE always from my earliest youth, rejoiced in the felicity
of my Fellow-men, and have ever consider'd it as the indispensible
duty of every member of society to promote, as far as in him lies,
the prosperity of every individual, but more especially of the community to which he belongs; and also, as a faithful subject of the
state, to use his utmost endeavours to detect, and having detected,
strenuously to oppose every traitorous plot which its enemies may
devise for its destruction. Security to the persons and properties of
the governed, is so obviously the design and end of civil government, that to attempt a logical proof of it, would be like burning
tapers at noon-day, to assist the sun in enlightening the world; and
it cannot be either virtuous or honorable, to attempt to support a
government, of which this is not the great and principal basis; and
it is to the last degree vicious and infamous to attempt to support
a government which manifestly tends to render the persons and
properties of the governed insecure. Some boast of being *friends
to government;* I am a friend to *righteous* government, to a government founded upon the principles of reason and justice; but I
glory in publickly avowing my eternal enmity to tyranny. Is the
present system which the British administration have adopted for
the government of the colonies, a righteous government? Or is it
tyranny? Here suffer me to ask (and would to Heaven there could
be an answer) What tenderness? what regard, respect, or consideration has *Great-Britain* shewn in their late transactions for the
security of the persons or properties of the inhabitants of the
colonies? or rather, What have they omitted doing to destroy that
security? They have declared that they have, ever had, and of right
ought ever to have, full power to make laws of sufficient validity
to bind the colonies in all cases whatever: They have exercised this
pretended right by imposing a tax on us without our consent; and
lest we should show some reluctance at parting with our property,
her fleets and armies are sent to inforce their mad pretensions. The
town of Boston, ever faithful to the British Crown, has been invested
by a British fleet: The troops of George III. have cross'd the wide
atlantick, not to engage an enemy, but to assist a band of
TRAITORS in trampling on the rights and liberties of his most
loyal subjects in America—those rights and liberties which as a

father he ought ever to regard, and as a King he is bound in honor to defend from violations, even at the risque of his own life.

LET not the history of the illustrious house of Brunswick inform posterity, that a King descended from that glorious monarch George the second, once sent his British subjects to conquer and enslave his subjects in America; but be perpetual infamy entail'd upon that villain who dared to advise his Master to such execrable measures; for it was easy to foresee the consequences which so naturally followed upon sending troops into America, to enforce obedience to acts of the British parliament, which neither God nor man ever empowered them to make. It was reasonable to expect that troops who knew the errand they were sent upon, would treat the people whom they were to subjugate, with a cruelty and haughtiness, which too often buries the honorable character of a *soldier,* in the disgraceful name of an *unfeeling ruffian.* The troops upon their first arrival took possession of our Senate House, and pointed their cannon against the Judgment-hall, and even continued them there whilst the Supreme Court of Judicature for this Province was actually sitting to decide upon the lives and fortunes of the King's subjects. Our streets nightly resounded with the noise of riot and debauchery; our peaceful citizens were hourly exposed to shameful insults, and often felt the effects of their violence and outrage. But this was not all: as though they thought it not enough to violate our civil Rights, they endeavoured to deprive us of the enjoyment of our religious privileges, to viciate our morals, and thereby render us deserving of destruction. Hence the rude din of arms which broke in upon your solemn devotions in your temples, on that day hallowed by Heaven, and set apart by God himself for his peculiar worship. Hence, impious oaths and blasphemies so often tortured your unaccustomed ears. Hence, all the arts which idleness and luxury could invent, were used to betray our youth of one sex into extravagance and effiminacy, and of the other to infamy and ruin; and did they not succeed but too well? Did not a reverence for religion sensibly decay? Did not our infants almost learn to lisp out curses before they knew their horrid import? Did not our youth forget they were Americans, and regardless of the admonitions of the wise and aged, servilely copy from their tyrants those vices which finally must overthrow the empire of Great Britain? And must I be compelled to acknowledge, that even the noblest, fairest part of all the lower creation did not entirely escape the cursed snare? When virtue has once erected her throne in the female breast, it is upon so solid a basis that nothing is able to expel the heavenly inhabitant. But have there not been some, few indeed, I hope, whose youth and inexperience have rendered them a prey to wretches whom, upon the least reflection, they would have despised and hated as foes to God and their country? I fear there have been some such unhappy instances; or why have I seen an honest father cloathed with shame? or why a virtuous mother drowned in tears?

BUT I forbear, and come reluctantly to the transactions of that dismal night, when in such quick succession we felt the extremes of grief, astonishment and rage; when Heaven in anger, for a dreadful moment, suffered Hell to take the reins; when Satan with his chosen band open'd the sluices of New-England's blood, and sacrilegiously polluted our land with the dead bodies of her guiltless sons. Let this sad tale of death never be told without a tear; let not the heaving bosom cease to burn with a manly indignation at the barbarous story, thro' the long tracts of further time: Let every parent tell the shameful story to his listening children till tears of pity glisten in their eyes, and boiling passion shakes their tender frames; and whilst the anniversary of that ill-fated night is kept a jubilee in the grim courts of pandaemonium, let all America join in one common prayer to Heaven, that the inhuman, unprovok'd murders of the Fifth of March 1770, planned by Hillsborough, and a knot of treacherous knaves in Boston, and executed by the cruel hand of Preston and his sanguinary coadjutors, may ever stand on history without a parallel. But what, my countrymen, with-held the ready arm of vengeance from executing instant justice on the vile assassins? Perhaps you fear'd promiscuous carnage might ensue, and that the innocent might share the fate of those who had performed the infernal deed. But were not all guilty? Were you not too tender of the lives of those who came to fix a yoke on your necks? But I must not too severely blame a fault, which great souls only can commit. May that magnificence of spirit which scorns the low pursuits of malice, may that generous compassion which often preserves from ruin, even a guilty villain, forever actuate the noble bosoms of Americans! But let not the miscreant host vainly imagine that we fear'd their arms. No; them we despis'd; we dread nothing but slavery. Death is the creature of a Poltroon's brains; 'tis immortality, to sacrifice ourselves for the salvation of our country. We fear not death. That gloomy night, the pale fac'd moon, and the affrighted stars that hurried through the sky, can witness that we fear not death. Our hearts, which at the recollection glow with rage that four revolving years have scarcely taught us to restrain, can witness that we fear not death; and happy 'tis for those who dared to insult us, that their naked bones are not now piled up an everlasting monument to Massachusett's bravery. But they retir'd, they fled, and in that flight they found their only safety. We then expected that the hand of publick justice would soon inflict that punishment upon the murderers, which by the laws of God and man they had incurred. But let the unbias'd pen of a Robertson, or perhaps of some equally fam'd American, conduct this trial before the great tribunal of succeeding generations. And though the murderers may escape the just resentment of an enraged people, though drowsy justice intoxicated by the poisonous draught prepared for her cup still nods upon her rotten seat, yet be assured such complicated crimes will meet their due reward. Tell me, ye bloody butcher, ye villians high and low, ye wretches who contrived, as well as you who executed the inhuman deed, do you not feel the goads and sting of conscious guilt pierce through your savage bosoms? Though some of you may think yourselves exalted to a heighth that bids defiance to human justice, and others shrowd yourselves beneath the mask of hypocrisy, and build your hopes of safety on the low arts of cunning, chicanery and false hood; yet, do you not sometimes feel the gnawings of that worm which never dies? Do not the injured shades of Maverick, Gray, Caldwell, Attucks, and Carr attend you in your solitary walks, arrest you even in the midst of your debaucheries, and fill even your dreams with terror? But if the unappeased manes of the dead should not disturb their murderers, yet surely even your obdurate hearts must shrink, and your guilty blood must chill within your rigid veins, when you behold the miserable Monk, the wretched victim of your savage cruelty. Observe his tottering knees which scarce sustain his wasted body, look on his haggard eyes, mark well the deathlike paleness on his fallen cheek, and tell me, does not the sight plant daggers in your souls? Unhappy Monk! Cut off, in the gay morn of manhood from all the joys which sweeten life, doom'd to drag on a pitiful existence without even a hope to taste the pleasures of returning health! Yet Monk, thou livest not in vain; thou livest a warning to thy country which sympathises with thee in thy sufferings; thou livest an affecting, an alarming instance of the unbounded violence which lust of power, assisted by a standing army, can lead a traitor to commit.

FOR us he bled, and now languishes. The wounds by which he is tortur'd to a lingering death were aim'd at our country! surely the meek-eyed charity can never behold such sufferings with indifference. Nor can her lenient hand forbear to pour oil and wine into these wounds; and to assuage, at least, what it cannot heal.

PATRIOTISM is ever united with humanity and compassion. This noble affection, which impels us to sacrifice every thing dear, even life itself, to our country, involves in it a common sympathy and tenderness for every citizen, and must ever have a *particular feeling* for one who suffers in a publick cause. Thoroughly persuaded of this, I need not add a word to engage your compassion and bounty toward a fellow citizen, who with lone-protracted anguish falls a victim to the relentless rage of our common enemies.

YE dark designing knaves, ye murderers, parricides! how dare you tread upon the earth, which has drank in the blood of slaughter'd innocents shed by your wicked hands? How dare you breathe that air which wafted to the ear of heaven the groans of those who fell a sacrifice to your accursed ambition? But if the labouring earth doth not expand her jaws, if the air you breathe is not commissioned to be the minister of death; yet, hear it, and tremble! the eye of Heaven penetrates the darkest chambers of the soul, traces the leading clue through all the labyrinths which your industrious folly has devised; and you, however you may have screen'd yourselves from human eyes, must be arraigned, must lift your hands, red with the blood of those whose death you have procur'd, at the tremendous bar of God.

BUT I gladly quit the gloomy theme of death, and leave you to improve the thought of that important day, when our naked Souls must stand before that Being from whom nothing can be hid. I would not dwell too long upon the horrid effects which have already follow'd from quartering regular troops in this town; let our misfortunes teach posterity to guard against such evils for the future. Standing armies are sometimes (I would by no means say generally, much less universally) composed of persons who have render'd themselves unfit to live in civil society; who have no other motives of conduct than those which a desire of the present gratification of their passions suggests; who have no property in any country; Men who have lost or given up their own liberties, and envy those who enjoy liberty; who are equally indifferent to the glory of a GEORGE or a Lewis; who for the addition of one peny [sic] a day to their wages would desert from the christian cross, and fight under the crescent of the Turkish Sultan; from such men as these, what has not a state to fear? With such as these, usurping Caesar pass'd the Rubicon; with such as these, he humbled mighty Rome, and forc'd the mistress of the world to own a master in a traitor. These are the men whom sceptr'd robbers now employ to frustrate the designs of God, and render vain the bounties which his gracious hand pours indiscriminately upon his creatures. By these, the miserable slaves of Turkey, Persia, and many other extensive countries, are render'd truly wretched, though their air is salubrious and their soil luxuriously fertile. By these France and Spain, tho' blessed by nature with all that administers to the convenience of life, have been reduc'd to that contemptible state in which they now appear; and by these, Britain—But if I was possess'd of the gift of prophecy, I dare not, except by divine command, unfold the leaves on which the destiny of that once powerful kingdom is inscrib'd.

BUT since standing armies are so hurtful to a state, perhaps, my countrymen may demand some substitute, some other means of rendering as secure against the incursions of a foreign enemy. But can you be one moment at a loss? Will not a *well disciplin'd militia* afford you ample security against foreign foes? We want not courage; it is discipline alone in which we are exceeded by the most formidable troops that ever trod the earth. Surely our hearts flutter no more at the sound of war than did those of the immortal band of Persia, the Macedonian phalanx, the invincible Roman legions, the Turkish Janissaries, the Gens des Armes of France, or the *well known Grenadiers of Britain.* A well disciplin'd militia is a safe, an honourable guard to a community like this, whose inhabitants are by nature brave, and are laudably tenacious of that freedom in which they were born. From a well regulated militia we have nothing to fear; their interest is the same with that of the state. When a country is invaded, the militia are ready to appear in it's defence; they march into the field with that fortitude which a consciousness of the justice of their cause inspires; they do not jeopard their lives for a master who considers them only as the instruments of his ambition, and whom them regard only as the daily dispenser of the scanty pittance of bread and water. No, they fight for their houses, their lands, for their wives, their children, for all who claim the tenderest names, and are held dearest in their hearts, they fight *pro aris & focis,* for their liberty, and for themselves, and for their God. And let it not offend if I say, that no militia ever appear'd in more flourishing condition, than that of this province now doth; and pardon me if I say—of this town in particular—I mean not to boast: I would not excite envy, but manly emulation. We have all one common cause; let it therefore be our only contest, who shall most contribute to the security of the liberties of America. And may the same kind providence which has watched over this country from her infant state, still enable us to defeat our enemies. I cannot here forbear noticing the signal manner in which the designs of those who wish not well to us have been discovered. The dark deeds of a treacherous Cabal have been brought to publick view. You now know the serpents who, whilst cherished in your bosoms, were darting their envenom'd stings into the vitals of the constitution. But the Representatives of the people have fixed a mark on these ungrateful monsters, which, though it may not make them so secure as Cain of old, yet renders them at least as infamous. Indeed, it would be affrontive to the tutelar deity of this country even to despair of saving it from all the snares which human policy can lay.

TRUE it is, that the British ministry have annexed a salary to the office of the Governor of this province, to be paid out of a revenue raised in America without our consent. They have attempted to render our Courts of Justice the instruments of extending the authority of acts of the British parliament over this colony, by making the judges dependent on the British administration for their support. But this people will never be enslaved with their eyes open. The moment they knew that the Governor was not such a Governor as the charter of the province points out, he lost his power of hurting them. They were alarmed; they suspected him, have guarded against him, and he has found that a wise and a brave people, when they know their danger, are fruitful in expedients to escape it.

THE Courts of Judicature also so far lost their dignity by being supposed to be under an undue influence, that our Representatives thought it absolutely necessary to Resolve, that they were bound to declare, that they would not receive any other salary besides that which the General Court should grant them; and if they did not make this declaration, that it would be the duty of the House to impeach them.

GREAT expectations were also formed from the artful scheme of allowing the East India Company to export Tea to America upon their own account. This certainly, had it succeeded, would have effected the purpose of the contrivers, and gratified the most sanguine wishes of our adversaries. We soon should have found our trade in the hands of foreigners, and taxes imposed on every thing we consumed; nor would it have been strange, if in a few years a company in London should have purchased an exclusive right of trading to America. But their plot was soon discovered. The people soon were aware of the poison which with so much craft and subtilty had been concealed: Loss and disgrace ensued; and perhaps this long concerted master-piece of policy, may issue in the total disuse of Tea in this country, which will eventually be the saving of the lives and the estates of thousands—yet while we rejoiced that the adversary has not hitherto prevailed against us, let us by no means put off the harness. Restless malice, and disappointed ambition will still suggest new measures to our inveterate *enemies*. Therefore let Us also be ready to take the field whenever danger calls, let us be united and strengthen the hands of each other, by promoting a general union among us. Much has been done by the Committees of Correspondence, for this and the other towns of this province toward uniting the inhabitants; let them still go on and prosper. Much has been done by the Committees of Correspondence for the Houses of Assembly in this and our Sister Colonies, for uniting the Inhabitants of the whole Continent for the security of their common interest. May success ever attend their generous endeavours. But permit me here to suggest a general Congress of Deputies from the several Houses of Assembly on the Continent, as the most effectual method of establishing such an Union as the present posture of our affairs requires. At such a Congress, a firm foundation may be laid for the security of our Rights and Liberties; a system may be formed for our common safety, by a strict adherence to which we shall be able to frustrate any attempt to overthrow our constitution; restore peace and harmony to America, and secure honor and wealth to Great-Britain, even against the inclinations of her ministers, whose duty it is to study her welfare; and we shall also free ourselves from those unmannerly pillagers who impudently tell us, that they are licensed by an act of the British parliament to thrust their dirty hands into the pockets of every American. But I trust, the happy time will come, when, with the besom of destruction, those noxious vermin will be swept forever from the streets of Boston.

SURELY you never will tamely suffer this country to be a den of thieves. Remember, my friends, from whom you sprang—Let not a meanness of spirit, unknown to those whom you boast of as your Fathers, excite a thought to the dishonor of your mothers. I conjure you, by all that is dear, by all that is honourable, by all that is sacred, not only that ye pray, but the ye act; that, if necessary, ye fight, and even die for the prosperity of our Jerusalem. Break in sunder, with noble disdain, the bonds with which the Philistines have bound you. Suffer not yourselves to be betrayed, by the soft arts of luxury and effeminacy, into the Pit digged for your destruction. Despise the glare of wealth. That people who pay greater respect to a wealthy villain than to an honest upright man in poverty, almost deserve to be enslaved; they plainly show that wealth, however it may be acquired, is in their esteem, to be preferr'd to virtue.

BUT I thank GOD, that America abounds in men who are superior to all temptation, whom nothing can divert from a steady pursuit of the interest of their country, who are at once it's ornament and its safe-guard. And sure I am, I should not incur your displeasure, if I paid a respect so justly due to their much honored characters in this place. But when I name an ADAMS, such a numerous host of Fellow-patriots rush upon my mind, that I fear it would take up too much of your time, should I attempt to call over the illustrious roll: But your grateful hearts will point you to the men; and their reverend names, in all succeeding times, shall grace the annals of America. From them, let us, my friends, take example; from them let us catch the divine enthusiasm; and feel, each for himself, the God-like pleasure of diffusing happiness on all around us; of delivering the oppressed from the iron grasp of tyranny; of changing the hoarse complaints and bitter moans of wretched slaves, into those cheerful songs, which freedom and contentment must inspire. There is a heart-felt satisfaction in reflecting on our exertions for the public weal, which all the sufferings an enraged tyrant can inflict, will never take away; which the ingratitude and reproaches of those whom we have sav'd from ruin cannot rob us of. The virtuous asserter of the Rights of mankind merits a reward, which even a want of success in his endeavors to save his country, the heaviest misfortune which can befall a genuine Patriot, cannot entirely prevent him from receiving.

I HAVE the most animating confidence that the present noble

struggle for liberty, will terminate gloriously for America. And let us play the man for our God, and for the cities of our God; while we are using the means in our power, let us humbly commit our righteous cause to the great Lord of the universe, who loveth righteousness and hateth iniquity. And having secured the approbation of our hearts, by a faithful and unwearied discharge of our duty to our country, let us joyfully leave our concerns in the hands of Him who raiseth up and putteth down the empires and kingdoms of the world as He pleases; and with cheerful submission to His sovereign will, devoutly say,

"*Although the Fig-Tree shall not Blossom, neither shall Fruit be in the vines; the Labour of the Olive shall fail, and the Fields shall yield no Meat; the Flock shall be cut off from the Fold, and there shall be no Herd in the Stalls; Yet we will rejoice in the LORD, we will joy in the GOD of our Salvation.*"

BOSTON MASSACRE ORATION

Peter Thacher

The Reverend Peter Thacher was born at Milton, Massachusetts, March 21, 1752. Like so many others who were deeply involved in the Revolutionary War, he was educated in the Boston Latin School and at Harvard College, from which he was graduated in 1769.

For a short time Peter Thacher was a school teacher at Chelsea, but in 1770 he was unanimously appointed pastor of the church at Molden. While a member of the Provincial Congress, he wrote a narrative of the Battle of Bunker Hill and also drafted resolutions and revolutionary instructions which were placed in the town records of Molden of 1775.

After the war, Rev. Thacher was invited to become the minister of the Brattle street church in Boston, a position he held until his death in 1802.

Peter Thacher delivered his memorial oration on the Boston Massacre at 10 A.M. on March 5, 1776, in the meeting house at Watertown, Massachusetts. It was presented here because, at that time, Boston was occupied by British regulars.

The text of the oration is taken from the edition published by Benjamin Edes in Watertown, 1776.

My Friends,

WHEN the ambition of Princes induces them to break over the sacred barriers of social compact, and to violate those rights, which it is their duty to defend, they will leave no methods unessayed to bring the people to acquiesce in their unjustifiable encroachments.

IN this cause, the pens of venal authors have in every age, been drawn: With Machiavelian subtility, they have labored to persuade mankind, that their public happiness consisted in being subject to uncontroled power; that they were incapable of judging concerning the mysteries of government; and that it was their interest to deliver their estates, their liberties, and their lives, into the hands of an absolute Monarch.

MITRED hypocrites, and cringing, base-souled Priests, have impiously dared to enlist the oracles of GOD into the service of despotism; to assert that, by the command of the supreme law-giver, we are bound to surrender our rights into the hands of the first bold Tyrant who dares to seize them; and that when they are seized, it

272

is rebellion against God, and treason against the prince, for us to attempt to resume them.

DEPRAVED as is the human understanding, it hath yet strength enough to discern the ridiculous fallacy of these assertions: The votaries of ignorance and superstition may, indeed, be imposed upon by them: When we place unlimited confidence in our civil or spiritual fathers, we can swallow, with ease, the most improbable dogmas: but there are feelings in the human heart, which compel men to recognize their own rights—to venerate the majesty of the people —and to despise the insult which is offered to their understandings by these doating absurdities. Had princes no other methods to accomplish their purposes, could they not establish their usurpation, without convincing men's judgments of their utility? They would be more harmless to mankind than they have ever yet been. They might be surrounded with the fascinating gewgaws of regal pomp; a few parasites might bow the knee before these idols of their own creating; the weak and the wicked might obey their mandates; but the baneful influence which they now have upon the interests of individuals, and of society, would come to a period: they would not revel in the spoils of nations, nor trample upon the ruins of public Liberty.

CONSCIOUS of this, they have used arguments, and pursued methods, entirely different from these, to effect their designs; instead of convincing the understandings, they have addressed themselves to the passions of men: The acts of bribery and corruption have been tried with a fatal success: Men, We know, have sold their children, their country, and their GOD, for a small quantity of painted dirt, *which will perish with the using.*

EXTENSIVE as are the revenues of princes, they are still inadequate to the purpose the bribing large communities to submit to their pleasure; corrupting therefore a few, they have overawed the rest; from small beginnings, and under specious pretences, they will raise a standing military force, the most successful engine ever yet wielded by the hand of lawless domination.

WITH such a force, it is easy for an ambitious prince, possessed by nature of very slender abilities, to subvert every principle of liberty in the constitution of his government, and to render his people the most abject of slaves: if any individual feels the injury done to his country, and wishes to restore it to a state of happiness, with a bayonet at his breast, a dragoon will compel him to silence; if the people, awakened to see their interest and their duty, assemble for the same purpose, a military force is at hand to subdue them, and by leaden arguments, to convince them of their error.

AN easy task would it be to enlarge upon the fatal consequences of keeping up such a standing army in time of peace, and of quartering a lawless body of men, who despise the just restraints of civil authority, in free and populous cities: that no vestige of freedom can remain in a state where such a force exists: that the morals of the people will be gradually corrupted: that they will contract such a habit of tame submission, as to become an easy prey to the brutal tyrant who rules them, hath been heretofore largely and plainly demonstrated, by persons so much more capable of doing it, than he who is speaking, that it would be presumption in him to attempt it now.

THERE is no need of recurring to the ancient histories of Greece and Rome for instances of these truths. The British nation, once famous for its attachment to freedom, and enthusiastically jealous of its rights, is now become a great tame beast, which fetches and carries for any minister who pleases to employ it.

ENGLISHMEN have been wont to boast of the excellence of their constitution; to boast that it contained whatever was excellent in every form of government hitherto, by the wit of man, devised: in their king, whose power was limited, they have asserted that they enjoyed the advantages of monarchy, without fear of its evils: while their house of commons, chosen by the suffrages of the people, and dependent upon them, represented a republic, their house of peers, forming a balance of power between the king and the people, gave them the benefit of an aristocracy. In theory, the British constitution is, on many accounts, excellent; but when we observe it reduced to practice, when we observe the British government, as it has been, for a long course of years administered, we must be convinced that its boasted advantages are not real: The management of the public revenue, the appointment of civil and military officers, are vested in the king: improving these advantages which these powers give him, he hath found means to corrupt the other branches of the legislature: Britons please themselves with the thought of being free; their tyrant suffers them to enjoy the shadow, whilst he himself grasps the substance of power. Impossible would it have been for the kings of England to have acquired such an exorbitant power, had they not had a standing army under their command: with the officers of this army, they have bribed men to sacrifice the rights of their country: having artfully got their arms out of the hands of the people, with their mercenary forces they have awed them into submission. When they have appeared, at any time, disposed to assert their freedom, these troops have been ready to obey the mandates of their sovereign, to imbrue their hands in the blood of their brethren.

HAVING found the efficacy of this method to quell a spirit of liberty in the people of Great-Britain, the righteous administration of the righteous king George the third, determined to try the experiment upon the people of America. To fright us into submission to their unjustifiable claims, they sent a military force to the town of Boston. This day leads us to reflect upon the fatal effects of the measure! by their intercourse with troops, made up in general of the most abandoned of men, the morals of our youth were corrupted: the temples and the day of our God were scandalously profaned: we experienced the most provoking insults; and at length saw the streets of Boston strewed with the corpses of five of its inhabitants, murdered in cool blood, by the British mercenaries.

THE indignant rage which swelled your bosoms upon this occasion—the fortitude and humanity which you discovered—the anguish of the friends and relatives of the dead and wounded, with all the horrors of that memorable night have been painted in vivid colors by an HANCOCK and a WARREN; they have shewn the necessity of those exertions made by the town, which defeated, at that time, the designs of the enemies to American liberty, and preserved us, for the present, from the calamities of war.

BUT the past year hath presented us with a tragedy more striking, because more extensive, than this: a tragedy, which more plainly proves the fatal effects of keeping up standing armies in time of peace, than any arguments whatsoever: we have seen the ground crimsoned with the gore of hundreds of our fellow-citizens—we have seen the first city in America, for wealth and extent, depopulated—we have seen others destroyed, and heard our savage enemies breathing out thirstings for our blood.

FINDING their arts insufficient to flatter, or their treasures to bribe, the people of America out of their freedom, the British government determined, by force, to subjugate them to their arbitrary will; in consequence of this determination, a large party of their troops marched from Boston, on the morning of the ever memorable nineteenth of April last: flushed with the hopes of certain victory, and defying the armies of the living God, they broke through every divine and political obligation; they wantoned in cruelty; they shed again American blood.

AROUSED by the uprovoked injury, like a lion awaking from his slumber, we sprang to arms! we felt ourselves inspired with the spirit of our ancestors; we heard our brethren's blood crying to us for vengeance; we rushed into the midst of battle: we compelled our enemies to betake themselves to disgraceful flight; we pursued them with avidity, and desisted not till they took refuge in that city, of which, by fraud and treachery, they had possessed themselves.

TRUSTING to the divine protection, from that hour we determined never to sheathe the sword, till we had reparation for our injuries; till we had secured our own freedom and the freedom of our posterity: from that hour the den of enemies hath been surrounded by an American army, *brave and determined*: although they had before boasted of their superiority to all the troops in the world, they have scarcely dared to set their feet out of their strong holds since that time, and instead of ravaging the American continent in a single campaign, with a single regiment, they have proceeded— *one mile and an half* in the conquest of it.

THE heights of Charlestown witnessed to the world, that Americans, fighting in the cause of freedom, were a formidable foe: although they were surrounded by troops hitherto deemed invincible; although they saw the habitations of their countrymen inveloped with flames; although cannon roared on every quarter, and they beheld scenes of desolation and bloodshed, to which they were entirely unused, yet they retired not till they had compelled their enemy twice to retreat, and had expended the whole of their ammunition: the British forces gained the ground, but they lost the flower of their army.

FROM one end of the continent to the other, a series of successes hath attended the American arms; instead of having troops of savages poured down to our frontiers (which the murderous policy of the tyrant of Britain induced him to attempt) we have, through the favor of heaven, carried our victorious arms into the very bowels of Canada; instead of having our stores and provisions cut off by the enemy, we have made important captures from them: success hath crowned our enterprises, while disappointment hath followed those who oppose us.

THAT elation of spirit, which is excited by our victories, is damped by our feeling the calamities of war. To hear the expiring groans of our beloved countrymen; to behold the flames of our habitations, once the abodes of peace and plenty, ascending to Heaven; to see the ruin and desolation spread over our fruitful villages, must occasion sensations in the hightest degree painful.

THIS Day, upon which the gloomy scene was first opened, calls upon us to mourn for the heroes who have already died in the bed of honor, fighting for GOD and their country. Especially, does it lead us to recollect the name and the virtues of general WARREN! the kind, the humane, the benevolent friend, in the private walks of life; the inflexible patriot, the undaunted commander in his public sphere, deserves to be recollected with gratitude and esteem! this audience, acquainted, in the most intimate manner, with his numberless virtues, must feel his loss, and bemoan their beloved, their entrusted fellow-citizen! oh! my countrymen, what tender, what excruciating sensations rush at once upon our burdened minds, when we recall his loved idea! when we reflect upon the manner of his death; when we fancy that we see his savage enemies exulting o'er his corpse, beautiful even in death, when we remember that, destitute of the rites of sepulture, he was cast into the ground, without the distinction due to his rank and merit; we cannot restrain the starting tear, we cannot repress the bursting sigh! we mourn thine exit, illustrious shade, with undissembled grief; we venerate thine exalted character; we will erect a monument to thy memory in each of our grateful breasts, and to the latest ages, will teach our tender infants to lisp the name of WARREN with veneration and applause!

WHEN we traverse the Canadian wilds, and come to the plains of Abraham, where WOLFE once fell, we are there again compelled to pay a tribute to exalted merit, and to lament the fall of the great MONTGOMERY! warmed with a spirit of patriotism, too little felt by his venal countrymen, he espoused the cause of American freedom: he left domestic ease and affluence: he girded on the sword which he had long laid aside, and *jeoparded his life in the high places of the field*: victory followed his standard; she hovered over his head, and crowned it with the laurel wreath; she was just ready to hail him the Conqueror of *Canada*, when the fatal sisters snapped, in a moment, the thread of life, and seized, from his eager grasp, the untasted conquest; Americans, bear witness to his humanity and his valor, for he died fighting in your cause, and the cause of mankind! let his memory live in your breasts; let it be handed down to your posterity, that millions yet unborn may *rise up and call him blessed!*

THE tender feelings of the human heart are deeply affected with the fate of these and the other heroes who have bled and died, that their country may be free; but at the same time, sensations of indignant wrath are excited in the breasts of every friend to freedom: he will listen to the voice of their blood, which cries aloud to heaven and to him, for vengeance! he will feel himself animated with new vigor in the glorious cause: nothing daunted by their untimely fate, he will rush into the midst of danger, that he may share their glory and avenge their death! every idea which can warm and animate him to glorious deeds, will rush at once upon his mind; and, when engaged in the warmest battle, he will hear them, from their heaven, urging him to action: he will feel their spirits transfused into his breast; he will sacrifice whole hecatombs of their murders to their illustrious *manes!*

INDEED, my countrymen, the people of America have everything to animate and encourage them in the present contest. Formidable as was once the power of the British lion, he hath now lost his teeth; universal dissipation hath taken place of that simplicity of manners, and hardiness of integrity, for which the nation was once remarkable: the officers of the British army, instead of inuring themselves to discipline, and seeking for glory in the blood-stained field, wish alone to captivate the softer sex, and triumph over their virtue. The legislature of Great-Britain is totally corrupt; her administration is arbitrary and tyrannical; the people have lost their spirit of resentment; and, like the most contemptible of animals, *bow the shoulder to bear and become servants unto tribute.* The national resources are cut off; she is loaded with an intolerable public debt; she is become the scorn of those foreigners to whom she was once terrible, and it is easy to see that her glory is in the wane.

HOW different from this is the present state of our country; descended from a race of hardy ancestors, who loved their freedom better than they loved their lives, the Americans are jealous of the least infringement of their rights; strangers to that luxury, which effeminates the mind and body, they are capable of enduring incredible hardships; with eagerness they rush into the field of battle, and brave, with coolness, every danger; they possess a rich and fruitful country, sufficient to supply them with every necessity and convenience of life; they have inexhaustible resources for carrying on war, and bid far soon to be courted for their alliance, by the proudest monarchs of the earth. Their statesmen are equal to the task of forming and defending a free and extensive empire: their generals are brave and humane, intrepid and prudent. When I name a WASHINGTON, my audience will feel the justice of the remark, and acquit me of the charge of flattery.

POSSESSED of these advantages, we should be inexcusable to God, to our posterity, to the whole world, if we hesitated, a single moment, in asserting our rights and repelling the attacks of lawless power. Freedom is offered to us, she invited us to accept her blessings; driven from the other regions of the globe, she wishes to find an asylum in the wilds of America; with open arms let us receive the persecuted fair; let us imitate the example of our venerable ancestors, who loved and courted her into these desert climes. With determined bravery, let us resist the attacks of her imprudent ravisher; by resolution and firmness we may defend her from their power, and transmit her blessings to millions upon millions of our posterity. Let us then arouse to arms; for, upon our exertions, under God, depends their freedom; upon our exertions depends the important question, whether the rising empire of America, shall be an empire of slaves or of freemen.

ANIMATED by these considerations, my friends and fellow-citizens, let us strain every nerve in the service of our country! what are our lives when viewed in competition with the happiness of such an empire! what is our private interest when opposed to that of three millions of men! let our bosoms glow with the warmth of patriotism; let us sacrifice our ease, our fortunes, and our lives that we may save our country.

THAT a spirit of public virtue may transcend every private consideration, you, the respected inhabitants of the town of Boston, have plainly manifested: with pleasure you have sacrificed what selfish men hold most dear, to save this oppressed land! with firmness you have resisted every attack of arbitrary power! like the sturdy oak, you have stood unmoved, and to you, under God, will be owing the salvation of this extensive continent.

WE feel, my beloved friends, our obligations to you! our hearts confess them; we cordially wish it were in our power to reward you for your patriotism; to restore you to that ease and affluence of which for our sakes, you have deprived yourselves; it is not. But our morning and evening petitions to the guardian God of America shall be, that he will bless and reward you.

WITH transport, my countrymen, let us look forward to the bright day, which shall hail us a free and independent state. With earnestness let us implore the forgiveness and the patronage of the Being of all beings, who holds the fate of empires in his hands! with zeal let us exert ourselves in the service of our country, in life: and when the earthly scene shall be closing with us, let us expire with this prayer upon our quivering lips, O GOD, LET AMERICA BE FREE!

SPEECH TO BOTH HOUSES

Thomas Hutchinson

Born in Boston September 9, 1711, Thomas Hutchinson was educated at the North Grammar School and at Harvard University, which he entered at the age of twelve. He was graduated in 1727 and three years later received his A.M. degree from the same institution. After entering his father's commercial house, Hutchinson moved into public life where he occupied a succession of offices beginning with that of selectman of Boston in 1737. In the next forty years he was to be elected or appointed as judge of probate for Suffolk County, lieutenant governor of Massachusetts, chief justice, and in 1771 governor of the colony.

Conservative, influential, wealthy, he was thought of as the leader of "the court party." It was his insistence that Parliament had the right to govern and to tax the colonies that stirred the anger of the citizens of Boston against him in 1765 and resulted in the destruction of his mansion by a mob. This action embittered Hutchinson and led him to take a more stringent position, finally resulting in his sending secret communications to the British government urging them to exercise greater authority over the colonies. The disclosure of the contents of these letters to the people of Boston further alienated Hutchinson from the colonists and particularly from the Council and House of Representatives. In 1774, Hutchinson was permitted to journey to England, and although he disliked England and was constantly homesick, he was never permitted to return. He died in England June 3, 1780.

On October 30, 1772, a committee of twenty-one persons was appointed by the town of Boston to state the right of the colonists. The report of this committee was sent to every town in the province and to every member of the House of Representatives. It was but the beginning of a series of communications between Governor Hutchinson and the Assembly, culminating in the address which Hutchinson gave to both houses on February 16, 1773. In it Hutchinson set forth clearly and explicitly his argument that the colonies derive their powers, not from the Crown, but from Parliament and were subject, therefore, to all its laws and authority.

The text of the address is a broadside printed by Draper in Boston in 1773.

Gentlemen of the Council, and
 Gentlemen of the House of Representatives,

THE Proceedings of such of the Inhabitants of the Town of Boston as assembled together and passed and published their

Resolves or Votes as the Act of the Town at a legal Town Meeting, denying in the most express terms the Supremacy of Parliament, and inviting every other Town and District in the Province to adopt the same Principle and to establish Committees of Correspondence to consult upon proper measures to maintain it, and the Proceedings of divers others Towns, in consequence of this invitation, appeared to me to be so unwarrantable and of such a dangerous nature and tendency, that I thought myself bound to call upon you in my Speech at opening the Session, to join with me in discountenancing and bearing a proper Testimony against such Irregularities and Innovations.

I stated to you fairly and truly, as I conceived, the Constitution of the Kingdom and of the Province so far as relates to the dependence of the latter upon the former; and I desired you, if you differed from me in Sentiments, to shew me with candour my own errors, and to give your reasons in support of your opinions, so far as you might differ from me. I hoped that you would have considered my Speech by your joint Committees, and have given me a joint Answer; but, as the House of Representatives have declined that mode of proceeding, and as your principles in Government are very different, I am obliged to make separate and distinct replies.

I shall first apply myself to you,

Gentlemen of the Council,

The two first parts of your Answer, which respect the disorders occasioned by the Stamp Act and the general nature of Supreme Authority, do not appear to me to have a tendency to invalidate any thing which I have said in my Speech; for, however the Stamp Act may have been the immediate occasion of any disorders, the authority of Parliament was notwithstanding, denied in order to justify or excuse them. And, for the nature of the Supreme authority of Parliament, I have never given you any reason to suppose that I intended a more absolute power in Parliament, or a greater degree of active or passive obedience in the People, than what is founded in the nature of Government let the form of it be what it may. I shall, therefore, pass over those parts of your Answer without any other remark. I would also have saved you the trouble of all those authorities which you have brought to shew, that all taxes upon English Subjects must be levied by virtue of the Act not of the King alone, but in conjunction with the Lords and Commons, for I should very readily have allowed it; and I should as readily have allowed that all other Acts of Legislation must be passed by the same joint Authority and not by the King alone.

Indeed, I am not willing to continue a controversy with you

upon any other parts of your Answer. I am glad to find that Independence is what you have not in contemplation; and that you will not presume to prescribe the exact limits of the authority of Parliament; only, as with due deference to it, you are humbly of opinion, that, as all human authority in the nature of it is and ought to be limited, it cannot constitutionally extend, for the reasons you have suggested, to the levying of Taxes in any form on His Majesty's Subjects of this Province.

I will only observe, that your attempts to draw a line as the limits of the Supreme authority in Government, by distinguishing some natural Rights, as more peculiarly exempt from such authority than the rest, rather tend to evince the impracticability of drawing such a line; and that some parts of your Answer seem to infer a Supremacy in the Province at the same time that you acknowledge the Supremacy of Parliament, for otherwise the Rights of the Subjects cannot be the same in all essential respects, as you suppose them to be, in all parts of the dominions, "under a like form of Legislature."

From these, therefore, and other considerations I cannot help flattering myself, that, upon more mature deliberation and in order to a more consistent plan of Government, you will chuse rather to doubt of the expediency of Parliament's exercising its authority in cases that may happen, than to limit the authority itself, especially as you agree with me in the proper method of obtaining a redress of grievances by constitutional representations, which cannot well consist with a denial of the authority to which the representations are made; and, from the best information I have been able to obtain, the denial of the authority of Parliament, expressly or by implication in those Petitions to which you refer was the cause of their not being admitted, and not any advice given by the Minister to the Agents of the Colonies.

I must enlarge and be more particular in my Reply to you. *Gentlemen of the House of Representatives,*

I shall take no notice of that part of your answer which attributes the disorders of the Province to an undue exercise of the power of Parliament, because you take for granted, what can by no means be admitted, that Parliament had exercised its power without just authority. The sum of your Answer so far as it is pertinent to my Speech, is this.

You alledge that the Colonies were an acquisition of foreign Territory not annexed to the Realm of England, and therefore at the *absolute* disposal of the Crown; the King having, as you take it, a constitutional right to dispose of and alienate any part of his Territories, not annexed to the Realm—that Queen Elizabeth accordingly conveyed the property, *dominion*, and *sovereignty* of Virginia to Sir Walter Raleigh to be held of the Crown *by homage and a certain render*, without receiving any share in the legislative and executive authority—that the subsequent grants of America were similar in this respect, that they were without any reservation for securing the subjection of the Colonists to the Parliament and future Laws of England—that this was the sense of the English Crown, the Nation and our Predecessors when they first took possession of this Country—that if the Colonies were not then annexed to the Realm they cannot have been annexed since that time—that if they are not now annexed to the Realm they are not part of the Kingdom, and consequently not subject to the Legislative authority of the Kingdom; for no Country, by the Common Law, was subject to the Laws or to the Parliament, but the Realm of England.

Now if this your foundation shall fail you in every part of it, as I think it will, the Fabrick which you have raised upon it must certainly fall.

Let me then observe to you that, as English Subjects, and agreeable to the doctrine of feudal Tenure, all our lands and Tenements are held mediately or immediately of the Crown, and although the possession and use or profits be in the Subject, there still remains a Dominion in the Crown. When any new Countries are discovered by English Subjects, according to the general law and usage of Nations, they become part of the State, and, according to the feudal System, the Lordship or Dominion is in the Crown and a right accrues of disposing of such Territories, under such Tenure or for such services to be performed as the Crown shall judge proper, and whensoever any part of such Territories, by Grant from the Crown, becomes the possession or property of private persons, such persons, thus holding under the Crown of England, remain, or become Subjects of England, to all intents and purposes, as fully as if any of the Royal Manors Forests or other Territory within the Realm had been granted them upon like Tenure. But that it is now, or was when the Plantations were first granted, the Prerogative of the Kings of England to alienate such Territories from the Crown, or to constitute a number of new Governments altogether independent of the Sovereign legislative authority of the English Empire, I can by no means concede to you. I have never seen any better authority to support such an opinion than an anonymous Pamphlet by which I fear you have too easily been misled, for I shall presently show you, that the declarations of King James the first and of King Charles the first, admitting they are truly related by the author of this Pamphlet, ought to have no weight with you; nor does the cession or restoration, upon a Treaty of Peace, of Countries which have been lost or acquired in War militate with these principles, nor may any particular act of power of a Prince, in selling, or delivering up any part of His Dominions to a foreign Prince or State against the general sense of the Nation be urged to invalidate them, and upon examination it will appear that all the Grants which have been made of America are founded upon them and are made to conform to them, even those which you have adduced in support of very different principles.

You do not recollect that, prior to what you call the first Grant by Q. Elizabeth to Sir Walter Raleigh, a Grant had been made by the same Princess, to Sir Humphrey Gilbert of all such Countries as he should discover, which were to be of the allegiance of her, her Heirs and Successors; but he dying in the prosecution of his voyage, a second Grant was made to Sir Walter Raleigh which, you say, conveyed the Dominion and Sovereignty, without any reserve of legislative or executive authority, *being held by homage and a render.* To hold by *homage*, which implies fealty, *and a render* is descriptive of Socage tenure as fully, as if it had been said to hold *as of our manor of East Greenwich* the words in your charter. Now this alone was a reserve of Dominion and Sovereignty in the Queen, her Heirs and Successors and, besides this, the Grant is made upon this express condition, which you pass over, *that the People remain Subject to the Crown of England*, the head of that legislative authority, which, by the English constitution, is equally extensive with the authority of the Crown throughout every Part of the Dominions. Now if we could suppose the Queen to have acquired separate from her relation to her Subjects or in her natural capacity, which she could not do, a Title to a Country discovered by her Subjects, and then to grant the same Country to English Subjects in her public capacity as Queen of England, still by this grant, she annexed it to the Crown. Thus by not distinguishing between the Crown of England and the Kings and Queens of England in their personal or natural capacities, you have been led into a fundamental error which must prove fatal to your System. It is not material whether Virginia reverted to the Crown by Sir Walter's attainder, or whether he never took any benefit from his Grant, though the latter is most probable seeing he ceased from all attempts to take possession of the Country after a few years trial. There were, undoubtedly, divers Grants made by King James the first of the Continent of America, in the beginning of the 17th century and similar to the grant of Q. Elizabeth in this respect, that they were dependent on the Crown. The Charter to the Council at Plimouth in Devon dated November 3, 1620 more immediately respects us, and of that we have the most authentic remains.

By this Charter, upon the petition of Sir Ferdinando Gorges a Corporation was constituted to be and continue by Succession forever in the town of Plimouth aforesaid, to which Corporation that part of the American Continent which lies between 40° and

48° degrees of Latitude was granted *to be held of the King, his Heirs and Successors as of the manor of East Greenwich,* with powers to constitute subordinate Governments in America and to make Laws for such Governments, *not repugnant to the Laws and Statutes of England.* From this Corporation your Predecessors obtained a Grant of the Soil of the Colony of Massachusetts-Bay, in 1627, and, in 1628, they obtained a Charter from K. Charles the first making them a distinct Corporation, also within the Realm, and giving them full powers within the limits of their Patent, and like to those of the Council of Plimouth throughout their more extensive Territory.

We will now consider what must have been the sense of the King of the Nation and of the Patentees at the time of granting these patents. From the year 1602, the Banks and Sea-Coasts of New-England had been frequented by English Subjects for catching and drying Cod-Fish. When an exclusive Right to the Fishery was claimed, by virtue of the Patent of 1620, the House of Commons were alarmed and a Bill was brought in for allowing a free Fishery and it was upon this occasion that one of the Secretaries of State declared, perhaps as his own opinion, that the Plantations were not annexed to the Crown and so were not within the Jurisdiction of Parliament. Sir Edwin Sandys, who was one of the Virginia Company and an eminent Lawyer, declared that he knew Virginia had been annexed and *was held of the Crown as of the Manor of East Greenwich* and he believed New-England was so also; and so it most certainly was. This declaration, made by one of the King's Servants, you say shewed the sense of the Crown and, being not secretly but openly declared in Parliament you would make it the sense of the Nation also, notwithstanding your own assertation that the Lords and Commons passed a Bill that shewed their sense to be directly the contrary. But if there had been full evidence of express declarations made by King James the first and King Charles the first they were declarations contrary to their own Grants, which declare this Country to be held of the Crown and consequently it must have been annexed to it. And may not such declarations be accounted for by other Actions of those Princes who when they were soliciting the Parliament to grant the Duties of Tonnage and Poundage with other aids and were, in this way, acknowledging the Rights of Parliament, at the same time were requiring the payment of those Duties with Ship Money, etc. by virtue of their Prerogative?

But to remove all doubts of the sense of the Nation, and of the Patentees of this Patent or Charter in 1620 I need only refer you to the account published by Sir Ferdinando Gorges himself of the proceedings in Parliament upon this occasion. As he was the most active Member of the Council of Plimouth, and, as he relates what came within his own knowledge and observation his Narrative, which has all the appearance of truth and sincerity, must carry conviction with it. He says that soon after the Patent was passed and whilst it lay in the Crown-Office he was summoned to appear in Parliament to answer what was to be objected against it, and the House being in a Committee, and Sir Edward Coke, that great oracle of the Law, in the Chair, he was called to the Bar and was told by Sir Edward that the House understood that a Patent had been granted to the said Ferdinando and divers other noble persons for establishing a Colony in New-England, that this was deemed a grievance of the Common-wealth *contrary to the Laws*, and to the privileges of the Subject, that it was a Monopoly, etc. and he required the delivery of the Patent into the House. Sir Ferdinando Gorges made no doubt of the authority of the House but submitted to their disposal the Patent as in their wisdom they thought good "not knowing, under favor, how any action of that kind could be a grievance to the Publick seeing it was undertaken for the advancement of Religion, *the enlargement of the bounds of our nation, etc.* —He was willing, however to submit the whole to their honorable censures." After divers attendances he imagined he had satisfied the House that the planting a Colony was of much more consequence than a simple disorderly course of Fishing. He was, notwithstanding, disappointed and, when the public grievances of the Kingdom were presented by the two Houses, that of the Patent for New-England was the first. I don't know how Parliament could have shewn more fully the sense they then had of their Authority over this new acquired Territory; nor can we expect better evidence of the sense which the Patentees had of it, for I know of no historical fact of which we have less reason to doubt.

And now, Gentlemen I will shew you how it appears from our Charter itself, which you say I have not yet been pleased to point out to you except from that Clause which restrains us from making Laws repugnant to the Laws of England, that it was the sense of our Predecessors, at the time when the Charter was granted that they were to remain subject to the supreme Authority of Parliament.

Besides this clause, which I shall have occasion further to remark upon before I finish, you will find that, by the Charter a grant was made of exemption from all taxes and impositions upon any goods imported *into New-England* or exported from thence into England for the space of twenty-one years, except the custom of five per Cent upon such goods as, after the expiration of seven years, should be brought into England. Nothing can be more plain than that the Charter, as well as the Patent to the Council of Plimouth, constitutes a Corporation in England with powers to create a subordinate government or governments within the Plantation, so that there would always be Subjects of taxes and impositions both in the Kingdom and in the Plantation. An exemption for twenty-one years implies a right of imposition after the expiration of the term, and there is no distinction between the Kingdom and the Plantation. By what authority, then, in the understanding of the Parties, were those impositions to be laid? If any, to support a System, should say by the King rather than to acknowledge the authority of Parliament, yet this could not be the sense of one of our principal Patentees Mr. Samuel Vassal who at that instant, 1628, the date of the Charter, was suffering the loss of his goods rather than submit to an imposition laid by the King without the authority of Parliament; and to prove that a few years after it could not be the sense of the rest, I need only to refer you to your own records for the year 1642 where you will find an Order of the House of Commons, conceived in such terms as discover a plain Reference to this part of the Charter, after fourteen years of the twenty-one were expired. By this Order the House of Commons declare that all goods and merchandize exported to New-England or imported from thence shall be free from all taxes and impositions both in the kingdom *and in New-England* until the House shall take further order therein to the contrary. The sense which our Predecessors had of the benefit which they took from this Order evidently appears from the Vote of the General Court, acknowledging their humble thankfulness and preserving a grateful remembrance of the honorable respect from that high Court, and resolving, that the Order sent unto them under the hand of the Clerk of the Honorable House of Commons shall be entered among their Publick Records to remain there unto Posterity: And, in an Address to Parliament, nine years after, they acknowledge, among other undeserved favors that of *taking off the Customs from them.*

I am at a loss to know what your Ideas could be when you say that if the Plantations are not Part of the *Realm*, they are not Part of the *Kingdom,* seeing the two words can properly convey but one idea and they have one and the same signification in the different languages from whence they are derived. I do not charge you with any design, but the equivocal use of the word Realm in several parts of your Answer makes them perplexed and obscure. Sometimes, you must intend the whole Dominion, which is subject to the authority of Parliament, sometimes only strictly the Territorial Realm to which other Dominions are or may be annexed. If you mean that no Countries but the ancient territorial Realm can constitutionally be subject to the Supreme authority of England, which you have very incautiously said is a rule of the Common Law of England; this is a doctrine which you will never be able to support. That the Common Law should be controuled and changed by Statutes, every day's experience teaches, but that the Common Law prescribes limits to the extent of the Legislative Power, I believe has never been said upon any other occasion. That Acts of Parliaments for several hundred Years past have respected Countries, which are not strictly within the Realm, you might easily have discovered by the statute Books. You will find Acts for regulating the Affairs of Ireland, though a separate and distinct Kingdom. Wales and Calais, whilst they sent no Representatives to Parliament, were subject to the like regulations; so are Guernsey, Jersey, Alderney, etc. which send no Members to this day. These Countries are not more properly a Part of the Ancient Realm, than the Plantations, nor do I know they can more properly be said to be annexed to the Realm, unless the declaring that Acts of Parliament shall extend to Wales, though not particularly named shall make it so, which I conceive it does not in the sense you intend.

Thus, I think, I have made it appear that the Plantations, though not strictly within the Realm, have from the beginning, been constitutionally subject to the Supreme Authority of the Realm and are so far annexed to it as to be, with the Realm and the other dependencies upon it one intire Dominion; and that the Plantation, or Colony of Massachusetts-Bay in particular is holden as feudatory of the Imperial Crown of England, deem it to be no Part of the Realm it is immaterial for, to use the words of a very great Authority in a Case in some respects analogous, "being feudatory the conclusion necessarily follows, that it is under the Government of the King's Laws and the King's Courts in Cases proper for them to interpose, though (like Counties Palatine) it has peculiar Laws and Customs, *Jura Regalia,* and complete jurisdiction at home."

Your remark upon and construction of the words, *not repugnant to the laws of England*, are much the same with those of the Council; but can any reason be assigned why the Laws of England as they stood just at that Period should be pitched upon as the Standard, more than at any other Period? If so, why was it not recurred to when the second Charter was granted, more than sixty Years after the first? It is not improbable, that the original intention might be a repugnancy in general and, *a fortiori,* such Laws as were made more immediately to respect us, but the statute of 7th and 8th, of King William and Queen Mary, soon after the second charter, favors the latter construction only; and the Province Agent, Mr. Dummer, in his much applauded defence of the Charter, says that *then* a Law in the Plantations may be said to be repugnant to a Law made in Great Britain, when it flatly contradicts it so far as the Law made there mentions and relates to the Plantations. But, gentlemen, there is another clause both in the first and second Charter which, I think will serve to explain this or to render all dispute upon the construction of it unnecessary.

You are enabled to impose such Oaths only as are warrantable by, or not repugnant to the Laws and Statutes of the Realm. I believe you will not contend that these Clauses must mean such Oaths only as were warrantable at the Respective times when the Charters were granted. It has often been found necessary, since the date of the Charters, to alter the forms of the Oaths to the Government by Acts of Parliament, and such alterations have always been conformed to in the Plantations.

Lest you should think that I admit the authority of King Charles the Second in giving his assent to an Act of the Assembly of Virginia, which you subjoin to the authorities of James the first and Charles the first, to have any weight, I must observe to you that I do not see any greater consistency with Magna Charta in the King's giving his assent to an Act of a subordinate Legislature immediately or in Person than when he does it mediately by His Governor or Substitute but, if it could be admitted that such an assent discovered the King's judgment that Virginia was independent, would you lay any stress upon it when the same King was from time to time giving his assent to Acts of Parliament which inferred the dependence of all the Colonies, and had by one of those Acts declared the Plantations to be inhabited and peopled by His Majesty's subjects of England?

I gave you no reason to remark upon the absurdity of a grant to Persons born within the Realm of the same liberties which would have belonged to them if they had been born within the Realm, but rather guarded against it by considering such grant as declaratory only, and in the nature of an assurance that the Plantations would be considered as the Dominions of England. But is there no absurdity in a grant from the King of England of the Liberties and Immunities of Englishmen to Persons born in and who are to inhabit other Territories than the Dominions of England, and would such grant, whether by charter, or other Letters Patent, be sufficient to make them inheritable, or to entitle them to the other Liberties and Immunities of Englishmen, in any Part of the English Dominions?

As I am willing to rest the Point between us upon the Plantations having been, from their first discovery and settlement under the Crown, a Part of the Dominions of England, I shall not take up any time in remarking upon your arguments to show that since that time, they cannot have been made a Part of those Dominions.

The remaining Parts of your Answer are principally intended to prove that, under both Charters, it hath been the sense of the People that they were not subject to the jurisdiction of Parliament, and, for this purpose, you have made large extracts from the History of the Colony. Whilst you are doing honor to the Book, by laying any stress upon its Authority, it would have been no more than justice to the Author if you had cited some other Passages which would have tended to reconcile the Passage, in my Speech to the History. I have said that, except about the time of the Anarchy which preceded the Restoration of King Charles the Second, I have not discovered that the Authority of Parliament had been called in question even by particular Persons. It was, as I take it, from the Principles imbibed in those times of Anarchy that the Persons of influence, mentioned in the History, disputed the authority of Parliament, but the Government would not venture to dispute it. On the contrary, in four or five Years after the Restoration, the Government declared to the King's Commissioners, that the Act of Navigation had been for some years observed here, that they knew not of its being greatly violated and that such Laws as appeared to be against it were repealed. It is not strange that these Persons of influence should prevail upon a great part of the people to fall in, for a time with their opinions and to suppose acts of the Colony necessary to give force to acts of Parliament; the government, however, several years before the Charter was vacated, more explicitly acknowledged the Authority of Parliament and voted that their Governor should take the Oath, required of him, faithfully to do and perform all matters and things enjoined him by the Acts of Trade. I have not recited in my Speech all these particulars, nor had I them all in my mind but, I think, I have said nothing inconsistent with them. My principles in Government are still the same with what they appear to be in the Book you refer to nor am I conscious that, by any part of my conduct, I have given cause to suggest the contrary.

Inasmuch as you say that I have not particularly pointed out to you the Acts and Doings of the General Assembly which relate to Acts of Parliament, I will do it now, and demonstrate to you that such Acts have been acknowledged by the Assembly, or submitted to by the People.

From your Predecessors Removal to America until the Year 1640 there was no Session of Parliament, and the first short Session of a few Days only in 1640, and the whole of the next Session, until the withdraw of the King, being taken up in the Disputes between the King and the Parliament, there could be no Room for Plantation Affairs. Soon after the King's withdraw the House of Commons passed memorable Order of 1642, and from that Time to the Restoration, this Plantation seems to have been distinguished from the rest, and the several Acts and Ordinances, which respected the other Plantations, were never enforced here, and, possibly, under Colour of the Exemption in 1642, it might not be intended they should be executed.

For 15 or 16 years after the Restoration, there was no Officer of the Customs in the Colony, except the Governor annually elected by the People, and the Acts of Trade were but little regarded, nor did the Governor take the Oath required of Governors, by the Act of the 12th of King Charles the Second, until the Time which I have mentioned. Upon the Revolution the Force of an Act of Parliament was evident in a Case of as great Importance as any which could happen to the Colony. King William and Queen Mary were proclaimed in the Colony, King and Queen of England, France, and Ireland, and *the Dominions thereunto belonging*, in the Room of King James, and this not by Virtue of an Act of Parliament which altered the Succession to the Crown, and for which the People waited several Weeks with anxious Concern. By force of another Act of Parliament, and that only, such Officers of the Colony as had taken the Oaths of Allegiance to King James deemed themselves at Liberty to take, and accordingly did take the Oaths to King William and Queen Mary. And that I may mention other Act of Parliament that the illustrious House of Hanover succeeded to the Throne of Britain and *its Dominions*, and by several other Acts, the Forms of the Oaths have from Time to Time, been altered, and by a late Act that Form was established which every one of us has complied with as the Charter in express Words requires and makes our Duty. Shall we now dispute whether Acts of Parliament have been submitted to when we find them submitted to in Points which are of the very Essence of our Constitution? If you should disown that Authority which has Power even to change the Succession to the Crown, are you in no Danger of denying the Authority of our most gracious Sovereign, which I am sure none of you can have in your Thoughts?

I think I have before shewn you, Gentlemen, what must have been the Sense of our Predecessors at the Time of the first Charter, let us now, whilst we are upon the Acts and Doings of the Assembly, consider what it must have been at the Time of the second Charter. Upon the first Advice of the Revolution in England, the Authority which assumed the Government instructed their Agents to petition *the Parliament* to restore the first Charter, and a Bill for that Purpose passed the House of Commons, but went no further. Was not this owning *the authority of Parliament?* By an Act of Parliament, passed in the first year of King William and Queen Mary, a form of Oaths was established, to be taken by those Princes and by all succeeding Kings and Queens of England at their Coronation, the first of which is, that they will govern the People of the Kingdom, *and the Dominions thereunto belonging, according to the Statutes in Parliament agreed on, and the Laws and Customs of the Same.* When the Colony directed their Agents to make their humble application to King William to grant the second Charter, they could have no other Pretence than as they were Inhabitants of Part *of the Dominions of England*, and they also knew the Oath the King had taken to govern them *according to the Statutes in Parliament*; surely then, at the time of this Charter also, it was the sense of our Predecessors, as well as of the King and of the Nation, that there was, and would remain a Supremacy in the Parliament. About the same time, they acknowledge, in an address to the King, that they have no Power to make Laws *repugnant to the Laws of England.* And, at the same Session, an Act passed establishing Naval Officers in several Ports of the Province, for which this reason is given, *that all undue trading contrary to an Act of Parliament made in the 15th year of King Charles the second may be prevented in this their Majesty's Province.* The Act of this Province passed so long ago as the second year of King George the first, for stating the Fees of the Custom House Officers, must have relation to the Acts of Parliament by which they are constituted, and the Provision made in that Act of the Province for extending the Port of Boston to all the Roads as far as Cape-Cod, could be for no other purpose than for the more effectual carrying the Acts of Trade into execution. And, to come nearer to the present time, when an Act of Parliament had passed, in 1741, for putting an end to certain unwarrantable schemes in this Province, did the Authority of Government, of those Persons more immediately affected by it, ever dispute the Validity of it? On the contrary, have not a number of Acts been passed in the Province, the Burdens to which such Persons were subjected might be equally apportioned, and have not all those Acts of the Province been very carefully framed to prevent their militating with the Act of Parliament? I will mention also an Act of Parliament made in the first year of Queen Anne, altho' the proceedings upon it, more immediately respected the Council. By this Act no Office civil or military shall be void by the death of the King, but shall continue six months, unless suspended or made void by the next successor. By force of this Act, Governor Dudley continued in the Administration six months from the demise of Queen Anne, and immediately after, the Council assumed the Administration and continued it until a Proclamation arrived from King George, by virtue of which Governor Dudley reassumed the government. It would be tedious to enumerate the Addresses, Votes and Messages of both the Council and House of Representatives to the same purpose. I have said enough to shew that this Government has submitted to Parliament from a Conviction of its constitutional Supremacy, and this not *from inconsideration, nor merely from reluctance at the idea of contending with the Parent State.*

If then I have made it appear, that both by the first and second Charters we hold our Lands and the Authority of Government not of the King but of the Crown of England, that being a Dominion of the Crown of England, we are consequently sub-

ject to the Supreme Authority of England, that this hath been the
sense of this Plantation, except in those few years when the principles of Anarchy which had prevailed in the Kingdom had not lost
their influence here; and if, upon a review of your Principles, they
shall appear to you to have been delusive and erroneous, as I think
they must, or if you shall only be in doubt of them, you certainly
will not draw that Conclusion which otherwise you might do,
and which I am glad you have hitherto avoided; especially when
you consider the obvious and inevitable distress and misery of
Independence upon our Mother Country, if such Independence
could be allowed or maintained, and the probability of much greater
distress which we are not able to foresee.

You ask me, if we have not reason to fear we shall soon be
reduced to a worse situation than that of the Colonies of France,
Spain, or Holland. I may safely affirm that we have not; that we
have no reason to fear any evils from a submission to the authority
of Parliament, equal to what we must feel from its authority
being disputed, from an uncertain Rule of Law and Government.
For more than seventy years together, the supremacy of Parliament
was acknowledged without complaints of Grievance. The effect of
every measure cannot be forseen by human wisdom. What can be expected more from any authority than when the unfitness of a
measure is discovered, to make it void? When upon the united
Representations and Complaints of the American Colonies any
Acts have appeared to Parliament to be unsalutary, have there not
been repeated instances of the repeal of such Acts? We cannot
expect these instances should be carried so far as to be equivalent
to a disavowal or relinquishment of the right itself. Why then shall
we fear for ourselves and our posterity, greater rigor of government for seventy years to come than what we and our predecessors
have felt, in the seventy years past.

You must give me leave, Gentlemen, in a few words to vindicate myself from a charge, in one part of your Answer, of having,
by my Speech, reduced you to the unhappy alternative of appearing
by your silence to acquiesce in my sentiments, or of freely discussing
this point of the supremacy of Parliament. I saw, as I have before
observed, the capital Town of the Province, without being reduced
to such an alternative, voluntarily not only discussing but determining this point, and inviting every other Town and District in the
Province to do the like. I saw that many of the principal Towns
had followed the example, and that there was imminent danger
of a compliance in most if not all the rest, in order to avoid being
distinguished. Was not I reduced to the alternative of rendering
myself justly obnoxious to the displeasure of my Sovereign by
acquiescing in such Irregularities, or of calling upon you to join
with me in suppressing them? Might I not rather have expected

from you an expression of your concern that any Persons should project and prosecute a plan of measure which would lay me under the necessity of bringing this point before you? It was so far from being my inclination, that nothing short of a sense of my duty to the King, and the obligations I am under to consult your true interest could have compelled me to it.

Gentlemen of the Council, and
   Gentlemen of the House of Representatives,

We all profess to be the loyal and dutiful subjects of the King of Great Britain. His Majesty considers the British empire as one entire Dominion, subject to one supreme legislative Power, a due submission to which is essential to the maintenance of the Rights, Liberties and Privileges of the several parts of this Dominion. We have abundant evidence of his Majesty's tender and impartial regard to the Rights of his Subjects; and I am authorised to say, that "his Majesty will most graciously approve of every constitutional Measure that may contribute to the Peace, the Happiness, and Prosperity of his Colony of Massachusetts-Bay, and which may have the effect to shew to the world, that he has no wish beyond that of reigning in the hearts and affections of his People."

"Let Us Look to the End"

Josiah Quincy, Jr.

Josiah Quincy, Jr. was born in Boston on February 23, 1744. He received his early schooling at Braintree. In 1759, he entered Harvard, taking his bachelor's degree in 1763 and his master's degree three years later. Immediately upon his graduation, he began the study of law in the office of Oxenbridge Thacher. When Thacher died, Quincy took charge of the office. After the attack by a Boston mob on the British soldiers had resulted in the "Boston Massacre," Quincy, with John Adams, undertook the task of defending the soldiers in court. Being one of the leaders of the patriot cause and having a gift of oratory, he was sent to England in 1774 where he interviewed leading men. His health failing, he set sail for home on March 16, 1775. He died a few hours before the ship entered Gloucester harbor, April 26, 1775.

Denying the right of Parliament to tax America, and especially condemning the tax on tea, the people of the Colonies were determined that tea shipments should not be landed but sent back to England.

With three ships, containing cargoes of tea, in the harbor of Boston, and with the day approaching when the Revenue officers could legally take possession of the ships and land the tea, the people from Boston and surrounding country held a meeting the morning of December 16, 1773. They voted unanimously that the tea should not be landed. Quincy gave his speech at that meeting. The Boston Tea Party occurred that evening.

The text is from the *Proceedings of the Massachusetts Historical Society, 1873–1875*. Boston: Massachusetts Historical Society, 1875, p. 197.

It is not, Mr. Moderator, the spirit that vapors within these walls that must stand us in stead. *The exertions of this day will call forth events* which will make a very different spirit *necessary* for our salvation. Look to the end. Whoever supposes that shouts and hosannas will terminate the trials of the day, entertains a childish fancy. We must be grossly ignorant of the importance and value of the prize for which we contend—we must be equally ignorant of the powers of those who have combined against us— we must be blind to that malice, inveteracy, and insatiable revenge, which actuate our enemies, public and private, abroad and in our bosom, to hope we shall end this controversy without the sharpest, the sharpest conflicts; to flatter ourselves that popular resolves, popular harangues, popular acclamations, and popular vapor, will vanquish our foes. Let us consider the issue. Let us look to the end. Let us weigh and consider before we advance to those measures which must bring on the most trying and terrible struggle, this country ever saw.

CHARGE

to the Grand Juries, November 5 & 15, 1774

William Henry Drayton

William Henry Drayton was born in September of 1742 near
Charleston, South Carolina. Educated in England at Westminster
School and Oxford, he returned to South Carolina and became a
planter. He entered the Assembly in 1765. From 1772 to 1775 he
sat on the Council of the province and served as assistant judge. A
member of the important revolutionary bodies in the province, and
chairman of several, he performed valuable service in the spring of
1775 in preparing for armed resistance. On November 1, 1775, he
was elected president of the provincial Congress. He was elected
chief justice under the state constitution of March, 1776. He represented the state of South Carolina in the Continental Congress
from March 30, 1778, until his death in September, 1779.

William Henry Drayton, as a judge for the districts of
Camden and Cheraws in South Carolina, delivered this charge to
the Grand Juries on his circuit through these districts.

The text is from Peter Force. *American Archives.* 4th ser.;
Vol. I, 959–60. Washington: M. St. Claire Clarke and Peter
Force, 1837.

Gentlemen of the Grand Jury:

You are now met to discharge one of the most important
duties in society, for you are assembled arbiters of the innocence
or guilt of such of your fellow citizens who are so unfortunate
as to have afforded occasion, however slight, for the laws to take
cognizance of their conduct. You are authorized to pass judgment,
in the first instance, upon the apparently guilty wretch, and by
your acquitting voice, to shield apparent innocence from a malicious
prosecution. Such powers have the Constitution of your country
vested in you, powers no less important than truly honourable,
when exercised with a fearless integrity.

It is your indispensable duty to endeavour to exercise these
powers with propriety; it is mine concisely to point out to you the
line of your conduct—a conduct which the venerable Constitution
of your country intends, by protecting the innocent and by delivering the guilty over to the course of law, should operate to nourish,
in its native vigour, even that Constitution itself, from whose
generous spirit we have a title to call ourselves freemen, an appel-
ation which peculiarly distinguishes the *English* subjects (those

unfortunately disappointed fellow-citizens in *Quebec* excepted) and ranks them above all the civilized Nations of the earth.

By as much as you prefer freedom to slavery, by so much ought you to prefer a generous death to servitude, and to hazard everything to endeavour to maintain that rank which is so gloriously pre-eminent above all other Nations. You ought to endeavour to preserve it, not only for its inestimable value, but from a reverence to our ancestors from whom we received it, and from a love of our children, to whom we are bound, by every consideration, to deliver down this legacy, the most valuable that ever was or can be delivered to posterity. It is compounded of the most generous civil liberty that ever existed, and the sacred Christian Religion released from the absurdities which are inculcated, the shackles which are imposed, the tortures which are inflicted, and the flames which are lighted, blown up and fed with blood by the Roman Catholick doctrines: doctrines which tend to establish a most cruel tyranny in Church and State—a tryanny under which all *Europe* groaned for many ages. And such are the distinguishing characters of this legacy, which may *God* of his infinite goodness and mercy long preserve to us and graciously continue to our posterity: but without our pious and unwearied endeavours to preserve these blessings, it is folly and presumption to hope for a continuance of them; hence, in order to stimulate your exertions in favour of your civil liberties, which protect your religious rights, instead of discoursing to you of the laws of other States, and comparing them to our own, allow me to tell you what your civil liberties are, and to charge you, which I do in the most solemn manner, to hold them dearer than your lives; a lesson and charge at all times proper from a Judge, but particularly so at this crisis, when *America* is in one general and generous commotion touching this truly important point.

It is unnecessary for me to draw any other character of those liberties than that great line by which they are distinguished; and happy is it for the subject that those liberties can be marked in so easy and in so distinguishing a manner. And this is the distinguishing character: *English* people cannot be taxed, nay, they cannot be bound by any law unless by their consent, expressed by themselves or their Representatives of their own election. This Colony was settled by *English* subjects; by a people from *England* herself; a people who brought over with them, who planted in this Colony, and who transmitted to posterity the invaluable rights of *English-men*—rights which no time, no contract, no climate can diminish. Thus possessed of such rights, it is of the most serious importance that you strictly execute those regulations which have arisen from such a parentage, and to which you have given the authority of laws, by having given your constitutional consent that they should operate as laws; for by your not executing what those laws require, you would weaken the force, and would shew, I may almost say, a treasonable contempt of those constitutional rights out of which your laws arise, and which you ought to defend and support at the hazard of your lives. Hence, by all the ties which mankind hold most dear and sacred; your reverence to your ancestors; your love to your own interests; your tenderness to your posterity; by the lawful obligations of your oath, I charge you to do your duty; to maintain the laws, the rights, the Constitution of your country, even at the hazard of your lives and fortunes.

Some courtly Judges style themselves the King's servants, a style which sounds harshly in my ears, inasmuch as the being a servant implies obedience to the orders of the master, and such Judges might possibly think that, in the present situation of *American* affairs, this charge is inconsistent with my duty to the King. But for my part, in my judicial character, I know no master but the law; I am a servant, not to the King, but to the Constitution; and, in my estimation, I shall best discharge my duty as a good subject to the King, and a trusty officer under the Constitution, when I boldly declare the law to the people and instruct them in their civil rights. Indeed, you gentlemen of the Grand Jury, cannot properly comprehend your duty, and your great obligation to perform it, unless you know those civil rights from which these duties spring, and, by knowing the value of those rights, thence learn your obligations to perform these duties.

Having thus generally touched upon the nature and importance of your civil rights, in order to excite you to execute those laws to which they have given birth, I will now point out to you the particular duties which the laws of your country require at your hands.

Unbiased by affection to, and unawed by fear of, any man, or any set of men, you are to make presentment of every person and of every proceeding militating against publick good. The law orders me particularly to give in charge, to watch carefully over our Negro Act, and our Jury Law—a law which cannot be too highly valued, whether we regard the excellency of its nature or the importance of its object. This law carries in itself an indelible mark of what high importance the Legislature thought it when they enacted it; and it carries in itself also a kind of prophecy that its existence in its native vigour would, in after times, be endangered, and therefore it is that the law orders the Judges ever to charge the Grand Juries to watch over it with care; indeed you ought to do so with the most jealous circumspection. A learned Judge says, "Every new tribunal erected for the decision of facts, without the intervention of a Jury, is a step towards aristocracy, the most oppressive of absolute Governments; and it is therefore a duty which every man owes to his country, his friends, his posterity, and himself, to maintain to the utmost of his power this valuable Constitution in all its rights, to restore it to its ancient dignity, if at all impaired; to amend it wherever it is defective, and above all to guard with the most jealous circumspection against the introduction of new and arbitrary methods of trial, which, under a variety of plausible pretences, may in time imperceptibly undermine this best preservative of *English* liberty." Mr. Justice *Blackstone* terms the *English* Trial by Jury, the glory of the *English* Law; let me tell you our Trial by Jury is that kind of glory in full meridian lustre, in comparison of which the *English* mode appears only with diminished splendour.

But let not your care of this great object occupy all your attention; you are to find all such bills of indictment as the examination of witnesses in support of them may induce you to think there is a probability that the fact charged is true; for you are not to exact such circumstancial and positive evidence as would be necessary to support the indictment before a Petit Jury. To make those presentments, and to find these bills, it is not necessary that you all agree in opinion; twelve united voices among you are sufficient to discharge the duties of a Grand Jury, but it is absolutely necessary that twelve of you agree in opinion upon every point under your consideration; and happy, happy, thrice happy are that people who cannot be made to suffer under any construction of the law, but by the united voices of twenty-four impartial men, having no interest in the cause, but that the laws be executed and justice be administered.

In short, that you may discharge your duty with propriety, and that you may pursue that course of conduct which the law requires, let me, in the strongest terms, recommend to you that you keep constantly in your mind the nature and particulars of the oath which you have just taken. To you this oath is of as much importance as the mariner's compass is to those who sail on the ocean; this points out the course of their voyage; your oath as clearly points out to you the course of your conduct. I dare say you are willing to discharge that duty which you owe to society; I make no doubt but that you will discharge it with advantage to the publick, and therefore with honour to yourselves.

AN ORATION

Thomas Bolton

In an effort to pass time and, perhaps, maintain their feeling of superiority, literate loyalists and British officers lampooned in verse, dramatic "production," and oratory the "misadventures" of their antagonists. Typical of the oratory is "An Oration Delivered March Fifteenth, 1775. At The Request of a Number of the Inhabitants OF The Town of Boston," a burlesque of Warren's second Boston Massacre oration.

According to Dr. Bolton, his audience was comprised of "several inhabitants of the town of Boston, legally assembled at the British Coffee House, on Wednesday the 15th day of March, Annoque Domini, 1775." The text is taken from a private printing of the oration in 1775.

Ye Friends to justice, equity, and truth,
Ye Foes to falsehood, treason, and rebellion,
- - - - - - - With patience hear me.

THE flourishes of rhetoric I cannot use—these will I leave to the SONS of LIBERTY of this degenerate age.

I cannot boast the ignorance of HANCOCK, the insolence of ADAMS, the absurdity of ROWE, the arrogance of LEE, the vicious life and untimely death of MOLLINEAUX, the turgid bombast of Warren, the treasons of QUINCY, the hypocrisy of COOPER, nor the principles of YOUNG—Nor can I with propriety pass over the characters of these *modern heroes,* (or, to use their own phrase, *Indians,*) without a few observations on their late conduct.

These *sachems,* or *Indian chiefs,* tho' of different titles, all proceeded from one and the same tribe; who being originally inhabitants of a country a thousand leagues to the eastward, were transplanted (or in the vulgar phrase, *transported*) hither, only for asserting that *claim,* which is the natural right of every man, to a share of the good things of this world; which good things, Fortune had most unjustly bestowed upon others in too large a proportion.

It was a matter of dispute for some time whether they were of the *Mohawk* kind or not; and this suspicion, I imagine, first arose from the observation of a learned physiognomist, who perceiving their *Os frontis* to be uncommonly flat, burst out into the following exclamation:

> *Your sapsculls are neither square, oval, nor round,*
> *A proof that their judgments can never be found:*
> *I really believe they are put* wrong way on,
> *As they seem to resemble a cobler's lap-stone.*

But notwithstanding the above assertion might border upon truth, yet several of these chiefs denied it, by openly declaring themselves to be neither more nor less than plain *Narragansets;* who scorn's to scalp any person who would submit to have his private property destroyed, without complaining.

With regard to their *political* schemes, I challenge all *Hell* to match them. Law they have none, nor any do they want; and could they send to Salem or Endor to procure a *witch* to bring MOLLINEAUX from the dead, even HE would condemn them.

The First of these chiefs is A——MS, a *sachem* of vast elocution; but being extremely poor, retails out syllables, sentences, eulogiums, etc. to draw in the multitude; and it can be attested, that what proceeds from the mouth of A——MS is sufficient to fill the mouths of millions in America. But it is prophesied that the time is near at hand, when the *frothy food* will fail them.

But generous JOHN scorns to let him starve—far from it; 'tis well known his purse-strings have been at SAM's disposal ever since he assisted in making the Oration delivered by JOHN on the 5th March 1774, to a crowded audience of Narraganset *Indians.*

The Second of these chiefs is H——CK, who having been possess'd of too much money for a private gentleman, resolved to make a public attempt to become a Monarch, and having courted popularity and power almost as long as he did Miss ——— Miss ——— or Mr Barnard's cook-maid, Betty Price, is at last likely to be jilted in his turn, and in the end to be wedded to beggary, contempt, and a g——s.

The Third of these incomparable *Indians* is ROWE; a chief (according to George Alexander Stevens) possess'd of a great fund of kn——owledge; but having a skull of an uncommon thickness, and the sutures of the *cranium* being closely compacted, he never has been able to display any rational faculties, except when he invented the new method of *making Tea.*

But, oh! for words to grace the character of the most traiterous of men!—a modern Bravo. Did not the name of *rebel* stain the *soldier,* I could have afforded him a more brilliant title, and have call'd him a General. His name is L——. Oh! beware my friends of his follies! He mounted to almost the height of preferment, but mazed with ambition, he fell from the precipice, burst himself asunder, and exposing his pride, proved Mr. Pope's assertion.

> *Pride still is aiming at the blest abodes,*
> *Men would be angels, angels would be gods;*
> *Aspiring to be gods, if angels fell,*
> *Aspiring to be angels, men REBELL.*

The Fifth of these chiefs is now no more. His name was M——x. He had a strong aversion to all order, civil or ecclesiastic; he swore the K—— was a tyrant, the Q—— a ————, the Prince a bastard, the bishops, papists, and the houses of lords and commons, *a den of thieves.* Thro' the strength of his own villainny, and the *laudanum* of Doctor W——n, he quitted this planet, and he went to a secondary one in search of LIBERTY.

The Sixth of these worthies is named W——RR——N; a man, who by his great skill in chemistry, could *turn water* into *milk,* and sell it for *six coppers* the quart. He was bound apprentice to an apothecary, and turn'd out a Quack; but thinking this profession too grovelling for so sublime a genius, he has lately changed it for that of *Orator,* and is already so great a proficient in the *sough,* or true *puritanic whine,* and his notes are so remarkably flat and productive of horror, that when he dismisses his hearers, you would swear they were just come out of the cave of Triphonius. - - - - - - - There's an Orator for you!

Oh! that some Son of Liberty would go to *hell,* and fetch a spark from the altar of *enthusiasm,* to kindle in me the reforming zeal of W——n!—then might I speak his language.

The Seventh of these pillars of the state is Q——CY, and tho' I have placed him only as the seventh *sachem,* yet it has been asserted that he is worthy of a higher rank; having lately composed a Treatise, in which he absolved all his Majesty's subjects from their allegiance; and was one of the first inventors of *mobbing, tarring and feathering,* and sundry other modes tending to the overthrow of all societies, civil and moral.

The Eighth of these heroes is Y——G, whose character cannot be drawn by any pen with the consistency that becomes a true limner. Could we raise up the spirit of one of the murderers of St Stephen, to tell us what a figure Paul cut, when he breathed out threatning and slaughter against his SAVIOUR, then might we form an idea of Dr Y——G; but since that is impossible, I can only refer you to—*his own countenance,* wherein you may read his true and genuine disposition. Suffice it to say, this man stands accused of rebellion, not only against his Sovereign, but against HIS GOD—he makes a mock at the merits of his Redeemer, and uses his God only *to swear by.*

Oh! my friends and fellow subjects! what infatuation must possess the deluded fools who depend on such a *race of rascals for their leaders!*

I shall pass over *many others* who are too insignificant to become the subject of my pen; - - - - - - -

> *And now to end th' infernal group here*
> *Who is so fit as Doctor C———?*
> *When gospel trumpeter surrounded*
> *With long-ear'd rout to battle sounded,*
> *And pulpit, drum ecclesiastic,*
> *Was beat with fist instead of a stick;*
> *He, prostituting his religion,*
> *Turns a dispenser of sedition;*
> *And to the greedy, gaping million,*
> *For holy writ, deals out rebellion;*
> *His sacred functions quite forsaking,*
> *Smells profit in oration making;*
> *And when with pangs and throws he's dropt it,*
> *Gets foolish, simple John t'adopt it:*
> *By me advis'd, ne'er mind the nation,*
> *But work at* home *a reformation;*
> *Leave, against kings and rulers railing,*
> *Give curtain lectures against* stealing.
> *Instead of making an Oration,*
> *Make sermons against fornication;*
> *And with uplifted voice and hand,*
> *Strongly enforce the seventh command.*
> *Of your black crimes 'gainst George and heav'n*
> *Repent; you may be yet forgiv'n.*
> *Reform the Rebel, Thief, and W———,*
> *And mercy suppliantly implore;*
> *Then entertain a ray of hope,*
> *T'escape d———mn———n and a Rope.*

"Give Me Liberty or Give Me Death"

Patrick Henry

Patrick Henry was born in Hanover County, Virginia, on May 29, 1736. He became a clerk in a crossroads store at the age of fifteen, and at sixteen he opened a store in partnership with his older brother. Within a year they had lost their capital. At the age of eighteen, he took up farming, later storekeeping, and then law. He began the practice of law in 1760. In 1765, he was chosen to the Virginia House of Burgesses. He was a delegate to both the First and Second Continental Congresses. He took part in the drafting of the new constitution of Virginia and on June 29, 1776, was elected governor. He was twice re-elected. He retired in 1779, but was again elected in 1784 and served until 1786, when his fifth term expired. He was elected to the Federal Constitutional Convention, but declined. When the Virginia convention met on October 20, 1788, he occupied a seat and took the leadership of those who opposed adoption of the proposed Federal Constitution. After this he again returned to the law. He was elected to the Virginia House of Delegates in 1799 but died on June 6 before he could assume his seat.

On the 23rd of March, 1775, the Virginia convention of delegates to the Continental Congress was meeting for the fourth anxious day in the Old Church in Richmond. That morning Mr. Henry introduced his resolution that the colony be put into a state of defense immediately. When several members raised objections, Mr. Henry answered them with this famous speech, reconstructed by William Wirt and published forty-two years after its original delivery.

The text is from William Wirt. *Life of Patrick Henry.* New York: Derby and Jackson, 1858, pp. 138–42.

Mr. President,

No man thinks more highly than I do of the patriotism, as well as abilities, of the very worthy gentlemen who have just addressed the house. But different men often see the same subject in different lights; and, therefore, I hope it will not be thought disrespectful to those gentlemen, if, entertaining as I do opinions of a character very opposite to theirs, I shall speak forth my sentiments freely and without reserve. This is no time for ceremony. The question before the house is one of awful moment to this country. For my own part, I consider it as nothing less than a question of freedom or slavery; and in proportion to the magnitude of the subject ought to be the freedom of the debate. It is only in this way that we can hope to arrive at truth, and fulfill the great responsibility which we hold to God and our country. Should I keep back my opinions at such a time through fear of giving offense, I should consider myself as guilty of treason towards my country, and of an act of disloyalty toward the Majesty of Heaven, which I revere above all earthly Kings.

Mr. President, it is natural to man to indulge in the illusions of hope. We are apt to shut our eyes against a painful truth, and listen to the song of that siren till she transforms us into beasts. Is this the part of wise men, engaged in a great and arduous struggle for liberty? Are we disposed to be of the number of those who, having eyes, see not, and having ears, hear not the things which so nearly concern their temporal salvation? For my part, whatever anguish of spirit it may cost, I am willing to know the whole truth, to know the worst, and to provide for it.

I have but one lamp by which my feet are guided, and that is the lamp of experience. I know of no way of judging of the future but by the past. And, judging by the past, I wish to know what there has been in the conduct of the British ministry for the last ten years to justify those hopes with which gentlemen have been pleased to solace themselves and the house. Is it that insidious smile with which our petition has been lately received? Trust it not, sir; it will prove a snare to your feet. Suffer not yourselves to be betrayed with a kiss. Ask yourselves how this gracious reception of our petition comports with those warlike preparations which cover our waters and darken our land. Are fleets and armies necessary to a work of love and reconciliation? Have we shown ourselves so unwilling to be reconciled that force must be called in to win back our love? Let us not deceive ourselves, sir. These are the implements of war and subjugation, the last arguments to which kings resort. I ask gentlemen, sir, What means this martial array, if its purpose be not to force us to submission? Can gentlemen assign any other possible motive for it? Has Great Britain any enemy, in this quarter of the world, to call for all this accumulation of navies and armies? No, sir, she has none. They are meant for us; they can be meant for no other. They are sent over to bind and rivet upon us those chains which the British ministry have been so long forging. And what have we to oppose to them? Shall we try argument? Sir, we have been trying that for the last ten years. Have we anything new to offer upon the subject? Nothing. We have held the subject up in every light of which it is capable, but it has been all in vain. Shall we resort to entreaty and humble supplication? What terms shall we find that have not been already exhausted? Let us not, I beseech you, sir, deceive ourselves longer. Sir, we have done everything that could be done to avert the storm which is now coming on. We have petitioned, we have remonstrated, we have supplicated, we have prostrated ourselves before the throne, and have implored its interposition to arrest the tyrannical hands of the ministry and parliament. Our petitions have been slighted, our remonstrances have produced additional violence and insult, our supplications have been disregarded, and we have been spurned with contempt from the foot of the throne! In vain, after these things, may we indulge the fond hope of peace and reconciliation. *There is no longer any room for hope.* If we wish to be free, if we mean to preserve inviolate those inestimable privileges for which we have been so long contending, if we mean not basely to abandon the noble struggle in which we have been so long engaged, and which we have pledged ourselves never to abandon until the glorious object of our contest shall be obtained, we must fight! I repeat it, sir, we must fight! An appeal to arms and to the God of Hosts is all that is left us.

They tell us, sir, that we are weak, unable to cope with so formidable an adversary. But when shall we be stronger? Will it be the next week or the next year? Will it be when we are totally disarmed, and when a British guard shall be stationed in every house? Shall we gather strength by irresolution and inaction? Shall we acquire the means of effectual resistance by lying supinely on our backs and hugging the delusive phantom of hope until our enemies shall have bound us hand and foot? Sir, we are not weak, if we make a proper use of those means which the God of nature hath placed in our power. Three millions of people, armed in the holy cause of liberty, and in such a country as that which we possess, are invincible by any force which our enemy can send against us. Besides, sir, we shall not fight our battles alone. There is a just God who presides over the destinies of nations, and who will raise up friends to fight our battles for us. The battle, sir, is not to the strong alone; it is to the vigilant, the active, the brave. Besides, sir, we have no election. If we were base enough to desire it, it is now too late to retire from the contest. There is no retreat but in submission and slavery! Our chains are forged! Their clanking may be heard on the plains of Boston! The war is inevitable—and let it come! I repeat, Sir, let it come!

It is in vain, sir, to extenuate the matter. Gentlemen may cry, Peace, Peace, but there is no peace. The next gale that sweeps from the north will bring to our ears the clash of resounding arms! Our Brethren are already in the field! Why stand we here idle? What is it that gentlemen wish? What would they have? Is life so dear, or peace so sweet, as to be purchased at the price of chains and slavery? Forbid it, Almighty God! I know not what course others may take, but as for me, give me liberty or give me death!

SPEECH

to the Convention of the Province of Pennsylvania

James Wilson

A "founding father" and theorist of federalism, James Wilson was born in Caskardy, Scotland, on September 14, 1742. From 1757 to 1765 he sporadically attended the Universities of St. Andrews, Glasgow, and Edinburgh. In February, 1776 he secured a position as Latin tutor at the College of Philadelphia and on May 19 received an honorary A.M. He studied law with John Dickinson for two years and was admitted to the bar in November, 1767. On July 12, 1774 he was made head of a Committee of Correspondence at Carlisle and elected to the first provincial conference at Philadelphia. In 1775 he was elected colonel of the fourth battalion of Cumberland County Associators but did not see active duty because of his election to the Second Continental Congress. Defeated in 1777, Wilson was re-elected in 1782 and, again, in 1785. An influential member of the Federal Convention, he was instrumental in drawing up the Constitution. In 1789 he was appointed by Washington to the Supreme Court. In 1790 he became the first professor of law at the College of Philadelphia. He died in Edenton, North Carolina, on August 21, 1798.

From January 23 to January 28, 1775 the provincial convention was held in Philadelphia. Its principal purpose was to approve the work of the Continental Congress. Wilson was asked to address the convention on the righteousness of the colonial cause and the tyrannies of Great Britain.

The text of the speech is from *The Works of the Honorable James Wilson, L.L.D.* Vol. III, 247–69. Philadelphia: Bronson and Chauncey, 1804.

Whence, Sir, proceeds all the invidious and ill-grounded clamour against the colonists of America? Why are they stigmatized, in Britain, as licentious and ungovernable? Why is their virtuous opposition to the illegal attempts of their governours, represented under the falsest colours, and placed in the most ungracious point of view? This opposition, when exhibited in its true light, and when viewed, with unjaundiced eyes, from a proper situation, and at a proper distance, stands confessed the lovely offspring of freedom. It breathes the spirit of its parent. Of this ethereal spirit, the whole conduct, and particularly the late conduct, of the colonists has shown them eminently possessed. It has animated and regulated every part of their proceedings. It has been recognised to be genuine, by all those symptoms and effects, by which it has been distinguished in other ages and other countries. It has been calm and regular: it has not acted without occasion: it has not acted disproportionately to the occasion. As the attempts, open or secret, to undermine or to destroy it, have been repeated or enforced; in a just degree, its vigilance and its vigour have been exerted to defeat or disappoint them. As its exertions have been sufficient for those purposes hitherto, let us hence draw a joyful prognostick, that they will continue sufficient for those purposes hereafter. It is not yet exhausted; it will still operate irresistibly whenever a necessary occasion shall call forth its strength.

Permit me, sir, by appealing, in a few instances, to the spirit and conduct of the colonists, to evince, that what I have said of them is just. Did they disclose any uneasiness at the proceedings and claims of the British parliament, before those claims and proceedings afforded a reasonable cause for it? Did they even disclose any uneasiness, when a reasonable cause for it was *first* given? Our rights were invaded by their regulations of our internal policy. We submitted to them: we were unwilling to oppose them. The spirit of liberty was slow to act. When those invasions were renewed; when the efficacy and malignancy of them were attempted to be redoubled by the stamp act; when chains were formed for us; and preparations were made for rivetting them on our limbs—what measures did we pursue? The spirit of liberty found it necessary now to act: but she acted with the calmness and decent dignity suited to her character. Were we rash or seditious? Did we discover want of loyalty to our sovereign? Did we betray want of affection to our brethren in Britain? Let our dutiful and reverential petitions to the throne—let our respectful, though firm, remonstrances to the parliament—let our warm and affectionate addresses to our brethren, and (we will still call them) our friends in Great Britain—let all those, transmitted from every part of the continent, testify the truth. By their testimony let our conduct be tried.

As our proceedings during the existence and operation of the stamp act prove fully and incontestably the painful sensations that tortured our breasts from the prospect of disunion with Britain; the peals of joy, which burst forth universally, upon the repeal of that odious statute, loudly proclaim the heartfelt delight produced in us by a reconciliation with her. Unsuspicious, because undesigning, we buried our complaints, and the causes of them, in oblivion, and returned, with eagerness, to our former unreserved confidence. Our connexion with our parent country, and the reciprocal blessings resulting from it to her and to us, were the favourite and pleasing topicks of our publick discourses and our private conversations. Lulled into delightful security, we dreamt of nothing but increasing fondness and friendship, cemented and strengthened by a kind and perpetual communication of good offices. Soon, however, too soon, were we awakened from the soothing dreams! Our enemies renewed their designs against us, not with less malice, but with more art. Under the plausible pretence of regulating our trade, and, at the same time, of making provision for the administration of justice, and the support of government, in some of the colonies, they pursued their scheme of depriving us of our property without our consent. As the attempts to distress us, and to degrade us to a rank inferiour to that of freemen, appeared now to be reduced into a regular system, it became proper, on our part, to form a regular system for counteracting them. We ceased to import goods from Great Britain. Was this measure dictated by selfishness or by licentiousness? Did it not injure ourselves, while it injured the British merchants and manufacturers? Was it inconsistent with the peaceful demeanour of subjects to abstain from making purchases, when our freedom and our safety rendered it necessary for us to abstain from them? A regard for our freedom and safety was our only motive; for no sooner had the parliament, by repealing part of the revenue laws, inspired us with the flattering hopes that they had departed from their intentions of oppressing and of taxing us, than we forsook our plan for defeating those intentions, and began to import as formerly. Far from being peevish or captious, we took no publick notice even of their declaratory law of dominion over us: our candor led us to consider it as a decent expedient of retreating from the actual exercise of that dominion.

But, alas! the root of bitterness still remained. The duty on tea was reserved to furnish occasion to the ministry for a new effort to enslave and to ruin us; and the East India Company were chosen, and consented, to be the detested instruments of ministerial despotism and cruelty. A cargo of their tea arrived at Boston. By a low artifice of the governour, and by the wicked activity of the tools of government, it was rendered impossible to store it up, or to send it back; as was done at other places. A number of persons unknown destroyed it.

Let us here make a concession to our enemies: let us suppose that the transaction deserves all the dark and hideous colours, in which they have painted it: let us even suppose—for our cause admits of an excess of candour—that all their exaggerated accounts of it were confined strictly to the truth: what will follow? Will it follow, that every British colony in America, or even the colony of Massachusetts Bay, or even the town of Boston in that colony, merits the imputation of being factious and seditious? Let the frequent mobs and riots that have happened in Great Britain upon much more trivial occasions shame our calumniators into silence. Will it follow, because the rules of order and regular government were, in that instance, violated by the offenders, that, for this reason, the principles of the constitution, and the maxims of justice, must be violated by their punishment? Will it follow, because those who were guilty could not be known, that, therefore, those who were known not to be guilty must suffer? Will it follow, that even the guilty should be condemned upon partial testimony, upon the representations of their avowed and embittered enemies? Why were they not tried in courts of justice known to their constitution, and by juries of their neighbourhood? Their courts and their juries were not, in the case of Captain Preston, transported beyond the bounds of justice by their resentment: why, then, should it be presumed, that, in the case of those offenders, they would be prevented from doing justice by their affection? But the colonists, it seems, must be stript of their judicial, as well as of their legislative powers. They must be bound by a legislature, they must be tried by a jurisdiction, not their own. Their constitutions must be changed: their liberties must be abridged: and those, who shall be most infamously active in changing their constitutions and abridging their liberties, must, by an express provision, be exempted from punishment.

I do not exaggerate the matter, sir, when I extend these observations to all the colonies. The parliament meant to extend the effects of their proceedings to all the colonists. The plan, on which their proceedings are formed, extends to them all. From an accident, of no very uncommon or atrocious nature, which happened in one colony, in one town in that colony, and in which only a few of the inhabitants of that town took a part, an occasion has been taken by those, who probably intended it, and who certainly prepared the way for it, to impose upon that colony, and to lay a foundation and a precedent for imposing upon all the rest, a system of statutes, arbitrary, unconstitutional, oppressive, in every view and in every degree subversive of the rights and inconsistent with even the name of freemen.

Were the colonists so blind as not to discern the consequences of these measures? Were they so supinely inactive as to take no steps for guarding against them? They were not. They ought not to have been so. We saw a breach made in those barriers, which our ancestors, British and American, with so much care, with so much blood, had erected, cemented, and established for the security of their liberties and—with filial piety let us mention it—of ours: we saw the attack actually begun upon one part: ought we to have folded our hands in indolence, to have lulled our eyes in slumbers, till the attack was carried on, so as to become irresistible, in every part? Sir, I presume to think not. We were roused; we were alarmed, as we had reason to be. But still our measures have been such as the spirit of liberty and of loyalty directed; not such as a spirit of sedition or of disaffection would pursue. Our counsels have

been conducted without rashness and function: our resolutions have
been taken without phrensy or fury.

That the sentiments of every individual concerning that
important object, his liberty, might be known and regarded, meetings have been held, and deliberations carried on in every particular
district. That the sentiments of all those individuals might gradually
and regularly be collected into a single point, and the conduct of
each inspired and directed by the result of the whole united, county
committees—provincial conventions—a continental congress have
been appointed, have met and resolved. By this means, a chain—
more inestimable, and, while the necessity for it continues, we hope,
more indissoluble than one of gold—a chain of freedom has been
formed, of which every individual in these colonies, who is willing
to preserve the greatest of human blessings, his liberty, has the
pleasure of beholding himself a link.

Are these measures, sir, the brats of disloyalty, of disaffection?
There are miscreants among us—wasps that suck poison from the
most salubrious flowers—who tell us they are. They tell us that
all those assemblies are unlawful, and unauthorized by our constitutions; and that all their deliberations and resolutions are so
many transgressions of the duty of subjects. The utmost malice
brooding over the utmost baseness, and nothing but such a hated
commixture, must have hatched this calumny. Do not those men
know—would they have others not to know—that it was impossible
for the inhabitants of the same province, and for the legislatures
of the different provinces, to communicate their sentiments to one
another in the modes appointed for such purposes, by their different
constitutions? Do not they know—would they have others not to
know—that all this was rendered impossible by those very persons,
who now, or whose minions now, urge this objection against us?
Do not they know—would they have others not to know—that
the different assemblies, who could be dissolved by the governours,
were, in consequence of ministerial mandates, dissolved by them,
whenever they attempted to turn their attention to the greatest
objects, which, as guardians of the liberty of their constituents,
could be presented to their view? The arch enemy of the human
race torments them only for those actions, to which he has tempted,
but to which he has not necessarily obliged them. Those men refine
even upon infernal malice: they accuse, they threaten us (superla-
tive impudence!) for taking those very steps, which we were laid
under the disagreeable necessity of taking by themselves, or by
those in whose hateful service they are enlisted. But let them know,
that our counsels, our deliberations, our resolutions, if not authorized by the forms, because that was rendered impossible by our
enemies, are nevertheless authorized by that which weighs much
more in the sacle of reason—by the spirit of our constitutions. Was

the convention of the barons at Running Meade, where the tyranny of John was checked, and magna charta was signed, authorized by the forms of the constitutions? Was the convention parliament, that recalled Charles the second, and restored the monarchy, authorized by the forms of the constitution? Was the convention of lords and commons, that placed King William on the throne, and secured the monarchy and liberty likewise, authorized by the forms of the constitution? I cannot conceal my emotions of pleasure, when I observe, that the objections of our adversaries cannot be urged against us, but in common with those venerable assemblies, whose proceedings formed such an accession to British liberty and British renown.

The resolutions entered into, and the recommendations given, by the continental congress, have stamped, in the plainest characters, the genuine and enlightened spirit of liberty upon the conduct observed, and the measures pursued, in consequence of them. As the invasion of our rights have become more and more formidable, our opposition to them has increased in firmness and vigour, in a just, and no more than a just, proportion. We will not import goods from Great Britain or Ireland: in a little time we will suspend our exportations to them: and, if the same illiberal and destructive system of policy be still carried on against us, in a little time more we will not consume their manufactures. In that colony where the attacks have been most open, immediate, and direct, some farther steps have been taken, and those steps have met with the deserved approbation of the other provinces.

Is this scheme of conduct allied to rebellion? Can any symptoms of disloyalty to his majesty, or disinclination to his illustrious family, or of disregard to his authority be traced to it? Those, who would blend, and whose crimes have made it necessary for them to blend, the tyrannick acts of administration with the lawful measures of government, and to veil every flagitious procedure of the ministry under the venerable mantle of majesty, pretend to discover, and employ their emissaries to punish the pretended discovery of such symptoms. We are not, however, to be imposed upon by such shallow artifices. We know, that we have not violated the laws or the constitution; and that, therefore, we are safe as long as the laws retain their force and the constitution its vigour, and that, whatever our demeanour be, we cannot be safe much longer. But another object demands our attention.

We behold—sir, with the deepest anguish we behold—that our opposition has not been as effectual as it has been constitutional. The hearts of our oppressors have not relented: our complaints have not been heard: our grievances have not been redressed: our rights are still invaded: and have we no cause to dread, that the invasions of them will be enforced in a manner, against which all reason and argument, and all opposition of every peaceful kind, will be in vain? Our opposition has hitherto increased with our oppression: shall it, in the most desperate of all contingencies, observe the same proportion?

Let us pause, sir, before we given an answer to this question: the fate of us; the fate of millions now alive; the fate of millions yet unborn depends upon the answer. Let it be the result of calmness and of intrepidity: let it be dictated by the principles of loyalty, and the principles of liberty. Let it be such, as never, in the worst events, to give us reason to reproach ourselves, or other reasons to reproach us for having done too much or too little.

Perhaps the following resolution may be found not altogether unbefitting our present situation. With the greatest deference I submit it to the mature consideration of this assembly.

> That the act of the British parliament for altering the charter and constitution of the colony of Massachusetts Bay, and those for the impartial administration of justice in that colony, for shutting the port of Boston, and for quartering soldiers on the inhabitants of the colonies, are unconstitutional and void; and can confer no authority upon those who act under colour of them. That the crown cannot, by its prerogative, alter the charter or constitution of that colony: that all attempts to alter the said charter or constitution, unless by the authority of the legislature of that colony, are manifest violations of the rights of that colony, and illegal: that all force employed to carry such unjust and illegal attempts into execution is force without authority: that it is the right of British subjects to resist such force: that this right is founded both upon the letter and the spirit of the British constitution.

To prove, at this time, that those acts are unconstitutional and void is, I apprehend, altogeher unnecessary. The doctrine has been proved fully, on other occasions, and has received the concurring assent of British America. It rests upon plain and indubitable truths. We do not send members to the British parliament: we have parliaments (it is immaterial what name they go by) of our own.

That a void act can confer no authority upon those, who proceed under colour of it, is a selfevident proposition.

Before I proceed to the other clauses, I think it useful to recur to some of the fundamental maxims of the British constitution; upon which, as upon a rock, our wise ancestors erected that stable fabrick, against which the gates of hell have not hitherto prevailed. Those maxims I shall apply fairly, and, I flatter myself, satisfactorily to evince every particular contained in the resolution.

The government of Britain, sir, was never an arbitrary government: our ancestors were never inconsiderate enough to trust those rights, which God and nature had given them, unreservedly into the hands of their princes. However difficult it may be, in other states, to prove an original contract subsisting in any other manner, and on any other conditions, than are naturally and necessarily implied in the very idea of the first institution of a state; it is the easiest thing imaginable, since the revolution of 1688, to prove it in our constitution, and to ascertain some of the material articles, of which it consists. It has been often appealed to: it has been often broken, at least on one part: it has been often renewed: it has been often confirmed: it still subsists in its full force: "it binds the king as much as the meanest subject." The measures of his power, and the limits, beyond which he cannot extend it, are circumscribed and regulated by the same authority, and with the same precision, as the measures of the subject's obedience, and the limits, beyond which he is under no obligation to practice it, are fixed and ascertained. Liberty is, by the constitution, of equal stability, of equal antiquity, and of equal authority with prerogative. The duties of the king and those of the subject are plainly reciprocal: they can be violated on neither side, unless they be performed on the other. The law is the common standard, by which the excesses of prerogative as well as the excesses of liberty are to be regulated and reformed.

Of this great compact between the king and his people, one essential article to be performed on his part is—that, in those cases where provision is expressly made and limitations set by the laws, his government shall be conducted according to those provisions, and restrained according to those limitations—that, in those cases, which are not expressly provided for by the laws, it shall be conducted by the best rules of discretion, agreeably to the general spirit of the laws, and subserviently to their ultimate end—the interest and happiness of his subjects—that, in no case, it shall be conducted contrary to the express, or to the implied principles of the constitution.

These general maxims, which we may justly consider as fundamentals of our government, will by a plain and obvious application of them to the parts of the resolution remaining to be proved, demonstrate them to be strictly agreeable to the laws and constitution.

We can be at no loss in resolving, that the king cannot, by his prerogative, alter the charter or constitution of the colony of Massachussetts Bay. Upon what principle could such an exertion of prerogative be justified? On the acts of parliament? They are already proved to be void. On the discretionary power which the king has of acting where the laws are silent? That power must be subservient to the interest and happiness of those, concerning whom it operates. But I go farther. Instead of being supported by law, or the principles of prerogative, such an alteration is totally and absolutely repugnant to both. It is contrary to express law. The charter and constitution we speak of are confirmed by the only legislative power capable of confirming them: and no other power, but that which can ratify, can destroy. If it is contrary to express law, the consequence is necessary, that it is contrary to the principles of prerogative: for prerogative can operate only when the law is silent.

In no view can this alteration be justified, or so much as excused. It cannot be justified or excused by the acts of parliament; because the authority of parliament does not extend to it: it cannot be justified or excused by the operation of prerogative; because this is none of the cases, in which prerogative can operate: it cannot be justified or excused by the legislative authority of the colony; because that authority never has been, and, I presume, never will be given for any such purpose.

If I have proceeded hitherto, as I am persuaded I have, upon safe and sure ground, I can, with great confidence, advance a step farther, and say, that all attempts to alter the charter of constitution of that colony, unless by the authority of its own legislature, are violations of its rights, and illegal.

If those attempts are illegal, must not all force, employed to carry them into execution, be force employed against law, and without authority? The conclusion is unavoidable.

Have not British subjects, then, a right to resist such force—force acting without authority—force employed contrary to law—force employed to destroy the very existence of law and of liberty? They have, sir, and this right is secured to them both by the letter and the spirit of the British constitution, by which the measures and the conditions of their obedience are appointed. The British liberties, sir, and the means and the right of defending them, are not the grants of princes; and of what our princes never granted they surely can never deprive us.

I beg leave, here, to mention and to obviate some plausible but ill founded objections, that have been, and will be, held forth by our adversaries, against the principle of the resolution now before us. It will be observed, that those employed for bringing about the proposed alteration in the charter and constitution of the colony of Massachusetts Bay act by the virtue of a commission for that purpose from his majesty: that all resistance of forces commissioned by his majesty, is resistance of his majesty's authority and government, contrary to the duty of allegiance, and treasonable. These objections will be displayed in their most specious colours: every artifice of chicanery and sophistry will be put in practice to establish them: law authorities, perhaps, will be quoted and tortured to prove them. Those principles of our constitution, which were designed to preserve and to secure the liberty of the people, and, for the sake of that, the tranquillity of government, will be perverted on this, as they have been on many other occasions, from their true intention; and will be made use of for the contrary purpose of endangering the latter, and destroying the former. The names of the most exalted virtues, on one hand, and of the most atrocious crimes, on the other, will be employed in contradiction to the nature of those virtues, and of those crimes: and, in this manner, those who cannot look beyond names, will be deceived; and those, whose aim it is to deceive by names, will have an opportunity of accomplishing it. But, sir, this disguise will not impose upon us. We will look to things as well as to names: and, by doing so, we shall be fully satisfied, that all those objections rest upon mere verbal sophistry, and have not even the remotest alliance with the principles of reason or law.

In the first place, then, I say, that the persons who allege, that those, employed to alter the charter and constitution of Massachusetts Bay, act by virtue of a commission from his majesty for that purpose, speak improperly, and contrary to the truth of the case. I say, they act by virtue of no such commission: I say, it is impossible they can act by virtue of such a commission. What is called a commission either contains particular directions for the purpose mentioned; or it contains no such particular directions. In neither case can those, who act for that purpose, act by virtue of a commission. In one case, what is called a commission is void; it has no legal existence; it can communicate no authority. In the other case, it extends not to the purpose mentioned. The latter point is too plain to be insisted on—I prove the former.

"Id rex potest," says the law, "quod de jure potest." The king's power is a power according to law. His commands, if the authority of Lord Chief Justice Hale may be depended upon, are under the directive power of the law; and consequently invalid, if unlawful. Commssions, says my Lord Coke, are legal; and are like the king's writs; and none are lawful, but such as are allowed by the common law, or warranted by some act of parliament.

Let us examine any commission expressly directing those to whom it is given, to use military force for carrying into execution the alterations proposed to be made in the charter and constitutions of Massachusetts Bay, by the foregoing maxims and authorities; and what we have said concerning it will appear obvious and conclusive. It is not warranted by any act of parliament; because, as has been mentioned on this, and has been proved on other occasions, any such act is void. It is not warranted, by the common law. It is not warranted by the royal prerogative; because, as has already been fully shown, it is diametrically opposite to the principles and the ends of prerogative. Upon what foundation, then, can it lean and be supported? Upon none. Like an enchanted castle, it may terrify those, whose eyes are affected by the magick influence of the sorcerers, despotism and slavery: but so soon as the charm is dissolved, and the genuine rays of liberty and of the constitution dart in upon us, the formidable appearance vanishes, and we discover that it was the baseless fabrick of a vision, that never had any real existence.

I have dwelt the longer upon this part of the objections urged against us by our adversaries; because this part is the foundation of all the others. We have now removed it; and they must fall of course. For if the force, acting for the purposes we have mentioned, does not act, and cannot act, by virtue of any commissions from his majesty, the consequence is undeniable, that it acts without his majesty's authority; that the resistance of it is no resistance of his majesty's authority; nor incompatible with the duties of allegiance.

And now, sir, let me appeal to the impartial tribunal of reason and truth—let me appeal to every unprejudiced and judicious observer of the laws of Britain, and of the constitution of the British government, let me appeal, I say, whether the principles on which I argue, or the principles on which alone my arguments can be opposed, are those which ought to be adhered to and acted upon— which of them are most consonant to our laws and liberties— which of them have the strongest, and are likely to have the most effectual, tendency to establish and secure the royal power and dignity.

Are we deficient in loyalty to his majesty? Let our conduct convict, for it will fully convict, the insinuation, that we are, of falsehood. Our loyalty has always appeared in the true form of loyalty— in obeying our sovereign according to law: let those, who would require it in any other form, know, that we call the persons who execute his commands, when contrary to law, disloyal and traitors. Are we enemies to the power of the crown? No sir: we are its best friends: this friendship prompts us to wish, that the power of the crown may be firmly established on the most solid basis: but we know, that the constitution alone will perpetuate the former, and securely uphold the latter. Are our principles irreverent to majesty? They are quite the reverse: we ascribe to it perfection, almost divine. We say, that the king can do no wrong: we say, that to do wrong is the property, not of power, but of weakness. We feel oppression; and will oppose it; but we know—for our constitution tells us—that oppression can never spring from the throne. We must, therefore, search elsewhere for its source: our infallible guide will direct us to it. Our constitution tells us, that all oppression springs from the ministers of the throne. The attributes of perfection, ascribed to the king, are, neither by the constitution, nor in fact, communicable to his ministers. They may do wrong; they have often done wrong: they have been often punished for doing wrong.

Here we may discern the true cause of all the impudent clamour and unsupported accusations of the ministers and of their minions, that have been raised and made against the conduct of the Americans. Those ministers and minions are sensible, that the opposition is directed, not against his majesty, but against them: because they have abused his majesty's confidence, brought discredit upon his government, and derogated from his justice. They see the publick vengeance collected in dark clouds around them: their consciences tell them, that is should be hurled, like a thunder bolt, at their guilty heads. Appalled with guilt and fear, they skulk behind the throne. Is it disrespectful to drag them into publick view, and make a distinction between them and his majesty, under whose venerable name they daringly attempt to shelter their crimes? Nothing can more effectually contribute to establish his majesty on the throne, and to secure to him the affections of his people, than this distinction. By it we are taught to consider all the blessings of government as flowing from the throne; and to consider every instance of oppression as proceeding, which in truth is oftenest the case, from the ministers.

If, now, it is true, that all force employed for the purposes so often mentioned, is force unwarranted by any act of parliament; unsupported by any principle of the common law; unauthorized by any commission from the crown—that, instead of being employed for the support of the constitution and his majesty's government, it must be employed for the support of oppression and ministerial tyranny—if all this is true—and I flatter myself it appears to be true—can any one hesitate to say, that to resist such force is lawful: and that both the letter and the spirit of the British constitution justify such resistance?

Resistance, both by the letter and the spirit of the British constitution, may be carried farther, when necessity requires it, than I have carried it. Many examples in the English history might be adduced, and many authorities of the greatest weight might be brought, to show, that when the king, forgetting his character and his dignity, has stepped forth, and openly avowed and taken part in such iniquitous conduct as has been described; in such cases, indeed, the distinction above mentioned, wisely made by the constitution for the security of the crown, could not be applied; because the crown had unconstitutionally rendered the application of it impossible. What has been the consequence? The distinction between him and his ministers has been lost: but they have not been raised to his situation: he has sunk to theirs.

ORATION

at the Reinterment of Warren

Perez Morton

Perez Morton was born at Plymouth, Massachusetts, on November 2, 1750. In 1760 he entered the Boston Latin School and then went to Harvard, graduating in 1771. He was admitted to the bar on July 27, 1774, and thereafter established a practice in Boston. In 1775 he was a member of the Committee of Correspondence and the Committee of Safety. From 1794 to 1796 he was a representative in the General Court of Massachusetts; he was elected again in 1800 and served until 1811. In 1806 he was the speaker of the General Court. From 1810 to 1832 he was Attorney General of Massachusetts. Retiring in 1832, he died five years later, October 14, 1837.

Perez Morton was asked by the Masons to give an oration at the reinterment of Dr. Warren's body. On April 8, 1776, a procession was formed at the State House, and Warren's remains were carried to King's Chapel. After a prayer by the Reverend Dr. Cooper, Morton gave this oration.

The text is from the edition published by Gill in Boston, 1776.

Illustrious Relicks:

WHAT Tidings from the Grave! Why hast thou left the peaceful mansions of the tomb, to visit again this troubled Earth! Art thou the welcome Messenger of peace! Art thou risen again to exhibit thy glorious Wounds, and thro' them proclaim Salvation to thy Country! Or art thou come to demand that last Debt of Humanity, to which your Rank and Merit have so justly entitled you—but which has been so long ungenerously withheld! And art thou angry at the barbarous usage? Be appealed, sweet Ghost! For tho' thy Body has long laid undistinguished among the vulgar Dead, scarce privileged with Earth enough to hide it from the Birds of Prey; tho' not a kindred Tear was dropt, tho' not a friendly Sigh was uttered, o'er thy Grave; and tho' the Execrations of an impious Foe, were all thy Funeral Knells; yet matchless Patriot! thy memory has been embalmed in the Affections of thy grateful Countrymen; who in their Breast have raised eternal Monuments to thy Bravery!

BUT let us leave the beloved Remains, and contemplate for a moment, those Virtues of the Man, the Exercise of which have so deservedly endeared him to the honest among the Great, and the Good among the humble.

IN the *private* Walks of Life, he was a Pattern for Mankind. The Tears of her, to whom the World's indebted for so much Virtue, are silent Heralds of his *filial Piety:* While his tender Off-spring, in lisping out their Father's Care, proclaim his *parential Affection:* And an ADAMS can witness with how much Zeal he loved, where he had formed the sacred Connection of a *Friend*— their kindred Souls were so closely twined, that both felt one Joy, both one Affliction. In Conversation he had the happy Talent of addressing his Subject both to the Understanding and the Passions; from the one he forced Conviction, from the other he stole Assent.

HE was blessed with a Complacency of Disposition, and Equality of Temper, which peculiarly endeared him to his Friends; and added to the Deportment of the Gentleman, commanded Reverence and Esteem even from his enemies.

SUCH was the tender Sensibility of his Soul, that he need but see Distress to feel it, and contribute to its Relief. He was deaf to the calls of Interest even in the Course of his Profession; and wherever he beheld an indigent Object, which claimed his healing Skill, he administered it, without even the Hope of any other Reward, than that which resulted from the Reflection of having so far promoted the Happiness of his Fellow Men.

IN the *social* Departments of Life, practicing upon the Strength of the Doctrine, he used so earnestly to inculcate himself, that nothing so much conduced to enlighten Mankind, and advance the great End of Society at last, as the frequent Interchange of Sentiments, in friendly Meetings; we find him constantly engaged in this eligible Labour; but on none did he place so high a Value, as on that *most honorable* of all detached Societies, THE FREE AND ACCEPTED MASONS: Into this Fraternity he was early initiated; and after having given repeated Proofs of a rapid Proficiency in the Arts, and after evidencing by his Life, the Professions of his Lips—finally, as the Reward of his Merit, he was commissioned *the most worshipful* GRAND MASTER of all the ancient Masons, thro' *North-America*. And you, Brethren, are living Testimonie, with how much Honor to himself, and Benefit to the Craft universal he discharged the Duties of his elevated Trust; with what sweetened Accents he courted your Attention, while with *Wisdom, Strength and Beauty,* he instructed his Lodges in the secret *Arts of Free masonry;* what perfect Order and Decorum he preserved in the Government of them; and in all his Conduct, what a bright Example he set us, *to live within Compass, and act upon the Square.*

WITH what Pleasure did he silence the Wants of poor and pennyless Brethren; yea of the Necessitous every where, tho' ignorant of the Mysteries of the Craft, from his Benefactions, felt the happy Effect of that Institution which is founded on *Faith,*

Hope, and Charity. And the World may cease to wonder, that he so readily offered up his Life, on the altar of his Country, when they are told, that the main Pillar of *Masonry*, is the love of mankind.

THE Fates, as tho' they would reveal, in the Person of our GRAND MASTER those Mysteries, which have so long lain hid from the World, have suffered him like the great Master-builder in the Temple of old, to fall by the Hands of Ruffians, and be again raised in Honor and Authority: We searched in the Field for the murdered Son of a Widow, and we found him, *by the Turf and the Twig,* buried on the Brow of a Hill, tho' not in a decent Grave. And tho' we must again commit his Body to the Tomb, yet our Breasts shall be the Burying Spot of his *Masonic Virtues,* and there—

> *An adamantine Monument we'll rear,*
> *With this Inscription,* Masonry *lies here.*

IN *public* Life, the sole Object of his Ambition was to acquire the Conscience of virtuous Enterprizes; *Amor Teteir* was the Spring of his Actions, and *Mens Conscia Recti* was his Guide. And on this Security he was on every occasion, ready to sacrifice his Health, his Interest and his Ease, to the sacred Calls of his Country. When the Liberties of America were attacked, he appeared an early Champion in the Contest; and tho' his Knowledge and Abilities would have insured Riches and Preferment (could he have stoop'd to Prostitution) yet he nobly withstood the fascinating Charm, tossed Fortune back her Plume, and persued the inflexible Purpose of his Soul, in guiltless Competence.

HE fought not the airy Honors of a Name, else, many of those Publications, which in the early Period of our Controversy served to open the Mind of the People, had not appeared anonymous. In every time of eminent Danger, his Fellow-Citizens flew to him for Advice; like the Orator of Athens, he gave it, and dispell'd their Fears—Twice did they call him to the Rostrum, to commemorate the Massacre of their Brethren; and from that Influence, in persuasive Language he taught them, not only the dangerous Tendency, but the actual Mischief, of stationing a Military Force, in a free City, in a Time of Peace. They learnt the profitable Lesson, and penned it among their Grievances.

BUT his Abilities were too great, his Deliberations too much wanted, to be confined to the Limits of a single City, and at a time when our Liberties were most critically in Danger from the secret Machinations and open Assaults of our Enemies, this Town, to their lasting Honor, elected him to take a Part in the Councils of the State. And with what Faithfulness he discharged the important Delegation, the Neglect of his private Concerns, and his unwearied Attendance on that Betrustment, will sufficiently testify, and the

Records of that virtuous Assembly will remain the Testimonials of his Accomplishments as a Statesman, and his Integrity and Services as a Patriots, thro' all Posterity.

THE Congress of our Colony could not observe so much Virtue and Greatness without honoring it with the highest Mark of their Favour; and the free Suffrages of that uncorrupted Body of Freemen, he was soon called to preside in the Senate. Where by his daily Councils and Exertions, he was constantly promoting the great Cause of *General Liberty*.

BUT when he found the Tools of Oppression were obstinately bent on Violence; when he found the Vengeance of the British Court must be glutted with Blood; he determined, that what he could not effect by his Eloquence or his Pen, he would bring to Purpose by his Sword. And on the memorable 19th of April, he appeared in the Field, under the united Characters of the General, the Soldier and the Physician. Here he was seen animating his Countrymen to Battle, and fighting by their Side, and there he was found administering healing Comforts to the wounded. And when he had repelled the unprovoked Assaults of the Enemy, and had driven them back into their Strongholds, like the virtuous Chief of Rome, he returned to the Senate, and presided again at the Councils of the Fathers.

WHEN the vanquished Foe had rallied their disordered Army, and by the Acquisition of fresh Strength, again presumed to fight against Freemen; our Patriot, ever anxious to be, where he could do the most good, again put off the Senator, and in Contempt of Danger flew to the field of Battle, where, after a stern, and *almost* victorious Resistance, ah! too soon for his Country! he sealed his Principles with his Blood—then—

> *Freedom wept, that* MERIT *could not save,*
> *But* WARREN'S *Manes must enrich the Grave.*

Enriched indeed! And the Heights of *Charlestown* shall be more memorable for thy Fall, than the *Plains of Abraham* are for that of the Hero of *Britain*. For while *he* died contending for a single Country, *You* fell in the Cause of Virtue and Mankind.

THE Greatness of his Soul shone even in the Moment of Death; for if Fame speaks true, in his last Agonies he met the insults of his Barbarous Foe, with his wonted Magnanimity, and with the true spirit of a soldier, frowned at the Impotence.

IN Fine, to complete the great Character—like HARRINGTON he wrote, like CICERO he spoke, like HAMPDEN he lived, and like WOLFE, he died.

AND can we, my Countrymen, with Indifference behold so much Worth and Valour laid prostrate by the Hand of *British Tyranny!* And can we ever grasp that Hand in Affection again? Are we not yet convinced "that he who hunts the Woods for Prey, the naked and untutored Indian is less a Savage than the *King of Britain*"! Have we not Proofs, rote in Blood, that the corrupted Nation, from whence we are stubbornly fixed on our Destruction! And shall we still court a *Dependence* on such a State? Still contend for a Connection with those, who have forfeited not only every kindred Claim, but even their Title to Humanity! Forbid it the Spirit of the brave MONTGOMERY! Forbid it the Spirit of immortal WARREN! Forbid it the Spirits of all our valiant Countrymen! Who fought, bled and died for far different Purposes; and who would have thought the Purchase *dear indeed!* to have paid their lives for the paltry Boon, of displacing one Set of Villains in Power, to make Way for another. No. They contended for the Establishment of Peace, Liberty and Safety to their Country, and we are unworthy to be called their Countrymen, if we flop at any Acquisition short of this.

NOW is the happy Season, to seize again those Rights, which as Men we are by Nature entitled to, and which by Contract never have and never could have surrendered—But which have been repeatedly and violently attacked by the *King, Lords, and Commons of Britain*. Ought we not then to disclaim forever the forfeited Affinity; and by a timely Amputation of that rotten Limb of the Empire, prevent the Mortification of the whole? Ought we not to listen to the Voice of our Slaughtered Brethren, who are now proclaiming aloud to their Country—

Go tell the King, and tell him from our Spirits,
That you and Britons can be Friends no more;
Tell him to you all Tyrants are the same:
Or if in Bonds, the never conquer'd soul
Can feel a Pang, more keen than Slavery's self,
'Tis where the Chains that crush you into Dust,
Are forg'd by Hands, from which you hop'd for Freedom.

YES, we ought and will—We will assert the Blood of our murdered Hero against thy hostile Oppressions, O shameless Britain! and when "thy Cloud cap'd Towers, thy gorgeous Palaces" shall by the Teeth of Pride and Folly be levell'd with the Dust— and when thy Glory shall have faded like the Western Sunbeam— the *Name and the Virtues of* WARREN shall remain immortal.

SPEECH TO BOTH HOUSES

John Rutledge

John Rutledge was born in Charlestown, South Carolina in September 1739. He received his early education from his father and a tutor. After studying in the Middle Temple, he was called to the English bar in February, 1760. He returned to Charlestown the same year. In 1761, he was elected to the Commons House from Christ Church parish and represented it in the provincial bodies until the Revolution placed him in the governor's chair. He was sent to the First Continental Congress and re-elected to the Second Continental Congress. He was one of the large committee which wrote the South Carolina constitution of 1776 and, when the Provincial Congress became the General Assembly, he was elected president. He was elected governor in 1779, held that office until 1782. In 1782, he was again a member of the House of South Carolina and at the same time he was elected to Congress and attended from May, 1782 to September of 1783. From 1785 to 1790, he sat in the House of Representatives. He was elected to the Federal Convention of 1787. He was appointed senior associate justice of the Supreme Court, accepted, but delayed taking his seat and then resigned in February, 1791 to accept the office of chief justice of the state of South Carolina. Washington offered him the position of chief justice of the Supreme Court in 1795, but the Senate rejected his appointment. He died on July 18, 1800.

On April 11, 1776 Rutledge, then Governor and Commander-in-Chief of the Colony of South Carolina, addressed the members of the Legislative Council and the General Assembly. The text of the speech is from Peter Force. *American Archives.* 4th ser.; Vol. V, 650–51. Washington: M. St. Claire Clarke and Peter Force, 1844.

Honourable Gentlemen of the Legislative Council,
   Mr. Speaker, and Gentlemen of the General Assembly:

It has afforded me much satisfaction to observe that, though the season of the year rendered your sitting very inconvenient, your private concerns (which must have suffered greatly by your long and close application in the late Congress to the affairs of this Colony) requiring your presence in the country; yet, continuing to prefer the publick weal to ease and retirement, you have been busily engaged in framing such laws as our peculiar circumstances rendered absolutely necessary to be passed before your adjournment. Having given my assent to them, I presume you are now desirous of a recess. On my part, a most solemn oath has been taken for the faithful discharge of my duty; on yours, a solemn assurance has been given to support me therein. Thus, a publick compact between us stands recorded. You may rest assured that I shall keep this oath ever in mind. The Constitution shall be the invariable rule of my conduct. My ears shall always be open to the complaints of the injured. Justice in mercy shall neither be denied or delayed. Our laws and religion, and the liberties of America, shall be maintained and defended to the utmost of my power. I repose the most perfect confidence in your engagement. And now, gentlemen, let me intreat that you will, in your several Parishes and Districts, use your influence and authority to keep peace and good order, and procure strict observance of and ready obedience to the law. If any persons therein are still strangers to the nature and merits of the dispute between Great Britain and the Colonies, you will explain it to them fully, and teach them, if they are so unfortunate as not to know their inherent rights. Prove to them that the privileges of being tried by a jury of the vicinage, acquainted with the parties and witnesses; of being taxed only with their own consent, given by their representatives, freely chosen by and sharing the burden equally with themselves—not for aggrandizing a rapacious Minister and his dependant favourities, and for corrupting the people and subverting their liberties, but for such wise and salutary purposes as they themselves approve; and of having their internal polity regulated only by laws consented to by competent judges of what is best adapted to their situation and circumstances—equally bound, too, by those laws, which are inestimable, and derived from the Constitution, which is the birthright of the poorest man, and the best inheritance of the most wealthy. Relate to them the various unjust and cruel statutes which the *British* Parliament, claiming a right to make laws binding the Colonies in all cases whatsoever, have enacted, and the many sanguinary measures which have been and are daily pursued and threatened, to wrest from them those invaluable benefits, and to enforce such an unlimited and destructive claim. To the most illiterate it must appear that no power on earth can of right deprive them of the hard-earned fruits of their honest industry, toil, and labour; even to them the impious attenpt to prevent many thousands from using the means of subsistence provided for man by the bounty of his Creator, and to compel them, by famine, to surrender their rights, will seem to call for Divine vengeance. The endeavours, by deceit and bribery, to engage barbarous nations to imbrue their hands in the innocent blood of helpless women and children; and the atempt by fair, but false promises, to make the ignorant domesticks subservient to the most wicked purposes, are acts at which humanity must revolt. Show your constituents, then, the indispensable necessity which there was for establishing some mode of Government in this Colony; the benefits of that which a full and free representation has established; and that the consent of the people is the origin, and their happiness the end, of Government. Remove the apprehensions with which honest and well-meaning, but weak and credulous minds may be alarmed, and prevent ill impressions by artful and designing enemies. Let it be known that this Constitution is but temporary, till an accommodation of the unhappy differences between Great Britain and America can be obtained; and that such an event is still desired by men who yet remember former friendships and intimate connections, though, for defending their persons and properties, they are stigmatized and treated as Rebels.

Truth being known, will prevail over artifice and misrepresentation. Conviction must follow its discovery. In such cases, no man, who is worthy of life, liberty, or property, will or can refuse to join with you in defending them to the last extremity; disdaining every sordid view, and the mean, paltry considerations of private interest and present emolument, when placed in competition with the liberties of millions; and seeing that there is no alternative but absolute, unconditional submission and the most abject slavery, or a defence becoming men born to freedom, he will not hesitate about the choice. Although superior force may, by the permission of Heaven, lay waste our towns and ravage our country, it can never eradicate from the breast of freemen those principles which are ingrafted in their very nature. Such men will do their duty, neither knowing or regarding consequences, but submitting them, with humble confidence, to the omniscient and omnipotent Arbiter and Director of the fate of Empires, and trusting that His almighty arm, which has been so signally stretched out for our defence, will deliver them in a righteous cause.

The eyes of *Europe,* nay, of the whole world, are on *America.* The eyes of every other Colony are on this—a Colony whose reputation, generosity, and Magnanimity, is universally acknowledged. I trust, therefore, it will not be diminished by our future conduct; that there will be no civil discord here; and that the only strife amongst brethren will be, who shall do most to serve and to save an oppressed and injured country.

V

On *Religious* Matters

The Unbeleevers Preparing for Christ

Thomas Hooker

Thomas Hooker, one of the most prominent of the Puritan preachers in the seventeenth century, was born in 1586, according to Cotton Mather, in Marfield, Leicestershire, England. He received his A.B. in 1608, and his A.M. in 1611 from Emmanuel College and became rector of Esher, Surrey, in 1620. While at Esher, he was greatly influenced by the Rev. John Rogers and his Puritan tendencies were nurtured. As a lecturer at St. Mary's Chelmsford in 1626, his preaching attracted much public attention and official disapproval. Forced into retirement, he established a school in Little Baddow near Chelmsford. In 1630, he fled to Holland where, successively, he was associated with the English nonconformist churches at Delft and Rotterdam.

On September 4, 1633, Hooker, John Cotton, and Samuel Stone landed in Boston. On October 21, Hooker became pastor of the church at Newton. Disturbed by affairs in Massachusetts, he accompanied the majority of his congregation to Hartford in 1636, where he became an acknowledged leader in the religious and political affairs of Connecticut.

Hooker's democratic views as contrasted with those of Winthrop and other magistrates and ministers in Massachuetts are exemplified in the following excerpts from the famous sermon before the General Court: "The foundation of all authority is laid . . . in the free consent of the people. . . . The privilege of election . . . belongs to the people. . . . They who have the power to appoint officers and magistrates . . . also have the power to set the bounds and limitations of the power and place unto which they call them."

The sermon "The Unbeleevers Preparing for Christ" was preached *Circa* 1638. The text of the sermon is taken from Thomas Hooker. *The Unbeleevers Preparing For Christ*. London: Andrew Crooke, 1638.

LUKE 1.17 *To make ready a people prepared for the Lord.*

I COR. 2.14 *The naturall man receiveth not the things of the Spirit of God, for they are foolishness unto him: neither can he know them, because they are spiritually discerned.*

Wee have propounded heretofore five generall circumstances of preparation. First a man must know that the offer of grace is free. Secondly that a man must will Christ and grace before hee shall

331

have Christ and grace. Thirdly, he that doth will Christ, shall have
Christ and salvation by him; all which we have already handled out
of that place *Revel.* 22.17. *Whosever will let him take of the water
of life freely.* And now wee are come to the fourth circumstance,
which is that no man by nature can will Christ and Grace; and for
this purpose I have chosen this Text. And a littel to make way for
ourselves, if you take your eyes backe to the beginning of the
Chapter, about the 3, 4, and 5. Verses, you may see how the holy
Apostle doth expresse his earnest desire to preach nothing, nor
know anything but Christ Jesus, and him crucified, and therefore
hee lookes not after the excellencie of humane eloquence, or wisedome of men, though hee could have had this too; and happily expressed this also, yet hee proclaimes it in the eares of the *Corinthian*
Doctours, that hee desired nothing in that University (for *Corinth*
was a famous University as *Cambridge* and *Oxford* is) but to know
the Lord Jesus and him crucified, and therefore his speech and
preaching was not with entising words of mans wisedome, but in
demonstration of the spirit and of power the *Corinthian* Doctours
bragged of, that humane wisedome and learning wherewith they
were endued, but hee tells them he desired not this, nor never lookt
after it. Now least some might cavill at the Apostles neglecting of
this elegance, whereby hee might sugar over his doctrine that was
to be delivered by him to the people, least by the not regarding of
this, he might bring a neglect upon himselfe and upon his doctrine;
the Apostle therefore to remoove these silly objections and secret
cavills, discovers unto us from the fift Verse to the end of the
Chapter, the excellency of the Gospell of the Lord, delivered in
the plainenesse of it in the sixt Verse; there faith he, howbeit we
speake wisedome among them that bee perfect. yet not the wisedome
of this world, nor of the Princes of this world that come to nought,
but wee speake the wisedome of God in a mystery, even the hidden
wisedome which God ordained before the world unto our glory, as
if he had said, though you thinke (O yee *Corinthians*) that there
is no learning but humane learning, yet you must know that wee
speake wisedome too, and that to those that are the perfectest men in
their owne understanding. I tell you, wee speake wisedome which
the world and the princes thereof, those that have the greatest
parts never knew, never obtained; you *Corinthian* Doctours bragge
much of your learning and knowledge, but you have received it of
other humane authors, but wee teach unto you the wisedome of
God and of the Gospell, which eye hath not seene nor eare heard,
neither hath it entred into the heart of man to conceive, for God
hath revealed them unto us by his spirit, where wee may observe
by the way, that hee which teacheth the Gospell in the plainenesse
of it, teacheth the deepest things that can be conceived; for here S.
Paul speaketh of things which the wise of the world never heard

of, never conceived. But then they might reply further, how can you
know these things, and why may not others know them as well as
you. These are the two objections that might bee made against that
which the Apostle had before spoken of. How came you to know
them, and why may not others know them as well as you? The
Apostle answereth these two questions. And he answeres the first,
how he came to know them, from the 10. Verse to the 14. *God* saith
he, *hath revealed them unto us by his Spirit, for the Spirit searcheth
all things, yea the deepe things of God;* now wee have received not
the spirit of the world, but the spirit which is of God, that wee
might know the things that are freely given to us of God, as if he
had sayd, The spirit of God knoweth these things, and teacheth a
poore soule these things as farre as is convenient for him; the Spirit
of God understandeth these things, and makes knowne these things
to his servants; they know not these things of themselves but by
the power of Gods Spirit, the Spirit of God assisting and working
effectually in them teacheth them these secrets. But then why doe
not wicked men come to understand these great matters also? To
this the Apostle answers in the Text, *The naturall man receiveth not
the things of the Spirit; for they are foolishnesse unto him,* etc.
they doe not know them because they cannot. A naturall man doth
not know these things, they are wonders and miracles unto him,
tell him how a poore soule comes to be humbled and broken, and
have his sinnes pardoned, and bee received to mercy, why these
things are wonders to a carnall man, the Text saith, *he doth not
understand these things,* because hee cannot, and the ground of
this is, because they have not the spirit to teach them; and this I
take to be the scope of the Apostle in the Text; and in the verse
we are to observe onely one point meete for our purpose, for as we
have sayd before there are five generall circumstances of preparation observable; three we have handled, and the fourth is this,
No man of himselfe by nature can will to receive Christ; and this
is here plainely set open in the test, and therein manifestly expressed, it is the maine scope of the holy Ghost in the words, a
naturall man receiveth not, nay he cannot receive the things of God;
but before wee can come to gather the point, two things must be
discovered unto us. First what is meant by a naturall man. Secondly
what is meant by the things of the spirit of God. First, what is
meant by a naturall man, the *Corinthians* might have replyed upon
the Apostle, what are you a man of the spirit onely, what meane
you by a naturall man? I answere, he is a naturall man, in phrase
of Scripture, which hath not the worke of grace soundly wrought
in him, which hath not the spirit of God; whosoever he be that
lyeth in the bosome of the Church, whosoever he be that hath a
name to live and yet is dead, all carnall Gospellers and hypocrites,
those that are coloured over with the name of Christians and reli-

gion, whosoever they be that have not that saving worke of grace, and the new frame of grace set up and reared in their soules, by the assistance of Gods Spirit, all these how ever they may be coloured over, if they have not had the sanctifying worke of God's Spirit upon them, all these are sayd according to the Phrase of the Apostle, to be naturall men, and voyd of the spirit, as may appeare by the words going before the Text, and following after. First compare them with the words going before in the 10. and 12. Verses, *Wee have receiveth the Spirit of God*, saith the Text; the naturall man and the spirituall are opposed one to another. Wee saith the Apostle have received the Spirit, so that hee that hath Gods Spirit is a spirituall man, and therefore hee that hath not the Spirit of God in him, hee that hath not the will of God revealed unto him by the Spirit he is a naturall man. Looke also in the words after the Text, Vers. 15. *He that is spirituall discerneth all things*, he that hath a heart truly humbled, and a soule truly sanctified; he that is adopted, he is a spirituall man, so that he which is voyd of the Spirit, he is a naturall man; the phrase is excellent in this kind *Jude* 19. these bee they saith the Text, that separate themselves, sensuall, not having the Spirit; the words there interpret one another, hee was speaking before of wicked wretches, and those that lived after their owne ungodly lusts; in the 18. Verse saith the Text, *there shall be mockers in the last time who shall walke after their owne ungodly lusts;* where we may note, that we shall never see a mocker, one that opposeth Christ and the Gospell, and is jearing at the Saints of God, but he walkes after ungodly lusts. They are sensuall men, who be those sensuall men; those that have not the Spirit of God, as wee may see Verse 19. and therefore whosoever he be or whatsoever hee be, be his appearance never so good, if hee be not truly sanctified by the spirit of God, though he be a new man outwardly, if hee be not found in his con-versation, hee is a naturall man; hee that hath not the Spirit of God ruling and domineering over his lusts, he is a naturall estate.

The second thing which is to bee discovered is this, *vid.* what is meant by the things of the Spirit of God, and then the point will fall faire and undeniable. To this I answere, there are some things of God that are revealed in the creation of the world, *Rom.* 1.20. there saith the text, *The invisible things of him* (meaning God) *from the creation of the world are cleerely seene, being understood by the things that are made, even his eternal power and Godhead;* that is, a man that looketh into the frame and fabricks of the world, and seeth the making of the earth, and the Sea, and all things therein, hee cannot say, but God hath beene here, an infinite wisdome, and an Almighty power hath beene here, and framed all these things, but these are not the things of God, which are meant in the text, but there are other things of God which we must looke after, and they cannot be discerned by the creation of the world, and therefore, 1 *Cor.* I.21. we shall observe this, *After that in the Wisedome of God*, saith the text, *the world by wisedome knew not God, it pleased God by the foolishnesse of Preaching, to save them that believe,* marke the naturall men might have knowne though they would not, that there was a God, by the wisedome of God, that is by the wisedome of God in creating of the World and by the observation of things in the same, but they could not take notice of him as a God reconciled, as a God that should appoint Christ as a redeemer, and as a God that should send Christ to bee a redeemer, these are the things which men could not know by the creation of the world and by the wisedome thereof, the things of grace and of our redemption, the favour and love that God beares towards his in Christ, these are the things of God the things of election, sanctification, justification and glorification; these are the things of God which are meant especially in the Text, as if they had sayd, God by the spirit can onely reveale these things, these come immediately from God by the meanes hee hath appointed; a man may know that God hath created heaven and earth, and that he hath made all, and provided for all, and yet goe to hell. But hee that hath found Gods love in Christ, God working graciously upon his soule, God humbling his heart and pulling downe his soule that hee might bee fit to receive mercy, and then bestowing mercy upon him; when a soule seeth these things, then these are the things of God here meant; Gods spirit must onely work these, the spirit onely must reveale these, and by the operation of the spirit wee are made partakers of these, these are the things of God which are to be understood in the Text; God is said to call and to sanctifie, it is the Spirit that converts, and adopts, and humbles mens soules, as who should say, These are the workes of the Spirit, there is no seeing, there is no perceiving of these, there is no way to be made partakers of these without the spirit, so that the doctrine now lieth open, and that is this; No man naturally is able of his owne power to receive the spirituall things of grace and salvation, no naturall man, that is, he that hath not the spirit of God working in him, no man that is in his naturall estate can receive the spirituall things of grace and salvation. Hee doth not receive them, nay he cannot receive them saith the Text, to put out all doubts, and to cast away all cavills; the Text doth not onely say he doth not receive them, but that he cannot receive them, doe hee what he will, doe he what he can, come to a naturall man; and aske him will you receive Christ and the worke of grace? why yes with all his heart, and he makes no doubt but he doth so, and hee hopes hee shall finde the comfort of it. The Text saith, God saith, the truth saith, you doe not, nay you cannot, you say you doe, whom shall wee beleeve in this case, God or you; I can prove you are a naturall man, you live in base wicked courses, the Spirit of

God is an holy Spirit; you live in ungodly and unlawful courses, the Spirit of God is a wise Spirit, you are ignorant and know not the things belonging to salvation, and therefore the world knowes, and you know that you are a naturall man, and the spirit, that saith a naturall man cannot receive the things of God, and yet you say you can, whom therefore shall we beleeve? So that the point is plaine, that a man by nature hath not power to will to receive Christ and grace and salvation by him, and we will make good the point in foure particulars, by way of explication, That a man hath not power to will to receive grace and salvation by Christ; First to omit that which the Papists themselves confesse in this case, namely that a naturall man of himselfe cannot finde out the meanes of life and Salvation, but God must give him some preventing grace, he must be enlightened, that is, God must reveale and make knowne the things that concerne his peace unto him out of the Word; hee must discover those things unto him, which appertaine to his peace and justification by Christ. I will omit this, and speake onely of the power which a naturall man hath to entertaine the things belonging to life and Salvation; and suppose it be granted that the things of Salvation must be made knowne unto a naturall man in this case, or else he can never of himselfe finde them out, yet when these things be set upon to mens eares by the ministers of God, when grace and Salvation are offered unto men, yet marke when these are proclamed, a naturall man cannot entertaine these things, but the heart of a naturall man will turne away from these things, which we may plainely see, if wee looke but into the 19 of *Mat. 22.* there was a young man made some good profession, he came unto Christ, and asked him, *Master, what good thing shall I doe to inherit eternall life?* Christ sayd unto him, *If thou wilt enter into life, keepe the Commandements,* the young man askes Christ, which Commandement he should keepe, our Saviour answers him, *Thou shalt not kill: Thou shall not commit adultery, etc.* The young man answers, *All these things have I observed from my youth, what lacke I yet;* Then Christ saith unto him, if thou wilt be perfect, *goe sell all that thou hast and give it to the poore, and thou shalt have treasure in heaven,* but the text saith, Vers. 23. *When the young man heard this, he went away sorrowfull, for he had great possessions:* All the while before our Saviour had not touched him to the quicke, but when he saith unto him, *Goe thy wayes sell all that thou hast and follow me, and thou shalt have treasure in heaven,* he then went away, why, marke here, Christ made him a brave offer, hee told him he should inherit heaven and happinesse if he would but doe this but saith the text, *he went away sorrowfull,* the text doth not say that he would dispute of it, and consider of it, but presently as soone as he heard it, he had a secret kind of distaste against it, and went away and with drew himself from

the offer of life and salvation. The phrase is pretty to observe in the
5 of *John* 40. There our Savior Christ was disputing with the
Scribes and Pharisees, and shewing unto them the meanes of Salvation, but marke what our Saviour saith of them, *Ye will not come
to me that ye might have life,* marke that phrase; for it is observeable in the 39 vers. the verse going before, our Saviour had sayd
unto them, *Search the Scriptures for in them ye thinke ye have eternall life and they are they which testifie of me*; the offer was faire,
if they would but have come to Christ, they might have hade life,
but marke what hee saith of them, of the Scribes and Pharisees,
and so of all naturall men, they will not come, though mercy and
salvation be offered and tendered.

But in the second place, when these things of life and salvation
are set before a naturall man, and offered unto him, and he will
not come to Christ, that he may have them; yet suppose Christ
come to him, imagine the Lord Jesus comes home to the soule
of a poore sinner, and knocketh and rappeth at the doore of his
heart, continually striving with him by his blessed Spirit, and the
use of meanes; although the Lord would winne him, and wooe
him as hee did *Jerusalem, O Jerusalem, Jerusalem, how often
would I have gathered thy children together, as a henne doth her
chickens under her wings, and yee would not:* Looke as the henne
clocketh her chickens together that so shee may gather them under
her wings, and therby prevent them from some mischance that may
befall them, so the Lord Jesus called after *Jerusalem, and wept
over it: Oh that thou hadst known at least in this thy day the things
belonging to thy peace,* and yet they would none of him; just so is
the case of all naturall men, God calleth after them, and knocketh
againe and againe, and yet notwithstanding they do not onely
decline from the truth, but if the Spirit of God still strive with them,
if they cannot goe away from Christ, but Christ followes them
home to their houses as it were, then they fall out with Christ, and
professe they will none of Christ and salvation, they resist and
oppose the Spirit of God, they take up armes against the Spirit in
this kinde. *Act.* 7.51. there saith the text, *Yee stiffenecked and un-
circumcised in heart and eares, ye doe alwayes resist the holy Ghost,
as your fathers did, so doe yee: which of the Prophets have not
your fathers persecuted, etc.* as who should say, the Lord sent his
spirit in the ministery of the Prophets (for so you must conceive of
Gods Ministers, though they bee poore soules, yet Gods spirit
labours through them, and when they strive with the soules of men,
and labour to plucke them out of their sinnes, then Gods Spirit
strives). God sent his spirit among these men here, and yet they
resisted it. And so, *Act.* 13.46. there saith the text of *Paul* and
*Barnabas, that they waxed bold and said, It was necessary that the
word of God should first have been spoken to you, but seeing ye*

*put it from you and judge your selves unworthy of everlasting life,
loe we turne to the Gentiles.* The text doth not say, because yee
have gone away from the word, *But because you have put it away
from you*: Thus the soule of a naturall man doth put away the word
of God, and opposeth salvation. In this kinde, in the 22. *Matt.* 5.
*When the King there had prepared a great feast of fatte tbings,
when he had killed his Oxen and his fatlings, and all things were
ready, hee sent forth his harbingers about to call them that were
bidden to the feast, but they* (saith the text) *made light of it, and
went their wayes, one to his farme, another to his merchandise, etc.*
Christ he sends his faithfull Ministers about to invite all people to
receive life and salvation, *Come yee that are hungry and thirstie and
buy without money*: but the truth is, they in the Parable spoken of,
would not come to the feast, so it is with all naturall men, though
our Savior followes them, and would perswade them to entertaine
the meanes of salvation, yet they refuse it, and stand out against
it; so that they doe not onely withdraw themselves from the truth,
but oppose it when they are pursued.

Thirdly, a naturall man doth not onely withdraw himselfe
from grace and salvation offered, and resist this grace pressed upon
him, but if the Lord follow him yet further, and course him, and
pursueth him that he may give him grace; yet considered in himselfe,
hee is not capable of this grace. In the 6. of *Mat.* 24. there saith
our Saviour, *Ye cannot serve God and Mammon,* Every man
naturally hath his Mammon, the proud man hath his Mammon, and
the covetous man hath his Mammon, and the prophane man hath
his Mammon, now these cannot serve God and Mammon, also to
serve them both, doth not imply onely a difficulty, but an impossibility also, so that we may plainely see, a naturall man is not
capable of grace, but understand this wisely, I doe not say, that a
man by nature is uncapable of grace, thus farre, that he is not a
fit subject to be wrought upon, and to be made capable, but this I
say, that a man having sinne, and remaining in his sinnes, is not
able to entertaine grace, things so considered for a while, as long
as he continueth in that estate, he is not capable of grace, but yet
God can make him fit, and disposed thereunto, he may be wrought
thereunto, and God by his spirit can make him able to entertaine
grace, but he must first be disposed therunto, looke as it is with a
vessel that is full of puddle, there is an unpossibility now in this
vessell, as long as it is full of that pudly and filthy water, that
it should receive cleane and pure water, but when it is emptied
of that filthy water, then it is capable to receive pure water, but
first the durty water must be put out, before it can receive the pure.
Just so it is here, though the soule may be made a vessell fit to
receive grace, yet now being full of abominations, full of convetous-
nesse, full of malice, full of pride, full of love of our selves, full

of hypocrisie, full of carelessenesse, loosenesse, and prophanenesse, full of all manner of lusts, and corruptions, and concupiscence of flesh, when the soule is brimme full of these, it is impossible that it should receive grace, it is impossible that grace and corruption should lodge in the same bosome, so that God must first empty the soule of these lusts, and abominations, and prepare him for grace, before grace can be put into him, before he can receive grace from God, the fallow ground that hath a great many thistles, and is full of weedes, and nettles, and grasse, this ground we use to say is yet arable ground, it may be plowed and made fit to receive seede, and beare fruite, but it must first be plowed, for all the while this trash is in it, it is not fit for seed, though it may be made fit by tilling of it, so the soule of a sinner is arable, God can fit it, and prepare it to receive grace and eternall life, but he must be first plowed and made fit, he is overrunne with all corruptions, and therefore of himselfe, for a while before the Lord humble him and fit him, and prepare him to entertaine Christ, and receive grace, he cannot receive it. *Joh. 5.44.* There saith the Text, *How can you beleeve which receive honour one of another and seeke not the honor which commeth from God onely.* As who should say, these things cannot stand together, that a man should be full of sinne, and at that time goe to the Spirit to have his sinnes crucified, these things cannot stand so, that there is a kinde of indisposition and impossibility, for the present, that a naturall man should receive grace, *Rom. 6.20.* There saith the Text, *When you were servants to sinne, you were free from righteousnesse,* that is, when a mans corruptions rule over him, when a man yeelds himselfe to be under the power of his lusts, when sinne is a mans master, insomuch that he must do everything which that commands him; if malice command him to hate, then he must obey malice, and hate, and envy his brother, when covetousnesse is a mans master, and if that bids him gripe, and cheate, and cozen, he must then doe it, if a man be thus a servant to sin, he is free from righteousnes, he cannot be made partaker of grace and salvation so long as he remaines in this estate and condition.

Fourthly, the fourth passage is this, as the soule of a naturall man declines from grace offered and revealed, as it opposeth grace, pressed so in the fourth place it is not willing to be wrought upon, that it may be fit to receive grace, and be made capable of it; there is no naturall man under heaven that is willing to be wrought upon, that hee may be capable to receive grace, hee would not have grace and Christ, and though he might in the 19 of *Luke* the 14. and 27. verses, our Saviour Compares himselfe to a master that was to goe into a farre Country to receive a kingdome, and therefore gives over his estate into the hands of his servants, hee called his ten servants and gave them ten pounds, saying, *Occupie till I come.*

Now when hee is gone marke what the Text saith in the 14. Verse, *We will not have this man to rule over us; the Citizens hated him and sent a messenger after him saying, We will not have this man to rule over us.* Herein is implyed two things, first that God would rule over the hearts, hee would informe their judgements, and fit their soules to receive grace, but marke what they say, We *will not have him to reigne over us, wee* will not have the Lord Jesus take possession of our hearts, and rule and guide them in the way of grace and salvation and so say all naturall men when the truth of God is followed and pressed, and their consciences awakened and their minds enlightned, then they cry out, we will not be troubled and pestered with these matters; in the *8.* of *Rom. 7.* there saith the Text *the carnall minde is enmitie against God, for it is not subject to the Law of God, neither indeede can be.* A naturall man is not subject to God he is not, nay hee cannot be subject to the Law of God, the Text doth not say he doth not obey the Law of God, but hee is not subject to it; for it is one thing to obey the word and Spirit of God, and another thing to be subject unto it, as for example, suppose a master command his servant to doe something that is unjust and unlawfull, and if hee will not doe it, then beats him; the servant is then said to be subject to his master, hee may beare the blow and endure the stripes of his master, but if he be honest and will not doe the thing, hee cannot bee sayd to obey his master; so likewise if it please a Prince to deale harshly with his subject and punish him unjustly, his subject may submit himselfe unto him, but he doth not obey him, but this is the madnesse of our sinfull natures that wee will not be subject to the Word of God, we will not beare the blow, nor indure the stroake of the Spirit, that so it may plucke us out of our corruptions, and frame us and fashion us in this case, and make us fit to receive grace; but when the word discovereth our sinnes unto us, and our misery in regard of the same, the soule beginns to swell and take up an indignation against the truth revealed, it endeavours what it may, and labours what it can to acquit it selfe of the word and to cast out the same, wee professe that we will not have our hearts informed and our minds enlightned, wee will not be humbled and prepared to receive grace and salvation offered by the Lord Jesus. If it bee not thus, what meane those swellings and bublings of heart against the word when it is preached, sometimes a mans conscience is opened and touched by the Word of God, and what followes? why presently hee professeth hee will never heare that Minister more, hee saith tis pittie hee should ever preach more, and tw'ere good hee were out of the Country, and that the kingdome were rid of him; alas, what doth the Minister this while, what doth he intend all it is while that you take such distaste at him, why you have a proud heart, hee would humble it, he would plucke you out of your corruptions that you may be prepared for grace, but your soules say you will not be wrought upon and framed, that you may receive grace and salvation; however you doe not professe so much with your mouthes, yet your actions testifie as much, there is never a faithfull Minister of God but speakes home to the con- sciences of men, and tells them of their beloved sinnes and bosome corruptions and hee doth this to prepare way for the Lord Jesus. He knowes you must be fitted to receive grace and salvation, before you shall be made partakers of grace and salvation; he knowes that there are many mountaines to bee levelled, and crooked things to bee made straight, and many rough things to bee made smooth and plaine, and therefore hee intends nothing but to have your soules broken and prepared for Christ, but you say you will not bee humbled and framed, and made fit to see the things that belong to your peace here, and your salvation hereafter, and therefore you cannot receive the things of God: so then to gather up all together, if it be so, that when the things of grace and salvation are revealed and offered, a naturall man doth turne away from them, if it bee so that though the Lord striveth with a naturall man, and labours by his Spirit to winne him and wooe him to receive grace, yet he resists the Spirit, and takes up armes against the offer of grace; if it bee so that when the Lord followes him with grace, yet a naturall man is not capable of grace, if it bee so that the heart of a naturall man is not subject to the Word of God, and would not bee wrought upon that he may be made fit to receive grace, than it is cleare, that a naturall man cannot receive the things of God if hee goes away from grace offered and resists grace pressed; if hee be not capable of grace, and is unwilling to be made capable, then the point is evident, and the doctrine undeniable, namely that a man in his naturall estate cannot receive the things of grace and salvation; and this is a thing so cleare to a gracious heart, as nothing more; wee see then the proofe of the point, a naturall man cannot receive the things of God, the reasons of the point why a naturall man cannot but doe thus, as he doth withdraw himselfe from grace offered, and resist and oppose the Word of God. The grounds of it are three, the first argument alledged is taken out of the words of the Text, and it stands thus, a naturall man cannot receive the things of God, why? because they are spiritually discerned, what is that? the meaning is this, hee that will receive spirituall things, must have some spirituall ability and power about him, some spirituall helpe vouchsafed unto him for the performance of this work; a man that will discern spirituall things must have a power answerable to that hee would discerne, a man must have spirituall helpe from heaven before hee can entertaine spirituall graces; for spirituall graces and the spirituall worke of the Lord are onely agreeable and fitting one for another, but now no naturall man hath any spirituall power, these two things are different in their kindes, namely nature and the Spirit, a naturall man hath nothing of the Spirit, no spirituall ability in him, but hee must have a spirituall ability that can discerne the things of the Spirit, and therefore a naturall man cannot discerne spirituall things; thus I reason, no naturall faculty can put forth a supernaturall worke, a thing that is barely within the compasse of nature cannot put forth an action above the nature of it, because every thing workes within its compasse; as the tree that growes, it cannot goe and walke as the beast doth; the beast that hath the sensuall facultie, that walkes, and sees, and heares and feeles, but it cannot reason; man hee hath the reasonable facultie, and he reasons and performes such actions as belong to him; now every one of these worke within their owne compasse, they have their severall kinds of operations; the tree growes, the beast feeles, and man reasons, and none of these can exceede their owne nature, or put forth a worke above their nature, so that then wee see no naturall power can performe a supernaturall worke, but a naturall man as hee came into the world hath nothing but nature in him, and therefore he cannot discerne the things of God, which is a supernaturall worke wrought by the Spirit of God, for so saith the Text, *they are spiritually discerned.*

The second argument is this, all naturall men are altogether fleshly, that is, wholly overpowred with sinne: marke that place in the third of *John* and sixt, there saith the Text, *whatsoever is borne of the flesh is flesh, and that which is borne of the spirit is spirit,* but now marke all the things of God, as first election, secondly conversion, thirdly sanctification, fourthly justification, fiftly glorification and the like, they are nothing else but spirituall, they are spirituall things, the grace of God is spirituall, and the Word of God is spirituall; now marke what followeth in the fift of *Galathians* the 17. there saith the Text, *The flesh lusteth against the Spirit, and the Spirit against the flesh, and these now are contrary the one to the other,* that is, a naturall corrupt heart resists and is contrary to the worke of Gods Spirit, they lust one against another, and are contrary one to another; then marke how I reason from the former ground, if the soule of a naturall man be professely opposite and contrary to the Spirit of grace, then the soule of a naturall man will not of itselfe, nay it cannot receive and entertaine Christ and grace, they that oppose and would destroy one another, they will not entertaine one another; as for example, fire and water are contrary one to another, and therefore they will not meete together and entertaine one another, but continually seeke to destroy one another, so light and darkenesse they are contrary, and therefore will not receive one another but seeke the destruction one of another, as when light comes darkenesse is gone, and when darkenesse comes light that must be gone; but now marke, the heart of a naturall man is all flesh, and the things of God are all Spirit, and therefore these two are contrary, and therefore oppose and would destroy one another; the heart of a naturall man is contrary to God and grace, and therefore cannot receive and entertaine God and grace, but seeke to destroy them, and therefore it is observeable in the 8 of *Rom. 7. the wisedome of the flesh is enmitie to the Spirit of God, it is not subject to the Law of God, neither indeede can be*; when the heart of a naturall man begins to feele the blow by the hand of Gods Spirit stirring and striving in him to humble him and make him fit for grace, it flyeth backe presently, and will by no means beare the blow of the Spirit it will not give way to the worke of God. Now marke how I dispute, that which will not, nay that which cannot be subject to the Spirit of God, that will never receive grace which is the worke of the Spirit of God, but a naturall man whatsoever he hath, even his wisedome is not subject to the Spirit, hee will not beare, hee will not away with the worke of the ministery, and therefore hee cannot receive grace, and this is the second passage. If the nature of a naturall man be altogether flesh, and is contrary to grace, and will not be subject to the Spirit, then it cannot receive grace; but all naturall men are contrary to grace, they are altogether flesh and resist the spirit and therefore they cannot entertaine grace.

The third Argument is this, a dead man hath no power to procure life unto himselfe, but all men by nature are dead in trespasses and sinnes, and therefore no naturall man is able to procure spirituall life unto himselfe; for the understanding of this argument, know thus much, that the nature of man since his fall is stripped of all that holinesse and righteousnesse whereby he might bee enabled to the performance of any spirituall worke, and not onely so, hee is not onely deprived of the image of God, but is altogether overspread with wickednesse and unrighteousnesse, which take the possession of every poore soule under heaven, *Joh. 3.6. Whatsoever is borne of the flesh is flesh*, now every man naturally is altogether flesh, the will of man and the heart of man is altogether fleshy; and therefore in the heart of man there is no good at all. And consider the reason of this, why the whole soule is thus defiled with sinne, wee must conceive that *Adam* was not onely a particular person, but he took the whole nature of mankind upon him; so that the nature of man in *Adam* while hee was in his innocencie might either bee carried to the obedience of the will of God, or else wholly against the will of God, and therefore by *Adams* fall man was altogether deprived of his righteousnesse, and caried against the will of God. Now to presse the Argument if it be so that all mens hearts are possessed with rebellions by nature, and turned away from God; then men naturally cannot turne unto God, but all men naturally are wholly possessed with sinne, and by rebellion, are turned from God, and therefore they cannot naturally turne unto God, Againe consider there must bee some spirituall power, some spirituall life put into a man before hee can performe any good, therefore a naturall man cannot doe any good, but is a dead man in respect of grace, because he hath lost that same soule of righteousnes whereby he should performe that good which God requireth, and so that holinesse being gone, the soule of the will is gone, and the power to doe any good or receive any good is gone. So then the case is cleare and the point evident by force of argument and Scripture; that a naturall man hath no power to receive the Lord Jesus, and grace, and salvation from him.

If this be true as hath beene prooved by reason plaine and undeniable arguments, that a naturall man cannot receive the things of God, then every soule may take notice of and condemne that sottish and foolish conceit that harbours in the minde of many silly poore ignorant soules, if any of you know such, take notice of them; there are many thinke that they brought grace into the world with them, and that they had grace from their mothers belly; aske them when did you receive grace, when did you receive faith, they will answer, they beleeved ever since they were borne, they had faith ever since they can remember; a great many poore ignorant soules thinke that grace came into the world with them; No, no, be not deceived, faith commeth by hearing, faith is the gift of God, and repentance is the gift of God, *narrow is the way, and straight is the gate that leadeth unto life, and few there be that finde it;* and therefore alas, if thou think'st thou broughtest faith with thee into the world, it is an argument that thou never hadst faith, it is an evidence that thou never hadst grace; for if every man should bring faith and grace into the world, then all should goe to heaven, and what is hell made for then? No, no, narrow is the way and exceeding straight is the gate; wee must not thinke to goe to heaven with our hands by our sides. No, no, it is a very narrow way, and few there be that finde it. But then they will pleade, though they had not grace by nature, yet grace is within a haires breadth of them, they have grace at command; and as it is with a man that leaves a commoditie at a mans house upon liking, if he like it, if it be for his turne he may buy it, if hee like it not hee may refuse it; now after it hath lien by him a while, if it doth not please him, he may returne it into the owners hand againe, he may say, I tooke your commoditie upon liking, and if it would have beene for my turne I would have bought it, but it will not serve for the use I thought to put it to, and therefore I returne it to you againe; So it is here, most men thinke that grace is left with them upon liking, and they may let it lie by them, and after they have lived in sinne, and tired themselves in their owne imaginations, and in following the sinfull desires of their owne wretched hearts, if after this when they become old, or lie upon their death beds, if then they like grace, they may take it, if not they may let it alone and refuse it. O poore creatures, you will perish and goe to hell hoodwinkt in this kind, you thinke you may have grace for calling for; hereafter when I am old then I will repent, and when I lie upon my death bed, then I will beginne to pray and humble myselfe before God, then you thinke to have grace at your owne liking; if you like the course of grace then you will take it, if you like it not, you will refuse it; must I pray with my family you will say? Well if I like the course happily I will doe it, if not I will neglect it; Alas, alas, I tell thee thou canst as well make a soule as convert a soule, thou canst as well create thy selfe as repent, is it in thy power to say, now I will have grace, now I will not? now I will repent and now I will not? Oh thinke of it, you shall finde it a harder taske then you are aware of, and if God bee pleased to open your eyes, you will then say, Oh what shall I doe to be saved, then you will see that something must bee done before you can bee saved, then you will finde it to be a hard matter to repent. Doe not think when you lie upon your death beds then you may repent if you will; is it in your power to repent and goe to heaven? no, no, all naturall men are under the power of Sathan, he ruleth them, he commandeth the hearts of the children of disobedience according to his will, and then for sinne and the power thereof looke, *Rom. 6.16. know yee not* saith the Apostle *that to whom yee yeeld your selves servants to obey, his servants yee are whether of sinne unto death, or of obedience unto righteousnesse?* every naturall man is a servant to sinne and a slave to his lusts, hee can doe nothing but that sinne will have him to doe. Take a proud man, whether are thou able to confesse thy pride, to see thy sinne, and humble thy selfe, and renounce thy folly, art thou able to doe this? No, thou must aske thy sin leave first: So take a covetous man, art thou able to set upen thy house, if thou hast wronged any man, or griped or cozened any man? art thou able to say, I will restore him fourefold? art thou able to doe this? No, no, thou must aske thy covetousnesse leave first; now whether you thinke that the divell will suffer you to goe out of his clutches when hee hath power over you, if you thinke sinne will give you leave to forsake your lusts when you are servants to it; I appeale to your owne consciences, and therefore whosoever he be that is a naturall man, let him not cosen himselfe, he hath no power in himselfe to forsake sinne; if heaven were layd downe before him and offered him for the leaving of one lust, hee could as well make a world, as part with one lust for heaven, and therefore every man should labour to see this and say, Lord heretofore I have beene deluded, I thought if I would have grace at any time, I might have grace when I would, if I would not have grace I might choose, and therefore I thought I would have profit now, and pleasures now, and corruptions, and hereafter I will repent, hereafter I will have Christ, but Lord I was deluded, what was it in my power then to entertaine the Lord Jesus? then it was in my power to goe to heaven, to make a world, and to create a soule also? I will assure you it is the almighty power of God that must doe this, in the first of *Ephesians* 19. there the Apostle giveth us to understand how God worketh in our conversion; *What is the exceeding greatnesse of his power*, saith hee, *to us ward that beleeve, according to the working of his mighty power, which he wrought in Christ, when hee raised him from the dead, and set him at his owne right hand in the heavenly places*. When the Lords body had lien in the grave three dayes, the selfe same power that raised Christ from the dead; this is the very same almighty power that workes in the heart of a man that is converted in this case; canst thou raise Christ from the dead? if thou canst doe this, then thou mayst repent, if not, then of thy selfe thou canst not repent; for the very same power that raised Christ from the dead, the same power must worke repentance in the heart of a man; be not therefore deceived, but now looke to it, many Christians have thought that they might have grace and salvation when they would at command, but when God opened their eyes, O then they saw no hope of this, they then knew that the same power that raised Christ out of the grave, the same power that must raise them out of the grave of their sinnes. I beseech you therefore to be informed, to yeeld to, to be convinced of this truth; the Text saith *a naturall man cannot receive the things of God*, you say you can, who shall we beleeve now? What will you be Atheists, the Lord saith, the word saith, *a naturall doth not receive the things of God, nay he cannot*, now whether thy word, or the word of God will stand, thou wilt one day know it to thy everlasting woe, and therefore now be perswaded to see your owne follies, and abandon this follish conceit.

The second use is an use of examination, namely from the former doctrine delivered, every soule that heareth the word this day, if they will deale plainely with their soules may understand what their conditions is, you may reade your owne estates, whether you bee naturall men or spirituall, whether gracious or gracelesse men; what wouldst thou know then, whether thou are a naturall man or no? and if thou beest so, woe be unto thee. The triall is easie in this kind, observe what disposition thou hast to the things of God, observe whether thy soule be affected with them, whether thy soule can give entertainement to them? the naturall man cannot receive the things of God, if thou beest a naturall man, thou then canst not receive grace nor entertaine Christ and salvation, so then canst thou finde that if pleasures come, then thy heart giveth way to them? if profits come, then thy heart is transported with the love thereof.

Is thy soule inlarged to these things? dost thou love and desire them? canst thou swallow downe all, entertaine all, digest all very willingly in this kind? never too much riches, never too much honour, never too much profit, never too much pleasure, is thy soule thus disposed? But when the word calleth for repentance, when the Gospell calleth for selfe deniall at thy hand, and the Lord Jesus would rule in thy heart, when the Lord would take away all thy sinnes, and all thy corruptions; is it so now that thy heart is weary to heare these? is it so that thou canst not give way to these? then the case is cleare, thou art in a naturall estate, for the Lords sake take notice of it; naturall things please thee, profits and pleasures, sinnes and corruptions please thee, but thou canst not away with the things of the Spirit, thou art therefore a naturall man, there is therefore no roome for Christ in thy soule, therefore there is no true grace yet wrought in they soule. In the 8. of the *Rom. 5.* there saith the Text, *They that are after the flesh doe mind the things of the flesh, but they that are after the Spirit, the things of the Spirit.* Now observe therefore what rellish thou findest in the things here below; canst thou rellish base courses and ill company? is any course or advice taken that may aduce thee unto wickednesse? canst thou sweare with the blasphemer, and swagger with the drunkard? canst thou rellish and approve of these courses? but when the Gospell comes and when a man checkes thee for drinking and swearing, and tells thee that these things stand not with the kingdome of God, the kingdome of Christ consists in righteousnesse and joy, and peace in the holy Ghost, and thou must deny thy selfe before thou canst receive the Lord Jesus; if a man shall tell thee that thou must be pure as Christ himselfe is pure, and that the Lord Christ Jesus did not come into the world to make men loose and carelesse, but holy and righteous, to live soberly in this present world, and deny all ungodly and worldly lusts, to renounce and abhorre these, when thou hearest that thou must become a foole that thou mayst bee made wise, and that the Lord came to refresh those onely that where laden with the burthen of their sinnes, when thou hearest these things, how canst thou take them, most men may give this answer, wee thinke not so, wee beleeve it not, nay wee cannot be perswaded of it; is it thus with thee? why then the case is ended, the tryall is done; whoever doth not nay cannot receive the things of God; the Gospell of God, and the things revealed therein; why the Text saith, and the Lord saith, *that man is a naturall man.* Now many a soule can say, I am not perswaded of these things which the Gospell reveales; why then the case is cleare, thou sayst plainely thou canst not receive the things of God, why then the Lord saith, the Text saith, and God of heaven saith, that *thou art a naturall man as thou camest into the world, and that thou hast not the grace and spirit of Christ.* But then

some may say if I be a natural man what then, what hurt is it, And
therefore in the fourth place it is an use of terrour; I presume many
that have heard this will say wee are so, and shall a man bee
ashamed because he is a naturall man? Therefore observe from the
former doctrine a word of terrour to all naturall creatures under
heaven, I am almost afraid to speake of the misery of a naturall
man, my tongue trembles to discover the wretched, fearefull,
damned, miserable estate that every naturall man is in, you thinke
it is nothing to be in a naturall estate; but I tell you, did you but
know what the Lord hath revealed concerning a naturall man, it
were enough to breake the backe of a man; a naturall man, why
it is enough to make thee goe sighing to thy grave, though thou
livest a thousand yeares; if thou beest a naturall man thou hast
not received Christ, nay thou art not neare the things of a better
life, nay you are not onely still to attaine those things, but you are
not able to receive the things of the Lord Jesus, whereby you may
be quickened to entertaine those things, and this is that which
maketh the soules of naturall men miserable, and the misery of
those soules the more miserable; because they are not onely unwilling to bee out of this condition, but they are unwilling to be
made willing to be out of it; they boast that still they remaine in
it, for marke what naturall men say, they bring a reproach upon
Gods Saints and children, what say they, you are a man of the
Spirit, you are a spirituall professor, one of the holy brethren,
are you miserable wretch; dost thou professe thy selfe that thou
art not so, but that thou art a naturall man? why then thou art a
miserable man, a naturall man, why then a damned man? a naturall
man why then an accursed man? thou that professest thou hast no
part and portion in the Lord Jesus, take heede that one day hee
doth not professe that hee hath no part in thee, *Rom. 8.9. If any
man hath not the Spirit of Christ, he is none of his;* thou that dost
make a matter of mocking at those that doe walke uprightly before
God, and that have the Spirit of God in them, thou that proclamest
to the world that thou hast not the Spirit of God, the Lord proclaimes it as openly to thee, that the Lord Jesus will not owne thee,
hee will have nothing to doe with thee, and then what shall become
of thee? the devill must take thee at the last day, when all flesh
shall appeare before the judgement seate of God, and the booke
shall be opened and the actions of men made manifest to Saints
and Angells! Oh one drop of mercy then, one dram of comfort then
will be worth a world; Oh then you will wish, Oh that Christ would
save us; no, no, you that were naturall men, Christ will not owne
you now, you had none at all of the Spirit, you have opposed the
good Spirit of God and flouted it, these are your spirituall men,
these are your holy ones, thus you have mocked and blasphemed,
you have sayd the Spirit of Christ is not mine, and therefore Christ

saith hee is none of thine; thy estate therefore here is miserable, but thrice wretched and miserable will it be hereafter; men may imagine great matters, and boast of themselves, of their riches, and their wisedome, and their honour and preferment in the world, but if they be naturall, there is small good at all in them, they may have lands, and preferments, and honours, but they have finall good in them, and therefore miserable needs must their estate bee here, but farre worse hereafter. Doe not thinke ye may climbe up to heaven by your owne imaginations; good Lord, how can a man that is in a naturall condition sleepe quietly? with what contentment can hee walke, when a man goeth into his fields to recreate and delight himselfe, and then considers the meanes that God hath offred him, whereby hee might attaine unto grace and salvation, when the soule thinks with it selfe, I may goe into my ground to be eased and refreshed, but alas I am but a naturall man, what therefore shall become of this poore soule of mine; he considers with himselfe I am but in a naturall condition, and therefore in a miserable, damned condition, and then when hee returnes home, still this strikes in his minde, I am but naturall, flesh and blood, and therefore never shall receive any spirituall comfort; but when these things shall neither helpe me nor I be helpefull unto them; Oh what then shall become of me? I have had no part in Christ here, and therefore I can never looke that hee will owne me hereafter; it is a great evill for a man to have no good, but this is the misery of a man that hee cannot procure any good, and this is the misery of all miseries, that he cannot desire to be out of this misery; and yet this is the condition of every naturall man, you therefore that are naturall goe into corners and mourne for your selves and those that belong unto you, and for those to whom you have relation; you husbands that have wives which be naturall, and you wives who have naturall husbands, goe and mourne for them and for your selves, and sigh to heaven for mercy, and pray to God that hee would be mercifull unto them and forgive them their sinnes, and bring them out of their naturall estate, and make them able to entertaine Christ, and grace, and salvation. Parents mourne for your children that are naturall, when thou lookest upon thy child whom thou dearely lovest, and whom perhaps hath good naturall parts, and is obedient unto thee in outward respects, when thou beholdest this child of thine, and considerest that hee is in a naturall estate, then this may peirce thee to the very heart, then thou mayst burst out and say, woe is me that this child of mine was ever borne, for he is in a naturall condition, and therefore in a miserable condition, hee is a naturall child, and therefore a child of the divell, truly he is my sonne, and for ought I know if God have not mercy upon him, the child of the divell also; a naturall child is a damned child, a naturall man is an accursed man; consider this, doth not the Word say this, doth not the Lord say this, that *a naturall man cannot receive the things of God,* and therefore deale with your owne soules, and with the soules of thy friends, as men use to doe with those that are sicke, hast thou a child or a husband sicke of any disease, thou goest to the Phisitian to aske his counsell concerning the diseases, he tells the disease is not dangerous and deadly, it may he helped, and if hee be but able to receive those things which he shall prescribe he will warrant his recovery, but now if the disease continue, and hee be not able to take any food, or receive any Phisicke, then the disease cannot bee helped, health cannot be procured; you that are naturall men you are sicke of corruptions, the disease I must confesse is not deadly, if you can but take mercy and receive grace, which is the phisick of the soule, then you may recover, but as long as you remaine in your naturall estate, you can receive no spirituall foode, no spirituall phisicke, but cast up all, and therefore you are gone, you are but dead men. I tell you, you have many brethren, many friends, many children that are sicke, I tell you, they are proud, and carelesse, and loose, and prophane; but this is their greatest miserie above all the rest, they cannot take any spirituall foode, they cannot receive any spirituall good thing, but cast up all, and vomit up all; the power of the Gospell prevailes not, your counsell they will not heare, the Ministers exhort, admonish, reprove, they will not regard, they cannot away with any spirituall phisicke; I tell you, this will be their death, and if God be not mercifull, their damnation also, and therefore goe and mourne for your children and for your friends if they be naturall, and pray for them. When a man is sicke of some disease, if hee can take no foode, if no phisicke will stay with him, nor worke upon him, but he casts up all, then his wife shee sits in one corner of the house weeping, and his children in another corner mourning and lamenting, now if one comes in and askes them how doth your husband, or how doth your father, Oh then they fall a wringing their hands, Oh my father or my husband is but a dead man, if hee could but take any thing, then there were some hope of life, but alas nothing will stay with him, but as soone as he takes it he vomits it up againe, and therefore now there is no expectation of his recovery, this is the condition of many of your friends and children, they can take nothing which should doe them good, they can receive no spirituall good things; no counsell can take place with them, the word of God prevails not with them, O mourne for them therefore, they are in a miserable estate, they are but dead men, they will be damned; if they could but receive the things of the Spirit, then there were some comfort; but alas, how can a man receive salvation? is it not by the Word? why then if the Word will not prevaile with them or take any place in them, nor worke upon them, how then shall they come to salvation, why they must therefore be damned, they must therefore perish, they must be cast into utter confusion and destruction for evermore, Oh mourne therefore and pray for those which belong unto you if they be in a naturall condition.

In the last place, if it be so dangerous to bee in a naturall condition, then it is a word of exhortation to you all, that you would labour to get out of this naturall corruption. I intreate you for the Lord Jesus sake, as you love your owne soules whoever you be that heare this doctrine if you be naturall men, give no sleepe unto your eyes, nor slumber unto your eye lids, give no rest to your soules nor contentment to your hearts, untill you have studied by all meanes possible to recover your selves out of your naturall condition, beginne speedily and persevere constantly in the meanes that God hath appointed, that the Lord may bestow that power upon you whereby you may bee enabled to receive grace and salvation offered you, that so it may goe well with you for ever, *John 3.27.* there saith the Text, *a man cannot receive any thing unlesse it be given him from heaven,* so then the case is cleare, though thou of thy selfe canst not receive grace and salvation, yet God can give abilitie to receive them; away therefore from your selves, and look up higher, flie unto God for strength and sufficiencie; I would have such a naturall man feare continually that God will cut him off, and than he is damned for ever; Oh consider of this, a naturall man, why hee may be affraid that Gods judgements will every moment, in every place fall upon him, both at home and abroad, within and without, hee may feare they will fall upon him upon every occasion hee meetes with all, when hee goeth in the way, when hee sitteth still, when hee eates, when he sleepes, what businesse soever hee is about, in every place, at all times, upon all occasions, hee may fear that the curse of God will fall upon him. A naturall man may continually stand in feare and consider, if God should cut me off by death, what then would become of me, my body must returne to the ground, and my soule that must go into everlasting torments in hell fire among the devill and his angels, *where the worme never dyeth, nor the fire never goeth out,* and therefore sure my estate is woefull, and my condition miserable. But you will say, a naturall man cannot receive any good, why should hee then be counselled to receive the things of God, as grace and salvation; this is a cavill of *Bellarmin* and thus I answer it, we have no spirituall abilitie in our selves to performe any spirituall duty, but yet wee have ability to performe some morall actions; a man hath restraining and preventing grace whereby he is able to waite upon God in the meanes, that so he may be enabled to receive grace, and therefore as long as the parts and members of your bodies and the faculties of your soules continue, as long as your understandings and memories indure, why cannot you bestow

your bodies to come to Church as well as to goe to the Alehouse?
why cannot you bestow your eyes as well in reading as in carding
and dicing? God hath given you liberty to use these meanes, that
so you might receive grace, and therefore this objection is onely
a cavill of *Bellarmine,* God doth not punish a man because he
cannot get faith, but because he will not use the meanes whereby
he might get faith, wee may waite upon God in his ordinances, wee
may attend upon the meanes, these things you may doe and those
things you have power to doe; you may doe naturall and civill
actions, and therefore you should imploy your selves in hearing
the Word, and reading, and praying; you should use the meanes
which God ordained for the working of grace in your soules, when
you come under the ministery of God; hereby you may be converted,
and therefore you must come, and so grace may be wrought in your
hearts, and that you may be converted.

And therefore I will advise you of three things which are in the
power of natural men to performe as directions to the use of the
former means appointed by God for the working of grace; First
I would have every naturall man throughly convinced of the misery
hee is in, and informed of his owne insufficiencie, *Jer. 10.23.* there
saith the Text, *O lord I know that the way of man is not in himselfe,
it is not in man that walketh to direct his owne steppes;* and the
Apostle *Paul* hee taketh it to himselfe, *I know* saith hee, *that in my
selfe there dwelleth no good thing,* this is a great matter that wee
presume of our selves; we thinke we can stand of our selves,
though we never use the meanes to have our weakenesse strengthned,
and this is the reason that wee never seeke to God in the use of the
meanes, take therefore the course of the Apostle, and say *in me
dwelleth no good thing,* suffer your selves to be throughly informed
and convinced of your owne miserie and weakenesse, and confesse
this truth; I confesse I am a naturall and carnall man, and therefore
in my flesh there is no good at all. Secondly, when you have thus
done, and when your hearts are perswaded of your owne misery, and
you confesse there is no good in you; when you can say, Lord what
a stout heart have I, what a many gracious promises and godly
councells have I had, and yet never would receive or give way to
any of them, and therefore there is no good in mee; and then
thirdly, when you have done this, then convince your owne hearts
that there is an All-sufficiencie in the promise that the Spirit is able to
doe good unto your soules, *Ezech. 11.18.* there saith the Text, *I
will give them one heart, and put a new Spirit within them, I will
take away their stony heart, and give them a heart of flesh,* so that
however it is true, that we have no sufficiencie in our selves, yet
the Lord Jesus hath enough; the spirit is able to doe that for us
which wee are not able to doe for our selves; and therefore in the
third place, when thou art throughly informed of these two things,

then come unto Gods ordinances, and looke up unto God, and waite upon him in the use of the meanes; it is a fine passage of *David,* *Lord* saith he, *teach me the way of the Spirit,* as if hee had sayd, Lord I have a naughtie spirit, I have a naughtie heart, but Lord thou hast a good Spirit, lead me by that good Spirit of thine in the wayes of uprightnesse; Thus doe you, waite upon God in his ordinances, and say, Lord thou hast promised that thou wilt put a new soule into thy people, and create a new heart in them, and throw their sinnes into the bottome of the sea, and that thou wilt cause them to walke in thy wayes. Thou hast promised to give thy Spirit to them that seeke it, Lord make good this thy promise unto mee; take away this wretched sinfull heart of mine, and create a new heart in me, and direct me by thy Spirit to walke in the wayes of thy Commandements. It is true Lord, a Leaper cannot take away his spots, a Blackamoore cannot change his hew, but Lord thou canst make a Blackamoore white, and thou canst cleanse the Leaper; though I be a dead man thou canst put life into me, though I can doe nothing, yet thou canst doe all things, I am a blackamore, but thou canst make me of a white hew, I am a Leaper, but thou canst take away my spots; I am naturall and carnall, *in me there is no* *good thing,* but Lord thou canst make me entertaine spirituall things; good Lord grant that thy blessed Spirit may teach me to know the things belonging to my everlasting peace; this doe, above all take heede that you doe not deferre the time; Oh deferre not the wayting upon God in the use of the meanes; Why? because you have no power in your selves to helpe your selves, it is not in your power to receive Christ, and entertaine salvation; and therefore begin speedily to attend upon Gods ordinances, that at length the Lord may put a new spirit into you, and worke upon you to your everlasting peace and comfort. I exhort you above all things not to deferre the time and say, wee will gather the flower while it is greene, while our youth continues we will follow our pleasures, and take up our sports, and when wee come to be old, then we will turne over a new leafe, and on our death beds then wee will repent; alas, alas, how wilt thou thinke to doe it in thine old age, when thou couldst never doe it in thy youth? and therefore doe not thus delude thy owne soule; thou thinkest when thou lyest on thy death bed, if thou doest but send for a Minister, then hee will bring salvation to thee presently; but I tell these though all the Ministers under heaven should preach mercy unto thee, though all the Angels in heaven should exhort and intreat thee to entertaine salvation, though thou shouldest have all glory and all happinesse layd downe as it were upon a table before thee, if the Lord should say here is all glory and happinesse, doe but beleeve and take it and it shall be thine, thou shalt be made partaker of it for ever; yet consider in thy naturall condition thou hast no power to receive happinesse and glory, thus offered; if God should open heaven gates, and bid thee goe into heaven, yet thou hast no power, if thou beest a naturall man to receive mercy and salvation upon those tearmes which God hath offered them, thou couldest not enter into heaven though God should open the gate wide, and intreate thee to enter in, what a thing is this then, when neither Minister can perswade thee, nor Angels exhort thee, nor Christ himselfe intreate thee to take mercy, yet thou shouldest thinke in thy old age or upon thy deathbed to have mercy and salvation at command; why deferre not therefore this worke untill the last, but make speede, beginne betime and hold on constantly to the end, that at last God may take away your corruptions, and give you his spirit, and raise you out of the grave of your sinnes, doe this because you see it is needfull to be done, it is not in your power to doe good unto your soules, or receive good, and therefore beginne betimes and wait upon God in the meanes, that so you may have grace and salvation thereby.

ELECTION SERMON

Thomas Shepard

Thomas Shepard, one of the most influential ministers of seventeenth-century Massachusetts, was born in 1604 or 1605 in Towcester, England. He received his A.B. in 1623, and his A.M. in 1627, from Emmanuel College, Cambridge. He was ordained deacon on July 12 and priest on July 13, 1627. Silenced for his nonconformity in 1630, by Archbishop Laud, he became a tutor and chaplain for Sir Richard Darley of Yorkshire.

After enduring a succession of hardships in his attempted ministry in England, Shepard sailed for the New England Colonies in 1635, arriving in Boston on October 3. Assisting in the establishment of the church at Newton, after Hooker's move to Hartford, Shepard became its pastor on February 1, 1636.

Intensely interested in education, Shepard was instrumental in locating Harvard College at Cambridge and by persuading the Commissioners to approve a small tax on able families for "the dyett of divers such students as may stand in neede," he helped found the tradition of scholarships in America. He died on August 25, 1649.

"Then sayd all the trees to the Bramble raine ouer vs &c" was the Election Sermon preached at the Court of Elections, May 3, 1638. The text is from the *New-England Historical & Genealogical Register,* XXIV (1870), 361–66.

JUDGES: 9:14:15: *"Then sayd all the trees to the Bramble raine ouer vs &c"*

When Gideon that famous generall & the judge of Israell was dead & the fickle minds of a heady multitude (as tis like) p'jecting who should be there gouernour now there judge was dead, Abimelech a yong courtier (being the son of Gideon yet begot of an ignoble concubine) yet very ambitious & exceeding subtill & well acquainted w^t the misteries of the market how to compasse his own ends & by aduancing himself he therefore fisheth for hims: in troubled waters & strikes in for the kingdom, & because he knew there was no rising to this glory w^{t}out craft & cruelty, as for cruelty he resolves to murder all his brethren that he knew might lay claime to it vpō better right than hims: & as for craft he has enough of that; for knowing he could never climbe so high but upon the backs of freends, & knowing freends could not help him wth out some strength and force; & knowing that this force could not be had without

355

mony to bribe, he therefore sets hims. to sale before his freends & makes y^m sure. v'se : 1 : by his friends he makes the town of Shechem sure; better on to gouern than many, v'se 3 & here hath his force; & frō y^m all he gets his mony to bribe his crue that should accomplish this bloody designe; & kills all but on vpō on stō :5 : & so comes to be kinge by faction not by lawful election : do not wonder if blood & cruelty do sometime p'sper :

Jotham who only escaped y^t was preserued frō death was reserved to be a p'phet (tho. not to be king) of Abimelechs ruine; & that they might w^h patience hear whiles he spake, & his words remembered w^h he was gone, he desires them to heare, vse. 7 : & begins w^h a fable : but it had a morall suting there conditiō to teach y^m their folly in choosinge Abimelech Kinge—The trees are ra-tionall men, in a Comōnwealth; their goinge to anoynt a kinge is y^r liberty of electiō of y^r Rulers ouer them : 1 : they goe to the oliue some thinke prudent wise men whose oyle in the lamp gives light to all the house, but he will not loose his fatness; 2 : they goe to the fig tree, rich men, who will help w^tout taxes, & prefer & giue gifts; for fig tree will growe in most base & barren soyle & h[ence]. scatters its roots & out of euery th. fetcheth moisture; he will not loose his sweetnes then they come to the vine; holy men; tho poor as vine whose trunke is poore yet flourishing familiar w^t trees & adorīg y^m, 4. Then they come frō on extreame to another to anoynt the bramble; & he accepts; the sume is this men of prudent holy hearts y^t have someth. in y^m will neuer come out of these places to be gouernors there where god hath already set his gouernment ouer them only a bramble will :

1] here is the last electiō that all the trees m^d of a bramble gouernour ouer them;

2] his accepting of there electiō : he denyes it not, but if you be serious in choosing, I shall not refuse;

3] the conditions he makes w^t them in accepting this honour they had conferred on hm; 1 : you must come vnder him & trust to his shadow; 2 : if not then look for fire to come out of ye bramble w^h shall destroy you; a speech beseeming the majesty of a bramble sharpe & bloody;

Obs. 1. the temper of the multitude especially in free states w^r the gouernment depends on popular electiō, how apt it is to desire & accept of change of gouernment; The trees will first have an oliue, if not the fig tree, if not him the vine & frō the vine they will fall to the bramble; Tho a people haue the beste gouernment of god ouer them, as Gideō told them tho they have 2 : tho they have had the best gouernors, Baraks, Deborahs, Gideons to judge them, & there-fore need no other m^c lesse a bramble yet they are apt to change frō the very best to the woorst : fro choosing oliues and vines to make choyce of brambles; especially when all the trees haue a hand in the choyce:

Reas. 1. this sometime ariseth from an aptness in men to change in matters of religion, & h: must make new walls & fences to preserue there seed plots; X[t] not being king ouer few in Israell eury man will thinke at least w[t] is good in his own eyes; Gideō had demolished the Idoll of Baal; the men of Shechem had set vp a Baal Berith ag.; & it not able to stand alone is glad to set vp an Abimelech tho it be by blood:

Reas. 2. bec: they are apt to looke no further than present respect & benefit; & cannot see the consequences of things no more than blind men pits afar off: 1 Sam: 18: [8] the Israelites will have a king; s[d] Samuel you must be slaues & times of trouble will come y[n] you shall cry bec. of yo[r] king. we care not let vs haue a king: so here the bramble could giue no shelter, but fire would destroy y[ts] all on, he is o[r] brother, but haue blood of these yet he is o[r] brother; naturall & priuate respects will dangerously corrupt all elections, & change y[e] gouernment:

Reas. 3. bec: the multitude are exceeding apt to be led by colours like birds by glasses & larkes by lures, & golden pretences w[c] Innouators euer have courtious Absalom that tooke euery man by the hand pretending the good of the cuntry p'fessing w[t] justice he would shew, steals away the harts of people to make change of that happy gouernment vnder his father Dauid: prudent Abimelech, foreseeing how dangerous it will be to haue 2 suns in heauen & many kings ouer on kingdō & that it was better for on y[n] many to rule; for public safety desires the Sechemites to looke about them:

Reas. 4. frō a spirit of discontent w[c] vsually ariseth in a people vnder the strict gouernment of god: whose bonds they therefore breake; for Sins of men are like raging Sea, w[c] would ouerwhelm all if they haue not bankes; the bankes are wholesō lawes these bankes will breake down vnles some keepe them h: magistrates; so y[t] magistrates must either not restrayne & then all goes to ruine or restrayne & y[n] the Sea rageth ag. her own bankes & weary of her own magistracy w[c] god hath set ouer them: & h: desire another that they may haue more liberty. Some thinke the Sechemites stomach did arise ag. Gideō w[m] his sō in his oratiō to y[m] calls as an odious tearme of Jerrubball & now it breakes out to choose a king: w[n] people in Egipt was discontent let vs make vs a captayne & goe down to Egipt:

Vse. 1. Let it teach vs to preserue o[r] freedō w[c] we haue in this country established by such a singular wisdō of god: for w[n] all the trees come to choose y^r gouernour its a 1000 to on tho they may desire if we have a new gouernour I pray god wee may have a good on an oliue a vine, & yet they will at last accept of a bramble:

Vse. 2. Let this shew freemen y^r harts w^t they are w^n god leaues them to joyne w^t the rest of the trees to change y^r gouernment y^t god hath set ouer them; (know y^t you are apt to change in y^r religiō: vngrounded & w^{t}out setled loue to the truth you haue rec: to looke only to present profit: to be fed & led by appearances; to fall to impatience vnder y^{or} yoke; & so to change; the Israelites had now yr standing counsell & yr other officers p'tic: judges the gouernment of god ouer y^m; & yet now will haue a king; not but the same state may haue change of gouernment & so may o^{rs} yet whiles it hath gods gouernment change it for no other; m^c lesse for a bramble, wch god neuer set vp: w^t is the best forme of gouerment, may plead; we shall obserue the Jewes had in a manner all & while they kept close god the Lord blest all; all th: are m^d to serue X^t whiles church doth y^t the state shall serue y^m, & subjects y^m, & all those subjects; whether you have now this gouernt. ye wine needs not my bush w^n lawes rule men do not: w^n any gouernment advanceth gods ends, in framing of common wealths y^r is the gouernmt of god: now that is 1. Tim. 2.2. w^n men may liue in peace, in godlines; 3: in all godlines; to deny this to be among vs was either great blindnes or vnthankfulnes:

Obs. 2. Who tis that accepts of a tyranicall gouernment of that people who are vnder the gouernment of the Lord & we find it here only to be the bramble; the oliue & vine refuse it not but that wise men should accept but w^n y^r is gouermnt of the Lord ouer a people, tis a bramble that hath neither fatnes nor sweetnes nor chearfulness to rejoyce the harts of god & men that will here accept: 1. the bramble is most base & empty of goodnes of any tree as we often obserue; so such vsurpers are vile & sinfull of debosht consciences as Abimelech was; 2: they are ambitious; like the bramble that catches hold on the sleeues of men to aduance & honer them: 3. cruell like bramble of bloody prickles; 4: audacious & bold to commit any lewdness to aduance y^r ends; as here the bramble Abimelech; 5: barren & vnfruitfull dig^g about it neuer make it better:

Reas. bec. the kingdō of god is not deuided ag. it selfe, if therefore any vsurpe and gouernment ouer y^t state w^c god hath set, tis not of god but Satan; such a man as is bewitcht by Satan that hath seene glory of a kingdō & now falls down to woorship it; fild w^t the blood & cruelty & craft of that dragō to pull down the gouernment of the L. ouer a people; & tho they may carry it smoothly & be no great actors in the business as Abimelech was not yet if once they haue the place they will appear to be brambles indeed:

Vse. Let this learne vs what to judge of those that may come to
vsurpe ouer the churches here or state here; how euer they may haue
sheepes clothing yet if they can come in by y^r factiō, you will then
find them to be indeed brambles; ambitious base & bloody; if they had
fatnes & sweetness w^r they are they would not leave it to walk vp &
down after trees; looke as X^t there s^d the shephard comes for the
sheepe he y^t enters not by the dore tis to kill & steale, so he y^t shall
attempt to come in by factiō as Abimelech rather y^n electiō: nay he y^t
by generall electiō shall by killing Gideons sons make hims: king,
know him to be an Abimelech, a bramble; & he comes to kill &
rend you not to helpe you: men y^t know the burden of a place will
not willingly accept.

Obs. 3. That a Bramble gouernour will be the mischiefe if not the
ruine of a people; especially of those who haue had a hand in his
choyce; Let the bramble speake out & it will tell you as m^c as I say:
either trust vnder my shadow & w^t shadow hath the bramble, w^t
shadow of protectiō frō him, w^t shadow of refreshing or benefit frō
them; 2: if w^n you find it not & now shall cast him off fire will come
out of him to burne the ceders especially the men of Shechem & the
house of Millo: do men gather grapes of Thornes or figs of thistles
do you looke for any good from a bramble?

Q: how will they hurt it & be a pest to it:

Answ: Let vs but looke vpō Abimelech & you may see somewhat of there workings; 2 th: he doth: 1: He makes a factiō, this is
the soyle w^r the bramble takes root; 2: he makes vse of his factiō
to rayse him this is his height:

1] Abimelech makes his factiō his freends & Schechemites tis not
strange to the bramble to come in by rending: so tis the funda-
mentall principle that all brambles hold, make a breach & then
enter, diuide & rule them; first rend & then rayne; a bramble
cannot hold vp its head alone vnles it hath its bushes & trees
vnder them to beare vp its head, its hard to ruine some states
tho weake without a factiō, & yet easy to do it by a small on.

The man that came to cut down the wood, w^n he had his
hatchet he could not hurt w^{t}out an helve frō some of the trees;
w^n he had got that then he did easily cut down all the wood: so
let the next ambitious sharpe vsurper in the world come to a
state they cannot hurt w^{t}out y^t helve; its not unknown y^t Armin:
doctrine m^d an Arminian factiō in Holland: & the end of the
brambles was to let in the Spanyard: but subtilly will he make
it; the bramble hangs down head till factiō is m^d. & y^n you will
see him so humble & for publicke good; y^t you would thinke him
far frō this—1: Abimelech pretends publicke good; w^n he
intends publicke ruine, so all brambles they pretend to make
lawes & settle peace & the good of the cuntry & seruants to it.

but yⁿ they intend to breake lawes & disturbe peace; do you thinke Herod was euer like to haue kild Xᵗ if he had not pretended to wise men that he would woorship him; or the Samaritan factiō so like to hurt Nehiemiah but by pretending to build wᵗ them & loue them.

do you thinke that in a cuntry full of professiō people will be mᵈ into a factiō but by shewes of religiō, in the p'ties yᵗ doe make it tis Jesuits principle ouercome religiō. by religiō. by it s: h: Featley relates a man swoorne at Roome; &c.

2] Abimelech drawes them by there own priuate benefit, I am yoʳ brother you shall haue these honours frō me you shall haue such p'tectiō. frō me; of all others I will seeke to make you p'sperous; you may lead a multitude wᶜ way you will by pretenting present benefit; & this is yᵗ wᶜ makes a strong yet fatall factiō wⁿ men respect yʳ own priuate aduantage tho it be wᵗ publicke losse: nullify such lawes & deliuer vp such & such men into its hands yⁿ peace protectiō—but if not, looke for none frō me, but swoord: private present good will sway.

3] He advanceth another religiō yⁿ wᵗ they had vnder Gideon, & stands for Baal-Berith, a god of a new couenant; & h: had his mony frō him; as noth. knits so fast as religiō. so noth. makes such deadly breaches as religiō: on condemng another thrash them vex them fight ag. them kill them they are woorse yⁿ Pilate & Scribes & Pharisees, oh but they be holy they be the woorse now a mans factiō. will stand fast to him out of conse: for wⁿ I see my priuate good tis publicke woe consc. cryes; &c.

4] he disgraceth & rayseth slanders of all Gideons sons; that they now sought to be petty kings; wⁿ its like they were mourning together for the death of yʳ father for tis thought yᵗ Gideō was scarce cold in his coffin but this vsurper began to pr'ject betimes, so wⁿ the bramble would aduance hims: people are loth in consc. to draw so mᶜ blood; h: scratch & rent & disfigure & disgrace all magistrates & ministers in a country; they are enuyous they seeke thems: & to take away yoʳ liberties, wᶜ god & the king hath giuen, &c.; & wᵗ tho. they have gouernd the cuntry in peace the strong man hath kept pallace; apostates persecutors.

5] He sows the seeds of underming principles of gouernment by way of question: 1: its very fit yʳ shoulde be now a king ouer you how euer Gideō in his humility refused it; & 2: its like you will have many not on, now wᶜ is better on or many; judge you: thus brambles behaue thems: you will find them lay seeds of ruine; is it not fit to make appeales is not the sentence ȯf a major pt of court w'out consent of minor a nullity:

Thus you see how they make y^r factiō, I could wish these last were lookd to: to make question before consult w^t them y^t can resolue.

2: How doth he make vse of his factiō: *Ans:* Dauid m^d hims. strong here; 1. he picks out a number of vaine (or empty men) & a beggarly crue that are fit for his turne; 2. he binds them sure to him by bribes & money & gifts; 3. he watches seasō carrys the businesse exceeding close & w^n all were together now he sacrifices y^m all vpon on stone: & now you see idolatry diuiseō betw. Abimeleh & Shechemites & swoord & blood; vntill they were vtterly consumed especially the conspirators;

Vse. 1. let this awaken this whole cuntry: consid. its possible a bramble may be annoynted ouer you; god forbid; why obserue do you see a man make a factiō. by those ways y^t haue been mentioned, then be sure he will vse it w^n he hath got his helue & he will pick some vaine beggarly discontented sp: here and there that will be m^d sure by money & gifts, & on of the first th: will be to take away magist: & minister frō you: & y^n looke for fire to come out of the brambles

Vse. 2. oh es^t be carefull in y^r choyce; at all times; brambles and bushes are not fit to be Kings ouer trees; if you at any time annoynt any ouer you let them be oliues or fig trees, or vines but not brambles; 2 th: to this end would I leaue w^t you.

1] maintayne the privelege to death w^{m}soeuer you shall choose let him be on frō among y^{r}selues; a member of some church; he y^t is shut out of the fellowship of churches will be an enemy vnto the strictnes of churches; & ruine church you ruine state; & X^t also: it was a plague not y^t y^r was no king ouer Israell but no king in Israell: Deut:17:15. let him be some tree not a bramble for tis s^d: all trees s^d to bramble, opposing y^m together

2] W^n he is so let him be well known: either for sweetnes or fruitfulnes or fatnes; for some eminency a wise people will neuer submit to y^m whō they cannot honour; the trees were so hasty to make the bramble a gouernour that they passed by many other trees y^t were better y^n the aspiring bramble; let any come ouer among vs neuer so nobly descended neuer so pious. let men seem to be neuer so fayre some good estate, it may be y^r judgmnts or hearts may be so corrupt & apt to be caryed by priuate respects y^t troublers not keepers of vineyard: & h: none chosen till the freemen know & giue y^r voluntary assent y^{r}to: known for wisdō holiness publicke sp:

Vse. 3. if the bramble will rayne remooue him; he will be ruine at last:

1] cleaue to the L. & loue his truth & ordinances; the strong oake
lifts vp the head of vines y^t they be not ouertopt by brambles;
god neuer sent oppressors but w^n men grow to loath him; Zach.
11 : 8 : despise messages of the L^d X^t will dept & yor house left
desolate till you say blessed is he that comes in name of L y^t
you may learne diffr. betw : y^r & your yoke X^ts yoke now set god
ag. the bramble.

2] let y^r be no bushes to beare him vp : cut them down y^t doe; &
the vigilancy of magistracy will looke to that to haue a strict
eye vpon them y^t may; y^rs many idle seruants y^t liue w^tout rule;
y^t the course they take the houses they haunt the company they
conuerse w^t may be taken; h. Dauid; Ps: 101 : 7; w^t could
Abimelech haue done had he not met w^t his crue; & knew y^m y^t w^r
agst. L.

3] w^n brambles do appeare call for hatchets do not deale gently it
will prick you; but let seuerity in this case, by vsed: the best
ornament of the despised magestracy in the day of y^r small th :

4] Take leaue of base feare, of rude brambles; for this will diuide
you in times of danger : w^n Saul was King, 1 : Sam : 13 : w^n
Philistians came people were distressed; v'se 6 : & some hid
y^ms. in caues; some went ouer riuer Jordan to Gilead; some followed Saul trembling; & these fell frō many 1000ds to 600 p'sns.
15 : oh remember; Is: 8 : 12 : 13 : 14 : let L be y^or feare; as men
feare no swoords but men y^t smite & he shall be y^r sanctuary :
frō fire; tho for a stō of ofence to others : the Lord hath brought
you by a strong hand & bought you & blest you, & he hath w^n
you cryed to him saued you frō sins frō stormes frō Pekoat
times y^t he could haue m^d to haue vex you. I say the judgem. is
betime only let him be y^or feare & yn shall not be hurt by
brambles for y^or feare will be y^or snare to deliuer you into the
hands of brambles.

Viall I

The Powring out of the Seven Vials:
or
An Exposition, with an Application, of the 16th Chapter of the Revelation

John Cotton

John Cotton was born on December 4, 1584, in Derby, England. He received an A.B. in 1603, and an A.M. in 1606, from Trinity College, then attended Emmanuel College on a fellowship, remaining six years as head lecturer and dean. He was ordained in 1610, and received his B.D. in 1613. In 1612, he became vicar of St. Botolph in Boston, Lincolnshire, where for twenty years he initiated many Puritan practices. In 1632, with other Puritan ministers, he was forced to flee from England. On September 4, 1633, he and Thomas Hooker arrived in Boston, Massachusetts, where he remained until his death as "teacher" or doctrinal authority in the First Church.

From the date of his arrival in Massachusetts, Cotton was active in both the religious and political affairs of the colony. A nonconformist in England, he became increasingly narrow and fixed in his views in America. He died on December 23, 1652.

"Viall I" was preached to his congregation *circa* 1642. The text of the sermon is from John Cotton. *The Powring Out of the Seven Vials.* . . . London, 1642.

REVELATION 16.1.2. *And I heard a great voyce out of the Temple, saying to the Seven Angels; Goe your wayes, and poure out the Vials of the wrath of God upon the earth.*
And the first went and poured out his Viall upon the Earth; and there fell a noysome, and grievous sore upon the men which had the Mark of the Beast, *and upon them which worshipped the* Image.

YOU have heard in the former Chapter, of the Preparation of the Seven Angels, to poure out the seven last *Plagues* of God upon the *Antichristian* State. In this Chapter, you read a large *Description* of their *Execution* of that worke, which is,

First, Commanded, *Verse* 1.

Secondly, Performed, in the sequell of the Chapter.

Commanded, wherein observe that Commandement met forth,

First by the *Instrumentall efficient Promulger* of it, a great voice [*I heard a great Voice.*]

Secondly, By the Subject-place, whence this Voice came forth, out of the Temple. [*A great voice out of the Temple.*]

Thirdly, By the matter commanded by the voice, [*Goe your waies and poure out the Vials of the wrath of God upon the earth.*]

This Commandement thus given, was accordingly performed by all the seven Angels, in this whole Chapter.

The first Angel poureth out his Viall, *ver.* 2. and that is, first set forth by the subject upon which he poured it, [*upon the earth.*]

Secondly, It is amplified by the effect it wrought, [*There fell a noysome and grievous sore upon the men*] What men? They are of two sorts:

First, [*Such as had the Marke of the Beast.*]

Secondly, [*Such as worshipped his Image.*]

The words are somewhat darke, and there is much variety in the Interpretation of them: I shall shortly open to you, what (by the comparing of this, and other Scriptures together) I take to be the meaning of the Words.

First, when he saith [*I heard a great voice*] It is a voice of Authority, and Power. And whose can that be, but his, that hath power over all these Plagues, even God himselfe, and the Lord Jesus Christ, who also have power in the Temple: It is not the voyce of one of the foure Beasts, the Officers of the Church alone, but a further power doth concur with this voice, such as carried Majestie, and authority with it.

Secondly [*Out of the Temple*] It implieth it was a voyce delivered not by one of the foure Officers in private, but came out of *Publike Administration*, where onely the Lord speaking, did with *Authority* set forward these Angels upon this work. And it may further Imply, that it sprung upon some Prayers of the Church in the Temple: for all the voices in the Temple, are either, the voice of the Church unto Christ, or of Christ unto the Church: And if the Lord speake graciously in the Temple. It is commonly obtained in the Praiers of the Church, craving answer from him,

[*To the seven Angels*] That is to say, Seven sorts of Gods Messengers, whether Magistrates or Ministers, or whosoever they be that poure out these Vials, they are Angels of God, as being the Messengers of his wrath. Neither is it meant of seven Individuall persons, but seven sorts of Persons, that set forward this worke. And withall I doe accord with those that say, that in all these administrations, there is some presence of the heavenly Angels accompaning the men in the worke.

[*Goe your waies*] [*your waies*] is not in the Originall, but [*Goe*] *poure out the Vials.*] The Vials are vessels of large content, but of narrow mouthes, they poure out slowly, but drench deeply, and distill effectually the wrath of God: Vessels they are of full and just measure, as all these judgements are dispensed in weight and measure.

Of the wrath of God] That argueth, that upon what subject soever these Vialls fell, the wrath of God fell together with them, upon the same. And that helpeth not a little to open the place, and to shew the danger of some interpretations, which doe expound the Sunne *vers.* 8. to be the Scriptures. If these Vials be the Vials of Gods wrath, how shall any of them be conceived to be poured out upon the Scripture, is the wrath of God kindled against the Scripture? And for the *Earth, vers.* 2. Some conceive it to be meant of the common sort of godly Christians; but though some soare plagues might befall some of them, yet how can the wrath of God be conceived to be powred upon them? It cannot therefore be meant (as some of good note say) of the *Waldenses,* and *Albugenses, Hugonets,* and *Lollards;* but the wrath of God falleth upon such, as worship the Beast and his Image: And therefore take that for certaine, that what things soever the Vials of Gods wrath are poured upon, they are such as God is deeply displeased withall.

Upon the earth] They thought right, that thought it to bee meant of common sort of Catholikes: but let us further consider how it commeth to passe that the first of these Angels poureth out his Viall upon the earth, and the rest upon other things, yet they all have a Commission to poure out the Vials of the wrath of God upon the earth. For the opening of this difficulty (which else might exercise some) we must know, that in this Prophecie sometimes [*earth*] is opposed to Heaven, and then as by Heaven is meant the pure Church, as *Revel.* 4.1. & 12.1. So by Earth is meant an earthly and corrupt Church. Sometimes also by *Heaven* is meant, a corrupt state of Religion, wherein heavenly and divine honour is given to Satan, or Idols, as *Revel.* 12.3.7. Againe, sometimes *Earth* is opposed not unto *Heaven*, but unto some other Element in the World, and so is it in this Chap. *The first Angel poureth forth his Viall upon the Earth, the second poureth his Viall on the Sea, &c.* So then in this case, the *Earth* is to be understood in a double sense. In generall, of the Antichristian state, or world, *Vers.* 1. And in the Antichristian World they have some things that represent the *Earth*, and some things the *Sea*, and some things represent the *Sunne* of that World, and some things represent that *Ayre* of that world; therefore in the particular execution of this Commission, *When the first Angel poureth out his Viall upon the Earth*, it is upon the lowest and basest Element in the *Antichristian* world, and that can bee no other, but the lowest sort of vulgar Catholicks, and they were the first that had the wrath of God pour'd upon them, which did afterwards arise higher to the Sea, and then to the Fountaines and Rivers of water, then to the Sunne, then to the throne of the Beast, then to the River *Euphrates,* and last of all to the *Ayre,* and in all these doth the wrath of God ascend higher and higher, as may afterwards more clearly appeare.

The first Angel went and poured out his Viall upon the earth.] This first *Angel* must be these first sort of Gods Messengers, that did poure out some wrath upon common Catholikes. And doubtlesse such wrath it was, as being poured out, did worke a *Noysome and grievous sore upon them that worshipped the Beast, and his Image* (as the Text expresseth) *They that had the Mark of the Beast* (you heard before out of the 13 Chapt.) are such as receive some indeliable Character of the *Beast;* such are their Secular, or Regular Priests, and all that receive religious Orders from the Church of *Rome.* Who then are they that worship his Image? *The Image of the first Beast* (you know) is all Nationall, and Diocesan, and Provinciall Churches; and they that rule them are the Image of the second *Beast:* So then they that worship the Image of the *Beast,* be such as are devoted to the Canons of Popish Churches, who drink them up, and receive them as Articles of their Faith; these are all afflicted with a noisome and grievous sore by the pouring out of this first Viall: For those who did poure it out, they were such as did convince them of the Damnable estate of a Catholike, and taught them that by their Religion they could go not beyond a Reprobate; and this was the common practise of the Martyrs of *Jesus Christ* in Queene *Maries* time, in *Edward* the sixth, and in *Henry* the eight's time, who discovered unto you, that all their Religion was but the worship of God after the devises of men, even Will-worship, such as they were led into by the Man of Sinne, who being himselfe blinde, leadeth those that are blinde, and both fall into the ditch; those that thus discovered the unsoundness of the Religion of these Catholikes, who before seemed to be good Churchmen, and good House-keepers, and good Christmas-keepers, they were the men that poured out this first Viall upon the earth. And upon this their discovery, there fell a noysome, and grieveous sore upon their *Catholike Priests,* who had borne the common sort in hand, *That ignorance was the mother of Devotion, and such ignorant Devotion was the way of Salvation,* when they see that all their People, who were heretofore their honest and good Neighbours, full of benevolence towards them, were now informed, that they lay under a state of deepe *Damnation,* it was an eye-sore to their *Catholike Priests,* and all of that religious Order, a double sore fell upon them.

First, a sore of Envy, and malice, against all the Martyrs of Christ, and all that fought for Reformation of Religion; against whom their spirits were so strongly embittered, that happy was he that could bring Fire and Faggot to execute vengeance upon them, that did discover the state of the common sort of Catholikes to be so dangerous. It was a publike speech of *Henry* the eight, when he sate in Parliament, Complaining of the stirs that were made about Religion, There are many (saith he) that are too busie with their new (*Sumpsimus*) meaning those that clave to that which he counted the new Religion, though withall others he taxed, who doated (as he said not amisse) much upon their old *Mumpsimus*. The new Religion (though true) Hee, and they all envied: the Old (though his owne)he despised.

Secondly, there was a noysome loathsomenesse discovered, by these true Witnesses, and Martyrs of Christ, unto the people. Whereby they began to see that the common sort of their Religious Orders were full of *Idlenesse,* of *Ignorance,* of *Covetousnes,* of *Pride,* and of *Hypocrysie,* and that they had laid such a foundation of Religion, as was not *Jesus Christ* the true Foundation, but had indeed reared up an Antichristian Religion, whereof (as it is said (*Isai.* 28.19.) it shall be a vexation to heare the Report. A grievous malignant ulcer it was, and the more they stirred in it, the more they were vexed. And this let me further adde, for opening the words, it is an allusion to that noysome sore of *Egypt* that fell upon the Common sort of the people, and upon the *Magitians* also, *Exod.* 9.11. So that they could not stand before *Moses;* and so it was here, these noisome sores of which wee have spoken, did so fall upon the common sort of Catholikes, and upon their common Religious Orders, that they fall before the Angell that poured out this Viall, as *Dagon* before the Arke. Thus you see the meaning of these words.

Now for the Notes that arise from them. You may observe that (*Chap.* 15.7.) *One of the foure Beasts gave unto the seven Angels, Seven golden Vialls full of the wrath of God, but they went not then, to poure them out, untill they heare a great voice out of the Temple, and now they goe.* So that the Doctrine in the first place to be observed, is this.

Doct: 1.

Though the counsell and instruction, and advise of a Church-Officer may be a good invitement, and inducement, and preparative unto a Calling: yet it is the mightie voice of Christ, specially in Publike Ordinances, that Effectually stirreth up a man to the execution of it. These Angels had councell and encouragement given them (as you have heard) to goe about this worke, and were furnished with the wrath of God for this ende: but were not effectually stirred up to fall upon the execution thereof, till they heare a great Voice of Christ out of the Temple, (that is in publike Ordinances) then they goe to poure out their Vialls. You shall find this a very ordinary Practise in some things sutable hereunto in

Scripture. *Isaack* gave *Jacob* a Commandment and Instruction to goe to *Padan-Aram, Gen.* 28.6. And thereupon *Jacob* went on his way, *Vers.* 7. But the first night that he lodged out of dores, when the Lord appeared to him in the House of God (*Vers.* 15.) and telleth him, That hee will bee with him, and keepe him in all places whithersoever hee goeth, and will bring him backe againe into this Land; Then *Jacob* (*Chap.* 29.1.) lifteth up his heeles, and goeth on his wayes; Like a Giant refreshed with Wine to runne his Course. And the like was the Practise of the same *Jacob,* when they told him that *Joseph* was yet alive, *Gen.* 45.27.28. his spirit revived, and he said, *He would goe down to see him;* but first he goeth to *Beersheba,* and there offereth *Sacrifices,* and consulteth with the Lord, *Gen.* 46.1, 2, 3, 4. and the Lord encourageth him to goe downe, bideth him not feare, *He will be with him, and there make a great Nation of him, and bring him back againe,* (and so he did to be buried) thus are his hands fully strengthned in his way: The like also was the case of the men of *Samaria, Joh.* 4. *When the woman had told them that Jesus was the Christ, because he had told her all that ever shee did, they beleeved, because of her saying, Vers.* 39. But when they came unto him, and talked with him, then they said unto her, *Vers.* 42. *Now we believe, not because of thy saying, for we have heard him our selves, and know that this is indeed the Christ, the Saviour of the World.* Thus the voice of Christ carrieth his people and end in the waies of their callings, with effectuall power unto sudden and speedy execution.

The Reason is taken first, from the greater power of the voice of Christ speaking by his Spirit, then when hee speaketh by the gifts of his Servants, and therefore *Paul* putteth a great difference in this case, *Acts* 19.21. The Text telleth us, *That he purposed in his Spirit to goe up to Hierusalem, afterwards going on his way, he meeteth with certaine Disciples,* Act. 21.4. *and they by reason of the Prophesie of Agabus concerning Paul, vers.* 11. *fell upon him and wept, and besought him not to goe up to Hierusalem, What meane you* (saith he) *to weepe, and to breake mine heart, for I am ready not to be bound onely, but to dye at Hierusalem for the name of the Lord Jesus.* Behold here the Spirit of God had revealed clearely himselfe in the heart of *Paul,* to strengthen him to goe up to *Hierusalem,* these Disciples (upon the Prophecie of *Agabus,* that he should be bound at *Hierusalem*) said to *Paul* through the Spirit, that he should not get up: By what Spirit? By the gifts of the Spirit, the spirit of love, and their care of the Churches; but *Paul* waves them all, for hee had the minde of Christ, by the voice of the Spirit himselfe; this was indeede in times of extraordinary Revelation: but it sheweth you neverthelesse the difference betweene the voyce of the Spirit, and of the gifts of the Spirit, he giveth the greater power to the Spirit, then to the gifts of the Spirit, being such kind of Gifts, wherein humane frailty might be mingled.

The second Reason is taken from the greater power of Gods voyce in Publike, then in private Administration; If one of these Elders speake unto them, it may be but a private incouragement: Such as the advice of *Nathan* was unto *David,* to build the Temple, *I Chro.* 17.2. But had he come, (as afterwards he did) in way of Publike Administration; Hee could not have beene so mistaken as then he was; For therein doth the Lord more specially reveale the presence, and the power of his Spirit, and grace, *Matth.* 18.18, 19, 20. Therefore it is, *That when there commeth a great voice out of the Temple,* it carrieth along the Seven Angels to a speedy dispatch of this great worke, *of pouring out the Vialls of the wrath of God upon the earth.*

Vse. 1. The first Vse may teach us all, that have any private inducements or incouragements to any calling, or worke of God, by any Church-Officer, or Church-Member, not to sleight the same; for these Angels did not sleight the motion, when one of the Church Officers gave unto them the seven golden Vialls, but they tooke the Vialls, and when they see their time, when there cometh a publike Voice out of the Temple, then doe they all follow on effectually with their worke, in their seasons. Sleight not therefore private encouragements to good callings, but looke for further provocation and strengthning in them, from the publike Ministry, even from the voyce of Christ in the publike Ordinances of his Church. Private Revelations without the Word, are out of date, but certaine it is, that God doth speake by his Spirit in private Meditation and Prayers, and conferences with Brethren; and in all these, comforteth his people with the manifestation of his fatherly goodnesse, yet speaketh nothing, but in his Word, and according to it. Now these be good hints, and good encouragements, which God giveth his people in them, and by no means to be sleighted, when God sheweth his presence in them: God forbid that any of the sonnes or daughters of God should put them away. Yet this let me say, though such be faire incouragements, (what private duty soever they come in) whether to beleeve on this or that gracious promise of God, or to stir us up unto any other Spirituall work, the servants of God are hereby led to attend the more upon the publike Administrations of the Church, for the further clearing of the mind and will of God; There will the Lord more clearely reveale himselfe by his Spirit in every Ordinance of his Worship, there doth he delight to poure out all his fresh Springs, *Psal.* 87. Last, For there the Lord commanded the blessing, *even life for evermore,* Psal. 133.3. Eternall life doth he give in the Publike fellowship of his Saints, there doth hee confirme their callings to them, looke unto the Lord therefore for his blessing in this way, and so shall you be faithfull followers of these holy Angels of God, who being privately incouraged, waite for a publike voice to carry them an end in their Administrations, wherein the Lord by the mighty power of his Spirit doth confirme al his Promises, threatnings, and Commandements, and more thoroughly stirreth up the hearts of all his people to take hold of al that is spoken unto them; therefore if ever you perceive any voyce of spirit to take off a man from Publike Ordinances, and cause him to sleight them, then ever looke at it as a manifest delusion, for every dispensation of God, doth but enkindle a more earnest longing that the Lord should confirme the same by his broad Letters Patents, the Publicke Word and Sacraments in the Church. Yea so farre doe the Saints of God stand hereupon, that whatsoever is in private onely brought unto them to beleeve, they will finde much adoe to rest satisfied in it, untill they see it confirmed in publike also. As when men have any speciall grant from their Prince, and have it confirmed by the Privy Seale, they will not rest therwith, but will go to the Lord Keeper for the Broad Seale, to confirme what was before Sealed to them, though either of them apart be sure, yet both joyned together will make it more sure: Shall men be so carefull for this world, and for temporall Patrimonies, and shall Christians take up every motion in private and sleight publicke Ordinances? Be not deceived, whatsoever is brought unto you by the spirit of God in private, will cause you to seeke for more cleare evidence from his loud voice in Publike, where His voice goeth on more strongly and powerfully, convincing the Conscience, and breaking downe all Temptations and discouragements that might hinder the comfort of Gods people. *Vse. 2.* The use in the 2. place serveth to reflect a just reprofe therefore upon any that shall despise or neglect the Publike ordinances of God in the Church, for you see here that what is confirmed in the whole Church is the great Voyce of God, and that without contradiction to the holy Saints and Angels, if therefore the Publick ordinances be undermined, and borne witnesse against by any that cometh not from the spirit of these Angels, but from some evill roote in the hearts of the sonnes and daughters of men, the report of which is a vexation of spirit to heare thereof. Thus much for the first note, *Goe poure out the vialls of the wrath of God upon the earth.*

And the first Angel went, and poured out his viall upon the Earth, &c.

Here is a world you see discribed, having an earth and sea, and rivers, and fountaines, and sunne, and aire, and they all belong unto the Beast, and therefore the first Viall is poured upon them that had the marke of the Beast, and the last brought in the fall of Babilon: So that from first to last, they are the judgments of

God upon the Roman Antichristian state; as sixe of the seven seales brought in judgements upon the Pagan Roman world, and the seven Trumpets, his Judgements upon the Christian world, as they were ruled by Christian Emperours: so are the seven last Vials poured out upon the Antichristian world; From hence therefore you may note thus much.

That the whole antichristian world, or state is but earthly and not heavenly. For all these Angels are commanded to poure the vials of the wrath of God upon the earth, and they went not beyond their Commission, in pouring them upon the sea, and Rivers, and fountaines, and upon the sunne, and upon the throne of the Beast, and the River *Euphrates,* and the Aire; whereby the Holy Ghost holdeth forth unto us, that all these are but earthly, the sea is but earthly, the fountaines and rivers earthly, their sunne an earthly sunne, and the throne earthly, &c. And though it is true, (as some say) poure out any judgement upon any element, and the earth fareth the worse for it: yet take the description of the Holy Ghost, as it is plaine, and it intendeth the antichristian world alone: They are of the world, therefore they speake of the world, and the world heareth them, *I. Job.* 4.5. *And hee that is of the earth, speaketh of the Earth, Job.* 3.31. And so also are all their ordinances earthly.

Doct. 2. The first Reason is taken from the efficient cause of all their frame and state, which is but from the Earth: all their Doctrine, worship and government, so farre as it is antichristian is but humane, if not devillish, *Rev.* 13.18. The whole number of the Beast, whatsoever is numbred to belong unto him, is but the number of a Man, humane inventions and will-wisdome, men will have it so, and this is the Summe of all Popish Religion.

Reas. 1. As the whole frame of their Religion cometh from the earth, so doeth it tend to the earth againe, for what doth all drive at, but the maintenance of an earthly Pompious, stately Prelacy; nothing in the world but devices to get money: they are full of covetousness and ambition; both which, what are they but an open doore to their earthly libertie? these are sensuall (saith *Jude, ver.* 19.) not having the spirit: There is nothing spirituall in all their orders, nor in their pleasant sights, sweet smells, delightfull musique, and many goodly Feasts they have, and what are they but to please the tastes of men; and all their carved and painted stocks, and stones, their goodly Images, what doe they but please mens fancies, And

Reason 2. This you shall finde in the third place, that their best devotions doe but leave a man in an earthly and carnall estate, and therefore the Holy Ghost speaketh boldly, *Rev.* 13.8. *That all that worship the Beast, their names are not written in the booke*

of life, of the Lambe slaine from the foundation of the world:
There is not a man of them, that knowing and beleeving no more
than what he hath from the Beast, can be saved, therefore they
thought no amisse, who have written, that a Papist by his Religion
cannot goe beyond a Reprobate, so then whatsoever is meant by
these things in the antichristian world, whereon these vials were
poured, all is but earthly; an earthly sea, an earthly sunne, an
earthly light, an earthly aire, fitter to choake men (so farre as it is
Antichristian) then to breath any life into the soules of Christians.

Vse. 1. To shew you the vanity of all their endeavours, that study
to reconcile Popish and Protestant Churches together, I will say
but thus much, you may as soone bring Heaven and earth together,
as you can draw Popish and Protestant Religion together; for
Popish Religion is all but earthly, and all the Churches of Christ
are Heavenly, and therefore when Heaven and earth meete, then
will Poperie and Protrolemy meete together,

Vse. 2. In the second place let all men beware, lest they have any
licourish affection towards the old Religion, as they call it, if you
shall hearken to the voyce of such charmers, charme they never
so wisely, your best Religion will be but earthly, your prayers
earthly, your faith earthly, your obedience will bee earthly, you
shall find nothing therein able to answer an Heavenly and spirituall
mind: what though they tell you that Protestant Religion loveth
ease; but as for them, they have their whippings, & scourgings, and
fastings, and these (they will say) are no such earthly dainties;
Truely these so farre as they are *Antichristian* are but earthly;
they fast from flesh indeed, and from white meats, but they have
the dainties of the Apothecaries shops, preserves, and conserves,
and such kind of pleasant meats, and what have they done all this
while? these their practises are not sanctified of God, and therefore doe leave the soules of men still under carnall delusions, being
no other, but earthly and bodily exercises. *Goe and poure out the*
vials of the wrath of God upon the Earth, and the first went and
poured out his viall upon the earth. This is upon the lowest and
basest element, in the antichristian world, Thence we may observe.

Doct. 3. That God in his Judgements upon wicked persons, and
states beginneth first with the least and lowest amongst them, this
is evident in the Text, first upon the earth, and the sea is next;
which like the naturall sea is above the earth, and the Rivers, and
fountaines are higher then it, and the sunne higher then they: and
then upon the throne of the Beast, and when we come to open the
sequell you shall see that all things goe in a gradation; And in this
sort did the Lord deale when hee brought antichrist into the world,
Rev. 8.7. The first judgement came upon the earth; The second

upon the sea; The third upon the rivers and fountaines of water; The fourth upon the Sunne, then cometh Antichrist the King of the Bottomlesse pit, *Rev.* 9.11. and here in the 5. Viall his throne is smitten, and upon the sounding of the sixt angell, the foure angels in the River *Euphrates* were loosened, and here pouring out the 6th Viall, the River *Euphrates* is dryed up. And the consideration yeeldeth great light to helpe us in the exposition of these seven vials: for by the same steps wherby antichrist came into the world, by the same steps doth the Lord undermine him and bring him downe. For at first the common sort of Christians were corrupted when antichrist was brought in, so first the Common sort of Catholiques are blasted, when antichrist beginneth to fall: The like course did the Lord take in the plagues of *Egypt, Exod.* 7.19. &c. He beginneth with the lowest, first to turne their waters into bloud, and thereby killeth their fish, but still men subsist well enough, but then he bringeth frogs into all the land of Egypt & they crawle into their kneading troughes, then he changeth the dust of the land into lice, and that was a great deale more loathsome to men, and at length hee killeth all their first borne, and at last overwhelmeth *Pharaoh* and his hoste in the bottome of the red sea; and all this is according to the old covenant of his justice, *Levit.* 26.18, 21, 24, 28. *If you will not for all this hearken unto me, I will punish you yet seven times more for your sins,* so he threatneth againe and againe in all those verses, untill at last he bring upon them such feareful and horrible Judgements, *that they become an hissing to all nations.*

Reas. 1. The Reason of Gods dealing thus, is to magnifie Gods patience unto all; knowest thou not that the long suffering of God leadeth thee to Repentance, *Rom.* 2.4. It becommeth the Lord to magnifie his patience and when he doeth strike he will not suddenly stirre up all his wrath, therefore when here he commeth to judge Antichrist, he first poureth out his wrath where it is least of all sensible to the great Lords of the Antichristian world, to magnifie the equity of his Justice, and that he might also leave them without excuse, if the lowest judgements doe not prevaile: this God doth that he might be justified when he judgeth, *Ps.* 51.4. Thus though *his wrath bee revealed from heaven against all ungodlinesse and unrighteousnesse of men, Rom.* 1.18. yet such is the holinesse of Gods proceedings, that hee will shew his patience, and will strike gently upon the least and lowest in estate first, and afterwards hee goeth on further in wasting to waste, untill he have overspread a state with punishment; thus doth hee together magnifie his patience, and justifie his justice, and leave men without excuse.

Vse. 1. This may serve in the first place to teach all men in the feare of God, to become wise by light Judgements and gentle afflictions, those which you would thinke may least of all concerne you sleight them not: nothing more distant, from the chiefe men in a State, then the common multitude. A Judgement upon them doth not matter much; if a Famine were upon the common sort of people, Princes and Great men would not be much affected therewith. But the least of his judgements should be warnings unto us, to teach us that the Lord hath taken his Sword into his hand, and will goe on in judgement, untill he make the soules of men to tremble. What if a judgement begin upon mens cattell? That is farre off: It will come next upon your servants and Children, and it may be, reach to the wife of your bosome; and if all this prevaile not, it may be, He will strike you with grievous diseases in your body; and if you hearken not for all this, what if he let the Devill loose upon the soules and consciences of men and women? What will the heart of a poore Creature doe in such a case? O consider this all ye that forget God! least hee teare you in pieces, and there be none to deliver. When the Lord striketh aloose from us, It is but the Viall of the first Angell, but when the Lord beginneth, he will goe on further; therefore it must be the wisdome of the sonnes of men to take heed of his stroakes afarre off. This also is the Method of Gods dealing with his owne Children: He did not fall upon the Conscience of his servant *Job* at the first, but upon his Cattell, then upon his Servants, after that upon his Children, and nextly, upon his Body, and at last, writeth bitter things against his soule. Be we warned therefore by the first hints of chastisements, by small and gentle visitations, and happy they that learne to profit by such, to turne unto God, and to make their peace with him, before his wrath breake forth like a devouring fire, and there be none to quench it.

Vse. 2. The second use is unto the common sort of Christians, if there by any more poore and common, and of lesse esteeme then other: Marke what I say, and take it from the word of the Lord, it behoveth you in speciall manner to take heed to your Religion; for if corruptions groe therein, you will be the first that will suffer by them. And Why so? It is because Religion concerneth the common sort of Christians, as well as any other: and yet they commonly leave their Religion, (as they say) to men that are wiser then themselves; well, if you cannot read in the Book of God the broade Characters of Salvation, and the way thereof, looke for it, that when the smarting providences of God come upon any State where you are, you shall first taste of them, and then shall you see the necessity of looking unto your Religion. And upon this ground it is that the Apostle *Jude, Vers.* 1.3. writeth unto all the faithfull, and exhorteth them, *That they should contend earnestly for the Faith once given to the Saints:* otherwise they shall have the first hanfell of Gods Judgements, for they will be soonest corrupted, and shall bee soonest punished.

That the discovery of the loathsome, and shamefull sinnes of men, is from the Viall of the wrath of God. For what was this Viall which is powred out upon the earth (that is upon the common sort of Christians). It was their conviction of their damnable Ignorance, and Superstition, Idolatry, and Hypocrisie; and this the Lord threatneth, as a judgement unto *Hierusalem, Ezeck.* 16.37. *That hee will discover her nakednesse, that those that loved her, and those that hated her should see her nakednesse,* Thus is his wrath revealed against all unrighteousnesse of men.

Reas. 1. For the Lord is the first cause of all the Evill that is done among the sonnes of men, *Amos* 3.6. So that, is mens wickednesse discovered, is their loathsome, sinfull, carnall, corrupt estate laid open? *The Lord hath done it.*

Reas. 2. Because it is the proper worke of the Spirit of God to convince the World of Sinne, *John* 16.8. and he worketh it by the Law, *For by the Law commeth the knowledge of sinne, Rom.* 7.7. And what the Law doth, the same doe the servants of God by the Ministry of it, yet all is the worke of the Spirit of God.

Vse. 1. The Use may be, first to teach the Sonnes of men, to take heede how you snarle at Instruments of Gods wrath, though it may be, they may sometimes deale disorderly; yet is it your part to see the righteous hand of God, and when men walke according to God, in discovering your wickednesse, there is it, the righteous hand of God much more. As when the Angels that poured out this Viall, were encouraged by the Officers of Christ in his Church, and so by the Lord himselfe, to shew man that they were full of palpable Ignorance, and superstition: Therefore let men learne in these cases, to sanctifie the Lord in their hearts, and to acknowledge his hand on them, in such convictions of their sinnefull and shamefull estate and course.

Vse. 2. Let it teach all such whose sinnes are discovered at any time, to humble their soules under the mighty hand of God, that as their sinnes have beene discovered by an Angel of wrath: so they may be covered againe by the Angel of peace.

Doct. 5. That the discovery of the sinnes of the Common sort of people doth inflict a noysome Boyle upon their corrupt leaders, and guides that allow them therein. *There fell, a noysome and grievous sore upon the men which had the Marke of the Beast, and upon them that worshipped his Image.* When all this wickednesse is discovered in the common Catholikes, then doth the leaudnesse of their leaders also grow notorious; what say you now to all the Catholicke Priests.

Their wickednesse appeareth, their Idlenesse, Hypocrisie, Covetousnesse, and wantonesse, breaketh forth. *A grievous sore lay upon
them all,* to see that all their labours are discovered, to be but a
building men up in wrath, the Spirits of the Popish Leaders were
greatly disturbed and troubled to see men so busie with their new
Sumpsimus. A noysome blemish was it to all their Religious Orders
and to all that did countenance them in the same. Evident this
is unto al those that reade the Stories of our owne times, or the
times of our Fathers, how this noysome sore fell upon their Guids
and Leaders, And so it hath done of Old, *Esay* 9.15, 16. *The Leaders of this People cause them to erre:* So *Jer.* 5.31. *The Prophets
prophecie falsely, and the Priests beare rule by their meanes, and my
people love to have it so:* Thus are their false guides blemished.

Reason   The Reason is taken from the duty of the guides of the
Church and People, which is to turn them from their evill waies,
Jer. 23.22. Therefore if they lead them into evil wayes, needs
must a noysome sore fall upon them, when the wickednesse of
the people is discovered.

This may teach all the servants of Christ, to whom the Church
of God is committed, to be the more vigilant in all the Administrations of the things of God in his House, that there may remain in
it no corruptions that are discerned; but that being discerned, they
may be also borne witnesse against, and be seasonably rooted out, and
the spirits of Gods people healed: else the sorenesse will fall upon
the guids of the Church, the people may perish in their sinnes, but
their blood will the Lord require at the hands of those that should
leade them in the way wherein they should goe. It is not enough
for the people to say, it is the fault of their guides, nor for Ministers to lay the blame upon the people, unlesse they warne them, then
indeed have they delivered their owne soules, but if the People perish
for lacke of knowledge, God will require their blood at the hand
of their Guides.

A DISCOURSE

Concerning the Uncertainty of the Times of Men . . .

Increase Mather

Increase Mather was born in Dorchester, Massachusetts, on June 21, 1639. He was graduated from Harvard College in 1656, and then attended Trinity College, Dublin. Disapproving of the Restoration's effect on religion, he returned to Massachusetts, in 1661, and became pastor of Boston's North Church. In 1662, he married Maria Cotton.

Mather was elected a fellow of Harvard in 1675, and ten years later became president of the college. He held this position until 1701.

In 1689, Mather was sent to England as agent of the province of Massachusetts, his function to secure redress for grievances. He had conferences with Charles II and with William and Mary. In 1692, he returned to Boston with a new crown charter which settled the matter of the government of the province.

After 1701, Mather devoted his time to writing and to the religious matters of the Congregational Church. Though his power in the Puritan colonies was indisputable, his attitude toward other sects became increasingly tolerant.

Mather published ninety-two volumes, one of which, *Cases of Conscience,* 1693, spoke his attitude toward the civil prosecution of witches in Massachusetts and was influential in bringing the witchcraft trials to a halt. He died in Boston on August 23, 1723.

"A Discourse Concerning the Uncertainty of the Times of Men, and the Necessity of being Prepared for Sudden Changes & Death" was preached at Cambridge on December 6, 1696, "on occasion of the sudden death of two scholars belonging to Harvard College." Increase Mather was then President of the college. The text is from the edition printed by Green and Allen for Samuel Phillips in Boston, 1697.

ECCLES. 9.12. *Man knoweth not his Time.*

SOLOMON in this book shews the Vanity and Uncertainty of all humane affairs, and the Misery which does on that account attend men whilst they are on the Earth. He takes notice of many Vanities, one whereof, is mentioned in the preceding Verse; namely, That Events & Successes are not alwayes as men Judging by Second Causes conclude they will be. One would think that the swiftest Runner should come to the End of the Race soonest; & that when there is a battel to be fought, they that have the greatest Number and

377

Strength should win the day; but sometimes it falls out to be quite contrary, that the race is not to the swift, nor the battel to the strong. For which there are two Reasons assigned. (1.) The over-ruling Providence of God. *Time and Chance happeneth to them all.* There is nothing that *Chanceth* in respect of God, who knoweth and has determined all Events : but as to man, *Casualties,* Accidents happen which cause things to fall out otherwise then according to probable rational Conjectures would have been; in all which there is a Providence, and sometimes there is a great Providence in a small Accident. (2.) Another Reason is in the words before us, because *Man knows not his Time:* which is not to be understood Universally, as if no man did ever in any thing know what Times should pass over him: but for the most part and in most things they are Ignorant thereof. So then the Doctrine at present before us, is,

That for the most part the Miserable Children of Men, know not Their Time.
There are three things for us here briefly to Enquire into. (1.) *What Times they are which Men know not?* (2.) *How it does appear that they are ignorant thereof.* (3.) The Reason *Why they are kept in Ignorance of their Time.*

Quest. 1. What Times are they which men know not?

Ans. 1. Time is sometimes put for the proper season for Action. For the fittest season for a man to Effect what he is undertaking. The Seventy Greek Interpreters translate the words KAIRON UTOU. There is a *Season,* a fit Time for men to go to work in. If they take hold of that nick of opportunity, they will prosper and succeed in their Endeavours. It is a great part of wisdom to know that season. Hence it is said, *A wise mans Heart discerneth both Time and Judgment.* Eccles. 8.5. but few have that wisdom or knowledge. Therefore it is added in the next verse. *because to every purpose there is Time and judgment, therefore the misery of man is great upon him.* The meaning is, because men discern not the proper Time for them to Effect what they purpose, their misery is great. If they would attempt such a thing just as such a Time, they would make themselves and others happy, but missing that Opportunity great misery comes upon them. So it is as to Civil Affairs very frequently. Men discern not the proper only season for them to obtain what they desire. Yea, and so it is as to Spirituals. Men are not aware of the proper season wherein they may obtain good for their Souls. There is a price put into their hands to get Wisdom, but they have no heart to know and improve it. There is a day of Grace in which if men seek to God for mercy they shall find it. Isa. 55.6. *Seek ye the Lord while he may be found.* The most of them that have such a day know it not until their finding Time is past. Thus it was with Israel of old. Jere. 8.7. *The Stork in the heaven knows her appointed Time, the Turtle, and the Crane and the Swallow observe the Time of their coming, but my People know not the Judgment of the Lord.* They discerned not the *Judgments,* that is the dispensations of God. They had a Summer of prosperity but did not improve it. There was a Winter of Adversity coming on them, but they knew it not, nor did they use the proper only means to prevent it. So the Jews when Christ was amongst them, had a blessed time if they had known it: but they knew not the things of their peace, in the day of their peace; they knew not the Time of their Visitation.

2] *A man knows not what Changes shall attend him whilest in this World.* Changes of Providence are in the Scripture called *Times.* It is said that the Acts of David, and *the Times that went over him,* and over Israel, and over all the Kingdoms of the Countries, were written by *Samuel,* and *Nathan* the Prophet, and in the Book of *Gad* the *Seer,* meaning the Changes of Providence which they were subject unto. 1 *Chron.* 29.30. A man knows not whether he shall see good or evil days for the Time to come: he knoweth what his past days have been; but does not know what they shall be for the time to come. It may be he is now in prosperity: he has Friends, Children, Relations, which he takes delight in, he has Health, an Estate, and Esteem in the World, he does not know that he shall have any of these things for the future. Indeed, men in Prosperity are apt to think (as they would have it) that they shall alwayes, or for a long time be so but very often they find themselves greatly mistaken. The Psalmist confesseth that it was so with him. Psal. 30.6, 7. *In my prosperity I said, I shall never be moved, Lord, by thy favour, thou hast made my Mountain to stand strong: thou didst hide thy face and I was troubled.* His Enemies were all subdued: his Mountain, that is his Kingdom, especially his Royal Palace in Mount Sion was become exceeding strong, that now he thought all dangers were over, but *Absaloms* unexpected Rebellion involved him and the whole Land in Trouble. The good People in *Josiahs* time promised themselves great happiness for many a year under the Government of such a King as he was. Lam. 4.20. *Of whom we said under his shadow we shall Live.* But his sudden Death made a sad Change in all the Publick Affairs. A man knows not *what* Afflictions shall come upon him whilst on the earth. This is true concerning particular persons: they may know in general, that Afflictions shall attend them in an evil Sinful World. But what those Afflictions in particular shall be they know not. Thus the Apostle speaks, Act 20.22, 23. *I go bound in Spirit to Jerusalem, not knowing what things shall befall me there, save that the holy Spirit witnesseth in every City, saying, the Bonds and Afflictions abide me.* So that he knew in general that he should meet with Affliction, but not in special what the Affliction would be. So it is true concerning a People, that they know not what *Times* or *Changes* may pass over them. Little was it thought that whilest *Hoshea* (who was the best of all the Nineteen Kings that had Ruled over the Ten Tribes) was Reigning, a Powerful forreign Enemy should invade the Land and make them all Slaves. Little did the Jews think that when *Josiah* was but Thirty nine years old, he should dy before that year was out, and they never see good day more after his Death. And as men know not *What* their Changes and Afflictions must be, so neither *When* they shall come upon them. Whether it will be a long or a short time before those Changes overtake them. Mar. 13.35. *You know not when the Master of the House comes, at even, or at mid-night, or at the Cock crowing, or in the morning.* Thus a man knoweth not whether the sharpest Afflictions which are reserved for him, shall come upon him in his Youth, or in his middle age, or in his old age; though for the most part mens greatest Afflictions overtake them in their old age. Nor can any man know whether his Afflictions shall be soon over, or continue for a longer time. Indeed, the Lords People knew that their Captivity in *Babylon* should last for Seventy years and no longer; but that knowledge was by divine Revelation. As for some other Perfections they knew not how long they would continue. Psal. 74.9. *There is no more a Prophet, neither is there any that knows how long.* Those words seem to respect the Persecution under *Antiochus,* when there was no Prophet.

3] *A man knows not the Time of his Death:* Often it is so, that when Death falls upon a man, he thinks no more of it, than the Fishes think of the Net before they are Caught in it; or then the Birds think of the Snare before they are taken in it, as *Solomon* here speaks. It useth to be said, (and it is a plain, weighty known Truth) that nothing is more certain then that every man shall Dy, and nothing more uncertain than the Time when. Old *Isaac* said, Gen. 27.2. *Behold, I know not the day of my Death.* Though he lived above twenty years after he spoke those words, he did not know that he should Live a day longer. A man cannot know how long himself or another shall live. It is true that *Hezekiah* was ascertained that he should not dy before fifteen years were expired. And the Prophet *Jeremy* knew that *Hananiah* should not live a year to an end. Jer. 28.16. *This year thou shalt Dy, because thou hast Taught Rebellion against the Lord.* But these were extraordinary cases. It is not a usual thing for a man to know before-hand how many months or years he shall live in this World: Nor may he desire to know it, but he ought to leave that with God. Although *David* prayed, saying, *Lord make me to know my End, and the*

number of my Dayes, what it is. Psal. 39.4. His meaning is, not
that he might know just how many dayes he should live, but that
he might be made duely sensible of his own frailty and mortality,
and lead his life accordingly. Oftentimes Death is nearest to men
when they least think of it; especially it is so with ungodly men: we
have an instance of it in *Agag.* He came before *Samuel, delicately,
and said, surely the bitterness of death is past.* 1 *Sam.* 15.32. Little
did he think, that within a few hours, he should be cut in pieces.
When *Haman* boasted of his being the chief Favourite at Court, and
that the Queen had invited no one but the King & himself to a
Banquet, he little thought of the destruction which was then preparing for him. When Belshazzar was in the beginning of the night
drinking and making merry, with his profane Companions, he little
thought that he should be a dead man before morning; but *that
night was Belshazzar slain. Dan.* 5.30. The Rich Fool in the Gospel
dream'd of a long life and merry: He said to his Soul, Eat, Drink
and be merry, thou hast Goods laid up for many years. But God
said, *This night thy Soul shall be required of thee:* He must appear
immediately before the dreadful Tribunal. Luk. 12.20. Thus we see
what Time it is which men know not.

The second thing to be Enquired into, is, *How it does appear
that men know not their Time.*

Answ. 1. It is evident, *In that all future Contingencies are known
to God only.* Hence Christ said to the Disciples, *It is not for you
to know the Times and the Seasons which the Father has put in
his own power. Act* 1.7. Future Times and Contingent Events, the
knowledge & disposal of them has God reserved to himself. There
are future things which happen necessarily, that a man may know
them long before they come to pass: *God has appointed Lights
in the Heaven to be for Signs and Seasons.* Gen. 1.14. These move
regularly and unfailably according to that Order which the Creator
has established. Therefore a man may know infallibly how many
hours or minutes such a day or night will be long before the Time
comes: He may know when there will be an *Eclipse* of the Sun
or of the Moon twenty, or an hundred years before it comes to
pass: but for Contingent Things, which have no necessary dependance on the constituted Order of Nature, but upon the meer
Pleasure and Providence of God, they are not known except unto
God, or to them unto whom he shall reveal them. The Lord chal-
lengeth this as his Prerogative. The Idols whom the Heathen
worshipped, could not make known future Contingencies. Isa.
41.22, 23. *Let them shew us what shall happen, or declare us things
for to come, shew the things that are to come hereafter, that we
may know they are Gods.* To do this was past their skill. The Devil

knows many future things which men are ignorant of; He could foretel *Sauls* ruin, and *Davids* coming to the Kingdom. Nevertheless, there are many future Events which he has no knowledge of. Therefore he often deludes those that Enquire of him with deceitful and uncertain Answers. But as for men they are ignorant of future things, which most mearly concern themselves, or their own Families. No man knows so much as who shall be his Heir, or Enjoy the Estate which he has laboured for. Psal. 39.6. *Surely every man walks in a vain shew, he heapeth up riches, and knows not who shall gather them.* He knows not whether one of his Relations, or a meer stranger shall possess that Estate which he has taken so much pains, and disquieted himself so much for the obtaining of it. This meditation made *Solomon* out of Love with this World. He knew as much as any man, and yet he confesseth that he did not know whether the man that should come after him, and enjoy all that he had Laboured for, would be a wise man or a fool, Eccles. 2.18, 19. And he sayes, *A man knows not that which shall be; for who can tell him when it shall be.* Eccles. 8.7, He knows neither what nor when it shall be. And again he saith, *A man cannot tell what shall be; and what shall be after him who can tell him!* Eccl. 10.14. This is to be understood concerning Contingent Events. Such as the particular Afflictions which are to befall a man, or the Time, Place, or manner of his Death.

2] *The Times of men are ordered according to the Decree of God.* There is nothing comes to pass in the Earth, but what was first determined by a wise decree in Heaven. Act. 15.18. *Known unto God are all his works from the beginning of the World.* God knows what he has to do. The Apostle speaks there concerning the Conversion of the Gentiles. This did God fore know and decree from the beginning of the World, yea from all Eternity. The like is to be said concerning every thing which happens in the World. Not a Sparrow falls to the Ground without his Providence, and therefore not without his decree, the one being an Infallible Effect of the other. He has decreed when and where every man that comes into the World shall be Born; and where he shall live, in what Country, and in what Town; yea, and in what House too. Act. 17.26. *He has determined the times before appointed, & the bounds of their Habitation.* He has decreed when every man shall dy. Eccl. 3.2. *There is a Time to be Born, and a Time to Dy.* That is to say, a Time decreed and appointed by God when every man shall be born, and when he shall dy. Not shall any man live a day longer than the Time which the Lord has appointed for him. Job 14.5. *His dayes are determined, the number of his months are with thee, thou hast appointed his bounds that he cannot pass.* All the Circumstances attending every mans Death, the place and the manner of it, whether he shall dy by Sickness, or by any other Accident, all is determined in Heaven before it comes to pass on the Earth. Now the decrees of God are Secret things until the Event or some divine Revelation shall discover them. Deut. 29.29. *Secret things belong unto the Lord our God.* His divine decrees are those secret things, which Himself alone knows. Rom. 11.34. *For who hath known the mind of the Lord? or, who has been his Counsellor?*

3] *The Conversations of men generally make it manifest, that they know not their Time.* They do many things which they would not do, and they neglect many things which they would certainly practice, if they knew what Times are near them. Math. 24.43. *If the good man of the house had known in what watch the Theef would come, he would have watched, and would not have suffered his house to be broken up.* Thus men live in a careless neglect of God, and of their own Souls and Salvation, but if they knew that Death will come stealing suddenly upon them, they would watch and pray. Did they know that before the next week, they shall be in another World, they would live after another manner than now they do. Most commonly Persons are light and vain in their spirits, when heavy Tidings is near to them. Did they know what sad News they shall hear shortly, they would be in a more solemn frame of Spirit. Isa. 5.12. *The harp and the viol, the tabret, and the pipe, and wine are in their feasts, but they regard not the work of the Lord, neither consider the operation of his hands.* Had they known what work God intended to make with them speedily, they would have minded something else besides their sensual pleasures and delights.

We proceed to Enquire 3. *Whence it is that men know not their Time.*

Answ. It is from God. He will have them to be kept in ignorance and uncertainties about their Time: And this for wise & holy Ends. *eg.*

1] That so his Children might live by Faith. That so they might live a life of holy dependance upon God continually. They must not know their Times, that so they might Trust in the Lord at all times. God would not have his Children to be anxiously solicitous about future Events, but to leave themselves and theirs with their Heavenly Father, to dispose of all their Concernments, as He in his Infinite Wisdom and Faithfulness shall see good.

2] That their Obedience may be tried. That they may follow the Lord, as it were blind fold whithersoever He shall lead them, though they do not see one step of their way before them, as *Abraham* did. Heb. 11.8. *When he was called to go out into a place which he* should after receive for an inheritance, he obeyed, and went out not *knowing whither he went.* We must follow God, tho' we know not what He will do with us, or how He will dispose of us, as to our Temporal Concerns, submitting our selves, yea, our lives and all entirely to the Will of God in every thing. That saying ought to be often in our mouths, *If the Lord will,* and we shall live, and do this or that. *Jam.* 4.15.

3] Men must not know their Time, that so they may be ever watchful. Math. 25.13. *Watch therefore, for you know neither the day nor the hour wherein the Son of Man comes.* The generality of men, if they had it revealed to them (as *Hezekiah*) that they should certainly live so many years they would in the mean time be careless about their Souls, and the World to come. We see that notwithstanding they are uncertain how short their Time may be, they are regardless about their future eternal Estate. How much more would they be so, if they knew that Death and Judgment were far off from them?

4] As to some they are kept in Ignorance of their Times, that so they may with the more comfort and composure of Spirit follow the work which they are called unto: That they may with diligence and chearfulness attend the duties of their general and particular Calling; which they could not do, if they knew what Evil Times and Things are appointed for them. The terror of what is coming on them, would be so dismal to them, that they could not enjoy themselves, nor take comfort in any thing they enjoy. As the Apostle speaks to the covetous Jews, Jam. 5.1. *Go to now you rich men, weep and howl for your miseries that shall come upon you.* So there are many in the World, that would spend their days in weeping and howling, did they not know what is coming on them and theirs. When the Prophet *Elisha* had it revealed to him, that sad things were coming on the Land, by reason of a bloody Neighbour Nation, which would break in upon them, and exercise barbarous Cruelties; the holy man wept at the foreknowledge of it. 2 King. 8.11. *The man of God wept.* So there would be nothing but weeping in many Families, weeping in many Towns, and in some whole Countries, did men but know their Times. Therefore they must be kept in ignorance thereof until the things come upon them.

We proceed to the USE of this Doctrine.

First by way of *Information.*

Inf. 1. *We see the Reason of those Meserable Disappointments which men frequently meet with;* It is because they know not their Time. If they had set about such an enterprize a little sooner, they had succeeded well, but not knowing that, all their labour is lost. So it is often as to matters wherein the Souls of men are concerned. How came *Esau* to be disappointed of the Blessing; if he had come but a few hours sooner, he had certainly attained it; but he knew not that, and so was eternally frustrated of all his hopes and expectations. The foolish Virgins cryed for Oyl when their Lamps were going out, they should have done that sooner. They came for Admission to the Marriage after the Door was shut. Thus by not knowing their Time they lost their Souls, and missed of Heaven for ever. Mat. 25.9, 10. Thus also it is as to Temporal Concerns. Some Accident not foreseen happens, and brings a frustration on all a mans Endeavours. Marriners go to Sea, and they meet with Enemies, where they least expected them. They come near home, a Storm happens, and they suffer Shipwrack. Had they been aware of those Evils, they would have been more careful to have avoided them. The Husbandman after much pains taken in Tilling the Ground, has an hopeful prospect of a good Harvest, but Blasting, or Mildew, or Droughts, or great Rains, or unseasonable Frost, disappoints all his hopes. These were things which he could not foresee nor avoid. A man Builds an House, hopes he shall Enjoy the Comfort of it many years: A Casualty never thought of, causeth the House to be Burnt: Had he known this, he would never have been at the Cost of such a Building.

Inf. II. *We may here see the Vanity and Impiety of those Persons who pretend to know their own or other mens Times.* There are some that will not ingage in a design on such or such dayes, because they are not (as they speak) *Lucky dayes.* Some (as Mr. *Cartwright* in his Commentary on the Text before us observes) will not undertake a matter on a *Saturday,* because they say *Saturn* has made that to be an unfortunate Time for Action. There are some wicked *Almanacks,* which tell men that such a day of the Month is *a Lucky Time,* to begin a Journey in: And that some other dayes are *Unlucky* ones. This is that which the Scripture calls *Observing Times;* and it is a most hainous Sin to do so. The Heathen of old did practise such things. But God in his Word declars them to be *Heathenish Abominations* and with the highest Severity has charged his People not to do thus. Deut. 18.10. It is mentioned as one of the Crying Sins of *Manassah,* that he *Observed Times,* 2 King. 21.6. And that wicked *Haman,* who designed the bloody destruction of the Lords People would go to Conjuring that he might know when would be a Lucky Time for him to Execute his purposed Mischief. Est. 3.7. And of this nature is that fallacious Art, which bears the Name of *Judicial Astrology,* when men will Calculate Nativities, & pretend to know by the Stars, what Times shall pass over such Persons. *Zanchy, Gassendus,* and other

Learned men have notably discovered the Vanity and Impiety of all such *Planetarians*. The old Chaldrans had as much skill as ever any man had in this Art or *Science falsly so called*. But how does the Prophet deride them? Isa. 47.13, 14. *Let now the Astrologers, the Stargazers, the Monthly Prognosticators stand up and save thee from those things, that shall come upon thee; behold they shall be a Stubble, the fire shall burn them, they shall not deliver themselves from the Power of the flame.* They pretended to know the Fate of Kingdoms, and yet could not tell their own and the Nations ruin before the day that it came upon them all. There are cursed *Fortune tellers,* who pretend to know what shall befal particular persons, how they shall be disposed of; when, and where they shall Dye. It is a sad thing, that ever any person should dare to do thus in *New-England*. Time was, when the Air of *New-England* was intollerable to such Vipers. Dreadful guilt is upon the Souls of them, that have gone to Enquire of such vile Creatures, and so of the Devil by them. That famous Gentlewoman, Mrs. *Honeywood,* who was a long Time under doleful desertions, the first Occasion of her sore Conflicts was that she had Enquired of a *Fortune-teller* concerning the Recovery of a sick Child. Much more is it Evil to be a *Practitioner* in this Iniquity. And it deserves to be Lamented with tears of Blood, that ever any one that has had a Standing in this *Colledge,* should be found in the number of those horrid Creatures. A late Writer observes, that persons who consult *Fortune-tellers,* or *Judicial Astrologers,* are many times visited with signal Judgments: And that this was an usual practice in *Jamaico,* a little before the late dreadful *Earthquake* there; and yet those Wretches could not foretel that Earthquake before they were swallowed up alive in it.

Inf. III. *If men know not their Time, then they are concerned to make a good use of the present Time.* How does it concern us to spend our Time well? And *Now* whilst we have Time, to do all the Service for God, and for Jesus Christ that possibly we can! we know not how soon our Opportunities for Service may be gone. Either Death or Sickness, or some other Providence may deprive us of them. We should therefore imitate the good Angel in *Thyatira,* unto whom the Lord Jesus Christ said, *I know thy Service and thy works, and that the last be more than the first.* Rev. 2.19. That thought will be a comfort to a man whatever Times or Changes may come upon him. It was so to *Hezekiah,* when he was Sick, and in his own Apprehension a dying man. Isa. 38.3. *Remember now, O Lord, I beseech thee, how I have walked before thee in truth, and with a perfect heart, and have done that which was good in thy sight.* If a man can say, as for the time past of my life, I have (through the grace of Christ) spent it well, &

this Sickness, this Death finds me walking with God, that's comfortable. And because we know not our Time, we should *do all the good we can for men:* And that in every respect wherein we are capable of doing good. If God has blessed any of us with Estates, let's do good with them. Eccl. 11.2. *Give a portion to seven, And also to eight, for thou knowest not what Evil shall be upon the Earth.* Such Evil Times may come as you shall loose your Estates. Therefore be liberal and charitable. If a man has lost his Estate, and can then say, when I had an Estate, I did good with it, I honoured God with my Substance, and was bountiful to his poor according to my ability; he may then be sure, that his Estate is taken from him, not in Judgment but in Mercy. But if his Conscience shall say to him, thou didst with hold more than is meet, and therefore Poverty is now come upon thee, that will be a sad thought. And because we know not our Time, we should be *alwayes doing good.* We should never be idle. When some would have had *Calvin,* because of his Bodily Infirmities to have ceased from his accustomed Studies, what (saith he) *vultis me dominum, me otiosum invenue.* Would you have the Lord find me Idle? When Death comes, would you have it find me doing nothing? Because we know not our Time, we should be careful not to Sin at any time. Luk. 21.34. *Take heed to your selves, lest at any time your hearts be overcharged with suffering and Drunkenness, and Cares of this Life, and so that day come upon you unawares.* If Death should come upon a man, presently after he has committed some grievous sin, how sad would that be; or if Death should find him acting sin, as it did *Zimre and Cozbi,* who were Slain in the act of wickedness, so *Nadah* and *Abihu,* at the time when they were profaning the Name of God, Lightning killed them. If Death should find a man profaning the Sabbath, or in Lewd Company it would be most uncomfortable; or if Death should find him in Drink, as very often it is so with notorious Drunkards: And altho' many a sober and godly man is Drowned, nevertheless, it is observable concerning Drunkards, that their sin is often seen in their punishment. They have used to drown themselves in Drink, and they often dy by Drowning; and are drowned too at the time of their being Drunk. This is very sad.

Let the Last USE be for
EXHORTATION

Be we *Prepared for a Change of Times, especially for the great Change of* DEATH *which will come upon us, we know not how soon, nor how suddenly.* Who can say what Changes may come upon us? It was said of *Moab,* Jer. 48.11. *Moab has been at ease from his Youth, and he has settled on his Lees, and has not been emptied from Vessel to Vessel.* It cannot be said so of *New-*

England. Altho we are too much settled on our Lees, yet we have
not been alwayes at Ease, but we have been emptied from Vessel
to Vessel. God has Rack't this Land: One Change after another
has come upon us, and some very awful ones. We have seen
Changes of Government in our Civil State: And some of them very
sad ones; when we were delivered into the hands of some that
hated us, and when we could call nothing our own, but our Civil
Liberties were gone, and our Sacred Liberties in utmost danger
of being taken from us also. *Changes and War have been against
us.* We had our Peace for many years together, but now the sound
of the Trumpet and the Alarum of War, and how long shall we hear
it! A long War has afflicted us now for eight years together. Our
Land has been changed from Plenty to Scarcity; we were wont to
supply other Plantations, but these two last years we stood in need
of supplies from other places. What the Lord will do with us for
the future we know not: According to Humane Judgment, either
there is to be a Peace among the Nations, or we shall fall into
the Hands of a formidable Enemy, before the next year is Expired;
but God has wayes which we know not of, to prevent what our
Sins deserve, and what we may rationally fear. There are awful
symptoms upon us: And in special the multiplied sudden Deaths
which have been of late. The last week two desirable young Scholars
were drowned here in *Cambridge.* The Week before that, seven
persons were Drowned in another place, and two the week before
that. And do you not hear of a very sad Accident, a young Child
eight years old happened to kill his Brother not above two years
old; besides some other awful Providences. Is there not a voice of
Heaven in these things! The words of Christ should be considered
by us. Luk. 13.4, 5. *Those Eighteen on whom the Tower of Siloam
fell and slew them, think ye that they were Sinners above all men
that dwell in Jerusalem, I tell you nay, but except you repent, you
shall likewise perish.* So do you suppose that those thirteen persons
who have been taken away by sudden strokes within these three
weeks last past, were greater Sinners than any in *New-England.*
Nay, but these *Evils falling suddenly upon them,* are Warnings
to all. God can as easily bring sudden Changes upon a whole Land
as upon a few particular persons.

But especially we are by such Providences called upon to *to
prepare for Death. I will wait all the days of my appointed time
until my Change come.* Job 14.14. Death brings a wonderful
Change with it. So it does as to the Bodies of men. They are turned
to Corruption; for the most part after they are dead, either Worms
or Fishes feed upon them. And a Change as to the Souls of men.
When once they are out of their Bodies, they know in a moment
where they must be to all Eternity. They then see Angels, and they

beheld the Majesty of the Terrible God. Consider but two things here.

Consider 1. Death may come on us suddenly. So does the Text and Context before us intimate. It is said, Numb: 69. *If any man die very suddenly.* That then is possible, and we see Instances of it before our Eyes frequently. The Scholars now gone, who were in this House the last Lords Day, hearing the Word of God, did not think that they should be dead the next day; no more then any of you think of being in another World before to morrow; sometimes Death does not give a days warning before it comes. Prov. 27.1. *Boast not thy self of to morrow, for thou knowest not what a day may bring forth.* You know not what shall be on the morrow, nor where you your selves shall be, no, not what World your Souls shall be in on the morrow. It may be, Death will not give an hours warning; nay, not a minutes warning. Have you not known some that the thunder of God has struck them dead in a moment? They were alive and in perfect health, and in less then a minute stark dead. Have you not heard of many in these late years, that fearful *Earthquakes* have swallowed them up in a moment? How many Hundreds did there so perish in *Jamaica!* You heard also how it was in *Sicily,* but a few years ago, above an hundred thousand Souls there went down alive into the pit. God by such things speaks to all that dwell on the Earth and hear thereof. Let none of you say, we are young, and Death is far from us. Were not they young and as likely to live as any of you, whose sudden Deaths has caused me to Preach this Sermon.

Consider 2. When Time is ended Eternity begins. Time ends with Death. Then as the Angel sayes concerning the *Fourth Monarchy, Time shall be no longer.* Rev. 10.6. When Time shall be no longer, Eternity begins. After *Dives* was dead and his Soul in Hell, *Abraham* told him, that there was a *great Gulf fixed,* that they that would go from Hell could not do it. Eternity is a great Gulf. When once a mans Soul is out of his body, he is got into a Gulf of Eternity: he is *fixed* where he must be forever. Rocks shall sooner move out of their places, than he shall stir from the place where he is. *If a man dy, shall he live again?* No, he shall never live again in this World as formerly. Suppose Death should come upon a man and find him wholly unprepared; if he could come into the World again to mend his Error that were another Case; but this shall never be. Job 7.9, 10. *He that goes down to the Grave, shall come up no more, he shall return no more to his house, neither shall his place know him any more.* Though a man would be willing to give never so much to live again, it shall not be granted to him. I have heard of one that when dying, said, *If I had Ten Thousand*

Worlds I would give them all that I might live one day longer.
Without doubt it is so, with the Souls in Hell. If they had Ten
Thousand Worlds to give, they would gladly part with them all,
that they might live one day longer on the Earth, to Repent and
Pray in, and earnestly endeavour that their peace might be made
with God through Jesus Christ.

You will say, but *What is to be done by us, that so we may be
prepared for Death?*

Ans. 1. Let us make sure that Death finds us in Christ. That was
Pauls great care, that he might be *found in him.* Phil. 3.9. If a man
was got into the City of Refuge, the Avenger of Blood could not
hurt him. Neither can Death hurt that man who is in Christ. There
are none of us all, but Death may come suddenly upon us. As
Eminent Saints, as ever lived have dyed suddenly: was it not so
with *Moses?* was he not well and dead in a Moment of Time,
without ever being sick? Have you not known or heard of many
Eminent Servants of the Lord with whom it has been thus? That
Holy Learned man, Mr. *Brightman,* was taken with Death as he
was Riding in a Coach, having a Greek Testament in his hand,
because he would loose no time. Our famous Mr. *Norton,* was
taken with Death as he was walking in his House, fell down, and
never spoke a word more. Those Worthy Governours, Mr. *Eaton,*
and *Haines* dyed in their sleep. So has it been with many a dear
Servant of God, that has gone to Bed well, and dyed in his sleep.
So did Mr. *Vines,* and Mr. *Capel,* after they had Preached twice
the Lords Day before. And therefore I do not advise you to pray
(as some do) that you may not dy suddenly, but to make sure of
your being in Christ, and then let Death come never so suddenly,
you shall receive no harm by it. There are Angels by you to take
care of your Souls. But if Death finds a man out of Christ, wo
unto him that ever he was born. What terrible work will Death
make with that man? It will tear him in pieces, Body & Soul, and
send both to Prison, his Body to the Prison of the Grave, and his
Soul to a worse Prison, there to remain in a certain fearful expectation of Judgment, and of Fiery Indignation at the Great Day.

2] *Live as you will wish you had lived when Time shall be no
longer with you.* I have read of a King that sent to a Minister,
desiring that he would tell him how he must live, that so he might
be sure to be a good and an happy man: Sir, (said he) *Live as you
wished you had lived the last time that you were Sick, and thought
you should dy,* and then you will certainly be a good and an happy
man. They that would dy well, must live well. Be alwayes serving
and glorifying God in Jesus Christ, & then if any body tells you
of Death, you may smile at it, and say, If Death comes it shall
be welcome, when ever the Lord pleases to send it.

AND now as I have spoken these things to all this Assembly, so let me apply them in a special manner to you the *Scholars* of this *Colledge,* who are here present before the Lord. I am concerned in my Spirit for you. All of you are my Children: And do you think that I can see my Children Drowned, and not be troubled for it? God has come among you this last week, & lessened two of your number by a sad & awful Providence. Do you think these two were greater Sinners than any amongst you. No, no, they were both of them hopeful youths. One of them (young *Eyres*) was an only Son, and a desirable dutiful Son, of a sweet amiable Temper, beloved by every body. He was observed to read the Scriptures constantly every day with great Alacrity. A sign that there was *some good thing in him towards the God of Israel.* As for the other (*Maxwell*) the Rebuke of Heaven in taking him away is the more solemn, in that his pious Relations sent him from far to be Educated in this Nursery, for Religion and good Literature. I took special notice of him; but could never observe any thing in him, but what was commendable. He was ingenious, and industrious, and I believe truly pious; had he lived, he was like to have been a choice Instrument of Service to the Church of God in his Time. And I am perswaded that his Soul is among the Angels of God. *But if this be done to the green Tree, what shall be done to the Dry?* This fatal blow looks ominously on the poor *Colledge.* Considering some other circumstances; there is cause to fear lest *suddenly* there will be no *Colledge* in *New-England;* and this as a sign that ere long there will be no Churches there. I know there is a blessed day to the visible Church not far off; but it is the Judgment of very Learned men, that in the Glorious Times promised to the Church on Earth, *America* will be Hell. And altho there is a number of the Elect of God yet to be born here, I am verily afraid, that in process of Time, *New-England* will be the wofullest place in all *America,* as some other parts of the World once famous for Religion, are now the dolefullest on the Earth, perfect Emblems and Pictures of Hell. When you see this little *Academy* fallen to the ground (as now it is shaking and most like to fall) then know it is a terrible thing which God is about to bring upon this Land. In the mean time, you the *Students* here, are concerned to bewail the Breach which the Lord has made among you. If you slight and make light of this hand of the Lord, or do not make a due improvement of it, you may fear, that God has not done with you, but that he has more arrows to shoot amongst you, that shall suddenly strike some of you ere long. But Oh that the Lord would sanctify what has hapned to awaken you unto serious thoughts about Death and Eternity. Who knows but that God may make these sudden Deaths, an occasion of promoting the Salvation, & Eternal Life of some amongst you. It is related concerning *Waldo,* (He from whom the

Waldenses have that Name given them) that the occasion of his Conversion was the *Sudden Death* of one of his Companions. The sight of that made him serious. He did not know, but that he might *dy suddenly* too, and that he was therefore concerned to be always fit to dy. So did he turn to the Lord, and became a great Instrument of Glory to God and good to his Church. Oh! that it might be so with you. Wherefore I pray you; yea, and I charge you in the Name of the Lord; *as my beloved Sons, I warn & charge you,* that every one of you endeavour that you may be able to give a good Answer to three plain, short Questions.

1] Let every one of you be able to give a good Answer to this Enquiry: *What am I?* Am I a true Believer, yea or no? Am I a Regenerate Person: it may be I am a Civil, Moral young Man, but what's that without Faith and Regeneration? If any man is in Christ, he is a new Creature, Am I so? The Apostle sayes that *in Christ Jesus neither Circumcision availeth any thing, nor Uncircumcision, but a new Creature.* Gal. 6.15. So it is not material to a mans Salvation whether he be a Learned or an Unlearned man, but whether he is in Christ and a new Creature. Tho' you should attain unto an Hundred Times more Learning than what you have, you may perish Eternally notwithstanding that, if you be not in Christ, or if you are not new Creatures. As *Austin* speaks, *Surgunt indocti et rapiunt Coelum, at nos cum omni doctrina nostra Mergimur in gehennam.* All your Parts and Learning will but aggravate your Misery at last, if you have not Christ and Grace in your Souls. If a man is Cast away with Bags of Gold about him, he will sink the faster and the deeper for it; so they that have Golden parts, but ungodly hearts and lives, will of all Persons sink the deepest into Hell. *Grotius,* who was one of the Learndest men that this age has produced, professed, that he would willingly part with all his Learning, for the Piety of a poor Godly Country man, who was wont to spend his Time every day, after this manner; Eight hours of the day he followed his Calling with diligence, he allowed himself eight hours for sleep; the other eight hours he spent in Reading the Scriptures, and in Prayer, Meditation & Communion with God. Then let your chief care be about matters wherein your Souls & Eternal Estates are concerned. Let every one of you think often with himself, If I should dy this day, is my Soul safe? He that knows not whether he is in Christ and as an effect thereof, a Sanctified Person, knows not what will become of his Soul to all Eternity. And how dare any of you live at peradventures about a matter of such Infinite Moment, one day to an end? It is related in the Life of that Eminent Saint, Mr. *Ignatius Jurdain,* that if he met any Scholar, & such an one especially as applied himself to the Study of Divinity (as there are some scores belonging to this

Academy, who are designed for the work of the Ministry) his usual question to such was, *What Evidence have you for Heaven? You Scholars* (said he) *have the best Opportunities of all men for the getting of Assurance: you are still looking into Gods Book, and into other good Books, and should acquaint your selves with your Spiritual Estate toward God.* Truly, it is a sad thing, when *Scholars* the design of whose life is to gain knowledge, yet know not what their Spiritual Estate is, or what shall become of their Souls for ever. Why! you cannot know what will become of your Bodies for a day; but you may know what will become of your Souls throughout an endless Eternity. Rest not then without being able to give a good Answer to that Question. I doubt many of you cannot say more than *Berengarius* did, (it may be some of you not so much) who when he was dying, thus expressed himself, *I am now going to appear before God the Judge of all; what will become of my Soul, I cannot tell; I have some hopes that I shall be Saved, but I am afraid that I shall be Damned.* Poor man! A sad word for so Learned a Person as he was to go out of the World with.

2] Let every one of you be always able to give a good Answer to this Question, *Where am I?* Have I allowance from God who sees me, to be in this place, and amongst this Company at this Time? Am I in a *Tavern* or in an *Ale house?* Is that a fit place for a *Scholar* to be in, except there be some special reason to induce & warrant him, since the *Statutes* of this and other Reformed *Universities* have prohibited *Students* from being seen in such places? Ought I not at this Time to be in my *Study* rather? What Company am I now Conversing with? Am I willing, that my life should be gathered with such Sinners? If Death should come upon us suddenly, am I willing that my Soul should be gathered where theirs must be? When Persons will be Venturing where they have no call, they are oftentimes surprised with Evils, *Like Fishes in an evil net,* which they least thought of. *Tertullian* speaks of a Christian Woman, that going to a *Stage Play,* an *Evil Spirit* there took possession of her, who when it was wondered at, that he should get possession of one that was a Christian, said, *I found her in my own ground,* and therefore might well take possession of her. Let not the Devil at any Time find any of you in his ground, or in any other place or Company, but where God in his Word giveth you leave to be.

3ly, and Finally, be always able to give a good Answer to this Question, *What am I doing?* Is the thing that I am about a Lawful thing? Am I using Recreations for my Health sake? And is it a Lawful Recreation, which no Law neither of God nor man has forbidden? The two young men that were Drowned the other day, Death found them in a Recreation: It's well, it was a Lawful one

Skating on the Ice is so, if used seasonably & with due discretion and moderation. But how dismal is it when Death shall surprise Persons when they are diverting themselves with *Scandalous Pastimes*. Histories tell us of some who whilest they have been *Playing at Cards,* the Lightning has struck them & they have been found Dead with the Cards in their hands. My dear Children! In the fear of God, let it never be so with any of you. Be often putting that Question to your selves, do I spend my Time well? Am I still attending some work either of my particular or my general Calling? Am I diligent in my Study? That was it which your Parents sent you hither for. As *Junius* his father used to direct Letters to him when in the University, as one that was *Missus ad Studendum?* If Death should come Suddenly on me, would it not find me squandering away my precious hours, in doing nothing? Do I Remember that an hours Idleness, is a Sin as well as an hours Drunkenness: I must give an account to Jesus Christ the Son of God concerning every hour of my life. Am I not forgetful of my Duty towards God every day? Do I read the Scriptures and Pray in Secret constantly? Do I often think how Christ lived in the World, and endeavour to be like him: Am I always doing the things that please God? Now if you can give a good Answer to these three Questions, *What am I? Where am I? What am I doing?* you need not be afraid of Death, let it come never so suddenly. Blessed is that *Servant,* yea Blessed is that Scholar, *Whom the Lord at His coming shall find so doing.*

The Bostonian Ebenezer

Cotton Mather

Cotton Mather, oldest son of Increase Mather, was born in Boston on February 12, 1663. He received his degree from Harvard at the age of fifteen and was promptly ordained as a colleague to his father in the North Church, Boston, where he spent the rest of his professional life laboring to establish the dominance of the New England clergy over the political life of New England.

An incredibly prolific writer and indefatigable publisher, Mather turned out over three-hundred volumes during his lifetime. One of these, *Memorable Providences Relating to Witchcraft and Possessions,* was used, apparently against his wishes, as a canon in the infamous Salem witchcraft trials.

A man of great courage as well as persistence, Mather supported the unpopular practice of innoculation and sponsored sodalities among college students at Harvard.

In 1710, Cotton Mather received the Doctor of Divinity degree from Glasgow. In 1713, he was made a Fellow of the Royal Society, the first American colonial to be so honored.

Mather died in Boston on February 13, 1728, with the reputation of being the great American scholar of his time.

The "Bostonian Ebenezer: Some Historical Remarks, On the State of Boston, The Chief Town of New England, And of the English America, With Some Agreeable Methods For Preserving and Promoting the Good State of That, as well as any Other Town, in the like Circumstance" was preached at Boston on Lecture Day on April 7, 1698. The text is from the edition printed by Green and Allen for Samuel Phillips, Boston, 1698.

I. SAM. vii. 12. *Then SAMUEL took a stone, and set it up, and called the Name of it EBENEZER, saying, Hitherto the Lord hath Helped us.*

THE Thankful Servants of God, have use sometimes to Erect Monuments of Stone, as durable Tokens of their *Thankfulness* to God, for *Mercies,* Received in the places thus distinguished. *Jacob* did so; *Joshua* did so, and *Samuel* did so; but they so did it, as to keep clear of the Transgression forbidden, in Lev. 26.1: *Ye shall not set up an Image of Stone in your Land, for to Bow down unto it.*

The *Stone* Erected by *Samuel,* with the Name of *Ebenezer,* which is as much as to say, *a Stone of Help;* I know not whether any Thing might be *Writt* upon it: but I am sure there is one thing to be now *Read* upon it, by our selves, in the Text where we find it: Namely, thus much,

That a People whom the God of Heaven hath Remarkably Helped, in their Distresses, ought Greatly and Gratefully to ac- knowledge what Help of Heaven they have Received.

Now, 'tis not my Design to lay the Scene of my Discourse, as far off as *Bethcar,* the place where *Samuel* set up his Ebenezer. I am immediately to Transfer it into the Heart of Boston, a place where the *Remarkable Help Received from Heaven,* by the People, does loudly call for an *Ebenezer.* And I do not ask you, to change the Name of the Town, into that of *Helpstone,* as there is a Town in *England* of that name, which may seem the English of Ebenezer; but my *Sermon* shall be this Day, your *Ebenezer,* if you will with a Favourable, and a Profitable Attention Entertain it. May the Lord Jesus Christ Accept me, and Assist me now to *Glorify Him,* In the Town, where I drew my First Sinful Breath; a Town whereto I am under Great Obligations for the precious opportunities to *Glorify Him,* which I have quietly and publickly enjoyed therein, for Near Eighteen years together. *O my Lord God, Remember me, I pray thee, and Strengthen me this once, to speak from thee unto thy People!*

And now, Sirs, That I may set up an EBENEZER among you, there are these Things to be Inculcated.

i] Let us Thankfully, and *Agreeably,* and *Particularly* Acknowl- edge *What* HELP we have Received from the God of Heaven, in the years that have Rolled over us. While the Blessed Apostle *Paul,* was, as it should seem, yet short of being *Threescore* years old, how affectionately did he set up an *Ebenezer,* with an Acknowl- edgment, in Acts 26.22: *Having obtained Help of God, I continue to This Day!* Our Town is now *Threescore and Eight* years old; and certainly 'tis Time for us, with all possible affection, to set up our *Ebenezer, saying Having obtained Help from God, the town is continued, until almost the Age of Man is passed over it!* The Town hath indeed three *Elder Sisters* in this Colony, but it hath Wonderfully Outgrown them all; and her Mother, Old Boston, in England also; Yea, within a Few years, after the first Settlement, it *grew* to be THE METROPOLIS OF THE WHOLE ENGLISH AMERICA. Little was This Expected, by them that First-Settled the Town, when, for a while BOSTON, was proverbially called *Lost-town,* for the mean and sad Circumstances of it. But, O *Boston,* it is because thou hast *Obtained Help from God;* even from the Lord Jesus Christ, who, for the sake of His *Gospel,* Preached and once prized here, undertook thy Patronage. When the World and the Church of God, had seen *Twenty-six* Generations, a Psalm was Compared, wherein that Note occurs with *Twenty-six* Repetitions; *His Mercy endureth for ever*. Truly, there has not one year passed over this Town, *Ab Urbe Condita,* upon the Story whereof, we might not make that Note our *Ebenezer: His Mercy endureth for ever*. It has been a Town of Great Experiences. There have been several years, wherein the Terrible famine, hath Terribly Stared the Town in the Face: We have been brought sometimes unto the *Last Meal* in the Barrel; We have cried out with the Disciples, *We have not Loaves enough to feed a Tenth part of us!* but the feared *Famine* has always been kept off; always, we have had Seasonable and Sufficient Supplies after a Surprising manner sent in unto us: Let the *Three Last years* in this thing most Eminently Proclaim the Goodness of our Heavenly *Shepherd* and *Feeder*. This has been the *Help* of our God; *because His Mercy endureth for ever!* The *Angels of Death,* have often Shot the *Arrows of Death* into the midst of the Town; the *Small Pox* has especially four Times, been a *Great Plague* upon us: How often have there been Bills desiring Prayers for more than an Hundred Sick, on one Day in one of our Assemblies? In *One Twelve-Month,* about one *Thousand* of our Neighbours, have one way or other been carried unto their long Home: And, yet we are after all, many more than Seven Thousand Souls of us, at this Hour, Living on the Spot. Why is not, a *Lord, Have Mercy upon us,* written on the Doors of our Abandoned Habitations? This hath been the Help of our God, *Because His Mercy Endureth for ever*. Never was any Town under the Cope of Heaven more liable to be laid in ASHES, either through the *Carelessness*, or through the *Wickedness* of them that *Sleep* in it. That such a *Combustible Heap,* of Contiguous Houses, yet Stands, it may be called, *A Standing Miracle*; it is not because *the Watch-man keeps the City*: Perhaps there may be too much cause of *Reflection* in that thing, and of *Inspection* too; No, *It is from thy Watchful Protection, O Thou keeper of* Boston, *who neither Slumbers nor Sleeps*. TEN TIMES has the *Fire* made Notable *Ruins* among us, and our *Good Servant* been almost our *Master*; But the *Ruins* have mostly and quickly been Rebuilt. I suppose, That many more than a *Thousand Houses* are to be seen, on this little piece of Ground, all filled with the undeserved Favours of God. Whence this preservation? This hath been the *Help* of our God; Because *His Mercy endureth for ever!* But if ever this Town saw a *Year of Salvations,* transcendently such was the LAST YEAR unto us. A Formidable *French Squadron*, hath not Shot one Bomb, into the midst of thee, O thou *Munition of Rocks*; Our streets have not Run with Blood, and Gore, and horribly Devouring Flames have not Raged upon our Substance: those are *Ignorant*, and *Unthinking*, and *Unthankful* men, who do not own, that we have narrowly escaped as dreadful Things as *Carthagena*, or *Newfoundland*, have Suffered. I am sure, our more considerate Friends beyond Sea, were very *Sus-*

picious, and well nigh *Despairing*, That Victorious *Enemies* had swallowed up the Town. But *thy Soul is Escaped, O Boston, as a Bird out of the Snare of the Fowlers*. Or, if you will be Insensible of *This, Ye Vain men*, yet be sensible that an *English Squadron*, hath not brought among us, the Tremendous *Pestilence*, under which a Neighbouring *Plantation*, hath undergone prodigious Desolations. *Boston,* 'tis a marvellous thing, a *Plague* has not Laid thee desolate! Our Deliverance from our *Friends*, has been as full of Astonishing *Mercy,* as our Deliverance from our *Foes*. We read of a certain city, in Isa. 19. 18, called, *The city of Destruction*. Why so? some say, Because: Delivered from Destruction. If that be so, then hast thou been a *City of Destruction*: or I will rather say, a *City of Salvation*: and this by the *Help* of God; because *His Mercy endureth for ever*. Shall I go on? I will. We have not had the *Bread of Adversity* and the *Water of Affliction*, Like many other places. But yet, all this while, *our Eyes have seen our Teachers*. Here are several *Golden Candlesticks* in the Town. *Shining and burning Lights*, have Illuminated them. There are gone to Shine in an *Higher Orb*, Seven Divines that were once the *Stars* of this Town, in the Pastoral Charge of it; besides many others, that for some years gave us transient Influences. *Churches* flourishing with much Love, and Peace, and many *Comforts of the Holy Spirit*, have hitherto been our greatest *Glory*. I wish that some sad *Eclipse* do not come ere long upon this *Glory*! The Dispensations of the *Gospel* were never Enjoyed by any Town, with more Liberty and Purity, for so long a while together. Our *Opportunities* to Draw near unto the Lord Jesus Christ, in His *Ordinances*, cannot be paralleled. *Boston,* Thou hast been *Lifted* up to Heaven; There is not a Town upon *Earth*, which on some Accounts has more to answer for. Such, O Such has been our *Help* from our God, Because *His Mercy Endureth forever*.

ii] Let us Acknowledge, WHOSE *Help* it is, that we have Received, & not *Give the Glory of our God unto another*. Poorly *Helped* had we been, I may tell you, if we had none but *Human Help,* all this while to depend upon. The Favours of our Superiors we Deny not; we Forget not the Instruments of our Help. Nevertheless, this Little *Outcast Zion*, shall with my consent, Engrave the Name of no MAN, upon her *Ebenezer*! It was well confessed in Psal. 108.12, *Vain is the Help of man*! It was well counselled in Psal. 146.3, *Put not your trust in Princes, nor in the Son of man, in whom there is no Help*.

Wherefore,

First, Let GOD in our Lord JESUS CHRIST, have the *Glory*, of *Bestowing* on us, all the *Help*, that we have had. When the Spirit of God came upon a Servant of His, he cried out unto *David,* in I

Chron. 12.18, *Thy God Helpeth thee.* This is the voice of God, from Heaven to *Boston* this Day, *thy God hath been thy Help.* A Great man, once Building an Edifice, caused an Inscription of this Importance, to be written on the Gates of it, *Such a place planted me, Such a place watered me, and Caesar gave the increase.* One that passed by, with a witty Sarcasm, wrote under it. *Hic Deus nihil fecit;* i.e. *God, it seems, did nothing for this man.* But the Inscription upon our *Ebenezer,* owning what *Help,* this Town hath had, shall say, *Our God hath done all that is done!* Say then, O Helped BOSTON, say as in Psal. 121.2, *My help is from the Lord, which made Heaven and Earth.* Say as in Psal. 94.17, *Unless the Lord had been my Help, my Soul had quickly dwelt in silence.* And boldly say, *'Tis only because the Lord has been my Helper, that Earth and Hell, have never done all that they would unto me.*

Let our Lord JESUS CHRIST, be praised as our Blessed *Helper:* That *Stone* which the *Foolish Builders* have *refused,* Oh! Set up that *Stone;* even that *High Rock,* Set Him on High in our praises, and say, That, *That is our Ebenezer.* 'Tis our Lord JESUS CHRIST, who in his Infinite Compassions for the Town, hath said, as in Isa. 63.5, *I Looked, and there was none to Help; Therefore my own Arm hath brought Salvation unto it.* It is foretold concerning the Idolatrous Roman Catholicks, That together with the Lord JesusChrist, they shall *Worship* other *Mauzzim;* that is to say, other *Protectors.* Accordingly, All their Towns, ordinarily have singled out their *Protectors,* among the *Saints* of Heaven; such a *Saint* is entitled unto the *Patronage* of such a Town among them, and such a *Saint* for another: old BOSTON, by name, was but St. BOTOLPH'S TOWN. Whereas, Thou, O *Boston,* shalt have but one *Protector* in Heaven, and that is our Lord JESUS CHRIST. Oh! Rejoice in Him alone, & say, *That Lord is my Fortress, and my Deliverer!* There was a Song, once made for a *Town,* which in its Distresses had been *Helped* wondrously; & the First Clause in that Song, (you have it in Isa. 26.1) may be so rendered: *We have a strong Town; Salvation* [of JESUS the Lord, whose Name hath *Salvation* in it] *Will appoint Walls and Bulwarks.* Truly, what *Help* we have had, we will Sing, *'Tis our JESUS that hath appointed them.* The old Pagan Towns, were sometimes mighty solicitous, to conceal the Name of the particular God, that they counted their *Protector, Ne ab hostibus Evocatus, alio commigraret.* But, I shall be far from doing my Town any Damage, by publishing the Name of its *Protector;* No, Let all Mankind know, That the Name of our *Protector,* is JESUS CHRIST: For *Among the Gods, there is none like unto thee, O* LORD: *Nor is any help like unto thine: And there is no Rock like to our God.*

Yea, When we ascribe the Name of *Helper,* unto our Lord JESUS CHRIST, Let us also acknowledge, that the Name is not sufficiently Expressive, Emphatical and Signficant. *Lactantius* of old, blamed the Heathen, for giving the Highest of their Gods, no Higher a Title, than that of, *Jupiter*, or, *Juvans Pater*, i.e. *An Helping Father*, and he says, *Non intelligit Divina Benefiecis, qui se a Deo tantummodo Juvari putat:* The *Kindnesses* of God, are not understood, by that man, who makes no more than an *Helper* of Him. Such indeed is the penury of our Language, that we cannot coin a more *Expressive Name*. Nevertheless, when we say, The Lord JESUS CHRIST hath been our *Helper*, Let us Intend more than we Express; *Lord, Thou hast been All unto us.*

Secondly; Let the SACRIFICE of our Lord Jesus Christ, most Explicitly, have the *Glory of Purchasing* for us all our *Help*. What was it, that procured, an *Ebenezer*, for the People of God? We read in 2 Sam. 7.9, *Samuel took a Sucking Lamb, and offered it a Burnt Offering wholly unto the Lord; and Samuel Cried unto the Lord for Israel, and the Lord Heard him.* Shall I tell you? Our Lord Jesus Christ is that *Lamb of God*; and he has been a *Lamb Slain as a Sacrifice*; and He is a *Sacrifice* pleadable, not only for *persons*, but also for *peoples*, that belong unto Him. To Teach us this Evangelical and Comfortable *Mystery*, there was, *A Sacrifice for the whole Congregation*, prescribed in the *Mosaic* Paedagogy. 'Tis notorious that the Sins of this Town have been many Sins, and mighty Sins; The Cry thereof hath *gone up to Heaven*. If the Almighty God should from Heaven Rain down upon the Town, an *horrible Tempest* of Thunderbolts, as He did upon the *Cities which He overthrew in His Anger, and repented not,* it would be no more than our Unrepented Sins deserve. How comes it then to pass that we have had so much *Help* from Heaven after all? Truly, The *Sacrifice* of our Lord Jesus Christ, has been pleaded for *Boston*, and *Therefore* say, *Therefore* it is, that the Town is not made a *Sacrifice* to the Vengeance of God. God sent *Help* to the Town, that was the very *Heart* and *Life* of the Land, that He had a pity for: But why so? He said, in Isa. 37.35, *I will defend this Town, to Save it, for my Servant David's sake.* Has this Town been *Defended*? It has been for the sake of the *Beloved* JESUS; Therefore has the Daughter of *Boston* shaken *her Head* at you, O ye Calamities, that have been Impending over her *Head*. O *Helped*, and Happy Town! Thou hast had those Believers in the midst of thee, that have pleaded this with the Great God: *Ah! Lord, Thou hast been more Honoured by the Sufferings of our Lord Jesus Christ, than thou couldst be Honoured by overwhelming this Town with all the plagues of thy Just Indignation. If thou wilt Spare, and Feed, and Keep, and Help this poor Town, the Sufferings of our Lord Jesus Christ, shall be owned, as the prize of all our Help.* 'Tis *This* that hath procured us all our *Help*: 'tis *This* that must have all our *praise*.

Thirdly, Let the Lord be in a special manner *Glorified* for the Ministry of His Good Angels, in that Help that has been ministered unto us. A *Jacob* lying on a *Stone*, saw the *Angels* of God *Helping* him. We are setting up an *Ebenezer*; but when we Lay our Heads and our Thoughts upon the *Stone*, let us then see, *The Angels of God have Helped us*. When *Macedonia*, was to have some Help from God, an *Angel*, whom the Apostle in Acts 16.9, Saw Habited like a *Man of Macedonia*, was a mean of its being brought unto them. There is abundant cause to think, That every Town in which the Lord Jesus Christ is worshipped, hath an *Angel* to watch over it. The Primitive Christians were persuaded from the Scriptures of Truth to make no Doubt of This, *Quod per Civitates distributae sunt Angelorum praefecturae*. When the Capital Town of *Judea* was rescued from an Invasion, we read in 2 Kings 19.35, *The Angel of the Lord* WENT OUT, *and smote the Camp of the Assyrians.* It should seem, There was an *Angel*, which did Reside in, and Preside over the Town, who *went out* for that amazing Exploit. And is it not likely, That *the Angel of the Lord* WENT OUT, *for to smite the Fleet of the Assyrians*, with a Sickness, which the Last Summer hindered their Invading of this Town? *The Angel of* BOSTON was concerned for it! Why have not the *Destroyers* broke in upon us, to prey upon us with sore *Destruction?* 'Tis because we have had *A Wall of Fire* about us; that is to say, a guard of *Angels*; those *Flames of Fire* have been as a *Wall* unto us. It was an *Angel*, that *Helped* a *Daniel*, when the Lions would else have swallowed him up. It was an *Angel* that *Helped* a *Lot*, out of the Fires that were coming to Consume his Habitation. It was an *Angel* that *Helped* an *Elias* to Meat when he wanted it. They were *Angels* that *Helped* the whole People of God, in the Wilderness, to their *Daily Bread*; Their *Manna*, was Angels Food: and it is nothing that such *Angels* have done for this Town. Think you? Oh!. Think not so. Indeed, if we should go to Thank the *Angels* for doing these things, They would zealously say, *See thou do it not*! But if we Thank their Lord and ours, for his Employing Them to Do these things, it will exceedingly gratifie them. Wherefore, *Bless ye the Lord, ye his Angels; And Bless the Lord, O my Town, for those His Angels.*

iii] Let the *Help* which we have *Hitherto* had from our God, Encourage us to *Hope* in Him for MORE HELP hereafter, as the Matter may Require. The *Help* that God had given to His People, of old was Commemorated, as with *Monumental Pillars,* conveying down the Remembrance of it, unto their Children. And what for? We are told in Psal 78.7, *That they might set their Hope in God, and not Forget the Works of God.* I am not willing to say, How much this Town may be Threatened, even with an *Utter Extirpation*. But

this I will say, the *Motto* upon all our Ebenezers is, HOPE IN GOD!
HOPE IN GOD! The Use of the *Former Help* that we have had
from God, should be an Hope for *Future Help*, from him that is
A present Help in the Time of Trouble. As in the Three First
Verses of the *Eighty-Fifth* Psalm, Six times over there occurs, *Thou
hast, Thou hast,* all to usher in this, *Therefore thou* WILT *still do
so,* O Let our *Faith* proceed in that way of Arguing in 2 Cor. 1.10,
*The Lord hath Delivered, and He doth Deliver, and in Him we
Trust, that He will still Deliver.* We are to Day Writing, *Hitherto
the Lord hath Helped us*; Let us write under it, *And we hope the
Lord has more Help for us in the Time of Need!* It may be, some
are purposing Suddenly and Hastily to Leave the Town, through
their Fears of the Straits that may come upon it. But I would not
have you be too Sudden and Hasty in your purposes, as too many
have been unto their *after-Sorrow.* There was a time when People
were so Discouraged about a *Subsistance* in the principal Town of
the Jews, that they talked of plucking up Stakes, and flying away;
but the Minister of God came to them, [and so do I to you, this
Day!] saying, in Isa. 30.7, *I Cried concerning This, Their Strength
is to Sit Still! Boston* was no sooner come to some Consistence
Threescore years ago, but the People found themselves plunged
into a sad *Non-plus* what way to take for a *Subsistence.* God then
Immediately put them into a way and, *Hitherto the Lord has
Helped us!* The Town is at this Day full of *Widows* and *Orphans*,
and a multitude of them are very *Helpless* Creatures. I am Astonished, how they Live! In that Church whereof I am the Servant, I
have counted The *Widows* make about a *Sixth Part* of our Com-
municants, and no doubt, in the whole Town the proportion differs
not very much. Now, stand still, my Friends, and Behold, the
Help of God! Were any of these ever *Starved* yet? No: These
Widows are every one in some sort provided for. And let me tell
you, Ye Handmaids of the Lord, You shall be *Still* provided for!
The Lord, whose *Family* you belong unto, will conveniently and
wonderfully provide for you; if you say, and Oh! Say! of Him,
The Lord is my Helper; I will not Fear!

What shall I say? When *Moses* was ready to faint, in his
Prayers for his People, we read in Exod. 17.12, *They took a stone,
and put it under him.* Christians, there are some of you, who
abound in *Prayers*, that the *Help* of God may be granted unto the
Town; the Town is much upheld by those *Prayers* of yours. Now,
that you may not faint in your *Prayers*, I bring you a *Stone*: the
Stone, 'tis our *Ebenezer*; or, the Relation of the *Help* that *hitherto*
the Lord hath given us.

iv] Let all that bear PUBLIC OFFICE in the Town, Contribute all
the *Help* they can, that may Continue the *Help* of God unto us.

Austin, in his *Confessions*, gives thanks to God, That when he was a *Helpless Infant*, he had a *Nurse* to *Help* him, and one that was both Able & Willing to *Help* him. Infant-*Boston*, Thou hast those, whom the Bible calls *Nursing-Fathers*. Oh, Be not *forward* as thou art, in thy Treating of thy Nurses; but give Thanks to God for them. I forget my self; 'Tis with the *Fathers* themselves, that I am concerned.

When it was demanded of *Demosthenes*, what it was, that so long Preserved *Athens* in a flourishing *State*, he made this answer: *The Orators are men of Learning and Wisdom; the Magistrates do Justice, the Citizens love Quiet, and the Laws are kept among them all.* May Boston flourish in such happy Order!

And first, You may assure yourselves That the MINISTERS of the Lord Jesus Christ among you will be *Joyful* to approve themselves, as the Book of God has called them, *The Helpers of your Joy*. O our dear Flocks, we owe you our *All*; All our *Love*, all our *Strength*, all our *Time*; We, Watch for you, as those that must give an Account; and I am very much mistaken if we are not willing to *Die* for you, too, if called unto it. If our Lord Jesus Christ should say, to us, *My Servant, if you'll Die to Night, you shall have this Reward: The People that you Preach to, shall be all Converted unto me!* I think, We should with Triumphing Souls Reply, *Ah! Lord, Then I'll Die with all my Heart.* Sirs, we should go away *Rejoycing with Joy unspeakable and full of Glory.* I am satisfied, That the most Furious and Foul-mouthed Reviler, that God may give any of us, to be *Buffeted* withal, if he will but come to sober Thoughts, he will say, That there is not any *One Man* in the Town, but the *Ministers* wish that man as well as they do their own Souls, and would gladly Serve that man by Day or by Night, in any thing that it were possible to do for him. Wherefore, O our Beloved People, I beseech you, Leave off, Leave off, to Throw *Stones* at your *Ebenezers*. Instead of That, *Pray for us,* and *Strive together with us, in your Prayers to God for us.* Then with the *Help* of Christ, we'll promise you; We will set our selves to observe what *Special Truths* may be most needful to be Inculcated upon you, and we will Inculcate them. We will set our selves to observe the *Temptations* that beset you, the *Afflictions* that assault you, and the *Duties* that are incumbent on you; and we will accomodate our selves unto them. We will set our selves to observe what Souls among you, do call for our more particular *Addresses*, and we will Address them faithfully and even *Travail* in *Birth* for them. Nor will we give over *Praying,* and *Fasting,* and *Crying* to our GREAT LORD for you, until we Die. Whatever other *Helpers* the Town Enjoys, they shall have that convenience in Ezra 5.2, *With them were the Prophets of God, Helping them.* Well, then, Let the rest of our Worthy *Helpers,* Lend an *Helping* Hand, for the promoting of those things, wherein the

Weal of the Town is wrapped up! When the *Jews* thought that a *Defiling* thing was breaking in among them, in Acts 21.28, *They cried out, Men of Israel, Help!* Truly, there is cause to make that Cry, *Men of Boston, Help!* for Ignorance, and Prophaneness, and Bad Living, and the worst things in the World, are breaking in upon us.

And now, Will the JUSTICE of the Town, set themselves to consider, *How they may Help to Suppress all Growing Vices among us?*

Will the CONSTABLES of the Town set themselves to consider, *How they may Help to Prevent all evil orders among us?*

There are some who have the Eye of the *Town* so much upon them, that the very Name of, TOWNS-MEN, is that by which they are distinguished. Sirs, Will *You* also consider, *How to Help the Affairs of the Town, so as that all Things may go well among us?*

Moreover, may not SCHOOL-MASTERS, *do much to* instil Principles of *Religion* and *Civility,* as well as other points of good Education into the Children of the *Town?* Only Let the *Town* well Encourage its Well Deserving *School-Masters.*

There are some *Officers*; But concerning *All*, there are these Two Things to be Desired: First, It is to be Desired, That such *Officers,* as are *Chosen* among us, may be Chosen in the *Fear* of God. May none but *Pious,* and *Prudent* men, and such as *Love* the Town, be Chosen to Serve it. And, Secondly, It is to be Desired, That *Officers* of several sorts, would often come together for *Consultation.* Each of the sorts by themselves, may they often come together, to Consult, *What shall we do to Serve the Town, in those Interests which are committed unto our Charge?* Oh! What a Deplorable Thing, will it be for persons to be Entrusted with *Talents,* [your Opportunities to Serve the *Town* are so many *Talents!*] and they never seriously consider, *What Good shall I do with my Talents, in the place where God hath Stationed me?*

And, Will the REPRESENTATIVES of the Town be considered among the rest, as Entrusted with some singular Advantages for our *Help?* The *Lord give you understanding in all Things!*

v] God *Help* the Town, to manifest all that PIETY, which a Town so *Helped* of Him is obliged unto! When the People of God, had been carried, by His *Help* through their Difficulties, they set up *Stones,* to keep in mind how He had *Helped* them; And something was written on the stones: But what was written? See Josh. 8.32, *Joshua wrote upon the Stones a Copy of the Law.* Truly, upon those *Ebenezers,* which we set up, we should write the Law of our God, and Recognize the Obligations which the help of our God has laid upon us to keep it.

We are a very Unpardonable Town, if, after all the *Help*

which our God has given us, we do not ingenuously Enquire, *What shall we Render to the Lord, for all His Benefits?* Render! Oh! Let us our selves thus answer the Enquiry: *Lord, we will Render all possible, and Filial Obedience unto thee, because Hitherto thou hast Helped us: Only do thou also Help us, to Render that Obedience!* Mark what I say: If there be so much as one *Prayerless House* in such a Town as this, 'tis Inexcusable! How Inexcusable then, will be all *Flagitious Outrages?* There was a Town, 'twas the town of Sodom! that had been wonderfully Saved out of the Hands of their Enemies. But after the *Help* that God sent unto them, the Town went on to Sin against God, in very prodigious Instances. At last, a provoked God sent a *Fire* upon the Town, that made it an Eternal Desolation. Ah, *Boston*, Beware, Beware, lest the Sins of *Sodom* get Footing in thee! And what were the Sins of *Sodom?* We find in Ezel. 16.49, *Behold, This the Iniquity of Sodom; Pride, Fulness of Bread, and Abundance of Idleness was in her; Neither did she Strengthen the Hand of the Poor and the Needy,* There was much Oppression there. If you know of any *Scandalous Disorders* in the Town, do all you can, to Suppress them, and Redress them; and let not those that send their Sons hither from other parts of the world, for to be improved in *Virtue*, have cause to Complain, *That after they came to Boston, they lost, what little Virtue was before Budding in them; That in Boston they grew more Debauched & more Malignant than ever they were before!* It was noted concerning the famous town of *Port-Royal* in *Jamaica*, which you know, was the other Day Swallowed up, in a Stupendous *Earthquake*, that just before the *Earthquake* the People were Violently and Scandalously set upon going to *Fortune-Tellers* upon all Occasions: much Notice was taken of this *Impiety* generally prevailing among the People: but none of those Wretched *Fortune-Tellers* could Foresee or Forestal the direful *Catastrophe.* I have heard, That there are *Fortune-Tellers* in this Town, sometimes consulted by some of the Sinful Inhabitants. I wish the Town could be made too Hot for these *Dangerous Transgressors.* I am sure the preservation of the Town, from horrendous Earthquakes, is one thing that bespeaks our, *Ebenezers*; 'Tis from the Merciful Help of our God unto us. But, beware, I beseech you, of those *Provoking Evils*, that may Expose us to a Plague, Exceeding all that are in the Catalogue of the *Twenty-Eighth of Deuteronomy.* Let me go on, to say, What! Shall there be any *Bawdy-Houses* in such a Town as This! It may be, the Neighbours, that could Smoke them, and Rout them, if they would, are loth to Stir, for fear of being reputed *Ill Neighbours.* But, I say unto you, That you are *Ill Neighbours*, because you do it not. All the Neighbours are like to have their Children and Servants poisoned, and their Dwellings laid in Ashes, because you do it not. And, Oh! that the DRINKING-HOUSES in the Town might once come under a laudable *Regulation*. The Town has an *Enormous Number* of them; Will the *Haunters* of those *Houses*, hear the Counsils of Heaven? For *You* that are the *Town-Dwellers*, to be oft, or long in your *Visits* of the *Ordinary*, 'twill certainly Expose you to Mischiefs more than ordinary. I have seen certain Taverns, where the Pictures of horrible *Devourers* were hanged out for the *Signs* and, thought I, 'twere well if such *Signs* were not sometimes too *Significant*: Alas, men have their Estates *Devoured*, their Names *Devoured*, their Hours *Devoured*, and their very Souls *Devoured*, when they are so besotted that they are not in their Element, except they be Tipling at such Houses. When once a man is Bewitched, with the *Ordinary*, what usually becomes of him? He is a *gone man*; and when he comes to Die, he will cry out, as many have done, *Ale-houses are Hell-houses*! *Ale-houses are Hell-Houses*! But let the *Owners* of those *Houses* also now hear our Counsils. *Oh! Hearken to me, that God may Hearken to you another Day!* It is an *Honest*, and a *Lawful*, though it may not be a very *Desirable*, Employment, that you have undertaken: You may *Glorifie* the Lord Jesus Christ in your Employment if you will, and Benefit the Town considerably. There was a very Godly man, that was an *Inn keeper*, and a Great Minister of God, could say to that man, in 3 John 2, *Thy soul prospereth*. O Let it not be said of you, since you are fallen into this Employment, *Thy soul withereth!* It is thus, with too many; Especially, when they that get a *License* perhaps to Sell Drink out of Doors, do stretch their *License* to Sell within Doors. Those *Private Houses*, when once a Professor of the Gospel, comes to *Steal* a Living out of them, it commonly precipitates them, into an abundance of wretchedness and confusion. But, I pray God, assist you that keep *Ordinaries*, to keep the Commandments of God, in them. There was an *Inn* at *Bethlehem;* where the Lord JESUS CHRIST was to be met withal. Can *Boston* boast of many such? Alas, Too ordinarily it may be said, *There is no Room for Him in the Inn*! My Friends, Let me beg it of you. Banish *the unfruitful works of Darkness* from your *Houses,* and then the *Sun of Righteousness* will shine upon them. Don't countenance *Drunkenness, Revelling,* & *Mispending* of precious Time in your Houses: Let none have the *Snares of Death* Laid for them in your Houses. You'll say, *I shall Starve then*! I say, *Better Starve than Sin*: But you, shall not. It is the Word of the Most High, *Trust in the Lord, and do Good, and verily* thou shalt be Fed. And is not *Peace of Conscience*, with a *Little*, better than those *Riches*, that will shortly melt away, and then run Like Scalding Metal down the very Bowels of thy Soul?

What shall I say more? There is one Article of *Piety* more to Recommended unto us all; and it is an Article which all *Piety* does exceedingly Turn upon, That is, THE SANCTIFICATION OF THE

LORD'S DAY. Some very Judicious Persons, have observed, That as *they Sanctified the Lord's day, Remisly or Carefully*, just so, their Affairs usually prospered all the Ensuing Week. Sirs, You cannot more consult the Prosperity of the Town, in all its Affairs, than by Endeavouring that the *Lord's Day* may be Exemplarily *Sanctified*. When People about *Jerusalem*, took too much Liberty on the *Sabbath*, the Ruler of the Town *Contended* with them, and said, *Ye bring wrath upon Israel, by prophaning the Sabbath*. I fear, I fear, There are many among us, to whom it may be laid, *Ye bring wrath upon Boston, by prophaning the Sabbath*. And what *Wrath*? *Ah, Lord, prevent it!* But there is an awful Sentence in Jer. 17.27, *If ye will not Hearken unto me, me, to Sanctify the Sabbath Day, then will I kindle a Fire* on the town, *and it shall Devour, and shall not be Quenched*.

Finally, Let the *Piety* of the town manifest it self in a due Regard unto the INSTITUTIONS of Him whose *Help* has *Hitherto* been a *Shield* unto us. Let the *Ark* be in the Town, and God will Bless the Town! I believe, it may be found, That in the *Mortal Scourges* of Heaven, which this Town has felt, there has been a *Discernable Distinction*, of those that have come up to Attend all the *Ordinances* of the Lord Jesus Christ, in the Communion of His *Churches*. Though these have had, as 'tis fit they should, a Share, in the Common Deaths, yet the *Destroying Angel*, has not had so great a proportion of thee in his Commission, as he has had of others. Whether *This* be so, or no, To Uphold, and Support and Attend the *Ordinances* of the Lord Jesus Christ in *Reforming Churches*, This will Entitle the Town to the *Help* of Heaven; for, *Upon the Glory there shall be a defence!* There were the Victorious Forces of *Alexander*, that in going backward and forward, passed by *Jerusalem*, without Hurting it. Why so? Said the Lord in Zech. 9.8, *I will Encamp about my House, because of the Army*. If our God have an *House* here, He'll Encamp about it. *Nazianzen*, a famous Minister of the Gospel, taking his Farewel of *Constantinople*, an old man, that had sat under his Ministry, cried out, *Oh! my Father, don't you dare to go away: You'll carry the whole Trinity with you!* How much more may it be cried out, *If we loose or sleight the Ordinances of the Lord Jesus Christ, we Foregoe the Help of all the Trinity with them!*

vi] Extraordinary EQUITY & CHARITY, as well as *Piety*, well becomes a Town that hath been by the *Help* of God so extraordinarily signalized. A Town marvellously *Helped* by God, has This Foretold concerning it, in Isa. 1.26, *Afterward thou shalt be called, The City of Righteousness, The Faithful City*. May the *Ebenezers* of this Town render it, *A Town of Equity*, and *A Town of Charity*! Oh! There should be none but fair dealings in a Town wherewith

Heaven has dealt so Favourably. Let us *Deal Fairly* in *Bargains*; *Deal Fairly* in *Taxes; Deal Fairly* in paying *Respects* to such as have been *Benefactors* unto the Town. 'Tis but *Equity*, that they, who have been *Old Standers* in the Town, and both with *Person* and *Estate* Served the Town unto the utmost for many years together, should on all Proper Occasions be considered. For *Charity,* I may indeed speak it without Flattery, this Town has not many Equals on the Face of the Earth. Our Lord Jesus Christ from Heaven, wrote, unto the good people of a Town in the lesser Asia, [Rev. 2.19,] *I know thy works, and Charity.* From that Blessed Lord, I may venture to bring that Message unto the Good people of this Town; *The Glorious Lord of Heaven, knows thy works, O Boston, and all thy Charity.* This is a *poor* Town, and yet it may be said of the *Bostonians*, as it was of the *Macedonians, Their Deep poverty hath abounded unto the riches of their Liberality.* O ye Bountiful people of God, all your *Daily Bounties* to the Needy, All your *Subscriptions* to Send the *Bread of Life* abroad unto places that are perishing in Wickedness, all your *Collections* in your Assemblies as often as they are called for; *All the Alms are come up for a Memorial before God!* The Lord Jesus Christ in Heaven hath Behold your *Helpfulness*, and *Readiness to every good Work*; and He hath Requited it, with His *Helpful Ebenezers*. It was said in Isa. 32.8, *The Liberal Deviseth Liberal Things, and by Liberal Things he shall stand.* There are some in this Town that are always *Devising Liberal Things*, and our Lord Jesus Christ, Lets the Town *Stand* for the sake of those! Instead of *Exhorting* you, to *Augment* your *Charity*, I will rather utter an *Exhortation*, or at Least a *Supplication*, that you may not *Abuse* your *Charity* by misapplying of it. I remember, I have Read, that an Inhabitant of the City *Pisa*, being asked, Why their Town so went, as it then did, unto Decay, he fetched a deep sigh, and said, *Our young men are too prodigal, our old men are too Affectionate, and we have no punishment for those that spend their years in Idleness.* Ah! The last stroak of that complaint I must here Sigh it over again. *Idleness*, alas! *Idleness* increases in the Town exceedingly; *Idleness*, of which there never came any *Goodness*; *Idleness*, which is a *Reproach to any people. We* work hard, all Summer, and the *Drones* count themselves wronged if they have it not in the Winter divided among them. The *Poor* that can't *Work*, are Objects for your Liberality. But the *Poor* that can *Work* and *won't*, the best *Liberality* to them is to *make* them. I beseech you, Sirs, Find out a method quickly, That the *Idle Persons* in the Town may Earn their *Bread*; it were the best piece of *Charity* that could be shown unto them, and *Equity*, unto us all. Our *Beggars*, do shamefully grow upon us, and such *Beggars* too, as our Lord Jesus Christ Himself hath Expressly forbidden us to countenance. I have Read a printed Sermon, which was Preached before *Both Houses of Parliament, the Lord Mayor and Aldermen of London, and the Assembly of Divines;* the Greatest Audience then in the World: And in that Sermon, the Preacher had this passage: *I have Lived in a Country, where, in seven years, I never saw a Beggar, nor heard an Oath, nor looked upon a Drunkard.* Shall I tell you where that *Utopia* was? 'Twas NEW ENGLAND! But they that go from hence, must now tell another story.

vii] May the CHANGES, and especially the JUDGMENTS, that have come upon the Town, direct us, what *Help* to petition from the *God of our Salvations.* The *Israelites* had formerly seen *dismal Things,* where they now set up their *Ebenezer: The Philistines* had no less than Twice beaten them there, and there taken from them the *Ark* of God. Now we are setting up our *Ebenezer,* Let us a little call to mind some *Dismal Things* that we have seen; the *Ebenezer* will go up the better for it.

We read in I Sam. 6.18, concerning *The Great Stone of Abel.* Some say, that *Adam* Erected that Stone, as a *Grave stone* for his *Abel,* and wrote that epitaph upon it, *Here was poured out the Blood of the Righteous* ABEL. I know nothing of *This;* The Names, I know, differ in the Original; But as we may Erect many a *Stone* for an *Ebenezer,* so, we may Erect many a *Great Stone of* ABEL, that is to say, We may write MOURNING and SORROW, upon the Condition of the Town in various Examples. Now, from the *Stones* of *Abel,* we will a little gather what we should wish to write upon the *Stones* of our *Ebenezer.*

What Changes have we seen, in point of RELIGION! It was Noted by *Luther, He could never see Good order in the Church, last more than Fifteen years together in the Purity of it.* Blessed be God, *Religion* hath here flourished in the *Purity* of it for more than *Fifteen years together.* But, certainly, the *Power of Godliness* is now grievously decayed among us. As the Prophet of old Exclaimed, in Joel 1.2, *Hear this, ye old men, and give Ear, ye Inhabitants; Has this been in your Days?* Thus may I say, *Hear this, ye old men, that are the Inhabitants of the Town:* Can't you Remember, that *in your Days,* a Prayerful, a Watchful, a Fruitful Christian, and a well Governed family, was a more common sight, than it is now in *our Days?* Can't you Remember, that *in your Days,* those Abominable Things did not *Show their Heads,* that are now *Bare-faced* among us? Here then is a Petition to be made unto our God: *Lord, help us to Remember whence we are Fallen, and to Repent, and to Do the First Works!*

Again; What *Changes* have we seen, in point of MORTALITY? by Mortality, almost all the *Old Race* of our *First Planters* here, are carryed off; the *Old Stock,* is in a manner Expired. We see the

Fulfilment of that word in Eccl. 1.4, *One Generation passeth away, and another Generation cometh.* It would be no unprofitable Thing for you, to pass over the several Streets, & call to mind, *Who lived here so many years ago*? Why? In *that place* lived such an one. But, *Where are they Now*? Oh! They are *Gone*; They are *Gone* into that Eternal World, whither *We* must quickly follow them. Here is another *Petition* to be made unto God: *Lord, Help us to Number our Days, and apply our Hearts unto Wisdom, that when the places that now know us, do know us no more, we may begone into the City of God!*

Furthermore; What *Changes* have we seen in point of POS-SESSIONS? If some that are now *Rich,* were once *Low* in the World, 'tis possible, more that were once *Rich* are now brought very *Low.* Ah! *Boston.* Thou hast seen the *Vanity* of all *Worldly Possessions.* One fatal Morning, which laid Fourscore of thy *Dwelling Houses*, and Seventy of thy *Ware houses*, in a Ruinous Heap, not Nineteen years ago, gave thee to Read it in Fiery Characters. And an huge *Fleet* of thy Vessels, which they would make if they were all together, that have miscarried in the late War, has given thee to Read more of it. Here is one Petition more, to be made unto our God; *Lord, Help us to Ensure a Better and a lasting Substance in Heaven, and the Good part that cannot be taken away.*

In fine; Now dreadfully have the *Young People of Boston,* perished under the Judgments of God! A Renowned Writer, among the Pagans, could make this Repay their *First-fruits* unto God; (which the *Light of Nature* taught the Pagans to do!) and says he, they were, by a Sudden Desolation so Strangely Destroyed, that there were no Remainders either of the *Persons*, or of the *Houses*, to be seen any more. Ah, *My Young Folks* there are few *First-fruits* paid unto the Lord Jesus Christ among you. From hence it comes to pass, that the Consuming Wrath of God, is every day upon you. *New England* has been like a *Tottering House*, the very *Foundations* of it have been Shaking; But the House thus overset-ting by the *Whirlwinds* of the Wrath of God, hath been like *Job's* House: *It falls upon the Young men, and they are Dead!* The Disasters on our *Young Folks* have been so multiplied, that there are few Parents among us, but what will go with *Wounded Hearts*, down unto their Graves: Their daily moans are, *Ah, My Son cut off in his Youth! My Son, my Son!* Behold then the Help that we are to ask of our God; and why do we, with no more Days of *Prayer* with *Fasting*, ask it? *Lord, Help the Young People of Boston, to Remember thee in the Days of their Youth, and Sanctify unto the Survivers, the Terrible Things that have come upon so many of that Generation.*

And now as *Joshua*, having Reasoned with his people, a little before he Died, in Josh. 24.26, 27, *Took a Great* STONE, *and set it up, and said unto all the people, Behold, this Stone shall be a witness unto you, Lest ye Deny your God.* Thus we have been this Day setting up a STONE, even an *Ebenezer,* among you; & I conclude, Earnestly testifying unto you, *Behold this Stone, shall be a witness unto you, that the Lord* JESUS CHRIST, *has been a Good Lord unto you, and if you Seek Him, He will be still found of you; but if you Forsake Him, He will cast you off for ever.*

The Piety & Duty of Rulers
To Comfort and Encourage the Ministry of Christ

Benjamin Colman

Benjamin Colman was born in Boston on October 19, 1673. He attended school under Ezekiel Cheever. In 1688, he entered Harvard and was graduated with high honors in 1692. He preached in Medford for six months, then returned to Harvard, receiving his A.M. degree in 1695. In that same year he sailed for England, was captured and made prisoner by the French, and eventually made his way to the British Isles. Here he associated himself with prominent nonconformist clergymen, preaching regularly at Bath.

Urgent invitations from William Brattle, John Leverett, and others brought Colman back to the colonies where he became the first pastor of the newly organized Brattle Street Church, whose leaders advocated doing away with the public recitation of religious experiences and substituting instead the reading of the Bible and repeating of the Lord's Prayer. As the years passed, however, Colman's theology took on a stronger conservative cast.

Colman was active in civil and religious affairs and was one of the most prominent clergymen of the time. He was a fellow of Harvard from 1717 to 1728, and was an Overseer until his death. Offered the presidency of Harvard in 1724, he refused it. He aided Yale College, took considerable interest in the Housatonic Indians, and believed strongly in the evangelical movement known as the Great Awakening. He died on August 29, 1747.

The sermon, "The Piety and Duty of Rulers to Comfort and Encourage the Ministry of Christ" was delivered at Boston on Lecture Day before the Governor and the General Court, June 10, 1708. The text is from the printed version of the sermon. Boston: Printed by B. Green, sold by Benj. Eliot, 1708.

II. CHRON. XXX. 22. *And Hezekiah spake Comfortably unto all the Levites, that taught the Good Knowledge of the* LORD.

IN the *Context* we have a Record of the glorious Beginning of King *Hezekiahs* Reign. The wicked *Abaz,* this pious *Prince* his *Father,* had *transgressed sore against the Lord,* forsaken His *Altars,* exhausted the Sacred Treasures of his *House, cut in pieces* the Holy *Vessels,* and at last *shut up the Doors* of it; making himself *Altars in every Corner of Jerusalem, and High Places in every City of Judah, to burn Incense unto other gods.* This was the forlorn State of the *Church* upon *Hezekiahs* Accession to the Throne, who immediately, even *in the first year of his Reign, in the*

*first Month, op'ned the doors of the House of the Lord and re-
paired them;* Summoning the *Priests* and the *Levites* to *Sanctify*
themselves and the *House;* to humble themselves for the Sins of
their *Fathers* (a), to renew their *Covenant with the Lord* (b), and
to offer a *Sin offering for the Kingdom* (c), to *make Reconciliation*
with the Blood upon the Altar, and *Attonement for all Israel* (d).
When this was done he proceeded to proclaim a (e) Solemn *Passover,* which was joyfully and religiously Solemniz'd: *With great
Gladness;* says the *verse* before the *Text, and the Levites and the
Priests praised the* LORD *day by day, singing with loud Instruments
unto the* LORD. It was at the Celebration of this *Passover,* the *Joy*
whereof had been never equal'd since the days of *Solomon* (f),
that the *Good King* among other Expressions of his Devotion gave
that which the *Text* records to his Immortal Honour; *And Hezekiah spake Comfortably unto all the Levites, that taught the good
Knowledge of the* LORD.

    We may here remark,

1] The Character of the *Persons* concerned, *Hezekiah* and the
   Levites: On both sides *Persons of Distinction,* the *One* in Civil,
   the *Other* in Ecclesiastical Office. *Hezekiah* was no less than
   the *King of Judah,* the Supream Civil Ruler: the *Levites* were
   Ministers of Religion, after the *Priests* the Sons of *Aaron*; the
   Tribe whom God had separated and consecrated to Himself
   out of all *Israel to do the Service of the Tabernacle.* So that the
   Civil & Sacred *Orders* are here together, the *Prince* and the
   Prophet, the Ruler in the *State,* and the Holy Teachers in
   the *Church.*

2] Let us attend unto the *thing related* as passing between them,
   which is the *Kings* speaking Comfortably unto the *Levites.* The
   like we read in the 35. *Chap.* 2.*v.* of *Josiah, that he set the
   Priests in their charges, and Encourag'd them to the service of
   the House of the Lord.* His Dignity made this Condescention
   in the fight of men, yet was it but strict Piety and Duty to God.
   He might have requir'd 'em only with the stern Majesty of a
   King, but as became his Devotion he mildly & kindly bespoke
   'em, with a sweet and gracious Affability. His Countenance, his
   Behaviour, and all his Words did abundantly express his Royal
   Favour & Grace toward 'em, for their Incouragement [sic] in
   their Holy Ministrations. Nor are we to interpret these Comfortable Expressions of *Good Words* only, *Be ye warmed, be
   ye filled;* without the substantial fruits of a *Princes* Favour &
   Care. Much less may we think them like the *Empty Respects,*
   flatteries & promises of *Modern Courtiers*; but all was Cordial,
   unfeigned & from the Heart: As we may read in the 31. *Chap.*

21.*v.* that *in every work, which he began in the Service of the House of God, and in the Law, and in the Commandments to seek his God, he did it with all his heart, and prospered.*

Wherefore,

3] The *real Reason of this Princely Grace* of the *King* is Subjoyned, and that is, *the Levites teaching the good Knowledge of the Lord.* The *Reason* is taken partly from their *Office,* more especially from their *Fidelity* therein: And so it answers the *Apostolick Precept, Esteeming them very highly in Love for their Works sake.* It was one part of the *Levites* Office to *instruct* the People in the Knowledge and Fear of God: their work was to *teach:* which reproves and condemns the *Idle Pastor,* who *Labours* not *in the Word and Doctrine,* to feed their Flocks with *Saving* Knowledge. And *King Hezekiahs* regard to the *Teaching Levite* may well call to Mind the like *Royal Examples,* which have blazon'd the *British Throne,* in our late *Sovereign Princes,* who have requir'd their *Highest Prelates* to be frequent in Preaching the *Word* Themselves; promoting at the same time such unto their Richest and Noblest *Sees,* as were desirous of teaching the People the Knowledge of God. In the day when *Popery abdicated the Throne, Princes* like holy *Hezekiah* ascended it, and they *spake Comfortably,* and to this day continue the same Gracious Expressions to all the *Levites* that teach the Good Knowledge of the Lord.

The Good Knowledge: Knowledge is Good: *Prov.* 19.2. *That the Soul be without Knowledge is not Good:* But of all Knowledge none is like that which we have of the *Blessed* GOD from his *Word:* Of *this* we may say, as our *Saviour* said of *God, Why call* we *any* other *Good? there is none Good save that One, which is* of GOD. They that teach this good Knowledge faithfully, are to be held among Men eminently Good, *Worthy of double Honour,* meriting to be spoken *Comfortably* unto by their *Princes & Rulers:* Each of them singly, and all of them together, do merit this treatment and a singular Regard: And accordingly, tho' the *Text denies not* but that the *King* might *frown* upon the *Idle and Vicious Levite,* if there were any One so; yet is it *expresd* on the other hand, that he spake comfortably to *all* those *Levites,* that did *faithfully* teach the Good Knowledge of the Lord.

The DOCTRINE I wou'd offer from the *Words* is this.

That it is a very Noble & Pious Disposition in Civil Rulers, and their Incumbent Duty, to Comfort and Encourage the faithful Ministers of CHRIST *in their Holy Work.*

Before I add a Word more, I have a double *Presumption* to *Apologize* for; that I shou'd presume to *Preach* to, or to *plead* for, my *Superiors* of *both Orders.* I am very sensible that a *Concio ad*

Magistratum calls for Learning, Gravity & Authority much beyond my Years, and that the *Noble Subject* (*Pro Clero*) does equally require the same. Yet I hope it will not be unacceptable at this time to Either *Order*, if I essay with all possible Deference and Humility, to assert the *Honours* which it has pleased God to entitle his *Ministry* unto, & which it will be the Care and *Pleasure* of Pious *Rulers* always to pay unto them.

Wherefore I beg the leave of this *Honourable Audience* to persue a little these two *Enquiries*.

1] *How* Civil Rulers are to endeavour the Comfort and Encouragement of the Gospel Ministry?

2] *Why* they shou'd do it, or what are their Obligations hereunto. The *Enquiries* are both *Copious*, and being to get *hastily* thro' them I must be brief and *general*.

¶i. *How, or which way, are Civil Rulers to endeavour the Comfort of the Ministry?* or, What is *the Comfort* which the *Ministry* craves or challenges of them by the Laws of the Gospel? What is it that will comfort the faithful *Dispensers* of the Word, and what are the *Regards* which for this end the *Civil Ruler* owes unto the *Ecclesiastical* Order?

To apprehend this aright, we must consider our *Rulers* in their *Legislative* power or Trust, and in their *Executive*, and finally in a *Personal* and more *Private* Character, as *Christians* of a *Superior Degree* only.

¶i. *In their Legislative power and trust,* it belongs to the Civil Ruler to speak comfortably to the Ministry, *by Enacting Good* LAWS *for the Honour and Establishment of Religion within their Government*. This lies near the heart of every good man; and one of the greatest Comforts he can have that wishes well to the Religion of a Place, aiming at the Glory of God and the Salvation of Souls, is to see a *Bulwark of good Laws* for the defence & propagation of the Truths and Laws of God. These Laws must needs respect, 1. The Publick *Worship* of God, both Natural and Instituted. 2. The Peace, Order, *Discipline* and Government of the Church. 3. The Honourable *Maintenance* of the Ministry. And 4. A Peoples *Morals*.

1] The Comfort of the Ministry depends very much on good and right *Laws respecting the Publick Worship of God, and that both Natural & Instituted:* that the *Holy Ordinances* of God be duly administered and attended according to His Appointment in His Word. Indeed *Magistrates* may not *frame* and invent at their pleasure *Modes* and Exercises of Divine Worship for their People: GOD by whom They rule has given Them & Us a *Law* how He will be Worship'd: to *alter* this or to *add* unto it were to offer *Strange*

Fire for Hallowed Incense, and with the face of Homage manifestly to kick at his Soverain Authority, despising his most perfect Word. Nor may the Ruler *invade the Priests Office to Officiate in their Holy Ministrations,* unto which they are *Ordain'd.* It was unto *Uzziahs* destruction that his *heart was lifted up to transgress against the Lord his God,* when he went into the Temple of the Lord *to burn Incense upon the Altar of Incense*: 2 Chron. XXVI. 16,—21. Nor was it Disloyalty or Rebellion in *Azariah the Priest* and his valiant *Brethren* when they *withstood* him, and said unto him, *It pertaineth not unto thee Ussiah to burn Incense unto the Lord, but to the Priests the Sons of Aaron, that are consecrated to burn Incense: Go out of the Sanctuary, for thou hast trespassed, neither shall it be for thine Honour from the Lord God:* And when he despis'd the faithful admonition, being *Inrag'd* at it, *The Lord smote him beside the Altar, with the Censer in his hand; the Leprosie rose up in his forehead,* and he *hasted* to leave the Sacred place he had invaded, *being a Leper to the day of his death,* and so cut off from the House of the Lord, whither he had gone so presumptuously. Now tho' this *Instance* alone be eno' to warn the *Highest Persons* unto all possible caution, not to trespass upon the *Inclosures of Gods Ministry,* consecrated to *Divine Service;* Nevertheless we must by no means think that the *Magistrate* has nothing to do, or to concern himself *ex Officio,* about the *Institutions of God.* The *Civil Powers* may Enact the very Laws of God about his own Worship under temporal *Penalties,* preserving an *Indulgence* unto tender Consciences: They may take Laws out of the Word of God and make 'em their *Own,* Commanding People to *regard* the holy *Ordinances* of God, to *get* & *uphold* his *Worship* among them, to *Sanctifie the Sabbath,* to *reverence* Gods *Sanctuary,* to *build* themselves *decent places* for the Publick Worship, and *frequent* them in the stated seasons thereof with Solemnity.

It belongs also to the Rulers Province, to provide that *Ministers do their Duty* in the Publick Administrations that pertain unto their Office; that neither by *gross Neglects,* Unreasonable *Absence* from their *Charge, Nonresidence,* open *Idleness,* or any Scandalous course of *Vice,* they *do not defeat* the glorious Design of their Ministry: in all which *Cases* the Civil Cognizance is merited, and needed to rebuke and remedy the Evil; and Rulers ought to provide accordingly in subordination to the Laws of *Christ,* provided in that case already. So that if the *Sons of Eli* will make themselves *Vile,* to cause men to *abhor* the Offering of the Lord, it is duty of the *Judge in Israel,* tho' he be their *Father,* to provide them not only a *light* Rebuke, but a severe Censure, Degradation and Punishment.

In all such Cases both Ministers and People *owe Obedience and Submission* to the Civil Ruler, as in our *Context* the *Priests* and the *Levites* obeyed the Summons of the *King,* and did the thing which he requir'd in the cause of God and agreeable to his Will: XXIX. *Chap.* 15.*v. And they gathered their Brethren, and Sanctify'd themselves, and came according to the Commandment of the King, by the Word of the Lord.* Being that the Kings Commandment was according to and grounded on the Law of God, they conscientiously obey'd it, in deference both to God and the King.

Nor are the Holy Sons of *Levi* and *Aaron* duly *comforted* in the work of the Lord, in their Serving at the Tabernacle and Temple, unless the Civil Power do thus engage on their side. For as the World goes, 'tis necessary for the Powers on Earth to enforce that under present *bodily Pains* & temporal Penalties, which the Great GOD has more awfully commanded on pain of *Eternal Damnation:* that bold Sinners who have no regard to their *Souls* may be restrain'd however by what they have for their *Bodies,* their *Name, Estates* and outward Interests; and that men who will not *Fear God* so as to be religious in secret and in heart, may however for *Fear of Man* at Least not be Audacious and Insolent, blaspheme the Name of God, nor spit at his Altars; which many profane Wretches wou'd do, if the Civil Sword did not defend and do Honour to the Worship of God.

2] The Comfort of the Ministry depends very much on Good and Right Laws with respect to *the Peace & Order, Discipline and Government of the Churches.* It is true, that the *Magistracy* are not to assume to themselves the Administration of *Church Censures,* but to preserve inviolate unto the *Ministry* the Power of *Judgment,* which *Christ* has lodg'd in them: Yet is it not to be tho't the Magistrate must sit by *Unconcerned,* and quietly see things run to *Confusion,* and the wounds of Churches to *Gangreen* and grow Incurable: Or if the State of the Church be visibly *Consumptive,* and it be sensibly pining and languishing away, the *Pastors* not eno' laying it to heart, and the *People* thro' Inadvertence willing to have it so; Is it not *Laudable* & a Duty for *Rulers* in such a case to take Care? to issue out their *Authoritative Orders,* to stir up Ministers and People to their Respective Duties? for the *Revival* of dying *Church Order,* and the Spirit of true *Devotion,* with practical Godliness, which depend so much thereupon.

As therefore it is the worthy Care of Rulers to *Admonish the Churches* of any gross defects and negligences, hazards and dangers, maladies and distempers, which they discern upon us at any time in Spiritual Respects; So also their Wisdom and Piety wou'd be greatly display'd at this day, and they wou'd do much to comfort the faithful Ministers of Christ thro' the Land, if they cou'd any way provide to heal the long *Unsettlement of bereaved Churches,* together with the criminal shameful *Quarrels* that occasion it; to give *Authority also to Ecclesiastical Councils* in their Determinations; and to make People know *that there must and shall be some End* to their Strifes & Discords, the Parents of every *Confusion & Evil Work,* the *bane* of all Religion.

It belongs also to the Civil Powers *to call Synods* upon Occasion for these Ends, and then to give their *Sanction* to their just and approved *Resolutions.* Not are the hands of *Aaron* strong, but when *Moses,* his Brother and his Lord, stands by and assists him.

3] The Comfort of the Ministry depends very much on Good and sufficient Laws *for the Honourable Support and Maintenance thereof,* and that in *a Wise and Right Manner.* So *Hezekiah* comforted the *Levites* in the *Text,* as we read in the XXXI. *Chap.* 4.*v. Moreover, he commanded the People that dwelt at Jerusalem, to give the portion of the Priests and the Levites, that they might be Encouraged in the Work of the Lord. The Wise King* knew that they cou'd not chearfully, diligently, wholly devote themselves to the *Study* of the Law, the Instruction of the People, and the Ministrations of the Sanctuary, without that Honourable *Subsistence,* which God had provided for them.

I need not say how *Noble the Provision* was that God made for the *Tribe of Levi,* nor how plain the *Gospel Institution* is, *That they that Preach the Gospel shou'd live of the Gospel.* So hath the *Lord Ordained,* even as we know that under the *Law,* They who did Minister about Holy things, *lived of the things of the Temple,* and they that waited at the Altar *were Partakers with the Altar.* I Cor. IX.13, 14. Which Institution has its foundation in strict Equity & Righteousness *v.* 7. *For who goeth a Warfare at his own Charges? who planteth a Vineyard and eateth not of the Fruit thereof? or who feedeth a Flock and eateth not of the Milk of the Flock?* Nay, the Advantage of the *Exchange* is so much on the side of the *People,* that after all they do by no means pay the Labours of their Faithful *Pastors,* nor recompence for the Profits received by those Labours if it be not their own fault: *v.*II. *If we have sown unto you spiritual things, is it a great thing if we shall reap your carnal things?* No truly, 'tis a small matter for People to subsist them in a few outward things, whom God has separated wholly from worldly things, to Serve them in their Spiritual and Soul concerns.

Now I need not labour much to prove to You, that *there can be no great Comfort* in the Ministerial Work without a decent outward Subsistence: Unless the *Angels of the Churches* were already ὡς αγγελοι *as the Angels of God* above, as the Saints will be in the *Resurrection* State; when as they shall no more *Marry,* so neither shall they need *Food* or *Raiment* for the Body. But while this

Treasure (the Gospel Ministration) is in *Earthen Vessels* and Spirits in Flesh, of as many necessities and bodily wants as their Nei'bours, are imploy'd in these holy Services for your Souls, there must be a laudable Provision for their Bodies and Families, or they must be left desolate and *Comfortless*. There can be no Comfort to be sure in *Pinching* and Starving Circumstances, in *Rags* and Nakedness, in the *Cryes* of hungry Children, or in the prospect of meaness and want for their Families after them. If it was Infamous in *Jeroboam* to make Priests of the *Lowest of the People,* 'twill be no less in us to degrade the *Sacred Order* to the *lowest,* by one *Method* or another, whether by Maintaining the Ministry so *Meanly* that none but the *Lowest* will come into it; or if they do, that according to humane prospect they shall be sure to have their Families among the *least in Israel.* [Which were as if all the *Sons of Aaron* were for ever to inherit the Curse of *Eli's House, crouching for a piece of Silver and a Morsel of Bread, and saying, Put me, I pray thee, into one of the Priests Offices, that I may eat a piece of bread.*]

Had I time I should here have added, *that* the Ministry alone is a *sufficient Care and Labour for the whole Life: that* our whole Time & Strength is too little for it to discharge it faithfully: *that* we need no *Avocations* or hindrances from the wants of Families, or from Worldly Secular Businesses: *That* the Office is *Generous* & Noble, as well as the Work Great and Heavy: *that the Minds* imploy'd in this Sublime and Holy Service shou'd be suppos'd *Superior,* and improved by a Learned Education: *that* their *Rank* and Place among men has always been next to the Civil Magistrate; and this not only by the *Custom* of all Nations, but by the *Grant* of God Himself, and therefore it is not of meer *Courtesy,* but of *Right* and Natural Decency: *that* where there has been any *Hierarchy,* whether of Gods Ordination among the *Jews,* or of Humane Establishment (we say) among *Christian Nations,* not to name the *Orders* of old in the Idolatrous *Heathen* World; I say, where-ever any *Hierarchy* has been set up in the World, distinguishing the *Clergy* into divers Orders & *Degrees,* the Superiour Order has been ever grac'd in the first *Rank of Nobles:* I might add. *That* the Ministerial Work is not to be levell'd wich [sic] *Mechanic* Labours, *Merchandize,* nor other more *Liberal* Imployments neither; the Practice of *Physick,* or the teaching of *Phylosophy,* not excepted: [To acknowledge which is but a meet Respect to the *Great God,* in whose immediate Service we are; as also 'tis but a decent respect to our own *Souls,* for the Improvment of which in Spiritual Knowledge, their Perfection, Conversion & Salvation, we are imployed; And surely, *to teach the Good Knowledge of the Lord* is of more Excellency & Use, than to be *Professors* of any *Secular Science,*

ignorant of which we may live and dy and yet be Saved.] Now if
the Office be so Superior, the Maintenance shou'd be also Honourable, or it is very Indecent and Unsightly.

I must needs add one thing more here: That the want of a
Comfortable Support for the Ministers of the Gospel is *a great
Wrong to Souls*. It is so very often to the Souls of your *Ministers:*
they can't be so faithful as they desire to be. I have heard some of our
Reverend Brethren complain of this with great Affliction, "That
they have not Time to *Study* as they wou'd, That they can't make
the *Pastoral Visits* which they gladly wou'd to the Families under
their Watch; because their own Families being Numerous, and their
Income Small, they must spend a great part of the Week in Secular
Affairs." Thus they are bereaved of the Comfort of the Sense of
having done their Duty to your Immortal Souls. *Again,* It is a
great Injury to the Souls of *People*, the precious Souls of your
Families & *Children*. These suffer in Spiritual respects, by Ministers
suffering in temporal things: They are not so *fed* and *watch'd* over
as else they might be: *And so in pinching their faithful Pastors,
People do eventually Starve the Souls of their Households.*

To Conclude, I know not how the *Publick can be Innocent,* if
Lawgivers do not make a just Provision for the Maintenance of the
Ministry: In a great part they must expect to answer to God for
the Neglect there is in the *Land* as to the Care of Souls; and if
Religion and Learning be lost, and our Souls after them, it will
be in a great measure owing to this, *That we have not hearts big
eno' to part with a few Carnal things to Save all.*

4] *And Lastly,* The Comfort of Gods Faithful Ministers does
very much depend on the Provision of a sufficient Body of Laws,
with respect unto Peoples Morals. This is a very wide and extensive *Head;* Namely, the Sobriety & Righteousness, Purity and
Blamelessness of People in Word and Action, in their whole Conduct and Behaviour, in every Relation and Circumstance of Life.
The Religion of a People appears in Practice, in Obedience to the
Moral Law. If this is religiously observed, if men lead Sober,
Righteous and Godly Lives, then have Ministers the Consolation
of their Labours, then have they not *spent their Strength for nought
and in vain;* but they behold the fruits of the Grace of God in their
Hearers hearts, *shown out of a Good Conversation:* Then is the
Gospel of *God our Saviour* visibly Adorned, and your *Apostolick
Pastors* have *no greater Joy.*

But if the Laws of a *Land* do not provide against all *Scandalous Immoralities,* Rulers do not speak *Comfortably* to any that
have the least Respect for Religion: they are grieved, scandaliz'd,
offended at bold and lawless Vice defying our Holy Religion: their

righteous Souls are *vexed* at the filthy unrestrained Conversation of the Wicked. 'Tis true, God will set a *Mark* on them that weep in Secret for the open Sins of others but by Man they are not *Comforted*. How cou'd our *Faces* and Hearts be otherwise than *Sad,* if there were not Good Laws for the Suppressing and Punishing all kinds of open *Profaness,* or secret *Frauds* and dishonesty, *Impurities* and Lusts. Our *Comfort* greatly depends on the *Laws* in force, and from time to time *Enacted,* against Blasphemy, Cursing and Swearing, Sabbath-breaking, Undutifulness of Children and Servants, Seditions, Murders, Pernicious Strifes, Uncleanness, Drunkenness, Thefts, Abuses of our Nei'bours Good Name, and whatever Moral *Turpitude* there is to pollute a Land and *corrupt Good Manners.*

And next to the good *Laws* in force among us against such *Scandals,* we have no greater Comfort than the *Royal* PROCLAMATIONS that have been issued out from the *Throne, For the Encouragement of Piety and Vertue, and for the Preventing and Punishing of Vice, Profaness and Immorality.* In this the Magistrate is the *Minister of God unto us for Good,* a *Terror* to the *Evil,* and a *Praise* to the *Good. Rom.* xiii.3, 4. He is by Office, as has been often said, *Custos utriusque Tabulae,* the *Defender* of both the *Tables* of the *Law,* as well as of the *Faith.* He succeeds in *Moses* Place, who having received the Law from God, then saw to it that the People kept it.

I have done with the *first thing* wherein Civil Rulers are to endeavour the Comfort of those that teach the good Knowledge of the LORD, *Namely, In their Legislative power and trust,* by *Enacting* good Laws for the Honour and Establishment of Religion within their Government. I will be more *brief* in the other *Instances.*

¶ii. It belongs to *Rulers,* and all *Publick Officers, Superior or Inferior,* in their *Executive* trust & power, to Comfort all those that stand up for GOD or are more immediately related to his Service, by the *Faithful Execution of those good Laws, that relate to Religion,* the Honour of God, the Observation of the Divine Law, and the Prosperity of the *Church of Christ.* We have *Good Laws* against Immoralities and Contempt of the Divine Ordinances; herein the *Legislative Power* have endeavour'd our Comfort: It now and always lies with the *Honourable Judges,* the *Worshipful Gentlemen in Commission for the Peace,* with *Inferior Officers* in every degree of Power or Trust, to the faithful discharge of which Respective Trusts they are *Sworn* and under the *Oath of God,* as *Revengers to execute Wrath upon him that doth Evil:* without which the Magistrate does at last *hold the Sword in vain,* and the *Penalties* threatned in the Law prove an *Empty Noise* and a *Lye*. *Laws* not duly Executed are but *Powder without Ball;* there's a terrible *blaze* and found but no *Execution* done: the *Wicked* have no Terror from them, nor the *Good* any Comfort.

More especially the *Ministry* wearing no *Secular Arms* for their own Defence, they *are more Peculiarly the Care of the Civil Sword,* to protect them from all Open Wrongs and Affronts; the wicked in the World being ready to trample them in the dust, and with hold their *Legal Rights:* And the more *backward* they are to *Assert* 'em, and fill their Superiors Ears with *Complaints;* of *Them* especially to whose Service in Spiritual Respects they are devoted; in this case the Magistrate shou'd not always *wait for a formal Complaint,* but find a Tongue for the *Dumb* and an Arm for the *Meek,* be Eyes to the *Blind,* and Feet to the *Lame,* and *Search out the Cause* Himself. For there is a *Modesty in Superior Minds* which restrains them from Complaints and causes 'em *rather to suffer wrong:* And there is a Regard to Mens Souls in many of Gods Servants so Superior to their Care about their own Temporal Concerns, *Seeking not theirs but them,* that they had rather Silently Suffer at home than their holy Ministrations shou'd suffer with unreasonable men abroad.

¶*iii. And Lastly,* Much is Incumbent on Civil Rulers for the Comfort and Encouragement of the Ministry, *in a Personal and more Private Character, as Christians of a Superior Degree only.* And under this Consideration of Themselves, they shou'd hold Themselves obliged to comfort the faithful Teachers of the good Knowledge of the Lord.

1] *In taking care to give a Vertuous and Religious Example in their own Conversation, both Private and Publick.* Authority and Dignity carries so much of the Stamp and Image of God upon it, that tho' it receives its highest Grace and Lustre from Religion, yet to the Eyes of Inferiors it reflects back also a great honour on Religion, and the Doctrine of God our Saviour is Eminently Adorn'd thereby. 'Tis a Comfortable thing to see Those, of whom it is said, *Ye are gods,* paying the profoundest Veneration and Homage to the Great GOD *by whom they Rule;* and they that give Laws to others paying Themselves the most careful Obedience to the Divine Law.

That when we come into your *Presence,* your Wise and Grave, your Pure and Devout *Discourse* may be long remembred with Reverence.

That the Vertue and *Order* of your Families, may like that of *Joshua* and *David* show the whole Land what the Fear of the Lord is.

That the Religious Sanctification of the *Sabbath* by your Housholds, and your constant reverent Attendance on the *Private and Publick Worship* of God, may visible testify your respect and honour to Gods holy Institutions.

For which End I cannot but wish, and with the lowest Deference wou'd earnestly commend it to the Consciences of Some whom I greatly honour in their Civil Character, *That all our Rulers might stand compleat in their Christian Profession:* And while they fill our Conspicuous *Seats* at the *Council Board,* in *Courts of Justice,* and in the *Assemblies* for Worship, their *Place* might not be left empty at the *Table of Christ:* An Example that must needs hurt our Churches, and the Souls of the *Vulgar,* from *Persons* of your Knowledge, Gravity, and believed Piety.

Magistrates shou'd be among the first at the Temple, and there and every where their *Lights* shou'd *Shine before Men;* Not in the vain Spirit of *Jehu,* who fought *Fame* from a *false Blaze, Come, see my Zeal for the Lord:* [Tho' it must be said, that it is as *Impolitick* as it is profane for Rulers to live in Irreligious Courses: And yet a meer *Mask* of Religion is a *Mean Disguize,* as well as *horrid;* to seek to establish our Power by abusing & affronting the Glorious and Fearful Name of God.]

2] It beseems the Christian Magistrate to speak Comfortably to the faithful Ministers of Christ, *by giving open Respects and Honours to their Persons, treating 'em always with distinction before the People.* As *Fathers,* says the *Apostle;* as *Children,* tho't the good King *Hezekiah, Chap.* xxix.v.11. *My Sons,* said he to the *Levites,* My Sons, *be not negligent.* And it is Remarkable with what Affability, Friendship and Love the *Pious Kings of Israel* were wont to treat the *Prophets of the Lord.*

A pious Ruler will never be a Stranger to his faithful *Pastor,* if it be not *his* own Will and Fault, which is not to be supposed neither. [Nor is it the single Comfort of a Venerable Superiors Respects, that we have in the Friendship of a Pious Ruler; but as *King Saul* himself once askt of the *Prophet,* it honours us before the People, and most effectually teaches them to venerate their *Teachers.*

Certainly our *Gracious* QUEEN has taught all in *Subordinate Place* their true Honour and Duty, promising in Her *Proclamation* against Vice, a *Distinction in Her Royal Favour to Persons of Piety and Vertue.* No Earthly *Prince* can go by a more perfect Rule, than this by which GOD governs His own Regards, which is *His Own Moral Image and Grace.*

3] It is expected of the Civil Ruler to speak Comfortably to those that teach the good Knowledge of God, *by excelling others in a chearful Readiness to Support the Divine Worship with their outward Estate.* 'Tis supposed, that generally they are distinguish'd by Providence with *Riches* as well as Honour and Power; and if so, they are *Poor Comforts* at last to their Respective Churches if they do not *lead in a Generous Contributing* to the Maintenance of the Ministry. If a rich Magistrate is seen to *Pinch,* what will not others do, who are of Estate as mean as their Quality? When the Building of the *Temple* was to be provided for, *King David* first exhausted his own *Royal Treasures,* and then the People gave largely. This also was one way wherein *Hezekiah* spake so comfortably to the *Levites* and the *Priesthood, v.*24. He gave *a Thousand Bullocks and Seven Thousand Sheep, and the Princes gave a Thousand Bullocks, and Ten Thousand Sheep, and a great number of Priests Sanctify'd themselves:* And in the xxxi. *Chap.* 3.*v.* we read further, that *Hezekiah appointed the Kings portion of his Substance for the Burnt-Offering.*

God has honour'd Rulers above others, and He expects that they do more than others to honour Him. Where He gives Riches in Abundance, He looks that Men do proportionably cast into his *Treasury* out of their Abundance; or else let the *Poor Widow* throw in her *Single Mite,* and Heaven will account that she has *done more than all* the Great and the Rich.

Having urg'd You so far, I will not Suppress two Tho'ts more, wherein the *Rich and Honourable* may greatly comfort the Churches & Ministry of Christ. The *One* is, *By devoting a Select Son* to the Service of the Temple, & leaving him an Inheritance equal with his *Brethren.* The *Other* is, That you wou'd employ some suitable parts of your *Estates,* as a *Tribute* to God and his Ministry in *Founding, Endowing, Establishing* and *Securing Schools for Literature and Religion:* More especially, our fair and lov'd *Mother* the COLLEDGE, which *Happy Foundation* God has signally bless'd and made the Great Glory of the *Land;* filling every *Chair of Honour* almost with her *Worthy Sons.* The flourishing of that *Society* is the Great Joy and Comfort of the *Ministry,* and so is the present *happy Settlement* thereof, as was abundantly testify'd to the *Honourable* COURT in the *united Addresses* of the *Ministers* the *last year.* And whatever it shall please God to direct the GREAT and GENERAL COURT further to do, in their present *Session* or hereafter, for the *Security* of that *Body* and the more Honourable Support of the *Reverend President,* it will greatly comfort the hearts of the present *Ministry:* So great a part of Whom must always own Him, with great Reverence and Love, a Wise and Careful *Father* to them, in their happy Education under his *Immediate Inspection and Institution.*

I have done with the *First Enquiry,* and it may be, almost presum'd too far on your Candour and Indulgence in some particulars; wherein at last I wou'd by no means be understood to pretend to direct my *Superiours.*

I will not enter on the *Second* thing Propounded, lest I trespass Egregiously on your Patience, Namely.

¶ii. *To give the Reasons of the Doctrine,* or to prove it to be the Rulers Incumbent Duty, to Comfort and Encourage the faithful Ministers of *Christ* in their holy Work. The *Word* of God *requires* this of Magistrates, [censures the wont of it, and brands those *Reigns* wherein Religion was not cared for, perverted, depraved, and the *Prophets* ill Treated.] Ministers *need* this Comfort and Help in their hard & difficult Work, [to oppose mens Lusts, & bear up under the double measure of Trouble that falls to their share.] The *Efficacy* and Success of the Ministerial Labours does under God very much depend on the Rulers Countenance and Influence. The *Nature of Magistracy* speaks it to be the Rulers incumbent Duty to encourage the *Ministry* of God, being the *Ordinance of God,* to rule and judge for Him, and accountable to Him, the Supream Governour and Judge of all the Earth. Not to add, that a Land has no more faithful *Friends* and richer *Blessings* in it, than the faithful Ministers of Christ: Nor the Magistracy any *surer Support* than the Encouragement of Religion; their Power being from God, the Reverence of Whom once failing the foundation of Government is ras'd.

But I hasten to some brief & particular *Application* of the *Doctrine.* And the USE may be in a *threefold Address.* I To our Honoured *Magistrates.*   II To *Ministers.*   III To the *People.*

¶i. *It addresses to our Civil Rulers, that Religion may always have this Countenance and Comfort from them.*

We cannot but own the Piety of our Rulers in their open and avowed Respects unto the *Churches* of *Christ,* and the holy *Pastors* of them. We give thanks to God, for the Great Comfort we have in the *Devotion* and bright *Vertue* of many of our *Magistrates;* for the Good *Laws* we have in defence of the Faith and Worship of *Christ;* and against Scandalous Immoralities; and that the *Seats of Judgment* are fill'd with Men of known Integrity and Religious Zeal.

We have Great *Consolation* in His EXCELLENCIES *Noble Example;* His Wise, Grave, and Occasionally Religious Conversation; the visible Order and Devotion of his House, and his tender Fatherly Carriage, toward the *Ministers of Christ;* Of the Body of *Whom* I have this most sure and certain Knowledge, that they are greatly comforted in Him.

In the Times of the *Romish* Superstition, I am told, it was the first Proposal or Enquiry at the opening of the *Parliament, What more is to be done for the Holy Mother the Church?* Far be it, that in our happyer Days of *Reform'd Religion,* the Ministry and *Pure* Worship of God shou'd have less of the *Legislators* Care. Suffer me then to pray that the Comfort of these Churches may always lye near Your hearts, and have some Consideration with You in every Session.

More especially, the more Honourable Support of *Ministers* thro' the Land wou'd be one most worthy Care of the *Assembly.* I speak not from Want, or for any *Self-Interest,* being by the good Providence of God, and the Care of my *Beloved Church,* equal in *Salary* with any of my *Brethren:* But I speak from a tender feeling of the *Slender* Circumstances of Many (my *Betters*) in other Places; and from an easy fore-fight of the Detriment that must come unto our Churches, if there be not an Inlargement in the Maintenance of the Ministry in most Places. For as this is in the People a too palpable Evidence of a *Lean* Profession, I mean of their not profiting by the Word; So is it the ready way to make lean and *Poor* Preaching, by Starving mens *Parts* & Oppressing their *Graces.*

The *Poverty of the Land is no Objection* against doing more than is done for the *Ministry.* People might do much more and not feel it. Nay it were the way to grow Rich, if we did our Duty in Supporting Honourably the Worship of God. For as it is the *Blessing* of God that maketh rich, so He has told his People that their defrauding Him is their own Impoverishment: *Mal. iii.*8, 9, 10. *Ye have robbed* ME,—*In Tithes and Offerings: Ye are cursed with a curse.—Bring ye all the Tithes into the Store-house, that there may be meat in my House, and prove me now here-with, saith the* LORD *of Hosts, if I will not open you the Windows of Heaven, and pour you out a Blessing, that there shall not be room eno' to receive it.*

Again, *There is no fear of the Idleness, Pride or Luxury of the Clergy,* from that decent and just Maintenance I am pleading for. I plead for no Sumptuousness or Excess, but bare Convenience. And if Professors of the Gospel are against this, their Devotion is too much like what the *Fable* tells of the *Illiberal Bishops* Blessing, not amounting in real Value unto the price of a *Farthing.*

We ought with Thankfulness to acknowledge the Piety of the *Government,* in the good Provision made to Pay out of the *Publick Treasury* the *Dues* of Ministers wrongfully detained from them; and to Tax the respective *Towns* or *Precincts* in proportion: And we may lay it down for a *Rule* to us, that the Ministry can never be Comfortable, while in the Settlement of *Ministers* there continues a necessity of *driving Sordid Bargains about a Salary,* or while after settlement they are forc'd either *abjectly to beg* and entreat, or *resolutely to scuffle* and fight for their Dues by solemn Engagements.

I shall not need to address You again about the *Colledge*; to speak comfortably always to the *Sons of the Prophets at Bethel,* which has indeed been to Us as *the House of* GOD *and the Gate of Heaven,* for the Heavenly *Issues* thence, which have refreshed the City of our God.

I will rather mention with great Honour the present Care that the *Government* is shewing, with respect unto the *Miserable Places of darkness and Irreligon,* that have hitherto *Shut out* the Ministry and Ordinances of *Christ* from among them, counting themselves unworthy of Eternal Life. Your Desires and Labours after a *Mission* of some Worthy *Persons* into such perishing Places, and for their Honourable Support in such difficult *Posts,* do greatly comfort us, and we Pray the *Great* LORD *of the Harvest* to prosper You, and to *send forth Labourers into his Harvest.*

And now, *Finally,* Need I again *Exhort You, Much Honoured, to be Religious Your Selves,* to fear the GOD by whom You rule, and to Serve Him who honours You among His People? You must needs think Your Selves Obliged to shine before Us, in all Vertue, in Devotion, in Faith, in Zeal; in a Publick respect to the Institutions of Christianity, and in an Abhorrence of all Immoral Practices; more especially let me say, of *Frauds* and dishonesty, of nauseous *Drunkenness,* of *Sabbath-breaking,* of *Unnatural Strifes* in Churches, and the *Contemptuous Spites of many against their holy Pastors.*

¶*ii.* My next Address is unto *my Reverend Fathers and Brethren in the* MINISTRY. If it be our *Rulers* Duty and Piety to comfort *Us,* we must needs think it *Our Own,*

1] *To endeavour in our Places to comfort our Faithful Rulers.* The Obligation is certainly mutual, and 'tis but a grateful Return unto the *Good and Gentle,* nay a Duty even to the *Froward.* Therefore let us fervently *Pray* for our Rulers, which is *Good and Acceptable in the fight of God our Saviour.* I *Tim.* ii.1, 2, 3. Let us be *Examples to our Flocks of Loyalty,* Humility, Peaceableness, Meekness, Love, Honour, Obedience and Submission in all just Cases: that if we are at any time falsely Accused, we may be able with Truth & Assurance to make the *Apostle's* Noble Defence, *Act.* xxv.8. *Neither against the Law, nor the Temple, nor yet against* CESAR *have I offended any thing at all.* Finally, let us be *Just to do our Rulers Honour* wherein they do well; owning it with Pleasure, and blessing God for it; influencing our respective *Charges* to do so likewise. We have no Liberty to grieve or disrest them, if They are bound to speak comfortable to us.

2] *Let us be comforted in the Countenance of our Rulers.* This is a Duty also which we owe unto GOD and *Them.* Let us take the

the Comfort which God gives us; *This also is the Gift of God.*
We have our *precious Opportunities* of Service : We enjoy great
Quietness; and may be *as Good* and *do* as much good as we
will, and have *Praise* of the *Powers that are* : This shou'd make
us the *Easier* under our Difficulties, and the more *Chearful* in
our Work. So were the *Levites* whom *Hezekiah* comforted,
*v.25. The Priests—the Levites—and all the Congregation—
—rejoyced. So there was great Joy in Jerusalem.*

3] If it is the Duty of the Civil Ruler to speak comfortably to the
Ministry of Christ, Then certainly *it is the Duty of Ministers
to comfort one another.* You must needs confess this *Inference*
to be very *Just and Natural,* and alas! it is no less *Necessary.*
We do not comfort and assist one another thro' this *Land* as we
ought : Some thro' *Negligence,* some thro' *Disaffection, Prejudices,* and *divers Interests.* Our *Independency,* in this sense,
is our *Woe* already, and will be our *Ruine* if it be not remedyed.
We shou'd *Unite* our Strength if we wou'd not be *Feeble* : By
Separateness we are *broken* one of another. We shou'd *Visit*
one another oft'ner, and be more *Open* and very *safe* in Communicating our Tho'ts to one Another. We shou'd tenderly
Sympathize with one another under Difficulties, and be ready
to *Succour* under Wrongs. We shou'd freely *Advise* and
Hearten one another when Aggrieved, and above all men *Bear*
with and *Forgive* one another, and he that is *Chief* shou'd be
Servant of all. We shou'd rejoyce in one anothers *Gifts* and
Graces, Credit and *Esteem. Use* and *Serviceableness*; and
whether we think the same thing in Smaller points of *Church
Order,* yet ought we to appear One in *Faith,* in *Charity,* & Zeal
for Practical Holiness. Finally, we shou'd beware of the Evil
Spirit of *Credulity* against *Elders,* lightly taking up Accusations
against *them*; but let our Religious Zeal be under the Restraints
of the Law of Charity.

¶iii. I will *Conclude,* with a brief *Exhortation to the People.*

1] *To Imitate their Good Rulers,* wherein They are Exemplary
in their Regards to the *Ministry of Christ. Inferiour People*
must needs hold themselves obliged in their Places to be *Comforts* to their *Ministers,* since the *Highest Orders* of Men are
bound to be so. Wherefore People ought conscientiously to
Love their Ministers, to *Pray* for 'em, to assist and *Support*
'em. They shou'd be very Careful not to *grieve* 'em, *contemn*
or *wrong* 'em, in *Word* or *Deed.*

2] *Obey the just and wise Laws made for the Comfort of the
Ministry.* As for *Instance,* Do but be *Just* to your *Aggreements*
with your *Ministers.* If we cou'd but obtain this in many Places

of the *Land,* it were a Great Point. Yet shou'd *Christians* blush to need this *Exhortation.* Read how the *People of Judah* obey'd the Command of the *King* in giving the *Levites* chearfully their *Portion*: xxxi. *Chap.* 5, 6. *verses*: *As soon as the Commandment came abroad, the Children of Israel bro't in Abundance the First-fruits of Corn, Wine and Oyl, and Honey, and of all the Increase of the Field, and the Tithe of all things bro't they in Abundantly—the Tithe of Holy things, which were Consecrated unto the* LORD *their God, and laid them by heaps.*

3] Let People learn from our *Doctrine,* to know *their own Happiness* when they have *Rulers* that set Themselves to Encourage the *Ministry* and Service of God. None but a *Sanballat* or *Tobiah* can be grieved at it, to see the *Civil Ruler* seeking the *Welfare of Israel.* It shou'd raise our Value, Esteem and Love, and put us on doubling our Prayers for, and our Endeavours to comfort Such *Rulers.* The *Good Job* was such a *Ruler; He chose out their Way, and sat Chief, and dwelt as a King in the Army; as one that Comforteth the Mourners*: and he tells us how it endear'd him to his People: *Job* xxix.23, 24. *They waited for me as for the Rain, and they op'ned their Mouth wide as for the latter Rain: If I laughed on them they believ'd it not, and the light of my Countenance they cast not down.* They were *refresh'd* by such a Rulers Presence and Countenance, Wisdom and Care, even as the *Thirsty Earth* is by the Showers of *Rain*: They priz'd his *Favour,* and were *Solicitous not to lose the light of his Countenance* shining upon them: They *Presum'd not* upon his *Condescentions* to diminish his Authority, and to *blow upon* the *Light* that cherish'd 'em: They were careful not to *Grieve* him, to make his *Countenance to fall,* or to make him *Change* his Looks and Carriage toward 'em: *The Light of my Countenance they cast not down.*

Thus I have endeavour'd to go thro' our respective *Duties* from the *Text,* and now will dismiss the ASSEMBLY as the *Levites* did the *Great Congregation of Israel and Judah,* in the *last Verse* of the *Chapter. Then the Priests the Levites arose, and blessed the People: and their Voice was heard, and their Prayer came up to His Holy Dwelling-place, even unto Heaven.*

Even so *Comfort* the Hearts of your faithful *Pastors,* and you will inherit their *louder and more fervent Blessing*: Their *Invigorated Prayers* for You and your Posterity will come up to the *Holy dwelling-place of* GOD, even unto *Heaven,* obtaining the *Effusion* of every *Sort,* and every *Measure,* of *Spiritual Blessing,* from on *High.*

The Defects of Preachers

Reproved

Solomon Stoddard

Solomon Stoddard, a member of one of the new world's leading mercantile families, was born in Boston in September, 1643. He was graduated from Harvard in 1662, and was called to the pastorate in the remote frontier fortress of Northampton, in 1670, a call he accepted in February, 1672. He was ordained September 11, 1672, and held this post until his death. Within a few years, he became known as "Pope Stoddard," the ecclesiastical autocrat of the entire Connecticut valley. He abolished the institutional and the theoretical covenant, forced the entire town's population into the church, and ruled through sheer force of personality.

Between 1700 and 1710, Increase and Cotton Mather initiated a violent pamphlet attack against Stoddard, accusing him of "Presbyterian" innovations. Although formally the battle ended in a draw, the outcome has been generally considered a defeat for the Mathers. This controversy indicates Stoddard's "radical" theological point of view, his willingness to do battle, and his spirit of self-reliance.

Stoddard died on February 11, 1728 (1729?).

"The Defects of Preachers *Reproved*" was preached at Northampton on May 19, 1723. The text is from the edition printed and sold by T. Green in New London, 1724.

MATTHEW XXIII. 2, 3. *The Scribes and the Pharisees sit in Moses seat. All therefore whatsoever they bid you observe, that observe and do.*

IN these Words is a Direction given by Christ unto the People: Where we have

First, The Foundation of the Rule. The Scribes & Pharisees sit on *Moses* Seat. Some take this as spoken of the Sanhedrim, who were the Successors of Moses and the Seventy Elders of Israel. Possibly that may be a mistake, for several of the Sanhedrim were not Pharisees. *Act.* 23.3. For the chief Priests did belong to that Society, *Act.* 4.6. And they are said to be Sadducees; but by Scribes & Pharisees I understand the Principal Teachers among the *Jews*. The Priests and Levites were more especially devoted to the study of the Law; Deut. 33.10. *They shall teach Jacob thy Judgments, and Israel thy Law—.* Yet others that were Learned in the Law, were made use of to Instruct the People, & were chosen to be Rulers of the Synagogues. The Pharisees were of any Tribe, *Paul* who was of the Tribe of *Benjamin* was a Pharisee by Education, as *he tells* Act. 23.6—*I am a Pharisee, the son of a Pharisee.*

Secondly, Here is the Rule given, What they bid you observe, that observe and do. This must needs be understood with that Limitation, when they Teach according to the Mind of God. Sometimes they taught for Doctrines the Commandments of Men, & then it was Sinful & Dangerous to observe their Directions. If the Blind lead the Blind, both shall fall into the ditch, *Mat.* 15.14. The Doctrine is,

¶DOCT. *There may be a great deal of good Preaching in a Country, and yet a Great want of good Preaching.*

It is a felicity to a People when there is good Preaching in the Land, yet there may in the same Land, be great want of good Teaching. Some things that are very useful may be plainly and fully taught, and other things that might be as useful may be Neglected; many sound Principles in Religion may be Taught, and other things that are of great Concernment unto Souls may be omitted. Ministers don't sufficiently do their Duty, if they Preach many sound Truths, and do it convincingly and with good affection, if they do it with great clearness and evidence, provided they neglect other things that are needful to Salvation. And so it falls out sometimes that men that make many good Sermons, are very defective in Preaching some other things that they ought to Preach.

I shall clear this in Three Instances.

1] Of the Scribes and Pharisees in Israel. They taught the People that there was only One God the Maker of all things; and were great Enemies to the Idolatry that their Fathers were guilty of, before the Babylonish Captivity; as the Scribe owned to Christ, Mark. 12.32. *Well, Master, thou hast said the truth: for there is one God, and there is none other but he.* They taught many Moral Duties, that men must love God & believe his Word; that they must be Just & Chast and men of Truth, and were very strict in the Observation of the Sabbath: They limited men how far they might go on the Sabbath. *Acts* 1.12. We read of a Sabbath days Journey. They taught truly the Doctrine of the Resurrection of the Dead: Act. 23.7, 8. The Pharisees dissented from the Sadducees, *the Sadducees say there is no Resurrection, nor Angel nor Spirit, but the Pharisees confess both.* They taught that the Messiah was to come; the Samaritans themselves received that Doctrine, *Joh.* 4.25 They were very punctual in teaching Circumcision & the Ceremonies of the Law of Moses, about Sacrifices, Tythes, and Legal Uncleanness.

But they were very faulty in Preaching in other particulars:

They were ignorant of the Doctrine of Regeneration, So Nicodemus, Joh. 3.4. he says, *How can a man be born when he is old?*
They taught that the first motions of lust, if the Will did not consent,
were not Sins. As we may gather from Rom. 7.7. *Paul* says, I had
not known Lust, except the Law had said thou shalt not Covet. And
from Mat. 5.27, 28. *It was said by them of old time, thou shalt
not commit Adultery. But I say whosoever looketh on a woman to
lust after her, hath committed Adultery in his heart.* They taught
also that dangerous Doctrine of Justification by Works, Rom. 10.3.
They went about to establish their own Righteousness. Rom. 9.2. 3
They sought it as it were by the works of the Law: They taught
the People that in case they devoted their Estates to the Temple,
they need not relieve their Fathers or Mothers, *Mat.* 15.4, 5, 6.
And above all they taught that JESUS of Nazareth was not the
Messiah, brought many Objections against Him; As that He came
out of Galilee, was a Gluttonous man and a Wine-bibber, *Mat.*
11.19. A friend of Publicans and Sinners: They Reproached Him
that by the Devil he cast out Devils: and they were very dull in
their Preaching, *Mat.* 7.29.

2] Of the Papists.   They teach the Doctrine of the Trinity truly,
   and the Attributes of God: So the Doctrine of the Incarnation
   of CHRIST, and that He died for our Redemption and is at the
   Right hand of God: They teach the Doctrine of the day of
   Judgment, of Heaven and of Hell, and many Moral Rules.

But they Preach a multitude of false Doctrines with these
Doctrines, that are pernicious to the Souls of men: They teach men
to seek the pardon of their Sin by afflicting their Bodies, by Pil-
grimage & paying a sum of Money: They teach many horrible
things with respect to their Pope, that he has power to forgive Sin,
to dispense with incestuous Marriages; that he has power over all
the Churches and may dispense with the Laws of GOD; that he is
infallible: They teach the Doctrine of Image-worship, abolishing
the Second Commandment: They teach Prayer to Saints departed,
the Unlawfulness of Priests Marriages, the Doctrine of Purgatory,
Justification by Works, a conditional Election, the power of Free-
will, falling from Grace, and Hundreds of other Erroneous Doctrines: They do indeed subvert the Faith of Christ.

3] Of the Arminians.   Many of them Preach very profitably,
   about GOD and the Person of CHRIST, about Justification by
   Faith and Universal Obedience, about the Day of Judgment &
   of Eternal Rewards and Punishments.

But there is a great deal of want of good Preaching among
them: They decry all absolute Decrees of Election and Reprobation,
making the Decrees of God to depend on the foresight of Repentance or Impenitence; they assert Universal Redemption, as if

Christ died to make all men Salvable: They deny the Propagation of Sin, saying men become sinners by Imitation: They hold a Power in Man to withstand the Grace of GOD; that after GOD has has done His work, it is in the power of Man to refuse to be Converted: They don't acknowledge the servitude of man to Sin, but hath power with that assistance that God affords, to Convert himself: They deny the Doctrine of Perseverance. These things draw a great train of Errors after them.

The *Reason of the Doctrine* is, Because some Preachers are men of Learning & Moral men, and they have drunk in some Errors, & they want Experience. Learning and Morality will qualify men to make many good and profitable Sermons, much for the Edification of the Hearers. Learning qualifies men to clear up many Principles of Religion; and a Moral disposition may fit men zealously to Reprove vicious Practices: But men may be Learned men, yet drink in very Corrupt Doctrines. Learning is no security against Erroneous Principles: The Pharisees and Sadducees were men of Liberal Education, yet leavened with many false Principles: Mat. 16.6 *Beware of the leaven of the Pharisees & Sadducees.* & ver. 12. *Then understood they that he bid them not beware of the leaven of bread; but of the doctrine of the Pharisees & of the Sadducees.* Learning will not cure those distempers of the Heart that do expose men to false Opinions; Learning will not cure the Pride & Conceitedness of mens Hearts. Men of Learning may lean too much to their own Understanding. Men of Learning may be led aside by Reading Erronious Books. Learned Education will not deliver men from Carnal Reason: Men of corrupt Affections are very inclinable to imbibe bad Principles: Men of Learning may be blind men. Christ says of the Pharisees, *They be blind, leaders of the blind,* Mat. 15.14. Most of the Errors in the world in matters of Religion, have been hatched by men of Learning. *Arius, Socinus,* and *Arminius,* and *Pelagius* were Learned men: Errors in Religion have been generally the Off-spring of great Scholars, have been propagated by them. And men may be Moral men that have no experience of the work of God upon their hearts. Men may be Zealous men against Drunkenness and Whoredom, they have no Saving Knowledge of Christ. Many Moral men have no Communion with God; no Experience of a Saving Change in their own Souls. Men may be very Moral & have no experience of a work of Humiliation, or being bro't off from their own Righteousness, or a work of Faith; of the difference that is between the Common and Special work of the Spirit; of the difference between Saving & Common Illumination, of the working of the heart under Temptation, of the way wherein godly men are wont to find Relief. Every Learned & Moral man is not a Sincere Convert, & so not able to speak exactly and experimentally to such things as Souls want to

be instructed in. It is as with a man that has seen a Map of a
Country, or has read a great deal about it; he can't tell the way
between Town and Town, and hundreds of particular Circumstances, as a man that has Travelled or Lived there is able to do.
Experience fits men to Teach others. A man that has himself had
only a common work of the Spirit and judges it saving, is very unfit
to judge of the State of other men. Men would not put their Lives
into the hands of an unskilful Physician, or trust their Ship with an
unskilful Pilot, or an intricate Case depending in the Law with an
unskilful Lawyer.

¶USE: *I.* Of *Examination.* Whether it be not thus in this Country?
It is notoriously known by those that are acquainted with the state
of the Christian World, that tho' there be many eminent Truths
taught, yet there is a great want of good Preaching; whence it
comes to pass, that among Professors a spirit of Piety runs exceeding low. But it is proper for us to take notice how it is among
our selves; and tho' it be very evident that there is a great deal of
good Preaching in the Land, and the way of Salvation is Preached
with a great deal of Plainness & power, and many men are very
faithful to declare all the Counsel of God; yet there may be cause
of Lamentation, that there is a great deal wanting in some places:
Some may be very much to blame in not Preaching as they ought to
do.

1] *If any be taught that frequently men are ignorant of the Time
of their Conversion, that is not good Preaching.* Some are of
that Opinion, and its like they may drink it in from their Ministers. This is a delusion, and it may do them a great deal of
hurt; it hardens men in their Natural Condition. *Paul* knew the
time of his Conversion; *At Midday, O King, I saw a Light from
Heaven, above the brightness of the Sun,* Act. 26.13. Men are
frequently at a loss whether their Conversion were true or
not; but surely men that are Converted must take some notice
of the Time when God made a Change in them: Conversion is
a great change, from darkness to light, from death to life, from
the borders of despair to a spirit of faith in Christ. As for the
outward Conversation, there is sometimes little difference; men
might carry very well before: But as to the frame of mens
Hearts, there is a very great difference. Formerly they were
under the reigning power of Objections against the Gospel,
when Converted they receive it as a Divine Truth; before they
were Converted they were under a sentence of Condemnation,
now they have Peace with God through Jesus Christ. Men are
generally a long time seeking Conversion, labouring to get an
interest in Christ; and it would be much if when God reveals
Christ to them, they should not take notice of it when the

change is made; Ten to one but Conscience will take notice of it. When a Seaman comes into the Harbour, when a Prisoner is pardoned, when a Victory is obtained, when a Disease is broke, it would be much if men should take no notice of them. Conversion is the greatest change that men undergo in this world, surely it falls under Observation. The Prodigal knew well enough the time of his return to his Fathers house: The Children of Israel knew the time of their passing over Jordan.

2] *If any be taught that Humiliation is not necessary before Faith, that is not good Preaching.* Such Doctrine has been taught privately and publickly, and is a means to make some men mistake their condition, and think themselves happy when they are miserable: For men must be brought off from their own Righteousness before they be brought to Christ. Men that think they have any thing to appease the Wrath of God and ingratiate themselves, will not accept the Calls of the Gospel in Sincerity. While People have a Foundation to build upon, they will not build upon Christ. A Self-righteous spirit is quite contrary to the Gospel: If men be Self-righteous men, they will not judge it fair for God to cast them off. Men that depend upon the Justice of God, will not depend upon the meer Mercy of God. Men that lay claim to Heaven from their own Works, will not depend on that Plea that Christ has given his life a Ransom for many, and has Redeemed us from the Curse being made a Curse for us. Multitudes of men are ruined by building upon a Sandy Foundation. Men must see their Malady, before they see their Remedy. Men must be led into the Understanding of the badness of their Hearts & the strictness of the Law, before they will be convinced of the Preciousness of Christ. Men that can heal their own Consciences, will not come to Christ for healing. Men must be driven by necessity indeed before they come to Christ. Tho' men feel great terrors and live a tormented Life, yet they will not come to Christ, till driven out of themselves. Men must feel themselves dead in sin, in order to their Believing; *Rom.* 7.9. *Sin revived, and I died.* Men must see themselves poor & miserable, wretched & blind and naked, before they receive that Counsel of buying of Christ gold tried in the fire, and white raiment, *Rev.* 3.17, 18.

3] When men don't Preach much about the danger of Damnation, there is want of good Preaching. Some Ministers Preach much about moral Duties and the blessed Estate of godly Men, but don't seek to awaken Sinners & make them sensible of their danger; they cry for Reformation: These things are very needful in their places to be spoken unto; but if Sinners don't hear often of Judgment and Damnation, few will be Converted.

Many men are in a deep Sleep and flatter themselves as if there was no Hell, or at least that God will not deal so harshly with them as to *Damn* them. Psal. 36.2. *He flattereth himself in his own eyes, until his iniquity be found to be hateful.* They need to be told of the Terrors of the Lord, that they may flee from Wrath to come: A little matter will not scare men, their hearts be as hard as a stone, as hard as a piece of the nether milstone, & they will be ready to laugh at the shaking of the Spear. Ministers must give them no rest in such a condition: They must pull them as Brands out of the burnings. It is well if Thunder and Lightning will awaken them: They had need to fear that they may work out their Salvation with fear & trem-*bling.* Ministers are faulty when they speak to them with gentleness, as *Eli* rebuked his Sons. Christ Jesus often warned them of the danger of Damnation: Mat. 5.29, 30. *It is better that one of thy members should perish, & not that thy whole body should be cast into hell.* Mat. 7.13. *Broad is the gate & wide is the way that leadeth to destruction, and many there be that go in thereat. Mat.* 13.42 *The Angels shall cast them into a furnace of fire, there shall be wailing and gnashing of teeth.* So also, *Mat.* 22.13. *Mat.* 25.41, 46. This for our imitation. Christ knew how to deal with Souls, and *Paul* followed His Example. Men need to be terrified and have the arrows of the Almighty in them that they may be Converted. Ministers should be Sons of Thunder: Men had need have Storms in their hearts, before they will betake themselves to Christ for Refuge: When they are pricked at the Heart, then they will say, What must we do to be Saved? Men must be fired out of their worldliness and sloth: Men must be driven as *Lot* was out of *Sodom.* Reason will govern men in other things; but it is Fear that must make them diligently to seek Salvation: If they be but thoroughly Convinced of their danger, that will make them go to God and take Pains.

4] *If they give a wrong account of the nature of Justifying Faith, that is not good Preaching.* Justifying Faith is set forth in the Scripture by many figurative Expressions; Coming to Christ, Opening to Him, sitting under his shadow, flying to Him for Refuge, building on Him as on a Foundation, feeding on Him, &c. These Expressions do imply not only an act of the Under-standing, but also an act of the Will, accepting of Him, depend-ing on Him. This Doctrine is despised by some, and Faith in Christ is said to be only a Perswasion of the truth of the Christian Religion. This is the way to make multitudes of Carnal men secure, and to flatter themselves as if they were in a good Condition: They say they are no Heathens, nor Turks,

nor Papists, nor Jews, but they believe that Jesus Christ is the
Eternal Son of God, they hope they are Believers; but multitudes of People have such a Faith that will fall short of Eternal
Life: Joh. 2.23, 24 *Many believed in his name, when they saw
the miracles that he did; but Jesus did not commit himself unto
them.* Joh. 12.42, 43. *Among the chief rulers many believed
on him, but because of the Pharisees they did not confess him.*
The Faith of some men is only a Perswasion from their Education: As Heathens do receive the Religion of their Fore-fathers
by Tradition, so these do receive the Christian Religion from
Hear-say. But Justifying Faith is wrought in men by the mighty
Power of God; 2 Thess. 1.11. *That he would work in you,
the work of faith with power.* Eph. 1.19, 20. *And what is the
exceeding greatness of his power to us-ward who believe, according to the working of his mighty power; which he wrought
in Christ when he raised him from the dead?* By Justifying
Faith, men answer the Calls of God, relinquishing their own
Righteousness, place their Dependance only on the Mediation of
Christ; Heb. 6.18 *They flee for refuge, to lay hold on the
hope that is set before them.* Justifying Faith is a living
Principle that Santifies men; Act 15.9. *Purifying their hearts by
faith.* Many men have a common Perswasion of the truth of
the Gospel, that are utterly destitute of Holiness: But true
Justifying Faith is always accompanied with an Holy Life.
Where there is Faith, there is every other Grace: Act. 26.18.
Sanctified by faith that is in me.

5] *If any do give false Signs of godliness, that is not good Preaching.* Signs of Grace are of two sorts: Some are Probable, and
they must be spoken of only as Probable; a Score of them may
make the thing more Probable, but don't make it Certain: Pro-
babilities make no Demonstration; Probable Signs are not
Conclusive. There are two Errors in laying down Signs; one is
when those things that may flow from Common Principles, as
natural Temper, natural Conscience, fear of Hell, false Imaginations, are given as sure Signs of Grace: But those things that
may flow from Common Principles, don't truly Distinguish between Saints & Hypocrites; As a good Conversation, savoury
Discourse, zeal against Sin, strong religious Affections, sorrow
for Sin, quietness under Afflictions, delight in Ordinances,
suffering for Religion, &c. From such loose Signs People are in
danger to take up a false Perswasion of their godliness. Such
signs are full of Delusion; and many men do bless themselves
who are in a miserable Condition. Such probable Signs may be,
where there be certain Signs of the contrary. Men are apt to
flatter themselves, and when they hear such Signs, they are

strengthned in their carnal Confidence. There is no infallible
Sign of Grace, but Grace. Grace is known only by intuition:
All the External Effects of Grace may flow from other Causes.
Another Error is when men are too strict in their Signs; As
when they give that as a Sign, that there is a constant care to
glorify GOD, and a continual living upon JESUS CHRIST, and a
constant watchfulness against the workings of Corruption.
There is no godly man but has at times ill frames of spirit:
David and *Jonah* and *Peter* had so. When *David* committed
Adultery, he had not a due care to glorify God; nor *Jonah* when
he was in a Fret, nor the *Psalmist* when he was as a Beast before
God, nor *Paul* when he was led into Captivity by the law of sin
that was in his Members. There is no godly man that can comfort
himself with such Signs as these: It is well if godly men do see
now and then the workings of a spirit of Grace: Grace is many
times under Hatches and invisible.

6] *If any teach men to build their faith about the Divine Authority
of the Scripture upon Probable Signs, that is not good Preaching.* There be many probable Arguments for the Authority of
the Sacred Scriptures; As the Eminency of the Penmen, and
they have had a mighty Efficacy to make a change in the
Hearts of men; it is said there were many Miracles wrought for
the confirmation of the Doctrine of them; there has been an
accomplishment of many of the Predictions in them. These
Arguments are preponderating and do outweigh all Objections
that are brought against the Authority of them: These Considerations may well strengthen the Faith of the People of
God; but these things cannot be the Foundation of our Faith:
it is only the certain Knowledge of their Authority, that can
be the foundation of Faith or any other Grace. Men cannot
believe them to be infallibly true upon probable Arguments:
Probable Arguments must be looked on but as Probable and
not Convincing. Men must have infallible Arguments for loving
God and believing His Word; the foundation of Believing the
Divine Authority of the Scripture, is the manifestation of
the Divine Glory in them. There is a Self-evidencing Light in the
Works of God: The Creation of the world shews God's Power
and God-head, *Rom.* 1.20. It is impossible that the World
should be made by any but an infinite God. So there is a Self-
evidencing light in the Word of God; there are such things
Revealed there as can be made known by none but God: 1 Cor.
2.9. *Eye hath not seen, nor ear heard, nor hath it entred into
the heart of man to conceive what God hath prepared for
them that love him.* Those Eternal Rewards that are spoken
of in the Scripture, those perfect Rules that are laid down there,

those accounts that are given of the Mercy of God, and the Justice of God, manifested in the way of our Salvation, would never have entred into the Heart of Man to conceive, if it had not been revealed by God; Men would never have thought of such a way of Salvation, if it had not been declared by God.

7] *If men preach for such Liberties as God doth not allow, that is no good preaching.* There are many Licentious Liberties that are taken by Men, in their Apparel, in their Drinking, in their Dancing and other Recreations, and in their Discourses upon the Sabbath, and in their Dealings with one another; and if Ministers either vindicate or connive at them, they don't Preach as they ought to do. Some men are but lax Casuists, and they take too great a Liberty themselves, & so do their Wives & Children, and they are afraid to anger men by Reproving some particular Evils that men are addicted to, that do prevail in the Land: The Pharisees were such Casuists; Mat. 5.43. *Ye have heard it hath been said of old, thou shalt love thy neighbour, and hate thine enemy.* Men should be solemnly Warned against all evil Carriages; and if this be omitted, it gives great increase to Sin in the Land. God complains of ill against Teachers for not Reproving Sinners; Isa. 56.10. *They are ignorant & blind, dumb dogs that cannot bark.* If men were duely Reproved for their Extravagancies, that would be a means to Reclaim them: Jer. 23.22. *If they had stood in my counsel I had caused my people to hear my words; then they should have turned them from their evil way and from the evil of their doings.* Faithful Preaching would be beneficial two ways; one way as it would cut off occasions of anger, and prevent those sins that bring down the Wrath of God on the Land; we should enjoy much more Publick Prosperity: The other is, that it would deliver men from those Vicious Practises that are a great hindrance to Conversion. As long as men live in ways of Intemperance, Injustice, and unsuitable Carriages on the Sabbath, it will be a great impediment to a thorough work of Conversion. There may be Conversion tho' men are not broken off from sins of Ignorance, but as long as they tolerate themselves in *Immoralitites,* that will be a mighty Bar in the way of their Conversion.

8] *If men preach for such Ceremonies in Worship as God doth not allow, that is not good Preaching.* There be those that plead for Humane Inventions in Worship; that would if they could, defend the Ceremonies of the Church of England, that would retain some *Jewish* Ceremonies that are abolished, and practise other Humane Appointments. *Jeroboam* was Condemned not only for Worshipping the Calves of *Dan* and *Bethel;* but for appointing a time of Worship in his own heart, 1 *King.* 12.32,

33. So it is noted as an imperfection, in the Reformation of *Asa,
Jehoshaphat* and *Manasseh:* That the high Places were not
taken away. This is spoken of as a great sign of Hypocrisy; Isa.
29.13. *This people draw near me with their mouth, and honour
me with their lips; but have removed their heart far from me:
and their fear towards me is taught by the precept of men.* When
men impose such Ceremonies, they usurp a Power that God has
not given them. It is God's Prerogative to appoint in what ways
we shall Worship Him: And men therein go quite beyond the
bounds of their Authority: Men therein impute *imperfection*
and *defect* to the Ordinances of God, as if they cou'd teach him
how it is fit that he shou'd be Worshipped; and they presume
on a Blessing without a Promise: Mat. 15.9. *In vain do they
worship me, teaching for doctrines the commandments of men.*
This is a way to make men Formal in their Worship; the multi-
plying of Ceremonies eats out the heart of Religion, and makes
a People Degenerate. Men that *multiply Ceremonies,* are apt
to content themselves with the *Form* without the *Life.*

 Quest. *Is the late Practice of some Ministers, in Reading their
  Sermons, Commendable?*
 Answ. There be some Cases wherein it may be tolerable. Per-
  sons through Age may loose the strength of their
  Memories, & be under a Necessity to make use of their
  Notes; but ordinarily it is not to be allowed.

Consider 1. *It was not the manner of the Prophets or Apostles.
Baruch* read the Roll that was written from the Mouth of *Jeremiah;*
but *Jeremiah* was not wont to read his Prophesies. It was the manner of the *Jews* to read the Scriptures in the Synagogues; but after
that it was their way to Instruct & Exhort men, not from any written Copy: Act, 13.15. *After the reading of the Law and the
Prophets, the Rulers of the Synagogue sent to them, saying, Men
and brethren, if ye have any word of Exhortation for the People,
say on.* This was according to the Example of Christ, *Luk.* 4.17, 20.
It was ordered in *England* in the Days of King *Edward* the Sixth,
That Ministers should Read Printed Homilies in Publick: And there
was great necessity of it, for there was not One in Ten, that were
able to make Sermons. But it has been the manner of worthy men
both here and in other Places, to deliver their Sermons without
their Notes.

2] *The Reading of Sermons is a dull way of Preaching.* Sermons
when Read are not delivered with Authority and in an affecting
way. It is Prophesied of Christ, Mic. 5.4. *He shall stand and
feed in the Strength of the Lord, in the Majesty of the Name
of the Lord his God.* When Sermons are delivered without

Notes, the looks and gesture of the Minister, is a great means to command Attention & stir up Affection. Men are apt to be Drowsy in hearing the Word, and the Liveliness of the Preacher is a means to stir up the Attention of the Hearers, and beget suitable Affection in them. Sermons that are Read are not delivered with Authority, they favour of the Sermons of the Scribes, *Mat.* 7.29. Experience shews that Sermons Read are not so Profitable as others. It may be Argued, that it is harder to remember Rhetorical Sermons, than meer Rational Discourses; but it may be Answered, that it is far more Profitable to Preach in the Demonstration of the Spirit, than with the enticing Words of mans wisdom.

¶ USE: II. *See the Reason why there is so little Effect of Preaching.* There is much good Preaching, and yet there is want of good Preaching. There is very good Preaching in *Old England,* yet there is great want of good Preaching, especially among the Conformists: And there is very good Preaching in *New-England,* and yet there is some want of good Preaching; especially in some places: And this is one Reason that there is no more good done. There is a great fault in Hearers, they are not studious of the mind of God; they are Enemies to the gospel: And when Christ Himself Preached among them, many did not Profit by it. Yet some Preachers are much to blame, and tho' they do Preach profitably many times, yet they have great cause to be Humbled for their Defects.

1] *For hence it is that there is so little Conversion.* There is great Complaint in one Country and in another, that there be few Converted; it is apparent by mens Unsanctified Lives & their unsavoury Discourses. This is one Reason, there is a great deal of Preaching that doth not much Promote it, but is an hindrance to it. To tell men that *they may be Converted tho' they don't know the time:* To teach that *there is no need of a work of Humiliation to prepare them for Christ;* and that *Faith is nothing else but a Perswasion that the Gospel is true,* is the very way to make many carnal men hope that they are converted. It makes other Preaching very ineffectual: It makes them think that it is needless to strive for Conversion. Such Preaching hardens men in their Sins: The want of dealing plainly with men is the reason, why there is seldom a noise among the *Dry Bones.* In some Towns there is no such thing to be Observed for *Twenty Years together.* And men continue in a senseless condition, come to Meeting & hear Preaching, but are never the better for it. In some Towns godly men are very thin sown. Most of the People are in as bad a condition as if they had never heard the Gospel: Go on in a still way, following their worldly Designs, carry on somewhat of the Form of godliness, but mind little but the World & the Pleasures of this Life. The Scribes did not Preach with Authority, *Mat.* 7.29. And they *entered not into the Kingdom of God themselves, and they that were entering in they hindred.* Such Preaching is not mighty *to the pulling down of strong Holds.* Conversion-work will fail very much where there is not Sound Preaching.

2] Hence many men that make an high profession, lead Unsanctified Lives: They are not dealt Plainly with; and so tho' they Profess high, they Live very Low: They are not dealt *Roundly with;* and they believe they are in a good Estate, and Conscience suffers them to Live after a Corrupt manner. Some of them live a Proud and Voluptuous Life, and they are not Searched as they should be. If they were told their own, that would keep them from saying that *they were Rich and increased in goods,* and had *need of nothing:* If they were *rebuked Sharply,* that might be a means *to make them Sound in the Faith,* Tit. 1.13. It might make them not only to Reform, but lay a better Foundation for Eternal Life, than ever yet was laid. *Paul* was very thorough in his work, & wherever he came he had the fulness of the blessing of the Gospel of Christ, *Rom.* 15.29.

A FAREWELL-SERMON

Jonathan Edwards

One of the most controversial figures in the Colonial period, Jonathan Edwards has been called variously a "devoted Christian," a "psychopath," and "the greatest of theologians." Together with George Whitefield and, perhaps, Gilbert Tennent, he was principally responsible for that tremendous surge in religious feeling and experience in the colonies during the first half of the eighteenth century now referred to as the "Great Awakening."

Born on October 5, 1703, in East Windsor, Connecticut, less than a century after New England was first settled, Edwards was educated first at home and later at Yale, from which institution he was graduated in 1720. His training had been a model of the education offered by the early New England colleges, strongly classical and theological in content, heavily Calvinistic in mood and outlook. An omnivorous and catholic reader, a prolific if not popular scholar, Edwards preferred his study to his parish, his books to his congregation, his theology to his fellow man. Early in his career, he was called to assist his grandfather, Solomon Stoddard, then pastor at Northampton, Massachusetts. Upon his grandfather's death, he succeeded him as pastor, a position he occupied until he was dismissed by the congregation more than twenty years later. He died on March 22, 1758, shortly after assuming the presidency of Princeton College.

During the greater part of his ministerial career, Edwards found himself out of step with his contemporaries. Preaching a doctrine of total depravity and of the imminence of eternal damnation, he failed to sense that there was a growing dissatisfaction with Calvinistic dogma because it did not square with human experience and because it was unable to survive the close scrutiny of rationalism. Nevertheless, for those who crowded into the rough pews of the church at Northampton, the sermons delivered by Edwards must have been vivid and moving experiences. Strongly logical, clearly arranged, plainly written, the sermons encouraged little hope; frequently, indeed, they drove the listeners to despair and, if stories are true, at times to suicide.

The "Farewell-Sermon" was his valedictory at the Northampton Church, delivered on July 2, 1750, ten days after his dismissal. It can scarcely be called a masterpiece of composition and on that score has never achieved great popularity. But more than most of Edward's sermons, it affords the reader a glimpse into the heart and mind of its author. The text is from the Kneeland edition, published in Boston, 1751.

443

II. COR. I. 14. *As also ye have acknowledged us in Part, that We are your Rejoycing, even as Ye also are ours, in the Day of the* **LORD JESUS.**

THE Apostle, in the preceeding Part of the Chapter, declares what great Troubles he met with in the Course of his Ministry. In the Text, and two foregoing Verses, he declares what were his Comforts and Supports under the Troubles he met with. There are four Things in particular.

1] That he had approved himself to his own Conscience. v.12. *For Our Rejoycing is this, the Testimony of our Conscience, that in Simplicity and godly Sincerity, not with fleshly Wisdom, but by the Grace of God, we have had our Conversation in the World, and more abundantly to-you-wards.*

2] Another Thing he speaks of as Matter of Comfort, is that as he had approved himself to his own Conscience, so he had also to the Consciences of his Hearers, the *Corinthians* whom he now wrote to, and that they should approve of him at the Day of Judgment.

3] The Hope he had of seeing the blessed Fruit of his Labours and Sufferings in the Ministry, in their Happiness and Glory, in that great Day of Accounts.

4] That in his Ministry among the *Corinthians,* he had approved himself to his Judge, who would approve and reward his Faithfulness in that Day.

These three last Particulars are signified in my Text and the preceding Verse; and indeed all the four are implied in the Text: 'Tis implied, that the *Corinthians* had acknowledged Him as their spiritual Father, and as one that had been faithful among them, and as the Means of their future Joy and Glory at the Day of Judgment, and one whom they should then see, and have a joyful Meeting with as such. 'Tis implied, that the Apostle expected at that Time to have a joyful Meeting with *Them* before the Judge, and with Joy to behold their Glory, as the Fruit of his Labours; and so they would be *his Rejoycing.* 'Tis implied also, that he then expected to be approved of the great Judge, when he and they would meet together before Him; and that he would then acknowledge his Fidelity, and that this had been the Means of their Glory; and that thus he would as it were give them to him as his *Crown of Rejoycing.* But this the Apostle could not hope for, unless he had the Testimony of his own Conscience in his Favour. And therefore the Words do imply in the strongest Manner, that he had approved himself to his own Conscience.

There is one Thing implied in each of these Particulars, and in every Part of the Text, which is that Point I shall make the Subject of my present Discourse, *viz.*

¶DOCT.   Ministers and the People that have been under their Care, must meet one another, before Christ's Tribunal, at the Day of Judgment.

Ministers and the People that have been under their Care, must be parted in this World, how well soever thay have been united: If they are not separated before, they must be parted by Death: And they may be separated while Life is continued. We live in a World of Change, where nothing is certain or stable; and where a little Time, a few Revolutions of the Sun, brings to pass strange Things, surprizing Alterations, in particular Persons, in Families, in Towns and Churches, in Countries and Nations. It often happens, that those who seem most united, in a little Time are most disunited, and at the greatest Distance. Thus Ministers and People, between whom there has been the greatest mutual Regard and strictest Union, may not only differ in their Judgments, and be alienated in Affection: But one may rend from the other, and all Relation between them be dissolved; the Minister may be removed to a distant Place, and they may never have any more to do one with another in this World. But if it be so, there is one Meeting more that they must have, and that is in the last great Day of Accounts.

Here I would shew,

¶*i.* In what Manner, Ministers and the People which have been under their Care, shall meet one another at the Day of Judgment.
¶*ii.* For what Purposes.
¶*iii.* For what Reasons God has so ordered it, that Ministers and their People shall then meet together in such a Manner, and for such Purposes.

¶*i.* I would shew, in some Particulars, in what Manner Ministers and the People which have been under their Care, shall meet one another at the Day of Judgment. Concerning this I would observe two Things in general.

1] That they shall not then meet only as all Mankind must then meet, but there will be something peculiar in the Manner of their Meeting.

2] That their Meeting together at that Time shall be very different from what used to be in the House of God in this World.

¶*i*. They shall not meet at that Day meerly as all the World must then meet together. I would observe a Difference in two Things.

(1) As to a clear actual View, and distinct Knowledge and Notice of each other.

Altho' the whole World will be then present, all Mankind of all Generations gathered in one vast Assembly, with all of the angelic Nature, both elect and fallen Angels; yet we need not suppose, that every one will have a distinct and particular Knowledge of each Individual of the whole assembled Multitude, which will undoubtedly consist of many Millions of Millions. Tho 'tis probable that Men's Capacities will be much greater than in their present State, yet they will not be infinite: Tho' their Understanding & Comprehension will be vastly extended, yet Men will not be deified. There will probably be a very enlarged View, that particular Persons will have of the various Parts and Members of that vast Assembly, and so of the Proceedings of that great Day: but yet it must needs be, that according to the Nature of finite Minds, some Persons and some Things, at that Day shall fall more under the Notice of particular Persons, than others; and this (as we may well suppose) according as they shall have a nearer Concern with some than others, in the Transactions of the Day. There will be special Reason, why those who have had special Concerns together in this World, in their State of Probation, and whose mutual Affairs will be then to be tried and judged, should especially be set in one another's View. Thus we may suppose, that Rulers and Subjects, earthly Judges and those whom they have judged, Neighbours who have had mutual Converse, Dealings and Contests, Heads of Families and their Children and Servants, shall then meet, and in a peculiar Distinction be set together. And especially will it be thus with Ministers and their People. 'Tis evident by the Text that these shall be in each others View, shall distinctly know each other, and shall have particular Notice one of another at that Time.

(2) They shall meet together, as having special Concern one with another in the great Transactions of that Day.

Altho they shall meet the whole World at that Time, yet they will not have any immediate and particular Concern with all. Yea, the far greater Part of those who shall then be gathered together, will be such as they have had no Intercourse with in their State of Probation, and so will have no mutual Concerns to be judged of. But as to Ministers, and the People that have been under their Care, they will be such as have had much immediate Concern one with another, in Matters of the greatest Moment, that ever Mankind have to do one with another in. Therefore they especially must meet, and be brought together before the Judge, as having special Concern one with another in the Design and Business of that great Day of Accounts.

Thus their Meeting, as to the Manner of it, will be diverse from the Meeting of Mankind in general.

¶*ii.* Their Meeting at the Day of judgment will be very diverse from their Meetings one with another in this World.

Ministers and their People, while their Relation continues, often meet together in this World: They are wont to meet from Sabbath to Sabbath, and at other Times, for the publick Worship of God, and Administration of Ordinances, and the solemn Services of God's House: And besides these Meetings, they have also Occasions to meet for the determining and managing their ecclesiastical Affairs, for the Exercise of Church-Discipline, and the settling and adjusting those Things which concern the Purity and good Order of publick Administrations. But their Meeting at the Day of Judgment will be exceeding diverse, in its Manner and Circumstances, from any such Meetings and Interviews as they have one with another in the present State. I would observe, how, in a few Particulars.

(1) Now they meet together in a preparatory mutable State, but then in an unchangeable State.

Now Sinners in the Congregation meet their Minister in a State wherein they are capable of a saving Change, capable of being turned, thro' God's Blessing on the Ministrations and Labours of their Pastor, from the Power of Satan unto God, and being brought out of a State of Guilt, Condemnation and Wrath, to a State of Peace and Favour with God, to the Enjoyment of the Privileges of his Children, and a Title to their eternal Inheritance. And Saints now meet their Minister with great Remains of Corruption, and sometimes under great spiritual Difficulties and Affliction: And therefore are yet the proper subjects of Means of an happy Alteration of their State, consisting in a greater Freedom from these Things; which they have Reason to hope for in the Way of an Attendance on Ordinances; and of which God is pleased commonly to make his Ministers the Instruments. And Ministers and their People now meet in Order to the bringing to pass such happy Changes; they are the great Benefits sought in their solemn Meetings in this World.

But when they shall meet together at the Day of Judgment, it will be far otherwise. They will not then meet in Order to the Use of Means for the bringing to Effect any such Changes; for they will all meet in an unchangeable State. Sinners will be in an unchangeable State: They who then shall be under the Guilt and Power of Sin, and have the Wrath of God abiding on them, shall be beyond all Remedy or Possibility of Change, and shall meet their Ministers without any Hopes of Relief or Remedy, or getting any Good by their Means. And as for the Saints, they will be already perfectly delivered from all their before remaining Corruption, Temptation and Calamities of every Kind, and set forever out of their Reach; and no Deliverance, no happy Alteration will remain to be accomplish'd in the Way of the Use of Means of Grace, under the Administrations of Ministers. It will then be pronounced, *He that is unjust, let him be unjust still; and he that is filthy, let him be filthy still;* and *he that is righteous, let him be righteous still*; and *he that is holy, let him be holy still.*

(2) Then they shall meet together in a State of clear, certain and infallible Light.

Ministers are set as Guides and Teachers, and are represented in Scripture as Lights set up in the Churches; and in the present State meet their People from Time to Time in Order to instruct and enlighten them, to correct their Mistakes, and to be a Voice behind them, when they turn aside to the right Hand or the left, saying, *This is the Way, walk in it;* to evince and confirm the Truth by exhibiting the proper Evidences of it, and to refute Errours and corrupt Opinions, to convince the erroneous and establish the doubting. But when Christ shall come to Judgment, every Errour and false Opinion shall be detected; all Deceit and Delusion shall vanish away before the Light of that Day, as the Darkness of the Night vanishes at the Appearance of the rising Sun; and every Doctrine of the Word of God shall then appear in full Evidence, and none shall remain unconvinced; all shall know the Truth with the greatest Certainty, and there shall be no Mistakes to rectify.

Now Ministers and their People may disagree in their Judgments concerning some Matters of Religion, and may sometimes meet to confer together concerning those Things wherin they differ, and to hear the Reasons that may be offered on one Side and the other; and all may be ineffectual, as to any Conviction of the Truth; they may meet and part again no more agreed than before; and that Side which was in the wrong, may remain so still: Sometimes the Meetings of Ministers with their People, in such a Case of disagreeing Sentiments, are attended with unhappy Debate and Controversy, managed with much Prejudice, and want of Candour; not tending to Light and Conviction, but rather to confirm and increase Darkness, and establish Opposition to the Truth, and Alienation of Affection one from another. But when they shall hereafter meet together, at the Day of Judgment, before the Tribunal of the great Judge, the Mind and Will of Christ will be made known; and there shall no longer be any Debate, or difference of Opinions; the Evidence of the Truth shall appear beyond all Dispute, and all Controversies shall be finally and forever decided.

Now Ministers meet their People in Order to enlighten and awaken the Consciences of Sinners; setting before them the great Evil and Danger of Sin, the Strictness of God's Law, their own Wickedness of Heart and Practice, the great Guilt they are under, the Wrath that abides upon them, and their Impotence, Blindness,

Poverty and helpless and undone Condition: But all is often in vain; they remain still, notwithstanding all their Ministers can say, stupid and unawakened, and their Consciences unconvinced. But it will not be so at their last Meeting at the Day of Judgment; Sinners, when they shall meet their Minister before their great Judge, will not meet him with a stupid Conscience: They will then be fully convinced of the Truth of those Things which they formerly heard from him, concerning the Greatness and terrible Majesty of God, his holiness and hatred of Sin, and his awful Justice in punishing of it, the Strictness of his Law, and the Dreadfulness and Truth of his Threatnings, and their own unspeakable Guilt and Misery: And they shall never more be insensible of these Things: The Eyes of Conscience will now be fully enlighten'd, and never shall be blinded again: The Mouth of Conscience shall now be open'd, and never shall be shut any more.

Now Ministers meet with their People, in publick and private, in Order to enlighten them concerning the State of their Souls; to open and apply the Rules of God's Word to them, in Order to their searching their own Hearts, and discerning the State that they are in: But now Ministers have no infallible discerning the State of the Souls of their People; and the most skilful of them are liable to Mistakes, and often are mistaken in Things of this Nature; nor are the People able certainly to know the State of their Minister, or one another's State; very often those pass among them for Saints, and it may be eminent Saints, that are grand Hypocrites: and on the other Hand, those are sometimes censured, or hardly received into their Charity, that are indeed some of God's Jewels. And nothing is more common than for Men to be mistaken concerning their own State: Many that are abominable to God, and the Children of his Wrath, think highly of themselves, as his precious Saints and dear Children. Yea, there is Reason to think, that often some that are most bold in their Confidence of their safe and happy State, and think themselves not only true Saints, but the most eminent Saints in the Congregation, are in peculiar Manner a Smoke in God's Nose. And thus it undoubtedly often is in those Congregations where the Word of God is most faithfully dispensed; notwithstanding all that Ministers can say in their clearest Explications, and most searching Applications of the Doctrines and Rules of God's Word to the Souls of their Hearers, in their Meetings one with another. But in the Day of Judgment they shall have another Sort of Meeting; then the Secrets of every Heart shall be made manifest, and every Man's State shall be perfectly known. I Cor. iv.5. *Therefore Judge nothing before the Time, until the Lord come; who both will bring to Light the hidden Things of Darkness, and will make manifest the Counsels of the Heart: And then shall every Man have praise of God.* Then none shall be deceived concerning his own State, nor shall be any more in Doubt about it. There shall be an eternal End to all the Self-conceit and vain Hopes of deluded Hypocrites, and all the Doubts and Fears of sincere Christians. And then shall all know the State of one another's Souls: The People shall know whether their Minister has been sincere and faithful, and the Minister shall know the State of every one of their People, and to whom the Word and Ordinances of God have been a Savour of Life unto Life, and to whom a Savour of Death unto Death.

Now in this present State, it often happens that when Ministers and People meet together to debate and manage their ecclesiastical Affairs, especially in a State of Controversy, they are ready to Judge and censure one another, with Regard to each other's Views and Designs, and the Principles and Ends that each is influenced by; and are greatly mistaken in their Judgment, and wrong one another in their Censures: But at that future Meeting, Things will be set in a true and perfect Light, and the Principles and Aims that every one has acted from, shall be certainly known; and there will be an End to all Errours of this Kind, and all unrighteous Censures.

(3) In this World Ministers and their People often meet together to hear of and wait upon an unseen Lord; but at the Day of Judgment, they shall meet in his most immediate and visible Presence.

Ministers, who now often meet their People to preach to 'em the King eternal, immortal and invisible, to convince 'em that there is a God, and declare to 'em what Manner of Being he is, and to convince 'em that he governs, and will judge the World, and that there is a future State of Rewards and Punishments, and to preach to 'em a Christ in Heaven, at the right Hand of God, in an unseen World, shall then meet their People in the most immediate sensible Presence of this great God, Saviour and Judge, appearing in the most plain, visible and open Manner, with great Glory, with all his holy Angels, before them and the whole World. They shall not meet them to hear about an absent Christ, an unseen Lord, and future Judge; but to appear before that Judge, and as being set together in the Presence of that supreme Lord, in his immense Glory and awful Majesty, whom they have heard so often of in their Meetings together on Earth.

(4) The Meeting, at the last Day, of Ministers and the People that have been under their Care, will not be attended, by any one, with a careless heedless Heart.

With such an Heart are their Meetings often attended in this World, by many Persons, having little Regard to Him whom they pretend unitedly to adore in the solemn Duties of his publick Worship, taking little heed to their own Thoughts or Frame of their Minds, not attending to the Business they are engaged in, or considering the End for which they are come together: But the Meeting at that great Day will be very different; there will not be one careless Heart, no sleeping, no wandring of Mind from the great Concern of the Meeting, no Inattentiveness to the Business of the Day, no Regardlessness of the Presence they are in, or of those great Things which they shall hear from Christ at that Meeting, or that they formerly heard from Him and of Him by their Ministers, in their Meetings in a State of Trial, or which they shall now hear their Ministers declaring concerning them before their Judge.

Having observed these Things, concerning the Manner and Circumstances of this future Meeting of Ministers and the People that have been under their Care, before the Tribunal of Christ at the Day of Judgment, I now proceed,

¶*iii.* To observe, to what Purposes they shall then meet.
(1) To give an Account before the great Judge, of their Behaviour one to another, in the Relation they stood in to each other in this World.

Ministers are sent forth by Christ to their People on his Business, are his Servants & Messengers; and when they have finished their Service, they must return to their Master to give him an Account of what they have done, and of the Entertainment they have had in performing their Ministry. Thus we find in *Luke* xiv.16–21. That when the Servant who was sent forth to call the Guests to the great Supper, had done his Errand, and finish'd his appointed Service, he returned to his Master and gave him an Account of what he had done, and of the Entertainment he had received. And when the Master, being angry, sent his Servant to others, he returns again, and gives his Master an Account of his Conduct and Success. So we read in *Heb.* xiii.17. of Ministers or Rulers in the House of God, *That watch for Souls, as those that must give Account.* And we see by the foremention'd *Luke* xiv. that Ministers must give an Account to their Master, not only of their own Behaviour in the Discharge of their Office, but also of their People's Reception of them, and of the Treatment they have met with among them.

And therefore as they will be called to give an Account of both, they shall give an Account at the great Day of Accounts, in the Presence of their People; they and their People being both present before their Judge.

Faithful Ministers will then give an Account with Joy, concerning those who have received them well, and made a good Improvement of their Ministry; and these will be given 'em, at that Day, as their Crown of Rejoycing. And at the same Time they will give an Account of the ill Treatment, of such as have not well received them and their Messages from Christ: they will meet these, not as they used to do in this World, to counsel and warn them, but to bear Witness against them, and as their Judges, and Assessors with Christ, to condemn them. And on the other Hand, the People will at that Day rise up in Judgment against wicked and unfaithful Ministers, who have sought their own temporal Interest, more than the Good of the Souls of their Flock.

(2) At that Time Ministers and the People who have been under their Care, shall meet together before Christ, that he may judge between them, as to any Controversies which have subsisted between them in this World.

So it very often comes to pass in this evil World, that great Differences and Controversies arise between Ministers and the People that are under their pastoral Care. Tho' they are under the greatest Obligations to live in Peace, above Persons in almost any Relation whatever; and altho' Contests and Dissentions between Persons so related, are the most unhappy and terrible in their Consequences, on many Accounts, of any Sort of Contentions; yet how frequent have such Contentions been? Sometimes a People contest with their Ministers about their Doctrine, sometimes about their Administrations and Conduct, and sometimes about their Maintenance; and sometimes such Contests continue a long Time; and sometimes they are decided in this World, according to the prevailing Interest of one Party or the other, rather than by the Word of God, and the Reason of Things; and sometimes such Controversies never have any proper Determination in this World.

But at the Day of Judgment there will be a full, perfect and everlasting Decision of them: The infallible Judge, the infinite Fountain of Light, Truth and Justice, will judge between the contending Parties, and will declare what is the Truth, who is in the Right, and what is agreable to his Mind and Will. And in Order hereto, the Parties must stand together before Him at the last Day; which will be the great Day of finishing and determining all Controversies, rectifying all Mistakes, and abolishing all unrighteous Judgments, Errors and Confusions, which have before subsisted in the World of Mankind.

(3) Ministers and the People that have been under their Care, must meet together at that Time, to receive an eternal Sentence & Retribution from the Judge, in the Presence of each other, according to their Behavior in the Relation they stood in one to another in the present State.

The Judge will not only declare Justice, but he will do Justice between Ministers and their People. He will declare what is right between them, approving him that has been just and faithful, and condemning the unjust; and perfect Truth and Equity shall take Place in the Sentence which He passes, in the Rewards He bestows, and the Punishments which He inflicts. There shall be a glorious Reward to faithful Ministers. To those who have been successful. Dan. xii.3. *And they that be wise shall shine as the Brightness of the Firmament, and they that turn many to Right-*

eousness, as the Stars for ever and ever: And also to those who have been faithful, and yet not successful; Isai. xlix.4. *Then I said, I have laboured in vain, I have spent my Strength for Nought; yet surely my Judgment is with the Lord, and my Reward with my God.* And those who have well receiv'd and entertain'd them shall be gloriously rewarded; Matth. x.40, 41. *He that receiveth you, receiveth me, and he that receiveth me, receiveth him that sent me. He that receiveth a Prophet, in the Name of a Prophet, shall receive a Prophet's Reward; and he that receiveth a righteous Man, in the Name of a righteous Man, shall receive a righteous Man's Reward.* Such People and their faithful Ministers shall be each other's Crown of rejoycing: I Thes. ii.19, 20. *For what is our Hope, or Joy, or Crown of Rejoycing? Are not even ye, in the Presence of our Lord Jesus Christ at his coming? For ye are our Glory and Joy.* And in the Text, *We are your Rejoycing, as ye also are ours, in the Day of the Lord Jesus.* But they that evil intreat Christ's faithful Ministers, especially in that wherein they are faithful, shall be severely punished; Matth. x.14, 15. *And whosoever shall not receive you, nor hear your Words, when ye depart out of that House or City, shake off the Dust of your Feet. Verily, I say unto you, It shall be more tolerable for the Sinners of* Sodom & Gomorrah, *in the Day of Judgment, than for that City.* Deut. xxxiii.8–11. *And of* Levi *he said, Let thy* Thummim *and thy* Urim *be with thy holy one.—They shall teach* Jacob *thy Judgments, and* Israel *thy Law.- - - -Bless, Lord, his Substance, and accept the Work of his Hands: smite through the Loins of them that rise up against him, and of them that hate him, that they rise not again.* On the other Hand, those Ministers who are found to have been unfaithful, shall have a most terrible Punishment. See *Ezek.* xxxiii.6. *Matt.* xxiii.1–33.

Thus Justice shall be administer'd at the great Day to Ministers and their People: And to that End they shall meet together, that they may not only receive Justice to themselves, but see Justice done to the other Party: For this is the End of that great Day, to *reveal,* or declare *the righteous Judgment of God*; Rom. ii.5. Ministers shall have Justice done them, and they shall see Justice done to their People: And the People shall receive Justice themselves from their Judge, and shall see Justice done to their Minister. And so all Things will be adjusted and settled for ever between them; every one being sentenced and recompensed according to his Works; either in receiving and wearing a Crown of eternal Joy and Glory, or in suffering everlasting Shame and Pain.

I come now to the next Thing proposed, *viz.*

¶*iv.* To give some Reasons why we may suppose God has so ordered it, that Ministers, and the People that have been under their Care, shall meet together at the Day of Judgment, in such a Manner and for such Purposes.

There are two Things which I would now observe.

(1) The mutual Concerns of Ministers and their People are of the greatest Importance.

The Scripture declares, that God will bring *every Work* into Judgment, with every secret Thing, whether it be Good, or whether it be Evil. 'Tis fit that all the Concerns, and all the Behaviour of Mankind, both publick and private, should be brought at last before God's Tribunal, and finally determin'd by an infallible Judge: But 'tis especially requisite that it should be thus, as to Affairs of very great Importance.

Now the mutual Concerns of a Christian Minister, and his Church and Congregation, are of the vastest Importance; in many Respects, of much greater Moment than the temporal Concerns of the greatest earthly Monarchs, and their Kingdoms or Empires. It is of vast Consequence how Ministers discharge their Office, and conduct themselves towards their People in the Work of the Ministry, and in Affairs appertaining to it. 'Tis also a Matter of vast Importance how a People receive and entertain a faithful Minister of Christ, and what Improvement they make of his Ministry. These Things have a more immediate and direct Respect to the great and last End for which Man was made, and the eternal Welfare of Mankind, than any of the temporal Concerns of Men, whether publick or private. And therefore 'tis especially fit that these Affairs should be brought into Judgment, and openly determin'd and settled in Truth and Righteousness; and that, to this End, Ministers and their People should meet together before the omniscient and infallible Judge.

(2) The mutual Concerns of Ministers and their People have a special Relation to the main Things appertaining to the Day of Judgment.

They have a special Relation to that great and divine Person who will then appear as Judge. Ministers are his Messengers, sent forth by Him; and in their Office and Administrations among their People, represent his Person, stand in his Stead, as those that are sent to declare his Mind, to do his Work, and to speak & act in his Name: And therefore 'tis especially fit that they should return to Him, to give an Account of their Work and Success. The King is Judge of *all* his Subjects, they are all accountable to Him: But 'tis more especially requisite that the *King's Ministers*, who are especially intrusted with the Administrations of his Kingdom, and that are sent forth on some special Negotiation, should return to Him, to give an Account of themselves, and their Discharge of their Trust, and the Reception they have met with.

Ministers are not only Messengers of the Person who at

the last Day will appear as Judge, but the Errand they are sent upon, and the Affairs they have committed to them as his Ministers, do most immediately concern his Honour, and the Interest of his Kingdom: The Work they are sent upon, is to promote the Designs of his Administration and Government; and therefore their Business with their People has a near Relation to the Day of Judgment; for the great End of that Day is compleatly to settle and establish the Affairs of his Kingdom, to adjust all Things that pertain to it, that every Thing that is opposite to the Interests of his Kingdom may be removed, and that every Thing which contributes to the Compleatness and Glory of it, may be perfected and confirmed, that this great King may receive his due Honour and Glory.

Again, the mutual Concerns of Ministers and their People have a direct Relation to the Concerns of the Day of Judgment, as the Business of Ministers with their People is to promote the eternal Salvation of the Souls of Men, and their Escape from eternal Damnation; and the Day of Judgment is the Day appointed for that End, openly to decide and settle Men's eternal State, to fix others in a State of everlasting Damnation and most perfect Misery. The mutual Concerns of Ministers and People have a most direct Relation to the Day of Judgment, as the very Design of the Work of the Ministry is the People's *Preparation for that Day*: Ministers are sent to warn them of the Approach of that Day, to forewarn them of the dreadful Sentence then to be pronounced on the Wicked, and declare to them the blessed Sentence then to be pronounced on the Righteous, and to use Means with them that they may escape the Wrath which is then to come on the ungodly, and obtain the Reward then to be bestowed on the Saints.

And as the mutual Concerns of Ministers and their People have so near and direct a Relation to that Day, 'tis especially fit that those Concerns should be brought *into that Day,* and there settled and issued; and that in Order to this, Ministers and their People should meet and appear together before the great Judge *at that Day.*

APPLICATION

The Improvement I would make of the Things which have been observed, is to lead the People here present, who have been under my pastoral Care, to some Reflections, and give them some Advice suitable to our present Circumstances; relating to what has been lately done in Order to our being separated, as to the Relation we have heretofore stood in one to another; but expecting to meet each other before the great Tribunal at the Day of Judgment.

The deep and serious Consideration of that our future most

solemn Meeting, is certainly most suitable at such a Time as this; there having so lately been that done, which in all Probability, will (as to the Relation we have heretofore stood in) be followed with an everlasting Separation.

How often have we met together in the House of God, in this Relation? How often have I spoke to you, instructed, counsel'd, warned, directed and fed you, and administred Ordinances among you, as the People which were committed to my Care, and whose precious Souls I had the Charge of? But in all Probability, this never will be again.

The Prophet *Jeremiah,* (Chapt. xxv.3.) puts the People in Mind how long he had laboured among them in the Work of the Ministry; *From the thirteenth Year of* Josiah, *the Son of* Amon, *King of* Judah, *even unto this Day (that is, the three and twentieth Year) the Word of the Lord came unto me, and I have spoken unto you, rising early and speaking.* I am not about to compare myself with the Prophet *Jeremiah*; But in this Respect I can say as he did, that *I have spoken the Word of God to you, unto the three and twentieth Year, rising early and speaking.* It was three and twenty Years, the 15th Day of last *February*, since I have laboured in the Work of the Ministry, in the Relation of a Pastor to this Church and Congregation. And tho' my Strength has been Weakness, having always laboured under great Infirmity of Body, besides my Insufficiency for so great a Charge in other Respects, yet I have not spared my feeble Strength, but have exerted it for the Good of your Souls. I can appeal to you, as the Apostle does to his Hearers, Gal. iv.13. *Ye know how through Infirmity of the Flesh, I preached the Gospel unto you.* I have spent the Prime of my Life and Strength in Labours for your eternal Welfare. You are my Witnesses, that what Strength I have had, I have not neglected in Idleness, nor laid out in persecuting worldly Schemes, and managing temporal Affairs, for the Advancement of my outward Estate, and aggrandizing my Self and Family; but have given myself to the Work of the Ministry, labouring in it Night and Day, rising early and applying myself to this great Business to which Christ appointed me. I have found the Work of the Ministry among you to be a great Work indeed, a Work of exceeding Care, Labour and Difficulty: Many have been the heavy Burdens, that I have borne in it, which my Strength has been very unequal to. GOD called me to bear these Burdens, and I bless his Name, that he has so supported me as to keep me from sinking under them, and that his Power herein has been manifested in my Weakness; so that altho' I have often been troubled on every Side, yet I have not been distressed; perplexed, but not in Despair; cast down, but not destroyed.

But now I have Reason to think, my Work is finish'd which

I had to do as your Minister: You have publickly rejected me, and my Opportunities cease.

How highly therefore does it now become us, to consider of that Time when we must meet one another before the chief Shepherd? When I must give an Account of my Stewardship, of the Service I have done *for,* and the Reception and Treatment I have had *among* the People he sent me to: And you must give an Account of your own Conduct towards me, and the Improvement you have made of these *three & twenty Years* of my Ministry. For then both you and I must appear together, and we both must give an Account, in Order to an infallible righteous and eternal Sentence to be pass'd upon us, by him who will judge us with Respect to all that we have said or done in our Meetings here, all our Conduct one towards another, in the House of God and elsewhere, on Sabbath-Days & on other Days; who will try our Hearts, and manifest our Thoughts, and the Principles and Frames of our Minds, will judge us with Respect to all the Controversies which have subsisted between us, with the strictest Impartiality, and will examine our Treatment of each other in those Controversies: There is nothing covered, that shall not be revealed, nor hid, which shall not be known; all will be examined in the searching penetrating Light of God's Omniscience and Glory, and by him whose Eyes are as a Flame of Fire; and Truth and Right shall be made plainly to appear, being stripped of every Veil; and all Error, Falshood, Unrighteousness and Injury shall be laid open, stripped of every Disguise; every specious Pretence, every Cavil, and all false Reasoning shall vanish in a Moment, as not being able to bear the Light of that Day. And then our Hearts will be turned inside out, and the Secrets of them will be made more plainly to appear than our outward Actions do now. Then it shall appear what the Ends are which we have aim'd at, what have been the governing Principles which we have acted from, & what have been the Dispositions, we have exercised in our ecclesiastical Disputes and Contests. Then it will appear, whether I acted uprightly, and from a truly conscientious careful Regard to my Duty to my great Lord and Master, in some former ecclesiastical Controversies, which have been attended with exceding unhappy Circumstances, and Consequences: It will appear whether there was any just Cause for the Resentment which was manifested on those Occasions. And then our late grand Controversy, concerning the Qualifications necessary for Admision to the Priviledges of Members, in compleat Standing, in the visible Church of Christ, will be examined and judged, in all its Parts and Circumstances, and the whole set forth in a clear certain and perfect Light. Then it will appear whether the Doctrine which I have preach'd and published concerning this Matter be Christ's own Doctrine, whether He won't own it as one of the precious

Truths which have proceeded from his own Mouth, and vindicate and honour as such before the whole Universe. Then it will appear what is meant by *the Man that comes without the Wedding Garment;* for that is the Day spoken of Mat. xxii.13. wherein such an one *shall be bound Hand and Foot, and cast into outer Darkness where shall be weeping and gnashing of Teeth.* And then it will appear whether in declaring this Doctrine, and acting agreable to it, and in my general Conduct in the Affair, I have been influenced from any Regard to my own temporal Interest, or Honour, or Desire to appear wiser than others; or have acted from any sinister secular Views whatsoever; and whether what I have done has not been from a careful, strict and tender Regard to the Will of my Lord and Master, & because I dare not offend Him, being satisfied what his Will was, after a long, diligent, impartial and prayerful Enquiry; Having this constantly in View and Prospect, to engage me to great Solicitude not rashly to determine Truth to be on this Side of the Question where I am now perswaded it is, that such a Determination would not be for my temporal Interest, but every Way against it, bringing a long Series of extream Difficulties, and plunging me into an Abyss of Trouble and Sorrow. And then it will appear whether my People have done their Duty to their Pastor with Respect to this Matter; whether they have shown a right Temper and Spirit on this Occasion; whether they have done me Justice in hearing, attending to, and considering what I had to say in Evidence of what I believed and taught as Part of the Counsel of God; whether I have been treated with that Impartiality, Candour and Regard which the just Judge esteem'd due; and whether, in the many Steps which have been taken, and the many Things that have been said and done in the Course of this Controversy, Righteousness and Charity & Christian Decorum has been maintain'd; or if otherwise, to how great a Degree these Things have been violated. Then every Step of the Conduct of each of us in this Affair, from first to last, and the Spirit we have exercised in all, shall be convinced, and the World shall know; and never shall there be any more Mistake, Misrepresentation or Misapprehension of the Affair to Eternity.

This Controversy is now probably brought to an Issue between you and me as to this World; it has issued in the Event of the Week before last: But it must have another Decision at that great Day, which certainly will come, when you and I shall meet together before the great Judgment Seat: And therefore I leave it to that Time, and shall say no more about it at present.

But I would now proceed to address my self particularly to several Sorts of Persons.

¶*i.* To those who are Professors of Godliness amongst us.

I would now call you to a serious Consideration of that great Day wherein you must meet him who has heretofore been your Pastor, before the Judge, whose Eyes are as a Flame of Fire.

I have endeavoured, according to my best Ability, to search the Word of God, with Regard to the distinguishing Notes of true Piety, those by which Persons might best discover their State, and most surely and clearly judge of themselves. And these Rules and Marks I have from Time to Time applied to you, in the Preaching of the Word, to the utmost of my Skill, and in the most plain and searching Manner that I have been able; in Order to the detecting the deceived Hypocrite, and establishing the Hopes and Comforts of the Sincere. And yet 'tis to be fear'd, that after all that I have done, I now leave some of you in a deceived deluded State; for 'tis not to be supposed that among several Hundred Professors, none are deceived.

Henceforward I am like to have no more Opportunity to take the Care and Charge of your Souls, to examine and search them. But still I intreat you to remember and consider the Rules which I have often laid down to you, during my Ministry, with a solemn Regard to the future Day when you and I must meet together before our Judge; when the Uses of Examination you have have [sic] heard from me must be rehearsed again before you, and those Rules of Trial must be tried, and it will appear whether they have been good or not; and it will also appear whether you have impartially heard them & tried your-selves by them; and the Judge himself who is Infallible will try both you and me: And after this none will be deceived concerning the State of their Souls.

I have often put you in Mind, that whatever your Pretences to Experiences, Discoveries, Comforts and Joys have been; at that Day every one will be judged according to his Works: And then you will find it so.

May you have a Minister of greater Knowledge of the Word of God, and better Acquaintance with Soul Cases, and of greater Skill in applying himself to Souls, whose Discourses may be more searching and convincing; that such of you as have held fast Deceit under my Preaching, may have your Eyes open'd by his; that you may be undeceived before that great Day.

What Means and Helps for Instruction & Self-Examination you may hereafter have is uncertain; but one Thing is certain that the Time is short, your Opportunity for rectifying Mistakes in so important a Concern will soon come to an End. We live in a World of great Changes. There is now a great Change come to pass; you have withdrawn yourselves from my Ministry, under which you have continued for so many Years: But the Time is coming, and will soon come, when you will pass out of Time into Eternity; and so will pass from under all Means of Grace whatsoever.

The greater Part of you who are Professors of Godliness have, (to use the Phrase of the Apostle) *acknowledged me in Part:* You have heretofore acknowledged me to be your spiritual Father, the Instrument of the greatest Good to you that ever is, or can be obtained by any of the Children of Men. Consider of that Day, when you and I shall meet before our Judge, when it shall be examined whether you have had from me the Treatment which is due to spiritual Children, and whether you have treated me as you ought to have treated a spiritual Father. As the Relation of a natural Parent brings great Obligations on Children in the Sight of God; so much more, in many Respects, does the Relation of a spiritual Father bring great Obligations on such, whose Conversion and eternal Salvation they suppose God has made them the Instruments of; I Cor. iv.15. *For tho' you have ten Thousand Instructors in Christ, yet have ye not many Fathers; for in Christ Jesus, I have begotten you through the Gospel.*

¶*ii.* Now I am taking my Leave of this People, I would apply my self to such among them as I leave in a Christless, Graceless Condition; and would call on such seriously to consider of that solemn Day when they and I must meet before the Judge of the World.

My parting with you is in some Respects in a peculiar Manner a melancholly parting; in as much as I leave you in most melancholly Circumstances; because I leave you in the Gall of Bitterness and Bond of Iniquity, having the Wrath of God abiding on you, and remaining under Condemnation to everlasting Misery and Destruction. Seeing I must leave you, it would have been a comfortable and happy Circumstance of our parting, if I had left you in Christ, safe and blessed in that sure Refuge and glorious Rest of the Saints. But it is otherwise, I leave you far off, Aliens & Strangers, wretched Subjects and Captives of Sin & Satan, and Prisoners of vindictive Justice; without Christ, and without God in the World.

Your Consciences bear me Witness, that while I had Opportunity, I have not ceased to warn you and set before you your Danger. I have studied to represent the Misery and Necessity of your Circumstances in the clearest Manner possible. I have tried all Ways that I could think of tending to awaken your Consciences, and make you sensible of the Necessity of your improving your Time, and being speedy in flying from the Wrath to come, and thorough in the Use of Means for your Escape and Safety. I have diligently endeavour'd to find out & use the most powerful Motives to perswade you to take Care for your own Welfare and Salvation. I have not only endeavoured to awaken you that you might be moved with Fear, but I have used my utmost Endeavours to win you: I have fought out acceptable Words, that if possible I might prevail upon you to forsake Sin, and turn to God, and accept of Christ as your Saviour & Lord. I have spent my Strength very much in these Things. But yet, with Regard to you whom I am now speaking to, I have not been successful: But have this Day Reason to complain in those Words, Jer. vi.29. *The Bellows are burnt, the Lead is consumed of the Fire, the Founder melteth in vain, for the Wicked are not plucked away.* 'Tis to be feared that all my Labours as to many of you have served to no other Purpose but to harden you; and that the Word which I have preach'd, instead of being a Savour of Life unto Life, has been a Savour of Death unto Death. Tho' I shall not have any Account to give for the future, of such as have openly and resolutely renounced my Ministry as of a Betrustment committed to me: Yet remember you must give Account for your selves, of your Care of your own Souls, and your Improvement of all Means past and future, through your whole Lives. God only knows what will become of your poor perishing Souls, what Means you may hereafter enjoy, or what Disadvantages & Temptations you may be under. May God in Mercy grant, that however all past Means have been unsuccessful, you may have future Means which may have a new Effect; and that the Word of God, as it shall be hereafter dispensed to you, may prove as the Fire and the Hammer that breaketh the Rock in Pieces. However, let me now at Parting exhort and beseech you not wholly to forget the Warning you have had while under my Ministry. When you and I shall meet at the Day of Judgment, then you will remember 'em: The Sight of me your former Minister, on that Occasion, will soon revive 'em in your Memory; and that in a very affecting Manner. O don't let that be the first Time that they are so revived.

You and I are now parting one from another as to this World; let us labour that we mayn't be parted after our Meeting at the last Day. If I have been your faithful Pastor (which will that Day appear, whither I have or no) then I shall be acquitted, and shall ascend with Christ. O do your Part, that in such a Case, it may not be so, that you should be forced eternally to part from me, and all that have been faithful in Christ Jesus. This is a sorrowful Parting that now is between you and me; but that would be a more sorrowful Parting to you than this. This you may perhaps bear without being much affected with it, if you are not glad of it; but such a Parting in that Day will most deeply, sensibly and dreadfully affect you.

¶*iii.* I would address my self to those who are under some Awakenings.

Blessed be God, that there are some such, and that (altho' I have Reason to fear I leave Multitudes in this large Congregation in a Christless State) yet I don't leave 'em all in total Stupidity and Carelessness about their Souls. Some of you, that I have Reason to hope are under some Awakenings, have acquainted me with your Circumstances; which has a Tendency to cause me, now I am leaving you, to take my Leave of you with peculiar Concern for you. What will be the Issue of your present Exercise of Mind I know not: But it will be known at that Day, when you and I shall meet before the Judgment Seat of Christ. Therefore now be much in Consideration of that Day.

Now I am parting with this Flock, I would once more press upon you the Counsels I have heretofore given, to take heed of being slightly in so great a Concern, to be thorough and in good earnest in the Affair, and to beware of Backsliding, to hold on and hold out to the End. And cry mightily to God that these great Changes that pass over this Church and Congregation don't prove your Overthrow. There is great Temptation in them; and the Devil will undoubtedly seek to make his Advantage of them, if possible to cause your present Convictions and Endeavours to be abortive. You had need to double your Diligence, and watch and pray least you be overcome by temptation.

Whoever may hereafter stand related to you as your spiritual Guide, my Desire and Prayer is, that the great Shepherd of the Sheep would have a special Respect to you, and be your Guide (for there is none teacheth like him) and that he who is the infinite Fountain of Light, would *open your Eyes, and turn you from Darkness unto Light, and from the Power of Satan unto God; that you may receive Forgiveness of Sins, and Inheritance among them that are sanctified, through Faith that is in Christ;* that so, in that great Day, when I shall meet you again before your Judge and mine, we may meet in joyful and glorious Circumstances, never to be separated any more.

¶*iv.* I would apply my self to the young People of the Congregation.

Since I have been settled in the Work of the Ministry in this Place, I have ever had a peculiar Concern for the Souls of the young People, and a Desire that Religion might flourish among them; and have especially exerted my self in Order to it; because I knew the special Opportunity they had beyond others, and that ordinarily those whom God intended Mercy for were brought to fear and love him in their Youth. And it has ever appear'd to me a peculiarly amiable Thing to see young People walking in the Ways of Vertue and Christian Piety, having their Hearts purified & sweeten'd with a Principle of divine Love. And it has appeared a Thing exceeding beautiful, and what would be much to the Adorning and Happiness of the Town if the young People could be perswaded, when they meet together, to converse as Christians, & as the Children of God; avoiding Impurity, Levity & Extravagance; keeping strictly to Rules of Vertue, and conversing together of the Things of God and Christ and Heaven. This is what I have longed for: And it has been exceeding grevious to me when I have heard of Vice, Vanity, and Disorder among our Youth. And so far as I know my Heart, it was from hence that I formerly led this Church to some Measures, for the suppressing Vice among our young People, which gave so great Offence, and by which I became so obnoxious. I have sought the Good and not the Hurt of our young People. I have desired their truest Honour and Happiness, and not their Reproach; knowing that true Vertue and Religion tended, not only to the Glory and Felicity of young People in another World, but their greatest Peace and Prosperity, and highest Dignity and Honour in this World, and above all Things to sweeten and render pleasant & delightful even the Days of Youth.

But whether I have loved you and sought your Good more or less, yet God in his Providence, now calling me to part with you, committing your Souls to Him who once committed the pastoral Care of them to me, nothing remains, but only (as I am now taking my Leave of you) earnestly to beseech you, from Love to your selves, if you have none to me, not to despise and forget the Warnings & Counsels I have so often given you; remembring the Day when you and I must meet again before the great Judge of Quick & Dead; when it will appear whether the Things I have taught you were true, whether the Counsels I have given you were good, and whether I truly sought your Good, and whether you have well improved my Endeavours.

I have, from Time to Time, earnestly warned you against Frolicking (as it is called) and some other Liberties commonly taken by young People in the Land. And whatever some may say in Justification of such Liberties and Customs, and may laugh at Warnings against them, I now leave you my parting Testimony against such Things; not doubting but God will approve and confirm it in that Day when we shall meet before Him.

¶v. I would apply my self to the Children of the Congregation, the Lambs of this Flock, who have been so long under my Care.

I have just now said that I have had a peculiar Concern for the young People: and in so saying, I did not intend to exclude you. You are in Youth, and in the most early Youth: And therefore I have been sensible, that if those that were Young had a precious Opportunity for their Souls good, you who are very Young had in many Respects a peculiarly precious Opportunity. And accordingly I have not neglected you: I have endeavoured to do the Part of a faithful Shepherd, in feeding the Lambs as well as the Sheep. Christ did once commit the Care of your Souls to me as your Minister;

and you know, dear Children, how I have instructed you, and warned you from Time to Time: You know how I have often called you together for that End: and some of you, sometimes, have seem'd to be affected with what I have said to you. But I am afraid it has had no saving Effect as to many of you; but that you remain still in an unconverted Condition, without any real saving Work wrought in your Souls, convincing you thoro'ly of your Sin & Misery, causing you to see the great Evil of Sin, and to mourn for it, and hate it above all Things; and giving you a Sense of the Excellency of the Lord Jesus Christ, bringing you with all your Hearts to cleave to Him as your Saviour; weaning your Hearts from the World; and causing you to love God above all, and to delight in Holiness more than in all the pleasant Things of this Earth: And so that I now leave you in a miserable Condition, having no Interest in Christ, and so under the awful Displeasure and Anger of God, and in danger of going down to the Pit of eternal Misery.

But now I must bid you Farewell: I must leave you in the Hands of God: I can do no more for you than to pray for you. Only I desire you not to forget, but often think of the Counsels & Warnings I have given you, and the Endeavours I have used, that your Souls might be saved from everlasting Destruction.

Dear Children, I leave you in an evil World, that is full of Snares & Temptations. God only knows what will become of you. This the Scripture has told us, that there are but few saved: and we have abundant Confirmation of it from what we see. This we see, that Children die as well as others: Multitudes die before they grow up; and of those that grow up, comparatively few ever give good Evidence of saving Conversion to God. I pray God to pity you, and take Care of you, and provide for you the best Means for the good of your Souls; and that God himself would undertake for you, to be your heavenly Father, and the mighty Redeemer of your immortal Souls. Don't neglect to pray for your selves: Take heed you ben't of the Number of those, who cast off Fear, and restrain Prayer before God. Constantly pray to God in Secret; and often remember that great Day when you must appear before the Judgment-Seat of Christ, and meet your Minister there, who has so often counsel'd and warned you.

I conclude with a few Words of Advice to all in general, in some Particulars, which are of great Importance in Order to the future Welfare and Prosperity of this Church and Congregation.

(1) One Thing that greatly concerns you, as you would be an happy People, is the maintaining of *Family Order*.

We have had great Disputes how the Church ought to be regulated; and indeed the Subject of these Disputes was of great Importance: But the due Regulation of your Families is of no less, and in some Respects, of much greater Importance. Every Christian Family ought to be as it were a little Church, consecrated to Christ, and wholly influenced & governed by his Rules. And Family Education and Order are some of the chief of the **Means of Grace**. If these fail, all other Means are like to prove ineffectual. If these are duly maintain'd, all the Means of Grace will be like to prosper and be successful.

Let me now therefore, once more, before I finally cease to speak to this Congregation, repeat and earnesty [sic] press the Counsel, which I have often urged on Heads of Families here, while I was their Pastor, to great Painfulness, in teaching, warning and directing their Chilldren; bringing them up in the Nurture & Admonition of the Lord; beginning early, where there is yet Opportunity; and maintaining a constant Diligence in Labours of this Kind: Remembring that, as you would not have all your Instructions and Counsels ineffectual, there must be Government as well as Instructions, which must be maintain'd with an even Hand, and steady Resolution; as a Guard to the Religion and Morals of the Family, and the Support of its good Order. Take heed that it ben't with any of you as it was with *Eli* of Old, who reproved his Children, but restrained them not; and that by this Means you don't bring the like Curse on your Families, as he did on his.

And let Children obey their Parents, and yield to their Instructions, and submit to their Orders, as they would inherit a Blessing and not a Curse. For we have Reason to think from many Things in the Word of God, that nothing has a greater Tendency to bring a Curse on Persons, in this World, and on all their temporal Concerns, than an undutiful, unsubmissive, disorderly Behaviour in Children towards their Parents.

(2) As you would seek the future Prosperity of this Society, 'tis of vast Importance that you should avoid *Contention*.

A contentious People will be a miserable People. The Contentions which have been among you, since I first became your Pastor, have been one of the greatest Burdens I have laboured under in the Course of my Ministry: Not only the Contentions you have had with me, but those which you have had one with another, about your Lands, and other Concerns. Because I knew that Contention, Heat of Spirit, Evil-speaking, & Things of the like Nature, were directly contrary to the Spirit of Christianity, and did in a peculiar Manner tend to drive away God's Spirit from a People, and to render all Means of Grace ineffectual, as well as to destroy a People's outward Comfort and Welfare.

Let me therefore earnestly exhort you, as you would seek your own future Good, hereafter to watch against a contentious Spirit. *If you would see good Days, seek Peace and ensue it*. I Pet.

iii.10, 11. Let the Contentions which has lately been about the Terms of Christian Communion, as it has been the greatest of your Contention, so be the last of them. I would, now I am preaching my Farewel-Sermon, say to you as the Apostle to the *Corinthians,* 2 Cor. xiii.11. *Finally, Brethren, Farewell. Be perfect: Be of one Mind: Live in Peace; and the God of Love & Peace shall be with you.*

And here I would particularly advise those that have adhered to me in the late Controversy, to watch over their Spirits, and avoid all Bitterness towards others. Your Temptations are in some Respects the greatest; because what has been lately done, is grievous to you. But however wrong you may think others have done, maintain, with great Diligence and Watchfulness, a Christian Meekness and Sedateness of Spirit: and labour, in this Respect, to excell others who are of the contrary Part: And this will be the best Victory: For *he that rules his Spirit, is better than he that takes a City.* Therefore let nothing be done through Strife or Vain-glory: Indulge no revengeful Spirit in any Wise; but watch and pray against it: and by all Means in your Power, seek the Prosperity of this Town: And never think you behave your selves as becomes Christians, but when you sincerely, sensibly and fervently love all Men of whatever Party or Opinion, & whether friendly or unkind, just or injurious, to you, or your Friends, or to the Cause and Kingdom of Christ.

(3) Another Thing that vastly concerns the future Prosperity of the Town, is that you should watch against the Encroachments of Error; and particularly *Arminianism,* and Doctrines of like Tendency.

You were many of you, as I well remember, much alarmed with the Apprehension of the Danger of the prevailing of these corrupt Principles, near sixteen Years ago. But the Danger then was small in Comparison of what appears now: These Doctrines at this Day are much more prevalent than they were then: The Progress they have made in the Land, within this seven Years, seems to have been vastly greater than at any Time in the like Space before: And they are still prevailing and creeping into almost all Parts of the Land, threatening the utter Ruin of the Credit of those Doctrines which are the peculiar Glory of the Gospel, and the Interests of vital Piety. And I have of late perceived some Things among your selves, that shew that you are far from being out of Danger, but on the contrary remarkably exposed. The elder People may perhaps think themselves sufficiently fortified against Infection: But 'tis fit that all should beware of Self-confidence and carnal Security, & should remember those needful Warnings of sacred Writ, *Be not high-minded but fear,* and *let him that stands, take heed least he fall.* But let the Case of the elder People be as it will, the rising Generation are doubtless greatly exposed. These Principles are exceeding taking with corrupt Nature, and are what young People, at least such as have not their Hearts establish'd with Grace, are easily led away with.

And if these Principles should greatly prevail in this Town, as they very lately have done in another large Town I could name, formerly greatly noted for Religion, and so for a long Time, it will threaten the spiritual and eternal Ruin of this People, in the present and future Generations. Therefore you have need of the greatest and most diligent Care and Watchfulness with Respect to this Matter.

(4) Another Thing which I would advise to, that you may hereafter be a prosperous People, is that you would give your selves much to Prayer.

God is the Fountain of all Blessing and Prosperity, and he will be sought to for his Blessing. I would therefore advise you not only to be constant in Secret and Family Prayer, and in the publick Worship of God in his House, but also often to assemble your selves in private praying Societies. I would advise all such as are grieved for the Afflictions of *Joseph,* & sensibly affected with the Calamities of this Town, of whatever Opinion they be with Relation to the Subject of our late Controversy, often to meet together for Prayer, and to cry to God for his Mercy to themselves, and Mercy to this Town, and Mercy to *Zion* and the People of God in general through the World.

(5) The last Article of Advice I would give (which doubtless does greatly concern your Prosperity) is, that you would take great Care with Regard to the Settlement of a Minister, to see to it who, or what Manner of Person he is that you settle; and particularly in these two Respects.

1. That he be a Man of thoroughly sound Principles, in the Scheme of Doctrine which he maintains.

This you will stand in the greatest Need of, especially as such a Day of Corruption as this is. And in Order to obtain such a one, you had need to exercise extraordinary Care and Prudence—I know the Danger—I know the Manner of many young Gentlemen of Corrupt Principles, their Ways of concealing themselves, the fair specious Disguises they are wont to put on, by which they deceive others, to maintain their own Credit, and get themselves into others Confidence & Improvement, and secure and establish their own Interest, 'till they see a convenient Opportunity to begin more openly to broach and propagate their corrupt Tenets.

2. Labour to obtain a Man who has an establish'd Character, as a Person of serious Religion, & fervent Piety.

'Tis of vast Importance that those who are settled in this Work should be Men of true Piety, at all Times, and in all Places;

but more especially at some Times, and in some Towns & Churches. And *this present Time*, which is a Time wherein Religion is in Danger, by so many Corruptions in Doctrine and Practice, is in a peculiar Manner a Day wherein such Ministers are necessary. Nothing else but sincere Piety of Heart, is at all to be depended on, at such a Time as this, as a Security to a young Man, just coming into the World, from the prevailing Infection, or thoroughly to engage him in proper and sucessful Endeavours to withstand and oppose the Torrent of Error, and Prejudice, against the high mysterious evangelical Doctrines of the Religion of Jesus Christ, and their genuine Effects in true experimental Religion. And *this Place* is a Place that does peculiarly need such a Minister, for Reasons obvious to all.

If you should happen to settle a Minister, who knows nothing truly of Christ, and the Way of Salvation by him, nothing experimentally of the Nature of vital Religion; alas, how will you be exposed as Sheep without a Shepherd! Here is need of One in this Place, who shall be eminently fit to stand in the Gap, and make up the Hedge, and who shall be as the Chariots of *Israel,* and the Horsemen thereof. You need One that shall stand as a Champion in the Cause of Truth and the Power of Godliness.

I Having briefly mentioned these important Articles of Advice, nothing remains; But that I now take my Leave of you, and bid you all, *farewell;* wishing and praying for your best Prosperity. I would now commend your immortal Souls to Him, who formerly committed them to me, expecting the Day, when I must meet you again before Him, who is the Judge of Quick and Dead. I desire that I may never forget this People, who have been so long my special Charge, and that I may never cease fervently to pray for your Prosperity. May God bless you with a faithful Pastor, one that is well acquainted with his Mind & Will, thoro'ly warning Sinners, wisely & skilfully searching Professors, & conducting you in the Way to eternal Blessedness. May you have truly a burning & shining Light set up in this Candlestick; and may you, not only for a Season, but during his whole Life, and that a long Life, be willing to rejoyce in his Light.

And let me be remember'd in the Prayers of all God's People that are of a calm Spirit, & are peaceable & faithful in *Israel,* of whatever Opinion they may be, with Respect to Terms of Church Communion.

And let us all remember, and never forget our future solemn Meeting, on that great Day of the Lord; the Day of infallible Decision, and of the everlasting & unalterable Sentence.

AMEN

The Danger of an Unconverted Ministry

Gilbert Tennent

Gilbert Tennent was born on February 5, 1703, in County Armagh, Ireland. He was the eldest of four sons, all ministers, of the Reverend William Tennent, founder of the Log College at Neshaminy, Pennsylvania. Fourteen years old when his family came to America, Gilbert Tennent never attended a regular school or college, but was educated entirely by his father. He received an honorary Master of Arts degree from Yale University at age twenty-two.

Tennent was licensed as a minister in 1725, and was formally accepted into the Presbyterian Church in New Brunswick, New Jersey. With the encouragement of George Whitefield, he successfully carried on Whitefield's work in a preaching tour of New England and became recognized as one of the leading preachers of the Great Awakening.

To promote revivalism Tennent became pastor of the Second Presbyterian Church in Philadelphia in 1743. He was elected trustee of Princeton College in 1747. He held this post until his death July 23, 1764. He is buried in his church in Philadelphia. "The Danger of an Unconverted Ministry" was preached at Nottingham, Pennsylvania, March 8, 1739 (1740?). The text is from the edition printed by Benjamin Franklin, Philadelphia, 1740.

MARK VI. 34. *And Jesus, when he came out, saw much People, and was moved with Compassion towards them, because they were as Sheep not having a Shepherd.*

AS a faithful Ministry is a great Ornament, Blessing, and Comfort, to the Church of GOD; even the Feet of such Messengers are beautiful: So on the contrary, and ungodly Ministry is a great Curse and Judgment: These Caterpillars labour to devour every green Thing.

THERE is nothing that may more justly call forth our saddest Sorrows, and make all our Powers and Passions mourn, in the most doleful Accents, the most incessant, insatiable, and deploring Agonies; than the melancholy Case of such, who have no faithful Ministry! This Truth is set before our Minds in a strong Light, in the Words that I have chosen now to insist upon; in which we have an Account of our LORD's Grief, with the Causes of it.

WE are informed, That our dear Redeemer was moved with Compassion towards them. The Original Word signifies the strongest and most vehement Pity, issuing from the innermost Bowels.

BUT what was the Cause of this great and compassionate Commotion in the Heart of Christ? It was because he saw much People as Sheep having no Shepherd. Why, had the People then no Teachers? O yes! they had Heaps of Pharisee-Teachers, that came out, no doubt after they had been at the Feet of *Gamaliel* the usual Time, and according to the Acts, Canons, and Traditions of the Jewish Church. But notwithstanding of the great Crowds of these Orthodox, Letter-learned and regular Pharisees, our Lord laments the unhappy Case of that great Number of People, who, in the Days of his Flesh, had no better Guides: Because that those were as good as none (in many Respects) in our Saviour's Judgment. For all them, the People were as Sheep without a Shepherd.

FROM the Words of our Text, the following Proposition offers itself to our Consideration, *viz.*

That the Case of such is much to be pitied, who have no other, but Pharisee-Shepherds, or uncoverted Teachers.

IN discoursing upon this Subject, I would

¶i. *Enquire into the Characters of the Old Pharisee-Teachers.*
¶ii. *Shew, why the Case of such People, who have no better, should be pitied.* And
¶iii. *Shew, how Pity should be expressed upon this mournful Occasion!* And

¶FIRST I am to enquire into the *Characters of the Old Pharisee-Teachers.* Now, I think the most notorious Branches of their Character, were these, viz. *Pride, Policy, Malice, Ignorance, Covetousness,* and *Bigotry to human Inventions in religious Matters.*

THE old Pharisees were very proud and conceity; they loved the uppermost Seats in the Synagogues, and to be called Rabbi, Rabbi; they were masterly and positive in their Assertions, as if forsooth Knowledge must die with them; they look'd upon others that differed from them, and the common People, with an Air of Disdain; and especially any who had a Respect for JESUS and his Doctrine, and disliked them; they judged such accursed.

THE old Pharisee-Shepherds were as crafty as Foxes; they tried by all means to ensnare our Lord, by their captious Questions, and to expose him to the Displeasure of the State; while in the mean Time, by sly and sneaking Methods, they tried to secure for themselves the Favour of the Grandees, and the People's Applause; and this they obtained to their Satisfaction. *Job.* 7.48.

BUT while they exerted the Craft of Foxes, they did not forget to breath forth the Cruelty of Wolves, in a malicious Aspersing the Person of Christ, and in a violent Opposing of the Truths, People, and Power of his Religion. Yea, the most stern and strict of them, were the Ring-leaders of the Party: Witness *Saul's* Journey to *Damascus,* with Letters from the Chief Priest, to bring bound to *Jerusalem,* all that he could find of that Way. It's true the Pharisees did not proceed to violent Measures with our Savior and his Disciples just at first; but that was not owing to their good Nature, but their Policy; for they feared the People. They must keep the People in their Interests: Ay, that was the main Chance, the Compass that directed all their Proceedings; and therefore such sly cautious Methods must be pursued as might consist herewith. They wanted to root vital Religion out of the World; but they found it beyond their Thumb.

ALTHOUGH some of the old Pharisee-Shepherds had a very fair and strict Out-side; yet were they ignorant of the New Birth: Witness Rabbi *Nicodemus,* who talk'd like a Fool about it. Hear how our LORD cursed those plaister'd Hypocrites, Mat. 23.27, 28. *Wo unto you, Scribes and Pharisees, Hypocrites; for ye are like whited Sepulchres, which indeed appear beautiful outward, but are within full of dead Bones, and of all Uncleanness. Even so ye also appear righteous unto Men, but within ye are full of Hypocrisie and Iniquity.* Ay, if they had but a little of the Learning then in Fashion, and a fair Outside, they were presently put into the Priests Office, though they had no Experience of the New Birth. O sad!

THE old Pharisees, for all their long prayers and other pious Pretences, had their Eyes, with *Judas,* fixed upon the Bag. Why, they came into the Priests Office for a Piece of Bread; they took it up as a Trade, and therefore endeavoured to make the best Market of it; they could: O Shame!

IT may be further observ'd, That the Pharisee-Teachers in Christ's Time, were great Bigots to small Matters in Religion. *Mat. 23.23. Wo unto you, Scribes and Pharisees, Hypocrites; for ye pay Tyth of Mint, and Anise, and Cumin, and have omitted the weightier Matters of the Law, Judgment, Mercy and Faith.* The Pharisees were fired with a Party-Zeal; they compassed Sea and Land to make a Proselyte; and yet when he was made, they made him twofold more the Child of Hell than themselves. They were also bigotted to Human Inventions in Religious Matters: *Paul* himself, while he was a natural Man, was wonderful zealous for the Traditions of the Fathers: Ay, those poor blind Guides, as our LORD testifies, strained at a Gnat, and swallowed a Camel.

AND what a mighty Respect had they for the Sabbath Day forsooth? in so much that Christ and his Disciples must be charged with the Breach thereof, for doing Works of Mercy and Necessity. Ah the Rottenness of those Hypocrites! It was not so much Respect to the Sabbath, as Malice against Christ; that was the Occasion of the Charge; they wanted some plausible Pretence to offer against him, in order to blacken his Character.

AND what a great Love had they in Pretence to those pious Prophets, who were dead before they were born? while in the mean Time they were persecuting the Prince of Prophets! Hear how the King of the Church speaks to them, upon this Head: *Matth.* 23.29– 33. *Wo unto you, Scribes and Pharisees, Hypocrites; because ye build the Tombs of the Prophets, and garnish the Sepulchres of the Righteous; and say, If we had been in the Days of our Father, we would not have been Partakers with them in the Blood of the Prophets. Ye Serpents, ye Generation of Vipers, how can ye escape the Damnation of Hell?* The

¶SECOND GENERAL HEAD of Discourse, is to shew, *Why such People, who have no better than the old Pharisee-Teachers, are to be pitied?* And

1] Natural Men have no Call of GOD to the Ministerial Work, under the Gospel-Dispensation.

Isn't it a principal Part of the ordinary Call of GOD to the Ministerial Work, to aim at the Glory of GOD, and, in Subordination thereto, the Good of Souls, as their chief Marks in their Undertaking that Work? And can any natural Man on Earth do this? No! no! Every Skin of them has an evil Eye; for no Cause can produce Effects above its own Power. Are not wicked Men forbid to meddle in Things sacred? *Ps.* 50.16. *But unto the Wicked,* GOD *saith, What hast thou to do to declare my Statutes, or that thou shouldst take my Covenant in thy Mouth?* Now, are not all uncoverted Men wicked Men? does not the Lord JESUS inform us, *John* 10.1. That *he who entreth not by the Door into the Sheep-fold, but climbeth up some other Way, the same is a Thief and a Robber?* In the 9th v. Christ tells us, That *He is the Door;* and that *if any Man enter in by him, he shall be saved, by him,* i. e. By Faith in him, says *Henry.* Hence we read of a *Door of Faith,* being opened to the *Gentiles.* Acts 14.27. It confirms this Gloss, that Salvation is annexed to the Entrance before-mentioned. Remarkable is that Saying of our Saviour, *Matth.* 4.19. *Follow me, and I will make you Fishers of Men.* See, our LORD will not make Men Ministers, 'til they follow him. Men that do not follow Christ, may fish faithfully for a good Name, and for worldly Pelf; but not for the Conversion of Sinners to God. Is it reasonable to suppose, that they will be earnestly concerned for others Salvation, when they slight their own? Our LORD reprov'd Nicodemus for taking upon him the Office of instructing others, while he himself was a Stranger to the New Birth, *Job.* 3.10. *Art thou a Master of Israel, and knowest not these Things?* The Apostle *Paul* (in 1 *Tim.* 1.12.) thanks GOD for counting him faithful, and putting him into the Ministry; which plainly supposes, That GOD Almighty does not send Pharisees and natural Men into the Ministry: For how can these Men be faithful, that have no Faith?

It's true, Men may put them into the Ministry, through Unfaithfulness, or Mistake; or Credit and Money may draw them, and the Devil may drive them into it, knowing by long Experience, of what special Service they may be to his Kingdom in that Office: But GOD sends not such hypocritical Varlets. Hence *Timothy* was directed by the Apostle *Paul,* to commit the ministerial Work to faithful Men. 2 *Tim.* 2.2. And do not these Qualifications, necessary for Church-Officers, specified 1 *Tim.* 3.7, 8, 9, 11. & *Tit.* 1.7, 8. plainly suppose converting Grace? How else can they hold the Mystery of Faith in a pure Conscience, and be faithful in all Things? How else can they be Lovers of Good, sober, just, holy, temperate?

2] The Ministry of natural Men is uncomfortable to gracious Souls.

The Enmity that is put between the Seed of the Woman and the Seed of the Serpent, will now and then be creating Jarrs: And no wonder; for as it was of old, so it is now, *He that was born after the Flesh, persecuted him that was born after the Spirit.* This Enmity is not one Grain less, in unconverted Ministers, than in others; tho' possibly it may be better polished with Wit and Rhetorick, and gilded with the specious Names of Zeal, Fidelity, Peace, good Order, and Unity.

Natural Men, not having true Love to Christ and the Souls of their Fellow-Creatures, hence their Discourses are cold and sapless, and as it were freeze between their Lips! And not being sent of GOD, they want that divine Authority, with which the faithful Ambassadors of Christ are clothed, who herein resemble their blessed Master, of whom it is said, That *He taught as one having Authority, and not as the Scribes.* Matth. 7.29.

And Pharisee-Teachers, having no Experience of a special Work of the Holy Ghost, upon their own Souls, are therefore neither inclined to, nor fitted for Discoursing, frequently, clearly, and pathetically, upon such important Subjects. The Application of their Discourses, is either short, or indistinct and general. They difference not the precious from the vile, and divide not to every Man his Portion, according to the Apostolical Direction to *Timothy.* No! they carelessly offer a common Mess to their People, and leave it to them, to divide it among themselves, as they see fit. This is indeed their general Practice, which is bad enough: But sometimes they do worse, by misapplying the Word, through Ignorance, or Anger. They often strengthen the Hands of the Wicked, by promising him Life. They comfort People, before they convince them; sow before they plow; and are busy in raising a Fabrick, before they lay a Foundation. These foolish Builders do but strengthen Men's carnal Security, by their soft, selfish, cowardly Discourses. They have not the Courage, or Honesty, to thrust the Nail of Terror into sleeping Souls; nay, sometimes they strive with all their Might, to fasten Terror into the Hearts of the Righteous, and so to make those sad, whom GOD would not have made sad! And this happens, when pious People begin to suspect their Hypocrisie, for which they have good Reason. I may add, That inasmuch as Pharisee-Teachers seek after Righteousness as it were by the Works of the Law themselves, they therefore do not distinguish as they ought, between *Law* and *Gospel,* in their Discourses to others. They keep Driving, Driving, to Duty, Duty, under this Notion, That it will recommend natural Men to the Favour of GOD, or entitle them to the Promises of Grace and Salvation: And thus those blind Guides fix a deluded World upon the false Foundation of their own Righteousness, and so exclude them from the dear Redeemer. All the Doings of unconverted Men, not proceeding from the Principles of Faith, Love, and a new Nature, nor being directed to the divine Glory as their highest End, but flowing from, and tending to Self, as their Principle and End; are doubtless damnably wicked in their Manner of Performance, and do deserve the Wrath and Curse of a Sin-avenging GOD; neither can any other Encouragement be justly given them, but this, That in the Way of Duty, there is a Peradventure or Probability of obtaining Mercy.

And natural Men, wanting the Experience of those spiritual Difficulties, which pious Souls are exposed to, in this Vale of Tears; they know not how to speak a Word to the Weary in Season.

Their Prayers are also cold; little Child-like Love to God, or Pity to poor perishing Souls, runs thro' their Veins.

Their Conversation hath nothing of the Savour of Christ, neither is it perfumed with the Spices of Heaven. They seem to make as little Distinction in their Practice, as Preaching. They love those Unbelievers, that are kind to them, better than many Christians, and chuse them for Companions: contrary to *Ps.* 15.4 *Ps.* 119.115 & *Gal.* 6.10. Poor Christians are stunted and starv'd, who are put to feed on such bare Pastures, and such dry Nurses; as the Rev. Mr. *Hildersham* justly calls them. It's only when the wise Virgins sleep, that they can bear with those dead Dogs, that can't bark; but when the LORD revives his People, they can't but abhor them! O! it is ready to break their very Hearts, with Grief, to see, how luke-warm those Pharisee-Teachers are in their publick Discourses, while Sinners are sinking into Damnation, in Multitudes! But

3] The Ministry of natural Men, is for the most part unprofitable; which is confirmed by a threefold Evidence, *viz.* of Scripture, Reason, and Experience. Such as the LORD sends not, he himself assures us, shall not profit the People at all. *Jer.* 23.32. Mr. *Pool* justly glosseth upon this Passage of sacred Scripture, thus,

viz. 'That none can expect God's Blessing upon their Ministry,
that are not called and sent of GOD into the Ministry. And right
Reason will inform us, how unfit Instruments they are to negoti-
ate that Work they pretend to. Is a blind Man fit to be a Guide
in a very dangerous Way? Is a dead Man fit to bring others to
Life? a mad Man fit to give Counsel in a Matter of Life and
Death? Is a possessed Man fit to cast out Devils? a Rebel, an
Enemy to GOD, fit to be sent on an Embassy of Peace, to bring
Rebels into a State of Friendship with GOD? a Captive bound in
the massy Chains of Darkness and Guilt, a proper Person, to
set others at Liberty? a Leper, or one that has Plague-sores
upon him, fit to be a good Physician? Is an ignorant Rustick,
that has never been at Sea in his Life, fit to be a Pilot, to keep
Vessels from being dashed to Pieces upon Rocks and Sand-
banks? Isn't an unconverted Minister like a Man who would
learn others to swim, before he has learn'd it himself, and so
is drowned in the Act, and dies like a Fool?'

I may add, that sad Experience verifies what has been now
observed, concerning the Unprofitableness of the Ministry of
unconverted Men. Look into the Congregations of unconverted
Ministers, and see what a sad Security reigns there; not a Soul
convinced that can be heard of, for many Years together; and
yet the Ministers are easy; for they say they do their Duty! Ay, a
small Matter will satisfy us, in the Want of that, which we have no
great Desire after. But when Persons have their Eyes opened, and
their Hearts set upon the Work of God; they are not so soon satisfied with their Doings, and with Want of Success for a Time. O!
they mourn with *Micah*, that they are as those that gather the
Summer-Fruits, as the Grape-gleaning of the Vintage. Mr. *Baxter*
justly observes, 'That those who speak about their Doings in the
aforesaid Manner, are like to do little Good to the Church of God.'
'But many Ministers (as Mr. *Bracel* observes) think the Gospel
flourishes among when the People are in Peace, and many come
to hear the Word, and to the Sacrament.' If with the other they get
their Salaries well paid; O then it is fine Times indeed! in their
Opinion. O sad! And they are full of Hopes, that they do good,
tho' they know nothing about it. But what Comfort can a con-
sciencious Man, who travels in Birth, that Christ may be formed in
his Hearers Hearts, take from what he knows not? Will a hungry
Stomach be satisfied with Dreams about Meat? I believe not; tho'
I confess a full one may.

What if some Instances could be shewn, of unconverted Ministers being Instrumental, in convincing Persons of their lost State?
The Thing is very rare, and extraordinary. And for what I know,
as many Instances may be given, of Satan's convincing Persons,
by his Temptations. Indeed it's a kind of Chance-medly, both in

respect of the Father, and his Children; when any such Event happens. And isn't this the Reason, why a Work of Conviction and Conversion has been so rarely heard of, for a long Time, in the Churches, till of late, *viz.* That the Bulk of her spiritual Guides, were stone-blind, and stone-dead!

4] The Ministry of natural Men is dangerous, both in respect of the Doctrines, and practice of Piety. The Doctrines of *Original Sin, Justification by Faith alone,* and the other Points of *Calvinism,* are very cross to the Grain of unrenewed Nature. And tho' Men, by the Influence of a good Education, and Hopes of Preferment, may have the edge of their natural Enmity against them blunted; yet it's far from being broken or removed; it's only the saving Grace of God, that can give us a true Relish, for those Nature-humbling Doctrines; and so effectually secure us from being infected by the contrary. Is not the Carnality of the Ministry, one great Cause of the general Spread of *Arminianism, Socinianism, Arianism,* and *Deism,* at this Day through the World?

And alas! what poor Guides are natural Ministers to those, who are under spiritual Trouble? they either slight such Distress altogether, and call it Melancholy, or Madness, or dawb those that are under it, with untemper'd Mortar. Our LORD assures us, That the Salt which hath lost its Savour, is good for nothing; some say, 'It genders Worms and Vermine.' Now, what Savour have Pharisee-Ministers? In Truth, a very stinking One, both in the Nostrils of God and good Men. 'Be these Moral Negroes never so white in the Mouth, (as one expresseth it) yet will they hinder, instead of helping others, in at the strait Gate.' Hence is that Threatning of our LORD, against them, *Mat.* 23.13. *Wo unto you, Scribes and Pharisees, Hypocrites; for ye shut up the Kingdom of Heaven against Men; for ye neither go in yourselves, nor suffer those that are entering, to go in.* Pharisee-Teachers will with the utmost Hate oppose the very Work of God's Spirit, upon the Souls of Men; and labour by all Means to blacken it, as well as the Instruments, which the Almighty improves to promote the same; if it comes near their Borders, and interferes with their Credit or Interest. Thus did the Pharisees deal with our Saviour.

If it be objected, against what has been offer'd, under this General Head of Discourse, That *Judas* was sent by Christ; I answer, (1) That *Judas's* Ministry was partly Legal, inasmuch as during that Period, the Disciples were subject to Jewish Observances, and sent only to the House of *Israel, Matth.* 10.5, 6. And in that they waited after Christ's Resurrection for another Mission, *Act.* 1.4. which we find they obtained, and that different from the former. *Matth.* 28.19. (2) *Judas's* Ministry was extraordinary necessary, in order to fulfil some antient Prophesies concerning him. *Acts* 1.16, 17, 18, 20. *Job*. 13.18. I fear that the Abuse of this Instance, has brought many *Judases* into the Ministry, whose chief Desire, like their great Grandfather, is to finger the Pence, and carry the Bag. But let such hireling murderous Hypocrites take Care, that they don't feel the Force of a Halter in this World, and an aggravated Damnation in the next.

Again, if it be objected, That *Paul* rejoyced, that the Gospel was preached, tho' of Contention, and not sincerely; I answer, The Expression signifies the Apostle's great Self-Denyal. Some laboured to eclipse his Fame and Character, by contentious Preaching, thinking thereby to afflict him; but they were mistaken; as to that, he was easy. For he had long before learned, to die to his own Reputation. The Apostle's Rejoycing was comparative only; he would rather that Christ should be preached out of Envy, than not at all. Especially considering the gross Ignorance of the Doctrinal Knowledge of the Gospel, which prevailed almost universally in that Age of the World. Besides the Apostle knew that that Tryal should be sanctified to him, to promote his spiritual Progress in Goodness, and perhaps prove a Mean of procuring his temporal Freedom; and therefore he would rejoyce. It is certain, we may both rejoyce and mourn, in relation to the same Thing, upon different Accounts, without any Contradiction.   But the

¶ THIRD GENERAL HEAD, was to shew, *How Pity should be expressed upon this mournful Occasion!*

My Brethren, we should mourn over those, that are destitute of faithful Ministers, and sympathize with them. Our Bowels should be moved with the most compassionate Tenderness, over those dear fainting Souls, that are *as Sheep having no Shepherd;* and that after the Example of our blessed LORD!

Dear Sirs! we should also most earnestly pray for them, that the compassionate Saviour may preserve them, by his mighty Power, thro' Faith unto Salvation; support their sinking Spirits, under the melancholy Uneasinesses of a dead Ministry; sanctify and sweeten to them the dry Morsels they get under such blind Men, when they have none better to repair to.

And more especially, my Brethren, we should pray to the LORD of the Harvest, to send forth faithful Labourers into his Harvest; seeing that the Harvest truly is plenteous, but the Labourers are few. And O Sirs! how humble, believing, and importunate should we be in this Petition! O! let us follow the LORD, Day and Night, with Cries, Tears, Pleadings, and Groanings upon this Account! For GOD knows, there is a great Necessity of it. O! thou Fountain of Mercy, and Father of Pity, pour forth upon thy poor Children a Spirit of Prayer, for the Obtaining this important Mercy! Help, help, O Eternal GOD and Father, for Christ's sake!

And indeed, my Brethren, we should join our Endeavours to our Prayers. The most likely Method to stock the Church with a faithful Ministry, in the present Situation of Things, the publick Academies being so much corrupted and abused generally, is, To encourage private Schools, or Seminaries of Learning, which are under the Care of skilful and experienced Christians; in which those only should be admitted, who upon strict Examination, have in the Judgment of a reasonable Charity, the plain Evidences of experimental Religion. Pious and experienced Youths, who have a good natural Capacity, and great Desires after the Ministerial Work, from good Motives, might be sought for, and found up and down the Country, and put to Private Schools of the Prophets; especially in such Places, where the Publick ones are not. This Method, in my Opinion, has a noble Tendency, to build up the Church of God. And those who have any Love to Christ, or Desire after the Coming of his Kingdom, should be ready according to their Ability, to give somewhat, from time to time, for the Support of such poor Youths, who have nothing of their own. And truly, Brethren, this Charity to the Souls of Men, is the most noble kind of Charity. O! if the Love of God be in you, it will constrain you to do something, to promote so noble and necessary a Work. It looks Hypocrite-like to go no further, when other Things are required, than cheap Prayer. Don't think it much, if the Pharisees should be offended at such a Proposal; these subtle selfish Hypocrites are wont to be fear'd about their Credit, and their Kingdom; and truly they are both little worth, for all the Bustle they make about them. If they could help it, they wou'dn't let one faithful Man come into the Ministry; and therefore their Opposition is an encouraging Sign. Let all the Followers of the Lamb stand up and act for GOD against all Opposers: Who is upon GOD's Side? who?

¶THE IMPROVEMENT of this Subject remains. And,

1] If it be so, That the Case of those, who have no other, or no better than Pharisee-Teachers, is to be pitied: Then what a Scrole and Scene of Mourning, and Lamentation, and Wo, is opened! because of the Swarms of Locusts, the Crowds of Pharisees, that have as covetously as cruelly, crept into the Ministry, in this adulterous Generation! who as nearly resemble the Character given of the old Pharisees, in the Doctrinal Part of this Discourse, as one Crow's Egg does another. It is true some of the modern Pharisees have learned to prate a little more orthodoxly about the New Birth, than their Predecessor *Nicodemus*, who are, in the mean Time, as great Strangers to the feeling Experience of it, as he. They are blind

who see not this to be the Case of the Body of the Clergy, of this
Generation. And O! that our Heads were Waters, and our
Eyes a Fountain of Tears, that we could Day and Night
lament, with the utmost Bitterness, the doleful Case of the poor
Church of God, upon this account.

2] From what has been said, we may learn, That such who are
contented under a dead Ministry, have not in them the Temper
of that Saviour they profess. It's an awful Sign, that they are as
blind as Moles, and as dead as Stones, without any spiritual
Taste and Relish. And alas! isn't this the Case of Multitudes?
If they can get one, that has the Name of a Minister, with a
Band, and a Black Coat or Gown to carry on a Sabbath-days
among them, although never so coldly, and insuccessfully; if he
is free from gross Crimes in Practice, and takes good Care to
keep at a due Distance from their Consciences, and is never
troubled about his Insuccessfulness; O! think the poor Fools,
that is a fine Man indeed; our Minister is a prudent charitable
Man, he is not always harping upon Terror, and sounding
Damnation in our Ears, like some rash-headed Preachers, who
by their uncharitable Methods, are ready to put poor People
out of their Wits, or to run them into Despair; O! how terrible
a Thing is that Despair! Ay, our Minister, honest Man, gives
us good Caution against it. Poor silly Souls! consider seriously
these Passages, of the Prophet *Jeremiah*, c.5.30, 31.

3] We may learn, the Mercy and Duty of those that enjoy a faithful Ministry. Let such glorify GOD, for so distinguishing a
Privilege, and labour to walk worthy of it, to all Well-pleasing;
lest for their Abuse thereof, they be exposed to a greater
Damnation.

4] If the Ministry of natural Men be as it has been represented;
Then it is both lawful and expedient to go from them to hear
Godly Persons; yea, it's so far from being sinful to do this,
that one who lives under a pious Minister of lesser Gifts, after
having honestly endeavour'd to get Benefit by his Ministry,
and yet gets little or none, but doth find real Benefit and more
Benefit elsewhere; I say, he may lawfully go, and that frequently, where he gets most Good to his precious Soul, after
regular Application to the Pastor where he lives, for his Consent, and proposing the Reasons thereof; when this is done in
the Spirit of Love and Meekness, without Contempt of any, as
also without rash Anger, or vain Curiosity.

Natural Reason will inform us, that Good is desireable for
its own sake. Now, as Dr. *Voetius* observes, Good added to Good,
makes it a greater Good, and so more desireable; and therefore

Evil as Evil, or a lesser Good, which is comparatively Evil, cannot be the Object of Desire.

There is a natural Instinct put even into the irrational Creatures, by the Author of their Being, to seek after the greater natural Good, as far as they know it. Hence the Birds of the Air fly to the warmer Climates, in order to shun the Winter-Cold, and also doubtless to get better Food; *For where the Carcass is, there the Eagles will be gathered together.* The Beasts of the Field seek the best Pastures, and the Fishes of the Ocean seek after the Food they like best.

But the written Word of God confirms the aforesaid Proposition, while God by it enjoins us, *to covet earnestly the best Gifts*; as also *to prove all Things, and hold fast that which is good.* I Cor. 12.21. I Thess. 5.2. And is it not the Command of God, that we should *grow in Grace?* 2 Pet. 3.18. and 1 Pet. 2.2. Now, does not every positive Command enjoin the Use of such Means, as have the directest Tendency to answer the End designed? namely, The Duty commanded. If there be a Variety of Means, is not the best to be chosen? else how can the Choice be called rational, and becoming an intelligent Creature? To chuse otherwise knowingly, is it not contrary to common Sense, as well as Religion, and daily confuted by the common Practice of all the rational Creation, about Things of far less Moment and Consequence?

That there is a Difference and Variety in Preachers Gifts and Graces, is undeniably evident, from the united Testimony of Scripture and Reason.

And that there is a great Difference in the Degrees of Hearers Edification, under the Hearing of these different Gifts, is as evident to the Feeling of experienced Christians, as any Thing can be to Sight.

It is also an unquestionable Truth, that ordinarily GOD blesses most the best Gifts, for the Hearers Edification, as by the best Food he gives the best Nourishment. Otherwise the best Gifts would not be desireable, and GOD Almighty in the ordinary Course of his Providence, by not acting according to the Nature of Things, would be carrying on a Series of unnecesary Miracles; which to suppose, is unreasonable. The following Places of holy Scripture, confirm what has been last observed. 1 *Cor.* 14.12. 1 *Tim.* 4.14, 15, 16. 2 *Tim.* 1.6. *& Act.* 11.24.

If God's People have a Right to the Gifts of all God's Ministers, pray, why mayn't they use them, as they have Opportunity? And if they should go a few Miles farther than ordinary, to enjoy those, which they profit most by; who do they wrong? Now, our LORD does inform his People, 1 *Cor.* 3.22. That *whether* Paul, *or* Apollos, *or* Cephas; *all was theirs.*

But the Example of our Dear Redeemer, will give farther

Light in this Argument. Tho' many of the Hearers, not only of the Pharisees, but of *John the Baptist*, came to hear our Saviour, and that not only upon Week-days, but upon Sabbath-days, and that in great Numbers, and from very distant Places; yet he reproved them not: And did not our Lord love the Apostle *John* more than the rest, and took him with him, before others, with *Peter* and *James*, to Mount *Tabor*, and *Gethsemany*? Matth. 17. and c.26.

To bind Men to a particular Minister, against their Judgment and Inclinations, when they are more edified elsewhere, is carnal with a Witness; a cruel Oppression of tender Consciences, a Compelling of Men to Sin: For he that doubts, is damn'd if he eat; and whatsoever is not of Faith, is Sin.

Besides it is an unscriptural Infringment on Christian Liberty; 1 *Cor.* 3.22. It's a Yoke worse than that of *Rome* itself. Dr. *Voetius* asserts, 'That even among the *Papists*, as to Hearing of Sermons, the People are not deprived of the Liberty of Choice.' It's a Yoke like that of *Egypt,* which cruel *Pharaoh* formed for the Necks of the oppressed *Israelites*, when he obliged them to make up their stated Task of Brick, but allowed them no Straw. So we must grow in Grace and Knowledge; but in the mean time, according to the Notion of some, we are confined from using the likeliest Means, to attain that End.

If the great Ends of Hearing may be attained as well, and better, by Hearing of another Minister than our own; then I see not, why we should be under a fatal Necessity of hearing him, I mean our Parish-Minister, perpetually, or generally. Now, what are, or ought to be, the Ends of Hearing, but the Getting of Grace, and Growing in it? *Rom.* 10.14. 1 *Pet.* 2.2. *As Babes desire the sincere Milk of the Word, that ye may grow thereby.* (Poor Babes like not dry Breasts, and living Men like not dead Pools.) Well then, and may not these Ends be obtained out of our Parish-line? *Faith* is said to come by *Hearing*, Rom. 10. But the Apostle doesn't add, *Your Parish-Minister.* Isn't the same Word preach'd out of our Parish? and is there any Restriction in the Promises of blessing the Word to those only, who keep within their Parish-line ordinarily? If there be, I have not yet met with it; yea, I can affirm, that so far as Knowledge can be had in such Cases, I have known Persons to get saving Good to their Souls, by Hearing over their Parish-line; and this makes me earnest in Defense of it.

That which ought to be the main Motive of Hearing any, *viz,* our Souls Good, or greater Good, will excite us, if we regard our own eternal Interest, to hear there, where we attain it; and he that hears with less Views, acts like a Fool, and a Hypocrite.

Now, if it be lawful to withdraw from the Ministry of a pious Man, in the Case aforesaid; how much more, from the Ministry of

a natural Man? Surely, it is both lawful and expedient, for the
Reasons offered in the Doctrinal Part of this Discourse: To which
let me add a few Words more.

To trust the Care of our Souls to those who have little or no
Care for their own, to those who are both unskilful and unfaithful,
is contrary to the common Practice of considerate Mankind, relating to the Affairs of their Bodies and Estates; and would signify,
that we set light by our Souls, and did not care what became of
them. For if the Blind lead the Blind, will they not both fall into
the Ditch?

Is it a strange Thing to think, that GOD does not ordinarily
use the Ministry of his Enemies, to turn others to be his Friends,
seeing he works by suitable Means?

I cannot think, that GOD has given any Promise, that he will
be with, and bless the Labours of natural Ministers: For if he had,
he would be surely as good as his Word. But I can neither see,
nor hear of any Blessing upon these Men's Labours; unless it be
a rare and wonderful Instance of Chance-medly! whereas the
Ministry of faithful Men blossoms and bears Fruit, as the Rod of
Aaron. Jer. 23.22. *But if they had stood in my Counsel, and had
caused my People to hear my Words, then they should have turned
them from their evil Way, and from the Evil of their Doings.*

From such as have a Form of Godliness, and deny the Power
thereof, we are enjoined to turn away, 2 *Tim.* 3.5. And are there
not many such?

Our LORD advised his Disciples, to beware of the Leaven of
the Pharisees, *Mat.* 16.6. by which he shews that he meant their
Doctrine and Hypocrisie, *Mark* 8.15. *Luke* 12.1. which were both
four enough.

Memorable is the Answer of our LORD to his Disciples, *Mat.*
15.12, 13, 14. *Then came his Disciples and said unto him, Knowest
thou, that the Pharisees were Offended? And he answered and
said, Every Plant which my Heavenly Father hath not planted, shall
be rooted up: Let them alone; they be blind Leaders of the Blind:
And if the Blind lead the Blind, both shall fall into the Ditch.*

If it is objected, That we are bid to go to hear those, that sit
in *Moses'* Chair, *Mat.* 23.2, 3. I would answer this, in the Words
of a Body of dissenting Ministers, *viz.* 'That Sitting in *Moses'*
Chair, signifies a Succeeding of *Moses* in the ordinary Part of his
Office and Authority; so did *Joshua*, and the 70 Elders, *Exod.* 18.
21–26. Now, *Moses* was no Priest, (say they) tho' of *Levi's*
Tribe, but King in *Jeshurun*, a civil Ruler and Judge, chosen by
God. *Exod.* 18.13.' Therefore no more is meant by the Scripture
in the Objection, but that it is the Duty of People to hear and obey
the Lawful Commands of the Civil Magistrate, according to *Rom.*
13.5.

If it be opposed to the preceeding Reasonings, That such an Opinion and Practice would be apt to cause Heats and Contentions among People;

I answer, That the aforesaid Practice, accompanied with Love, Meekness, and Humility, is not the proper *Cause* of those Divisions, but the *Occasion* only, or the Cause by Accident, and not by itself. If a Person exercising Modesty and Love in his Carriage to his Minister and Neighbours, through Uprightness of Heart, designing nothing but his own greater Good, repairs there frequently where he attains it; is this any reasonable Cause of Anger? will any be offended with him, because he loves his Soul, and seeks the greater Good thereof, and is not like a senseless Stone, without Choice, Sense, and Taste? Pray, must we leave off every Duty, that is the Occasion of Contention or Division? Then we must quit powerful Religion altogether. For *he that will live godly in Christ Jesus, shall suffer Persecution*. And particularly we must carefully avoid faithful Preaching: For that is wont to occasion Disturbances and Divisions, especially when accompanied with divine Power. 1 *Thess.* 1.5,6. *Our Gospel came not unto you in Word only, but in Power:* And then it is added, That they *received the Word in much Affliction*. And the Apostle *Paul* informs us, 1 *Cor.* 16.9. That a great Door and effectual was open'd unto him, and that there were many Adversaries. Blessed Paul was accounted a common Disturber of the Peace, as well as *Elijah* long before him: And yet he left not off Preaching for all that. Yea, our blessed LORD informs us, That he came not to send Peace on Earth, but rather a Sword, Variance, Fire, and Division, and that even among Relations. *Matth.* 10.34, 35, 36. *Luke* 12.49, 51, 52, 53. As also, That while the strong Man armed keeps the House, all the Goods are in Peace. It is true the Power the Gospel is not the proper Cause of those Divisions, but the innocent Occasion only: No; the proper Cause of sinful Divisions, is that Enmity against GOD, and Holiness, which is in the Hearts of natural Men, of every Order; being stirred up by the Devil, and their own proud and selfish Lusts. And very often natural Men, who are the proper Causes of the Divisions aforesaid, are wont to deal with God's Servants, as *Potiphar's* Wife did by *Joseph*; they lay all the Blame of their own Wickedness at their Doors, and make a loud Cry!

Such as confine Opposition and Division, as following upon living Godliness and successful Preaching, to the first Ages of Christianity; it is much to be fear'd neither know themselves, nor the Gospel of Christ. For surely the nature of true Religion, as well as of Men and Devils, is the same in every Age.

Is not the visible Church composed of Persons of the most contrary Characters? While some are sincere Servants of God, are not many Servants of Satan, under a religious Mask? and have not these a fixed Enmity against the other? How is it then possible, that a Harmony should subsist between such, till their Nature be changed? Can Light dwell with Darkness?

Undoubtedly it is a great Duty, to avoid giving just Cause of Offence to any; and it is also highly necessary, that pious Souls should maintain Union and Harmony among themselves; notwithstanding of their different Opinions in lesser Things. And no doubt this is the Drift of the many Exhortations which we have to Peace and Unity in Scripture.

Surely, it cannot be reasonably suppos'd, that we are exhorted to a Unity in any Thing that is wicked, or inconsistent with the Good, or greater Good of our poor Souls: For that would be like the Unity of the Devils, a Legion of which dwelt peaceably in one Man: Or like the Unity of *Ahab's* false Prophets; all these four Hundred Daubers were very peaceable and much united, and all harped on the pleasing String: Ay, they were moderate Men, and had the Majority on their Side.

But possibly some may again object against Persons going to hear others, besides their own Ministers; the Scripture about *Paul* and *Apollos*, 1 Cor. 1.12. and say, that it is carnal. Dr. *Voetius* answers the aforesaid Objection, as follows: 'The Apostle reproves (says he) such as made Sects, saying, *I am of Paul, and I of Apollos* —and we with him reprove them. But this is far from being against the Choice, which one hath of Sermons and Preachers; seeing at one time we cannot hear all, neither doth the Explication and Application of all, equally suit such a Person, in such a Time, or Condition, or equally quicken, and subserve the Encrease of Knowledge.' Thus far he.

Because that the Apostle, in the aforesaid Place, reproves an excessive Love to, or Admiration of particular Ministers, accompanied with a sinful Contention, Slighting and Disdaining of others, who are truly godly, and with Sect-making: To say that from hence it necessarily follows, That we must make no Difference in our Choice, or in the Degrees of our Esteem of different Ministers, according to their different Gifts and Graces; is an Argument of as great Force, as to say, Because Gluttony and Drunkenness are forbidden, therefore we must neither eat nor drink, or make any Choice in Drinks or Victuals, let our Constitution be what it will.

Surely the very Nature of Christian Love inclines those that are possessed of it, to love others chiefly for their Goodness, and therefore in Proportion thereto. Now, seeing the Inference in the Objection is secretly built upon this Supposition, That we should love all good Men alike; it strikes at the Foundations of that Love to the Brethren, which is laid down in Scripture, as a Mark of true Christianity, 1 *Job.* 5. and so is carnal, with a Witness.

Again it may be objected, That the aforesaid Practice tends to grieve our Parish-Minister, and to break Congregations in Pieces.

I answer, If our Parish-Minister be grieved at our greater Good, or prefers his Credit before it; then he has good Cause to grieve over his own Rottenness and Hypocrisie. And as for Breaking of Congregations to Pieces, upon the Account of People's Going from Place to Place, to hear the Word, with a View to get greater Good; that spiritual Blindness and Death, that so generally prevails, will put this out of Danger. It is but a very few, that have got any spiritual Relish; the most will venture their Souls with any Formalist, and be well satisfied with the sapless Discourses of such dead Drones.

Well, doesn't the Apostle assert, That *Paul and Apollos are nothing*? Yes, it is true, they and all others are nothing as Efficient Causes; they could not change Men's Hearts. But were they nothing as Instruments? The Objection insinuates one of these two Things, either that there is no Difference in Means, as to their Suitableness; or that there is no Reason to expect a greater Blessing upon the most suitable Means: Both which are equally absurd, and before confuted.

But it may be further objected, with great Appearance of Zeal, That what has been said about People's Getting of Good, or greater Good, over their Parish-line, is a meer Fiction; for they are out of God's Way.

I answer, That there are Three monstrous Ingredients in the Objection, namely, A Begging of the Question in Debate, rash Judging, and Limiting of God.

It is a mean Thing in Reasoning, to beg or suppose that, which should be prov'd, and then to reason from it. Let it be prov'd, that they are out of God's Way; and then I will freely yield: But till this be done, bold Saysoes will not have much Weight with any but Dupes or Dunces. And for such who cry out against others for Uncharitableness, to be guilty of it themselves in the mean time in a very great Degree, is very inconsistent. Isn't it rash to judge of Things they have never heard? But those that have received Benefit, and are sensible of their own Uprightness, they will think it a light Thing, to be judged of Man's Judgment. Let *Tertullus* ascend the Theatre, and gild the Objection with the most mellifluous Ciceronean Eloquence; it will no more perswade them, that what they have felt is but a Fancy (unless they be under strong Temptations of Satan, or scared out of their Wits by frightful Expressions) than to tell a Man, in proper Language, that sees, That it is but a Notion, he does not see: Or to tell a Man that feels Pleasure or Pain, That it's but a deluded Fancy; they are quite mistaken.

Besides there is a Limiting the Holy One of Israel, in the aforesaid Objection, which sinful Sin the *Hebrews* were reproved for. It is a Piece of daring Presumption, to pretend by our finite Line, to fathom the infinite Depths that are in the Being and Works of God. The Query of *Zophar* is just and reasonable, *Job* 11.7, 8. *Canst thou by Searching find out* GOD? The humble Apostle with Astonishment acknowledged, that the Ways of GOD were past finding out. *Rom.* 11.33. Surely the Wind blows where it listeth, and we cannot tell whence it cometh, nor whither it goeth. Doesn't JEHOVAH ride upon a gloomy Cloud? and make Darkness his Pavilion? and isn't his Path in the great Waters? *Ps.* 18. *Ps.* 77.19.

I would conclude my present Meditations upon this Subject, by Exhorting All those who enjoy a faithful Ministry, to a speedy and sincere Improvement of so rare and valuable a Privilege; lest by their foolish Ingratitude the Righteous GOD be provok'd, to remove the Means they enjoy, or his Blessing from them, and so at last to expose them in another State to Enduring and greater Miseries. For surely, these Sins which are committed against greater Light and Mercy, are more presumptuous, ungrateful, and inexcusable; there is in them a greater Contempt of GOD's Authority, and Slight of his Mercy; those Evils do awfully violate the Conscience, and declare a Love to Sin as Sin; such Transgressors do rush upon the Bosses of GOD's Buckler, they court Destruction without a Covering, and embrace their own Ruin with open Arms. And therefore according to the Nature of Justice, which proportions Sinners Pains, according to the Number and Heinousness of their Crimes, and the Declaration of divine Truth, you must expect an enflamed Damnation: Surely, it shall be more tolerable for *Sodom* and *Gomorrah,* in the Day of the LORD, than for you, except ye repent.

And let gracious Souls be exhorted, to express the most tender Pity over such as have none but Pharisee-Teachers; and that in the Manner before described: To which let the Example of our LORD in the Text before us, be an inducing and effectual Incitement; as well as the gracious and immense Rewards, which follow upon so generous and noble a Charity, in this and the next State.

And let those who live under the Ministry of dead Men, whether they have got the Form of Religion or not, repair to the Living, where they may be edified. Let who will, oppose it. What famous Mr. *Jenner* observes upon this Head, is most just, 'That if there be any godly Soul, or any that desires the Salvation of his Soul, and lives under a blind Guide, he cannot go out (of his Parish) without giving very great Offence; it will be tho't a Giddiness, and a Slighting of his own Minister at home. When People came out of every Parish round about, to *John,* no Question but this bred Heart-burning against *John*, ay, and Ill-will against those People, that would not be satisfied with that Teaching they had in their own Synagogues.' Thus far he. But tho' your Neighbours growl against you, and reproach you for doing your Duty, in seeking your Souls Good; bear their unjust Censures with Christian Meekness, and persevere; as knowing that Suffering is the Lot of Christ's Followers, and that spiritual Benefits do infinitely overbalance all temporal Difficulties.

And O! that vacant Congregations would take due Care in the Choice of their Ministers! Here indeed they should hasten slowly. The Church of *Ephesus* is commended, for Trying them which said they were Apostles, and were not; and for finding them Liars. Hypocrites are against all Knowing of others, and Judging, in order to hide their own Filthiness; like Thieves they flee a Search, because of their stolen Goods. But the more they endeavour to hide, the more they expose their Shame. Does not the spiritual Man judge all Things? Tho' he cannot know the States of subtil Hypocrites infallibly; yet may he not give a near Guess, who are the Sons of *Seeva*, by their Manner of Praying, Preaching, and Living? Many Pharisee-Teachers have got a long fine String of Prayer by Heart, so that they are never at a Loss about it; their Prayers and Preachings are generally of a Length, and both as dead as a Stone, and without all Savour. I beseech you, my dear Brethren, to consider, That there is no Probability of your getting Good, by the Ministry of Pharisees. For they are no Shepherds (no faithful ones) in Christ's Account. They are as good as none, nay, worse than none, upon some Accounts. For take them first and last, and they generally do more Hurt than Good. They serve to keep better out of the Places where they live; nay, when the Life of Piety comes near their Quarters, they rise up in Arms against it, consult, contrive and combine in their Conclaves against it, as a common Enemy, that discovers and condemns their Craft and Hypocrisie. And with what Art, Rhetorick, and Appearances of Piety, will they varnish their Opposition of Christ's Kingdom? As the Magicians imitated the Works of *Moses*, so do false Apostles, and deceitful Workers, the Apostles of Christ.

I shall conclude this Discourse with the Words of the Apostle *Paul*, 2 *Cor.* 11.14, 15.

And no Marvel; for Satan himself is transformed into an Angel of Light: Therefore it is no great Thing if his Ministers also be transformed as the Ministers of Righteousness; whose End shall be according to their Works.

A *Caveat Against* Enthusiasm

Charles Chauncy

Charles Chauncy was born in Boston, January 1, 1705. The great-grandson of Charles Chauncy, the second president of Harvard University, he was graduated from Harvard with an A.B. degree in 1721, and an A.M. degree in 1724. He was ordained minister of the First Church of Boston in 1727, and continued in that position until his death on February 10, 1787.

Chauncy became famous throughout the colonies for his opposition to the revivalists. He wrote numerous pamphlets against those who preached with "enthusiam," instilling in his own sermons a "studied plainness . . . being averse to all effort of the imagination." The "Sermon Cautioning Against Enthusiasm" is an example of his plain style and his closely reasoned method of attack. It was preached at the Old Brick Meeting House in Boston, "the Lord's Day after the Commencement, 1742." The text is from the S. Eliot edition, Boston, 1742.

COR. XIV, xxxvii. *If any Man among you think himself to be a* PROPHET, *or* SPIRITUAL, *let him acknowledge that the Things that I write unto you are the Commandments of the* LORD.

MANY Things were amiss in the *Church* of *Corinth*, when *Paul* wrote this Epistle to them. There were envyings, strife and divisions among them, on account of their ministers. Some cried up one, others another: one said, I am of PAUL, another I am of APPOLLOS. They had form'd themselves into parties, and each party so admired the teacher they followed, as to reflect unjust contempt on the other.

Nor was this their only fault. A spirit of pride prevailed exceedingly among them. They were conceited of their gifts, and too generally dispos'd to make an ostentatious shew of them. From this vain glorious temper proceeded the forwardness, of those that had the *gift* of *tongues*, to speak in languages which others did not understand, to the disturbance, rather than edification of the church: And from the same principle it arose, that they spake not by turns, but several at once, in the same place of worship, to the introducing such confusion, that they were in danger of being tho't mad.

Nor were they without some pretence to justify these disorders. Their great plea was, that in these things they were guided by the Spirit, acted under his immediate influence and direction.

This seems plainly insinuated in the words I have read to you. *If any man think himself to be a prophet, or spiritual, let him acknowledge that the things that I write unto you are the commandments of the Lord.* As if the apostle had said, you may imagine your selves to be *spiritual* men, to be under a divine afflatus in what you do; but 'tis all imagination, meer pretence, unless you pay a due regard to the *commandments* I have here *wrote to you*; receiving them not as the *word of man, but of* GOD. Make trial of your spiritual pretences by this rule: If you can submit to it, and will order your conduct by it, well; otherwise you only cheat yourselves, while you think yourselves to be *spiritual* men, or, *prophets*: You are nothing better than *Enthusiasts*; your being acted by the SPIRIT, immediately guided and influenced by him, is meer pretence; you have no good reason to believe any such thing.

From the words thus explained, I shall take occasion to discourse to you upon the following Particulars.

¶*i.* I shall give you some account of *Enthusiasm*, in its *nature* and *influence.*

¶*ii.* Point you to a rule by which you may judge of persons, whether they are under the influence of *Enthusiasm.*

¶*iii.* Say what may be proper to guard you against this unhappy turn of mind.

The whole will then be follow'd with some suitable Application.

¶*i.* I am in the first place, to give you some account of *Enthusiasm.* And as this is a thing much talk'd of at present, more perhaps than at any other time that has pass'd over us, it will not be tho't unreasonable, if I take some pains to let you into a true understanding of it.

The word, from it's Etymology, carries in it a good meaning, as signifying *inspiration from* GOD: in which since, the prophets under the old testament, and the apostles under the new, might properly be called *Enthusiasts.* For they were under a divine influence, spake as moved by the HOLY GHOST, and did such things as can be accounted for in no way, but by recurring to an immediate extraordinary power, present with them.

But the word is more commonly used in a bad sense, as intending an *imaginary*, not a *real* inspiration: according to which sense, the *Enthusiast* is one, who has a conceit of himself as a person favoured with the extraordinary presence of the *Deity.* He mistakes the workings of his own passions for divine communications, and fancies himself immediately inspired by the SPIRIT of GOD, when all the while, he is under no other influence than that of an over-heated imagination.

The cause of this *enthusiasm* is a bad temperament of the blood and spirits; 'tis properly a disease, a sort of madness: And there are few; perhaps, none at all, but are subject to it; tho' none are so much in danger of it as those, in whom *melancholy* is the prevailing ingredient in their constitution. In these it often reigns; and sometimes to so great a degree, that they are really beside themselves, acting as truly by the blind impetus of a wild fancy, as tho' they had neither reason nor understanding.

And various are the ways in which their *enthusiasm* discovers itself.

Sometimes, it may be seen in their countenance. A certain wildness is discernable in their general look and air; especially when their imaginations are mov'd and fired.

Sometimes, it strangely loosens their tongues, and gives them such an energy, as well as fluency and volubility in speaking, as they themselves, by their utmost efforts, can't so much as imitate, when they are not under the enthusiastick influence.

Sometimes, it affects their bodies, throws them into convulsions and distortions, into quakings and tremblings. This was formerly common among the people called *Quakers*. I was myself, when a Lad, an eye-witness to such violent agitations and foamings, in a boisterous female speaker, as I could not behold but with surprize and wonder.

Sometimes, it will unaccountably mix itself with their conduct, and give it such a tincture of that which is freakish or furious, as none can have an idea of, but those who have seen the behavior of a person in a phrenzy.

Sometimes, it appears in their imaginary peculiar intimacy with heaven. They are, in their own opinion, the special favourites of GOD, have more familiar converse with him than other good men, and receive immediate, extraordinary communications from him. The tho'ts, which suddenly rise up in their minds, they take for suggestions of the SPIRIT; their very fancies are divine illuminations; nor are they strongly inclin'd to any thing, but 'tis an impulse from GOD, a plain revelation of his will.

And what extravagances, in this temper of mind, are they not capable of, and under the specious pretext too of paying obedience to the authority of GOD? Many have fancied themselves acting by immediate warrant from heaven, while they have been committing the most undoubted wickedness. There is indeed scarce any thing so wild, either in *speculation* or *practice*, but they have given into it: They have, in many instances, been blasphemers of GOD, and open disturbers of the peace of the world.

But in nothing does the *enthusiasm* of these persons discover it self more, than in the disregard they express to the Dictates of

reason. They are above the force of argument, beyond conviction
from a calm and sober address to their understandings. As for them,
they are distinguish'd persons; GOD himself speaks inwardly and
immediately to their souls. "They see the light infused into their
understanding, and cannot be mistaken; 'tis clear and visible there,
like the light of bright sunshine; shews it self and needs no other
proof but its own evidence. They feel the hand of GOD moving them
within, and the impulses of his SPIRIT; and cannot be mistaken in
what they feel. Thus they support themselves, and are sure reason
hath nothing to do with what they see and feel. What they have a
sensible experience of, admits no doubt, needs no probation." And
in vain will you endeavour to convince such persons of any mistakes
they are fallen into. They are certainly in the right; and know
themselves to be so. They have the SPIRIT opening their understandings and revealing the truth to them. They believe only as he has
taught them: and to suspect they are in the wrong is to do dishonour
to the SPIRIT; 'tis to oppose his dictates, to set up their own wisdom
in opposition to his, and shut their eyes against that light with which
he has shined into their souls. They are not therefore capable of
being argued with; you had as good reason with the wind.

And as the natural consequence of their being thus sure of
every thing, they are not only infinitely stiff and tenacious, but impatient of contradiction, censorious and uncharitable: they encourage
a good opinion of none but such as are in their way of thinking and
speaking. Those, to be sure, who venture to debate with them about
their errors and mistakes, their weaknesses and indiscretions, run
the hazard of being stigmatiz'd by them as poor unconverted
wretches, without the SPIRIT, under the government of carnal
reason, enemies to GOD and religion, and in the broad way to hell.

They are likewise positive and dogmatical, vainly fond of
their own imaginations, and invincibly set upon propagating them:
And in the doing of this, their Powers being awakened, and put as
it were, upon the stretch, from the strong impressions they are under,
that they are authorized by the immediate command of GOD himself,
they sometimes exert themselves with a sort of *extatic* violence: And
'tis this that gives them the advantage, among the less knowing
and judicious, of those who are modest, suspicious of themselves,
and not too assuming in matters of conscience and salvation. The
extraordinary fervour of their mind, accompanied with uncommon
bodily motions, and an excessive confidence and assurance, gains
them great reputation among the populace; who speak of them as
men of GOD in distinction from all others, and too commonly hearken
to, and revere their dictates, as tho' they really were, as they pretend, immediately comunicated to them from the DIVINE SPIRIT.

This is the nature of *Enthusiasm,* and this its operation, in a less or greater degree, in all who are under the influence of it. 'Tis a kind of religious Phrenzy, and evidently discovers it self to be so, whenever it rises to any great height.

And much to be pitied are the persons who are seized with it. Our compassion commonly works towards those, who, while under distraction, fondly imagine themselves to be Kings and Emperors: And the like pity is really due to those, who, under the power of *enthusiasm,* fancy themselves to be *prophets; inspired of God,* and *immediately called* and *commissioned by him to deliver his messages to the world:* And tho' they should run into disorders, and act in a manner that cannot but be condemned, they should notwithstanding be treated with tenderness and lenity; and the rather, because they don't commonly act so much under the influence of a *bad mind* as a *deluded imagination.* And who more worthy of christian pity than those, who, under the notion of serving GOD and the interest of religion, are filled with zeal, and exert themselves to the utmost, while all the time they are hurting and wounding the very cause they take so much pains to advance. 'Tis really a pitiable case: And tho' the honesty of their intentions won't legitimate their bad actions, yet it very much alleviates their guilt: We should think as favourably of them as may be, and be dispos'd to judge with mercy, as we would hope to obtain mercy.

But I come

¶*ii.* In the second place, to point you to a *rule* by which you may judge of persons, whether they are *enthusiasts,* meer pretenders to the immediate guidance and influence of the SPIRIT. And this is, in general, *a regard to the bible, an acknowledgment that the things therein contained are the commandments of* GOD. This is the rule in the text. And 'tis an infallible rule of tryal in this matter: We need not fear judging amiss, while we keep closely to it.

'Tis true, it wont certainly follow, that a man, pretending to be a *prophet,* or *spiritual,* really is so, if he owns the *bible,* and receives the truths therein revealed as the mind of GOD: But the conclusion, on the other hand, is clear and certain; if he pretends to be conducted by the SPIRIT, and disregards the scripture, pays no due reverence to *the things there delivered as the commandments of* GOD, he is a meer pretender, be his pretences ever so bold and confident, or made with ever so much seeming seriousness, gravity, or solemnity.

And the reason of this is obvious; viz that the things contained in the scripture were wrote by holy men as they were moved by the HOLY GHOST; they were received from GOD, and committed to writing under his immediate, extraordinary influence and guidance. And the divine, ever-blessed SPIRIT is consistent with himself. He cannot be suppos'd to be the author of any *private* revelations that

are contradictory to the *public standing* ones, which he has preserved in the world to this day. This would be to set the SPIRIT of
truth at variance with himself; than which a greater reproach can't
be cast upon him. 'Tis therefore as true, that those are *enthusiastical,*
who pretend to the SPIRIT, and at the same time express a disregard
to the scripture, as that the SPIRIT is the great revealer of the things
therein declared to us. And we may depend upon the certainty of
this conclusion. We have warrant to do so from the *inspired Paul;*
and we have the more reason to rely upon the rule he has given us,
as he had made it evident to the world, that he was a *prophet,* and
spiritual, by signs and wonders which he did before the people, by
the power of the SPIRIT of GOD.

But the *rule* in the text is yet more particular. It refers especially to *the things wrote by the apostle* PAUL, and which he wrote
to the *church* of *Corinth,* to rectify the *disorders* that had crept in
among them. And whoever the person be, that pretends to be *spiritual,* to be under the extraordinary guidance of the SPIRIT, and yet
acts in contradiction to what the apostle has here wrote, he vainly
imagines himself to be under the special guidance of the SPIRIT;
he is a downright *enthusiast.*

And here suffer me to make particular mention of some of the
things, the apostle has wrote in *this Epistle,* which, whoever will not
acknowledge, in *deed* as well as *word,* to be the *commandments* of
GOD, they are not guided by the SPIRIT, but vainly pretend to be so.

The first thing, in this kind, I would mention, is that which relates to *Ministers;* condemning an undue preference of one to another, the holding one in such admiration as to reflect disgrace on
another. This was one of the disorders the Apostle takes notice of,
as prevailing in the *church* of *Corinth;* and he is particular in his
care to give check to this unchristian spirit, which had crumbled them
into parties, and introduced among them faction and contention.

Now, whoever, under the pretence of being guided by the
spirit, set up one minister in opposition to another, glory in this
minister to the throwing undue contempt on that, thereby obstruct-
ing his usefulness, and making way for strife and divisions, they are
not really acted by the SPIRIT, whatever they may pretend. For
they evidently contradict what the apostle has wrote upon this
very head: And if *he* was inspired, the spirit they are influenced by,
cannot be the SPIRIT of GOD.

Not that one minister may not be preferr'd to another; this is
reasonable: But no minister ought to be regarded, as tho' he was
the author of our faith; nor, let his gifts and graces be what they
will, is he to be so esteemed, as that others must be neglected, or
treated in an unbecoming manner. But I shall not enlarge here, having spoken fully to this point, in a Sermon you may, some of you,
have in your hands.

Another thing the apostle is particular in writing upon, is the *commandment of charity*. And this he declares to be a matter of such essential importance in true christianity, that if a man is really destitute of it, he is nothing in the sight of GOD: Nay, tho' his pretences, his attainments, his gifts, be ever so extraordinary or miraculous; still, if he is without charity he will certainly be rejected of GOD and the LORD JESUS CHRIST. This is beautifully represented in the three first verses of the 13th chapter of this Epistle, in some of the boldest figures. "Tho' I speak, says the apostle, with the tongues of men and of angels, and have not charity, I am become as sounding brass, or a tinkling cymbal. And tho' I have the gift of prophecy, and understand all mysteries and all knowledge; and tho' I have all faith, so that I could remove mountains, and have not charity, I am nothing. And tho' I bestow all my goods to feed the poor, and tho' I give my body to be burned, and have not charity, it profiteth me nothing." As if the apostle had said, tho' a man had the languages of all nations, and could speak with the eloquence of angels; tho', like an inspired prophet, he had understanding in the deep counsels of GOD, and knew even all things sacred and divine; tho' he had the faith of miracles, and could do impossibilities; tho' he had the zeal of a martyr, and should give his body to be burned; tho' he had a disposition to alms-giving, and should bestow upon the poor his whole substance; still, if he was without charity, "that charity which suffereth long, and is kind; that charity which envyeth not, vaunteth not it self, is not puffed up; that charity which behaveth not it self unseemly, seeketh not her own, is not easily provoked, thinketh no evil, rejoiceth not in iniquity, but rejoiceth in the truth; that charity, in fine, which beareth all things, believeth all things, hopeth all things, endureth all things": I say, if he was without this charity, this love of his neighbour, these things would be all nothing; he would notwithstanding be out of favour with GOD, without any interest in CHRIST, and in such circumstances, as that unless there was a change in them, he would certainly perish.

This, in sum, is what the apostle has, in a distinct and peremptory manner, delivered concerning charity.

And in vain may any pretend to be under the extraordinary guidance of the SPIRIT, while in their practice they trample upon this law of christian love. Men may talk of their *impulses* and *impressions,* conceive of them as the call of GOD, and go about, as moved by them, from place to place, imagining they are sent of GOD, and immediately commissioned by him: But if they are censorious and uncharitable; if they harbour in their minds evil surmisings of their brethren; if they slander and reproach them; if they claim a right to look into their hearts, make it their business to judge of their state, and proclaim them hypocrites, carnal unregenerate sinners, when at the same time they are visibly of a good conversation in CHRIST; I say, when this is the practice of any, they do not acknowledge what the inspired PAUL has here *wrote as the commandment of* GOD: They are not therefore acted by the same SPIRIT with which he spake; but are evidently under a spirit of delusion: And this is so obviously the case, that there is no reasonable room to doubt upon the matter.

Charity, my brethren, is the commandment of the gospel by way of eminence. 'Tis the grand mark by which christians are to distinguish themselves from all others. By *this,* says our SAVIOUR, *shall all men know that ye are my disciples, if ye have love to one another:* Yea, this is the grand criterion by which we are to judge, whither GOD *dwelleth in us by his* SPIRIT. *If we love one another,* GOD *dwelleth in us.* And in the following Verse, *Hereby,* i.e. by our loving one another, *we know that we dwell in him, and he in us, because he hath given us of his* SPIRIT. To pretend therefore that we are led by the SPIRIT, and are under his extraordinary influence, when, in contradiction to the plain laws of JESUS CHRIST, revealed by the SPIRIT, we *judge our brother,* and *set at naught our brother,* and plead a right to do so, and are in a disposition TO THANK GOD, THAT WE ARE ENABLED TO DO SO; there is not a more sure mark, in all the revelations of GOD, of a BAD HEART, or a DISTEMPERED MIND. If any thing will evidence a man to be a *prophet* and *spiritual,* only in his own conceit, this must do it: And if this is not allow'd to be sufficient proof, there is no knowing, when a man is under the influence of *enthusiastick* heat and zeal.

Another thing the apostle bespeaks this church upon, is that *self-conceit* which appear'd among them in the exercise of *spiritual gifts:* And 'tis more than probable, there were those among them, who being vainly puffed up in their minds, behaved as tho' they were *apostles,* or *prophets,* or *teachers;* leaving their own station, and doing the work that was proper to others. It was to rectify such disorders, that the apostle, in the 12th chapter, addresses to them in that language, v.29. *Are all apostles? Are all prophets? Are all teachers?* The question carries with it it's own answer, and means the same thing, as when he affirms in the foregoing verse *God hath set some in the church, first apostles, secondarily prophets, thirdly teachers,* and so on. 'Tis evident from what the apostle here writes, and indeed from the current strain of this whole chapter, that there is in the body of CHRIST, the Church, a distinction of members; some intended for one use, others for another; and that it would bring confusion into the *body mystical,* for one member to be employed in that service which is adapted to another, and is its proper business.

'Tis not therefore the pretence of being moved by the SPIRIT, that will justify *private christians* in quitting their own proper station, to act in that which belongs to another. Such a practice as this naturally tends to destroy that order, GOD has constituted in the church, and may be followed with mischiefs greater than we may be aware of.

'Tis indeed a powerful argument with many, in favour of these persons, their pretending to *impulses,* and a call from GOD; together with their insatiable thirst to do good to souls. And 'tis owing to such pretences as these, that encouragement has been given to the rise of such numbers of *lay exhorters and teachers,* in one place and another, all over the land. But if 'tis one of the things wrote by the apostles as the *commandment of* GOD, that there should be *officers* in the church, an *order of men* to whom it should belong, as their *proper, stated work,* to exhort and teach, this cannot be the business of others: And if any who think themselves to be *spiritual,* are under *impressions* to take upon them *this ministry* they may have reason to suspect, whether their *impulses* are any other than the workings of their own imaginations: And instead of being under any divine extraordinary influence, there are just grounds of fear, whether they are not acted from the vanity of their minds: Especially, if they are but beginners in religion; men of weak minds, babes in understanding: as is most commonly the case. The apostle speaks of *novices,* as in danger of being *lifted up with pride, and falling into the condemnation of the devil:* And it is a seasonable caution to this kind of persons. They should study themselves more, and they will see less reason to think their disposition to exhort and teach to be from the SPIRIT OF GOD. And indeed, if the SPIRIT has bid men to *abide in their own callings,* 'tis not conceivable he should influence them to *leave their callings:* And if he has set a mark of disgrace upon *busiy-bodies in other men's matters,* 'tis impossible he should put men upon *wandring about from house to house, speaking the things they ought not.*

And it deserves particular consideration, whether the suffering, much more the encouraging WOMEN, yea, GIRLS to speak in the assemblies for religious worship, is not a plain breach of that *commandment of the* LORD, wherein it is said, *Let your* WOMEN *keep silence in the churches; for it is not permitted to them to speak—* *It is a shame for* WOMEN *to speak in the church.* After such an express constitution, designedly made to restrain WOMEN from speaking in the church, with what face can such a practice be pleaded for? They may pretend, they are moved by the SPIRIT, and such a tho't of themselves may be encouraged by others; but if the apostle *spake by the* SPIRIT, when he delivered *this commandment,* they can't *act by the* SPIRIT when they break it. 'Tis a plain case, these FEMALE EXHORTERS are condemned by the apostle; and if 'tis the *commandment of the* LORD, that they should not speak, they are *spiritual* only in their own tho'ts, while they attempt to do so.

The last thing I shall mention as written by the apostle, is that which obliges to a *just decorum in speaking* in the *house of* GOD. It was an extravagance these *Corinthians* had fallen into, their speaking many of them together, and upon different things, while in the same place of worship. *How is it, brethren*, says the apostle? *When ye come together, every one hath a psalm; hath a doctrine; hath a tongue; hath a revelation; hath an interpretation*. It was this that introduced the confusion and noise, upon which the apostle declares, if an unbeliever should come in among them, he would take them to be mad. And the *commandment* he gives them to put a stop to this disorder, is, that they should *speak in course, one by one*, and so as that *things might be done to edifying*.

And whoever the persons are, who will not acknowledge what the apostle has here said is the *commandment of* GOD, and act accordingly, are influenced by another spirit than that which moved in him, be their impressions or pretences what they will. The disorder of EXHORTING, and PRAYING, and SINGING, and LAUGHING, *in the same house of worship, at one and the same time*, is as great as was that, the apostle blames in the *church of Corinth*: And whatever the persons, guilty of such gross irregularity may imagine, and however they may plead their being under the influence of the SPIRIT, and mov'd by him, 'tis evidently a breach upon common order and decency; yea, a direct violation of the *commandment of* GOD, written on purpose to prevent such disorders: And to pretend the direction of the SPIRIT in such a flagrant instance of extravagant conduct, is to reproach the blessed SPIRIT, who is not, as the apostle's phrase is, *the author of confusion, but of peace, as in all the churches of the saints.*

In these, and all other instances, let us compare men's pretences to the SPIRIT by the SCRIPTURE: And if their conduct is such as can't be reconcil'd with an *acknowledgment of the things therein revealed, as the commandments of* GOD, their pretences are vain, they are *prophets* and *spiritual*, only in their own proud imaginations. I proceed now to

¶*iii.* The third thing, which is to caution you against giving way to *enthusiastic impressions*. And here much might be said,

I might warn you from the *dishonour* it reflects upon the SPIRIT of GOD. And perhaps none have more reproach'd the blessed SPIRIT, than men pretending to be under his extraordinary guidance and direction. The veryest fancies, the vainest imaginations, the strongest delusions, they have father'd on him. There is scarce any absurdity in *principle*, or irregularity in *practice*, but he has been made the patron of it. And what a stone of stumbling has the wildness of *Enthusiasm* been to multitudes in the world? What prejudices have been hereby excited in their minds against the very being of the SPIRIT? What temptations have been thrown in their way to dispute his OFFICE as the SANCTIFYER and COMFORTER of GOD's people? And how have they been over-come to disown HIS WORK, when it has been really wro't in the hearts of men?

I might also warn you from the damage it has done in the world. No greater mischiefs have arisen from any quarter. It is indeed the genuine source of infinite evil. Popery it self han't been the mother of more and greater blasphemies and abominations. It has made strong attempts to destroy all property, to make all things common, *wives* as well as *goods*. It has promoted faction and contention; filled the church oftentimes with confusion, and the state sometimes with general disorder. It has, by its pretended spiritual interpretations, made void the most undoubted laws of GOD. It has laid aside the *gospel sacraments* as weak and carnal things; yea, this *superior light within* has, in the opinion of thousands, render'd the *bible* a *useless dead letter*. It has made men fancy themselves to be *prophets* and *apostles*; yea, some have taken themselves to be CHRIST JESUS; yea, the blessed GOD himself. It has, in one word, been a pest to the church in all ages, as great an enemy to real and solid religion, as perhaps the grossest *infidelity*.

I might go on and warn you from the danger of it to yourselves. If you should once come under the influence of it, none can tell whither it would carry you. There is nothing so wild and frantick, but you may be reconcil'd to it. And if this shou'd be your case, your recovery to a right mind would be one of the most difficult things in nature. There is no coming at a thorow pac'd *enthusiast*. He is proof against every method of dealing with him. Would you apply to him from reason? That he esteems a carnal thing, and flees from it as from the most dangerous temptation. Would you rise higher, and speak to him from *Scripture*? It will be to as little purpose. For if he pays any regard to it, 'tis only as it falls in with his own pre-conceiv'd notions. He interprets the scripture by *impulses* and *impressions*, and sees no meaning in it, only as he explains it from his own fancy. 'Tis infinitely difficult convince a man grown giddy and conceited under the false notion, that the good SPIRIT teaches him every thing. His apprehended inspiration sets him above all means of conviction. He rather despises than hearkens to the most reasonable advices that can be given him.

But as the most suitable guard against the first tendencies towards *enthusiasm*, let me recommend to you the following words of counsel.

1] Get a true understanding of the *proper work of the* SPIRIT; and don't place it in those things wherein the gospel does not make it to consist. The work of the SPIRIT is different now from what it was in the first days of christianity. Men were then favoured with the extraordinary presence of the SPIRIT. He came upon them in miraculous gifts and powers; as a spirit of prophecy, of knowledge, of revelation, of tongue, of miracles: But the SPIRIT is not now to be expected in these ways. His grand business lies in preparing men's minds for the grace of GOD, by true *humiliation,* from an apprehension of sin, and the necessity of a *Saviour;* then in working in them faith and *repentance,* and such a *change* as shall *turn them from the power of sin and satan unto* GOD; and in fine, by carrying on the good work he has begun in them; assisting them in duty, strengthening them against temptation, and in a word, preserving them blameless thro' faith unto salvation: And all this he does by the *word* and *paayer,* [sic] as the great means in the accomplishment of these purposes of mercy.

Herein, in general, consists the work of the SPIRIT. It does not lie in giving men *private revelations,* but in opening their minds to understand the *publick ones* contained in the scripture. It does not lie in *sudden impulses* and *impressions,* in *immediate calls* and *extraordinary missions.* Men mistake the business of the SPIRIT, if they understand by it such things as these. And 'tis, probably, from such unhappy mistakes, that they are at first betrayed into *enthusiasm.* Having a wrong notion of the *work of* the SPIRIT, 'tis no wonder if they take the uncommon sallies of their own minds for his influences.

You cannot, my brethren, be too well acquainted with what the *bible* makes the *work* of the HOLY GHOST, in the affair of salvation: And if you have upon your minds a clear and distinct understanding of this, it will be a powerful guard to you against all *enthusiastical impressions.*

2] Keep close to the *Scripture,* and admit of nothing for an impression of the SPIRIT, but what agrees with that unerring rule. Fix it in your minds as a truth you will invariably abide by, that the *bible* is the grand test, by which every thing in religion is to be tried; and that you can, at no time, nor in any instance, be under the guidance of the SPIRIT of GOD, much less his *extraordinary* guidance, if what you are led to, is inconsistent with the things there revealed, either in point of *faith* or *practice.* And let it be your care to compare the motions of your minds, and the workings of your imaginations and passions, with the *rule* of GOD's *word.* And see to it, that you be impartial in this matter: Don't make the rule bend to your pre-conceiv'd notions and inclinations; but repair to the *bible,* with a mind dispos'd, as much as may be, to know the truth as it lies nakedly and plainly in the *scripture* it self. And whatever you are moved to, reject the motion, esteem it as nothing more than a vain fancy, if it puts you upon any method of *thinking,* or *acting,* that can't be evidently reconcil'd with the *revelations* of GOD in *his word.*

This adherence to the bible, my brethren, is one of the best preservatives against enthusiasm. If you will but express a due reverence to this *book* of GOD, making it the great rule of judgment, even in respect of the SPIRIT's *influences* and *operations,* you will not be in much danger of being led into delusion. Let that be your inquiry under all suppos'd *impulses* from the SPIRIT, *What faith the scripture? To the law, and to the testimony:* If your impressions, and imagined spiritual motions agree not therewith, 'tis because there is no hand of the SPIRIT OF GOD in them: They are only the workings of your own imaginations, or something worse; and must at once, without any more ado, be rejected as such.

3] Make use of the *Reason* and *Understanding* GOD has given you. This may be tho't an ill-advised direction, but 'tis as necessary as either of the former. Next to the *Scripture,* there is no greater enemy to *enthusiasm,* than *reason.* 'Tis indeed impossible a man shou'd be an *enthusiast,* who is in the just exercise of his understanding; and 'tis because men don't pay a due regard to the sober dictates of a well inform'd mind, that they are led aside by the delusions of a vain imagination. Be advised then to shew yourselves men, to make use of your reasonable powers; and not act as the *horse* or *mule,* as tho' you had no understanding.

'Tis true, you must not go about to set up your own *reason* in *opposition* to *revelation:* Nor may you entertain a tho't of making *reason* your *rule* instead of *scripture.* The *bible,* as I said before, is the *great rule* of religion, the grand test in matters of salvation: But then, you must use your reason in order to understand the *bible:* Nor is there any other possible way, in which, as a reasonable creature, you shou'd come to an understanding of it.

You are, it must be acknowledged, in a corrupt state. The fall has introduc'd great weakness into your reasonable nature. You can't be too sensible of this; nor of the danger you are in of making a wrong judgment, thro' prejudice, carelessness, and the undue influence of sin and lust. And to prevent this, you can't be too sollicitous to get your *nature sanctified:* Nor can you depend too strongly upon the divine grace to assist you in your search after truth: And 'tis in the way of due dependance on GOD, and the influences of his SPIRIT, that I advise you to the use of your reason: And in this way, you must make use of it. How else will you know what is a revelation from GOD? What shou'd hinder your entertaining the same tho't of a *pretended* revelation, as of a *real* one, but your reason discovering the falshood of the one, and the truth of the other? And when in the enjoyment of an undoubted revelation from GOD, as in the case of the *scripture*, How will you understand its meaning, if you throw by your reason? How will you determine, that this, and not that, is its true sense, in this and the other place? Nay, if no reasoning is to be made use of, are not all the senses that can be put on scripture equally proper? Yea, may not the most contrary senses be receiv'd at the same time since reason only can point out the inconsistency between them? And what will be sufficient to guard you against the most monstrous extravagancies, in *principle* as well as *practice*, if you give up your understandings? What have you left, in this case, to be a check to the wantoness of your imaginations? What shou'd hinder your following every idle fancy, 'till you have lost yourselves in the wilds of falshood and inconsistency?

You may, it is true, misuse your reason: And this is a consideration that shou'd put you upon a due care, that you may use it well; but no argument why you shou'd not use it at all: And indeed, if you shou'd throw by your reason as a useless thing, you would at once put your selves in the way of all manner of delusion.

But, it may be, you will say, you have committed yourselves to the *guidance* of the SPIRIT; which is the best preservative. Herein you have done well; nothing can be objected against this method of conduct: Only take heed of mistakes, touching the SPIRIT's *guidance*. Let me enquire of you, how is it the SPIRIT preserves from delusion? Is it not by opening the understanding, and enabling the man, in the due use of his reason, to perceive the truth of the things of GOD and religion? Most certainly: And, if you think of being led by the SPIRIT without understanding, or in opposition to it, you deceive yourselves. The SPIRIT of GOD deals with men as *reasonable* creatures: And they ought to deal with themselves in like manner: And while they do thus, making a wise and good use of the understanding, GOD has given them, they will take a proper means to prevent their falling into delusions; nor will there be much danger of their being led aside by *enthusiastic* heat and imagination.

4] You must not lay too great stress upon the *workings* of your *passions* and *affections*. These will be excited, in a less or greater degree, in the business of religion: And 'tis proper they shou'd. The passions, when suitably mov'd, tend mightily to awaken the *reasonable powers*, and put them upon a lively and vigorous exercise. And this is their proper use: And when address'd to, and excited to this purpose, they may be of good service: whereas we shall mistake the right use of the passions, if we place our religion *only* or *chiefly*, in the heat and fervour of them. The *soul* is the *man*: And unless the *reasonable nature* is suitably wro't upon, the *understanding* enlightned, the *judg-ment* convinc'd, the *will* perswaded, and the *mind* intirely chang'd, it will avail but to little purpose; tho' the passions shou'd be set all in a blaze. This therefore you shou'd be most concern'd about. And if while you are solicitous that you may be in transports of affection, you neglect your more noble part, your reason and judgment, you will be in great danger of being carried away by your imaginations. This indeed leads directly to *Enthusiasm:* And you will in vain, endeavour to preserve yourselves from the influence of it, if you a'nt duly careful to keep your passions in their proper place, under the government of a well inform'd understanding. While the passions are uppermost, and bear the chief sway over a man, he is in an unsafe state: None knows what he may be bro't to. You can't therefore be too careful to keep your passions under the regiment of a *sober judgment.* 'Tis indeed a matter of necessity, as you would not be led aside by delusion and fancy.

5] In the last place here, you must not forget to go to GOD by *prayer.* This is a duty in all cases, but in none more than the present. If left to yourselves, your own wisdom and strength, you will be insufficient for your own security; perpetually in danger from your *imaginations,* as well as the other enemies of your *souls.* You can't be too sensible of this; nor can you, from a sense of it, apply with too much importunity to the FATHER of *mercies,* to take pity upon you, and send you such a supply of grace as is needful for you. You must not indeed think, that your duty lies in the business of prayer, and nothing else. You must use your own endeavours, neglect nothing that may prove a guard to you: But together with the use of other means, you must make known your request to GOD by prayer and supplica-tion. You must daily commit the keeping of your soul to him; and this you must particularly be careful to do in times of more special hazard; humbly hoping in GOD to be your help: And if he shall please to undertake for you, no delusion shall ever have power over you, to seduce you; but, possessing a sound mind, you shall go on in the uniform, steady service of your maker and generation, till of the mercy of GOD, thro' the merits of the REDEEMER, you are crowned with eternal life.

But I shall now draw towards a close, by making some suitable *application* of what has been said, And,

1] Let us beware of charging GOD *foolishly,* from what we have heard of the *nature,* and *influence* of *enthusiasm.* This may appear a dark article in GOD's government of the world; but it stands upon the same foot with his permission of other evils, whether *natural* or *moral.* And, if we shou'd not be able to see perfectly into the reason of this dispensation, we shou'd rather attribute it to our own ignorance, than reply against GOD. We may assure ourselves, a wise, and good, and holy GOD, would not have suffered it thus to be, if there were not some great and valuable ends to be hereby answered.

Greater advantages may, in the end, accrue to true religion, by the sufferance of an *enthusiastic* spirit, and the prevalence of it, at certain times, than we may be capable of discerning at present.

It may furnish both opportunity and occasion for the trial of those, who call themselves christians; whether they have just notions of religion, and courage and faithfulness to stand up for *real* truths, against meer *imaginary* ones. It may serve as a foil to set off the beauty and glory of true, genuine christianity. It may tend to the encouragement of reasonable and solid religion; and, in the run of things, recommend it, in the most effectual manner, to men's choice and practice—In a word, It may put men upon a more thorough examination into the ground of the christian religion, and be the means of their being, more generally, established in its truth, upon the best and most reasonable evidence.

These are some of the ends capable of being answered by the permission of a *spirit of enthusiasm,* and the prevalence of it, for a while. And as to the persons themselves led aside by it, it is, in the same way to be reconcil'd with the general goodness of GOD towards men, as in the case of *distraction,* and the evil effects consequent thereupon. The persons, heated with *enthusiastic* imaginations, are either, in a faulty sense, accessary to this unhappy turn of mind, or they are not: If the *latter,* they may depend upon the pity and mercy of GOD, notwithstanding the extravagancies they may run into; yea, if they are good men, as is, doubtless, sometimes the case, it may be hoped, that this evil which has happened to them, will, after the manner of other sufferings, work together for good to them: But if thro' the pride of their hearts, a vainglorious temper, accompanied with rashness and arrogance, or the like, they are really accessary to their own delusion, and mad conduct following therefrom, let them not think to cast the blame on GOD: They do but reap the fruit of what they themselves have sown. And if they shou'd be totally delivered up, as has sometimes been the case, to the devices of their own hearts, and the *lying inspirations* of *wicked spirits,* they can fault no body but themselves. GOD is just while he makes them an example for the warning of others, lest they also be given up to believe lies. And he is *good* as well as just; good to others, in putting them hereby upon their guard, tho' he is severe towards them.

2] Let none, from what has been offered, entertain prejudices in their minds against the *operations* of the SPIRIT. There is such a thing as his influence upon the hearts of men. No consistent sense can be put upon a great part of the *bible,* unless this be acknowledged for a truth: Nor is it any objection against its being so, that there has been a great deal of *enthusiasm* in the world, many who have mistaken the motions of their own passions for divine operations. This, it must be acknowledged, shou'd make us cautious; putting us upon a careful examination of whatever offers itself, as a communication from the SPIRIT, that we deceive not ourselves: But its no argument, why we shou'd conceive a flighty tho't, either of the SPIRIT, or his influences, really made upon the minds of men. Much less is it a just ground of exception against the SPIRIT's *operations*, that they may be counterfeited; that men may make an appearance, as if they were acted by the SPIRIT, when, all the while, they have no other view in their pretences, but to serve themselves. This has often been the case; and points it out as a matter of necessity, that we take heed to ourselves, if we would not be impos'd upon by a *fair shew,* and *good words:* But at the same time, 'tis no reason, why we shou'd think the worse of the blessed SPIRIT, or of those influences that are really *his.*

Let us be upon our guard as to this matter. Many, from what they have seen or heard of the strange conduct of men, pretending to be under *divine impressions,* have had their minds insensibly leaven'd with prejudices against the things of the SPIRIT. O let it be our care, that we be not thus wro't upon! And the rather, least it shou'd prove the ruin of our souls. This, perhaps, we may not be afraid of: But the danger is great, if we take up wrong notions of the SPIRIT, or encourage an unbecomming tho't of his influences in the business of salvation, least we shou'd grieve the *good* SPIRIT, and he shou'd leave us to perish in a state of alianation from GOD, and true holiness. 'Tis worthy our particular remark, it is by the powerful operation of the holy SPIRIT on the hearts of men, that they are chang'd from the love and practice of sin, to the love and practice of holiness; and have those tempers form'd in them, whereby they are made meet for the glory to be hereafter revealed: Nor can this be done, in any way, without the *special influence* of the blessed SPIRIT.

And is it likely, *He* shou'd be present with men to such gracious purposes, if they suffer their minds to be impressed with contemptuous tho'ts of him? If they begin to call in question his *office,* as the *great dispenser of divine grace,* or look upon his operations as all delusion and imagination.

We must have upon our minds a just tho't of the good SPIRIT, and of his *influences*. This is a matter of necessity. O let us encourage a steady faith in him, as that glorious person, by whom, and by whom alone, we can be prepared in this world, for happiness in the world that is come. And let nothing, no wildness of enthusiasm, ever be able to tempt us to call this in question. And let us so believe in the HOLY GHOST, as to put ourselves under his guidance; and let our dependance be on him for grace to help us in every time of need.

Only let us look to it, that we take no *impressions* for his but such as really are so: And let us not be satisfied, 'till we experience within ourselves the *real effects* of the SPIRIT's operations; such as are common to all that are in CHRIST JESUS; and always have been, and always will be, accompanied with a *holy frame of soul,* and a *conversation becoming the Gospel.*

3] Let not any think *ill* of religion, because of the *ill* representation that is made of it by *enthusiasts.* There may be danger of this; especially, in regard of those who have not upon their minds a serious sense of GOD and the things of another world. They may be ready to judge of religion from the *copy* given them of it, by those who are too much led by their fancies; and to condemn it, in the gross, as a wild, imaginary, inconsistent thing. But this is to judge too hastily and rashly. Religion ought not to suffer in the opinion of any, because of the imprudencies or extravagancies of those, who call themselves the friends of it. Any thing may be abused: Nor is there any thing but has actually been abused. And why shou'd any think the worse of religion, because some who make more than ordinary pretences to it, set it forth in an ugly light by their conduct relative to it?

There is such a thing as real religion, let the conduct of men be what it will; and 'tis, in it's nature, a sober, calm, reasonable thing: Nor is it an objection of any weight against the sobriety or reasonableness of it, that there have been *enthusiasts,* who have acted as tho' it was a wild, imaginary business. We should not make our estimate of religion as exhibited in the behaviour of men of a *fanciful* mind; to be sure, we should not take up an ill opinion of it, because in the example they give of it, it don't appear so amiable as we might expect. This is unfair. We shou'd rather judge of it from the conduct of men of a *sound judgment;* whose lives have been such a uniform, beautiful transcript of that which is just and good, that we can't but think well of religion, as display'd in their example.

But however religion may appear as viewed in the lives, even of the best men, 'tis a lovely thing, as required by GOD, and pourtrayed in the bible. We shou'd take our sentiments of it from this *book of* GOD; and this, in the calm and sober exercise of our understandings: And if we view it as 'tis here delineated, we can't but approve of it, the *doctrines* it teaches, and the *duties* it requires, whether they relate to GOD, our selves, or our neighbour; they are all so reasonable in themselves, and worthy of the GOD, the stamp of whose authority they bear.

Let us fetch our notions of religion from the scripture: And if men, in their practice, set it in a disadvantageous light, let us be upon our guard, that we don't take up prejudices against it. This will blind our eyes, and may, by degrees, prepare the way to our throwing off all concern about religion: vea, we may be bro't to treat it even with contempt; than which, nothing can be more dangerous, or put our salvation to a greater risque.

4] Let us esteem those as *friends* to religion, and not *enemies,* who warn us of the danger of *enthusiasm,* and would put us upon our guard, that we be not led aside by It. As the times are, they run the hazard of being call'd *enemies* to the *holy* SPIRIT, and may expect to be ill-spoken of by many, and loaded with names of reproach: But they are notwithstanding the best friends to religion: and it may be, it will more and more appear, that they have all along been so. They have been stigmatised as OPPOSERS of the WORK OF GOD: but 'tis a great mercy of GOD, there have been such OPPOSERS: This land had, in all probability, been over-run with confusion and distraction, if they had acted under the influence of the same *heat* and *zeal,* which some others have been famous for.

'Tis really best, people shou'd know there is such a thing as *enthusiasm,* and that it has been, in all ages, one of the most dangerous enemies to the church of GOD, and has done a world of mischief: And 'tis a kindness to them to be warn'd against it, and directed to the proper methods to be preserved from it. 'Tis indeed, one of the best ways of doing service to *real* religion, to distinguish it from that which is *imaginary:* Nor shou'd ministers be discouraged from endeavouring this, tho' they shou'd be ill-tho't, or evil-spoken of. They shou'd beware of being too much under the influence of that *fear of man, which bringeth a snare;* which is evidently the case, where they are either silent, or dare not speak out faithfully and plainly, lest they shou'd be called PHARISEES or HYPOCRITES, and charged with LEADING SOULS TO THE DEVIL. 'Tis a *small matter* to be thus *judged* and *reviled;* and we shou'd be above being affrighted from duty by this, which is nothing more than the *breath* of poor, ignorant, frail man.

There is, I doubt not, a great deal of *real, substantial* religion in the land. The SPIRIT of GOD has wro't effectually on the hearts of many, from one time to another: And I make no question he has done so of late, in more numerous instances, it may be, than usual. But this, notwithstanding, there is, without dispute, a *spirit of enthusiasm,* appearing in one place and another. There are those, who make great pretences to the SPIRIT, who are carried away with their imaginations: And some, it may be, take themselves to be *immediately and wonderfully conducted by him;* while they are led only by their own fancies.

Thus it has been in other parts of the world. *Enthusiasm,* in all the *wildness,* and *fury,* and *extravagance* of it, has been among them, and sometimes had a most dreadfully extensive spread. *Ten thousand* wild *enthusiasts* have appear'd in arms, at the same time; and this too, in defence of *gross opinions,* as well as *enormous actions.* The first discovery therefore of such a spirit, unless due care is taken to give check to its growth and progress, is much to be feared; for there is no knowing, how high it may rise, nor what it may end in.

The good LORD give us all wisdom; and courage, and conduct, in such a Day as this! And may both *ministers* and *people* behave after such a manner, as that religon may not suffer; but in the end, gain advantage, and be still more universally established.

And, may that grace of GOD, which has appeared to all men, bringing salvation, teach us effectually, to deny ungodliness and worldly lusts, and to live soberly, and righteously, and godlily in the world: so may we look with comfort for the appearing of our SAVIOUR JESUS CHRIST: And when he shall appear in the glory of his FATHER, and with his holy angels, we shall also appear with him, and go away into everlasting life: Which GOD, of his infinite mercy grant may be the portion of us all; for the sake of CHRIST JESUS.

AMEN.

Unlimited Submission and Non-Resistance to The Higher Powers

Jonathan Mayhew

Jonathan Mayhew was born in Chilmark, Martha's Vineyard, on October 8, 1720. It is thought that he received his initial education from his father. Mayhew was graduated from Harvard *cum laude* in 1744, and became pastor of West Church, Boston, in 1747.

Because of his liberal opinions in government and church matters, Mayhew was unpopular with many prominent people in Boston. Fortunately for his career, a group of Boston ministers extended their support despite his Unitarianism and his propounding of the doctrine of free will.

Mayhew's tracts and sermons attracted attention in Great Britain as well as in the colonies. The University of Aberdeen awarded him the degree of Doctor of Divinity in 1750. Shortly afterwards, he was elected Scribe of the Massachusetts Convention of Congregational Ministers.

Mayhew soon became aligned with such political leaders as Otis, Quincy, and Samuel Adams. John Adams held him in great respect and called him a "transcendent genius."

His short but eventful career as a minister lasted only nineteen years. At the age of forty-six he died on July 9, 1766.

The discourse concerning "Unlimited Submission and Non-Resistance to the Higher Powers" was preached in the West Meeting House in Boston "the Lord's Day after the 30th of January, 1749" [1750?]. The text is from the D. Fowle edition printed in Boston, 1750.

Let every soul be subject unto the Higher Powers. For there is no power but of God: The Powers that be are ordained of God. Whosoever therefore resisteth the Power, Resisteth the ordinance of God; and they that resist shall receive to themselves Damnation. For rulers are not a terror to good works, but to the evil. Wilt thou then not be afraid of the Power? Do that which is good, and thou shalt have praise of the same; for he is the Minister of God to thee for good. But if thou do that which is evil, be afraid; for he beareth not the sword in vain: for he is the Minister of God, a revenger to execute wrath upon him that doeth evil. Wherefore Ye must needs be subject, not only for wrath, but also for conscience' sake. For, for, this cause pay you tribute also: for they are God's ministers, attending continually upon this very thing. Render therefore to all their dues: Tribute to whom tribute is due; custom

to whom custom; fear to whom fear; honor to whom honor.—
ROMANS xiii. 1–8.

IT is evident that the affairs of civil government may properly fall under a moral and religious consideration, at least so far forth as it relates to the general nature and end of magistracy, and to the grounds and extent of that submission which persons of a private character ought to yield to those who are vested with authority. This must be allowed by all who acknowledge the divine original of Christianity. For, although there be a sense, and a very plain and important sense, in which Christ's kingdom is not of this world, his inspired apostles have, nevertheless, laid down some general principles concerning the office of civil rulers, and the duty of subjects, together with the reason and obligation of that duty. And from hence it follows, that it is proper for all who acknowledge the authority of Jesus Christ, and the inspiration of his apostles, to endeavor to understand what is in fact the doctrine which they have delivered concerning this matter. It is the duty of Christian magistrates to inform themselves what it is which their religion teaches concerning the nature and design of their office. And it is equally the duty of all Christian people to inform themselves what it is which their religion teaches concerning that subjection which they owe to the higher powers. It is for these reasons that I have attempted to examine into the Scripture account of this matter, in order to lay it before you with the same freedom which I constantly use with relation to other doctrines and precepts of Christianity; not doubting but you will judge upon everything offered to your consideration with the same spirit of freedom and liberty with which it is spoken.

The passage read is the most full and express of any in the New Testament relating to rulers and subjects; and therefore I thought it proper to ground upon it what I had to propose to you with reference to the authority of the civil magistrate, and the subjection which is due to him. But, before I enter upon an explanation of the several parts of this passage, it will be proper to observe one thing, which may serve as a key to the whole of it.

It is to be observed, then, that there were some persons amongst the Christians of the apostolic age, and particularly those at Rome, to whom St. Paul is here writing, who seditiously disclaimed all subjection to civil authority; refusing to pay taxes, and the duties laid upon their traffic and merchandise; and who scrupled not to speak of their rulers without any due regard to their office and character. Some of these turbulent Christians were converts from Judaism, and others from Paganism. The Jews in general had, long before this time, taken up a strange conceit, that, being the peculiar and elect people of God, they were therefore exempted from the jurisdiction of any heathen princes or governors. Upon this ground it was that some of them, during the public ministry of our blessed Saviour, came to him with that question, "Is it lawful to give tribute unto Caesar, or not?" And this notion many of them retained after they were proselyted to the Christian faith. As to the Gentile converts, some of them grossly mistook the nature of that liberty which the gospel promised, and thought that by virtue of their subjection to Christ, the only king and head of his church, they were wholly freed from subjection to any other prince; as though Christ's kingdom had been of this world in such a sense as to interfere with the civil powers of the earth, and to deliver their subjects from that allegiance and duty which they before owed to them. Of these visionary Christians in general, who disowned subjection to the civil powers in being where they respectively lived, there is mention made in several places in the New Testament. The apostle Peter, in particular, characterizes them in this manner: them that "despise government, presumptuous are they; self-willed; they are not afraid to speak of evil dignities." Now, it is with reference to these doting Christians that the apostle speaks in the passage before us. And I shall now give you the sense of it in a paraphrase upon each verse in its order; desiring you to keep in mind the character of the persons for whom it is designed, that so, as I go along, you may see how just and natural this address is, and how well suited to the circumstances of those against whom it is levelled.

The apostle begins thus: "Let every soul be subject unto the higher powers; for there is no power but of God; the powers that be are ordained of God;" *q.d.,* "Whereas some professed Christians vainly imagine that they are wholly excused from all manner of duty and subjection to civil authority, refusing to honor their rulers and to pay taxes; which opinion is not only unreasonable in itself, but also tends to fix a lasting reproach upon the Christian name and profession—I now, as an apostle and ambassador of Christ, exhort every one of you, be he who he will, to pay all dutiful submission to those who are vested with any civil office; for there is, properly speaking, no authority but what is derived from God, as it is only by his permission and providence that any possess it. Yea, I may add, that all civil magistrates, as such, although they may be heathens, are appointed and ordained of God. For it is certainly God's will that so useful an institution as that of magistracy should take place in the world for the good of civil society." The apostle proceeds: "Whosoever, therefore, resisteth the power, resisteth the ordinance of God; and they that resist shall receive to themselves damnation." *q.d.,* "Think not, therefore, that ye are guiltless of any crime or sin against God, when ye factiously disobey and resist the civil authority. For magistracy and government being, as I have said, the ordinance and appointment of God, it follows, that to resist magistrates in the execution of their offices, is really to resist the will and ordinance of God himself; and they who thus resist will accordingly be punished by God for this sin, in common with others." The apostle goes on: "For rulers are not a terror to good works, but to the evil. Wilt thou, then, not be afraid of the power? Do that which is good, and thou shalt have praise of the same; for he is the minister of God to thee for good." *q.d.*, "That you may see the truth and justness of what I assert (viz., that magistracy is the ordinance of God, and that you sin against him in opposing it), consider that even pagan rulers are not, by the nature and design of their office, enemies and a terror to the good and virtuous actions of men, but only to the injurious and mischievous to society. Will ye not, then, reverence and honor magistracy, when ye see the good end and intention of it? How can ye be so unreasonable? Only mind to do your duty as members of society, and this will gain you the applause and favor of all good rulers. For, while you do thus, they are by their office, as ministers of God, obliged to encourage and protect you: it is for this very purpose that they are clothed with power." The apostle subjoins: "But if thou do that which is evil, be afraid; for he beareth not the sword in vain. For he is the minister of God, a revenger, to execute wrath upon him that doeth evil." *q.d.*, "But, upon the other hand, if ye refuse to do your duty as members of society; if ye refuse to bear your part in the support of government; if ye are disorderly, and do things which merit civil chastisement—then, indeed, ye have reason to be afraid. For it is not in vain that rulers are vested with the power of inflicting punishment. They are, by their office, not only the ministers of God for good to those that do well, but also his ministers to revenge, to discountenance, and punish those that are unruly, and injurious to their neighbors." The apostle proceeds: "Wherefore ye must needs be subject not only for wrath, but also for conscience' sake." *q.d.*, "Since, therefore, magistracy is the ordinance of God, and since rulers are by their office benefactors to society, by discouraging what is bad and encouraging what is good, and so preserving peace and order amongst men, it is evident that ye ought to pay a willing subjection to them; not to obey merely for fear of exposing yourselves to their wrath and displeasure, but also in point of reason, duty, and conscience. Ye are under an indispensable obligation, as Christians, to honor their office, and to submit to them in the execution of it." The apostle goes on: "For, for this cause pay you tribute also; for they are God's ministers attending continually upon this very thing." *q.d.*, "And here is a plain reason also why ye should pay tribute to them—for they are God's ministers, exalted above the common level of mankind—not that they may indulge themselves in softness and luxury, and be entitled to the servile homage of their fellow-men, but that they may execute an office no less laborious than honorable, and attend continually upon the public welfare. This being their business and duty, it is but reasonable that they should be requited for their care and diligence in performing it; and enabled, by taxes levied upon the subject, effectually to prosecute the great end of their institution, the good of society." The apostle sums all up in the following words: "Render, therefore, to all their dues; tribute to whom tribute is due; custom to whom custom; fear to whom fear; honor to whom honor." *q.d.,* "Let it not therefore be said of any of you hereafter, that you contemn government, to the reproach of yourselves and of the Christian religion. Neither you being Jews by nation, nor your becoming the subjects of Christ's kingdom, gives you any dispensation for making disturbances in the government under which you live. Approve yourselves, therefore, as peaceable and dutiful subjects. Be ready to pay to your rulers all that they may, in respect of their office, justly demand of you. Render tribute and custom to those of your governors to whom tribute and custom belong; and cheerfully honor and reverence all who are vested with civil authority, according to their deserts."

The apostle's doctrine, in the passage thus explained, concerning the office of civil rulers, and the duty of subjects, may be summed up in the following observations, viz.:

That the end of magistracy is the good of civil society, *as such*.

That civil rulers, *as such,* are the ordinance and ministers of God; it being by his permission and providence that any bear rule, and agreeable to his will that there should be *some persons* vested with authority in society, for the well-being of it.

That which is here said concerning civil rulers extends to all of them in common. It relates indifferently to monarchical, republican, and aristocratical government, and to all other forms which truly answer the sole end of government—the happiness of society; and to all the different degrees of authority in any particular state; to inferior officers no less than to the supreme.

That disobedience to civil rulers in the due exercise of their authority is not merely a political sin, but a heinous offence against God and religion.

That the true ground and reason of our obligation to be subject to the higher powers is, the usefulness of magistracy (when properly exercised) to human society, and its subserviency to the general welfare.

That obedience to civil rulers is here equally required under all forms of government which answer the sole end of all government—the good of society; and to every degree of authority, in any state, whether supreme or subordinate. From whence it follows—

That if unlimited obedience and non-resistance be here required as a duty under any one form of government, it is also required as a duty under all other forms, and as a duty to subordinate rulers as well as to the supreme.

And, lastly, that those civil rulers to whom the apostle enjoins subjection are the persons *in possession; the powers that be;* those who are actually vested with authority.

There is one very important and interesting point which remains to be inquired into, namely, the *extent* of that subjection to the higher powers which is here enjoined as a duty upon all Christians. Some have thought it warrantable and glorious to disobey the civil powers in certain circumstances, and in cases of very great and general oppression, when humble remonstrances fail of having any effect; and, when the public welfare cannot be otherwise provided for and secured, to rise unanimously even against the sovereign himself, in order to redress their grievances; to vindicate their natural and legal rights; to break the yoke of tyranny, and free themselves and posterity from inglorious servitude and ruin. It is upon this principle that many royal oppressors have been driven from their thrones into banishment, and many slain by the hands of their subjects. It was upon this principle that Tarquin was expelled from Rome, and Julius Caesar, the conqueror of the world and the tyrant of his country, cut off in the senate-house. It was upon this principle that King Charles I. was beheaded before his own banqueting-house. It was upon this principle that King James II. was made to fly that country which he aimed at enslaving; and upon this principle was that revolution brought about which has been so fruitful of happy consequences to Great Britain. But, in opposition to this principle, it has often been asserted that the Scripture in general, and the passage under consideration in particular, makes all resistance to princes a crime, in any case whatever. If they turn tyrants, and become the common oppressors of those whose welfare they ought to regard with a paternal affection, we must not pretend to right ourselves, unless it be by prayers, and tears, and humble entreaties. And if these methods fail of procuring redress, we must not have recourse to any other, but all suffer ourselves to be robbed and butchered at the pleasure of the "Lord's anointed," least we should incur the sin of rebellion and the punishment of damnation—for he has God's authority and commission to bear him out in the worst of crimes so far that he may not be withstood or controlled. Now, whether we are obliged to yield such an absolute submission to our prince, or whether disobedience and resistance may not be justifiable in some cases, notwithstanding anything in the passage before us, is an inquiry in which we all are concerned; and this is the inquiry which is the main design of the present discourse.

Now, there does not seem to be any necessity of supposing that an absolute, unlimited obedience, whether active or passive, is here enjoined, merely for this reason—that the precept is delivered in absolute terms, without any exception or limitation expressly mentioned. We are enjoined to be "subject to the higher powers;" and to be "subject for conscience' sake." And because these expressions are absolute and unlimited, or, more properly, general, some have inferred that the subjection required in them must be absolute and unlimited also—at least so far forth as to make passive obedience and non-resistance a duty in all cases whatever, if not active obedience likewise—though, by the way, there is here no distinction made betwixt active and passive obedience; and if either of them be required in an unlimited sense, the other must be required in the same sense also, by virtue of the present argument, because the expressions are equally absolute with respect to both. But that unlimited obedience of any sort cannot be argued merely from the indefinite expressions in which obedience is enjoined, appears from hence, that expressions of the same nature frequently occur in Scripture, upon which it is confessed on all hands that no such absolute and unlimited sense ought to be put. For example: "Love not the world, neither the things that are in the world," "Lay not up for yourselves treasures upon earth," "Take therefore no thought for the morrow," are precepts expressed in at least equally absolute and unlimited terms; but it is generally allowed that they are to be understood with certain restrictions and limitations; some degree of love to the world and the things of it being allowable. Nor, indeed, do the *Right Reverend Fathers in God,* and other *dignified clergymen* of the Established Church, seem to be altogether averse to admitting of restrictions in the latter case, how warm soever any of them may be against restrictions and limitations in the case of submission to authority, whether civil or ecclesiastical. It is worth remarking, also, that patience and submission under private injuries are enjoined in much more preemptory and absolute terms than any that are used with regard to submission to the injustice and oppression of civil rulers. Thus: "I say unto you, that ye resist not evil; but whosoever shall smite thee on the right cheek, turn to him the other also. And if any man will sue thee at the law, and take away thy coat, let him have thy cloak also. And whosoever shall compel thee to go a mile with him, go with him twain." Any man may be defied to produce such strong expressions in favor of a passive and tame submission to unjust, tyrannical rulers, as are here used to enforce submission to private injuries. But how few are there that understand those expressions literally! And the reason why they do not, is because (with submission to the Quakers) common sense shows that they were not intended to be so understood.

But, to instance in some Scripture precepts which are more directly to the point in hand: Children are commanded to obey their parents, and servants their masters, in as absolute and unlimited terms as subjects are here commanded to obey their civil rulers. Thus this same apostle: "Children, obey your parents in the Lord; for this is right. Honor thy father and mother, which is the first commandment with promise. Servants, be obedient to them that are your masters according to the flesh, with fear and trembling, with singleness of your heart, as unto Christ." Thus, also, wives are commanded to be obedient to their husbands: "Wives, submit yourselves unto your own husbands, as unto the Lord; for the husband is head of the wife, even as Christ is the head of the church. Therefore, as the church is subject unto Christ, so let the wives be to their own husbands in everything." In all these cases, submission is required in terms at least as absolute and universal as are ever used with respect to rulers and subjects. But who supposes that the apostle ever intended to teach that children, servants, and wives, should, in all cases whatever, obey their parents, masters, and husbands respectively, never making any opposition to their will, even although they should require them to break the commandments of God, or should causelessly make an attempt upon their lives? No one put such a sense upon these expressions, however absolute and unlimited. Why, then, should it be supposed that the apostle designed to teach universal obedience, whether active or passive, to the higher powers, merely because his precepts are delivered in absolute and unlimited terms? And if this be a good argument in one case, why is it not in others also? If it be said that resistance and disobedience to the higher powers is here said positively to be a sin, so also is the disobedience of children to parents, servants to masters, and wives to husbands, in other places of Scripture. But the question still remains, whether, in all these cases, there be not some exceptions. In the three latter it is allowed there are; and from hence it follows, that barely the use of absolute expressions is no proof that obedience to civil rulers is in all cases a duty, or resistance in all cases a sin. I should not have thought it worth while to take any notice at all of this argument, had it not been much insisted upon by some of the advocates for passive obedience and non-resistance; for it is in itself perfectly trifling, and rendered considerable only by the stress that has been laid upon it for want of better.

There is, indeed, one passage in the New Testament where it may seem, at first view, that an unlimited submission to civil rulers is enjoined: "Submit yourselves to every ordinance of man for the Lord's sake." To *every ordinance of man.* However, this expression is no stronger than that before taken notice of with relation to the duty of wives: "So let the wives be subject to their own husbands in *everything*." But the true solution of this difficulty (if it be one) is this: "By every ordinance of man" is not meant every command of the civil magistrate without exception, but every order of magistrates appointed by man, whether superior or inferior; for so the apostle explains himself in the very next words: "Whether it be to the king as supreme, or to governors, as unto them that are sent," etc. But although the apostle had not subjoined any such explanation, the reason of the thing itself would have obliged us to limit the expression "every ordinance of man" to such human ordinances and commands as are not inconsistent with the ordinances and commands of God, the Supreme Lawgiver, or with any other higher and antecedent obligations.

It is to be observed, in the next place, that as the duty of universal obedience and non-resistance to the higher powers cannot be argued from the absolute, unlimited expressions which the apostle here uses, so neither can it be argued from the scope and drift of his reasoning, considered with relation to the persons he was here opposing. As was observed above, there were some professed Christians in the apostolic age who disclaimed all magistracy and civil authority in general, despising government, and speaking evil of dignities; some, under a notion that Jews ought not to be under the jurisdiction of Gentile rulers, and others that they were set free from the temporal powers by Christ. Now, it is with persons of this licentious opinion and character that the apostle is concerned; and all that was directly to his point was to show that they were bound to submit to magistracy in general. This is a circumstance very material to be taken notice of, in order to ascertain the sense of the apostle; for, this being considered, it is sufficient to account for all that he says concerning the duty of subjection and the sin of resistance to the higher powers, without having recourse to the doctrine of unlimited submission and passive obedience in all cases whatever. Were it known that those in opposition to whom, the apostle wrote, allowed of civil authority in general, and only asserted that there were some cases in which obedience and non-resistance were not a duty, there would then indeed be reason for interpreting this passage as containing the doctrine of unlimited obedience and non-resistance, as it must, in this case, be supposed to have been levelled against such as denied that doctrine. But since it is certain that there were persons who vainly imagined that civil government in general was not to be regarded by them, it is most reasonable to suppose that the apostle designed his discourse only against them; and, agreeable to this supposition, we find that he argues the usefulness of civil magistracy in general, its agreeableness to the will and purpose of God, who is over all, and so deduced from hence the obligation of submission to it. But it will not follow that because civil government is, in general, a good institution, and necessary to the peace and happiness of human society, therefore there are no supposable causes in which resistance to it can be innocent. So that the duty of unlimited obedience, whether active or passive, can be argued neither from the manner of expression here used, nor from the general scope and design of the passage.

And if we attend to the nature of the argument with which the apostle here enforces the duty of submission to the higher powers, we shall find it to be such a one as concludes not in favor of submission to all who bear the title of rulers in common, but only to those who actually perform the duty of rulers by exercising a reasonable and just authority for the good of human society. This is a point which it will be proper to enlarge upon, because the question before us turns very much upon the truth or falsehood of this position. It is obvious, then, in general, that the civil rulers whom the apostle here speaks of, and obedience to whom he presses upon Christians as a duty, are good rulers, such as are, in the exercise of their office and power, benefactors to society. Such they are described to be throughout this passage. Thus, it is said that they are not a terror to good words, but to the evil; that they are God's ministers for good; revengers to execute wrath upon him that doeth evil; and that they attend continually upon this very thing. St. Peter gives the same account of rulers: They are "for a praise to them that do well, and the punishment of evil doers." It is manifest that this character and description of rulers agrees only to such as are rulers in fact, as well as in name; to such as govern well, and act agreeably to their office. And the apostle's argument for submission to rulers is wholly built and grounded upon a presumption that they do in fact answer this character, and is of no force at all upon supposition of the contrary. If rulers are a terror to good words, and not to the evil; if they are not ministers for good to society, but for evil and distress, by violence and oppression; if they execute wrath upon sober, peaceable persons, who do their duty as members of society, and suffer rich and honorable knaves to escape with impunity; if, instead of attending continually upon the good work of advancing the public welfare, they attend continually upon the gratification of their own lust and pride and ambition, to the destruction of the public welfare—if this be the case, it is plain that the apostle's argument for submission does not reach them; they are not the same, but different persons from those whom he characterizes, and who must be obeyed, according to his reasoning. Let me illustrate the apostle's argument by the following similitude (it is no matter how far it is from anything which has, in fact, happened in the world) : Suppose, then it was allowed, in general, that the clergy were a useful order of men; that they ought to be "esteemed very highly in love for their works' sake, and to be decently supported by those they serve," the laborer being worthy of his reward. Suppose, further, that a number of reverend and right reverend drones, who worked not; who preached, perhaps, but once a year, and then not the gospel of Jesus Christ, but the divine right of tithes, the dignity of their office as ambassadors of Christ, the equity of sinecures and a plurality of benefices, the excellency of the devotions in that prayer-book which some of them hired chaplains to use for them, or some favorite point of church-tyranny and anti-Christian usurpation—suppose such men as these, spending their lives in effeminacy, luxury, and idleness—or, when they were not idle, doing that which is worse than idleness—suppose such men should, merely by the merit of ordination and consecration, and a peculiar, odd habit, claim great respect and reverence from those whom they civilly called the beasts of the laity, and demand thousands per annum for that service which they never performed, and for which, if they had performed it, this would be more than a *quantum meruit*—suppose this should be the case (it is only by way of simile, and surely it will give no offence), would not everybody be astonished at such insolence, injustice, and impiety? And ought not such men to be told plainly that they could not reasonably expect the esteem and reward due to the ministers of the gospel unless they did the duties of their office? Should they not be told that their title and habit claimed no regard, reverence, or pay, separate from the care and work and various duties of their function—and that, while they neglected the latter, the former served only to render them the more ridiculous and contemptible? The application of this similitude to the case in hand is very easy. If those who bear the title of civil rulers do not perform the duty of civil rulers, but act directly counter to the sole end and design of their office; if they injure and oppress their subjects, instead of defending their rights and doing them good, they have not the least pretence to be honored, obeyed, and rewarded, according to the apostle's argument. For his reasoning, in order to show the duty of subjection to the higher powers, is, as was before observed, built wholly upon the supposition that they do, in fact, perform the duty of rulers.

If it be said that the apostle here uses another argument for submission to the higher powers besides that which is taken from the usefulness of their office to civil society when properly discharged and executed, namely, that their power is from God, that they are ordained of God, and that they are God's ministers; and if it be said that this argument for submission to them will hold good, although they do not exercise their power for the benefit, but for the ruin and destruction of human society—this objection was obviated, in part, before. Rulers have no authority from God to do mischief. They are not God's ordinance, or God's ministers, in any other sense than as it is by his permission and providence that they are exalted to bear rule; and as magistracy duly exercised, and authority rightly applied, in the enacting and executing good laws— laws attempered and accommodated to the common welfare of the subjects—must be supposed to be agreeable to the will of the ben- ficient Author and supreme Lord of the universe, whose "kingdom ruleth over all," and whose "tender mercies are over all his works." It is blasphemy to call tyrants and oppressors God's ministers. They are more properly "the messengers of Satan to buffet us." No rulers are properly God's ministers but such as are "just, ruling in the fear of God." When once magistrates act contrary to their office, and the end of their institution—when they rob and ruin the public, instead of being guardians of its peace and welfare— they immediately cease to be the ordinance and ministers of God, and no more deserve that glorious character than common pirates and highwaymen. So that, whenever that argument for submission fails which is grounded upon the usefulness of magistracy to civil society—as it always does when magistrates do hurt to society instead of good—the other argument, which is taken from their being the ordinance of God, must necessarily fail also; no person of a civil character being God's minister, in the sense of the apostle, any further than he performs God's will by exercising a just and reasonable authority, and ruling for the good of the subject.

This in general. Let us now trace the apostle's reasoning in favor of submission to the higher powers a little more particularly and exactly; for by this it will appear, on one hand, how good and conclusive it is for submission to those rulers who exercise their power in a proper manner, and, on the other, how weak and trifling and inconnected it is if it be supposed to be meant by the apostle to show the obligation and duty of obedience to tyrannical, oppressive rulers, in common with others of a different character.

The apostle enters upon his subject thus: "Let every soul be subject unto the higher powers; for there is no power but of God: the powers that be are ordained of God." Here he urges the duty of obedience from this topic of argument: that civil rulers, as they are supposed to fulfil the pleasure of God, are the ordinance of God. But how is this an argument for obedience to such rulers as do not perform the pleasure of God by doing good, but the pleasure of the devil by doing evil; and such as are not, therefore, God's ministers, but the devil's? "Whosoever, therefore, resisteth the power, resisteth the ordinances of God; and they that resist shall receive to themselves damnation." Here the apostle argues that those who resist a reasonable and just authority, which is agreeable to the will of God, do really resist the will of God himself, and will, therefore, be punished by him. But how does this prove that those who resist a lawless, unreasonable power, which is contrary to the will of God, do therein resist the will and ordinance of God? Is resisting those who resist God's will the same thing with resisting God? Or shall those who do so "receive to themselves damnation? For rulers are not a terror to good works, but to the evil. Wilt thou then not be afraid of the power? Do that which is good, and thou shalt have praise of the same. For he is the minister of God to thee for good." Here the apostle argues, more explicitly than he had before done, for revering and submitting to magistracy, from this consideration, that such as really performed the duty of magistrates would be enemies only to the evil actions of men, and would befriend and encourage the good, and so be a common blessing to society. But how is this an argument that we must honor and submit to such magistrates as are not enemies to the evil actions of men, but to the good, and such as are not a common blessing, but a common curse to society? "But if thou do that which is evil, be afraid: for he is the minister of God, a revenger, to execute wrath upon him that doth evil." Here the apostle argues, from the nature and end of magistracy, that such as did evil, and such only, had reason to be afraid of the higher powers; it being part of their office to punish evil-doers, no less than to defend and encourage such as do well. But if magistrates are unrighteous—if they are respecters of persons—if they are partial in their administration of justice—then those who do well have as much reason to be afraid as those that do evil: there can be no safety for the good, nor any peculiar ground of terror to the unruly and injurious; so that, in this case, the main end of civil government will be frustrated. And what reason is there for submitting to that government which does by no means answer the design of government? "Wherefore ye must needs be subject not only for wrath, but also for conscience' sake." Here the apostle argues the duty of a cheerful and conscientious submission to civil government from the nature and end of magistracy, as he had before laid it down; *i.e.,* as the design of it was to punish evil-doers, and to support and encourage such as do well; and as it must, if so exercised, be agreeable to the will of God. But how does what he here says prove the duty of a cheerful and conscientious subjection to those who forfeit the character of rulers—to those who encourage the bad and discourage the good? The argument here used no more proves it to be a sin to resist such rulers than it does to resist the devil, that he may flee from us. For one is as truly the minister of God as the other. "For, for this cause pay you tribute also; for they are God's ministers, attending continually upon this very thing." Here the apostle argues the duty of paying taxes from this consideration, that those who perform the duty of rulers are continually attending upon the public welfare. But how does this argument conclude for paying taxes to such princes as are continually endeavoring to ruin the public; and especially when such payment would facilitate and promote this wicked design? "Render therefore to all their dues; tribute to whom tribute is due; custom to whom custom; fear to whom fear; honor to whom honor." Here the apostle sums up what he has been saying concerning the duty of subjects to rulers; and his argument stands thus: "Since magistrates who execute their office well are common benefactors to society, and may in that respect properly be called ministers and ordinance of God, and since they are constantly employed in the service of the public, it becomes you to pay them tribute and custom, and to reverence, honor, and submit to them in the execution of their respective offices." This is apparently good reasoning. But does this argument conclude for the duty of paying tribute, custom, reverence, honor, and obedience to such persons as, although they bear the title of rulers, use all their power to hurt and injure the public— such as are not God's ministers, but Satan's? such as do not take care of and attend upon the public interest, but their own, to the ruin of the public—that is, in short, to such as have no just claim at all to tribute, custom, reverence, honor, and obedience? It is to be hoped that those who have any regard to the apostle's character as an inspired writer, or even as a man of common understanding, will not represent him as reasoning in such a loose, incoherent manner, and drawing conclusions which have not the least relation to his premises. For what can be more absurd than an argument thus framed: "Rulers are, by their office, bound to consult the public welfare and the good of society; therefore, you are bound to pay them tribute, to honor, and to submit to them, even when they destroy the public welfare, and are a common pest to society by acting in direct contradiction to the nature and end of their office"?

Thus, upon a careful review of the apostle's reasoning in this passage, it appears that his arguments to enforce submission are of such a nature as to conclude only in favor of submission to such rulers as he himself describes; *i.e.,* such as rule for the good of society, which is the only end of their institution. Common tyrants and public oppressors are not entitled to obedience from their subjects by virtue of anything here laid down by the inspired apostle.

I now add, further, that the apostle's argument is so far from proving it to be the duty of people to obey and submit to such rulers as act in contradiction to the public good, and so to the design of their office, that it proves the direct contrary. For, please to observe, that if the end of all civil government be the good of society; if this be the thing that is aimed at in constituting civil rulers; and if the motive and argument for submission to government be taken from the apparent usefulness of civil authority—it follows, that when no such good end can be answered by submission, there remains no argument or motive to enforce it; and if, instead of this good end's being brought about by submission, a contrary end is brought about, and the ruin and misery of society effected by it, here is a plain and positive reason against submission in all such cases, should they ever happen. And therefore, in such cases, a regard to the public welfare ought to make us withhold from our rulers that obedience and submission which it would otherwise be our duty to render to them. If it be our duty, for example, to obey our king merely for this reason, that he rules for the public welfare (which is the only argument the apostle makes use of), it follows, by a parity of reason, that when he turns tyrant, and makes his subjects his prey to devour and destroy, instead of his charge to defend and cherish, we are bound to throw off our allegiance to him, and to resist; and that according to the tenor of the apostle's argument in this passage. Not to discontinue our allegiance in this case would be to join with the sovereign in promoting the slavery and misery of that society, the welfare of which we ourselves, as well as our sovereign, are indispensably obliged to secure and promote, as far as in us lies. It is true the apostle puts no case of such a tyrannical prince; but, by his grounding his argument for submission wholly upon the good of civil society, it is plain he implicitly authorizes, and even requires us to make resistance, whenever this shall be necessary to the public safety and happiness. Let me make use of this easy and familiar similitude to illustrate the point in hand: Suppose God requires a family of children to obey their father and not to resist him, and enforces his command with this argument, that the superintendence and care and authority of a just and kind parent will contribute to the happiness of the whole family, so that they ought to obey him for their own sakes more than for his; suppose this parent at length runs distracted, and attempts in his mad fit to cut all his children's throats. Now, in this case, is not the reason before assigned why these children should obey their parent while he continued of a sound mind—namely, their common good— a reason equally conclusive for disobeying and resisting him, since he is become delirious and attempts their ruin? It makes no altera- tion in the argument whether this parent, properly speaking, loses his reason, or does, while he retains his understanding, that which is as fatal in its consequences as anything he could do were he really deprived of it. This similitude needs no formal application.

But it ought to be remembered that if the duty of universal obedience and non-resistance to our king or prince can be argued from this passage, the same unlimited submission, under a re- publican or any other form of government, and even to all the subordinate powers in any particular state, can be proved by it as well, which is more than those who allege it for the mentioned pur- pose would be willing should be inferred from it; so that this passage does not answer their purpose, but really overthrows and confutes it. This matter deserves to be more particularly considered. The advocates for unlimited submission and passive obedience do, if I mistake not, always speak with reference to kingly and monarchical government as distinguished from all other forms, and with reference to submitting to the will of the king in distinction from all subordinate officers acting beyond their commission and the authority which they have received from the crown. It is not pretended that any persons besides kings have a divine right to do what they please, so that no one may resist them without incurring the guilt of factiousness and rebellion. If any other powers oppress the people, it is generally allowed that the people may get redress by resistance, if other methods prove ineffectual. And if any officers in a kingly government go beyond the limits of that power which they have derived from the crown (the supposed original source of all power and authority in the state), and attempt illegally to take away the properties and lives of their fellow-subjects, they may be forcibly resisted, at least till application can be made to the crown. But as to the sovereign himself, he may not be resisted in any case, nor any of his officers, while they confine themselves within the bounds which he has prescribed to them. This is, I think, a true sketch of the principles of those who defend the doctrine of passive obedience and non-resistance. Now, there is nothing in Scripture which supports this scheme of political principles. As to the passage under consideration, the apostle here speaks of civil rulers in general—of all persons in common vested with authority for the good of society, without any particular reference to one form of government more than to another, or to the supreme power in any particular state more than to subordinate powers. The apostle does not concern himself with the different forms of goverment. This he supposes left entirely to human prudence and discretion. Now, the consequence of this is, that unlimited and passive obedience is no more enjoined in this passage under monarchical government, or to the supreme power in any state, than under all other species of government which answer the end of government, or to all the subordinate degrees of civil authority, from the highest to the lowest. Those, therefore, who would from this passage infer the guilt of resisting kings in all cases whatever, though acting ever so contrary to the design of their office, must, if they will be consistent, go much further, and infer from it the guilt of resistance under all other forms of government, and of resisting any petty officer in the state, though acting beyond his commission in the most arbitrary, illegal manner possible. The argument holds equally strong in both cases. All civil rulers, as such, are the ordinance and ministers of God, and they are all, by the nature of their office, and in their respective spheres and stations, bound to consult the public welfare.

With the same reason, therefore, that any deny unlimited and passive obedience to be here enjoined under a republic or aristocracy, or any other established form of civil government, or to subordinate powers acting in an illegal and oppressive manner; with the same reason others may deny that such obedience is enjoined to a king or monarch, or any civil power whatever. For the apostle says nothing that is *peculiar to kings;* what he says extends equally to all other persons whatever vested with any civil office. They are all, in exactly the same sense, the ordinance of God and the ministers of God, and obedience is equally enjoined to be paid to them all. For, as the apostle expresses it, there is *no power* but of God; and we are required to render to all their *dues,* and not *more* than their dues. And what these dues are, and to whom they are to be rendered, the apostle saith not, but leaves to the reason and conscience of men to determine.

Thus it appears that the common argument grounded upon this passage in favor of universal and passive obedience really overthrows itself, by proving too much, if it proves anything at all—namely, that no civil officer is, in any case whatever, to be resisted, though acting in express contradiction to the design of his office—which no man in his senses ever did or can assert.

If we calmly consider the nature of the thing inself, nothing can well be imagined more directly contrary to common sense than to suppose that millions of people should be subjected to the arbitrary, precarious pleasure of one single man, who has naturally no superiority over them in point of authority—so that their estates, and everything that is valuable in life, and even their lives also, shall be absolutely at his disposal, if he happens to be wanton and capricious enough to demand them. What unprejudiced man can think that God made *all* to be thus subservient to the lawless pleasure and frenzy of *one,* so that it shall always be a sin to resist him? Nothing but the most plain and express revelation from heaven could make a sober, impartial man believe such a monstrous, unaccountable doctrine; and, indeed, the thing itself appears so shocking, so out of all proportion, that it may be questioned whether all the miracles that ever were wrought could make it credible that this doctrine really came from God. At present there is not the least syllable in Scripture which gives any countenance to it. The hereditary, indefeasible, divine right of kings, and the doctrine of non-resistance, which is built upon the supposition of such a right, are altogether as fabulous and chimerical as transubstantiation, or any of the most absurd reveries of ancient or modern visionaries. These notions are fetched neither from divine revelation nor human reason; and, if they are derived from neither of those sources, it is not much matter from whence they came or whither they go. Only it is a pity that such doctrines should be propagated in society, to raise factions and rebellions, as we see they have, in fact, been, both in the last and in the present reign.

But, then, if unlimited submission and passive obedience to the higher powers, in all possible cases, be not a duty, it will be asked, "How far are we obliged to submit? If we may innocently disobey and resist in some cases, why not in all? Where shall we stop? What is the measure of our duty? This doctrine tends to the total dissolution of civil government, and to introduce such scenes of wild anarchy and confusion as are more fatal to society than the worst of Tyranny."

After this manner some men object; and, indeed, this is the most plausible thing that can be said in favor of such an absolute submission as they plead for. But the worst, or, rather, the best of it is, that there is very little strength or solidity in it; for similar difficulties may be raised with respect to almost every duty of natural and revealed religion. To instance only in two, both of which are near akin, and indeed exactly parallel to the case before us: it is unquestionably the duty of children to submit to their parents, and of servants to their masters; but no one asserts that it is their duty to obey and submit to them in all supposable cases, or universally a sin to resist them. Now, does this tend to subvert the just authority of parents and masters, or to introduce confusion and anarchy into private families? No. How, then, does the same pjrinciple tend to unhinge the government of that larger family the body politic? We know, in general, that children and servants are obliged to obey their parents and masters respectively; we know also, with equal certainty, that they are not obliged to submit to them in all things without exception, but may, in some cases, reasonably, and therefore innocently, resist them. These principles are acknowledged upon all hands, whatever difficulty there may be in fixing the exact limits of submission. Now, there is at least as much difficulty in stating the measure of duty in these two cases as in the case of rulers and subjects; so that this is really no objection—at least, no reasonable one—against resistance to the higher powers. Or, if it is one, it will hold equally against resistance in the other cases mentioned. It is indeed true, that turbulent, vicious-minded men may take occasion, from this principle that their rulers may in some cases be lawfully resisted, to raise factions and disturbances in the state, and to make resistance where resistance is needless, and therefore sinful. But is it not equally true that children and servants, of turbulent, vicious minds, may take occasion, from this principle that parents and masters may in some cases be lawfully resisted, to resist when resistance is unnecessary, and therefore criminal? Is the principle, in either case, false in itself merely because it may be abused, and applied to legitimate disobedience and resistance in those instances to which it ought not to be applied? According to this way of arguing, there will be no true principles in the world; for there are none but what may be wrested and perverted to serve bad purposes, either through the weakness or wickedness of men.

A people, really oppressed in a great degree by their sovereign, cannot well be insensible when they are so oppressed; and such a people—if I may allude to an ancient fable—have, like the hesperian fruit, a dragon for their protector and guardian. Nor would they have any reason to mourn if some Hercules should appear to dispatch him. For a nation thus abused to arise unanimously and resist their prince, even to the dethroning him, is not criminal, but a reasonable way of vindicating their liberties and just rights: it is making use of the means, and the only means, which God has put into their power for mutual and self defense. And it would be highly criminal in them not to make use of this means. It would be stupid tameness and unaccountable folly for whole nations to suffer *one* unreasonable, ambitious, and cruel man to wanton and riot in their misery. And in such a case, it would, of the two, be more rational to suppose that they that did not resist, than that they who did, would receive to themselves damnation.

And this naturally brings us to make some reflections upon the resistance which was made, about a century since, to that unhappy prince King Charles I., and upon the anniversary of his death. This is a point which I should not have concerned myself about, were it not that some men continue to speak of it, even to this day, with a great deal of warmth and zeal, and in such a manner as to undermine all the principles of liberty, whether civil or religious, and to introduce the most abject slavery both in church and state—so that it is become a matter of universal concern. What I have to offer upon this subject will be comprised in a short answer to the following queries, viz.:

¶For what reason the resistance to King Charles the First was made.
¶By whom it was made.
¶Whether this resistance was rebellion, or not.
¶How the anniversary of King Charles's death came at first to be solemnized as a day of fasting and humiliation. And, lastly,
¶Why those of the Episcopal clergy who are very high in the principles of ecclesiastical authority continue to speak of this unhappy man as a great saint and a martyr.

For what reason, then, was the resistance to King Charles made? The general answer to this inquiry is, that it was on account of the tyranny and oppression of his reign. Not a great while after his accession to the throne, he married a French Catholic, and with her seemed to have wedded the politics, if not the religion of France, also. For afterwards, during a reign, or, rather, a tyranny of many years, he governed in a perfectly wild and arbitrary manner, paying no regard to the constitution and the laws of the kingdom, by which the power of the crown was limited, or to the solemn oath which he had taken at his coronation. It would be endless, as well as needless, to give a particular account of all the illegal and despotic measures which he took in his administration—partly from his own natural lust of power, and partly from the influence of wicked counsellors and ministers. He committed many illustrious members of both Houses of Parliament to the Tower for opposing his arbitrary schemes. He levied many taxes upon the people without consent of Parliament, and then imprisoned great numbers of the principal merchants and gentry for not paying them. He erected, or at least revived, several arbitrary courts, in which the most unheard-of barbarities were committed with his knowledge and approbation. He supported that more than fiend, Archbishop Laud, and the clergy of his stamp, in all their church-tyranny and hellish cruelties. He authorized a book in favor of sports upon the Lord's day; and several clergymen were persecuted by him and the mentioned *pious* bishop for not reading it to the people after divine service. When the Parliament complained to him of the arbitrary proceedings of his corrupt ministers, he told that august body, in a rough, domineering, unprincely manner, that he wondered any one should be so foolish and insolent as to think that he would part with the meanest of his servants upon their account. He refused to call any Parliament at all for the space of twelve years together, during all which time he governed in an absolute, lawless, and despotic manner. He took all opportunities to encourage the Papists, and to promote them to the highest officers of honor and trust. He (probably) abetted the horrid massacre in Ireland, in which two hundred thousand Protestants were butchered by the Roman Catholics. He sent a large sum of money, which he had raised by his arbitrary taxes, into Germany, to raise foreign troops, in order to force more arbitrary taxes upon his subjects. He not only, by a long series of actions, but also in plain terms, asserted an absolute, uncontrollable power—saying, even in one of his speeches to Parliament, that, as it was blasphemy to dispute what God might do, so it was sedition in subjects to dispute what the king might do! Towards the end of his tyranny he came to the House of Commons, with an armed force, and demanded five of its principal members to be delivered up to him; and this was a prelude to that unnatural war which he soon after levied against his own dutiful subjects, whom he was bound, by all the laws of honor, humanity, piety, and, I might add, of interest also, to defend and cherish with a paternal affection. I have only time to hint at these facts in a general way, all which, and many more of the same tenor, may be proved by good authorities. So that the figurative language which St. John uses concerning the just and beneficent deeds of our blessed Saviour may be applied to the unrighteous and execrable deeds of this prince, viz.: "And there are also many other things which" King Charles "did, the which, if they should be written every one, I suppose that even the world itself could not contain the books that should be written." Now, it was on account of King Charles's thus assuming a power above the laws, in direct contradiction to his coronation oath, and governing, the greatest part of his time, in the most arbitrary, oppressive manner—it was upon this account that resistance was made to him, which at length issued in the loss of his crown, and of that head which was unworthy to wear it.

But by whom was this resistance made? Not by a private junto, not by a small seditious party, not by a few desperadoes, who to mend their fortunes would embroil the state; but by the Lords and Commons of England. It was they that almost unanimously opposed the king's measures for overturning the constitution, and changing that free and happy government into a wretched, absolute monarchy. It was they that, when the king was about levying forces against his subjects in order to make himself absolute, commissioned officers, and raised an army to defend themselves and the public; and it was they that maintained the war against him all along, till he was made a prisoner. This is indisputable; though it was not, properly speaking, the Parliament, but the army, which put him to death afterwards. And it ought to be freely acknowledged that most of their proceeding, in order to get this matter effected, and particularly the court by which the king was at last tried and condemned, was little better than a mere mockery of justice.

The next question which naturally arises is, whether this resistance which was made to the king by the Parliament was properly rebellion or not? The answer to which is plain—that it was not, but a most righteous and glorious stand, made in defence of the natural and legal rights of the people, against the unnatural and illegal encroachments of arbitrary power. Nor was this a rash and too sudden opposition. The nation had been patient under the oppressions of the crown, even to long-suffering, for a course of many years, and there was no rational hope of redress in any other way. Resistance was absolutely necessary, in order to preserve the nation from slavery, misery, and ruin. And who so proper to make this resistance as the Lords and Commons—the whole representative body of the people —guardians of the public welfare; and each of which was, in point of legislation, vested with an equal, coordinate power with that of the crown? Here were two branches of the legislature against one; two, which had law and equity and the constitution on their side, against one which was impiously attempting to overturn law and equity and the constitution, and to exercise a wanton, licentious sovereignty over the properties, consciences, and lives of all the people—such a sovereignty as some inconsiderately ascribe to the Supreme Governor of the world. I say, inconsiderately, because God himself does not govern in an absolutely arbitrary and despotic manner. The power of this almighty King—I speak it not without caution and reverence —the power of this almighty King is limited by law; not indeed by acts of Parliament, but by the eternal laws of truth, wisdom, and equity, and the everlasting tables of right reason—tables that cannot be repealed, or thrown down and broken like those of Moses. But King Charles set himself up above all these, as much as he did above the written laws of the realm, and made mere humor and caprice, which are no rule at all, the only rule and measure of his administration. And now is it not perfectly ridiculous to call resistance to such a tyrant by the name of *rebellion*—the grand rebellion? Even that—Parliament which brought King Charles II. to the throne, and which run loyally mad, severely reproved one of their own members for condemning the proceedings of that Parliament which first took up arms against the former king. And upon the same principles that the proceedings of this Parliament may be censured as wicked and rebellious, the proceedings of those who, since, opposed King James II., and brought the Prince of Orange to the throne, may be censured as wicked and rebellious also. The cases are parallel. But, whatever some men may think, it is to be hoped that, for their own sakes, they will not dare to speak against the Revolution, upon the justice and legality of which depends, in part his present majesty's right to the throne.

If it be said that although the Parliament which first opposed King Charles's measures, and at length took up arms against him, were not guilty of rebellion, yet certainly those persons were who condemned and put him to death—even this, perhaps, is not true; for he had, in fact, unkinged himself long before, and had forfeited his title to the allegiance of the people. So that those who put him to death were, at most, only guilty of murder—which indeed is bad enough, if they were really guilty of *that*—which is, at least, disputable. Cromwell, and those who were principally concerned in the (nominal) king's death, might possibly have been very wicked and designing men. Nor shall I say anything in vindication of the reigning hypocrisy of those times, or of Cromwell's mal-administration during the interregnum; for it is truth, and not a party, that I am speaking for. But still, it may be said that Cromwell and his adherents were not, properly speaking, guilty of rebellion, because he whom they beheaded was not, properly speaking, their king, but a lawless tyrant; much less are the whole body of the nation at that time to be charged with rebellion on that account: for it was no national act; it was not done by a free Parliament. And much less

still is the nation at present to be charged with the great sin of
rebellion for what their ancestors did, or, rather, did not, a century
ago.

But how came the anniversary of King Charles's death to be
solmnized as a day of fasting and humiliation? The true answer
in brief to which inquiry is, that this fact was instituted by way of
court and compliment to King Charles II. upon the restoration. All
were desirous of making their court to him, of ingratiating themselves, and of making him forget what had been done in opposition
to his father, so as not to revenge it. To effect this they ran into
the most extravagant professions of affection and loyalty to him,
insomuch that he himself said that it was a mad and hair-brained
loyalty which they professed. And, amongst other strange things
which his first Parliament did, they ordered the thirtieth of January
—the day on which his father was beheaded—to be kept as a day
of solemn humiliation, to deprecate the judgments of Heaven for
the rebellion which the nation had been guilty of, in that which
was no national thing, and which was not rebellion in them that
did it. Thus they soothed and flattered their new king at the expense
of their liberties, and were ready to yield up freely to Charles II.
all that enormous power which they had justly resisted Charles I.
for usurping to himself.

The last query mentioned was, Why those of the Episcopal
clergy who are very high in the principles of ecclesiastical authority
continue to speak of this unhappy man as a great saint and a martyr.
This we know is what they constantly do, especially upon the thirtieth of January—a day sacred to the extolling of him, and to the re-
proaching of those who are not of the Established Church. "Out of
the same mouth," on this day, "proceedeth blessing and cursing;"
therewith bless they their God, even Charles, and therewith curse
they the dissenters. And their "tongue can no man tame; it is an
unruly evil, full of deadly poison." King Charles is upon this
solemnity frequently compared to our Lord Jesus Christ, both in
respect of the holiness of his life and the greatness and injustice
of his sufferings; and it is a wonder they do not add something concerning the merits of his death also: but "blessed saint" and "royal
martyr" are as humble titles as any that are thought worthy of him.

Now this may, at first view, well appear to be a very strange
phenomenon; for King Charles was really a man black with
guilt, and "laden with iniquity," as appears by his crimes before
mentioned. He lived a tyrant; and it was the oppression and violence
of his reign that brought him to his untimely and violent end at
last. Now, what of saintship or martyrdom is there in all this? What
of saintship is there in encouraging people to profane the Lord's
day? What of saintship in falsehood and perjury? What of saintship in repeated robberies and depredations? What of saintship in

throwing real saints and glorious patriots into jails? What of saintship in overturning an excellent civil constitution, and proudly
grasping at an illegal and monstrous power? What of saintship in
the murder of thousands of innocent people, and involving a nation
in all the calamities of civil war? And what of martyrdom is there
in a man's bringing an immature and violent death upon himself
by "being wicked overmuch"? Is there any such thing as grace without goodness; as being a follower of Christ without following him;
as being his disciple without learning of him to be just and beneficent;
or as saintship without sanctity? If not, I fear it will be hard to
prove this man a saint. And verily one would be apt to suspect that
church must be but poorly stocked with saints and martyrs which
is forced to adopt such enormous sinners into her calendar in order
to swell the number.

But to unravel this mystery of (nonsense as well as of) iniquity,
which has already worked for a long time amongst us, or, at least,
to give the most probable solution of it, it is to be remembered that
King Charles—this burlesque upon saintship and martyrdom—
though so great an oppressor, was a true friend to the church—so
true a friend to her that he was very well affected towards the
Roman Catholics, and would probably have been very willing to
unite Lambeth and Rome. This appears by his marrying a true
daughter of that true "mother of harlots," which he did with a
dispensation from the Pope, that supreme bishop, to whom, when
he wrote, he gave the title of Most Holy Father. His queen was
extremely bigoted to all the follies and superstitions, and to the
hierarchy, of Rome, and had a prodigious ascendency over him all
his life. It was in part owing to this that he (probably) abetted the
massacre of the Protestants in Ireland—that he assisted in extir-
pating the French Protestants at Rochelle—that he all along encouraged Papists and popishly affected clergymen, in preference to
all other persons—and that he upheld that monster of wickedness,
Archbishop Laud, and the bishops of his stamp, in all their church
tyranny and diabolical cruelties. In return to his kindness and indulgence in which respects they caused many of the pulpits throughout the nation to ring with the divine, absolute, indefeasible right
of kings—with the praise of Charles and his reign, and with the
damnable sin of resisting the "Lord's anointed," let him do what
he would; so that not Christ, but Charles, was commonly preached
to the people. In plain English, there seems to have been an impious
bargain struck up betwixt the sceptre and the surplice for enslaving
both the bodies and souls of men. The king appeared to be willing
that the clergy should do what they would—set up a monstrous
hierarchy like that of Rome, a monstrous Inquisition like that of
Spain or Portugal, or anything else which their own pride and the
devil's malice could prompt them to—provided always that the

clergy would be *tools* to the crown; that they would make the people believe that kings had God's authority for breaking God's law— that they had a commission from Heaven to seize the estates and lives of their subjects at pleasure—and that it was a damnable sin to resist them, even when they did such things as deserved more than damnation. This appears to be the true key for explaining the mysterious doctrine of King Charles's saintship and martyrdom. He was a saint, not because he was in his life a good man, but a good Churchman; not because he was a lover of holiness, but the hierarchy; not because he was a friend to Christ, but the craft. And he was a martyr in his death, not because he bravely suffered death in the cause of truth and righteousness, but because he died an enemy to liberty and the rights of conscience; *i.e.*, not because he died an enemy to sin, but dissenters. For these reasons it is that all bigoted clergymen and friends to church power paint this man as a saint in his life, though he was such a mighty, such a *royal sinner*; and as a martyr in his death, though he fell a sacrifice only to his own ambition, avarice, and unbounded lust of power. And, from prostituting their praise upon King Charles, and offering him that incense which is not his due, it is natural for them to make a transition to the dissenters—as they commonly do—and to load them with that reproach which they do not deserve—they being generally professed enemies both to civil, and ecclesiastical, tyranny. We are commonly charged, upon the thirtieth of January, with the guilt of putting the king to death, under a notion that it was our ancestors that did it; and so we are represented in the blackest colors, not only as schismatics, but also as traitors and rebels, and all that is bad. And these lofty gentlemen usually rail upon this head in such a manner as plainly shows that they are either grossly ignorant of the history of those times which they speak of, or—which is worse—that they are guilty of the most shameful prevarication, slander, and falsehood. But every petty priest with a roll and a gown thinks he must do something in imitation of his betters in lawn, and show himself a true son of the church: and thus, through a foolish ambition to appear considerable, they only render themselves contemptible.

But, suppose our forefathers did kill their mock saint and martyr a century ago, what is that to us now? If I mistake not, these gentlemen generally preach down the doctrine of the imputation of Adam's sin to his posterity as absurd and unreasonable, notwithstanding they have solemnly subscribed what is equivalent to it in their own articles of religion; and therefore one would hardly expect that they would lay the guilt of the king's death upon us, although our forefathers had been the only authors of it: but this conduct is much more surprising when it does not appear that *our* ancestors had any more hand in it than *their own*. However, bigotry is sufficient to account for this and many other phenomena which cannot be accounted for in any other way.

Although the observation of this anniversary seems to have been at least superstitious in its original; and although it is often abused to very bad purposes by the established clergy, as they serve themselves of it to perpetrate strife, a party spirit, and divisions in the Christian church; yet it is to be hoped that one good end will be answered by it, quite contrary to their intention: It is to be hoped that it will prove a standing momento that Britons will not be slaves, and a warning to all corrupt counsellors and ministers not to go too far in advising to arbitrary, despotic measures.

To conclude: Let us all learn to be free and to be loyal; let us not profess ourselves vassals to the lawless pleasure of any man on earth; but let us remember, at the same time, government is sacred, and not to be trifled with. It is our happiness to live under a prince who is satisfied with ruling according to law, as every other good prince will. We enjoy under his administration all the liberty that is proper and expedient for us. It becomes us, therefore, to be contented and dutiful subjects. Let us prize our freedom, but not "use our liberty for a cloak of maliciousness." There are men who strike at liberty under the term licentiousness; there are others who aim at popularity under the disguise of patriotism. Be aware of both. Extremes are dangerous. There is at present amongst us, perhaps, more danger of the latter than of the former; for which reason I would exhort you to pay all due regard to the government over us, to the king, and all in authority, and to "lead a quiet and peaceful life." And, while I am speaking of loyalty to our earthly prince, suffer me just to put you in mind to be loyal also to the Supreme Ruler of the universe, "by whom kings reign and princes decree justice"—to which King, eternal, immortal, invisible, even to "the only wise God," be all honor and praise, dominion and thanksgiving, through Jesus Christ our Lord.

AMEN

The Curse of Cowardice

Samuel Davies

Samuel Davies was born in New Castle County, Delaware, on November 3, 1723. He was trained for the ministry at the school of Samuel Blair in Pennsylvania and was licensed to preach by the Presbytery of New Castle in 1746. In 1747, he was sent to Virginia as an evangelist. He settled in Hanover County and very shortly became the spokesman for the religious dissenters who were frequently harassed by the authorities.

Davies worked diligently to build a strong Presbyterian membership in Virginia, serving as pastor for seven different churches located in five separate counties, as well as traveling throughout the state actively engaged in the work of the church.

In 1753, the Synod of New York sent Davies, together with Gilbert Tennent, to England to raise money for the College of New Jersey. The two ministers were highly successful. Not only was a considerable sum of money raised, but Davies himself had the opportunity to preach more than sixty sermons throughout the British Isles.

Returning to Virginia, widely acclaimed and highly respected, the Rev. Davies once more plunged into the work of the church. Following the untimely deaths in rapid succession of Aaron Burr and Jonathan Edwards as presidents of the College of New Jersey, Davies accepted the offer of the board of trustees to fill the vacancy in the presidency of the college. But Samuel Davies did not vary the pattern set by his predecessors, for shortly after assuming office, he, too, died in 1761.

The *Dictionary of National Biography* comments that Davies had "achieved the reputation of being the greatest pulpit orator of his generation. For fifty years after his death, his sermons were more widely read than those of any of his contemporaries." "The Curse of Cowardice" is an example of the master sermon, addressed to soldiers and potential soldiers alike, in an effort to get citizens to "take up Arms for the Defence of their Country." It was preached at Hanover County, Virginia, on May 8, 1758. The text is from the J. Buckland edition printed in London in 1758.

JER. XLVIII. 10. *Cursed be he that doth the Work of the Lord deceitfully; and cursed be he that keepeth back his Sword from Blood.*

NOTHING can be more agreeable to the God of Peace, than to see universal Harmony and Benevolence prevail among his Creatures: and He has laid them under the strongest Obligations to cultivate a pacific Temper towards one another, both as *Individuals*, and as *Nations*. *"Follow Peace with all Men,"* is one of the principal Precepts of our holy Religion. And the great Prince of Peace has solemnly pronounced, *"Blessed are the Peace-makers."*

But when, in this corrupt disordered State of Things, where the Lusts of Men are perpetually embroiling the World with Wars and Fightings, and throwing all into Confusion; when Ambition and Avarice would rob us of our Property, for which we have toiled, and on which we subsist; when they would enslave the free-born Mind, and compel us meanly to cringe to Usurpation and Arbitrary Power; when they would tear from our eager Grasp the most valuable Blessing of Heaven. I mean our RELIGION : when they invade our Country, formerly the Region of Tranquillity, ravage our Frontiers, butcher our Fellow-Subjects, or confine them in a barbarous Captivity in the Dens of Savages; when our *earthly* All is ready to be seized by rapacious Hands, and even our *Eternal* All is in Danger by the Loss of our Religion: When this is the Case, what is then the Will of God? Must Peace then be maintained? maintained with our perfidious and cruel Invaders? maintained at the Expence of Property, Liberty, Life, and every Thing dear and valuable? maintained, when it is in our Power to vindicate our Right, and do ourselves Justice? Is the Work of Peace then our only Business? No; in such a Time even the God of Peace proclaims by his Providence, "TO ARMS!" Then the *Sword* is, as it were, *consecrated* to God; and the Art of WAR becomes a Part of our *Religion*. Then happy is he that shall reward our Enemies, as they have served us. Blessed is the brave Soldier: blessed is the Defender of his Country, and the Destroyer of its Enemies. Blessed are they who offer themselves willingly in this Service, and who faithfully discharge it. But on the other Hand, "Cursed is he that doth the Work of the Lord deceitfully; and cursed is he that keepeth back his Sword from Blood."

As to the original Reference and Meaning of these Words, it is sufficient to my Purpose to observe, That the Moabites, against whom this Prophecy was immediately denounced, were a troublesome and restless Nation in the Neighbourhood of the *Jews,* who, though often subdued by them, as *France* has been by England, yet upon every Occasion struggled to recover their Power, and renewed their Hostilities. By this, and various other Steps, they were arrived to the highest Pitch of national Guilt, and ripe for Execution. The *Babylonians* were commissioned for this Work of Vengeance: and they were bound to execute the Commission faithfully, under Penalty of a Curse. To them this Denunciation was immediately directed, "Cursed to be that doth the Work of the Lord deceitfully or negligently; and cursed be he that keepeth back his Sword from Blood." This is expressed in the Form of an Imprecation, or an authoritative Denunciation of a Curse: And in this Form it might be used, consistently with Benevolence, by a Prophet speaking as the Mouth of God. But this is not a Pattern for our Imitation, who are peculiarly obliged under the Gospel to *"Bless, and curse not,"* and to *"pray for all Men."* However, it may be pronounced even by our Lips as a *Declaration* of the righteous Curse of God against a dastardly Refusal to engage in War, when it is our Duty; or a deceitful negligent Discharge of that Duty, after we have engaged in it. These are the Crimes that seem intended in my Text: and against each of these the tremendous Curse of JEHOVAH is still in full Force in all Ages, even under the mild and gentle Dispensation of the Gospel. Cowardice and Treachery are now as execrable as ever.

"Cursed be he that keepeth back his Sword from Blood." This Denunciation, like the Artillery of Heaven, is leveled against the mean, sneaking Coward, who, when God, in the Course of his Providence, calls him to Arms, refuses to obey, and consults his own Ease and Safety, more than his Duty of God and his Country.

"Cursed be he that doth the Work of the Lord deceitfully." This seems to be leveled against another Species of Cowards; sly, hypocritical Cowards, who undertake the Work of the Lord, that is, take up Arms; but they do the work of Lord *deceitfully,* that is, they do not faithfully use their Arms for the Purposes they were taken. They commence Soldiers, not that they may serve their country, and do their Duty to God, but that they may live in Ease, Idleness and Pleasure, and enrich themselves at the public Expence. *Cursed is he that doth the Work of the Lord deceitfully,* and serves himself under Pretence of serving his Country.

You Gentlemen and others, whom I this Day behold with peculiar Pleasure engaged in the Cause of your neglected Country, and who have done me the Honour of inviting me to this Service; a Service, which I am sure I should perform to your Satisfaction, if my Preparations and Abilities were proportioned to my Benevolence for you, and my Concern for your Success: *You* are peculiarly interested in the remarks I have made upon the Text. And that I may contribute all in my Power both to increase your Number, and direct you to a proper Conduct in the honourable Character you sustain, I shall lay before you a brief View of the present Circumstances of our Country, from which it will appear, that the War in which we are engaged is a Duty, or THE WORK OF THE LORD; and consequently, that we are all obliged, according to our respective Characters, to carry it on with Vigour, under Penalty of falling under the Curse of God. And then I shall shew you what is the deceitful Performance of the Lord's Work, or unseasonably keeping back to the Sword from Blood, which exposes to the Curse.

¶i.   I am to lay before you a brief View of the Present Circumstances of our Country, which render the War in which we are engaged the Work of the Lord, which consecrate Swords as Instruments of Righteousness, and call us to the dreadful, but important Duty of shedding human Blood, upon Penalty of falling under the tremendous Curse of God.

Need I inform you what Barbarities and Depredations a mongrel Race of Indian Savages and French Papists have perpetrated upon our Frontiers? How wide an Extent of Country abandoned! How many poor Families obliged to fly in Consternation, and leave their All behind them! What Breaches and separations between the nearest Relations! What painful Ruptures of Heart from Heart! What shocking Dispersions of those once united by the strongest and most endearing Ties! Some lie dead, mangled with savage Wounds, consumed to Ashes with outrageous Flames, or torn and devoured by the Beasts of the Wilderness, while their Bones lie whitening in the Sun, and serve as tragical Memorials of the fatal Spot where they fell. Others have been dragged away Captives, and made the Slaves of imperious and cruel Savages. Others have made their Escape, and live to lament their butchered or captivated Friends and Relations. In short, our Frontiers have been drenched with the Blood of our Fellow-Subjects, through the Length of a thousand Miles: and new Wounds are still opening. We, in these inland Parts of the Country, are as yet unmolested, through the immerited Mercy of Heaven. But let us glance a Thought to the Western Extremities of our Body Politick; and what melancholy Scenes open to our View! Now, perhaps, while I am speaking; now, while you are secure and unmolested, our Fellow-Subjects there may be feeling the calamities I am describing. Now, perhaps, the savage Shouts and Whoops of Indians, and the Screams and Groans of some butchered Family, may be mingling their Horrors, and circulating their horrendous Echoes thro' the Wilderness of Rocks and Mountains. Now, perhaps some tender delicate Creature may be suffering an involuntary Prostitution to savage Lust; and perhaps debauched and murdered by the same Hand. Now, perhaps, some miserable Briton or Virginian may be passing through a tedious Process of Experiments in the infernal Art of Torture. Now some helpless Children may be torn from the Arms of their murdered Parents, and dragged away weeping and wringing their Hands, to receive their Education among Barbarians, and to be formed upon the Model of a ferocious Indian Soul.

And will these Violences cease without a vigorous and timely Resistance from us? Can Indian Revenge and Thirst for Blood be glutted? or can French Ambition and Avarice be satisfied? No, we have no Method left, but to repel Force with Force, and give them Blood to drink in their Turn, who have drunk ours. If we sit still and do nothing, or content ourselves, as alas we have hitherto, with feeble dilatory Efforts, we may expect these Barbarities will not only continue, but that the Indians, headed by the French, those eternal Enemies of Peace, Liberty and Britons, will carry their Inroads still farther into the Country, and reach even to us. By the Desertion of our remote Settlements, the Frontiers are approaching every Day nearer and nearer to us: and if we cannot stand our Ground now, when we have above an hundred Miles of a thick-settled Country between us and the Enemy, much less shall we be able, when our Strength is weakened by so vast a Loss of Men, Arms and Riches, and we lie exposed to their immediate Incursions. Some cry, "Let the Enemy come down to us, and then we will fight them." But this is the trifling Excuse of Cowardice or Security, and not the Language of Prudence and Fortitude. Those who make this Plea, if the Enemy should take them at their Word, and make them so near a Visit, would be as forward in Flight, as they are now backward to take up Arms.

Such, my Brethren, such, alas! is the present State of our Country: it bleeds in a thousand Veins; and without a timely Remedy, the Wound will prove mortal. And in such Circumstances, is it not our Duty in the Sight of God, is it not a Work to which the Lord loudly calls us, to take up Arms for the Defence of our Country? Certainly it is: and "cursed is he," who having no Ties sufficiently strong to confine him at Home, "keepeth his Sword from Blood." The mean, sneaking Wretch, that can desert the Cause of his Country in such an Exigency; his Country, in the Blessings of which he shared, while in Peace and Prosperity; and which is therefore intitled to his Sympathy and Assistance in the Day of its Distress; that cowardly ungrateful Wretch sins against God and his Country, and deserves the Curse of Both. Such a Conduct in such a Conjuncture, is a *moral Evil*, a gross Wickedness; and exposes the Wretch to the heavy Curse of God both in this and the eternal World.

And here I cannot but observe, that among the various and numberless Sins under which our Country groans, and which must be looked upon as the Causes of our public Calamities, by every one that believes a divine Providence; (a Doctrine so comfortable, and so essential both in Natural and Revealed Religion; an Article in the Creed of Heathens and Mahometans, as well as Jews and Christians;) I say among these various Sins, Cowardice and Security are none of the least. He that hath determined the Bounds of our Habitation, hath planted us in a Land of Liberty and Plenty; a Land, till lately, unalarmed with the Terrors of War, and unstained with human Blood: Indeed, all Things considered, there are but few such happy spots upon our Globe. And must it not highly provoke our divine Benefactor, to see a People thus distinguished with Blessings, so insensible of their Worth, so ungrateful for them, and so unacquainted with their own Unworthiness to receive them? What can be more evidential of their undue Apprehensions of the Worth of these Blessings, than their being so little concerned to secure and recover them? The Generality among us have acted, as if their Interests at State were so trifling, that it would not be worth while to take Pains, or encounter Dangers, to preserve them. What greater Evidence can be given of Ingratitude, than a supine Neglect of these Blessings, and such a stupidly tame and irresisting Resignation of them into bloody and rapacious Hands? And what can be more evidential of a proud Insensibility of our Unworthiness of such Blessings, than our being so inapprehensive of losing them, even in the most threatening and dangerous Circumstances? Our Countrymen in general have acted, as if Beings of their Importance and Merit might certainly rest in the quiet unmolested Possession of their Liberty and Property, without any one daring to disturb them, and without their doing any Thing for their own Defence: or as if neither God nor Man could strip them of their Enjoyments. What a vain self-confident Presumption, What intolerable Insolence is this, in a sinful Nation, a People laden with Iniquity, who have forfeited every Blessing, even the Ground they tread upon, and the Air they breathe in; and who live merely by the immerited Grace, and Bounty of God? Is not Cowardice and Security, or an Unwillingness to engage with all our Might in the Defence of our Country, in such a Situation, an enormous *Wickedness* in the Sight of God, and worthy of his Curse, as well as a scandalous dastardly *Meanness* in the Sight of Men, and worthy of public Shame and Indignation? Is it not fit, that those who so contemptuously depreciate the rich and undeserved Bounties of Heaven, and who swell so insolently with a vain Conceit of their own Importance and Worth, should be punished with the Loss of those Blessings? What Discipline can be more seasonable or congruous? May we not suppose, that divine Providence has permitted our Body Politick to suffer Wound after Wound, and baffled all our languid Efforts, in order to give it Sensibility, and rouse us to exert our Strength in more vigorous Efforts? Has not the Curse of God lain heavy upon our Country, because we have *done the Work of the Lord deceitfully, and kept back our Swords from Blood?*

And shall this Guilt increase from Year to Year, till we are entirely crushed with the enormous Load? Shall neither the Fear of JEHOVAH's Curse, nor the Love of our Country, nor even the love of ourselves, and our own personal Interest, constrain us at Length to relieve our ravaged Country, and defend the Blessings which God has entrusted to our *Custody*, as well as lent to us to *enjoy*?—Blessed be God, and Thanks to you, brave Soldiers, for what I now see. I see you engaged in this good Cause: and may the effectual *Blessing* of Heaven be upon you, instead of the Curse entailed upon Cowardice and Treachery! But are there no more to join with you? what! none more in this Crowd? None more in Hanover? Hanover! which I think should shew itself worthy of Precedence, and exhibit a brave Example to other Counties: This is what may reasonably be expected, from the Number of our Militia, the high Price of our Staple Commodity, the Frequency and Variety of our religious Instructions; and I may add, from our own former good Conduct in such an Emergency. Hanover had the Honour of sending out the first Company of Volunteers, that were raised in the Colony. And are we degenerated so soon? Or is our Danger less now, than immediately after Braddock's Defeat? Or are we now inured and hardened to bad News, so that the Calamities of our Frontiers, which have been growing every Year, have now ceased to be Objects of our Compassion?

I am sorry to tell you, that the Company now forming, is not yet compleated, tho' under Officers from among yourselves, from whom you may expect good Usage; and the Encouragement is so unusually great, and the Time of Service so short. May I not reasonably insist upon it, that the Company be made up this very Day before we leave this Place? Methinks your King, your Country, nay, your own Interests command me: and therefore I must insist upon it. Oh! for the all-prevailing Force of Demosthenes's Oratory —but I recall my Wish, that I may correct it—Oh! for the Influence of the Lord of Armies, the God of Battles, the Author of true Courage, and every heroic Virtue, to fire you into Patriots and Soldiers this Moment! Ye young and hardy Men, whose very Faces seem to speak that God and Nature formed you for Soldiers, who are free from the Incumbrance of Families depending upon you for Subsistence, and who are perhaps but of little Service to Society, while at Home, may I not speak for you, and declare as your Mouth, "Here we are, all ready to abandon our Ease, and rush into the glorious Dangers of the Field, in Defence of our Country?" Ye that love your Country, enlist: for Honour will follow you in Life or Death in such a Cause. You that love your Religion, enlist: for your Religion is in Danger. Can Protestant Christianity expect Quarters from Heathen Savages and French Papists? Sure in such an Alliance, the Powers of Hell make a third Party. Ye that love your Friends and Relations, enlist: lest ye see them enslaved or butchered before your eyes. Ye that would catch at Money, here is a proper Bait for you; ten Pounds for a few Months Service, besides the usual Pay of Soldiers. I seriously make the Proposal to you, not only as a Subject of the best of Kings, and a Friend to your Country, but as *a Servant of the most High God*: for I am fully persuaded what I am recommending, is his Will; and Disobedience to it may expose you to his Curse.

This Proposal is not liable to the Objections that have been urged against former Measures for raising Men. You can no longer object, "that you are dragged away like Slaves against your Wills, while others are without Reason exempted:" for now it is left to your own Honour, and you may act as free Men. Nor can you object, "that you are arbitrarily thrust under the Command of foreign, unknown, or disagreeable Officers:" for the Gentleman that has the immediate Command of this Company, and his subordinate Officers, are of yourselves, your Neighbours Children, and perhaps your old Companions. And I hope I may add, you need not object, that you shall be badly used: for, GENTLEMEN-OFFICERS, may I not promise for you, that not one Man in your Company shall be treated with Cruelty or Injustice, as far as your Authority or Influence can prevent? May I not be your Security, that none but the Guilty shall be punished, and only according to the Nature of the Offence? Perhaps some may object, that should they enter the Army, their morals would be in Danger of Infection, and their Virtue would be perpetually shocked with horrid Scenes of Vice. This may also be a Discouragement to Parents to consent to their Childrens engaging in so good a Cause. I am glad to hear this Objection, when it is sincere, and not an empty Excuse: and I wish I could remove it, by giving you an universal Assurance, that the Army is a School of Religion; and that Soldiers, as they are more exposed to Death than other Men, are proportionably better prepared for it than others. But alas! the Reverse of this is too true; and the Contagion of Vice and Irreligion is perhaps no where stronger than in the Army; where, one would think, the supreme Tribunal should be always in View, and it should be their chief Care to prepare for Eternity, on the slippery Brink of which they stand every Moment. But, GENTLEMEN-OFFICERS, I must again appeal to you, that as for this Company, you will not willingly allow any Form of Vice to be practised in it with Impunity; but will always endeavour to recommend and enforce Religion and good Morals by your Example and Authority, and to suppress the contrary? May I not give the Public the Satisfaction of such an Assurance concerning you, that whatever others do, as for you and your Company you will serve the Lord? Do you not own yourselves bound to this in Honour and Duty? Such a Conduct I can assure you, will render you popular among the Wise and Good; tho' perhaps it may expose you to the senseless Contempt of Fools, who *make a Mock of Sin*, and who esteem it Bravery to insult that God, *in whose Hand their Breath is*, and *whose are all their Ways*. Such a Conduct will afford you Pleasure in the Review, when the Terrors of the bloody Field are spread round you, and Death starts up before you in a thousand shocking Forms. Such a Conduct will be a Source of true Courage, and render you nobly indifferent about Life or Death in a good Cause. And let me honestly warn you, that if you do not maintain such a Conduct, you will bitterly repent it either in Time, or Eternity.

But I return to invite others to join with you in this important Expedition. What a Crowd of important Arguments press you on every Hand? What can our Legislature do more, than they have done to engage you? If such unusual Encouragement does not prevail upon you to enlist as *Volunteers*, what remains but that you must be *forced* to it by Authority? For our Country *must* be defended: and if nothing but *Force* can constrain you to take up Arms in its Defence, then Force *must* be used: Persons of such a sordid unmanly Spirit, are not to expect the Usage of *Freemen*. Think what the paternal Care of our Sovereign has done for us: and how many Millions of Money, and Thousands of Men our Mother-Country has furnished for our Defence. And shall we do nothing for ourselves? Great-Britain, I own, is interested in our Protection: but can she be as much interested as ourselves? Consider what the brave New-England Men have done, after so many Mortifications and Disappointments, and their Treasury so much exhausted. By the best Accounts I have had, the little Colony of Massachusetts-Bay has raised no less than 7000 Men, tho' not larger perhaps than 15 or 20 of those 53 Counties contained in Virginia. And since we have the same Interests at Stake, shall not we chearfully furnish our Quota for the public Service? We all admire the Bravery and Success of the King of Prussia: but his Success must be greatly owing to the Bravery of his *Subjects*, as well as his *own*. He has almost as many Soldiers as Subjects. And he has almost *miraculously* stood his Ground against such superior Numbers, shall we, with the Advantage of Numbers on our Side, be perpetually flying before a pitiful Enemy, and tamely give up our Country to their Ravages? Let us strenuously exert that superior Force, which a gracious Providence has put in our Hands: and we may soon expect, thro' the Concurrence of Heaven, that we shall again enjoy the Blessings of Peace. Whatever Intelligence our artful Enemies may send, or the Cowardly among ourselves may believe, there is no Reason to conclude, that the French Regulars upon this Continent are half so many as ours: and as to the *Coloni*, or Country-militia, we are certainly 20, perhaps 40, to one. Let us then, in the Name of the Lord of Hosts, the God of the Armies of Israel, let us collect our whole Strength, and give one decisive Blow; and we may humbly hope Victory will be ours.

Every one can complain of the bad Management of our public Undertakings, and lament the general Security and Inactivity that prevails. Every one can wish that Something were effectually done, and that this and that Person would enlist. Every one can tell, what great Atchievements he *would* perform, were it not for this and that, and a hundred Obstructions in his Way. But this idle Complaining, Wishing and Lamenting, and Boasting, will answer no End. SOMETHING MUST BE DONE! must be done BY YOU! Therefore, instead of assuming the State of Patriots and Heroes at home, TO ARMS! and away to the Field, and prove your Pretensions sincere. Let the Thunder of this Imprecation rouse you out of your Ease, and Security, "Cursed be he that doth the Work of the Lord deceitfully; and cursed be he that keepeth back his Sword from Blood." God sent an Angel from Heaven to curse the dastardly Inhabitants of Meroz, who refused to take up Arms for the Defence of their Country. (Judges v.23.) "Curse ye Meroz, said the Angel of the Lord, curse ye bitterly the Inhabitants thereof: because they came not to the Help of the Lord, to the Help of the Lord against the Mighty." And shall this Curse fall upon Virginia? no, fly from it by venturing your lives for your Country: for this Curse is far more terrible than any Thing that can befal you in the Field of Battle. But it is not enough for you to *undertake* this Work: you are also obliged *faithfully to perform* it, as the Work of the Lord. And this leads me,

¶ii. To shew you, what is that deceitful Performance of the Lord's Work, or unseasonable keeping back the Sword from Blood, which exposes to his Curse.

If Soldiers, instead of abandoning their Ease and Pleasure, and risquing their Lives in Defence of their Country, should unman themselves with sensual Pleasures and Debauchery; if, instead of searching out the Enemy, they keep out of their Way, lest they should search out and find them; if they lie sleeping or rioting in Forts and Places of Safety, while their Country is ravaged, perhaps in their very Neighborhood: when they waste their Courage in Broils and Duels among themselves, or in tyrannizing over those that are under their Command: when they lay themselves open to false Alarms, by being credulous to every Account that magnifies the Force of the Enemy: when they are tedious or divided in their Consultations, and flow and faint in the Execution: when they consult rather what may be most *safe for themselves*, than most *beneficial to their Country*: when they keep skirmishing at a Distance, instead of making a bold Push, and bringing the War to a speedy Issue by a decisive Stroke: when they are fond of prolonging the War, that they may live and riot the longer at the public Expence: when they sell themselves and their Country to the Enemy for a Bribe: in short, when they do not conscientiously exert all their Power to repel the Enemy, and protect the State that employs them, but only seek to serve themselves, then they do the Work of the Lord deceitfully; and his Curse lights upon them as their heavy Doom. I leave others to judge, whether the Original of this ugly Picture is to be found any where in the Universe. But as for you of this Company, may I not presume that you will behave in a nobler Manner? Shall not Sobriety, public Spirit, Courage, Fidelity, and good Discipline be maintained among you? This I humbly recommend to you; and may God enable you to act accordingly!

Thus far have I addressed you as *Soldiers*, or at least as Persons concerned in your Stations to do all in your Power to save your Country. But we must not part thus. It is possible we may never meet more, till we mingle with the assembled Universe before the supreme Tribunal: Therefore, before I dismiss you, I must address myself to you as *Sinners*, and as *Candidates for Eternity*. You are concerned to save your *Souls*, as well as your *Country*; and should you save or gain a Kingdom, or even the whole World, and lose your Souls, your Loss will be irreparable.

None of you I hope will reply, "I am now a Soldier, and have nothing more to do with Religion?" What! has a Soldier Nothing to do with Religion? Is a Soldier under no Obligations to the God that made him, and that furnishes him with every Blessing? Is not a Soldier as much exposed to Death as other Men? May not a Soldier be damned for Sin, as well as other Sinners? And will he be able to dwell with devouring Fire and everlasting Burnings? Are these Things so? Can any of you be so stupid as to think them so? If not, you must own, that even a *Soldier* has as much Concern with Religion, as another. Therefore hear me seriously upon this Head.

You are about entering into *the School of Vice*: for such the Army has generally been. And are any of you already initiated into any of the Mysteries of Iniquity there practised? Must I so much as suppose, that some of you, who have bravely espoused the Cause of your Country, are addicted to Drunkenness, Swearing, Whoredom, or any gross Vice? I cannot now take Time to reason with you for your Conviction: it may suffice to appeal to your own Reason and Conscience, Do you do well in indulging these Vices? Will you aprove of it in the honest Hour of Death? Will this Conduct prove a Source of Courage to you, when the Arrows of Death are flying thick around you, and Scores are falling on every Side? No, you are self-condemned; and may I not reasonably hope, you will endeavour to reform, what you cannot but condemn? Soldiers indeed, are too commonly addicted to such Immoralities: but are they the better Soldiers on that Account? Can an Oath or a Debauch inspire them with a rational Fortitude against the Fears of Death? Would not Prayer and a Life of Holiness better answer this Purpose? Their Courage, if they have any, must be the Effect, not of Thought, but of the *Want* of Thought; it must be a brutal Stupidity, or Ferocity; but not the rational Courage of a Man or a Christian.

Some of you, I doubt not, are happily free from these gross Vices; and long may you continue so! But I must tell you, this *negative* Goodness is not enough to prepare you for Death, or to constitute you true Christians. The temper of your Minds must be changed by the Power of divine Grace; and you must be turned from the Love and Practice of all Sin, to the Love and Practice of universal Holiness. You must become humble, broken-hearted Penitents, and true Believers in Jesus Christ. You must be enabled to live righteously, soberly, and godly, in this present evil World. This is Religion: this is Religion that will keep you uncorrupted in the midst of Vice and Debauchery: this is Religion, that will befriend you, when Cannons roar, and Swords gleam around you, and you are every Moment expecting the deadly Wound: this is Religion, that will support you in the Agonies of Death, and assure you of a happy Immortality.

But are not some of you conscious, that you are destitute of such a Religion as this? Then it is high Time for you to think on your Condition in sober Sadness. Pray to that powerful and gracious Being, who can form your Hearts and Lives after this sacred Model. Oh! pray earnestly, pray frequently, for this Blessing: and use all the Means of Grace in that Manner which your Circumstances will permit. Remember also, that if you try to prolong your Life by a dastardly Conduct, your life will lie under the Curse of Heaven; and you have little Reason to hope, you will ever improve it as a Space for Repentance. Remember also to put your Confidence in God; who keeps the Thread of your Life, and the Event of War, in his own Hand. Devoutly acknowledge his Providence in all your Ways, and be sensible of your Dependance upon it.

And now, to conclude my Address to you, as the Mouth of this Multitude, and of your Countrymen in general, I heartily bid you farewel. Farewel, my dear Friends, my brave Fellow-Subjects, the Guardians of your poor ravaged Country. God grant you may return in Safety and Honour, and that we may yet welcome you Home, crowned with Laurels of Victory! Or if any of you should lose your Lives in so good a Cause, may you enjoy a glorious and blessed Immortality in the Region of everlasting Peace and Tranquility! Methinks I may take upon me to promise you the Prayers and good Wishes of Thousands. Thousands, whom you leave behind, will think of you with affectionate Anxiety, will wish you Success, and congratulate your Return, or lament your Death. Once more I pour out all my Heart in another affectionate Farewel. May the Lord preserve your Going out, and your Coming in, from this Time forth and even for evermore. Amen.

Here I thought to have concluded. But I must take up a few Minutes more to ask this Crowd, Is there Nothing to be done by us who stay at Home, towards the Defence of our Country, and to promote the success of the Expedition now in Hand? Shall we sin on still impenitent and incorrigible? Shall we live as if we and our Country were *self-dependent*, and had Nothing to do with the Supreme Ruler of the Universe? Can an Army of *Saints* or of *Heroes* defend an obnoxious People, ripe for Destruction, from the righteous Judgment of God? The Cause in which these brave Men, and our Army in general, are engaged, is not so much their own as *ours*: Divine Providence considers them not so much in their *private personal* Character, as in their *public* Character, as the *Representatives*, and Guardians of their Country: and therefore they will stand or fall, not so much according to their own *personal* Character, as according to the *public* Character of the People, whose Cause they have undertaken. Be it known to you, then, their Success depends upon *us*, even more than upon themselves. Therefore let us all turn every one from his evil Ways. "Let the Wicked forsake his Way, &c." Let us humble ourselves under the mighty Hand of God, which is lifted up over our guilty Heads, that we may be exalted in due Time. I could venture the Reputation of my Judgment and Veracity, that it will never be well with our Country, till there be more of the Fear and Love of God in it, and till the Name of Jesus be of more Importance among us. I could prescribe a Method for our Deliverance, which is at once infallible, and also cheap, and safe, and so far from endangering the Life of any, that it would secure the everlasting Life of all that comply with it. Ye that complain of the Burden of our public Taxes; ye that love Ease, and shrink from the Dangers of War; ye that wish to see Peace restored once more; ye that would be happy beyond the Grave, and live for ever, attend to my Proposal: It is this, A THOROUGH NATIONAL REFORMATION. This will do, what Millions of Money and Thousands of Men, with Guns and Swords and all the dreadful Artillery of Death, could not do; it will procure us Peace again; a lasting well-established Peace. We have tried other Expedients without this long enough: Let us now try this new Expedient, the Success of which I dare to warrant. And do not object, that such a *general* Reformation is beyond your Power; for a general Reformation must begin with *Individuals*: therefore do you, through the Grace of God, do your Part; Begin *at Home*, and endeavour to reform yourselves, and those under your Influence.

It is a natural Inference from what has been said, that if the Defence of our Country, in which we can stay but a few Years at most, and from which we must ere long take our Flight, be so important a Duty, then how much more are we obliged to "seek a better Country, i.e. an heavenly;" and to carry on a vigorous War against our spiritual Enemies, that would rob us of our heavenly Inheritance? Therefore in the Name of JESUS, the Captain of your Salvation, I invite you all to enlist in the spiritual Warfare. Now proclaim eternal War against all Sin. Now "take to you the whole Armour of God: quit you like Men, be strong." And for your En-

couragement, remember, "He that overcometh, shall inherit all
Things:" He shall enter into a Kingdom that cannot be shaken—
cannot be shaken with those Storms of Public Calamities which toss
and agitate this restless Ocean of a World. In that blessed Harbour may we all rest at last!

You Are to Take These Free Booters and Desperadoes

Charles Woodmason

From the little that is recorded of Woodmason's early life, it is surmised that he was born in England about 1720, and that he lived in London for a time. In 1752, he left his family in England and settled in South Carolina where he amassed a considerable estate in lower Prince Frederick Winyaw Parish. In 1756, he became church warden for the parish and for a period of six years, while the congregation searched for a resident minister, he read prayers and delivered the Sunday sermon. In 1761, he added to his duties the posts of coroner and collector of the general tax.

In 1762 or 1763, after returning to England to settle his wife's estate, Woodmason settled in Charleston and quickly rose in the social and literary circles of that important colonial city. A fall from favor which accompanied his acquisition of the post of stamp distributor was followed by his application in 1765 for the position of itinerant Anglican minister in the upper part of St. Mark's Parish.

Ordained in England in 1766, Woodmason was licensed to work in St. Mark's and eagerly took to the back country where he struggled against the prevailing Presbyterians and Baptists and set himself up as a missionary of English civilization.

In 1772, his congregations overwhelmed by the New Light Baptists, Woodmason moved to Maryland where he was suspected of being a government spy and an enemy to American liberty. His refusal to read the "Brief for collecting Money for relief of the poor of Boston" resulted in his fleeing to England in 1774. In 1776 he sought aid from the Bishop of London as a loyalist refugee. Little is known of his later activity.

"You Are to Take These Free Booters and Desperadoes" was delivered in December, 1767, or January, 1768, at Swift Creek, Wateree River before Captain Joseph Kirkland and Captain Henry Hunter and their two companies of Rangers. The text of the sermon is from Woodmason's Sermon Book, IV, 329–58.

Gentlemen

The present Audience is met to congratulate You, on opening the Important Commission Granted You by Government; For Your taking those Steps by Legal Authority, wch Necessity, & the Principles of Self Defence, forc'd You (& all of us) lately upon unauthoriz'd, & unempowered. The King has now drawn his Sword & put it into Yr Hands for Protection of his Subjects in these Parts; and freeing the Country from a lawless Banditti, that has laid us all under Contribution—the Particulars of wch are too well felt, for me to bring now before You. & As Your Officers have requested me to give You a Word of Exhortation before You set out on this so long wish'd for Expedition, I shall from the Words of the Text, consider the Nature of the Kingly Office, and that of Yr Commission under it.

Your Commision is of a mix'd Nature Partly Civil, partly *Military*. You are to take these Free booters and Desperadoes, Alive if possible and deliver them to the Magistrates. But if they make resistance, and act either Defensively or Offensively, Then You are to treat them as Rebels—Outlaws, and an abandon'd Crew. And as You may be oblig'd to pursue them thro' many Provinces It was proper that You should be invested with the Character of the Kings Troops that Your March might not be impeded by delays in formal Applications to the Kings Courts. For *Celerity*, is one Article of Your Commission. And You are stil'd *Rangers*, because Your Progress is not confin'd to any particular District.

For when under Sentence of Death and saved from the Gallows by Clemency of a New Administration—they [the thieves] not [only] flew in the Face of Justice by returning again to their old Trade, but this with redoubled Vigour Cruelty and Villany. They added the Shocking Sin of Ingratitude to their former Crimes by spoiling those who were their Benefactors and Intercessors for them. They dealt treacherously with their Deliverers from an Halter—by robbing them at the very first Hour of deliverance and in the Sight of the Gibbet they escaped from. And now the Sword is drawn against them for their demerits, and saith *Spare not.*

Adultery and Fornication are gloried in, and practic'd in open Noon Day—The Almighty therefore permitted Your Wives to be ravished and Your Daughters Stollen, or deflower'd. Lying Cheating filching, Jockeying are made a Trade of, and He is accounted the cleverest fellow who is the best Trickster. Gaming and Gambling—Rioting and Drunkenness—Gambling and Wagering—Fighting and Brawling take up most of Your Time and Attention. No wonder then that Providence should punish You in Your own way, by such vile Instruments born and rais'd among Your Selves—Spawn of the Pillory and Whipping Post. They are really Plants of Your own Growth. Not one *European*, or Foreigner among them and what better fruit from such Trees could You expect than what You have received?

But they would have met their Deserts long ago had it not been fear'd that at the Gallows they would have told Tales of some Folk—And made Confessions, as would have affected the Hypocrites—the Venal—and the Receivers. They therefore were set adrift, in hope that they would have gone to some very great Distance. And this will still be the saving of many of them Whether You shew Mercy, or not.

We are sensible that many Women and Girls are very deep in the foulest of Crimes, and Deeds of darkness not to be mention'd —And that they have been very Instrumental in aiding, abetting— Watching—Secreting—Trafficking and in ev'ry Manner support- ing and assisting these Villains. While there are others who tho' now bold in Sin—Yet were either Stollen—debauch'd—trepann'd or forcibly made to take on with them. As many Females will fall into Your Hands, You will be very careful to distinguish rightly, in these Particulars.

From the Dispersion of the Gang (many of which begin al- ready to shrink) numberless Children of all Ages Sexes and Condi- tions must be thrown on the Public. Pity and Compassion will incline You to fall on proper Methods that they never more return to their Relations, lest their Minds be perverted, and We should see New Shoots of Thieves arise from the Old Roots. In this Respect it will be proper totally, and wholly to separate the Children from aged Persons, if they read them no Lectures of Revenge, or sow the Seeds of Malice or Vice in their Hearts. They should for ever be kept very wide asunder—Never more to see, or Converse with each Other.

As for the Elderly Persons, who have harbour'd Entertain'd, and Embolden'd these fellows, and taught them the Rudiments of ev'ry Vice, The Legislature doubtless will take some thought con- cerning them, by depriving them of their Lands and dwellings— Yet so as not to bring down their Grey Hairs with Sorrow, (tho' it will be with Infamy) to the Grave.

I know that many among You have personally been injur'd by the Rogues. Some in their Wives—Others in their Sisters, or Daughters—By loss of Horses, Cattle, Goods and Effects. But all these things must not be thought of—and should You come upon the Villains. You are not to vent Your rage against them so much for what You have suffered as for what they have made the Province suffer, and the Expence they have occasion'd to the Public.

In the Act of Assembly that incorporated You, and in the Commission to Your Officers—Ye are call'd *Rangers*. A Term al- most of Reproach among us, from the bad Conduct of those so stil'd in the last War. Who instead of protecting the Country, dam- aged it almost as much as the Enemy. Indeed, had they not behav'd so bad, the Indians would not. It is well known that this War originated from the Ill Conduct and Licentiousness of the Garrison of Fort Prince George to the Towns of *Keowee* and *Satochee*. And it must also be infer'd, that the Indians rather acted defensively (in their way) than offensively for they could have done 50 times the Murder and Mischief than they did. And had the Rangers not been as Licentious as the Garrisons, the War might soon have been terminated. But after the withdrawing and return of the Regulars,

These Rangers, instead of annoying the Enemy, fell to plundering
of, and living at free quarter on the poor Scatter'd Inhabitants: The
Forts into which they retir'd were fill'd with Whores and Prostitutes
and there maintain'd at the Public Expense. The Stores were
pillag'd to bestow Cloathing on them—They plunder'd the Settlers,
and all others for Liquors Wasted the Ammunition and Provisions
of the Troops, and there liv'd in an open, scandalous debauch'd
Manner with their Doxies, instead of going on Duty. So that many
complain'd That they sustain'd more damage from their Protectors
than from the Enemy, as they stript them of the little the other
had left and their prophaneness and Immorality was as Notorious, as their Debauchery—for they far exceeded the Kings
Troops in all degrees of Wickedness. And notwithstanding all
this Rioting and Wantonness—their Plunder—and High Pay,
Yet (You know it) they all returned Poor and Penny less, with
Shame and Contempt. But from the Known Vertue, Experience and
Honour of these Worthy Officers under whose Command You are,
I am morally certain that no such Complaints will ever arise against
the meanest Individual among You, as Ye are all chosen Persons,
and of Estate and Credit. Therefore You'l act as becometh Gentlemen. Not when You have been kindly entertain'd in a Plantation, to
make Waste, and do damage. To lye with the Negro Wenches and
Servants To debauch the Daughters or pervert the Wife, or any
other such ungodly Practices.

On Civil Liberty, Passive Obedience, and Non-Resistance

Jonathan Boucher

Jonathan Boucher, Anglican clergyman and outspoken loyalist, was born in Blencogo, England, on March 12, 1737 (1738?). After preliminary training at home, he attended a small free-school at Bromfield and then another school at Wigton. Two years later he obtained a position as Usher at a school at St. Bees. Through the efforts of the Rev. John James, he secured a tutorial position in Port Royal, Virginia, in 1759.

In hopes of bettering his position, Boucher returned to England in 1762, and was ordained. Soon afterwards he returned to the colonies and established a school in Caroline County, Virginia. In 1770, he was made rector at St. Anne's in Annapolis, and because active in the social life of the "genteelest town in North America." After several years of increasing good fortune during which he became the chaplain of the lower house of the Assembly, rector of the Queen Anne's Parish in Prince George's County, and recipient of an honorary A.M. from King's College in New York, his outspoken defense of the crown and attacks on the sentiments of the colonies forced him to flee to England, in September, 1775.

In England, Boucher became a curate at Paddington and received a small pension from the government. Around 1785, he became vicar of Epson, a post he retained until his death on April 27, 1804.

The sermon, "On Civil Liberty, Passive Obedience, and Non-Resistance," preached with a brace of pistols lying on the cushion, was delivered in Queen Anne's Parish in 1775. The text is from Jonathan Boucher. *A View of the Causes and Consequences of the American Revolution* . . . . London: G. G. and J. Robinson, 1797, pp. 495–560.

GALATIANS, *ch.* v. ver. i. *Stand fast, therefore, in the liberty wherewith Christ hath made us free.*

It is not without much sincere concern that I find myself thus again constrained to animadvert on the published opinions of another Clergyman, of great worth and amiableness of character—a Clergyman whom I have the pleasure to know, and who, I believe, is not more generally known than he is beloved. If his opinions had been confined to points of little moment, and on which even mistakes could have done no great harm, I could have been well contented to have let this pass down the stream of time, with a long list of similar patriotic publications, without any animadversions of mine. But if what he had published, even with good intentions, be, as I think it clearly is, of a pernicious and dangerous tendency, (and the more so, perhaps, from it's being delivered in the form of a sermon,) I owe no apology either to him, or to any man, for thus endeavouring to furnish you with an antidote to the poison which has been so industriously dispersed among you.

To have become noted either as a political writer or preacher, as some (who at least are unacquainted with my preaching) are pleased to tell you I now am, is a circumstance that gives me no pleasure. I was sorry to hear the observation; not (I thank God!) from any consciousness of my having ever written or preached any thing, of which (at least in point of principle) I have reason to be ashamed; but because it is painful to reflect, that it should have fallen to my lot to live in times, and in a country, in which such subjects demand the attention of every man. Convinced in my judgment that it is my duty to take the part which I have taken, though I cannot but lament it's not having produced all the beneficial consequences which I fondly flattered myself it might, I dare not allow myself to discontinue it. The time, I know, has been, when addresses of this sort from English pulpits were much more frequent than they now are. Even now, however, they are not wholly discontinued: sermons on political topics, on certain stated days, are still preached, and with the authority of Government. This is mentioned to obviate a charge, that I am singular in continuing this practice; as it proves that such preaching is not yet proscribed from our pulpits. That a change, indeed, in this respect, as well in the principles as in the conduct of modern preachers, has taken place among us, is readily confessed: but that it is a change for the better, has no where yet been proved. A comparison of the 30th of January sermons of the present times, with those of our older Divines, might suggest many not uninteresting reflections: but as it is no part of my purpose to seat myself in a censorial chair, I enter not into the disquisition; but shall content myself with cursorily observing, that if the political sermons of the present day be more popular than those of our predecessors, it is owing, too probably, to their being also more frivolous (not to say more unsound, and less learned) than such compositions used to be.

But, without being influenced by the principles or the practices of other preachers, I must, for myself, be permitted to think it incumbent on me to watch and attend to circumstances as they arise; such, more especially, as nearly concern the welfare of the people committed to my charge. In any such politics as do not touch the conscience, nor trench upon duty, I hope I neither feel nor take more interest than mankind in general do: but there is a sense in which politics, properly understood, form an essential branch of Christian duty. These politics take in a very principal part, if not the whole, of the second table of the Decalogue, which contains our duty to our neighbour. It is from this second table that the compilers of our Catechism have very properly deduced the great duty of *honouring and obeying the king, and all that are put in authority under him.* Reverently to submit ourselves to *all our governors, teachers, spiritual pastors, and masters,* is indeed a duty so essential to the peace and happiness of the world, that St. Paul thinks no Christian could be ignorant of it: and therefore, when he recommends it to Titus as a topic on which he should not fail frequently to insist, he supposes it would be sufficient if his converts were *put in mind to be subject to principalities and powers, to obey magistrates, and to be ready to every good work.* This, however, is as direct and clear a commission for a Christian minister's preaching on politics, in the just sense of the word, on all proper occasions, as can be produced for our preaching at all on any subject. Let me hope, then, that I now stand sufficiently vindicated as a preacher of politics (if such an one I am to be deemed) by having proved, that, in thus preaching, I do no more than St. Paul enjoined: all I pretend to, all I aim at, is to *put you in mind* only of your *duty to your neighbour.*

It is, however, not a little mortifying to the few friends of the good old principles of the Church of England yet left among us to observe (as it is impossible they should fail to observe) that offence is taken, not so much because some of us preach on politics, as because we preach what are called unpopular politics. Preachers who are less anxious to *speak right,* than *smooth things,* are now hardly less numerous among us, in proportion to our population, than such men were among the puritans in the last century: and their discourses are not only preached, but published, "at the request of battalions, generals, and commanders in chief." But, wo unto that people who studiously place temptations in the way of the ministers of God to *handle the word of God deceitfully!* and wo unto those ministers who are thus tempted to *cause the people to err, by their lies and their lightness!*

Let me humbly hope, then, that, whilst I thus continue to plead in behalf of Government, I may continue to experience the same indulgence which those persons do who speak against it. The ground I have taken, I am aware, is deemed untenable; but, having now just gone over the ground with great care, I feel a becoming confidence that I shall not easily be driven from it. The same diligence, the same plain honest course of proceeding which I have taken, will, I trust, produce the same effects with all of you, who, not being yet absorbed within the vortex of party, are still happy in the possession of minds open to conviction. With no others do I presume to argue. That I am persevering in the pursuit of this unpopular course, I readily own; yet I feel I want spirits to enter on any such discussions with those persons among us, who, setting controverted points with their hands rather than with their tongues, demonstrate with tar and feathers, fetch arguments from prisons, and confute by confiscation and exile.

To find out the true and precise meaning of any passage of Scripture, it is in general necessary to know the circumstances of the writer, and his end and aim in writing. St. Paul, the author of my text, was deeply involved in that very natural but perplexing dispute which soon arose among the first converts, and even among the Disciples, concerning the observance of the ritual services; and how far they were, or were not, obligatory on Christians. There are few of his writings, in some part or other of which this great question does not come forward. It evidently runs through the whole of this epistle to the Galatians, as well as through this particular verse.

The Jewish zealots (like their ancestors in the wilderness, who ever and anon murmured for want of the flesh-pots in Egypt) were perpetually troubling the infant church on the subject of this question. It became our Apostle, then, diligently to labour after the removal of this difficultly. This he undertakes to do; and very satisfactorily obviates the difficulty by a comparison of the two dispensations, the former of which he proves to have been *a yoke of bondage* when put in competition with that perfect *law of liberty* now promulged to the world. The law of Moses was no doubt well contrived and adapted to the singular circumstances of the people to whom it was given; yet, when a revelation still better adapted to the general circumstances of mankind was made known, it was a most unaccountable instance of folly and perverseness in that people to wish to be again *entangled* in a yoke which neither they nor their forefathers were well able to bear. Emancipated as they now were from so burthersome a service, it was to act the part of madmen still to hug their chains.

Freely offered, however, as the Gospel of uncircumcision now was *to the Jew first and also to the Gentile,* it behoved the latter also (who, as well as their brethren of the law, were *called unto liberty*) *to stand fast.* It is true they were not, as the Jews were, *made free* from the servile observance of *days, and months, and times, and years*; to which they had never been subjected. But there was another kind of subjection or slavery, not less oppressive, from which they were now released; I mean the slavery of sin. Heretofore they were *the servants of sin*; but now, they were *no more servants, but sons; and if sons, then heirs of God through Christ.* Admitted to this blessed privilege, and no longer the children of Hagar and of Ishmael, but of Sarah and of Isaac, the exhortation is with great propriety addressed to them also: *Stand fast in the liberty wherewith Christ hath made you free.*

As the liberty here spoken of respected the Jews, it denoted an exemption from the burthensome services of the ceremonial law: as it respected the Gentiles, it meant a manumission from bondage under the *weak and beggarly elements of the world*, and an admission into the covenant of grace: and as it respected both in common, it meant a freedom from the servitude of sin. Every sinner is, literally, a slave; for, *his servants ye are, to whom ye obey*: and the only true liberty is the liberty of being the servants of God; for, *his service is perfect freedom*. The passage cannot, without infinite perversion and torture, be made to refer to any other kind of liberty; much less to that liberty of which every man now talks, though few understand it. However common this term has been, or is, in the mouths chiefly of those persons who are as little distinguished for the accuracy as they are for the paucity of their words; and whatever influence it has had on the affairs of the world, it is remarkable that it is never used (at least not in any such sense as it is elsewhere used) in any of the laws either of God or men. Let a minister of God, then, stand excused if (taught by him who knoweth what is fit and good for us better than we ourselves, and is *wont also to give us more than either we desire or deserve*) he seeks not to amuse you by any flowery panegyrics on liberty. Such panegyrics are the productions of ancient heathens and modern patriots: nothing of the kind is to be met with in the Bible, nor in the Statute Book. The word *liberty*, as meaning civil liberty, does not, I believe, occur in all the Scriptures. With the aid of a concordance I find only two or three passages, in two apocryphal writers, that look at all like it. In the xivth chapter and 26th verse of the 1st of Maccabees, the people are said to owe much gratitude to Simon, the highpriest, for having renewed a friendship and league with the Lacedemonians, confirmed the league with the Romans, established Israel, and *confirmed their liberty*. But it is evident that this expression means, not that the Jews were then to be exempted from any injunctions, or any restraints, imposed upon them by their own lawful government; but only that they were delivered from a foreign jurisdiction and from tributary payments, and left free to live under the law of Moses. The only circumstance relative to government, for which the Scriptures seem to be particularly solicitous, is in inculcating obedience to lawful governors, as well knowing where the true danger lies. Nevertheless, as occasion has lately been taken from this text, on which I am now to discourse, to treat largely on civil liberty and government (though for no other reason that appears but that the word *liberty* happens to stand in the text), I entreat your indulgence, whilst, without too nicely scrutinizing the propriety of deducing from a text a doctrine which it clearly does not suggest, I once more adopt a plan already chalked out for me, and deliver to you what occurs to me as proper for a Christian audience to attend to on the subject of Liberty.

It has just been observed, that the liberty inculcated in the Scriptures (and which alone the Apostle had in view in this text) is wholly of the spiritual or religious kind. This liberty was the natural result of the new religion in which mankind were then instructed; which certainly gave them no new civil privileges. They remained subject to the governments under which they lived, just as they had been before they became Christians, and just as others were who never became Christians; with this difference only, that the duty of submission and obedience to Government was enjoined on the converts to Christianity with new and stronger sanctions. The doctrines of the Gospel make no manner of alteration in the nature or form of Civil Government; but enforce afresh, upon all Christians, that obedience which is due to the respective Constitutions of every nation in which they may happen to live. Be the supreme power lodged in one or in many, be the kind of government established in any country absolute or limited, this is not the concern of the Gospel. It's single object, with respect to these public duties, is to enjoin obedience to the laws of every country, in every kind or form of government.

The only liberty or freedom which converts to Christianity could hope to gain by becoming Christians, was the being exempted from sundry burthensome and servile Jewish ordinances, on the one hand; and, on the other, from Gentile blindness and superstition. They were also in some measure perhaps made more *free* in the *inner man*; by being endowed with greater firmness of mind in the cause of truth, against the terrors and the allurements of the world; and with such additional strength and vigour as enabled them more effectually to resist the natural violence of their lusts and passions. On all these accounts it was that our Saviour so emphatically told the Jews, that *the truth* (of which himself was now the preacher) would *make them* free. And on the same principle St. James terms the Gospel *the perfect law of liberty.*

In the infancy of Christianity, it would seem that some rumour had been spread (probably by Judas of Galilee, who is mentioned in the Acts) that the Gospel was designed to undermine kingdoms and commonwealths; as if the intention of our Saviour's first coming had been the same with that which is reserved for the second, viz. to *put down all rule, and all authority, and all power.* On this supposition the apparent solicitude of our Saviour and his Apostles, in their frequent and earnest recommendation of submission to *the higher powers*, is easily and naturally accounted for. Obedience to Government is every man's duty, because it is every man's interest: but it is particularly incumbent on Christians, because (in addition to it's moral fitness) it is enjoined by the positive commands of God: and therefore, when Christians are disobedient to human ordinances, they are also disobedient to God. If the form of government under which the good providence of God has been pleased to place us be mild and free, it is our duty to enjoy it with gratitude and with thankfulness; and, in particular, to be careful not to abuse it by licentiousness. If it be less indulgent and less liberal than in reason it ought to be, still it is our duty not to disturb and destroy the peace of the community, by becoming refractory and rebellious subjects, and *resisting the ordinances of God*. However humiliating such acquiescence may seem to men of warm and eager minds, the wisdom of God in having made it our duty is manifest. For, as it is the natural temper and bias of the human mind to be impatient under restraint, it was wise and merciful in the blessed Author of our religion not to add any new impulse to the natural force of this prevailing propensity, but, with the whole weight of his authority, altogether to discountenance every tendency to disobedience.

If it were necessary to vindicate the Scriptures for this their total unconcern about a principle which so many other writings seem to regard as the first of all human considerations, it might be observed, that, avoiding the vague and declamatory manner of such writings, and avoiding also the useless and impracticable subtleties of metaphysical definitions, these Scriptures have better consulted the great general interests of mankind, by summarily recommending and enjoining a conscientious reverence for law whether human or divine. To respect the laws, is to respect liberty in the only rational sense in which the term can be used; for liberty consists in a subserviency to law. "Where there is no law," says Mr. Locke, "there is no freedom." The mere man of nature (if such an one there ever was) has no freedom: *all his lifetime he is subject to bondage*. It is by being included within the pale of civil polity and government that he takes his rank in society as a free man.

Hence it follows, that we are free, or otherwise, as we are governed by law, or by the mere arbitrary will, or wills, of any individual, or any number of individuals. And liberty is not the setting at nought and despising established laws—much less the making our own wills the rule of our own actions, or the actions of others—and not bearing (whilst yet we dictate to others) the being dictated to, even by the laws of the land; but it is the being governed by law, and by law only. The Greeks described Eleutheria, or Liberty, as the daughter of Jupiter, the supreme fountain of power and law. And the Romans, in like manner, always drew her with the pretor's wand (the emblem of legal power and authority) as well as with the cap. Their idea, no doubt, was, that liberty was the fair fruit of just authority, and that it consisted in men's being subjected to law. The more carefully well-devised restraints of law are enacted, and the more rigorously they are executed in any country, the greater degree of civil liberty does that country enjoy. To pursue liberty, then, in a manner not warranted by law, whatever the pretence may be, is clearly to be hostile to liberty: and those persons who thus *promise you liberty*, are themselves *the servants of corruption.*

"Civil liberty (says an excellent writer) is a severe and a restrained thing; implies, in the notion of it, authority, settled subordinations, subjection, and obedience; and is altogether as much hurt by too little of this kind, as by too much of it. And the love of liberty, when it is indeed the love of liberty, which carries us to withstand tyranny, will as much carry us to reverence authority, and to support it; for this most obvious reason, that one is as necessary to the being of liberty, as the other is destructive of it. And, therefore, the love of liberty which does not produce this effect, the love of liberty which is not a real principle of dutiful behaviour towards authority, is as hypocritical as the religion which is not productive of a good life. Licentiousness is, in truth, such an excess of liberty as is of the same nature with tyranny. For, what is the different betwixt them, but that one is lawless power exercised under pretence of authority, or by persons vested with it; the other, lawless power exercised under pretence of liberty, or without any pretence at all? A people, then, must always be less free in proportion as they are more licentious; licentiousness being not only different from liberty, but directly contrary to it—a direct breach upon it."

True liberty, then, is a liberty to do every thing that is right, and the being restrained from doing any thing that is wrong. So far from our having a right to do every thing that we please, under a notion of liberty, liberty itself is limited and confined—but limited and confined only by laws which are at the same time both it's foundation and it's support. It can, however, hardly be necessary to inform you, that ideas and notions respecting liberty, very different from these, are daily suggested in the speeches and the writings of the times; and also that some opinions on the subject of government at large, which appear to me to be particularly loose and dangerous, are advanced in the sermon now under consideration; and that, therefore, you will acknowledge the propriety of my bestowing some farther notice on them both.

It is laid down in this sermon, as a settled maxim; that the end of government is "the common good of mankind." I am not sure that the position itself is indisputable; but, if it were, it would by no means follow that, "this common good being matter of common feeling, government must therefore have been instituted by common consent." There is an appearance of logical accuracy and precision in this statement; but it is only an appearance. The position is vague and loose; and the assertion is made without an attempt to prove it. If by men's "common feelings" we are to understand that principle in the human mind called common sense, the assertion is either unmeaning and insignificant, or it is false. In no instance have mankind ever yet agreed as to what is, or is not, "the common good." A form or mode of government cannot be named, which these "common feelings" and "common consent," the sole arbiters, as it seems, of "common good," have not, at one time or another, set up and established, and again pulled down and reprobated. What one people in one age have concurred in establishing as the "common good," another in another age have voted to be mischievous and big with ruin. The premises, therefore, that "the common good is matter of common feeling," being false, the consequence drawn from it, viz. that government was instituted by "common consent," is of course equally false.

This popular notion, that government was originally formed by the consent or by a compact of the people, rests on, and is supported by, another similar notion, not less popular, nor better founded. This other notion is, that the whole human race is born equal; and that no man is naturally inferior, or, in any respect, subjected to another; and that he can be made subject to another only by his own consent. The position is equally ill-founded and false both in it's premises and conclusions. In hardly any sense that can be imagined is the position strictly true; but, as applied to the case under consideration, it is demonstrably not true. Man differs from man in every thing that can be supposed to lead to supremacy and subjection, *as one star differs from another star in glory*. It was the purpose of the Creator, that man should be social: but, without government, there can be no society; nor, without some relative inferiority and superiority, can there be any government. A musical instrument composed of chords, keys, or pipes, all perfectly equal in size and power, might as well be expected to produce harmony, as a society composed of members all perfectly equal to be productive of order and peace. If (according to the idea of the advocates of this chimerical scheme of equality) no man could rightfully *be compelled to come in* and be a member even of a government to be formed by a regular compact, but by his own individual consent; it clearly follows, from the same principles, that neither could he rightfully be made or compelled to submit to the ordinances of any government already formed, to which he has not individually or actually consented. On the principle of equality, neither his parents, nor even the vote of a majority of the society (however virtuously and honourably that vote might be obtained) can have any such authority over any man. Neither can it be maintained that acquiescence implies consent; because acquiescence may have been ex-

torted from impotence or incapacity. Even an explicit consent can
bind a man no longer than he chooses to be bound. The same
principle of equality that exempts him from being governed without
his own consent, clearly entitles him to recall and resume that consent whenever he sees fit; and he alone has a right to judge when
and for what reasons it may be resumed.

Any attempt, therefore, to introduce this fantastic system into
practice, would reduce the whole business of social life to the
wearisome, confused, and useless talk of mankind's first expressing,
and then withdrawing, their consent to an endless succession of
schemes of government. Governments, though always forming,
would never be completely formed: for, the majority to-day, might
be the minority tomorrow; and, of course, that which is now fixed
might and would be soon unfixed. Mr. Locke indeed says, that, "by
consenting with others to make one body-politic under government,
a man puts himself under an obligation to every one of that society
to submit to the determination of the majority, and to be concluded
by it." For the sake of the peace of society, it is undoubtedly reasonable and necessary that this should be the case: but, on the
principles of the system now under consideration, before Mr. Locke
or any of his followers can have authority to say that it actually
is the case, it must be stated and proved that every individual man,
on entering into the social compact, did first consent, and declare
his consent, to be concluded and bound in all cases by the vote of
the majority. In making such a declaration, he would certainly
consult both his interest and his duty; but at the same time he
would also completely relinquish the principle of equality, and eventually subject himself to the possibility of being governed by ignorant and corrupt tyrants. Mr. Locke himself afterwards disproves
his own position respecting this supposed obligation to submit to
the "determination of the majority," when he argues that a right
of resistance still exists in the governed: for, what is resistance but
a recalling and resuming the consent heretofore supposed to have
been given, and in fact refusing to submit to the "determination of
the majority?" It does not clearly appear what Mr. Locke exactly
meant by what he calls "the determination of the majority:" but
the only rational and practical public manner of declaring "the
determination of the majority," is by law: the laws, therefore, in all
countries, even in those that are despotically governed, are to be
regarded as the declared "determination of a majority" of the
members of that community; because, in such cases, even ac-
quiesecence only must be looked upon as equivalent to a declaration.
A right of resistance, therefore, for which Mr. Locke contends, is
incompatible with the duty of submitting to the determination of
"the majority," for which he also contends.

It is indeed impossible to carry into effect any government

which, even by compact, might be framed with this reserved right of reistance. Accordingly there is no record that any such government ever was so formed. If there had, it must have carried the seeds of it's decay in it's very constitution. For, as those men who make a government (certain that they have the power) can have no hesitation to vote that they also have the right to unmake it; and as the people, in all circumstances, but more especially when trained to make and unmake governments, are at least as well disposed to do the latter as the former, it is morally impossible that there should be any thing like permanency or stability in a government so formed. Such a system, therefore, can produce only perpetual dissensions and contests, and bring back mankind to a supposed state of nature; arming every man's hand, like Ishmael's, against every man, and rendering the world an *aceldama*, or field of blood. Such theories of government seem to give something like plausibility to the notions of those other modern theorists, who regard all governments as invasions of the natural rights of men, usurpations, and tyranny. On this principle it would follow, and could not be denied, that government was indeed fundamentally, as our people are sedulously taught it still is, an evil. Yet it is to government that mankind owe their having, after their fall and corruption, been again reclaimed, from a state of barbarity and war, to the conveniency and the safety of the social state: and it is by means of government that society is still preserved, the weak protected from the strong, and the artless and innocent from the wrongs of proud oppressors. It was not without reason, then, that Mr. Locke asserted, that a greater wrong cannot be done to prince and people, than is done by "propagating wrong notions concerning government."

Ashamed of this shallow device, that government originated in superior strength and violence, another party, hardly less numerous, and certainly not less confident than the former, fondly deduce it from some imaginary compact. They suppose that, in the decline perhaps of some fabulous age of gold, a multitude of human beings, who, like their brother beasts, had hitherto ranged the forests, *without guide, overseer, or ruler*—at length convinced, by experience, of the impossibility of living either alone with any degree of comfort or security, or together in society, with peace, without government, had (in some lucid interval of reason and reflection) met together in a spacious plain, for the express purpose of framing a government. Their first step must have been the transferring to some individual, or individuals, some of those rights which are supposed to have been inherent in each of them: of these it is essential to government that they should be divested; yet can they not, rightfully, be deprived of them, otherwise than by their own consent. Now, admitting this whole supposed assembly to be perfectly equal as to rights, yet all agreed as to the propriety of ceding

some of them, on what principles of equality is it possible to determine, either who shall relinquish such a portion of his rights, or
who shall be invested with such new accessory rights? By asking
another to exercise jurisdiction over me, I clearly confess that I do
not think myself his equal; and by his consenting to exercise such
authority, he also virtually declares that he thinks himself superior.
And, to establish this hypothesis of a compact, it is farther necessary
that the whole assembly should concur in this opinion—a concurrence so extremely improbable, that it seems to be barely possible.
The supposition that a large concourse of people, in a rude and
imperfect state of society, or even a majority of them, should
thus rationally and unanimously concur to subject themselves to
various restrictions, many of them irksome and unpleasant, and
all of them contrary to all their former habits, is to suppose them
possessed of more wisdom and virtue than multitudes in any
instance in real life have ever shewn. Another difficulty respecting
this notion may yet be mentioned. Without a power of life and
death, it will, I presume, be readily admitted that there could be
no government. Now, admitting it to be possible that men, from
motives of public and private utility, may be induced to submit to
many heavy penalties, and even to corporal punishment, inflicted
by the sentence of the law, there is an insuperable objection to any
man's giving to another a power over his life: this objection is,
that no man has such a power over his own life; and cannot therefore transfer to another, or to others, be they few or many, on
any conditions, a right which he does not himself possess. He only
who gave life, can give the authority to take it away: and as such
authority is essential to government, this argument seems very
decidedly to prove, not only that government did not originate in
any compact, but also that it was originally from God.

This visionary idea of a government by compact was, as Filmer
says, "first hatched in the schools; and hath, ever since, been fostered
by Papists, for good divinity." For some time, the world seemed
to regard it merely as another Utopian fiction; and it was long
confined to the disciples of Rome and Geneva, who, agreeing in
nothing else, yet agreed in this. In an evil hour it gained admittance
into the Church of England; being first patronized by her during
the civil wars, by "a few miscreants, who were as far from being
true Protestants, as true Subjects." Mankind have listened, and
continue to listen to it with a predilection and partiality, just as they
do to various other exceptionable notions, which are unfavourable to
true religion and sound morals; merely from imagining, that if
such doctrines be true, they shall no longer be subjected to sundry
restraints, which, however wholesome and proper, are too often
unpalatable to our corrupt natures. What we wish to be true, we
easily persuade ourselves is true. On this principle it is not difficult

to account for our thus eagerly following these *ignes fatui* of our own fancies or "feelings," rather than the sober steady light of the word of God; which (in this instance as well as in others) lies under this single disadvantage, that it proposes no doctrines which may conciliate our regards by flattering our pride.

If, however, we can even resolve no longer to be bewildered by these vain imaginations, still the interesting question presses on us, "Where," in the words of Plato, "where shall we look for the origin of government?" Let Plato himself instruct us. Taught then by this oracle of Heathen wisdom, "we will take our stations there, where the prospect of it is most easy and most beautiful." Of all the theories respecting the origin of government with which the world has ever been either puzzled, amused, or instructed, that of the Scriptures alone is accompanied by no insuperable difficulties.

It was not to be expected from an all-wise and all-merciful Creator, that, having formed creatures capable of order and rule, he should turn them loose into the world under the guidance only of their own unruly wills; that, like so many wild beasts, they might tear and worry one another in their mad contests for preeminence. His purpose from the first, no doubt, was, that men should *live godly and sober lives*. But, such is the sad estate of our corrupted nature, that, ever since the Fall, we have been averse from good, and prone to evil. We are, indeed, so disorderly and unmanageable, that, were it not for the restraints and the terrors of human laws, it would not be possible for us to dwell together. But as men were clearly formed for society, and to dwell together, which yet they cannot do without the restraints of law, or, in other words, without government, it is fair to infer that government was also the original intention of God, who never decrees the end, without also decreeing the means. Accordingly, when man was made, his Maker did not turn him adrift into a shoreless ocean, without star or compass to steer by. As soon as there were some to be governed, there were also some to govern: and the first man, by virtue of that paternal claim, on which all subsequent governments have been founded, was first invested with the power of government. For, we are not to judge of the scriptures of God, as we do of some other writings; and so, where no express precept appears, hastily to conclude that none was given. On the contrary, in commenting on the Scriptures, we are frequently called upon to find out the precept from the practice. Taking this rule, then, for our direction in the present instance, we find, that, copying after the fair model of heaven itself, wherein there was government even among the angels, the families of the earth were subjected to rulers, at first set over them by God: *for, there is no power, but of God; the powers that be are ordained of God.* The first father was the first king: and if (according to the rule just laid down) the law may be inferred from the practice, it was thus that all government originated; and monarchy is it's most ancient form.

Little risque is run in affirming, that this idea of the patriarchal origin of government has not only the most and best authority of history, as far as history goes, to support it; but that it is also by far the most natural, most consistent, and most rational idea. Had it pleased God not to have interfered at all in the case, neither directly nor indirectly, and to have left mankind to be guided only by their own uninfluenced judgments, they would naturally have been led to the government of a community, or a nation, from the natural and obvious precedent of the government of a family. In confirmation of this opinion, it may be observed, that the patriarchal scheme is that which always has prevailed, and still does prevail, among the most enlightened people: and (what is no flight attestation of it's truth) it has also prevailed, and still does prevail, among the most unenlightened. According to Vitruvius, the rudiments of architecture are to be found in the cottage: and, according to Aristotle, the first principles of government are to be traced to private families. Kingdoms and empires are but so many larger families: and hence it is that our Church, in perfect conformity with the doctrine here inculcated, in her explication of the fifth commandment, from the obedience due to parents, wisely derives the congenial duty of *honouring the king and all that are put in authority under him.*

It is from other passages of Scripture, from the nature of the thing, from the practice of Adam, and from the practice of all nations (derived from and founded on this precedent) that we infer that Adam had an exercised sovereign power over all his issue. But the first instance of power exercised by one human being over another is in the subjection of Eve to her husband. This circumstance suggests sundry reflections, of some moment in this argument. In the first place, it shews that power is not a natural right. Adam could not have assumed, nor could Eve have submitted to it, had it not been so ordained of God. It is, therefore, equally an argument against the domineering claims of despotism, and the fantastic notion of a compact. It proves too, that there is a sense in which it may, with truth, be asserted, that government was originally founded in weakness and in guilt: that it may and must be submitted to by a fallen creature, even when exercised by a fallen creature, lost both to wisdom and goodness. The equality of nature (which, merely as it respects an ability to govern, may be admitted, only because God, had he so seen fit, might have ordained that the man should be subjected to the woman) was superseded by the actual interference of the Almighty, to whom alone original underived power can be said to belong.

Even where the Scriptures are silent, they instruct: for, in general, whatever is not therein commanded is actually forbidden. Now, it is certain that mankind are no where in the Scriptures commanded to resist authority; and no less certain that, either by direct injunction, or clear implication, they are commanded to *be subject to the higher powers:* and this subjection is said to be enjoined, not for our sakes only, but also *for the Lord's sake.* The glory of God is much concerned, that there should be good goverment in the world: it is, therefore, the uniform doctrine of the Scriptures, that it is under the deputation and authority of God alone that *kings reign and princes decree justice.* Kings and princes (which are only other words for supreme magistrates) were doubtless created and appointed, not so much for their own sakes, as for the sake of the people committed to their charge: yet are they not, therefore, the creatures of the people. So far from deriving their authority from any supposed consent or suffrage of men, they receive their commission from Heaven; they receive it from God, the source and original of all power. However obsolete, therefore, either the sentiment or the language may now be deemed, it is with the most perfect propriety that the supreme magistrate, whether consisting of one or of many, and whether denominated an emperor, a king, an archon, a dictator, a consul, or a senate, is to be regarded and venerated as the vicegerent of God.

But were the texts usually appealed to on this topic more dubious than (we bless God!) they are, the example of the Christian legislator may, at least to Christians well stand in the place of all precepts. There are not many questions, in which the interests of mankind are more nearly concerned than they are in ascertaining their duty as subjects. It is therefore very improbable, that the Saviour of the world should have left the world in the dark, in an affair of so much moment: but that he should have misled his followers, and that Christians should have been exposed to the hazard of becoming bad subjects even through the inadvertence of their founder, it is little less than blasphemy to suppose. We are therefore deeply interested to find out, if we can, what it was that our Saviour really thought, said, and did, in the case; and for what purpose.

It is readily acknowledged, that his history (in which alone his laws are contained) does not dwell copiously on the duties of sovereigns and subjects. This appearance of inattention, we may be assured, was not permitted without design: nor, in fact, is our duty on this point (any more than it is in others) the less forcibly inculcated by our having been left to find out the precept from his practice. On one point, however, of great moment in this discussion, the gospel history, when properly understood, is full and decided; viz. that every thing our blessed Lord either said or did, pointedly tended to discourage the disturbing a settled government.

Hence it is fair to infer the judgment of Jesus Christ to have been, that the most essential duty of subjects with respect to government was (in the phraseology of a prophet) *to be quiet, and to sit still*. Yet, had he judged of questions of this nature as we do, he certainly did not want motives to induce him to excite commotions in the government of Judea; and such motives too as (according to human reckoning) are highly meritorious and honourable. At the time when he was upon earth, his country groaned under an unjust and most oppressive bondage. It had just been subdued by a people, whose chief motive for over-running the world with their conquests was a lust of dominion: and it was as arbitrarily governed, as it had been iniquitously acquired. The Jews, it is true, were not then eminent, at least as a nation, for their virtues: but they were not chargeable with that "un-Roman spirit," as one of our orators expressed himself, or (to borrow the congenial phraseology of another) that "degeneracy of soul," which led them tamely to submit to their oppressors. A general opinion prevailed in the nation, that the expected Messiah would deliver them from this galling vassalage; that he was to be, not a spiritual, but a temporal, prince —a prince who should restore to Israel the supremacy, of which the Romans had deprived it—who should reign in all secular pomp and power in the throne of David—and, having subdued the rest of the world, make Jerusalem the seat of an universal monarchy. The very name given to him imports royalty and sovereignty: and he really was the legal heir to the crown of Judea.

In support of this assertion, it is to be observed, that the Jews had two ways of tracing their genealogies, by a kind of double descent; the one natural, the other legal. The natural descent was when a person by natural generation, descends from another; the legal, when one not naturally descended from another, yet succeeded, as nearest of kin, to the inheritance. St. Luke deduces the natural line of Christ from David; and shews how Christ, by Nathan, is the son of David, according to the flesh, by natural descent: whereas St. Matthew deduces the legal line of Christ also from David, shewing how Christ, as Solomon's heir, and lawful king of the Jews, succeeded, as nearest of kin, to sit upon the throne of David his father: and the Evangelist is so satisfied with the legality of this genealogy, that he calls Christ *"the born* king of the Jews," that is to say, the person who was their king by birth. The Jews themselves could name none of their nation who was nearer than he was. None of them ever produced any legal exception against him; and therefore, whilst a large party, convinced of the validity of his title to the throne by birth, wished to confirm it by election, and to make him a king, all that the friends of the Power who was in possession, or his enemies, could do to defeat his claim, was to get the Romans on their side, by artfully insinuating that the best of all titles was that which had been obtained by conquest: hence, their cry was, *We will have no king but Caesar!*

Add to this—It is well known that in no instance whatever did our Saviour give greater offence to his countrymen than he did by not gratifying them in their expectations of a temporal deliverance. For this opinion of his title to the throne was not taken up at random; nor only by a few persons, merely to serve some bye-ends of their own. The idea pervades his whole history. It was one of the chief grounds of the enmity of his countrymen towards him, and the only plausible pretence on which he could be arraigned. And, notwithstanding his repeated declarations that his *kingdom was not of this world,* yet it was on this account that at last he was *brought as a lamb to the slaughter.*

When it is asserted that Christianity made no alteration in the civil affairs of the world, the assertion should neither be made, nor understood, without some qualification. The injunction to *render unto Caesar the things that are Caesar's,* is no doubt very comprehensive; implying that unless we are good Subjects, we cannot be good Christians: but then we are to *render unto Caesar,* or the supreme magistrate, that obedience only to which God has given him a just claim: our paramount duty is to God, to whom we are to render *the things that are God's.* If, therefore, in the course of human affairs, a case should occur (and no doubt such cases do often occur) in which the performance of both these obligations becomes incompatible, we cannot long be at a loss in determining that it is our duty to obey God rather than men. The worship of idols, as well as sacrifices and auguries, certainly entered into, and made a part of, the civil policy of ancient Rome. Temples dedicated to a variety of false deities were under the peculiar care of the Senate. The office of Pontifex Maximus, or High Priest, was annexed to the title of Emperor. Now, surely, it was the intention of the Founder of Christianity, and it is the natural tendency of it's doctrines, to produce some alteration in things of this sort. In Mahometan countries, a plurality of wives is allowed by law: in many countries still Pagan, the worship of images is enjoined by the State: in several parts of Africa, parents who are past labour are, by the laws of the land, exposed by their children to be torn in pieces by wild beasts: and even in so civilized a country as China, children are thus exposed by their parents, with the sanction and authority of the laws. Would Christianity endure such shocking outrages against all that is humane, moral, or pious, though supported by Government? It certainly would not: for the spirit of St. Paul, when he saw the city of Athens *wholly given to idolatry,* was so *stirred in him,* that, for disputing publicly with *certain philosophers of the Epicureans and of the Stoics,* they carried him unto Areopagus; where, far from shrinking from his duty, he openly arraigned all the people of Athens, of being *too superstitious*. This charge he founded on his having seen *an altar with this inscription, To the unknown God;* which yet was not set up contrary to law. Sundry improprieties, sanctioned by legal authority, were censured by Christ himself. Was it not by virtue of his regal power that, as *one having authority,* he cast the buyers and sellers out of the temple; who yet were there, and pursuing their usual callings, with the public permission? Still, though they certainly were not restrained by any idea that all interference with the civil affairs of the world was contrary to Christianity, it no where appears, that either our saviour, or any of his apostles, ever did interfere with the affairs of any government, or the administration of any government, otherwise than by submitting to them. Yet, let it not be said, that he who could have commanded *more than twelve legions of angels,* wanted power or means to have resisted, and with effect, that pusillanimous Roman governor, who, from the basest of all motives, *gave sentence,* that a person in whom he declared he *found no fault,* should be put to death, merely to gratify a senseless, malicious, and clamorous multitude. Let it not be said, that his pretensions to sovereignty were either romantic or dubious: *a great multitude* of his contemporaries and countrymen, *being in number about five thousand,* thought so favourably of them, that they would have set him on their throne in that way by which alone we are now told authority over a free people can properly be obtained, viz. by the suffrages of the people. To assert his claim *de jure* against those who held it *de facto,* they would fain have *taken him by force* (that is, no doubt, in opposition to the Romans and their adherents) *to make him a king.* That he was not restrained from gratifying these natural wishes of so large a number of his impatient countrymen, by any apprehensions of his being evil-spoken of, as a *pestilent fellow,* one who *perverted the people, forbidding to give tribute to Caesar, and saying that he himself was king,* may very rationally be inferred from his having submitted to no less unmerited aspersions with invincible fortitude: and his yielding at last to the ignominy of the cross, proves that he was not to be deterred from doing any thing which he knew would rebound either to the glory of God, or the good of mankind, by the dread of any calumnies, or the terrors of any sufferings.

His constant discouragement, therefore, of a scheme so well calculated not only to promote his own elevation, but to emancipate his country (had he estimated either worldly grandeur, or the conditon of subjects under government, according to our ideas) would have been inconsistent with that love to mankind which he manifested in every other action of his life. The only rational conclusion, therefore, that the case will admit of, is, that he thought it would be better, both for Judea in particular, and for the world in general, that in the former case the people should not be distracted by a revolution, and in the latter that there should be no precedent to which revolutionists might appeal: his words were not meant to bear merely a local and circumscribed, but a general and extended application, when he directed his followers to *render unto Caesar the things that are Caesar's:* his practice was comformable to this precept; and so would ours be, were we but practically convinced that *it is enough for the disciple to be as his master, and the servant as his lord.* As Christians, solicitous to tread in the steps in which our saviour trod, the tribute of civil obedience is as much due to our civil rulers, even though they should happen to be invaders like the Romans, and though, like Herod, the ministers of government should chance to be oppressors, as the duty of religious obedience is a debt which we owe to *the King of kings, and Lord of Lords.*

Nor let this be deemed a degrading and servile principle: it is the very reverse; and it is this it's superior dignity which proves it's celestial origin. For, whilst other doctrines and other systems distract the world with disputes and debates which admit of no decision, and of *wars and fightings* which are almost as endless as they are useless, it is the glory of Christianity to teach her votaries patiently to bear imperfections, inconveniences and evils in government, as in every thing else that is human. This patient acquiescence under some remediless evils is not more our duty than it is our interest: for, the only very intolerable grievance in government is, when men allow themselves to disturb and destroy the peace of the world, by vain attempts to render that perfect, which the laws of our nature have ordained to be imperfect. And there is more magnanimity, as well as more wisdom, in enduring some present and certain evils, than can be manifested by any projects of redress that are uncertain; but which, if they fail, may bring down irretrievable ruin on thousands of others, as well as on ourselves: since to suffer nobly indicates more greatness of mind than can be shewn even by acting valiantly. Wise men, therefore, in the words of a noted philosopher, will "rather choose to brook with patience some inconveniences under government (because human affairs cannot possibly be without some) than self-opinionatedly disturb the quiet of the public." And, weighing the justice of those things you are about, not by the persuasion and advice of private men, but by the laws of the realm, you will no longer suffer ambitious men, through the streams of your blood, to wade to their own power; but esteem it better to enjoy yourselves in the present state, though perhaps not the best, than, by waging war, endeavour to procure a reformation in another age, yourselves "in the meanwhile either killed, or consumed with age."

This long enquiry concerning the divine origin and authority of government might perhaps have been deemed rather curious than useful, were it not of acknowledged moment, that some dangerous inferences which are usually drawn from the contrary opinion should be obviated. One of these dangerous inferences it seems to have been the aim of the sermon now before me to inculcate. Government being assumed to be a mere human ordinance, it is thence inferred, that "rulers are the servants of the public:" and, if they be, no doubt it necessarily follows, that they may (in the coarse phrase of the times) be *cashiered* or continued in pay, be reverenced or resisted, according to the mere whim or caprice of those over whom they are appointed to rule. Hence the author of this sermon also takes occasion to enter his protest against "passive obedience and non-resistance."

It really is a striking feature in our national history, that, ever since the Revolution, hardly any person of any note has preached or published a sermon, into which it was possible to drag this topic, without declaring against this doctrine. It seems to have been made a kind of criterion or test of principle, and the watch-word of a party. For, it cannot well be said, that the circumstances of the times, or the temper of men's minds, either lately have been, or now are, such as particularly to call for these studied and repeated protestations. What is not less remarkable is, that whilst the right of resistance has thus incessantly been delivered from the pulpit, insisted on by orators, and inculcated by statesmen, the contrary position is still (I believe) the dictate of religion, and certainly the doctrine of the established Church, and still also the law of the land.

You are not now to learn my mind on this point. As, however, the subject has again been forced on me, let me be permitted again to obviate, if I can, some fresh misrepresentations, and again to correct some new mistakes.

All government, whether lodged in one or in many, is, in it's nature, absolute and irresistible. It is not within the competency even of the supreme power to limit itself; because such limitation can emanate only from a superior. For any government to make itself irresistible, and to cease to be absolute, it must cease to be supreme; which is but saying, in other words, that it must dissolve itself, or be destroyed. If, then, to resist government be to destroy it, every man who is a subject must necessarily owe to the government under which he lives an obedience either active or passive: active, where the duty enjoined may be performed without offending God; and passive (that is to say, patiently to submit to the penalties annexed to disobedience) where that which is commanded by man is forbidden by God. No government upon earth can rightfully compel any one of it's subjects to an active compliance with any thing that is, or that appears to his conscience to be, inconsistent with, or contradictory to, the known laws of God: because every man is under a prior and superior obligation to *obey God in all things*. When such cases of incompatible demands of duty occur, every well-informed person knows what he is to do; and every well-principled person will do what he ought, viz. he will submit to the ordinances of God, rather than comply with the commandments of men. In thus acting he cannot err and this alone is "passive obedience;" which I entreat you to observe is so far from being "unlimited obedience" (as it's enemies wilfully persist to miscall it) that it is the direct contrary. Resolute not to disobey God, a man of good principles determines, in case of competition, as the lesser evil, to disobey man: but he knows that he should also disobey God, were he not, at the same time, patiently to submit to any penalties incurred by his disobedience to man.

With the fancies or the follies of the injudicious defenders of this doctrine, who, in the heat of controversy, have argued for the exclusive irresistibility of kings, merely in their personal capacity, I have no concern. Such arguments are now to be met with only in the answers of those equally injudicious, but less candid, opposers of the doctrine, who (as though there were any gallantry in taking a fortress that is no longer defended) persist to combat a phantom which, now at least, may be said to be of their own creating. In the present state of things, when a resistance is recommended, it must be, not against the king alone, but against the laws of the land. To encourage undistinguishing multitudes, by the vague term of resistance, to oppose all such laws as happen not to be agreeable to certain individuals, is neither more nor less than, by a regular plan, to attempt the subversion of the government: and I am not sure but that such attacks are more dangerous to free than to absolute governments.

Even the warmest advocates for resistance acknowledge, that, like civil liberty, the term is incapable of any accurate definition. Particular cases of injury and oppression are imagined: on which arguments are founded, to shew that mankind must be determined and governed, not by any known and fixed laws, but "by a law antecedent and paramount to all positive laws of men; by their natural sense and feelings." These unwritten, invisible, and undefinable "antecedent laws;" this indescribable "natural sense and feelings;" these "hidden powers and mysteries" in our Constitution, are points too refined and too subtle for argument. Indeed it can be to little purpose to argue, either on resistance or on any other subject, with men who are so weak as to declaim, when it is incumbent on them to reason.

Without any encouragement, mankind, alas! are, of themselves, far too *prone to be presumptuous and self-willed;* always disposed and ready to *despise dominion,* and *to speak evil of dignities*. There is, says a learned writer, such a "witchcraft in rebellion, as to tempt men to be rebels, even though they are sure to be damned for it." What dreadful confusions and calamities must have been occasioned in the world, had such strong and dangerous natural propensities been directly encouraged by any positive law! It was surely, then, merciful and wise in the Almighty Ruler of the world, to impose on his creatures the general law of obedience without any exceptions. A non-resisting spirit never yet made any man a bad subject. And if men of such mild and yielding tempers have shewn less ardour, than many others do, in the pursuit of that liberty which makes so conspicuous a figure in the effusions of orators and poets, it can be only for this reason, that they think it is precisely that kind of liberty which has so often set the world in an uproar, and that therefore it would be better for the world if it were never more heard of. If they are mistaken, their mistakes are at least harmless: and there is much justice, as well as great good sense, in Bishop Hall's remark, that "some quiet errors are better than some unruly truths."

When, not long since, a noted patriot declared, in his place in Parliament, that he knew no difference between a revolution and a rebellion, excepting that in the former an attempt to alter the form of government succeeded, and in the latter it did not, the sentiment was objected to as licentious and seditious. Yet, on the principles of the advocates of resistance, he said no more than he might easily have defended: nor am I sure but that (notwithstanding the pains which the public men of that period took to guard against such an inference, in their debates on the word *abdication*) on these principles the promoters of the revolution itself, emphatically so called, must submit to the imputation of having effected it by resistance. It was clearly a successful revolution. If, then, this was the case as to the revolution, how, it may be asked, did it differ, in point of principle, either from the grand rebellion that preceded it, or either of the subsequent rebellions for the purpose of restoring the abdicated family? and how, on the same principles, can we condemn the murder of the father, and vindicate the expulsion of the son? Mr. Locke, like many inferior writers, when defending resistance, falls into inconsistencies, and is at variance with himself. "Rebellion being," as he says, "an opposition not to persons, but to authority, which is founded only in the constitution and laws of the government, those, whoever they be, who by force break through, and by force justify their violation of them, are truly and properly rebels." To this argument no one can object: but it should be attended to, that, in political consideration, it is hardly possible to dissociate the ideas of authority in the abstract from persons vested with authority. To resist a person legally vested with authority, is, I conceive, to all intents and purposes, the same thing as to resist authority. Nothing, but it's success, could have rescued the revolution from this soul imputation, had it not been for the abdication. Accordingly this great event has always hung like a mill-stone on the necks of those who must protest against rebellions; whilst yet their system of politics requires that they should approve of resistance, and the revolution.

The resistance which your political counsellors urge you to practice (and which no doubt was intended to be justified by the sermon which I have now been compelled to notice), is not a resistance exerted only against the persons invested with the supreme power either legislative or executive, but clearly and literally against *authority*. Nay, if I at all understand the following declaration made by those who profess that they are the disciples of Mr. Locke, you are encouraged to resist not only all authority over us as it now exists, but any and all that it is possible to constitute. "Can men who exercise their reason believe, that the Divine Author of our existence intended a part of the human race to hold an absolute property in, and an unbounded power over, others, marked out by his infinite wisdom and goodness as the objects of a legal domination never rightfully resistible, however severe and oppressive?" It might be hazardous, perhaps, for me, even under the shelter of a Scripture phrase, to call these words *great swelling words;* because they are congressional words. That they have excited a very great general panic, and many apprehensions of a real impending slavery, is no more than might have been expected in a country where there is literally "absolute property in, and unbounded power over, human beings." How far this was intended, I presume not to judge. But, involved and obscure as the language (in which these extraordinary sentiments are couched) must be confessed to be, the declaration certainly points at all government: and it's full meaning amounts to a denial of that just supremacy which "the Divine Author of our existence" has beyond all question given to "one part of the human race" to hold over another. Without some paramount and irresistible power, there can be no government. In our Constitution, this supremacy is vested in the King and the Parliament; and, subordinate to them, in our Provincial Legislatures. If you were now released from this constitutional power, you must differ from all others "of the human race," if you did not soon find yourselves under a necessity of submitting to a power no less absolute, though vested in other persons, and a government differently constituted. And much does it import you to consider, whether those who are now so ready to promise to make *the grievous yoke of your fathers lighter,* may not themselves verify Rehoboam's assertion, and make you feel that *their little fingers are thicker than your father's loins.*

Be it (for the sake of argument) admitted, that the government under which till now you have lived happily, is, most unaccountably, all at once become *oppressive and severe;* did you, of yourselves, make this discovery? No: I affirm, without any apprehension of being contradicted, that you are acquainted with these oppressions only from the report of others. For what, then (admitting you have a right to resist in any case), are you now urged to resist and rise against those whom you have hitherto always regarded (and certainly not without reason) as your *nursing fathers and nursing mothers?* Often as you have already heard it repeated without expressing any disapprobation, I assure myself it will afford you no pleasure to be reminded, that it is on account of an insignificant duty on tea, imposed by the British Parliament; and which, for aught we know, may or may not be constitutionally imposed; but which, we well know, two thirds of the people of America can never be called on to pay. Is it the part of an *understanding people,* of loyal subjects, or good Christians, instantly to resist and rebel for a cause so trivial? O my brethren, consult your own hearts, and follow your own judgments! and learn not your "measures of obedience" from men who weakly or wickedly imagine there can be liberty unconnected with law—and whose aim it is to drive you on, step by step, to a resistance which will terminate, if it does not begin, in rebellion! On all such trying occasions, learn the line of conduct which it is your duty and interest to observe, from our Constitution itself: which, in ths particular, is a fair transcript or exemplification of the ordinance of God. Both the one and the other warn you against resistance: but you are not forbidden either to remonstrate or to petition. And can it be humiliating to any man, or any number of men, to ask, when we have but to *ask and it shall be given?* Is prayer an abject duty; or do men ever appear either so great, or so amiable, as when they are modest and humble? However meanly this privilege of petitioning may be regarded by those who claim every thing as a right, they are challenged to shew an instance, in which it has failed, when it ought to have succeeded. If, however, our grievances, in any point of view, be of such moment as that other means of obtaining redress should be judged expedient, happily we enjoy those means. In a certain sense, some considerable portion of legislation is still in our own hands. We are supposed to have chosen "fit and able" persons to represent us in the great council of our country: and they only can constitutionally interfere either to obtain the enacting of what is right, or the repeal of what is wrong. If we and our fellow-subjects, have been conscientiously faithful in the discharge of our duty, we can have no reason to doubt that our delegates will be equally faithful in the discharge of theirs. Our Provincial Assemblies, it is true, are but one part of our Colonial Legislature: they form, however, that part which is the most efficient. If the present general topic of complaint be, in their estimation, well founded, and a real and great grievance, what reason have you to imagine that all the Assemblies on the Continent will not concur and be unanimous in so representing it? And if they should all concur so to represent it, it is hardly within the reach of supposition that all due attention will not be paid to their united remonstrances. So many and such large concessions have often been made, at the instance only of individual Assemblies, that we are warranted in relying, that nothing which is reasonable and proper will ever be withheld from us, provided only it be asked for with decency, and that we do not previously forfeit our title to attention by becoming refractory and rebellious.

Let it be supposed, however, that even the worst may happen, which can happen; that our remonstrances are disregarded, our petitions rejected, and our grievances unredressed: what, you will naturally ask—what, in such case, would I advise you to do? Advice, alas! is all I have to give; which, however, though you may condescend to ask and to regard it, will neither be asked, nor accepted, by those who alone can give it great effect. Yet, circumscribed as our sphere of influence is, we are not wholly without influence; and therefore, even in our humble department, we have some duties to perform. To your question, therefore, I hesitate not to answer, that I wish and advise you to act the part of reasonable men, and of Christians. You will be pleased to observe, however, that I am far from thinking that your virtue will ever be brought to so severe a test and trial. The question, I am aware, was an ensnaring one, suggested to you by those who are as little solicitous about your peace, as they are for my safety: the answer which, in condescension to your wishes, I have given to it, is direct and plain; and not more applicable to you, than it is to all the people of America. If you think the duty of threepence a pound upon tea, laid on by the British Parliament, a grievance, it is your duty to instruct your members to take all the constitutional means in their power to obtain redress: if those means fail of success, you cannot but be sorry and grieved; but you will better bear your disappointment, by being able to reflect that it was not owing to any misconduct of your own. And, what is the whole history of human life, public and private, but a series of disappointments? It might be hoped that Christians would not think it grievous to be doomed to submit to disappointments and calamities, as their Master submitted, even if they were as innocent. His disciples and first followers shrunk from no trials nor dangers. Treading in the steps of him who, *when he was reviled, blessed, and when he was persecuted, suffered it,* they willingly laid down their lives, rather than resist some of the worst tyrants that ever disgraced the annals of history. Those persons are as little acquainted with general history, as they are with the particular doctrines of Christianity, who represent such submission as abject and servile. I affirm, with great authority, that "there can be no better way of asserting the people's lawful rights, than the disowning unlawful commands, by thus patiently suffering." When this doctrine was more generally embraced, our holy religion gained as much by submission, as it is now in a fair way of losing for want of it.

Having, then, my brethren, thus long been *tossed to and fro* in a wearisome circle of *uncertain traditions*, or in speculations and projects still more uncertain, concerning government, what better can you do than, following the Apostle's advice, *to submit yourselves to every ordinance of man, for the Lord's sake; whether it be to the King as supreme, or unto* GOVERNORS, *as unto them that are* SENT *by him for the punishment of evildoers, and for the praise of them that do well? For, so is the will of God, that with well-doing ye may put to silence the ignorance of foolish men: as free, and not using your liberty for a cloke of maliciousness, but as the servants of God. Honour all men: love the brotherhood: fear God: honour the king.*

ELECTION-SERMON

Samuel West

Samuel West, American patriot and theologian, was born at Yarmouth, Cape Cod, March 3, 1730. Soon after his birth, his family moved to Barnstaple. West worked as a farmer until he was twenty. He was privately tutored by a minister for six months before he entered Harvard in 1750. He was graduated from Harvard in 1754, was ordained June 3, 1761, and received the degree of Doctor of Divinity from Harvard in 1793.

After leaving college, West explored almost every branch of science, though theology remained his main interest. He devoted much of his learning and religious zeal to serving the emerging nation. He was a chaplain in the army, and an influential member of the convention that wrote the Constitution of the State of Massachusetts, and the convention for the adoption of the Constitution of the United States, where, it is said, he personally persuaded John Hancock to sign.

West felt that sermons should be simple rather than pompous and rhetorical, and that they should show good sense and sublime theology. He was distinguished for his mastery of many difficult subjects, and for his profound thought.

During his late years, West became increasingly absent-minded, and before his death, his memory failed entirely.

He retired in 1803, because of poor health. He died in his son's home in Tiverton, Rhode Island, September 24, 1807.

The following election sermon was preached before the Council and the House of Representatives of the Colony of Massachusetts Bay on May 29, 1776, "being the anniversary for the election of the honorable Council for the Colony." The text is from the edition printed in Boston in 1776, for John Gill.

Titus, Chapter 3d. Verse 1st. *Put them in mind to be subject to principalities and powers, to obey magistrates, to be ready to every good work.*

THE great Creator, having design'd the human race for society, has made us dependent on one another for happiness; he has so constituted us, that it becomes both our duty and interest, to seek the public good; and that we may be the more firmly engaged to promote each others welfare, the Deity has endowed us with tender and social affections, with generous and benevolent principles: hence the pain, that we feel in seeing an object of distress: Hence the satisfaction, that arises in relieving the afflicted, and the superior pleasure, which we experience in communicating happiness to the miserable. The Deity has also invested us with moral powers and faculties, by which we are enabled to discern the difference between right and wrong, truth and falsehood, good and evil: Hence the approbation of mind, that arises upon doing a good action, and the remorse of conscience, which we experience, when we counteract the moral sense, and do that which is evil. This proves, that in what is commonly called a state of nature, we are the subjects of the divine law and government, that the Deity is our supreme magistrate, who has written his law in our hearts, and will reward, or punish us, according as we obey or disobey his commands. Had the human race uniformly persevered in a state of moral rectitude, there would have been little, or no need of any other law, besides that which is written in the heart, for every one in such a state would be a law unto himself. There could be no occasion for enacting or enforcing the penal laws, for such are *not made for the righteous man, but for the lawless and disobedient, for the ungodly, and for sinners, for the unholy and profane, for murderers of fathers, and murderers of mothers, for manslayers, for whoremongers, for them that defile themselves with mankind, for men-stealers, for liars, for perjured persons, and if there be any other thing, that is contrary to* moral rectitude, and the happiness of mankind. The necessity of forming ourselves into politic bodies, and granting to our rulers, a power to enact laws for the public safety, and to enforce them by proper penalties, arises from our being in a fallen, and degenerate state. The slightest view of the present state and condition of the human race, is abundantly sufficient to convince any person of common sense, and common honesty, that civil government is absolutely necessary for the peace and safety of mankind, and consequently that all good magistrates, while they faithfully discharge the trust reposed in them, ought to be religiously and conscientiously obeyed. An enemy to good government is an enemy not only to his country, but to all mankind; for he plainly shows himself to be divested of those tender and social sentiments which are characteristic of a human temper, even of that generous and benevolent disposition which is the peculiar glory of a rational creature. An enemy to good government has degraded himself below the rank and dignity of a man, and deserves to be classed with the lower creation. Hence we find, that wise and good men of all nations, and religions, have even inculcated subjection to good government, and have borne their testimony against the licentious disturbers of the public peace.

NOR has Christianity been deficient in this capital point. We find our blessed Saviour directing the Jews to render to Caesar the things that were Caesar's: And the apostles and first preachers of the gospel not only exhibited a good example of subjection to the magistrate, in all things that were just and lawful, but they have also in several places in the new-testament, strongly enjoined upon christians the duty of submission to that government under which providence had placed them. Hence we find, that those, who despise government, and are not afraid to speak evil of dignities, are by the apostles Peter and Jude, class'd among those presumptuous, self-willed sinners that are reserved to the judgment of the great day. And the apostle Paul judg'd submission to civil government, to be a matter of such great importance, that he tho't it worth his while to charge Titus, to put his hearers in mind to be submissive to principalities and powers, to obey magistrates, to be ready to every good work: As much as to say, none can be ready to every good work, or be properly dispos'd to perform those actions, that tend to promote the public good, who do not obey magistrates, and who do not become good subjects of civil government. If then obedience to the civil magistrates is so essential to the character of a christian, that without it he cannot be disposed to perform those good works that are necessary for the welfare of mankind; if the despisers of governments are those presumptuous, self-willed sinners who are reserv'd to the judgment of the great day; it is certainly a matter of the utmost importance to us all, to be thoroughly acquainted with the nature and extent of our duty, that we may yield the obedience requir'd; for it is impossible that we should properly discharge a duty when we are strangers to the nature and extent of it.

IN order therefore, that we may form a right judgment of the duty enjoin'd in our text, I shall consider the nature and design of civil government, do equally oblige us to resist tryanny; or that tyranny and magistracy are so opposite to each other that where the one begins, the other ends. I shall then apply the present discourse to the grand controversy, that at this day subsists between Great-Britain and the American colonies.

THAT we may understand the nature and design of civil government, and discover the foundation of the magistrates authority to command, and the duty of subjects to obey, it is necessary to derive civil government from its orginal; in order to which we must consider what *state all men are naturally in, and that is as* (*Mr. Lock observes*) *a state of perfect freedom to order all their actions, and dispose of their possessions and persons as they think fit, within the bounds of the law of nature, without asking leave, or depending upon the will of any man.* It is a state wherein all are equal, no one having a right to controul another, or oppose him in what he does, unless it be in his own defence, or in the defence of those that being injured stand in need of his assistance.

HAD men persevered in a state of moral rectitude, every one would have been disposed to follow the law of nature, and pursue the general good; in such a state, the wisest and most experienced would undoubtedly be chosen to guide and direct those of less wisdom and experience than themselves; there being nothing else that could afford the least show or appearance of any one's having the superiority or precedency over another; for the dictates of conscience, and the precepts of natural law being uniformly and regularly obey'd, men would only need to be informed what things were most fit and prudent to be done in those cases, where their inexperience, or want of acquaintance, left their minds in doubt what was the wisest and most regular method for them to pursue. In such cases it would be necessary for them to advise with those, who were wiser and more experienced than themselves. But these advisers could claim no authority to compel, or to use any forcible measures to oblige any one to comply with their direction, or advice; there could be no occasion for the exertion of such a power; for every man, being under the government of right reason, would immediately feel himself constrain'd to comply with everything that appeared reasonable or fit to be done, or that would any way tend to promote the general good. This would have been the happy state of mankind, had they closely adhered to the law of nature, and persevered in their primitive state.

THUS we see, that a state of nature, tho' it be a state of perfect freedom, yet is very far from a state of licentiousness; the law of nature gives men no right to do anything that is immoral, or contrary to the will of GOD, and injurious to their fellow-creatures; for a state of nature is properly a state of law and government, even a government founded upon the unchangeable nature of the Deity, and a law resulting from the eternal fitness of things; sooner shall heaven and earth pass away, and the whole frame of nature be dissolved, than any part, even the smallest iota of this law shall ever be abrogated; it is unchangeable as the Deity himself, being a transcript of his moral perfections. A revelation, pretending to be from GOD, that contradicts any part of natural law, ought immediately to be rejected as an imposture; for the Deity cannot make a law contrary to the law of nature, without acting contrary to himself. A thing in the strictest sense impossible, for that which implies contradiction is not an object of the divine power. Had this subject been properly attended to and understood, the world had remained free from a multitude of absur'd and pernicious principles, which have been industriously propagated by artful and designing men, both in politics and divinity. The doctrine of non-resistance, and unlimited passive obedience to the worst of tyrants, could never have found credit among mankind, had the voice of reason been hearkened to for a guide, because such a doctrine would immediately have been discerned to be contrary to natural law.

IN a state of nature we have a right to make the persons that have injured us, repair the damages that they have done us; and it is just in us to inflict such punishment upon them, as is necessary to restrain them from doing the like for the future: The whole end and design of punishing being either to reclaim the individual punished, or to deter others from being guility of similar crimes: Whenever punishment exceeds these bounds, it becomes cruelty and revenge, and directly contrary to the law of nature. Our wants and necessities being such, as to render it impossible in most cases to enjoy life in any tolerable degree, without entering into society, and there being innumerable cases, wherein we need the assistance of others, which if not afforded, we should very soon perish; hence the law on nature requires, that we should endeavor to help one another, to the utmost of our power in all cases, where our assistance is necessary. It is our duty to endeavor always to promote the general good; to do to all, as we would be willing to be done by, were we in their circumstances, to do justly, to love mercy, and to walk humbly before GOD. These are some of the laws of nature, which every man in the world is bound to observe, and which whoever violates, exposes himself to the resentment of mankind, the lashes of his own conscience, and the judgment of heaven. This plainly shews, that the highest state of liberty subjects us to the law of nature, and the government of GOD. The most perfect freedom consists in obeying the dictates of right reason, and submitting to natural law. When a man goes beyond, or contrary to the law of nature and reason, he becomes the slave of base passions, and vile lusts, he introduces confusion and disorder into society, and brings misery and destruction upon himself. This therefore cannot be called a state of freedom, but a state of the vilest slavery, and the most dreadful bondage: The servants of sin and corruption are subjected to the worst kind of tyranny in the universe. Hence we conclude, that where licentiousness begins, liberty ends.

THE law of nature is a perfect standard and measure of action for beings that persevere in a state of moral rectitude. But the case is far different with us, who are in a fallen and degenerate estate. We have a law in our members, which is continually warring against the law of the mind; by which we often become enslaved to the basest lusts, and are brought into bondage to the vilest passions. The strong propensities of our animal nature often overcome the sober dictates of reason and conscience, and betray us into actions injurious to the public, and destructive of the safety and happiness of society. Men of unbridled lusts, were they not restrained by the power of the civil magistrate, would spread horror and desolation all around them. This makes it absolutely necessary, that societies should form themselves into politick bodies, that they may enact laws for the public safety, and appoint particular penalties for the violation of their laws, and invest a suitable number of persons with authority to put in execution and enforce the laws of the state; in order that wicked men may be restrained from doing mischief to their fellow-creatures, that the injured may have their rights restored to them, that the virtuous may be encouraged in doing good, and that every member of society may be protected and secured in the peaceable, quiet possession and enjoyment of all those liberties and privileges, which the Deity has bestowed upon him, i.e. that he may safely enjoy, and pursue whatever he chooses, that is consistent with the publick good. This shews that the end and design of civil government, cannot be to deprive men of their liberty, or take away their freedom; but on the contrary the true design of civil government is to protect men in the enjoyment of liberty.

FROM hence it follows that tyranny and arbitrary power are utterly inconsistent with, and subversive of the very end design of civil government, and directly contrary to natural law, which is the true foundation of civil government and all politick law: Consequently the authority of a tyrant is of itself null and void; for as no man can have a right to act contrary to the law of nature, it is impossible that any individual, or even the greatest number of men, can confer a right upon another, of which they themselves are not possessed; i.e. no body of men can justly and lawfully authorize and person to tyrannize over, and enslave his fellow creatures, or do anything contrary to equity and goodness. As magistrates have no authority, but what they derive from the people, whenever they act contrary to the public good, and pursue measures destructive of the peace and safety of the community, they forfeit their right to govern the people. Civil rulers and magistrates are properly of human creation; they are set up by the people to be the guardians of the rights, and to secure their persons from being injured, or oppressed; the safety of the publick being the supreme law of the state, by which the magistrates are to be governed, and which they are to consult upon all occasions. The modes of administration may be very different, and the forms of government may vary from each other in different ages and nations; but under every form, the end of civil government is the same, and cannot vary: It is like the laws of the Medes and Persians, it altereth not.

THOUGH magistrates are to consider themselves as the servants of the people, seeing from them it is, that they derive their power and authority; yet they may also be considered as the ministers of GOD ordain'd by him for the good of mankind: For under him as the supreme magistrate of the universe they are to act; and it is GOD who has not only declared in his word, what are the necessary qualifications of a ruler, but who also raises up and qualifies men for such an important station. The magistrate may also in a more strict and proper sense, be said to be ordained of GOD, because reason, which is the voice of GOD, plainly requires such an order of men to be appointed for the public good; now whatever right reason requires as as necessary to be done, is as much the will and law of GOD as tho' it were enjoin'd us by an immediate revelation from heaven, or commanded in the sacred scriptures.

FROM this account of the origin, nature and design of civil government, we may be very easily led into a thorough knowledge of our duty; we may see the reason why we are bound to obey magistrates, viz. because they are the ministers of GOD for good unto the people. While therefore they rule in the fear of GOD, and while they promote the welfare of the state, i.e. while they act in the character of magistrates, it is the indispensable duty of all to submit to them, and to oppose a turbulent, factious, and libertine spirit, whenever and wherever it discovers itself. When a people have by their free consent conferr'd upon a number of men, a power to rule and govern them, they are bound to obey them: Hence disobedience becomes a breach of faith, it is violating a constitution of their own appointing, and breaking a compact for which they ought to have the most sacred regard: Such a conduct discovers so base and disengenuous a temper of mind, that it must expose them to contempt in the judgment of all the sober thinking part of mankind. Subjects are bound to obey lawful magistrates by every tender tie of human nature, which disposes us to consult the public good, and to seek the good of our brethren, our wives, our children, our friends and acquaintances; for he that opposes lawful authority, does really oppose the safety and happiness of his fellow creatures. A factious, seditious person, that opposes good government, is a monster in nature; for he is an enemy to his own species, and destitute of the sentiments of humanity.

SUBJECTS are also bound to obey magistrates, for conscience sake, out of regard to the divine authority, and out of obedience to the will of GOD: For if magistrates are the ministers of GOD, we cannot disobey them without being disobedient to the law of GOD; and this extends to all men in authority, from the highest ruler to the lowest officer in the state. To oppose them when in the exercise of lawful authority, is an act of disobedience to the Deity, and as such will be punished by him. It will doubtless be readily granted by every honest man, that we ought cheerfully to obey the magistrate and submit to all such regulations of government, as tend to promote the publick good; but as this general definition may be liable to be misconstrued, and every man may think himself at liberty to disregard any laws that do not suit his interest, humor, or fancy; I would observe, that in a multitude of cases, many of us, for want of being properly acquainted with affairs of state, may be very improper judges of particular laws, whether they are just or not: In such cases it becomes us, as good members of society, peaceably and conscientiously to submit, tho' we cannot see the reasonableness of every law to which we submit; and that for this plain reason, that if any number of men should take it upon themselves to oppose authority for acts, which may be really necessary for the public safety, only because they do not see the reasonableness of them, the direct consequence will be introducing confusion and anarchy into the state.

IT is also necessary, that the minor part should submit to the major; e.g. when legislators have enacted a set of laws, which are highly approved by a large majority of the community, as tending to promote the publick good, in this case, if a small number of persons are so unhappy as to view the matter in a very different point of light from the public, tho' they have an undoubted right to shew the reasons of their dissent from the judgment of the publick, and may lawfully use all proper arguments to convince the public of what they judge to be an error, yet if they fail in their attempt, and the majority still continue to approve of the laws that are enacted, it is the duty of those few that dissent, peaceably and for conscience sake to submit to the publick judgment; unless something is required of them which they judge would be sinful for them to comply with; for in that case they ought to obey the dictates of their own consciences, rather than any human authority whatever. Perhaps also some cases of intolerable oppression, where compliance would bring on inevitable ruin and destruction, may justly warrant the few to refuse submission to what they judge inconsistent with their peace and safety; for the law of self-preservation will always justify opposing a cruel and tyrannical imposition, except where opposition is attended with greater evils than submission, which is frequently the case where a few are oppressed by a large and powerful majority. Except the above-named cases, the minor ought always to submit to the major; otherwise there can be no peace nor harmony in society. And besides, it is the major part of a community that have the sole right of establishing a constitution, and authorizing magistrates; and consequently it is only the major part of the community that can claim the right of altering the constitution, and displacing the magistrates; for certainly common sense will tell us, that it requires as great an authority to set aside a constitution, as there was at first to establish it. The collective body, not a few individuals, ought to constitute the supreme authority of the state.

THE only difficulty remaining is to determine, when a people may claim a right of forming themselves into a body politick, and assume the powers of legislation. In order to determine this point, we are to remember, that all men being by nature equal, all the members of a community have a natural right to assemble themselves together, and act and vote for such regulations, as they

judge are necessary for the good of the whole. But when a community is become very numerous, it is very difficult, and in many
cases impossible for all to meet together to regulate the affairs of the
state : Hence comes the necessity of appointing delegates to represent
the people in a general assembly. And this ought to be look'd upon
as a sacred and inalienable right, of which a people cannot justly
divest themselves, and which no human authority can in equity ever
take from them, viz. that no one be obliged to submit to any law,
except such as are made either by himself, or by his representative.

IF representation and legislation are inseparably connected,
it follows, that when great numbers have emigrated into a foreign
land, and are so far removed from the parent state, that they
neither are or can be properly represented by the government from
which they have emigrated, that then nature itself points out the
necessity of their assuming to themselves the powers of legislation,
and they have a right to consider themselves as a separate state
from the other, and as such to form themselves into a body politick.

IN the next place,

WHEN a people find themselves cruelly oppressed by the parent
state, they have an undoubted right to throw off the yoke, and to
assert their liberty, if they find good reason to judge that they
have sufficient power and strength to maintain their ground in
defending their just rights against their oppressors : For in this
case by the law of self-preservation, which is the first law of nature,
they have not only an undoubted right, but it is their indispensable
duty, if they cannot be redressed any other way, to renounce all
submission to the government that has oppressed them, and set up
an independent state of their own; even tho' they may be vastly
inferior in numbers to the state that has oppress'd them. When
either of the aforesaid cases takes place, and more especially when
both concur, no rational man (I imagine) can have any doubt in
his own mind, whether such a people have a right to form themselves into a body politick, and assume to themselves all the powers
of a free state. For can it be rational to suppose, that a people
should be subjected to the tyranny of a set of men, who are perfect
strangers to them, and cannot be supposed to have that fellow
feeling for them, that we generally have for those with whom we
are connected and acquainted; and besides, thro' their unacquainted-
ness with the circumstances of the people over whom they claim the
right of jurisdiction, are utterly unable to judge, in a multitude of
cases, which is best for them.

IT becomes me not to say what particular form of government is best for a community, whether a pure democracy, artistoc-
racy, monarchy, or a mixture of all the three simple forms. They
have all their advantages & disadvantages; and when they are
properly administred, may any of them answer the design of civil

government tolerably well. Permit me however to say, that an unlimited absolute monarchy, and an aristocracy not subject to the control of the people, are two of the most exceptionable forms of government:

1st, BECAUSE in neither of them is there a proper representation of the people, and,

2dly, BECAUSE each of them being entirely independent of the people, they are very apt to degenerate into tryranny. However, in this imperfect state, we cannot expect to have government formed upon such a basis, but that it may be perverted by bad men to evil purposes. A wise and good man would be very loth to undermine a constitution, that was once fixed and established, altho' he might discover many imperfections in it; and nothing short of the most urgent necessity would ever induce him to consent to it; because the unhinging a people from a form of government to which they had been long accustomed, might throw them into such a state of anarchy and confusion as might terminate in their destruction, or perhaps in the end, subject them to the worst kind of tyranny.

HAVING thus shown the nature, end and design of civil government, and pointed out the reasons, why subjects are bound to obey magistrates, viz. because in so doing, they both consult their own happiness as individuals, and also promote the public good, and the safety of the estate: I proceed,

IN the next place, to shew, That the same principles that oblige us to submit to civil government, do also equally oblige us, where we have power and ability, to resist and oppose tyranny; and that where tyranny begins, government ends. For if magistrates have no authority but what they derive from the people, if they are properly of human creation; if the whole end and design of their institution is to promote the general good, and to secure to men their just rights, it will follow, that when they act contrary to the end and design of their creation, they cease being magistrates, and the people, which gave them their authority, have the right to take it from them again. This is a very plain dictate of common sense, which, universally obtains in all similar cases: For who is there, that having employ'd a number of men to do a particular piece of work for him, but what would judge that he had a right to dismiss them from his service, when he found that they went directly contrary to his orders; and that instead of accomplishing the business he had set them about, they would infallibly ruin and destroy it. If then men, in the common affairs of life always judge, that they have a right to dismiss from their service such persons as counteract their plans and designs, tho' the damage will affect only a few individuals, much more must the body politick have a right to depose any persons, tho' appointed to the highest place of power and authority, when they find, that they are unfaithful to the trust reposed in them, and that instead of consulting the general good, they are disturbing the peace of society by making laws cruel and oppressive, and by depriving the subjects of their just rights and privileges. Whoever pretends to deny this proposition, must give up all pretence of being master of that common sense and reason by which the Deity has distinguished us from the brutal herd.

AS our duty of obedience to the magistrate is founded upon our obligation to promote the general good, our readiness to obey lawful authority will always arise in proportion to the love and regard that we have for the welfare of the publick; and the same love and regard for the public will inspire us with as strong a zeal to oppose tyranny, as we have to obey magistracy. Our obligation to promote the publick good extends as much to the opposing every exertion of arbitrary power, that is injurious to the State, as it does to the submitting to good and wholesome laws. No man therefore can be a good member of the community, that is not as zealous to oppose tyranny, as he is ready to obey magistracy. A slavish submission to tyranny is a proof of a very sordid and base mind: Such a person cannot be under the influence of any generous human sentiments, nor have a tender regard for mankind.

FURTHER, if magistrates are no farther ministers of GOD, than they promote the good of the community, then obedience to them neither is, nor can be unlimited; for it would imply a gross absurdity to assert, that, when magistrates are ordained by the people solely for the purpose of being beneficial to the State, they must be obeyed, when they are seeking to ruin and destroy it. This would imply, that men were bound to act against the great law of self-preservation, and to contribute their assistance to their own ruin and destruction, in order that they may please and gratify the greatest monsters in nature, who are violating the laws of GOD and destroying the rights of mankind. Unlimited submission and obedience is due to none but GOD alone: He has an absolute right to command: He alone has an uncontrollable sovereignty over us, because he alone is unchangeably good: He never will, nor can require of us consistent with his nature and attributes, anything that is not fit and reasonable; his commands are all just and good: And to suppose that he has given to any particular set of men a power to require obedience to that, which is unreasonable, cruel and unjust, is robbing the Deity of his justice and goodness, in which consists the peculiar glory of the divine character; and it is representing him, under the horrid character of a tyrant.

IF magistrates are ministers of GOD only because the law of GOD and reason points out the necessity of such an institution for the good of mankind; it follows that whenever they pursue measures directly destructive of the publick good, they cease being GOD'S ministers; they forfeit their right to obedience from the subject, they become the pests of society; and the community is under the strongest obligation of duty, both to GOD and to its own members, to resist and oppose them, which will be so far from resisting the ordinance of GOD, that it will be strictly obeying his commands. To suppose otherwise, will imply, that the Deity requires of us an obedience, that is self-contradictory and absurd, and that one part of his law is directly contrary to the other, i.e. while he commands us to pursue virtue, and the general good, he does at the same time require us to persecute virtue, and betray the general good, by enjoyning us obedience to the wicked commands of tyrannical oppressors. Can any one not lost to the principles of humanity undertake to defend such absurd sentiments as these? As the public safety is the first and grand law of society, so no community can have a right to invest the magistrate with any power, or authority that will enable him to act against the welfare of the state, and the good of the whole. If men have at any time wickedly, and foolishly given up their just rights into the hands of the magistrate, such acts are null and void of course; to suppose otherwise will imply, that we have a right to invest the magistrate with a power to act contrary to the law of GOD, which is as much as to say, that we are not the subjects of divine law and government. What has been said, is (I apprehend) abundantly sufficient to show that tyrants are no magistrates, or that whenever magistrates abuse their power and authority, to the subverting the publick happiness, their authority immediately ceases, and that it not only becomes lawful, but an indispensable duty to oppose them: That the principle of self-preservation, the affection, and duty, that we owe to our country, and the obedience we owe the Deity, do all require us to oppose tyranny.

IF it be asked, who are the proper judges to determine, when rulers are guilty of tyranny and oppression? I answer, the publick; not a few disaffected individuals, but the collective body of the state, must decide this question; for as it is the collective body that invests rulers with their power and authority, so it is the collective body that has the sole right of judging, whether rulers act up to the end of their institution or not. Great regard ought always to be paid to the judgment of the publick. It is true the publick may be imposed upon by a misrepresentation of facts; but this may be said of the publick, which can't always be said of individuals, viz. that the public is always willing to be rightly informed, and when it has proper matter of conviction laid before it, its judgment is always right.

THIS account of the nature and design of civil government, which is so clearly suggested to us by the plain principles of common sense and reason, is abundantly confirmed by the sacred scriptures, even by those very texts, which have been brought by men of slavish principles to establish the absurd doctrine, of unlimited passive obedience and non-resistance: As will abundantly appear, by examining the two most noted texts, that are commonly bro't to support the strange doctrine of passive obedience. The first that I shall cite is in 1 Peter 2d. c. ver. 13, 14. *Submit yourselves to every ordinance of man, or rather as the words ought to be rendered from the Greek submit yourselves to every human creation, or human constitution for the Lord's sake, whether it be to the king as supreme, or unto governors, as unto them, that are sent by him for the punishment of evil-doers, and for the praise of them, that do well.* Here we see, that the apostle asserts, that magistracy is of human creation or appointment, that is, that magistrates have no power or authority, but what they derive from the people; that this power they are to exert for the punishment of evil-doers, and for the praise of them that do well, i.e. the end and design of the appointment of magistrates, is to restrain wicked men by proper penalties from injuring society, and to encourage and honor the virtuous and obedient. Upon this account, christians are to submit to them for the Lord's sake, which is, as if he had said; Tho' magistrates are of mere human appointment, and can claim no power, or authority, but what they derive from the people, yet as they are ordained by men to promote the general good by punishing evil-doers, and by rewarding and encouraging the virtuous and obedient, you ought to submit to them out of a sacred regard to the divine authority; for as they in the faithful discharge of their office to fulfil the will of GOD, so ye, by submitting to them, do fulfil the divine command. If the only reason assign'd by the apostle, why magistrates should be obey'd out of a regard to the divine authority, is because they punish the wicked and encourage the good: It follows, that when they punish the virtuous, and encourage the vicious, we have a right to refuse yielding any submission or obedience to them; i.e., whenever they act contrary to the end and design of their institution, they forfeit their authority to govern the people, and the reason for submitting to them out of regard to the divine authority immediately ceases; and they being only of human appointment, the authority which the people gave them, the publick have a right to take from them, and to confer it upon those who are more worthy. So far is this text from favoring arbitrary principles, that there is nothing in it, but what is consistent with, and favorable to the highest liberty, that any man can wish to enjoy; for this text requires us to submit to the magistrate no further than he is the encourager and protector of virtue, and the punisher of vice; and this is consistent with all that liberty which the Deity has bestowed upon us.

THE other text which I shall mention, and which has been made use of, by the favourers of arbitrary government, as their great sheet anchor and main support, is in Rom 13th the first six verses. *Let every soul be subject to the higher powers; for there is no power but of* GOD: *The powers that be are ordained of* GOD. *Whosoever therefore resisteth the power, resisteth the ordinance of* GOD; *and they that resist shall receive to themselves damnation: For rulers are not a terror to good works but to the evil. Wilt thou then not be afraid of the power? Do that which is good, and thou shalt have praise of the same. For he is the minister of* GOD *to thee for good. But if thou do that which is evil be afraid, for he beareth not the sword in vain, for he is the minister of* GOD, *a revenger to execute wrath upon him, that doth evil. Wherefore ye must needs be subject not only for wrath, but also for conscience sake. For, for this cause pay you tribute also; for they are* GOD's *ministers, attending continually upon this very thing.* A very little attention (I apprehend) will be sufficient to shew, that this text is so far from favoring arbitrary government, that on the contrary, it strongly holds forth the principles of true liberty. Subjection to the higher powers is enjoined by the apostle, because there is no power but of GOD; the powers that be are ordained of GOD, consequently, to resist the power is to resist the ordinance of GOD: And he repeatedly declares that the ruler is the minister of GOD. Now, before we can say, whether this text makes for, or against the doctrine of unlimited passive obedience, we must find out in what sense the apostle affirms, that magistracy is the ordinance of GOD, and what he intends when he calls the ruler the minister of GOD.

I CAN think but of three possible senses, in which magistracy can with any propriety be called GOD's ordinance, or in which rulers can be said to be ordained of GOD as his ministers. The first is a plain declaration from the word of GOD, that such a one, and his descendants are, and shall be the only true and lawful magistrates; thus we find in scripture, the kingdom of Judah to be settled by divine appointment in the family of David, or,

2dly, BY an immediate commission from GOD, ordering and appointing such a one by name to be the ruler over the people; thus Saul and David were immediately appointed by GOD to be kings over Israel. Or,

3dly, MAGISTRACY may be called the ordinance of GOD; and rulers may be called the ministers of GOD, because the nature and reason of things, which is the law of GOD requires such an institution for the preservation and safety of civil society. In the two first senses, the apostle cannot be supposed to affirm, that magistracy is GOD's ordinance, for neither he, nor any of the sacred writers have entailed the magistracy to any one particular family under the gospel dispensation. Neither does he, nor any of the inspired writers give us the least hint, that any person should ever be immediately commissioned from GOD to bear rule over the people: The third sense then is the only sense, in which the apostle can be supposed to affirm, that the magistrate is the minister of GOD, and that magistracy is the ordinance of GOD, viz. that the nature and reason of things, require such an institution for the preservation and safety of mankind. Now if this be the only sense in which the apostle affirms, that magistrates are ordained of GOD as his ministers, resistance must be criminal only so far forth, as they are the ministers of GOD, i.e. while they act up to the end of their institution, and ceases being criminal, when they cease being the ministers of GOD, i.e. when they act contrary to the general good, and seek to destroy the liberties of the people.

THAT WE have gotten the apostle's sense of magistracy, being the ordinance of GOD, will plainly appear from the text itself: For, after having asserted, that to resist the power is to resist the ordinance of GOD, and they that resist, shall receive to themselves damnation; he immediately adds, as the reason of this assertion, *For rulers are not a terror to good works, but to the evil: Wilt thou then not be afraid of the power? Do that which is good, and thou shalt have praise of the same: For he is the minister of* GOD *to thee for good. But if thou do that which is evil be afraid; for he beareth not the sword in vain: For he is the minister of* GOD, *a revenger to execute wrath upon him that doth evil.* Here is a plain declaration of the sense, in which he asserts, that the authority of the magistrate is ordained of GOD, viz. because rulers are not a terror to good works, but to the evil, therefore we ought to dread offending them, for we cannot offend them but by doing evil, and if we do evil, we have just reason to fear their power; for they bear not the sword in vain, but in this case, the magistrate is a revenger to execute wrath upon him that doeth evil: but if we are found doers of that which is good, we have no reason to fear the authority of the magistrate, for in this case, instead of being punished we shall be protected and encouraged: The reason why the magistrate is called the minister of GOD, is, because he is to protect, encourage and honor them that do well, and to punish them that do evil; therefore it is our duty to submit to them, not merely for fear of being punished by them, but out of regard to the divine authority, under which they are deputed to execute judgment, and to do justice. For this reason (according to the apostle) tribute is to protect every man in the enjoyment of his just rights and privileges, and to punish every evil-doer.

IF the apostle then asserts, that rulers are ordain'd of GOD, only because they are a terror to evil works, and a praise to them that do well, if they are ministers of GOD only because they encourage virtue and punish vice; if for this reason only they are to be obey'd for conscience sake; if the sole reason, why they have a right to tribute is because they devote themselves wholly to the business of securing to men their just rights, and to the punishing of evil doers;

it follows, by undeniable consequence, that when they become the pests of human society; when they promote and encourage evil doers, and become a terror to good works, they then cease being the ordinance of GOD; they are no longer rulers, nor ministers of GOD; they are so far from being the powers that are ordain'd of GOD, that they become the ministers of the powers of darkness: And it is so far from being a crime to resist them, that in many cases it may be highly criminal in the sight of heaven to refuse resisting and opposing them to the utmost of our power; or in other words, that the same reasons that require us to obey the ordinance of GOD, do equally oblige us, when we have power and opportunity, to oppose and resist the ordinance of satan.

HENCE we see that the apostle Paul instead of being a friend to tyranny and arbitrary government, turns out to be a strong advocate for the just rights of mankind; and is for our enjoying all that liberty, with which GOD has invested us: For no power (according to the apostle) is ordained of GOD, but what is an encourager of every good and virtuous action, *do that which is good and thou shalt have praise of the same:* No man need to be afraid of this power, which is ordained of GOD who does nothing but what is agreeable to the law of GOD; for this power will not restrain us from exercising any liberty, which the Deity has granted us; for the minister of GOD is to restrain us from nothing, but the doing of that which is evil, and to this we have no right: To practise evil is not liberty, but licentiousness. Can we conceive of a more perfect, equitable and generous plan of government, than this which the apostle has laid down, viz. to have rulers appointed over us, to encourage us to every good and virtuous action, to defend and protect us in our just rights and privileges; and to grant us everything that can tend to promote our true interest and happiness; to restrain every licentious action, and to punish every one that would injure or harm us; to become a terror of evil doers; to make and execute such just and righteous laws, as shall effectually deter and hinder men from the commission of evil; and to attend continually upon this very thing; to make it their constant care and study day and night to promote the good and welfare of the community, and to oppose all evil practices. Deservedly may such rulers be called the ministers of GOD for good. They carry on the same benevolent design towards the community which the great governor of the universe does towards his whole creation. 'Tis the indispensable duty of a people to pay tribute, and to afford an easy and comfortable subsistence to such rulers, because they are the ministers of GOD, who are continually labouring and employing their time for the good of the community. He that resists such magistrates, does in a very emphatical sense resist the ordinance of GOD; he is an enemy to mankind, odious to GOD, and justly incurs the sentence of condemnation from the great judge of quick and dead. Obedience to such magistrates is yielding obedience to the will of GOD; and therefore ought to be performed from a sacred regard to the divine authority.

FOR any one from hence to infer, that the apostle enjoins in this text unlimited obedience to the worst of tyrants, and that he pronounces damnation upon those that resist the arbitrary measures of such pests of society, is just as good sense, as if one should affirm, that because the scripture enjoins us obedience to the laws of GOD, therefore we may not oppose the power of darkness, or because we are commanded to submit to the ordinance of GOD, therefore we may not resist the ministers of satan. Such wild work must be made with the apostle before he can be brought to speak the language of oppression. It is as plain (I think) as words can make it, that according to this text, no tyrant can be a ruler; for the apostle's definition of a ruler is, that he is not a terror to good works, but to the evil; and that he is one who is to praise and encourage those that do well; whenever then, the ruler encourages them that do evil, and is a terror to those that do well, i.e., as soon as he becomes a tyrant, he forfeits his authority to govern, and becomes the minister of satan, and as such ought to be opposed.

I know, it is said, that the magistrates were at the time when the apostle wrote, heathens; and that Nero, that monster of tyranny was then emperor of Rome; that therefore the apostle, by enjoining submission to the powers that then were, does require unlimited obedience to be yielded to the worst of tyrants. Now not to insist upon what has been often observed, viz. that this epistle was written most probably about the beginning of Nero's reign, at which time he was a very humane and merciful prince, did everything that was generous and benevolent to the publick, and shewed every act of mercy, and tenderness to particulars; and therefore might at that time justly deserve the character of the minister of GOD for good to the people: I say, waiving this; we will suppose that this epistle was written after that Nero was become a monster of tyranny and wickedness, it will by no means follow from thence, that the apostle meant to enjoin unlimited subjection to such an authority, or that he intended to affirm, that such a cruel, despotick authority was the ordinance of GOD. The plain, obvious sense of his words (as we have already seen) forbids such a construction to be put upon them; for they plainly imply a strong abhorrence and disapprobation of such a character, and clearly prove that Nero, so far forth as he was a tyrant, could not be the minister of GOD, nor have a right to claim submission from the people; so that this ought perhaps rather to be view'd as a severe satyr upon Nero, than as enjoyning any submission to him.

IT is also worthy to be observed, that the apostle prudently wav'd mentioning any particular persons that were then in power; as it might have been construed in an invidious light, and exposed the primitive christians to the severe resentments of the men that were then in power. He only in general requires submission to the higher powers, because the powers that be are ordain'd of GOD; now tho' the emperor might at that time be such a tyrant, that he could with no propriety be said to be ordain'd of GOD, yet it would be somewhat strange if there were no men in power among the Romans, that acted up to the character of good magistrates, and that deserved to be esteemed as the ministers of GOD for good unto the people: If there were any such, notwithstanding the tyranny of Nero, the apostle might with great propriety enjoin submission to those powers that were ordain'd of GOD, and by so particularly pointing out the end and design of magistrates, and giving his definition of a ruler, he might design to shew that neither Nero, nor any other tyrant, ought to be esteemed as the minister of GOD.

OR, rather, which appears to me to be the true sense, the apostle meant to speak of magistracy in general, without any particular reference to the emperor, or any other person in power, that was then at Rome; and the meaning of this passage is, as if he had said, it is the duty of every christian to be a good subject of civil government, for the power and authority of the civil magistrate are from GOD, for the powers that be are ordained of GOD, i.e. the authority of the magistrates that are now either at Rome, or elsewhere, is ordained of the Deity; wherever you find any lawful magistrates, remember, they are of divine ordination; but that you may understand what I mean, when I say, that magistrates are of divine ordination, I will shew you how you may discern, who are lawful magistrates and ordained of GOD, from those who are not: Those only are to be esteemed lawful magistrates, and ordain'd of GOD, who pursue the publick good by honoring and encouraging those that do well, and punishing all that do evil, such and such only, wherever they are to be found, are the ministers of GOD for good; to resist such, is resisting the ordinance of GOD, and exposing yourselves to the divine wrath and condemnation.

IN either of these senses, the text cannot make any thing in favour of arbitrary government. Nor could he with any propriety tell them, that they need not be afraid of the power, so long as they did that which was good, if he meant to recommend an unlimited submission to a tyrannical Nero; for the best characters were the likeliest to fall a sacrifice to his malice. And besides, such an injunction would be directly contrary to his own practice, and the practice of the primitive christians, who refused to comply with the sinful commands of men in power; their answer in such cases being this, we ought to obey GOD rather than men: Hence the Apostle Paul himself suffered many cruel persecutions, because he would not renounce christianity, but persisted in opposing the idolatrous worship of the pagan world.

THIS text being rescued from the absurd interpretations, which the favourers of arbitrary government have put upon it, turns out to be a noble confirmation of that free and generous plan of government, which the law of nature and reason points out to us. Nor can we desire a more equitable plan of government, than what the apostle has here laid down: For if we consult our happiness and real good, we can never wish for an unreasonable liberty, viz. a freedom to do evil, which according to the apostle, is the only thing that the magistrate is to refrain us from. To have a liberty to do whatever is fit, reasonable or good, is the highest degree of freedom, that rational beings can possess. And how honorable a station are those men placed in, by the providence of GOD, whose business it is, to secure to men this rational liberty, and to promote the happiness and welfare of society, by suppressing vice and immorality, and by honouring and encouraging everything that is amiable, virtuous and praiseworthy? Such magistrates ought to be honored and obeyed as the ministers of GOD, and the servants of the king of heaven. Can we conceive of a larger and more generous plan of government than this of the apostle? Or can we find words more plainly expressive of a disapprobation of an arbitrary and tyrannical government? I never read this text without admiring the beauty and nervousness of it: And I can hardly conceive how he could express more ideas in so few words, than he has done. We see here, in one view, the honor that belongs to the magistrate, because he is ordain'd of GOD for the publick good. We have his duty pointed out, viz. to honor and encourage the virtuous, to promote the real good of the community, and to punish all wicked and injurious persons. We are taught the duty of the subject, viz. to obey the magistrate for conscience sake, because he is ordain'd of GOD; and that rulers being continually employed under GOD for our good, are to be generously maintained, by the paying them tribute; and that disobedience to rulers is highly criminal, and will expose us to the divine wrath. The liberty of the subject is also clearly asserted, viz. that subjects are to be allowed to do everything that is in itself just and right, and are only to be restrained from being guilty of wrong actions. It is also strongly implied, that when rulers become oppressive to the subject, and injurious to the state, their authority, their respect, their maintenance, and the duty of submitting to them, must immediately cease; they are then to be considered as the ministers of satan, and, as such it becomes our indispensable duty to resist and oppose them.

THUS we see that both reason and revelation perfectly agree in pointing out the nature, end and design of government, viz. that it is to promote the welfare and happiness of the community; and

that subjects have a right to do everything that is good, praiseworthy, and consistent with the good of the community, and are
only to be restrain'd when they do evil, and are injurious either to
individuals or the whole community; and that they ought to submit
to every law, that is beneficial to the community for conscience
sake, altho' it may in some measure interfere with their private
interest; for every good man will be ready to forego his private
interest for the sake of being beneficial to the publick. Reason and
revelation (we see) do both teach us, that our obedience to rulers
is not unlimited; but that resistance is not only allowable, but an
indispensable duty in the case of intolerable tyranny and oppression.
From both reason and revelation, we learn, that as the public safety
is the supreme law of the state, being the true standard and measure
by which we are to judge whether any law or body of laws are
just or not, so legislators have a right to make, and require subjection to, any set of laws that have a tendency to promote the good
of the community.

OUR governors have a right to take every proper method to
form the minds of their subjects so, that they may become good
members of society. The great difference that we may observe
among the several classes of mankind, arises chiefly from their
education, and their laws; hence men become virtuous or vicious;
good common-wealthsmen or the contrary, generous, noble, and
courageous, or base, mean spirited, and cowardly; according to the
impression that they have received from the government that they
are under, together with their education, and the methods that
have been practised by their leaders to form their minds in early
life: Hence the necessity of good laws to encourage every noble
and virtuous sentiment, to suppress vice and immorality; to promote
industry, and to punish idleness, that parent of innumerable
evils; to promote arts and sciences, and to banish ignorance from
among mankind.

AND as nothing tends like religion and the fear of GOD to make
men good members of the common wealth: it is the duty of magistrates to become the patrons and promoters of religion and piety,
and to make suitable laws for the maintaining publick worship, and
decently supporting the teachers of religion: Such laws (I apprehend) are absolutely necessary for the well-being of civil society.
Such laws may be made consistent with all that liberty of conscience,
which every good member of society ought to be possessed of; for as
there are few, if any religious societies among us, but what profess
to believe and practise all the great duties of religion and morality,
that are necessary for the well-being of society, and the safety of
the state; let every one be allow'd to attend worship in his own
society, or in that way, that he judges most agreeable to the will of
GOD, and let him be obliged to contribute his assistance to the sup-

porting and defraying the necessary charges of his own meeting. In this case no one can have any right to complain that he is depriv'd of liberty of conscience, seeing that he has a right to choose and freely attend that worship, that appears to him to be most agreeable to the will of GOD; and it must be very unreasonable for him to object against being obliged to contribute his part towards the support of that worship, which he has chosen. Whether some such method as this might not tend in a very eminent manner to promote the peace and welfare of society, I must leave to the wisdom of our legislators to determine; be sure it would take off some of the most popular objections against being obliged by law to support public worship, while the law restricts that support only to one denomination.

BUT for the civil authority to pretend to establish particular modes of faith, and forms of worship, and to punish all that deviate from the standard which our superiors have set up, is attended with the most pernicious consequences to society: It cramps all free and rational inquiry; fills the world with hypocrites and superstitious bigots; nay with infidels and skeptics: It exposes men of religion and conscience to the rage and malice of fiery blind zealots; and dissolves every tender tie of human nature: In short, it introduces confusion and every evil work. And I cannot but look upon it as a peculiar blessing of heaven, that we live in a land where every one can freely deliver his sentiments upon religious subjects, and have the privilege of worshipping GOD, according to the dictates of his own conscience, without any molestation or disturbance: A privilege which I hope, we shall ever keep up, and strenuously maintain. No principles ought ever to be discountenanced by civil authority, but such as tend to the subversion of the state. So long as a man is a good member of society, he is accountable to GOD alone for his religious sentiments: But when men are found disturbers of the publick peace, stirring up sedition, or practising against the state, no pretence of religion or conscience, ought to screen them from being brought to condign punishment. But then, as the end and design of punishment is either to make restitution to the injured, or to restrain men from committing the like crimes for the future, so when these important ends are answered, the punishment ought to cease; for whatever is inflicted upon a man under the notion of punishment, after these important ends are answered, is not a just and lawful punishment, but is properly cruelty and base revenge.

FROM this account of civil government we learn, that the business of magistrates is weighty and important: It requires both wisdom and integrity: When either are wanting, government will be poorly administered; more especially if our governours are men of loose morals, and abandoned principles; for if a man is not

faithful to GOD and his own soul, how can we expect that he will
be faithful to the publick. There was a great deal of propriety in
the advice that Jethro gave to Moses to provide able men; men of
truth, that feared GOD, and that hated covetousness, and to appoint
them for rulers over the people. For it certainly implies a very gross
absurdity to suppose, that those who are ordain'd of GOD for the
public good, should have no regard to the laws of GOD; or that the
ministers of GOD should be despisers of the divine commands. David
the man after GOD's own heart, makes piety a necessary qualification
in a ruler; *He that ruleth over men (says he) must be just, ruling
in the fear of* GOD: It is necessary it should be so, for the welfare
and happiness of the state; for to say nothing of the venality and
corruption, of the tyranny and oppression, that will take place
under unjust rulers; barely their vicious and irregular lives will
have a most pernicious effect upon the lives and manners of their
subjects; their authority becomes despicable in the opinion of discerning men: And besides, with what face can they make, or execute
laws against vices, which they practise with greediness? A people
that have a right of choosing their magistrates are criminally guilty
in the sight of heaven when they are govern'd by caprice and humor,
or are influenced by bribery to choose magistrates, that are irreligious men, who are devoid of sentiment, and of bad morals and
base lives. Men cannot be sufficiently sensible, what a curse they
may bring upon themselves, and their posterity, by foolishly and
wickedly choosing men of abandoned characters and profligate
lives for their magistrates and rulers.

WE have already seen, that magistrates who rule in the fear
of GOD, ought not only to be obey'd as the ministers of GOD; but
that they ought also to be handsomely supported, that they may
cheerfully and freely attend upon the duties of their station; for it
is a great shame and disgrace to society, to see men that serve the
publick laboring under indigent and needy circumstances; and
besides, it is a maxim of eternal truth, that the laborer is worthy
of his reward.

IT is also a great duty incumbent on people to treat those in
authority with all becoming honor and respect, to be very careful
of casting any aspersion upon their characters. To despise government and to speak evil of dignities is represented in scripture as
one of the worst of characters; and it was an injunction of Moses,
Thou shalt not speak evil of the ruler of thy people. Great mischief
may ensue upon reviling the character of good rulers; for the unthinking herd of mankind are very apt to give ear to scandal: And
when it falls upon men in power, it brings their authority into
contempt, lessens their influence, and disheartens them from doing
that service to the community of which they are capable: Whereas,
when they are properly honored, and treated with that respect

which is due to their station; it inspires them with courage and a noble ardor to serve the publick; their influence among the people is strengthened, and their authority becomes firmly established. We ought to remember, that they are men like to ourselves, liable to the same imperfections and infirmities with the rest of us, and therefore so long as they aim at the public good, their mistakes, misapprehensions and infirmities ought to be treated with the utmost humanity and tenderness.

BUT tho' I would recommend to all christians, as a part of the duty that they owe to magistrates, to treat them with proper honor and respect; none can reasonably suppose, that I mean that they ought to be flattered in their vices, or honored and caressed while they are seeking to undermine and ruin the state: For this would be wickedly betraying our just rights, and we should be guilty of our own destruction: We ought ever to persevere with firmness and fortitude in maintaining and contending for all that liberty, that the Deity has granted us: It is our duty to be ever watchful over our just rights, and not suffer them to be wrested out of our hands by any of the artifices of tyrannical oppressors. But there is a wide difference between being jealous of our rights, when we have the strongest reason to conclude, that they are invaded by our rulers, and being unreasonably suspicious of men that are zealously endeavoring to support the constitution, only because we do not thoroughly comprehend all their designs: The first argues a noble and generous mind, the other a low and base spirit.

THUS have I considered the nature of the duty enjoin'd in the text, and have endeavored to shew, that the same principles that require obedience to lawful magistrates, do also require us to resist tyrants; this I have confirm'd from reason, and scripture.

IT was with a particular view to the present unhappy controversy that subsists between us, and Great-Britain, that I chose to discourse upon the nature and design of government, and the rights and duties both of governors, and governed, that so, justly understanding our rights and privileges, we may stand firm in our oppositon to ministerial tyranny, while at the same time we pay all proper obedience and submission to our lawful magistrates; and that, while we are contending for liberty, we may avoid running into licentiousness; and that we may preserve the due medium between submitting to tyranny, and running into anarchy. I acknowledge that I have undertaken a difficult task; but, as it appear'd to me, the present state of affairs loudly call'd for such a discourse; and, therefore, I hope the wise, the generous, and the good will candidly receive my good intentions to serve the public. I shall now apply this discourse to the grand controversy that at this day subsists between Great-Britain and the American colonies.

AND here in the first place, I cannot but take notice, how

wonderfully providence has smiled upon us by causing the several colonies to unite so firmly together against the tyranny of Great-Britain, tho' differing from each other in their particular interest, forms of government, modes of worship, and particular customs and manners; besides several animosities that had subsisted among them. That under these circumstances such a union should take place, as we now behold, was a thing that might rather have been wished than hoped for.

AND, in the next place, Who could have thought, that when our charter was vacated, when we became destitute of any legislative authority; and when our courts of justice in many parts of the country were stopp'd so that we could neither make, nor execute laws upon offenders, who, I say would have thought, that in such a situation, the people should behave so peaceably, and maintain such good order and harmony among themselves! This is a plain proof, that they having not the civil law to regulate themselves by, became a law unto themselves; and by their conduct they have shewn, that they were regulated by the law of GOD written in their hearts. This is the Lord's doing, and it ought to be marvellous in our eyes.

FROM what has been said in this discourse, it will appear, that we are in the way of our duty, in opposing the tyranny of Great-Britain; for if unlimited submission is not due to any human power; if we have an undoubted right to oppose and resist a set of tyrants, that are subverting our just rights and privileges, there cannot remain a doubt in any man, that will calmly attend to reason, whether we have a right to resist and oppose the arbitrary measures of the King and Parliament; for it is plain to demonstration, nay it is in a manner self-evident, that they have been, and are endeavoring to deprive us not only of the privileges of Englishmen, and our charter rights, but they have endeavor'd to deprive us of what is much more sacred, viz. the privileges of men and christians, i.e. they are robbing us of the inalienable rights, that the GOD of nature has given us, as men, and rational beings, and has confirmed to us in his written word as christians, and disciples of that Jesus, who came to redeem us from the bondage of sin, and the tyranny of satan, and to grant us the most perfect freedom, even the glorious liberty of the sons and children of GOD; that here they have endeavor'd to deprive us of the sacred charter of the king of heaven. But we have this for our consolation, the Lord reigneth, he governs the world in righteousness, and will avenge the cause of the oppressed, when they cry unto him. We have made our appeal to heaven, and we cannot doubt, but that the *judge of all the earth will do right*.

NEED I upon this occasion descend to particulars? Can any one be ignorant what the things are of which we complain? Does not every one know, that the King and Parliament have assumed the right to tax us without our consent? And can any one be so lost to the principles of humanity and common sense, as not to view their conduct in this affair as a very grievous imposition? Reason and equity require that no one be obliged to pay a tax that he has never consented to, either by himself, or by his representative: But as divine providence has placed us at so great a distance from Great-Britain, that we neither are, nor can be properly represented in the British parliament; it is a plain proof that the Deity design'd, that we should have the powers of legislation and taxation among ourselves: For can any suppose it to be reasonable, that a set of men that are perfect strangers to us, should have the uncontrollable right to lay the most heavy and grievous burdens upon us that they please, purely to gratify their unbounded avarice and luxury? Must we be obliged to perish with cold and hunger to maintain them in idleness, in all kinds of debauchery and dissipation? But if they have the right to take our property from us without our consent, we must be wholly at their mercy for our food and raiment, and we know by sad experience, that their tender mercies are cruel.

BUT because we were not willing to submit to such an unrighteous and cruel decree, tho' we modestly complain'd and humbly petition'd for a redress of our grievances, instead of hearing our complaints, and granting our requests, they have gone on to add iniquity to transgression, by making several cruel and unrighteous acts. Who can forget the cruel act to block up the harbor of Boston, whereby thousands of innocent persons must have been inevitably ruin'd had they not been supported by the continent? Who can forget the act for vacating our charter, together with many other cruel acts which it is needless to mention? But not being able to accomplish their wicked purposes by mere acts of parliament, they have proceeded to commence open hostilities against us; and have endeavor'd to destroy us by fire and sword; our towns they have burnt, our brethren they have slain, our vessels they have taken, and our goods they have spoiled. And after all this wanton exertion of arbitrary power, is there the man that has any of the feeling of humanity left, who is not fired with a noble indignation against such merciless tyrants; who have not only brought upon us all the horrors of a civil war, but have also added a piece of barbarity unknown to Turks and Mohammedan infidels; yea such as would be abhorred and detested by the savages of the wilderness: I mean their cruelly forcing our brethren, whom they have taken prisoners, without any distinction of whig or tory, to serve on board their ships of war, thereby obliging them to take up arms against their brethren, their wives, and their children, and to assist in plundering their own estates. This my brethren, is done by men who call themselves christians against their christian brethren, against men who till now gloried in the name of Englishmen, and who were ever ready to spend their lives and fortunes in the defence of British rights: Tell it not in Gath, publish it not in the streets of Askelon, lest it cause our enemies to rejoice, and our adversaries to triumph. Such a conduct as this, brings a great reproach upon the profession of christianity, nay it is a great scandal even to human nature itself.

IT would be highly criminal not to feel a due resentment against such tyrannical monsters. It is an indispensable duty my brethren which we owe to GOD, and our country, to rouse up and bestir ourselves, and, being animated with a noble zeal for the sacred cause of liberty, to defend our lives, and fortunes, even to the shedding the last drop of blood. The love of our country, the tender affection that we have for our wives and children, the regard we ought to have for unborn posterity, yea everything that is dear and sacred, do now loudly call upon us, to use our best endeavors to save our country: We must *beat our plough-shares into swords, and our pruning-hooks into spears,* and learn the art of self-defence against our enemies. To be careless, and remiss, or to neglect the cause of our country thro' the base motives of avarice, and self-interest, will expose us not only to the resentments of our fellow creatures, but to the displeasure of GOD Almighty: For to such base wretches in such a time as this, we may apply with the utmost propriety that passage in Jer. 48 chap. ver. 10: *Cursed be he that doth the work of the Lord deceitfully, and cursed be he, that keepeth back his sword from blood.* To save our country from the hands of our oppressors, ought to be dearer to us, even than our own lives, and, next the eternal salvation of our own souls, is the thing of the greatest importance: A duty so sacred, that it cannot justly be dispensed with for the sake of our secular concerns: Doubtless for this reason GOD has been pleased, to manifest his anger against those who have refused to assist their country against its cruel oppressors. Hence in a case similar to ours, when the Israelites were struggling to deliver themselves from the tyranny of Jabin the king of Canaan, we find a most bitter curse denounced against those, who refused to grant their assistance in the common cause; see Judges 5th, ver. 23. *Curse ye Meroz (said the angel of the Lord) curse ye bitterly the inhabitants thereof because they came not to the help of the Lord, to the help of the Lord against the mighty.*

NOW if such a bitter curse is denounced against those, who refused to assist their country against its oppressors, what a dreadful doom are those exposed to, who have not only refused to assist their country in this time of distress, but have thro' motives of interest or ambition shown themselves enemies to their country by opposing us in the measures that we have taken, and by openly favoring the British parliament. He that is so lost to humanity, as to be willing to sacrifice his country for the sake of avarice or ambition, has arrived to the highest stage of wickedness, that human nature is capable of, and deserves a much worse name, than I at present care to give him; but I think I may with propriety say, that such a person has forfeited his right to human society, and that he ought to take up his abode not among the savage men but among the savage beasts of the wilderness.

NOR can I wholly excuse from blame those timid persons, who thro' their own cowardice, have been induced to favor our enemies, and have refused to act in defence of their country: For a due sense of the ruin and destruction that our enemies are bringing upon us, is enough to raise such a resentment in the human breast, that would (I should think) be sufficient to banish fear from the most timid make: And, besides, to indulge cowardice in such a cause, argues a want of faith in GOD; for can he that firmly believes and relies upon the providence of GOD, doubt, whether he will avenge the cause of the injured when they apply to him for help: For my own part, when I consider the dispensations of providence towards this land, ever since our fathers first settled in Plymouth, I find abundant reason to conclude, that the great sovereign of the universe, has planted a vine in this American wilderness which he has caused to take deep root, and it has filled the land, and that he will never suffer it to be plucked up, or destroyed.

OUR fathers fled from the rage of prelatical tyranny and persecution, and came into this land in order to enjoy liberty of conscience; and they have encreased to a great people: Many have been the interpositions of divine providence on our behalf, both in our fathers days and ours: And though we are now engaged in a war with Great-Britain, yet we have been prospered in a most wonderful manner: And can we think, that he, who has thus far helped us, will give us up into the hands of our enemies? Certainly he, that has begun to deliver us, will continue to show his mercy towards us, in saving us from the hands of our enemies; he will not forsake us, if we do not forsake him. Our cause is so just and good, that nothing can prevent our success, but only our sins. Could I see a spirit of repentance and reformation prevail through the land, I should not have the least apprehension, or fear of being brought under the iron rod of slavery, even though all the powers of the globe were combined against us: And though I confess, that the irreligion and profaneness, which are so common among us, gives something of a damp to my spirits, yet I cannot help hoping, and even believing, that providence has designed this continent for to be the asylum of liberty and true religion; for can we suppose, that the GOD who created us free agents and designed that we should glorify and serve him in this world, that we might enjoy him forever hereafter, will suffer liberty and true religion to be banished from off the face of the earth? But do we not find that both religion and liberty seem to be expiring and gasping for life in the other continent, where then can they find a harbour, or place of refuge but in this?

THERE are some who pretend that it is against their consciences to take up arms in defense of their country; but can any rational being suppose, that the Deity can require us to contradict the law of nature, which he has written in our hearts, a part of which I am sure is the principle of self-defence, which strongly prompts us all to oppose any power that would take away our lives, or the lives of our friends: Now for men to take pains to destroy the tender feelings of human nature, and to eradicate the principles of self preservation, and then to persuade themselves that in so doing, they submit to, and obey the will of GOD, is a plain proof how easily men may be led to pervert the very first and plainest principles of reason and common sense, and argues a gross corruption of the human mind. We find such persons are very inconsistent with themselves, for no men are more zealous to defend their property, and to secure their estates from the encroachments of others, while they refuse to defend their persons, their wives, their children, and their country against the assaults of the enemy. We see to what unaccountable lengths men will run, when once they leave the plain road of common sense, and violate the law, which GOD has written in their heart: Thus some have thought, they did GOD service, when they unmercifully butchered and destroyed the lives of the servants of GOD; while others upon the contrary extreme believe, that they please GOD while they sit still, and quietly behold their friends and brethren killed by their unmerciful enemies, without endeavoring to defend, or rescue them. The one is a sin of omission, and the other is a sin of commission, and it may perhaps be difficult to say, under certain circumstances, which is the most criminal in the sight of heaven; of this I am sure, that they are both of them, great violations of the law of GOD.

HAVING thus endeavored to show the lawfulness and necessity of defending ourselves against the tyranny of Great-Britain, I would observe, that providence seems plainly to point to us the expedience, and even necessity of our considering ourselves as an independent state: For not to consider the absurdity implied, in making war against a power, to which we profess to own subjection, to pass by the impracticability of our ever coming under subjecting to Great-Britain upon fair and equitable terms; we may observe, that the British parliament has virtually declared us an independent state by authorizing their ships of war to seize all American property, wherever they can find it, without making any distinction between the friends of administration, and those that have appeared in opposition to the acts of parliament. This is making us a distinct nation from themselves; they can have no right any longer to style us rebels; for rebellion implies a particular faction risen up in opposition to lawful authority, and, as such, the factious party ought to be punished, while those that remain loyal are to be protected: But when war is declared against a whole community without distinction, and the property of each party is declared to be seizable; this, if anything can be, is treating us as an independent state: Now, if they are pleased to consider us, as in a state of independency, who can object against our considering ourselves so too.

BUT while we are nobly opposing with our lives and estates, the tyranny of the British parliament, let us not forget the duty which we owe to our lawful magistrates; let us never mistake licentiousness for liberty. The more we understand the principles of liberty, the more readily shall we yield obedience to lawful authority: For no man can oppose good government, but he that is a stranger to true liberty. Let us ever check and restrain the factious disturbers of the peace; whenever we meet with persons, that are loth to submit to lawful authority, let us treat them with the contempt, which they deserve, and ever esteem them as the enemies of their country, and the pests of society. It is with peculiar pleasure, that I reflect upon the peaceable behavior of my country-men, at a time when the courts of justice were stopped, and the execution of laws suspended; it will certainly be expected of a people, that could behave so well, when they had nothing to re-strain them, but the laws written in their hearts, that they will yield all ready and cheerful obedience to lawful authority: There is at present, the utmost need of guarding ourselves against a seditious and factious temper; for when we are engaged with so powerful an enemy from without, our political salvation under GOD does in an eminent manner depend upon our being firmly united to-gether in the bonds of love to one another, and of due submission to lawful authority. I hope we shall never give any just occasion to our adversaries to reproach us as being men of turbulent dispositions, and licentious principles, that cannot bear to be restrained by good and wholesome laws, even though they are of our own making, not submit to rulers of our own choosing: But I have reason to hope much better things of my countrymen, though I thus speak. How-ever, in this time of difficulty and distress, we cannot be too much guarded against the least approaches to discord and faction. Let us while we are jealous of our rights, take heed of unreasonable suspicions, and evil surmises, which have no proper foundation. Let us take heed, lest we hurt the cause of liberty by speaking evil of the ruler of the people.

LET us treat our rulers, with all that honor and respect, which the dignity of their station requires; but let it be such an honor and respect as is worthy of the sons of freedom to give: Let us ever abhor the base arts, that are used by fawning parasites, and cringing courtiers, who by their low artifices, and base flatteries, obtain offices and posts, which they are unqualified to sustain; and honors of which they are unworthy, and oftentimes have a greater number of places assigned them, than any one person of the greatest abilities can ever properly fill; by means of which the community becomes greatly injured, for this reason, that many an important trust remains undischarg'd, and many an honest and worthy member of society is deprived of those honors and privileges to which he has a just right; whilst the most despicable, worthless courtier is loaded with honorable and profitable commissions. In order to avoid this evil, I hope, our legislators will always despise flattery as something below the dignity of a rational mind, and that they will ever scorn the man that will be corrupted, or take a bribe. And let us all resolve with our selves, that no motives of interest, nor hopes of preferment, shall ever induce us to act the part of fawning courtiers towards men in power. Let the honor and respect, which we show our superiors, be true and genuine, flowing from a sincere upright heart.

THE honors that have been paid to arbitrary princes, have often been very hypocritical and insincere: Tyrants have been flattered in their vices, and have often had an idolatrous reverence paid them. The worst princes have been the most flattered and adored: And many such, in the pagan world, assumed the title of gods; and had divine honors paid them. This idolatrous reverence has ever been the inseparable concomitant of arbitrary power, and tyrannical government: For even christian princes, if they have not been adored under the character of gods, yet the titles given them, strongly savor of blasphemy, and the reverence paid them is really idolatrous. What right has a poor sinful worm of the dust to claim the title of his most sacred Majesty; most sacred certainly belongs only to GOD alone, for there is none holy as the Lord; yet how common is it to see this title given to kings? And how often have we been told, that the king can do no wrong, even though he should be so foolish and wicked as hardly to be capable of ever being in the right? yet still it must be asserted and maintained, that it is impossible for him to do wrong?

THE cruel savage disposition of tyrants, and the idolatrous reverence that is paid them, are both most beautifully exhibited to view by the apostle John in the revelation, 13th chap. from the first to the tenth ver. where the apostle gives a description of a horrible wild beast which he saw rise out of the sea, having seven heads and ten horns, and upon his heads the names of blasphemy. By heads are to be understood forms of government, and by blasphemy, idolatry; so that it seems implied, that there will be a degree of idolatry in every form of tyrannical government. This beast is represented as having the body of a leopard, the feet of a bear, and the

mouth of a lion, i.e. a horrible monster possessed of the rage and
fury of the lion, the fierceness of the bear, and the swiftness of the
leopard to seize and devour its prey; can words more strongly
point out or exhibit in more lively colours the exceeding rage,
fury and impetuosity of tyrants in their destroying and making
havoc of mankind. To this beast we find the dragon gave his power,
seat and great authority, i.e. the devil constituted him to be his
vicegerent on earth; this is to denote that tyrants are the ministers
of satan, ordained by him for the destruction of mankind.

SUCH a horrible monster we should have thought, would have
been abhorred and detested of all mankind, and that all nations
would have joined their powers and forces together to oppose and
utterly destroy him from off the face of the earth: But so far are
they from doing this, that on the contrary, they are represented as
worshipping him, ver. 8. *and all that dwell on the earth shall
worship him, viz. all those whose names are not written in the
lamb's book of life,* i.e. the wicked world shall pay him an idolatrous
reverence, and worship him with a godlike adoration. What can in
a more lively manner show the gross stupidity and wickedness of
mankind, in thus tamely giving up their just rights into the hands of
tyrannical monsters, and in so readily paying them such an unlimited obedience, as is due to GOD alone.

WE may observe further, that these men are said, ver. 4. *to
worship the dragon;* not that it is to be supposed that they in direct
terms paid divine homage to satan, but that the adoration paid to
the beast, who was satan's vicegerent, did ultimately centre in him.
Hence we learn that those who pay an undue and sinful veneration
to tyrants, are properly the servants of the devil, they are worshippers of the prince of darkness, for in him all that undue homage
and adoration centers, that is given to his ministers. Hence that
terrible denunciation of divine wrath against the worshippers of
the beast and his image. Rev. 14th, ver. 9th, 10th, and 11th, *If
any man worship the beast and his image, and receive his mark in
his forehead, or in his hand, the same shall drink of the wine of
the wrath of* GOD *which is poured out without mixture into the cup
of his indignation, and he shall be tormented with fire and brimstone
in the presence of the holy angels, and in the presence of the Lamb;
and the smoke of their torment ascendeth for ever and ever: And
they have no rest day nor night, who worship the beast and his image,
and who receive the mark of his name.* We have here set forth in
the clearest manner, by the inspired apostle, GOD's abhorrence of
tyranny and tyrants, together with the idolatrous reverence, that
their wretched subjects are wont to pay them, and the awful denunciation of divine wrath, against those who are guilty of this
undue obedience to tyrants.

DOES it not then highly concern us all to stand fast in the

liberty wherewith Heaven hath made us free, and to strive to get the victory over the beast and his image, over every species of tyranny. Let us look upon a freedom from the power of tyrants, as a blessing, that cannot be purchased too dear; and let us bless GOD that he has so far delivered us from that idolatrous reverence, which men are so very apt to pay to arbitrary tyrants; and let us pray that he would be pleased graciously to perfect the mercy he has begun to show us by the confounding the devices of our enemies, and bringing their counsels to nought, and by establishing our just rights and privileges, upon such a firm and lasting basis, that the powers of earth and hell shall not prevail against it.

UNDER GOD, every person in the community ought to contribute his assistance to the bringing about so glorious and important an event; but in a more eminent manner does this important business belong to the gentlemen, that are chosen to represent the people in this general assembly, including those, that have been appointed members of the honorable council board.

HONORED fathers, we look up to you in this day of calamity and distress, as the guardians of our invaded rights, and the defenders of our liberties against British tyranny; you are called in providence to save your country from ruin. A trust is reposed in you of the highest importance to the community, that can be conceived of, its business the most noble and grand, and a task the most arduous and difficult to accomplish, that ever engag'd the human mind. (I mean as to things of the present life.) But as you are engaged in the defence of a just and righteous cause, you may with firmness of mind commit your cause to GOD, and depend on his kind providence for direction and assistance. You will have the fervent wishes and prayers of all good men, that GOD would crown all your labors with success, and direct you into such measures as shall tend to promote the welfare and happiness of the community, and afford you all that wisdom and prudence, which is necessary to regulate the affairs of state, at this critical period.

HONORED fathers of the house of Representatives: We trust to your wisdom and goodness, that you will be led to appoint such men to be in Council, whom you know to be men of real principle, and who are of unblemished lives, that have shown themselves zealous and hearty friends to the liberties of America, and men, that have the fear of GOD before their eyes; for such only are men, that can be depended upon uniformly to pursue the general good.

MY reverend Fathers and Brethren in the ministry will remember, that according to our text, it is part of the work and business of a gospel minister, to teach his hearers the duty they owe to magistrates. Let us, then, endeavor to explain the nature of their duty faithfully, and show them the difference between liberty and licentiousness; and while we are animating them to oppose tyranny and arbitrary power, let us inculcate upon them the duty of yielding due obedience to lawful authority. In order to the right and faithful discharge of this part of our ministry, it is necessary, that we should thoroughly study the law of nature, the rights of mankind, and the reciprocal duties of governors and governed: By this means, we shall be able to guard them against the extremes of slavish submission to tyrants on one hand, and of sedition and licentiousness on the other. We may I apprehend, attain a thorough acquaintance with the law of nature, and the rights of mankind while we remain unacquainted with the obscure and barbarous latin, that was so much used in the ages of popish darkness and superstition.

TO conclude, WHILE we are fighting for liberty, and striving against tyranny, let us remember to fight the good fight of faith, and earnestly seek to be delivered from that bondage of corruption, which we are brought into by sin, and that we may be made partakers of the glorious liberty of the sons and children of GOD: Which may the Father of Mercies grant us all, thro' Jesus Christ.

AMEN.

The Law of Liberty

John Joachim Zubly

John Joachim Zubly was born August 27, 1724, in St. Gall, Switzerland. He was a Presbyterian minister, ordained at the German Church in London, August 19, 1744. In 1760, he became the first pastor of what is now known as the Independent Presbyterian Church of Savannah. He preached to his own and to neighboring congregations in German, French, and English. He was granted the degree of Doctor of Divinity by the College of New Jersey in 1770.

Zubly took an active part in the War for Independence, strongly supporting the Colonial cause. A man of intellect and patriotism, he was appointed delegate to the Continental Congress in 1775 and 1776. But, he was afraid of the extreme path of separation from England, and quit his congressional post, returning to Georgia. He here took sides against the colonies, and was asked to leave Savannah, though he did return in time to die in that city, July 23, 1781.

"The Law of Liberty" was preached at the opening of the second Provincial Congress of Georgia in the meeting house at Savannah on July 4, 1775. The text is from the Henry Miller edition printed in Philadelphia, 1775.

JAMES II. 12. *So speak ye, and so do, as they that shall be judged by the Law of Liberty.*

THERE was a time when there was no king in Israel, and every man did what was good in his own eyes. The consequence was a civil war in the nation, issuing in the ruin of one of the tribes, and a considerable loss to all the rest.

And there was a time when there was a king in Israel, and he also did what was right in his own eyes, a foolish son of a wise father; his own imprudence, the rashness of his young counsellors, his unwillingness to redress the grievances of the nation, and the harsh treatment he gave to those who applied for relief, also brought on a civil war, and issued in the separation of the ten tribes from the house of DAVID. He sent his treasurer to gather an odious duty or tribute, but the children of Israel stoned him that he died; and when he gathered one hundred and four score thousand men, that he might bring again the kingdom unto Roboam, GOD sent him a message, "ye shall not go up, nor fight against your brethren, return every man to his house, for this thing is done of me." GOD disapproved of the oppressive measures and ministry of Roboam, and that king's army appears more ready to obey the command of their

GOD, than slay their brethren by orders of a tyrant. "They obeyed the voice of the LORD, and returned from going against Jeroboam." —2 Chron. x:18. xi:4.

The things that happened before are written for our learning. By comparing past times and proceedings with these that are present, prudence will point out many salutary and religious lessons. The conduct of Roboam verifies the lamentation of his father, "Woe to thee, o land, when thy king is a child." Eccles. x:16. A very small degree of justice and moderation might have preserved his kingdom, but he thought weapons of war better than wisdom; he hearkened not, neither to the people, nor to some of his more faithful counsellors, and the consequence was that, instead of enslaving the ten tribes who stood up for their liberty, GOD gave Judah to be servants to the king of Egypt, that they might learn the difference between his service and the service of the kingdoms of the nations. A people that claim no more than their natural rights, in so doing, do nothing displeasing unto GOD; and the most powerful monarch that would deprive his subjects of the liberties of man, whatever may be his success, he must not expect the approbation of GOD, and in due time will be the abhorrence of all men.

In a time of public and general uneasiness, it behoves both superiors and inferiors to consider. It is easy to extinguish a spark, it is folly to blow up discontent into a blaze; the beginning of strife is like the letting out of waters, and no man may know where it will end. There is a rule given to magistrates and subjects; which, if carefully attended to, would secure the dignity and safety of both; which, if not duly regarded, is usually attended with the worst consequences. The present, my hearers, will easily be allowed is a day of trouble, and surely in this day of adversity we ought to consider. When a people think themselves oppressed, and in danger, nothing can be more natural than that they should enquire into the real state of things, trace their grievances to their source, and endeavour to apply the remedies which are most likely to procure relief: This I take to be the design of the present meeting of persons deputed from every part of the country; and as they have thought proper to open and begin their deliberations with a solemn address unto GOD, and the consideration of his holy word, I most chearfully comply with their request to officiate on this occasion, and shall endeavour, as I may be enabled, to point out such directions from the holy scriptures as may make us wise in the knowledge of time, and direct us how to carry ourselves worthy of the character of good subjects and Christians: Whatever may be necessary for this purpose, I take to be comprehended in the apostolical rule, which I have laid down as the subject of this discourse, "So speak, and so do, as they that shall be judged by the law of liberty."

There are two things which properly come before us, viz.

I. That we are to be judged by the law of liberty; and

II. The exhortation to act worthy, and under the influence, of this important truth on every occasion.

A law is a rule of behaviour, made under proper authority, and with penalties annexed, suitable to deter the transgressions. As all laws suppose man to be in a social state, so all laws ought to be made for the good of man: A law that is not made by such as have authority for so doing, is of no force; and if authority makes laws destructive in themselves, no authority can prevent things from finally taking their natural course.

Wherever there is society, there must also be law; it is impossible that society should subsist without it. The will, minds, tempers, dispositions, views, and interests of men are so very different, and sometimes so opposite, that without law, which cements and binds all, every thing would be in endless disorder and confusion. All laws usually wear the complexion of those by whom they were made, but it cannot be denied that some bad men, from a sense of necessity, have made good laws, and that some good men, from mistake, or other weaknesses, have enacted laws bad in themselves, and pernicious in their consequence.

All human laws partake of human imperfection; it is not so with the laws of GOD. He is perfect, and so are all his works and ways. "The law of the LORD is perfect, converting the soul. The testimony of the LORD is sure, making wise the simple. The statutes of the LORD are right, rejoicing the heart. The commandment of the LORD is pure, enlightening the eyes. All his judgments are truth, and righteousness altogether." Psalm xix.

Among men society and country has its own laws and form of government, which may be very different, and cannot operate beyond their limits; but those laws and that form of government is undoubtedly best which has the greatest tendency to make all those that live under it secure and happy. As soon as we consider man as formed into society, it is evident that the safety of the whole must be the grand law which must influence and direct every other: Men did not pass from a state of nature into a state of society, to render their situation more miserable, and their rights more precarious. That government and tyranny is the hereditary right of some, and that slavery and oppression is the original doom of others, is a doctrine that would reflect dishonour upon GOD; it is treason against all mankind, it is indeed an enormous faith that millions were made for one; transubstantiation is but a harmless absurdity, compared with the notion of a divine right to govern wrong, or of making laws which are contrary to every idea of liberty, property, and justice.

The law which the apostle speaks of in our text, is not a law of man, but of Him who is the only lawgiver, that can save and condemn, to whom all owe obedience, and whose laws none can transgress with impunity.

Though all the laws that GOD ever gave unto man are worthy of GOD, and tend to promote the happiness of those to whom they are given, yet we may observe a very striking variety in the different laws which he gave at different times and to different people. "He shewed his word unto Jacob, his statutes and his judgments unto Israel; he has not dealt so with any other nation." Psalm cxlvii.18, 19.

To the generality of mankind he gave no written law, but yet left not himself without a witness among them; the words of the law were written in their hearts, their conscience also bearing witness, and their thoughts the mean while excusing or else accusing one another: It cannot be said they were without law, whilst what they were to do, and what they were to forbear, was written in their hearts.

To Israel GOD came with a fiery law in his hands, it was given with the most awful solemnity upon mount Sinai; and as the sum and substance of all their ceremonial, political and moral law centered in the ten commandments, so the sum and substance of these is comprehended in love to GOD and love to man, which, as our LORD himself informs us, contains all the law and all the prophets.

All manifestations of the will of GOD have been gradual, and it is probable the means of knowing GOD will be progressive through different ages, till eternity gives the good man a full sight of GOD in his immediate presence. During the dispensation of the old testament and the ceremonial law, a spirit of bondage obtained unto fear, the law was a schoolmaster to bring us unto CHRIST; neither did the law make any thing perfect, but the bringing in of a better hope: Grace and truth was brought to light by JESUS CHRIST; and hence the dispensation of the gospel, under which we live, is called the law of LIBERTY.

Though there is manifest distinction between law and gospel, and sometimes these two things are even opposed to one another, yet the doctrine of the gospel is also called "the law of faith;" Rom. iii: 17. partly because it was usual with the Jewish writers to call every doctrine a law, and partly also because the doctrine of the gospel presents us with a rule of life, which all its professors are bound to obey; hence they are said to be "not without law, but under the law of CHRIST;" 1 Cor. ix:11. and hence our apostle speaks of a royal law, which, though we cannot obey in perfection, nor derive any merit from our imperfect obedience, we cannot neglect without danger, nor disobey without shewing our disregard to the doctrine of the gospel in general.

It deserves very particular attention that the doctrine of the gospel is called a law of LIBERTY. Liberty and law are perfectly consistent; liberty does not consist in living without all restraint; for were all men to live without restraint, as they please, there would soon be no liberty at all; the strongest would be master, the weakest go to the wall; right, justice and property must give way to power, and, instead of its being a blessing, a more unhappy situation could not easily be devised unto mankind than that every man should have it in his power to do what is right in his own eyes: well regulated liberty of individuals is the natural offspring of laws, which prudentially regulate the rights of whole communities; and as laws which take away the natural rights of men, are unjust and oppressive, so all liberty which is not regulated by law, is a delusive phantom, and unworthy of the glorious name.

The gospel is called a law of liberty, because it bears a most friendly aspect to the liberty of man; it is a known rule, *Evangelium non tollit politias,* the gospel makes no alternation in the civil state; it by no means renders man's natural and social condition worse than it would be without the knowledge of the gospel. When the Jews boasted of their freedom, and that they never were in bondage, our LORD does not reprove them for it, but only observes, that national freedom still admits of improvement: "If the Son shall make you free, then you are free indeed." John viii: 16. This leads me to observe that the gospel is a law of liberty in a much higher sense: By whomsoever a man is overcome, of the same he is brought into bondage; but no external enemy can so completely tyrannize over a conquered enemy, as sin does over all those who yield themselves its servants; vicious habits, when once they have gained the ascendant in the soul, bring man to that unhappy pass that he knows better things and does worse; sin, like a torrent, carries him away against knowledge and conviction, while conscience fully convinceth him that he travels the road of death, and must expect, if he so continues, to take up his abode in hell; though his decaying body clearly tells him sin breaks his constitution, as well as wastes his substance, though he feels the loss of credit and wealth, still sin has too strong a hold of him to be forsaken, though he faintly resolves to break off, yet, till the grace of GOD brings salvation, when he would do good, evil is present with him; in short, instead of being under a law of liberty, he is under the law of sin and death, but whenever he feels the happy influence of the grace of the gospel, then this "law of liberty makes him free from the law of sin and death;" Rom. viii:2. it furnisheth him only with motives to resist but with power also to subdue sin; sin reigns no longer in his mortal body, because he is not under the law, but under grace. By this law of liberty he is made free from sin, and has his fruit unto holiness, and the end of it eternal life. There is another reason why the gospel is called a law of liberty, which is to distinguish it from the ceremonial law under the Mosaic dispensation; a yoke, of which an apostle saith, neither they nor their fathers were able to bear; it was superadded on account of their transgressions, and suited to the character of a gross and stubborn nation, to whom it was originally given; they were so prone to idolatry, and so apt to forget their GOD, their notions were so gross and carnal, that a number of external rites and ceremonies became necessary, to put them in mind of him, and to attach them to some degree of his worship and service. This, however necessary, was a heavy burden; it bid them "touch not, taste not, handle not;" it required of them expensive sacrifices, and a costly and painful service; it was attended with the most fearful threatnings, if any man brake Moses law, he died under two or three witnesses; and the very spirit they then received, was a spirit of bondage unto fear: Whereas the gospel dispensation breatheth a spirit of confidence, and under the law of liberty we call upon GOD as Abba Father. By this law of liberty the professors of the gospel will be judged.

Every man is a rational, and therefore accountable, creature. As a creature he must needs depend on his Creator, and as a rational creature he must certainly be accountable for all his actions. Nothing is more evident than that man is not of himself; and if once we admit that he holds his existence, his faculties and favours from GOD, that made him, it becomes a very obvious conclusion, that his Maker must have had some view in giving him existence, and more understanding than to the beasts of the field, neither can it be a matter of indifference to him whether man acts agreeably or contrary to his designs. The Creator of the natural world, is also its moral ruler; and if he is now the proprietor and ruler of intelligent beings, at some time or other he must also be their judge.

If GOD had not made his will known unto man, there could have been neither transgression nor judgment. If it should be said that GOD has not manifested himself alike unto all men, and that some have much smaller opportunities to know his will and their duty than others, it is enough to observe, that no man will be judged by a rule of which it was impossible he should have any knowledge. Every work and every man will be brought into judgment, and the judgment of GOD will never be otherwise than according to truth; but those that never had the law of liberty, will not be judged by that law, and those that have been favoured with the revelation of the gospel will be more inexcusable than any others, if they neglect the day of their visitation. "As many as have sinned without law, shall also perish without law, and as many as have sinned in the law, shall be judged by the law." Rom. ii:12. All men are under some law, they feel, they are conscious, that they are so; the thoughts which already excuse or condemn one another, are an anticipation of a final and decisive judgment, when every man's reward will be according to his works.

That all those who heard and professed to believe the gospel, will be finally judged by that, we have the fullest assurance. GOD will judge the secrets of men by JESUS CHRIST, according to his gospel. "The word that I have spoke," saith CHRIST, "the same will judge them that heard it, on the last day." John xii :48. It greatly interests us clearly to know what is the import and consequence of being judged by the gospel as a law of liberty; and it contains the following things,

The general character, all the thoughts, words and actions, together with the general conduct of all those who professed the gospel, will be brought to the test, and tried by this rule. Man's own opinion of himself, the good opinion of others, will here stand him in no stead; his character will not be determined by his external appearance, but by his inward reality. "Man looketh on the outward appearance, but the LORD looketh on the heart." I Sam. xvii :7. The self-righteous pharisee will be rejected, notwithstanding his fair appearance and boasting; the penitent publican will be received, though he has nothing to plead but LORD have mercy on me a sinner. The law is spiritual, and no law more so than the law of the gospel; it requires not merely an external obedience, but an internal conformity to the will of GOD; it demands truth in the inward part, it looks not only to the actions that are done, but to the principle from which they flow, we must judge of man's inward disposition by his visible action, but GOD judges of the actions of men according to their invisible spring; thoughts are out of the reach of human cognizance, but they are the first object of divine notice; there is not a word that drops from our tongue but what our judge hears, whatever we do or whatever we neglect, is all under his immediate eye, and he not only attends to our general character, but also to every thought, word or action, and the prevailing complexion of all these taken together form our true and real character.

In the judgment, according to this law, our character, words, thoughts and actions will be brought to the test of this rule, our conduct will be compared with these precepts, this is the balance of the sanctuary, in which the professors of the gospel shall be weighed, and as they shall be found approved or deficient, their case must be determined. Those whose temper and actions shall be found conformable to the law of liberty, will be acquitted, graciously accepted, and made every happy, and those who turned the grace of GOD into wantonness, and made the liberty of the gospel a cloak for their sins, will be finally rejected. The gospel informs us, that a day is already appointed for that purpose; it acquaints us with the person of our judge, and every circumstance, as well as the rule according to which he will proceed in judgment. Perhaps on that day when all nations shall appear before the judge, and he will divide them as a shepherd divideth the sheep from the goats, distinct places will also be allotted to those who are to be judged by natural conscience and the law of nature, and those who have been favoured with a divine revelation, and especially with the light of the gospel: The people of Niniveh will arise against empty professors of the gospel, and will condemn them. Those who have been exalted above others in means and privileges, will sit proportionably lower than those who have made a better improvement of lesser means; and notwithstanding the fondest hope and finest profession, it is a determined rule of the law of liberty, that "except our righteousness shall exceed that of the scribes and pharisees, we shall in no case enter into the kingdom of heaven."

It deserves our peculiar attention, that the apostle considers the gospel as a law of liberty, at the same time when he sets it before us as the rule by which we are to be judged. We are not to imagine because the gospel is a law of liberty, therefore men will not be judged; on the contrary judgment will be the more severe against all who have heard and professed the gospel, and yet walked contrary to its precepts and doctrine. As the transgression of a law of liberty must be more inexcusable, than the transgression of a law unjust or oppressive in itself, or even the ceremonial law, which was given only for a certain period, and to answer temporary purposes, so their judgment and doom must be proportionably heavier, who have sinned against love and liberty, as well as against power and justice.

According to this law the fate of men will not only be determined, but sentence will also be put into execution. GOD sitteth on the throne of judgment every day, and judgeth righteously, but he hath moreover appointed a particular day when he will manifest his power and justice before the whole creation; when the dead both small and great will stand before GOD, when those that acted agreeable to the law of liberty, will attain the fulness of glory of the freedom of the sons of GOD, and when he will also take vengeance on all that have not known GOD, and have not obeyed his holy gospel. This naturally leads to the second thing proposed, to take a nearer view of the importance of the exhortation, "So speak, and so do, as they that shall be judged by the law of liberty."

It seems as though the apostle had an eye to some particular branch of the law of liberty, *i.e.* the love which we owe unto our neighbour, and that his design is to obviate the mistake as though men might be considered as fulfilling the law of CHRIST, in paying respect to some of its commands and prohibitions, at the same time that they were entirely regardless of the rest. He assures them, that "whosoever shall keep the whole law, but shall transgress in one point" (*e.g.* having respect of persons) "is guilty of all." On this principle the apostle builds the general exhortation, "So speak, and so do, as they that shall be judged by the law of liberty." This implies:

1] Be thoroughly convinced of the certainty of a judgment to come, and that it extends to you, to all your thoughts, words, and actions. There is not any truth of greater moment, nor perhaps more easily forgotten. The belief or unbelief of this important doctrine must have the most sensible effects. All the apostles frequently put their hearers in mind of a judgment to come; and there is not any truth more necessary to be frequently inculcated and daily thought on, and wherever this truth is really believed and felt, it will have a constant and natural influence on the behavior of those who truly believe it.

2] See to it that in judgment you may stand. All men will be brought into judgment, but few will be able to stand; none will be excused, or be able to withdraw, and only those who have acted worthily, will meet with the divine acceptance. The difference will be amazing and beyond all conception: An eternity of happiness, which eye has not seen, ear has not heard, and which never entered into the heart of any man, lies on the one side, and despair, misery and torment on the other. Those that are able to stand, will meet with the smiles and approbation of their judge, and to all the rest the king will say, "These mine enemies that would not have me to bear rule over them, bring them here, and slay them before mine eyes." Those that believe and are convinced of this awful alternative, should certainly make it their care that they may be able to stand in judgment; neither should the persuasion of this only influence their conduct in general, but these words ought to be considered as a rule, which we ought to have constantly before our eyes in all our discourses and every undertaking; we should ever "so speak, and so act, as they that shall be judged by the law of liberty."

I shall draw a few inferences, before I conclude with a more particular address to the worthy Gentlemen at whose request I preach on this occasion.

1. The gospel is a law of Liberty

A late writer asserts, "Every religion countenances despotism, but none so much as the Christian." This is a very heavy charge against religion in general, but bears hardest on the Christian. Whether it proceeds from malice, ignorance, or misapprehension, it is needless to determine; but if Christianity be a law of liberty, it must be obvious how ill-grounded is such a charge against it. It cannot be denied but some Christian writers have wrote against the rights of mankind. All those who stand up for unlimited passive obedience and non-resistance, may have given but too much cause for such surmises and suspicions; but the truth is, that both those which make this charge, and those who gave occasion for it, were alike ignorant of the spirit and temper of Christianity; and it may well be doubted whether the venders of such odious doctrines, who foisted tenets, so abominable and injurious to mankind, into the system of Christian religion, have not done that holy religion greater hurt under the pretence of friendship and defence than its most barefaced enemies by all their most violent attacks. Some Christian divines have taught the enormous faith, that millions were made for one, they have ascribed a divine right to kings to govern wrong; but what then? Are such abominable doctrines any part of christianity, because these men say so? does the gospel cease to be a law of liberty, because some of its professors pervert it into an engine of tyranny, oppression and injustice.

The assertion, that all religion countenances despotism, and christianity more than any other, is diametrically opposite to fact. Survey the globe, and you will find that liberty has taken its seat only in Christendom, and that the highest degree of freedom is pleaded for and enjoyed by such as make profession of the gospel.

There are but two religions, which are concerned in this charge; the Jewish and the Christian. Natural religion writers of this kind I suppose would not include in their charge; if they do, they set all religion at variance with the rights of mankind, contrary to the sense of all nations, who are generally agreed, that, abstractly of a world to come, religion is of real service and necessity to mankind, for their better government and order.

As to the Jewish religion, it seems really strange that any should charge it with favouring despotism, when by one of its express rites at certain times it proclaimed "liberty throughout the land, to the inhabitants thereof." Levit. xxv:10. It required their kings "not to be lifted up in their hearts above their brethren." Deut. xvii:20. And the whole system of that religion is so replete with laws against injustice and oppression, it pays such an extraordinary regard to property, and gives such a strict charge to rule in justice and the fear of GOD, and to consider those, over whom they judge, as their brethren, even when dispensing punishments, and forbids all excess in them, that it is really surprising any one acquainted with its precepts, should declare it favourable to despotism or oppression.

The Christian religion, while it commands due respect and obedience to superiors, no where requires a blind and unlimited obedience on the part of the subjects; nor does it vest any absolute and arbitrary power in the rulers. It is an institution for the benefit, and not for the distress, of mankind. It preacheth not only "glory to GOD on high," but also "peace on earth, and good will among men."

The gospel gives no higher authority to magistrates than to be "the ministers of GOD, for the good of the subject." Rom. xiii. From whence it must surely follow, that their power is to edify, and not to destroy: When they abuse their authority, to distress and destroy their subjects, they deserve not to be thought ministers of GOD for good; nor is it to be supposed, when they act so contrary to the nature of their office, that they act agreeable to the will of GOD, or in conformity to the doctrine of the gospel.

The gospel recommends unto masters to forbear threatnings, and to remember that they also have a master in heaven; it assures them that the eye of GOD is equally upon the servant and the master, and that with GOD there is no respect of persons: It commands masters, from the most solemn considerations, to give unto servants that which is just and equal; it saith to the meanest slave: "Art thou called being a servant, care not for it, but if thou mayest be made free, use it rather." 1 Cor. vii:21.

The doctrine of the gospel has that regard to property, that it commands even soldiers, "Do violence to no man, and be content with your wages:" Luke iii:14—that a Paul sent back a run-away slave, though now converted, and belonging to his intimate friend, and at a time when he seems to have stood in real need of his service, from a delicacy that he would do nothing without the owner's mind, less his benefit should appear as if it were of necessity, and not willingly. Philem. 14. From the same spirit of justice a Zacheus, after his conversion, restored fourfold what before he had taken from any by false accusation: Surely, then the spirit of the gospel is very friendly to the rights and property of men.

The gospel sets conscience above all human authority in matters of faith, and bids us to "stand fast in that liberty wherewith the Son of GOD has made us free." Gal. v:1. Freedom is they very spirit and temper of the gospel: "He that is called in the LORD being a servant, is the LORD's freeman. Ye are bought with a price, be ye not the servants of men." 1 Cor. vii:22, 23. At the same time that it commands us to submit to every ordinance of men, it also directs us to act "as free, and not using liberty as a cloak of maliciousness, but as the servants of GOD." 1 Pet. iii:13–18.

Those therefore that would support arbitrary power, and require an unlimited obedience, in vain look for precedents or precepts for such things in the gospel, an institution equally tending to make men just, free, and happy here, and perfectly holy and happy hereafter.

2. The main design of the gospel is not to direct us in our external and civil affairs, but how we may at last stand with comfort before GOD, *the judge of all.*

Human prudence is to be our guide in the concerns of time: the gospel makes us wise unto salvation, and points out the means to be pursued that it may be well with us in the world to come. As rational creatures we are to make use of our reason; as Christians we are to repent and believe the gospel. Motives of a worldly nature may very properly influence us in our worldly concern, we are created not only for eternity, but also for time: It is not at all improper for us to have a due regard for both. The gospel will regulate our desires and restrain our passions as to earthly things, and will raise us at the same time above time and sense, to objects of a nature more worthy of ourselves. A due regard for, and a frequent meditation on, a judgment to come, will greatly assist us in all our concerns; and this very consideration the gospel holds out to us in the clearest manner. It not only affirms as a truth, what reason and conscience might consider only as probably, but it takes away as it were the veil from between us and things to come; it gives us a present view of the future bliss of saints, and the terrors and despair of sinners; rather an historical account than a prophetic description of all the proceedings of the dreadful pleasing day; it clearly points out the road to destruction, and the way to escape; it affords us a plain and general rule to obtain safety and comfort, when it bids us, "So speak, and so do, as they that shall be judged by the law of liberty."

This general rule may also be of considerable service in extraordinary and particular cases. It is impossible to provide express directions for every particular case, and in the course of things circumstances may happen when a good man may be at a loss to know his duty, and find it difficult so to act as to obtain his own approbation. There may be danger of going beyond, and danger in not coming up to, the mark. To act worthy of GOD, who has called us, is the general rule of the Christian at all times, and upon every occasion, and did we but always follow this rule, what manner of persons should we then be! But in cases of intricacy we may still be in doubt what may be most for the glory of GOD, and most consistent with our duty. Sometimes also our relative duties may seem to come in competition with one another, and we may hesitate in our own mind which for the present has the strongest call. We would fain obey our superiors, and yet we cannot think of giving up our natural, our civil and religious rights, nor acquiesce in or contribute to render our fellow-creatures or fellow-citizens slaves and miserable. We would willingly follow peace with all men, and yet

would be very unwilling that others should take the advantage of a
pacific disposition, to injure us in hopes of impunity. We would express duty, respect and obedience to the king, as supreme, and yet
we would not wish to strengthen the hands of tyranny, nor call oppression lawful: In such a delicate situation it is a golden rule, "So
to speak, and so to do, as they that shall be judged by the law of
liberty." Nothing has a greater tendency to make men act wrong
than the disbelief of a future judgment, and nothing will more effectually restrain and direct them than the full persuasion that such an
event will certainly take place; nothing would have a happier
tendency to make us act with prudence, justice and moderation than
the firm persuasion that GOD will bring every work into judgment,
and every secret thing, whether it be good or bad.

Neither could I think on any direction more applicable to the
design of our present meeting, or which I might more properly recommend to the respectable Gentlemen, now met together to consult
on the recovery and preservation of the liberties of America, and
who chose to begin their deliberations with a solemn act of worship
to almighty GOD who has established government as his ordinance,
and equally abhors licentiousness and oppression; whose singular
blessing it is if subjects enjoy a righteous government, and under
such a government lead a quiet and peaceable life in all godliness
and honesty.

You are met, Gentlemen, in a most critical time, and on a most
alarming occasion, not in a legislative capacity, but (while the
sitting of the usual representation is not thought for the king's
service, or necessary for the good of this province) you are chosen
by the general voice of this province to meet on their behalf, to consult on such measures as in our local circumstances may be most to
the real advantage and tend to the honour of our gracious sovereign,
as well as the good and safety of this province, and of all this great
continent. For the sake of the auditory, I shall briefly state the immediate causes that have given rise to this Provincial and a general
American Congress, and then offer such humble advice as appears to
me most suitable to our circumstances.

To enforce some Acts for laying on a duty to raise a perpetual
revenue in America, which the Americans think unjust and unconstitutional, which all America complains of, and some provinces
have in some measure opposed. A fleet and army has been sent to
New England, and after a long series of hardships by that province
patiently endured, it is now out of all question that hostilities have
been commenced against them; blood has been shed, and many lives
have been taken away; thousands, never so much as suspected of
having any hand in the action which is made the pretence of all the
severity now used against that province, have been and still are
reduced to the greatest distress. From this other provinces have

taken the alarm; an apprehension of nearer foes, not unlikely to appear as auxiliaries in an unjust cause, has thrown our neighbours into arms; how far and wide the flame so wantonly kindled may be permitted to spread, none can tell; but in these alarming circumstances the liberty of this continent, of which we are a part, the safety and domestick peace of this province will naturally become subject of your deliberations; and here I may well adapt the language of old, "There was no such deed done nor seen from the day that America was first settled unto this day; consider of it, take advice, and speak your minds." Judges xix:30. I mean not to anticipate and direct your counsels, but from your desire I should speak on this occasion; I take it for granted you will permit me to offer such hints as may appear suitable to the place and design of our present meeting.

In the first place, as there is no evil in a city in which the hand of GOD may not be seen, so in vain is salvation looked for from the hills and from the mountains, but can come from him only who has made heaven and earth. This undoubtedly is a day of trouble, but GOD saith to his people, "Call upon me in a day of trouble, and I will deliver thee." Ps. 1:15. "What nation has GOD so nigh unto them, as the LORD our GOD is in all things that we call upon him for." Deut. iv:7. If this be our first step, if first of all we look unto him from whom our help cometh, we may hope all will be well at last. Let us be thoroughly convinced of this, we must stand well with GOD, else it can never be well with us at all; without him and his help we can never prosper. The LORD is with you, if you are with him; "If you seek him, you will find him, but if you forsake him, you will be forsaken by him." 2 Chron. xv:2. If GOD be for us, who can be against us? if he be against us, who can be for us? Before we think on, or look any where else, may our eyes be unto GOD, that he may be gracious unto us. Let us humbly confess and speedily turn from our sins, deprecate his judgment, and secure his favour. "Rent your hearts, and not your garments, and turn unto the LORD your GOD, for he is gracious and merciful, slow to anger and of great kindness, and repenteth him of the evil, who knoweth if he will return and repent, and leave a blessing behind him, even a meat-offering and a drink-offering unto the LORD your GOD." Joel ii:13, 14.

Let it be a standing rule with every one that is to sit in council upon this occasion, "so to speak, and so to do, as one that is to be judged by the law of liberty." Let us most carefully avoid every thing that might make us incur the displeasure of GOD and wound our own consciences. The effects of your deliberation may become very serious and extensive, and the consequences extremely important: Think therefore before you speak, deliberate before you execute, and let the law of liberty, by which you are hereafter to be judged, be the constant rule of all your words and actions: Far be it from us to be reduced under laws inconsistent with liberty, and as far to wish for liberty without law; let the one be so tempered with the other that when we come to give our account to the supreme lawgiver, who is the great judge of all, it may appear we had a due regard to both, and may meet with his approbation.

Such always hath been, and such is still, the attachment of America to the illustrious house of Hanover, that I need not put you in mind of our duty to the king as supreme. By our law the king can do no wrong; but of his present Majesty, who is universally known to be adorned with many social virtues, may be not justly conclude that he would not do any wrong, even though he could. May we not hope that to the greatness of a monarch, he will super-add the feelings of the man, the tenderness of a father. May we not hope that when the truth of things, the tears of his suffering sub-jects, the distresses caused by Acts extremely ill advised, once reach his notice, a generous pity will force his heart, and that pity, when he feels it, will command redress? "The heart of the king is in the hand of the LORD, as the rivers of water, and he turneth it as he pleaseth;" Prov. xxi:1. most earnestly therefore let us pray that in this great and most important matter also GOD may give unto the king an understanding heart, that power may be governed by wis-dom, and the wheels of government roll on with justice and moder-ation.

Should you think that all our present distress is owing to evil counsellors, nothing need to hinder you from praying that GOD would turn their counsels into foolishness; you may make it your earnest request both in public and in private, that the wicked being removed from before the king, his throne may be established in righteousness, that the rod of the oppressor may be broke, and justice and equity take place of tyranny and oppression.

It may be owing to nothing but the firm attachment to the reigning family that so many Americans look upon the present measures as a deep laid plan to bring in the Pretender. Perhaps this jealousy may be very groundless, but so much is certain, that none but Great-Britain's enemies can be gainers in this unnatural contest.

Never let us loose out of sight that our interest lies in a perpetual connection with our mother country. Notwithstanding the present unwise and harsh measures, there are thousands in Great-Britain that think with us, and wish well to the American cause, and make it their own; let us convince our enemies that the struggles of America have not their rise in a desire of independency, but from a warm regard to our common constitution; that we esteem the name of Britons, as being the same with freemen; let every step we take afford proof how greatly we esteem our mother country, and that, to the wish of a perpetual connexion, we prefer this only consideration, that we may be virtuous and free.

Let me entreat you, Gentlemen, think coolly, and act deliberately; rash counsels are seldom good ones: ministerial rashness and American rashness can only be productive of untoward compounds; inconsiderate measures, framed on the other side of the atlantic, are the cause of all our mischiefs, and it is not in the least probable that inconsiderate measures in America can be productive of any good. Let nothing be done through strife and vain glory; let no private resentment or party zeal disgrace your honest warmth for your country's welfare: Measures determined on by integrity and prudence, are most likely to be carried into execution by steadiness and moderation. Let neither the frowns of tyranny, nor the pleasure of popularity, sway you from what you clearly apprehend just and right, and to be your duty. Consider how much lies at stake, how greatly your religion, your liberty, your property, your posterity, is interested. Endeavour to act like freeman, like loyal subjects, like real Christians, and you will "so speak, and so act, as they that shall be judged by the law of liberty." Act conscientiously, and with a view to GOD, then commit your ways to him, leave the event with GOD, and you will have great reason to hope that the event will be just, honourable and happy.

And now, Gentlemen, you have the wishes and prayers of every thoughtful person, that your deliberations may be carried on with candour, unanimity and prudence, may be blessed to preserve the quietness of this province, and co-operate in restoring the rights and tranquillity of all America, as well as promote the prosperity of the whole British empire. This will afford you a heartfelt satisfaction, and transmit your name to posterity with honour, when all those who had opposite views, and sought their greatness in the ruin of others, will be held in abhorrence and detestation.

I have but a few hints to give to my hearers in general

The times are evil; this is a day of adversity, and in a time of adversity we ought to consider. It may perhaps soon become impossible, even to the most indolent, to continue unconcerned, and those that wish no more than to hide themselves in quiet obscurity, may not always have it in their power to remain neuter: To know the signs of the time, is a considerable part of human prudence, and it is a still greater to walk circumspectly, and redeem the time, because the days are evil. Whatever part you may think yourselves obliged to take, "So speak, and so do, as they that shall be judged hereafter, and judged by the law of liberty."

In these times of confusion I would press on my hearers a most conscientious regard to the common laws of the land. Let our conduct shew that we are not lawless; by well-doing let us put to silence the reproaches of our adversaries. Let us convince them that we do not complain of law, but of oppression; that we do not abhor these acts because we are impatient to be under government, but being destructive of liberty and property, we think them destructive also of all law. Let us act "as free, and yet not make liberty a cloke of maliciousness, but as the servants of GOD."

While it is yet peace and quietness with us, let us not think ourselves inaccessible to the evils which are already come upon others; there are some evils which we would rather deprecate in private than speak of in public, against which, being forewarned, we should be forearmed; every trifling report should not alarm us, but it would be folly still greater not to be on our guard against sudden dangers.

Remember them that suffer adversity, as being yourselves also in the body. Think on those who are driven from their habitations and all their conveniences of life, or confined in their own houses by an enraged soldiery, to starve in their own country, in the midst of property and plenty, not permitted to enjoy their own, and distressed in every connexion, and this without any cause alleged against numbers of them, without complaint, suspicion or a legal trial: The like was never heard since the cruel siege of Londonderry, and is a species of cruelty at which even that hardhearted bigot James II relented.

Above all, let every one earnestly pray that HE that is higher than the highest would soon make a righteous end of all their confusion; that he would incline the king to hear the cries of his subjects, and that no more innocent blood may be shed in America.

One thing more: Consider the extreme absurdity of struggling for civil liberty, and yet to continue slaves to sin and lust. "Know ye not to whom ye yield yourselves servants to obey, his servants ye are, to whom ye obey, whether of sin unto death, or of obedience unto righteousness." Rom. vi:16. Cease from evil, and do good, seek peace, and pursue it, who will hurt you while you follow that which is good; become the willing servants of the LORD JESUS CHRIST, hearken to and obey the voice of his gospel; for "where the spirit of the LORD is, there is liberty;" and "if the Son makes you free, THEN, and not till then, "SHALL YOU BE FREE INDEED."

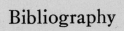

Bibliography

An Introductory Bibliography

General

Adams, Charles Francis. *Three Episodes of Massachusetts History.* 2 vols. Boston: Houghton, Mifflin and Co., 1883.

Andrews, Charles M. *The Colonial Period of American History.* 4 vols. New Haven: Yale University Press, 1934–38.

Bailyn, Bernard. *The Ideological Origins of the American Revolution.* Cambridge: The Belknap Press of Harvard University Press, 1967.

Baldwin, Alice M. *The New England Clergy and the American Revolution.* New York: Frederick Ungar, 1958.

Beam, Jacob N. *The American Whig Society.* Princeton: American Whig Society, 1933.

Bohman, George V. "The Colonial Period," in *History and Criticism of American Public Address,* ed. William N. Brigance, Vol. I, 1–54. New York: McGraw-Hill, 1943.

Boorstin, Daniel J. *The Americans: The Colonial Experience.* New York: Random House, 1958.

Bushman, Richard L. *From Puritan to Yankee: Character and the Social Order in Connecticut, 1690–1768.* Cambridge: Harvard University Press, 1967.

Davidson, Philip. *Propaganda and the American Revolution.* Chapel Hill: University of North Carolina Press, 1941.

Gaustad, Edwin S. *The Great Awakening in New England.* New York: Harper and Brothers, 1957.

Gewehr, Wesley. *The Great Awakening in Virginia, 1740–1790.* Durham: Duke University Press, 1930.

Heimert, Alan. *Religion and the American Mind: From the Great Awakening to the Revolution.* Cambridge: Harvard University Press, 1966.

Hudson, Roy Fred. "Rhetorical Invention in Colonial New England," *Speech Monographs,* XXV (August, 1958), 215–21.

Kerr, Harry P. "The Election Sermon: Power for Revolutionaries," *Speech Monographs,* XXIX (March, 1962), 13–22.

Lengyel, Cornel. *Four Days in July.* New York: Doubleday Co., 1958.

Levy, Babette May. *Preaching in the First Half Century of New England History.* Hartford: American Society of Church History, 1945.

Maxson, Charles H. *The Great Awakening in the Middle Colonies.* Gloucester: Peter Smith, 1958.

Meriwether, Colyer. *Our Colonial Curriculum, 1607–1776.* Washington: Capital Publishing Co., 1907.

Miller, Helen Hill. *The Case for Liberty.* Chapel Hill: The University of North Carolina Press, 1965.

Miller, John C. *Origins of the American Revolution.* Boston: Little, Brown, and Company, 1943.

631

————. *Sam Adams, Pioneer in Propaganda.* Stanford: Stanford University Press, 1960.

Miller, Perry. *New England Mind: The Seventeenth Century.* Cambridge: Harvard University Press, 1954.

————. *Orthodoxy in Massachusetts, 1630–1650.* Cambridge: Harvard University Press, 1933.

Minnick, Wayne C. "The New England Execution Sermon, 1639–1800," *Speech Monographs,* xxxv (March, 1968), 77–89.

Morrison, Samuel E. *The Founding of Harvard College.* Cambridge: Harvard University Press, 1935.

————. *Harvard in the Seventeenth Century.* 2 vols. Cambridge: Harvard University Press, 1936.

————. *The Intellectual Life of Colonial New England.* New York: New York University Press, 1956.

Nelson, William H. *The American Tory.* Oxford: Oxford University Press, 1961.

Oliver, Robert T. *History of Public Speaking in America.* Boston: Allyn and Bacon, Inc., 1965.

Osgood, Herbert L. *The American Colonies in the Seventeenth Century.* 3 vols. New York: The MacMillan Co., 1904-7.

Parrington, Vernon L. *Main Currents in American Thought: The Colonial Mind.* New York: Harcourt, Brace and Co., 1927.

Potter, David. *Debating in the Colonial Chartered College.* New York: Bureau of Publications, Teachers College, Columbia University, 1944.

Rossiter, Clinton. *Seed Time of the Republic.* New York: Harcourt, Brace and Co., 1953.

Schlesinger, Arthur M. *Prelude to Independence.* New York: Alfred A. Knopf, 1958.

Tyler, Moses C. *The Literary History of the American Revolution, 1763–1783.* G. P. Putnam's Sons, 1957.

Wallace, Karl R., (ed.) *History of Speech Education in America.* Parts 1 and 2, pp. 1–258. New York: Appleton-Century-Crofts, Inc., 1954.

Warren, Charles. *A History of the American Bar.* Boston: Little, Brown and Company, 1913.

Wertenbaker, Thomas J. *The Founding of American Civilization.* 3 vols. New York: Charles Scribner's Sons, 1938–47.

Winslow, Ola E. *Meetinghouse Hill, 1630–1783.* New York: The MacMillan Co., 1952.

Specific

Adams, John

Adams, Charles F. *The Works of John Adams, with Life (1850–56).* Philadelphia: J. B. Lippincott & Co., 1871.

Bowen, Catherine D. *John Adams and the American Revolution.* Boston: Little, Brown and Company, 1950.

Chinard, Gilbert. *Honest John Adams.* Boston: Little, Brown and Company, 1933.

Smith, Page. *John Adams.* 2 vols. Garden City, New York: Doubleday & Company, Inc., 1962.

Berkeley, Governor William

Bruce, Philip Alexander. "Governor William Berkeley," *Dictionary of American Biography,* Vol. II, 217–18. New York: Charles Scribner's Sons, 1929.

Dowdey, Clifford. *The Great Plantation*. New York: Rhinehart & Company, Inc., 1957, pp. 57–100.

Bernard, Governor Francis
Adams, James Truslow. "Governor Bernard," *Dictionary of Ameican Biography*, Vol. II, 221–22. New York: Charles Scribner's Sons, 1929.
Hutchinson, Thomas. *The History of the Colony and Province of Massachusetts-Bay*, ed. Lawrence S. Mayo, Vol. III, 60–183. Cambridge: Harvard University Press, 1936.

Boucher, Jonathan
Boucher, Jonathan. *Reminiscences of an American Loyalist, 1738–1789*. Boston and New York: Houghton Mifflin Co., 1925.
Johnson, Allen. "Jonathan Boucher," *Dictionary of American Biography*, Vol. II, 473–75. New York: Charles Scribner's Sons, 1929.

Chauncy, Charles
Eliot, Samuel A. *Heralds of a Liberal Faith*. Vol. I, 20–34. Boston: American Unitarian Association, 1910.
Fenn, William W. "Charles Chauncy," *Dictionary of American Biography*, Vol. IV, 42–43. New York: Charles Scribner's Sons, 1930.
Sprague, William B. *Annals of the American Unitarian Pulpit*. New York; Robert Carter & Brothers, 1865, pp. 8–13.

Church Benjamin
Lorring, James Spear. *The Hundred Boston Orators*. Boston: John P. Jewett and Company, 1854, pp. 37–44.
Mallock, Archibald C. "Benjamin Church," *Dictionary of American Biography*, Vol. IV, 100–101. New York: Charles Scribner's Sons, 1931.

Colman, Benjamin
Adams, James Truslow. "Benjamin Colman," *Dictionary of American Biography*, Vol. IV, 311. New York: Charles Scribner's Sons, 1930.
———. "Memoir of Rev. Benjamin Colman D.D.," *New England Historical and Genealogical Register*, III, 105–22, 220–32.
Sprague, William B. *Annals of the American Pulpit*. Vol. I, pp. 223–29. New York: Robert Carter & Brothers, 1857.
Turell, Ebenezer. *Life and Character of the Rev. Benjamin Colman*. Boston: Rogers and Fowle, 1749.

Cotton, John
Adams, James Truslow. "John Cotton," *Dictionary of American Biography*, Vol. IV, 460–62. New York: Charles Scribner's Sons, 1930.
Come, Donald. "John Cotton, Guide of the Chosen People," Unpublished dissertation, Princeton, 1949.
Hirsch, E. F. "John Cotton and Roger Williams: their controversy concerning religious liberty," *Church History*, X (March, 1941), 38–51.
Ziff, Larzer. *The Career of John Cotton: Puritanism and the American Experience*. Princeton: Princeton Univ. Press, 1962.

Davies, Samuel
Egbert, Donald Drew and D. M. Lee. *Princeton Portraits*. Princeton: Princeton University Press, 1947, pp. 42–45.
Sprague, William B. *Annals of the American Pulpit*. Vol. III, 140–46. New York: Robert Carter and Brothers, 1860.

Dickinson, John

Adams, James Truslow. "John Dickinson," *Dictionary of American Biography,* Vol. V, 299–300. New York: Charles Scribner's Sons, 1930.

Egbert, Donald Drew and D. M. Lee. *Princeton Portraits.* Princeton University Press, 1947, pp. 47–215.

Powell, John H. "John Dickinson, Penman of the American Revolution," Unpublished Ph.D. Dissertation, State University of Iowa, 1938.

Stillé, Charles Janeway. *The Life and Times of John Dickinson, 1732–1808.* Philadelphia: J. B. Lippincott Company, 1891.

Drayton, William Henry

Dargon, Marion. "William Henry Drayton," *Dictionary of American Biography,* Vol. V, 448–49. New York: Charles Scribner's Sons, 1930.

Drayton, John. *Memoirs of the American Revolution.* Vol. I. Charleston: A. E. Miller, 1821.

McCrady, Edward. *The History of South Carolina in the Revolution, 1775–1780.* London: The Macmillan Co., 1901.

Edwards, Jonathan

Davidson, F. "Three Patterns of Living," *American Association of University Professors Bulletin,* XXXIV (Summer 1948), 364–74.

Elwood, Douglas J. *The Philosophical Theology of Jonathan Edwards.* New York: Columbia University Press, 1960.

Hitchcock, Orville A. "Jonathan Edwards," in *History and Criticism of American Public Address.* Ed. William N. Brigance. Vol. I, 213–37. New York: McGraw-Hill Book Co., 1934.

Miller, Perry. *Jonathan Edwards.* New York: W. Sloane Association, 1949.

Winslow, Ola Elizabeth. *Jonathan Edwards, 1703–1758: A Biography.* New York: The Macmillan Co., 1940.

Galloway, Joseph

Van Tyne, Claude H. *The Loyalists in the American Revolution.* New York: P. Smith, 1929, pp. 85, 87, 160–62, 255.

Werner, Raymond C. "Joseph Galloway," *Dictionary of American Biography,* Vol. VII, 116–17. New York: Charles Scribner's Sons, 1931.

Hancock, John

Allan, Herbert Sanford. *Patriot in Purple.* New York: Macmillan Co., 1948.

Baxter, William T. *The House of Hancock: Business in Boston.* Cambridge: Harvard University Press, 1945.

Brown, Abram English. *John Hancock, His Book.* Boston: Lee and Shepard, 1898.

Loring, James Spear. *The Hundred Boston Orators.* Boston: John P. Jewett and Company, 1854, pp. 72–122.

Magoon, Elias L. *Orators of the Revolution.* New York: Charles Scribner's Sons, 1857, pp. 139–54.

Henry, Patrick

Axelrod, Jacob. *Patrick Henry: The Voice of Freedom.* New York: Random House, 1947.

Dodd, William E. "Patrick Henry," *Dictionary of American Biography,* Vol. VIII, 554–59. New York: Charles Scribner's Sons, 1932.

Henry, William W. *Patrick Henry: Life, Correspondence and Speeches.* 3 vols. New York: Charles Scribner's Sons, 1891.

Mallory, Louis. "Patrick Henry," in *History and Criticism of American Public Address*. Ed. William N. Brigance. Vol. II, 580–602. New York: McGraw-Hill, 1943.

Tyler, Moses Coit. *Patrick Henry*. Boston: Houghton Mifflin Company, 1887.

Hooker, Thomas

Adams, James Truslow. "Thomas Hooker," *Dictionary of American Biography*, Vol. IX, 199–200. New York: Charles Scribner's Sons, 1932.

Miller, Perry. "Thomas Hooker and the Democracy of Early Connecticut," *New England Quarterly*, IV (October, 1931), 663–712.

Walker, George L. *Thomas Hooker, Preacher, Founder, Democrat*. New York: Dodd, Mead and Co., 1891.

Hutchinson, Thomas

Becker, Carl L. "Thomas Hutchinson," *Dictionary of American Biography*, Vol. IX, 439–42. New York: Charles Scribner's Sons, 1932.

Hosmer, J. K. *The Life of Thomas Hutchinson, Royal Governor of the Province of Massachusetts Bay*. Boston and New York: Houghton Mifflin & Co., 1896.

Morgan, E. S. "Thomas Hutchinson and the Stamp Act," *New England Quarterly*, XXI (December, 1948), 459–92.

Lovell, James

Drake, Samuel Adams. *Old Landmarks and Historic Personages of Boston*. Boston: Little, Brown and Company, 1900.

Loring, James Spear. *The Hundred Boston Orators*. Boston: John P. Jewett, 1854, pp. 29–37.

Lovell, John

Mays, Lawrence S. "John Lovell," *Dictionary of American Biography*, Vol. XI, 439–40. New York: Charles Scribner's Sons, 1933.

Seybolt, Robert E. *The Private Schools of Colonial Boston*. Cambridge: Harvard University Press, 1935, pp. 22–76.

Sibley, John Langdon. *Biographical Sketches of Those Who Attended Harvard*. Cambridge: Massachusetts Historical Society, 1873–79, pp. 441–46.

Mather, Cotton

Boas, R. P. and Louise Boas. *Cotton Mather, Keeper of the Puritan Conscience*. New York and London: Harper Brothers, 1928.

Murdock, Kenneth B. "Cotton Mather," *Dictionary of American Biography*, Vol. XII, 836–89. New York: Charles Scribner's Sons, 1933.

Wendell, Barrett, *Cotton Mather: The Puritan Priest*. Cambridge: Harvard University Press, 1926.

Mather, Increase

Murdock, Kenneth B. *Increase Mather, The Foremost American Puritan*. Cambridge: Harvard University Press, 1925.

Murdock, Kenneth B. "Increase Mather," *Dictionary of American Biography*, Vol. XII, 390–94. New York: Charles Scribner's Sons, 1933.

Sprague, William B. *Annals of the American Pulpit*. Vol. I. 151–59. New York: Robert Carter & Brothers, 1857.

Mayhew, Jonathan

Akers, Charles W. *Called Unto Liberty: A Life of Jonathan Mayhew, 1720–1776*. Cambridge: Harvard University Press, 1964.

Baldwin, A. M. *The New England Clergy and the American Revolution*. Durham: Duke University Press, 1928, pp. 69–70, 91–92.

Bradford, Alden. *Memoir of the Life and Writings of Rev. Jonathan Mayhew.* Boston: C. C. Little and Co., 1838.
Eliot, Samuel. *Heralds of a Liberal Faith.* Vol. I, pp. 34–48. Boston: American Unitarian Association, 1910.
Mood, Fulmer. "Jonathan Mayhew," *Dictionary of American Biography,* Vol. XII, 454–55. New York: Charles Scribner's Sons, 1933.
Sprague, William B. *Annals of the American Unitarian Pulpit.* New York: Robert Carter and Brothers, 1857, pp. 22–29.

Morton, Perez
Loring, James Spear. *The Hundred Boston Orators.* Boston: John P. Jewett and Company, 1854, pp. 127–30.

Otis, James
Morison, Samuel Eliot. "James Otis," *Dictionary of American Biography,* Vol. XIV, 103–5. New York: Charles Scribner's Sons, 1934.
Tudor, William. *The Life and Times of James Otis of Massachusetts.* Boston: Wills and Lilly, 1823.
Tyler, Moses C. *The Literary History of the American Revolution, 1763–1783.* Vol. I. 30–90. New York: Barnes and Noble Inc., 1941.

Pearson, Eliphalet
Fuess, Claude M. "Eliphalet Pearson," *Dictionary of American Biography,* Vol. XIV, 358. New York: Charles Scribner's Sons, 1934.
Sprague, William B. *Annals of the American Pulpit.* Vol. II, 126–31. New York: Robert Carter & Brothers, 1857.

Quincy, Josiah, Jr.
Adams, James T. "Josiah Quincy," *Dictionary of American Biography,* Vol. XV, 307–8. New York: Charles Scribner's Sons, 1935.
Magoon, Elias L. *Orators of the American Revolution.* New York: C. Scribner, 1857, pp. 121–38.
Quincy, Josiah. *Memoirs of the Life of Josiah Quincy, Jr.* Boston: Cummings, Hilliard, & Company, 1825.

Rittenhouse, David
Ford, Edward. *David Rittenhouse, Astronomer-Patriot, 1732–96.* Philadelphia, University of Pennsylvania Press, 1946.
Hindle, Brooke *David Rittenhouse.* Princeton: Princeton University Press, 1964.
Rufus, W. Carl. "David Rittenhouse," *Dictionary of American Biography,* Vol. XV, 630–32. New York: Charles Scribner's Sons, 1935.

Rutledge, John
Barry, Richard H. *Mr. Rutledge of South Carolina.* New York: Sican & Pearce, 1942.
Meriwether, Robert L. "John Rutledge," *Dictionary of American Biography,* Vol. XVI, 258–60. New York: Charles Scribner's Sons, 1935.
Peterson, Clarence Stewart. *First Governors of the Forty-eight States.* New York: Hobson Book Press, 1947, pp. 19–20.

Shepard, Thomas
Albro, John A. *The Life of Thomas Shepard.* Boston: Sabbath School Society, 1847.
Dewey, Edward H. "Thomas Shepard," *Dictionary of American Biography,* Vol. XVII, 75–76. New York: Charles Scribner's Sons, 1935.

Morison, Samuel Eliot. *Builders of the Bay Colony*. Boston: Houghton Mifflin Company, 1930, pp. 105–34.

Shepard, Thomas. "Autobiography," *Colonial Society of Massachusetts, Publications*, XXVII (1932), 345–47.

Smith, William

Gegenheimer, Albert Frank. *William Smith, Educator and Churchman, 1727–1803*. Philadelphia: University of Pennsylvania Press, 1943.

Smith, Horace W. *The Life and Correspondence of the Rev. William Smith, D. D.* 2 vols. Philadelphia: Ferguson Brothers & Company, 1880.

Starr, Elwood Harris. "William Smith," *Dictionary of American Biography*, Vol. XVII, 353–57. New York: Charles Scribner's Sons, 1935.

Stillé, Charles Janeway. *A Memoir of the Rev. William Smith, D. D. Provost of the College Academy and Charitable School of Philadelphia*. Philadelphia: Moore & Sons, Printers, 1869.

Stoddard, Solomon

Parkes, Henry B. "Solomon Stoddard," *Dictionary of American Biography*, Vol. XVIII, 59. New York: Charles Scribner's Sons, 1936.

Spague, William B. *Annals of the American Pulpit*. Vol. I, 718–23. New York: Robert Carter & Brothers, 1857.

White, Eugene E. "Solomon Stoddard's Theories of Persuasion," *Speech Monographs*, XXIX (March, 1962), 235–59.

Tennent, Gilbert

Alexander, Archibald. *Biographical Sketches of the Founder and Principal Alumni of the Log College*. Princeton: J. T. Robinson, 1845, pp. 33–107.

Egbert, Donald Drew, and D. M. Lee. *Princeton Portraits*. Princeton: Princeton University Press, 1947, pp. 32–34.

Maxson, C. H. *The Great Awakening in the Middle Colonies*. Chicago: University of Chicago Press, 1920, pp. 21–40.

Starr, Harris E. "Gilbert Tennent," *Dictionary of American Biography*, Vol. XVIII, 366–69. New York: Charles Scribner's Sons, 1936.

Thacher, Peter

Dewey, Edward. "Peter Thacher," *Dictionary of American Biography*, Vol. XVIII, 390–91. New York: Charles Scribner's Sons, 1936.

Loring, James Spear. *The Hundred Boston Orators*. Boston: John P. Jewett and Company, 1854, pp. 122–26.

Sprague, William B. *Annals of the American Pulpit.* Vol. 1, 718–23. New York: Robert Carter & Brothers, 1857.

Varnum, James Mitchell

Coburn, Frederick N. "James Mitchell Varnum," *Dictionary of American Biography*, Vol. XIX, 227–28. New York: Charles Scribner's Sons, 1936.

Warren, Joseph

Adams, James Truslow. "Joseph Warren," *Dictionary of American Biography*, Vol. XIX, 482–83. New York: Charles Scribner's Sons, 1936.

Cary, John. *Joseph Warren, Physician, Politician, Patriot*. Urbana: University of Illinois Press, 1961.

Frothingham, Richard. *Life and Times of Joseph Warren*. Boston: Little, Brown and Company, 1865.

Loring, James Spear. *The Hundred Boston Orators.* Boston: P. Jewett and Company, 1854, pp. 45–71.

Washington, George
Fitzpatrick, John C. "George Washington," *Dictionary of American Biography*, Vol. XIX, 509–27. New York: Charles Scribner's Sons, 1936.
Freeman, Douglas S. *George Washington, A Biography*. 6 vols. New York: Charles Scribner's Sons, 1948–54.
Stephenson, Nathaniel W., and Waldo H. Dunn. *George Washington*. 2 vols. New York: Oxford University Press, 1940.

West, Samuel
Dewey, Edward H. "Samuel West," *Dictionary of American Biography*, Vol. XX, 12. New York: Charles Scribner's Sons, 1936.
Eliot, Samuel A., ed. *Heralds of a Liberal Faith*. Vol. 1, 49–59. Boston: American Unitarian Association, 1910.
Sprague, William B. *Annals of the American Unitarian Pulpit*. New York: Robert Carter & Brothers, 1865, pp. 37–50.

Wigglesworth, Michael
Crowder, Richard. *No Featherbed to Heaven*. East Lansing: Michigan State University Press, 1963.
Dean, John Ward. *Sketch of the Life of Rev. Michael Wigglesworth*. Albany: J. Munsell, 1863.
Matthiessen, F. O. "Michael Wigglesworth, A Puritan Priest," *New England Quarterly*, I (1929), 491–504.
Murdock, Kenneth B. "Michael Wigglesworth," *Dictionary of American Biography*, Vol. XX, 194–95. New York: Charles Scribner's Sons, 1936.

Wilson, James
Boyd, Julian F. "James Wilson," *Dictionary of American Biography*, Vol. XX, 326–30. New York: Charles Scribner's Sons, 1936.
Quattrocchi, Anna M. "James Wilson and the Establishment of the Federal Government," *Historian*, I (1940), 105–17.
Rahskopf, Horace G. "The Oratory of James Wilson of Pennsylvania," *Speech Monographs*, V (1938), 40–61.
Smith, Charles P. *James Wilson, Founding Father: 1742–1798*. Chapel Hill: University of North Carolina Press, 1956.
Smith, William C. "James Wilson and the Philosophy of Freedom in the American Revolution," *American Catholic Historical Society Records*, LI (1939), 65–71.

Winthrop, John
Morison, Samuel Eliot. *Builders of the Bay Colony*. Boston and New York: Houghton Mifflin Company, 1930, pp. 51–104.
Winthrop, John. *The History of New England from 1630–1649*, James Savage, Vol. II, 270–86. Boston: Little, Brown and Company, 1853.
Winthrop, Robert C. *Life and Letter of John Winthrop*. 2 vols. Boston: Ticknor and Fields, 1864–67.
Truslow, James Adams, "John Winthrop," *Dictionary of American Biography*, Vol. XX, 408–11. New York: Charles Scribner's Sons, 1936.

Witherspoon, John
Collins, Varnum L. *President Witherspoon*. 2 vols. Princeton: Princeton University Press, 1925.
Egbert, Donald D. and D. M. Lee. *Princeton Portraits*. Princeton: Princeton University Press, 1947, pp. 45–50.
Paul, Wilson, B. "John Witherspoon's Theory & Practice of Public Speaking," *Speech Monographs*, XVI (1949), 272–89.

Wertenbaker, Thomas Jefferson. "John Witherspoon, Father of American Presbyterianism," in *Lives of Eighteen From Princeton,* ed. Willard Thorp, pp. 68–85. Princeton: Princeton University Press, 1946.

Woodmason, Charles
Hooker, Richard J. *The Carolina Backcountry on the Eve of the Revolution.* Chapel Hill: University of North Carolina Press, 1953.

Zubly, John T.
Daniel, Marjorie. "John J. Zubly," *Dictionary of American Biography,* Vol. XX, 660–61. New York: Charles Scribner's Sons, 1936.
Jones, Charles C. *Biographical Sketches of the Delegates from Georgia to the Continental Congress.* Boston: Houghton Mifflin and Company, 1891, pp. 203–11.
Sprague, William B. *Annals of the American Pulpit.* Vol. III, 219–22. New York: Robert Carter & Brothers, 1860.